MW01486980

Copyright © 2024

Table of Contents

INTRO:

The bustling emergency department fell silent as Dr. Sarah Chen, Chief Nursing Officer, strode through the doors. Her face was a mask of determination, belying the weight of the crisis at hand. A ransomware attack had crippled the hospital's electronic health records system, threatening patient safety and operational continuity.

"Team, we're facing an unprecedented challenge," Sarah began, her voice steady and reassuring. "But I have complete faith in our ability to overcome this together."

Over the next 72 hours, Sarah's leadership would be put to the ultimate test. She swiftly assembled a cross-functional crisis team, leveraging her deep understanding of hospital operations and information technology infrastructure. Her strategic thinking shone as she implemented a temporary paper-based documentation system, ensuring uninterrupted patient care while IT worked to restore the network.

Ethical dilemmas arose as limited resources strained the hospital's capacity. Sarah navigated these treacherous waters with grace, making difficult decisions that prioritized patient safety while considering staff well-being and legal implications. Her transparent communication style and ability to articulate a clear vision kept staff motivated and focused amidst the chaos.

As dawn broke on the third day, systems gradually flickered back to life. Sarah's tireless efforts had not only averted disaster but had transformed the crisis into an opportunity for growth. The hospital emerged stronger, with improved cybersecurity protocols and a renewed sense of teamwork.

This is the caliber of leadership you aspire to embody. As you embark on your journey toward the ANCC Nurse Executive Advanced certification, envision yourself confidently steering your organization through similarly daunting challenges. The knowledge and skills you'll gain from this study guide will be your compass, guiding you through the complex landscape of modern healthcare leadership.

In these pages, you'll master the intricacies of healthcare policy, unraveling the web of regulations that shape our industry. You'll delve into financial management, learning to balance budgets and allocate resources with precision. Evidence-based practice will become your north star, informing every decision with the latest research and data.

But leadership is more than just knowledge – it's about inspiring others to achieve greatness. You'll explore advanced communication strategies, learning to build and lead high-performing teams across diverse disciplines. Ethical leadership will be your foundation, ensuring your decisions always put patients and staff first.

As you progress through this guide, imagine yourself confidently presenting to your board of directors, implementing transformative quality improvement initiatives, or deftly navigating your organization through a public health crisis. Each chapter will bring you closer to realizing your potential as a visionary nurse executive.

The challenges facing healthcare are immense, but so is the impact you can make. Armed with the comprehensive knowledge this study guide provides, you'll be poised to drive meaningful change, elevate patient care, and shape the future of healthcare delivery. Your journey to becoming an exceptional nurse executive starts now – let's begin.

The ANCC Nurse Executive Advanced certification exam stands as the pinnacle of recognition for nurse leaders, validating the highest level of competencies required to excel in complex healthcare environments. This rigorous assessment evaluates your ability to drive organizational strategy, foster innovation, and lead transformational change across diverse healthcare settings.

Exam Structure and Format: The test comprises 175 questions, with 150 scored items and 25 pretest questions. You'll have 3.5 hours to complete this computer-based examination. Questions primarily appear in multiple-choice format, but be prepared for alternative item types such as drag-and-drop, hot spot, or chart/exhibit questions that assess your ability to apply knowledge in practical scenarios.

Content Domains:

1. Organizational and Systems Leadership (40% - 60 questions) • Strategic planning and execution • Financial management and budgeting • Human resource management • Technology and information management • Change management and innovation
2. Quality Improvement and Safety (25% - 37 questions) • Quality improvement methodologies (e.g., Lean, Six Sigma) • Patient safety initiatives • Risk management and mitigation • Performance measurement and benchmarking • Regulatory compliance and accreditation
3. Healthcare Policy (20% - 30 questions) • Health policy development and advocacy • Legislative and regulatory processes • Ethical and legal considerations in healthcare • Population health management • Healthcare economics and reimbursement models
4. Professional Practice (15% - 23 questions) • Evidence-based practice implementation • Interprofessional collaboration and team leadership • Professional development and mentoring • Nursing research and innovation • Ethical decision-making in leadership

Cognitive Levels: The exam assesses your abilities across three cognitive levels:

1. Knowledge Recall (15%): Basic recall of facts, concepts, and principles.
2. Application (60%): Applying knowledge to specific situations or problems.
3. Analysis and Synthesis (25%): Evaluating complex scenarios, integrating information from multiple sources, and developing strategic solutions.

Eligibility Requirements:

- Hold a current, active RN license
- Possess a master's degree or higher in nursing (or a bachelor's in nursing and a master's in another field)
- Have held a mid-level or higher administrative position OR a faculty position teaching graduate students executive leadership OR a nursing executive advanced-level practice role for at least 24 months full-time equivalent within the last 5 years
- Have completed 30 hours of continuing education in nursing administration within the last 3 years

Scoring and Passing: The exam uses a scaled scoring system, with scores ranging from 0 to 500. A score of 350 or higher is required to pass. The exact number of correct answers needed to achieve a passing score may vary slightly between exam versions due to differences in question difficulty.

Renewal and Continuing Education: Certification is valid for 5 years. To renew, you must either retake the exam or fulfill the following requirements:

- 1,000 practice hours in the specialty area
- 75 continuing education hours, with at least 25 in your specialty area
- Fulfill one or more professional development categories (e.g., academic credits, presentations, publications)

Distinguishing Factors: Unlike entry-level leadership certifications, the Nurse Executive Advanced exam delves into complex, system-wide issues that senior leaders face. It assesses your ability to:

- Drive organizational strategy and culture change
- Navigate complex financial and policy landscapes
- Lead quality improvement initiatives across entire health systems
- Foster innovation and evidence-based practice at an organizational level
- Make high-stakes decisions with far-reaching implications

This certification is considered the gold standard for nurse executives because it comprehensively evaluates the multifaceted skills required to lead in today's dynamic healthcare environment. It demonstrates to employers, colleagues, and stakeholders that you possess the expertise to navigate the challenges of modern healthcare leadership and drive positive change at the highest levels of an organization.

Mastering the ANCC Nurse Executive Advanced exam demands a strategic approach. Let's dive into comprehensive preparation and test-taking techniques to maximize your performance.

Preparation Strategies:

1. Structured Study Schedule: Create a 12-week study plan. Allocate specific time blocks for each content domain, weighted according to their exam representation. For example, dedicate 40% of your study time to Organizational and Systems Leadership.
2. Diverse Learning Resources: Combine textbooks, online courses, and practice exams. Utilize ANCC's test content outline as your roadmap. Supplement with current healthcare journals to stay abreast of industry trends.
3. Collaborative Learning: Form a study group with fellow nurse leaders. Meet weekly to discuss complex topics, share real-world experiences, and quiz each other on key concepts.
4. Simulated Exam Environment: Take full-length practice tests under exam-like conditions. This builds stamina and familiarizes you with the exam format.

Managing Test Anxiety:
1. Progressive Muscle Relaxation: Practice tensing and relaxing muscle groups sequentially. This technique can be discreetly used during the exam to release tension.
2. Visualization: Regularly visualize yourself successfully navigating the exam, maintaining calm and focus throughout.
3. Positive Self-Talk: Develop a mantra that reinforces your competence and preparation. Repeat it during study sessions and on exam day.

Time Management During the Exam:
1. Strategic Pacing: Allocate 1.3 minutes per question on average. Use the on-screen timer to track your progress.
2. Two-Pass Approach: First, answer all questions you're confident about. Flag challenging questions for review in a second pass.
3. Complex Question Strategy: For scenario-based questions, allocate up to 2 minutes. If you're stuck, flag it and move on to avoid time sink.

Tackling Different Question Types:
1. Scenario-Based Questions:
- Read the entire scenario before looking at answer choices.
- Identify the core issue or challenge presented.
- Consider how leadership principles apply to the specific context.
- Evaluate each answer choice against both the scenario and broader leadership best practices.
2. Data Interpretation Questions:
- Quickly scan the data to identify the type of information presented (financial statements, quality metrics, etc.).
- Read the question carefully to understand exactly what's being asked.
- Look for trends, outliers, or significant discrepancies in the data.
- Consider how a nurse executive would use this information to make decisions.
3. Policy and Regulatory Questions:
- Focus on the intent and broad implications of policies rather than minute details.
- Consider how policies intersect with ethical principles and organizational goals.

Elimination Techniques:
1. Absolute Statements: Be wary of answer choices with words like "always" or "never." In leadership, context often matters.
2. Scope of Practice: Eliminate options that fall outside the scope of a nurse executive's responsibilities.
3. Ethical Considerations: When in doubt, lean towards answers that prioritize patient safety and ethical practice.

Maintaining Focus and Energy:
1. Strategic Breaks: Plan two 5-minute breaks during the exam. Use these to stretch, hydrate, and reset your focus.
2. Mindful Breathing: Practice 4-7-8 breathing (inhale for 4 seconds, hold for 7, exhale for 8) to re-center yourself.

3. Positive Anchoring: Bring a small object that reminds you of your strengths and accomplishments. Touch it when you need a confidence boost.

Day-Before Exam Preparation:

1. Light Review: Skim through summary notes or flashcards. Avoid deep dives into new material.
2. Prepare Exam Kit: Gather necessary identification, snacks, and water. Lay out comfortable clothing.
3. Relaxation: Engage in a calming activity like gentle yoga or reading for pleasure.
4. Early Bedtime: Aim for 8 hours of sleep to ensure peak cognitive function.

Exam Day Strategies:

1. Nourishing Breakfast: Eat a balanced meal with complex carbohydrates and protein for sustained energy.
2. Arrival: Plan to arrive at the test center 30 minutes early to allow for check-in procedures and to settle your nerves.
3. Positive Affirmations: Before beginning the exam, take a moment to silently affirm your readiness and capability.

Remember, this exam is the culmination of your extensive experience and dedicated preparation. Trust in your abilities as a nurse leader. Each question is an opportunity to demonstrate your expertise. Approach the exam with confidence, knowing that you're well-equipped to join the ranks of advanced nurse executives. Your strategic preparation and wealth of leadership experience have prepared you for this moment. Embrace the challenge and let your executive acumen shine.

Leadership

Transformational leadership stands as a cornerstone of effective healthcare management, particularly in the dynamic and complex environment of modern healthcare organizations. Let's dissect its core components and their specific applications in healthcare settings.

Core Components of Transformational Leadership:

1. Idealized Influence: In healthcare, idealized influence manifests as the leader's ability to embody the values and mission of the organization. Nurse executives who demonstrate this quality consistently model ethical behavior, patient-centered care, and evidence-based practice.

Example: A Chief Nursing Officer who regularly rounds on units, engaging with staff and patients, demonstrating best practices in patient communication and safety protocols.

2. Inspirational Motivation: This component involves articulating a compelling vision for the future of healthcare delivery and inspiring staff to strive for excellence.

Example: Rallying nursing staff around a goal to achieve Magnet status, emphasizing how this recognition will improve patient outcomes and professional satisfaction.

3. Intellectual Stimulation: In healthcare, this translates to encouraging innovation in care delivery, quality improvement initiatives, and problem-solving.

Example: Implementing a nurse-led innovation program where staff can propose and pilot new approaches to common healthcare challenges.

4. Individualized Consideration: This aspect focuses on recognizing and developing the unique potential of each team member.

Example: Creating personalized professional development plans for nurses based on their career aspirations and the organization's needs.

Application of Transformational Leadership in Healthcare:

Idealized Influence and Organizational Culture Change: Idealized influence plays a crucial role in shaping organizational culture by setting the tone from the top. When nurse executives consistently demonstrate commitment to excellence, ethical decision-making, and patient-centered care, it permeates throughout the organization.

Example: A nurse executive champions a "Just Culture" initiative, consistently modeling behavior that prioritizes learning from errors rather than punitive actions. Over time, this approach leads to increased error reporting, improved patient safety, and a more collaborative work environment.

Individualized Consideration in Nurse-Patient Interactions: While typically discussed in terms of leader-follower relationships, the principle of individualized consideration can be extended to nurse-patient interactions, enhancing the quality of care.

Examples:

1. Tailored Communication: A nurse assesses a patient's health literacy level and adapts their education approach accordingly, ensuring the patient fully understands their care plan.

2. Cultural Competence: A nurse takes time to understand a patient's cultural background and adjusts care practices to align with the patient's beliefs and values, fostering trust and improving adherence to treatment plans.

3. Personalized Care Goals: Working collaboratively with patients to set achievable health goals based on their individual circumstances, priorities, and challenges.

4. Emotional Support: Recognizing and addressing the unique emotional needs of each patient, whether it's providing extra reassurance to an anxious patient or respecting the stoicism of another.

5. Family Involvement: Tailoring the level and type of family involvement in care based on patient preferences and family dynamics.

Implementing Transformational Leadership in Healthcare:

1. Leadership Development Programs: Invest in programs that cultivate transformational leadership skills among nurse managers and executives.

2. Mentorship Initiatives: Pair experienced transformational leaders with emerging nurse leaders to model and reinforce these practices.

3. Feedback Mechanisms: Implement 360-degree feedback systems that assess leaders' effectiveness in embodying transformational leadership principles.
4. Align Rewards and Recognition: Ensure that performance evaluation and reward systems reinforce transformational leadership behaviors.
5. Storytelling and Celebration: Regularly share stories that highlight successful applications of transformational leadership principles, reinforcing their value and impact.

By embracing and effectively implementing transformational leadership, nurse executives can drive significant positive change in healthcare organizations. This leadership style fosters a culture of continuous improvement, empowers staff at all levels, and ultimately leads to enhanced patient outcomes and organizational performance.

Servant leadership and traditional hierarchical leadership models represent two distinct approaches to leadership in healthcare, each with its own set of principles and implications for both patient outcomes and staff satisfaction.

Servant Leadership vs. Traditional Hierarchical Leadership

Traditional hierarchical leadership in healthcare typically follows a top-down approach, where decision-making power is concentrated at the upper levels of the organization. In this model, directives flow from executives and managers down to frontline staff, with a clear chain of command. Leaders are seen as authority figures who set the vision and direction, and employees are expected to follow orders and execute tasks within their defined roles. This approach can create a highly structured environment, which is beneficial in ensuring compliance with protocols, but it can also stifle creativity and limit the empowerment of lower-level staff.

In contrast, servant leadership flips the traditional hierarchy by prioritizing the needs of employees and patients above the leader's own agenda. Servant leaders focus on empowering their teams, fostering collaboration, and facilitating the personal and professional growth of their staff. Rather than issuing commands, a servant leader listens, provides resources, and supports their team in achieving collective goals. This model encourages a more inclusive and participatory culture, where every team member's voice is valued, potentially leading to higher engagement and innovation.

Application of Servant Leadership to Improve Patient Outcomes and Staff Satisfaction

Servant leadership can have a profound impact on both patient outcomes and staff satisfaction when applied in healthcare settings. By prioritizing the needs of the team, servant leaders create an environment where healthcare professionals feel supported and valued. This can lead to higher job satisfaction, reduced burnout, and a stronger commitment to patient care.

For example, a nurse leader who practices servant leadership might focus on ensuring that nurses have adequate resources, manageable workloads, and opportunities for professional development. This attention to staff well-being directly impacts the quality of care they provide. Nurses who feel supported are more likely to engage in patient-centered care, communicate effectively with patients and colleagues, and go the extra mile to ensure positive patient outcomes.

Additionally, servant leadership encourages collaboration and shared decision-making, which can lead to more holistic and innovative approaches to patient care. For instance, involving nurses and other frontline staff in developing care protocols can result in procedures that are more practical and effective, ultimately improving patient safety and outcomes.

Challenges of Implementing Servant Leadership in High-Stress Medical Environments

While the benefits of servant leadership are clear, implementing this approach in high-stress medical environments can present challenges. One of the primary difficulties is the inherent tension between the urgent, high-stakes nature of medical work and the time-consuming processes of listening, mentoring, and consensus-building that servant leadership requires. In emergency situations, the need for quick, decisive action can conflict with the servant leadership's focus on collaboration and employee empowerment.

Another challenge is the resistance to change from those accustomed to traditional hierarchical models. Shifting to a servant leadership approach may be met with skepticism by both leaders and staff who are more comfortable with clear directives and established chains of command. Overcoming this resistance requires a cultural shift within the organization, which can be difficult to achieve without strong buy-in from all levels of leadership.

Moreover, servant leaders must be careful to balance the needs of their staff with the operational demands of the healthcare environment. In some cases, prioritizing staff needs might lead to perceptions of favoritism or unequal treatment, which can undermine team cohesion. Leaders must ensure they apply servant leadership principles consistently and transparently to maintain trust and fairness.

In conclusion, while servant leadership offers a promising approach to improving patient outcomes and staff satisfaction, it must be carefully adapted to the realities of healthcare environments. Leaders who can navigate these challenges and foster a supportive, inclusive culture stand to make a significant positive impact on their organizations.

The Situational Leadership Model, developed by Paul Hersey and Ken Blanchard, emphasizes that there is no one-size-fits-all approach to leadership. Instead, effective leaders adapt their style based on the competence and commitment of their team members. This model outlines four leadership styles: directing, coaching, supporting, and delegating. These styles range from highly directive to highly supportive, and their application varies depending on the team's development level.

Directing (High Directive, Low Supportive)

The directing style is most effective when managing a newly formed team, especially during a challenging period like a hospital merger. In this scenario, team members may be enthusiastic but lack the experience or knowledge required to navigate the complexities of the merger. The nurse executive would take on a more hands-on approach, providing clear instructions, setting specific goals, and closely monitoring progress. For example, during the initial phase of the merger, the executive might outline the new organizational structure, define roles, and establish detailed action plans to ensure everyone understands their responsibilities.

Coaching (High Directive, High Supportive)

As the team begins to gain some experience but still requires guidance, the nurse executive might shift to a coaching style. This style involves not only providing direction but also offering support and encouragement. The leader would still make key decisions but would engage team members in the process, explaining the rationale behind choices and seeking their input. During a hospital merger, the nurse executive might use coaching to help the team understand the merger's strategic objectives, encouraging them to contribute ideas for integrating the two organizations while still providing the necessary oversight.

Supporting (Low Directive, High Supportive)

When managing a more experienced team, the nurse executive can adopt a supporting leadership style. Here, the focus shifts from directing tasks to facilitating the team's performance and offering encouragement. The executive would provide less instruction and more empowerment, allowing the team to take on greater responsibility. In the context of a hospital merger, a nurse executive might rely on the supporting style to foster collaboration between teams from both organizations, encouraging them to share best practices and develop integrated workflows while remaining available to address concerns or obstacles.

Delegating (Low Directive, Low Supportive)

Finally, for a highly experienced team, particularly one that has successfully navigated previous challenges, the delegating style is most appropriate. This approach involves minimal supervision, as the team is fully capable of working independently. The nurse executive would trust the team to make decisions and manage their own tasks, stepping in only when necessary. During a hospital merger, this could involve delegating the integration of specific departments to senior managers who have the expertise to handle the transition smoothly, while the nurse executive focuses on overarching strategic goals.

Application in a Hospital Merger

In a newly formed team, the nurse executive would likely start with a directing style to establish clear expectations and ensure that everyone is aligned with the merger's objectives. As the team gains experience and confidence, the executive might transition through coaching and supporting styles, gradually empowering the team to take on more responsibility. For a highly experienced team, the nurse executive could begin with a supporting style, quickly moving to delegating as the team demonstrates its capability to manage the merger independently. This adaptability in leadership ensures that the team's development is matched with the appropriate level of guidance and support, leading to a smoother, more effective merger process.

Authentic leadership, characterized by self-awareness, transparency, balanced processing, and moral integrity, has a significant impact on nurse retention and job satisfaction. In the high-stress environment of healthcare, where burnout and turnover rates are high, authentic leadership can play a crucial role in creating a supportive and trustworthy work atmosphere, directly influencing nurses' willingness to stay in their roles and their overall job satisfaction.

Impact of Authentic Leadership on Nurse Retention and Job Satisfaction

Nurses working under authentic leaders often report higher job satisfaction and are more likely to remain in their positions for extended periods. This leadership style fosters a culture of trust and respect, where nurses feel valued and understood. Authentic leaders are consistent in their actions, aligning their decisions with core values and openly communicating the rationale behind their choices. This approach reduces ambiguity and creates a sense of security among staff, which is essential for job satisfaction.

For example, an authentic nurse leader who consistently acknowledges the challenges their team faces, such as understaffing or high patient acuity, and works actively to address these issues—whether by advocating for more resources or adjusting workload distributions—can significantly enhance nurse morale. When nurses see that their leaders are not only aware of their struggles but also committed to mitigating them, they are more likely to feel appreciated and less inclined to leave the organization.

Moreover, authentic leadership promotes a work environment where nurses are encouraged to voice their opinions and concerns without fear of retribution. This open dialogue leads to greater engagement, as nurses feel their contributions are meaningful and valued. The resulting empowerment further increases job satisfaction, as nurses see the direct impact of their input on patient care and organizational practices.

Role of Self-Awareness in Effective Authentic Leadership

Self-awareness is the cornerstone of authentic leadership. A self-aware leader understands their strengths, weaknesses, values, and the impact of their behavior on others. This insight enables them to lead with empathy and integrity, ensuring that their actions are consistent with their professed values and that they are genuinely attuned to the needs and concerns of their team.

In practice, a self-aware nurse leader might recognize when their stress or frustration could negatively impact their interactions with staff. By being conscious of these emotions, the leader can take steps to manage them—such as taking a moment to decompress before engaging with the team—thereby maintaining a calm and supportive presence. This ability to regulate emotions and respond thoughtfully is critical in maintaining the trust and respect of the team.

Additionally, self-aware leaders are more likely to seek feedback and reflect on their leadership practices. This openness to learning and growth allows them to adapt and improve, ensuring they continue to meet the evolving needs of their staff. For example, a leader who regularly solicits and acts on feedback about their communication style or decision-making processes demonstrates a commitment to personal and professional development, which can inspire similar behaviors in their team.

Examples of Transparent Decision-Making in Critical Care Settings

Transparent decision-making is a key aspect of authentic leadership, particularly in critical care settings where decisions often carry significant consequences. Transparent leaders ensure that their decisions are made openly, with input from relevant stakeholders, and that the rationale behind decisions is clearly communicated to the team.

For instance, in a critical care unit facing a sudden surge in patient volume, an authentic leader might gather input from frontline nurses to understand their perspective on resource allocation. Instead of unilaterally deciding to reassign staff or redistribute workloads, the leader could involve the team in discussions about the best approaches to manage the increased demand. By explaining the factors influencing the final decision—such as staffing levels, patient acuity, and available resources—the leader ensures that the team understands and supports the chosen course of action.

Another example could be during the implementation of a new protocol for managing critically ill patients. An authentic leader would involve the nursing staff in the development and refinement of the protocol, soliciting feedback on potential challenges and areas for improvement. Once the protocol is finalized, the leader would transparently communicate the reasons for specific changes, such as aligning with evidence-based practices or meeting new regulatory requirements. This transparency helps build trust and ensures that nurses are fully informed and engaged in the implementation process.

By embracing authentic leadership and fostering self-awareness, nurse leaders can create a work environment where transparency, trust, and open communication thrive, leading to higher nurse retention, greater job satisfaction, and ultimately, improved patient care.

Mnemonic Device: "TRUST Leadership"
Transformational
Results through
Uplifting
Servant
Teamwork
This mnemonic—**TRUST**—captures the essence of how nurse executives can remember the key aspects of each leadership style:

- **Transformational**: Focuses on achieving **Results** by inspiring and motivating the team to exceed expectations.
- **Servant**: Prioritizes **Uplifting** team members by putting their needs first, empowering them to grow and succeed.
- **Situational**: Adapts leadership approach to the **Teamwork** required in each situation, providing guidance and support as needed.
- **Authentic**: Builds **Trust** through genuine relationships, self-awareness, and transparency.

Combining Leadership Styles in Real-World Healthcare Scenarios
In a real-world healthcare setting, these leadership styles are often combined to address complex challenges and drive positive outcomes.

1. **Transformational and Servant Leadership**: During a major change initiative, such as implementing a new patient care model, a nurse executive might use **transformational leadership** to inspire the team with a compelling vision for the future. Simultaneously, they could employ **servant leadership** to ensure that individual team members have the support and resources they need to adapt to the new model. This combination fosters a motivated and empowered workforce, aligned with both the organization's goals and personal development.
2. **Situational and Authentic Leadership**: When managing a crisis, like a sudden outbreak of infection within the hospital, a nurse executive might rely on **situational leadership** to quickly assess the team's competence and commitment, adjusting their leadership style accordingly—perhaps starting with a more directive approach and then shifting to supportive or delegating as the team gains control over the situation. **Authentic leadership** would also be critical here, as the executive's transparency and integrity would build trust and keep the team focused and cohesive in a high-pressure environment.
3. **Transformational and Authentic Leadership**: In a scenario where the organization is aiming for Magnet recognition, the nurse executive could use **transformational leadership** to drive the pursuit of excellence, fostering a culture of innovation and continuous improvement. **Authentic leadership** would be essential to maintain credibility and trust throughout this process, ensuring that the team feels genuinely supported and valued as they work towards this prestigious achievement.

By integrating these leadership styles, nurse executives can navigate the complexities of healthcare with a flexible, responsive approach that meets both organizational goals and the needs of their teams.

Emotional intelligence (EI) is a critical component of effective nurse leadership, particularly in navigating the complexities of healthcare environments. EI encompasses the ability to understand and manage one's own emotions, as well as to recognize and influence the emotions of others. For nurse leaders, high emotional intelligence facilitates better communication, decision-making, and team management, especially during high-pressure situations like public health crises.

Role of Emotional Intelligence in Nurse Leadership
Nurse leaders with strong emotional intelligence are better equipped to lead their teams through challenging situations. They can maintain composure under stress, empathize with their team members, and foster a positive work environment even in the face of adversity. EI is essential for building trust and rapport within the team, which is crucial for maintaining morale and ensuring cohesive, efficient team performance.
For example, during a hospital-wide emergency, a nurse leader with high EI would be able to assess the emotional climate of the team, recognizing signs of burnout or anxiety. By addressing these emotions proactively, perhaps

through supportive communication or by providing stress-relief resources, the leader can help maintain team stability and focus on patient care.

Contribution of Self-Regulation to Effective Team Management

Self-regulation, a core aspect of emotional intelligence, involves the ability to manage one's emotions, particularly in stressful situations. For nurse leaders, self-regulation is vital in maintaining a calm and composed demeanor, which can significantly impact the team's ability to function effectively during a crisis.

In the midst of a public health crisis, such as a pandemic, nurse leaders are often required to make quick decisions and manage complex logistical challenges. If a leader is prone to panic or frustration, it can lead to confusion, errors, and a decrease in team morale. However, a leader who can self-regulate will approach these challenges with a clear mind, making rational decisions and providing stable guidance to the team.

For instance, when dealing with a sudden influx of patients during a public health emergency, a nurse leader who practices self-regulation might take a few moments to assess the situation calmly before directing resources and assigning tasks. This measured approach not only prevents rash decisions but also sets a tone of calmness and control that can help the team remain focused and effective.

Role of Social Awareness in Team Management

Social awareness, another key component of emotional intelligence, involves the ability to understand and respond to the emotions of others. For nurse leaders, social awareness is crucial in recognizing the needs, concerns, and emotional states of their team members, which is especially important during a public health crisis when stress levels are high.

A socially aware nurse leader can detect when a team member is overwhelmed or struggling and can offer support or reassign tasks as needed to prevent burnout. This understanding fosters a supportive environment where team members feel valued and cared for, which can enhance overall team performance and resilience.

For example, during an outbreak of a contagious disease, a nurse leader with high social awareness might notice that some team members are particularly anxious about their safety. Recognizing this, the leader could take extra steps to provide reassurance, such as reinforcing safety protocols, offering additional personal protective equipment, or simply providing a space for staff to express their concerns. This attentiveness helps to alleviate anxiety and keeps the team focused on their critical tasks.

Application During a Public Health Crisis

During a public health crisis, the combination of self-regulation and social awareness enables nurse leaders to manage their teams more effectively. Self-regulation allows leaders to navigate the crisis with clear-headedness, making sound decisions without being clouded by stress or emotional reactions. Social awareness, on the other hand, ensures that leaders are attuned to the emotional needs of their team, allowing them to provide the necessary support and maintain high levels of morale and engagement.

For instance, in a scenario where a healthcare facility is overwhelmed by a sudden surge in patients, a nurse leader with strong EI might recognize that the team is nearing its breaking point. By exercising self-regulation, the leader can calmly reassess the situation, perhaps reallocating resources or adjusting shift schedules to better distribute the workload. Simultaneously, social awareness enables the leader to check in with individual team members, providing encouragement, and ensuring that no one feels neglected or unsupported.

This balanced approach, where both the leader's own emotions and the emotions of the team are managed effectively, can make a significant difference in the team's ability to navigate the crisis successfully. It not only helps maintain operational efficiency but also preserves the well-being of the staff, ultimately leading to better patient care and outcomes.

In summary, emotional intelligence, with its components of self-regulation and social awareness, is indispensable for nurse leaders, especially in the context of a public health crisis. It allows leaders to maintain stability, support their teams, and ensure that even in the most challenging circumstances, the highest standards of care are upheld.

Strategies for Building Trust and Credibility Among Diverse Healthcare Teams

1. **Active Listening and Open Communication**
   - **Strategy**: Engage team members in open, two-way communication. Encourage them to express their concerns, ideas, and perspectives without fear of judgment. Use active listening techniques, such as summarizing their points and asking clarifying questions, to ensure understanding.

- o **Application**: In team meetings or one-on-one sessions, a nurse executive could invite feedback on current challenges and genuinely consider input from all levels of staff. This approach not only shows respect for diverse perspectives but also fosters a culture of inclusivity and collaboration.

2. **Consistent and Transparent Decision-Making**
   - o **Strategy**: Make decisions based on clear, consistent criteria that align with the organization's values and mission. When decisions are made, especially those that are difficult or controversial, explain the reasoning behind them openly and honestly.
   - o **Application**: When deciding to allocate resources, a nurse executive might outline the criteria used (e.g., patient safety, staff workload) and share the rationale with the team. Transparency in decision-making helps reduce uncertainty and builds trust in leadership.

3. **Visible Support and Advocacy**
   - o **Strategy**: Act as a visible advocate for team members' professional growth and well-being. Support their needs by providing resources, opportunities for advancement, and recognition of their contributions.
   - o **Application**: A nurse executive could implement a mentorship program where more experienced staff guide newer employees, demonstrating a commitment to both individual and team development.

4. **Cultural Competence and Sensitivity**
   - o **Strategy**: Recognize and respect the diverse cultural backgrounds and values within the team. Tailor communication and leadership approaches to be culturally sensitive and inclusive.
   - o **Application**: When addressing a multicultural team, a nurse executive could consider language preferences, cultural norms, and religious practices to ensure that all team members feel respected and understood. This might involve offering multilingual resources or scheduling meetings around important cultural or religious observances.

5. **Lead by Example**
   - o **Strategy**: Model the behaviors and values that you expect from your team. Demonstrating integrity, accountability, and a strong work ethic sets a standard that others are likely to follow.
   - o **Application**: If the organization is facing budget cuts, a nurse executive might take personal steps to reduce expenses or prioritize front-line staff needs over administrative luxuries. This shows the team that the executive is willing to share in the challenges they face.

Demonstrating Competence and Integrity When Implementing a Controversial New Policy
1. **Thorough Preparation and Expertise**
   - o **Strategy**: Before implementing a controversial policy, thoroughly research its implications, benefits, and potential drawbacks. Demonstrating a deep understanding of the policy and its impact on various stakeholders shows competence.
   - o **Application**: If a nurse executive is introducing a new electronic health record (EHR) system that some staff are resistant to, they could prepare by mastering the system, understanding its long-term benefits, and being ready to address specific concerns with data and evidence. This might involve running pilot programs and gathering feedback from early adopters.

2. **Involving Key Stakeholders Early**
   - o **Strategy**: Involve key stakeholders from the beginning of the policy development process. This not only builds buy-in but also allows the executive to anticipate resistance and address concerns early on.
   - o **Application**: When introducing a policy to change nurse-to-patient ratios, a nurse executive might form a task force of representatives from different departments to provide input and help shape the policy. By involving them in the process, the executive demonstrates a collaborative approach and respects the team's expertise.

3. **Transparency and Open Dialogue**
   - o **Strategy**: Be transparent about the reasons for the policy change, including any external pressures (e.g., regulatory requirements) or internal goals (e.g., improving patient outcomes). Openly discuss the potential challenges and how they will be managed.

- **Application**: A nurse executive could hold town hall meetings or Q&A sessions where staff can voice concerns about the new policy. The executive would respond candidly, acknowledging potential difficulties and outlining steps to mitigate them. This transparency helps build credibility, even when the policy is unpopular.

4. **Ethical Considerations and Fairness**
   - **Strategy**: Ensure that the policy is implemented fairly and ethically, with consideration for how it affects all members of the team and patient care. Address any ethical concerns directly and make adjustments if necessary.
   - **Application**: If a new overtime policy is introduced that might reduce overtime pay, the nurse executive should carefully consider how it affects staff morale and work-life balance. By being upfront about the reasons for the change and offering support, such as flexible scheduling options, the executive demonstrates a commitment to fairness.

5. **Follow-Through and Accountability**
   - **Strategy**: After implementing the policy, monitor its impact and be willing to make adjustments based on feedback and results. Show accountability by taking responsibility for the outcomes, whether positive or negative.
   - **Application**: After rolling out a new staffing policy, the nurse executive might conduct regular reviews to assess its effectiveness and listen to ongoing feedback from staff. If issues arise, the executive should be ready to make necessary changes and communicate these adjustments transparently.

By combining these strategies, a nurse executive can build trust and credibility across diverse teams while demonstrating competence and integrity in the face of challenging or controversial decisions.

Networking and stakeholder management are essential skills for healthcare leaders, particularly nurse executives, who are responsible for influencing and driving change within complex healthcare systems. Effective networking and stakeholder engagement enable nurse leaders to build strategic alliances, garner support for initiatives, and collaborate across sectors to improve population health outcomes.

Importance of Networking and Stakeholder Management in Healthcare Leadership

In healthcare, networking extends beyond internal relationships within an organization; it includes connecting with a broad range of stakeholders such as community leaders, government officials, industry partners, and other healthcare providers. These relationships are vital for advancing organizational goals, securing resources, and implementing health initiatives that require multi-sector collaboration.

Effective stakeholder management allows nurse executives to align the interests of various stakeholders with the mission and vision of their healthcare organization. By understanding and addressing the needs and priorities of different stakeholders, nurse leaders can gain their support and participation, which is crucial for the successful implementation of health programs and policies.

For example, when a hospital is looking to launch a new community health initiative, the success of the project often hinges on the support of local community leaders and government officials. These stakeholders can provide the necessary funding, policy backing, and community buy-in needed to implement the initiative effectively.

Engaging with Community Leaders

Community leaders are pivotal in shaping public opinion and mobilizing local resources. Nurse executives can engage with these leaders by participating in community events, serving on local boards, or collaborating on health-related projects. Building strong relationships with community leaders can help nurse executives gain insight into the health needs and concerns of the population, enabling them to tailor services and programs more effectively.

For instance, a nurse executive aiming to reduce diabetes rates in a community might partner with local religious leaders who can help disseminate health information and encourage participation in screening and educational programs. By involving community leaders in the planning and implementation process, the nurse executive can ensure the program is culturally sensitive and more likely to be embraced by the community.

Collaborating with Government Officials

Government officials, at both the local and state levels, play a significant role in healthcare through the regulation of services, allocation of funds, and implementation of public health policies. Nurse executives can effectively engage with government officials by participating in policy discussions, providing testimony on healthcare issues, and advocating for policies that align with their organization's goals.

For example, during the COVID-19 pandemic, many nurse executives worked closely with government officials to coordinate the distribution of vaccines and ensure that vulnerable populations received timely care. By establishing strong lines of communication with government officials, nurse executives can influence public health policies and secure the necessary support for large-scale health initiatives.

Partnering with Industry

Industry partners, including pharmaceutical companies, medical device manufacturers, and health technology firms, are crucial stakeholders in healthcare. These partnerships can provide access to new technologies, funding for research, and innovative solutions to healthcare challenges.

Nurse executives can engage industry partners by participating in joint ventures, attending industry conferences, and exploring opportunities for collaboration on research and development projects. For instance, a nurse executive might partner with a health technology company to pilot a telehealth program aimed at improving access to care in rural areas. Through such collaborations, nurse executives can bring cutting-edge solutions to their organizations, enhancing the quality of care and improving population health outcomes.

Strategies for Effective Stakeholder Engagement

1. **Identify Key Stakeholders:** The first step in effective stakeholder management is to identify the key stakeholders who have a vested interest in the outcome of a health initiative. This includes internal stakeholders such as staff and physicians, as well as external stakeholders like community leaders, government officials, and industry partners.
2. **Build and Maintain Relationships:** Establishing trust and rapport with stakeholders is critical. Nurse executives should engage in regular communication, attend relevant meetings and events, and demonstrate a genuine interest in the concerns and priorities of their stakeholders.
3. **Align Goals and Interests:** To gain stakeholder support, nurse executives must align their organization's goals with the interests of the stakeholders. This might involve finding common ground on issues such as improving access to care, reducing healthcare costs, or addressing social determinants of health.
4. **Communicate Clearly and Transparently:** Transparent communication is key to building trust and managing expectations. Nurse executives should provide regular updates on the progress of initiatives, share data and results, and be open about challenges and setbacks.
5. **Leverage Stakeholder Expertise:** Stakeholders often bring valuable expertise and resources to the table. Nurse executives should actively seek input from stakeholders during the planning and implementation of initiatives, ensuring that their perspectives are considered and incorporated.

Improving Population Health Outcomes Through Stakeholder Engagement

Effective engagement with stakeholders can lead to significant improvements in population health outcomes. By leveraging the expertise, resources, and influence of community leaders, government officials, and industry partners, nurse executives can implement comprehensive health initiatives that address the root causes of health disparities and promote long-term wellness.

For example, a nurse executive leading a campaign to reduce childhood obesity might collaborate with local schools, government agencies, and food industry partners to implement a multi-faceted program that includes nutrition education, physical activity initiatives, and changes to school meal programs. By coordinating efforts across different sectors, the nurse executive can create a more impactful and sustainable program that reaches a larger segment of the population.

In summary, networking and stakeholder management are essential skills for nurse executives aiming to improve population health outcomes. By effectively engaging with community leaders, government officials, and industry partners, nurse executives can build the coalitions necessary to drive meaningful change in healthcare.

Relationship-centered care (RCC) significantly enhances patient satisfaction and health outcomes by emphasizing the quality of the interactions between healthcare providers, patients, and their families. This approach shifts the focus from a purely biomedical model to one that acknowledges the importance of emotional, social, and psychological factors in the healing process.

Impact of Relationship-Centered Care on Patient Satisfaction and Health Outcomes

1. **Enhanced Patient Satisfaction**

- o **Empathy and Understanding**: Patients who feel understood and cared for are more likely to express higher satisfaction levels. RCC fosters empathetic communication, where providers actively listen, validate patients' feelings, and engage in meaningful dialogue. This helps patients feel valued and respected, which directly contributes to their overall satisfaction with care.
- o **Personalized Care**: RCC enables personalized care plans tailored to the individual's unique needs and preferences. When patients are involved in their care decisions, they are more likely to adhere to treatment plans, leading to better health outcomes. For example, a patient with chronic illness might feel more motivated to manage their condition if they feel their concerns are genuinely heard and addressed by their healthcare team.

2. **Improved Health Outcomes**
   - o **Stronger Patient-Provider Relationships**: Strong relationships between patients and healthcare providers lead to better communication, which in turn improves diagnosis accuracy, treatment adherence, and follow-up care. For instance, a patient who trusts their nurse is more likely to disclose important information, such as non-adherence to medication, allowing for timely intervention.
   - o **Reduction in Readmission Rates**: RCC can reduce hospital readmission rates by ensuring that patients fully understand their discharge instructions and feel comfortable reaching out to their healthcare team if issues arise. Effective communication and patient engagement help prevent complications that might otherwise lead to readmissions.
   - o **Better Mental Health and Well-being**: By addressing the emotional and psychological needs of patients, RCC reduces anxiety, stress, and depression, which are often associated with chronic illness or hospitalization. Patients who feel emotionally supported are more likely to experience positive health outcomes, as stress and anxiety can negatively impact recovery.

Fostering a Culture of Empathetic Communication and Patient Engagement

1. **Lead by Example**
   - o **Nurse Executives' Role**: Nurse executives should model empathetic communication and relationship-building in their interactions with staff and patients. By demonstrating these behaviors, they set a standard for others to follow. For instance, regularly engaging with front-line staff and showing genuine concern for their well-being can inspire similar behavior towards patients.
   - o **Personal Engagement**: Executives can take time to visit patient care areas, listen to patient stories, and engage in conversations with both patients and families. This not only reinforces the importance of RCC but also provides executives with firsthand insights into patient experiences.

2. **Training and Education**
   - o **Communication Skills Training**: Implement ongoing training programs focused on developing communication skills, including active listening, empathy, and conflict resolution. Role-playing scenarios can be particularly effective, allowing staff to practice these skills in a safe environment.
   - o **Patient-Centered Care Workshops**: Offer workshops that educate staff on the principles of RCC and how to apply them in daily practice. These sessions can include real-life examples and testimonials from patients, illustrating the impact of empathetic care.

3. **Interdisciplinary Collaboration**
   - o **Team-Based Approach**: Encourage collaboration across disciplines to ensure that all aspects of a patient's care are coordinated and that communication remains consistent. Regular interdisciplinary meetings can help align team members on RCC goals and patient-centered care strategies.
   - o **Shared Decision-Making**: Promote shared decision-making practices, where patients are actively involved in their care choices alongside their healthcare team. This can be facilitated by creating care plans that reflect patient preferences and by involving patients in care conferences.

4. **Supportive Work Environment**
   - o **Creating a Compassionate Culture**: Cultivate a work environment that values and rewards compassionate care. Recognize and celebrate staff members who exemplify empathetic

communication and patient engagement. This could be done through awards, public recognition, or professional development opportunities.
- o **Staff Well-being Programs**: Implement programs that support the emotional and mental well-being of staff, such as mindfulness training, counseling services, and stress management workshops. When staff feel supported, they are better equipped to provide compassionate care to patients.

5. **Patient Feedback and Involvement**
   - o **Patient Advisory Councils**: Establish patient advisory councils to gather feedback on care practices and involve patients in the development of policies and procedures that affect their care. This not only improves care practices but also strengthens the bond between patients and providers.
   - o **Regular Surveys and Follow-Ups**: Conduct regular patient satisfaction surveys that specifically assess the quality of communication and relationship-building efforts. Use this feedback to make continuous improvements in care delivery.

6. **Technology Integration**
   - o **Use of Patient Portals**: Encourage the use of patient portals where patients can communicate with their healthcare providers, access their medical records, and participate in their care plans. These tools can enhance engagement by making it easier for patients to stay informed and involved in their care.
   - o **Telehealth and Remote Monitoring**: Leverage telehealth to maintain regular communication with patients, especially those with chronic conditions. Remote monitoring devices can also be used to keep track of patients' health status and engage them in their care.

By integrating these strategies, nurse executives can foster a culture that prioritizes empathetic communication and patient engagement, leading to higher patient satisfaction and better health outcomes. This approach not only benefits patients but also enhances the overall quality of care provided by the healthcare organization.

SWOT Analysis for a Hypothetical Rural Hospital

Strengths

1. **Strong Community Ties:** The hospital has deep-rooted connections with the local community, fostering trust and loyalty among residents.
2. **Dedicated Staff:** Despite staffing shortages, the existing staff is committed, often going above and beyond their duties to provide quality care.
3. **Critical Access Designation:** The hospital benefits from a critical access designation, which provides enhanced Medicare reimbursement rates.
4. **Niche Services:** The hospital offers specialized services not readily available in the region, such as telehealth for chronic disease management, which is highly valued by the community.

Weaknesses

1. **Financial Instability:** The hospital is struggling with cash flow issues, high operational costs, and declining reimbursements, leading to significant financial strain.
2. **Staffing Shortages:** Chronic understaffing, particularly in nursing and specialized roles, is leading to burnout and potentially impacting the quality of care.
3. **Aging Infrastructure:** The hospital's facilities and equipment are outdated, requiring significant investment to meet modern healthcare standards.
4. **Limited Access to Advanced Technology:** The hospital lacks access to the latest medical technologies and electronic health records (EHR) systems, hindering operational efficiency and patient care.

Opportunities

1. **Telehealth Expansion:** There is growing demand for telehealth services, which could help the hospital reach more patients and reduce operational costs.
2. **Partnerships with Larger Healthcare Systems:** Forming strategic alliances with larger hospitals or healthcare networks could bring in resources, expertise, and potentially improve financial stability.
3. **Grant Funding and Government Support:** The hospital could pursue federal or state grants aimed at supporting rural healthcare facilities, particularly for infrastructure upgrades and staff training.

4. **Community Health Initiatives:** The hospital could lead preventive care and wellness programs that address local health issues, which may attract additional funding and improve population health outcomes.

Threats

1. **Increased Competition:** Nearby hospitals or urgent care centers may draw patients away, particularly if they offer more advanced services or better facilities.
2. **Regulatory Changes:** Potential changes in healthcare policy or reimbursement structures could further strain the hospital's financial situation.
3. **Continued Staff Attrition:** Ongoing staffing challenges could lead to further burnout, increased turnover, and ultimately, compromised patient care.
4. **Economic Downturn:** A worsening local or national economy could reduce patient volumes and lead to increased uncompensated care, exacerbating financial difficulties.

Prioritizing Strategies Based on the SWOT Analysis

1. **Address Staffing Shortages (Critical and Immediate Priority)**
   - **Strategy:** Focus on recruiting and retaining staff, particularly in critical areas such as nursing and specialized care. Consider offering competitive salaries, signing bonuses, flexible scheduling, and professional development opportunities. Additionally, implementing well-being programs to reduce burnout could help retain current staff.
   - **Rationale:** Staffing is directly linked to patient care quality and staff morale. Resolving this issue will stabilize operations and reduce the risk of further staff attrition, which is crucial for maintaining patient safety and service quality.

2. **Expand Telehealth Services (High Priority)**
   - **Strategy:** Invest in expanding telehealth capabilities, particularly for chronic disease management and mental health services. This can be done through partnerships with technology providers or leveraging government grants aimed at enhancing rural healthcare infrastructure.
   - **Rationale:** Telehealth can alleviate some of the operational pressures by extending care without the need for additional physical infrastructure or extensive staffing increases. It also opens new revenue streams by attracting patients from a broader geographic area.

3. **Seek Partnerships with Larger Healthcare Systems (Strategic Priority)**
   - **Strategy:** Actively pursue affiliations or partnerships with larger healthcare systems that can provide financial support, shared services, and access to advanced medical technologies. This might include joint ventures, shared service agreements, or becoming part of a larger health network.
   - **Rationale:** Partnerships can bring much-needed resources, including capital for infrastructure improvements, access to advanced technologies, and specialized staff, thereby enhancing the hospital's service offerings and operational efficiency.

4. **Pursue Grant Funding for Infrastructure and Technology Upgrades (Moderate Priority)**
   - **Strategy:** Identify and apply for federal and state grants that are available for rural healthcare facilities, focusing on funds that support infrastructure improvements, technology upgrades, and staff training programs.
   - **Rationale:** Securing grants can help address the hospital's aging infrastructure and outdated technology without further straining its financial resources. Upgrading these areas is essential for long-term viability and improving patient care standards.

5. **Develop Community Health Initiatives (Long-Term Priority)**
   - **Strategy:** Launch community health initiatives focused on preventive care, such as wellness programs, health screenings, and education on managing chronic diseases. These programs can be developed in partnership with local organizations, schools, and public health agencies.
   - **Rationale:** By addressing prevalent local health issues, the hospital can improve overall community health outcomes, potentially reducing the demand for acute care services and enhancing its role as a community health leader. This could also attract additional funding and support from local and state governments.

Implementation Approach

Given the pressing financial challenges and staffing shortages, the hospital should first stabilize its operations by addressing these critical issues. The focus should then shift to strategic growth areas such as telehealth and partnerships, which have the potential to improve financial stability and service offerings. Lastly, long-term strategies like community health initiatives and infrastructure upgrades should be pursued to ensure sustained growth and relevance in the community.

By prioritizing these strategies based on the SWOT analysis, the hospital can create a roadmap to overcome its challenges, enhance its strengths, and capitalize on emerging opportunities, ultimately ensuring its long-term survival and success in the rural healthcare landscape.

Balanced Scorecard Design for a Large Urban Healthcare System

A Balanced Scorecard (BSC) is a strategic management tool that helps organizations translate their mission and vision into actionable goals across four key perspectives: Financial, Customer, Internal Processes, and Learning and Growth. Below is a comprehensive BSC tailored for a large urban healthcare system, with an emphasis on aligning key performance indicators (KPIs) to the organization's mission and vision.

Mission Statement

"To provide high-quality, compassionate care to our diverse urban community while advancing medical knowledge through research and education."

Vision Statement

"To be a leader in innovative healthcare delivery, improving the health of our community through exceptional service, cutting-edge research, and continuous professional development."

1. Financial Perspective

Objective: Ensure the financial health and sustainability of the healthcare system while supporting its growth and innovation goals.

Key Performance Indicators (KPIs):

- **Operating Margin**: Target a specific percentage to ensure profitability while reinvesting in patient care and innovation.
- **Cost per Patient Visit**: Track and reduce costs through efficiency improvements without compromising care quality.
- **Revenue Growth Rate**: Monitor year-over-year revenue increases, focusing on expanding services in high-demand areas.
- **Return on Investment (ROI) in Technology and Infrastructure**: Evaluate the financial returns from investments in new technologies and facilities.

Alignment with Mission and Vision:

- The financial KPIs ensure that the healthcare system remains financially robust, enabling it to invest in cutting-edge research and provide high-quality care. A strong operating margin and controlled costs support the mission of delivering compassionate care sustainably.

2. Customer Perspective

Objective: Enhance patient satisfaction and improve community health outcomes by delivering high-quality, accessible care.

Key Performance Indicators (KPIs):

- **Patient Satisfaction Scores**: Measure patient satisfaction using surveys (e.g., HCAHPS) to assess the quality of care and patient experience.
- **Patient Retention Rate**: Monitor the percentage of patients who return for future care, indicating trust and satisfaction with services.
- **Community Health Improvement Metrics**: Track health outcomes in the community, such as reduced rates of chronic disease or improved vaccination rates.
- **Access to Care**: Measure wait times for appointments and emergency services to ensure timely care delivery.

Alignment with Mission and Vision:

- These KPIs reflect the healthcare system's commitment to compassionate, high-quality care that meets the needs of a diverse urban population. Improving patient satisfaction and community health aligns directly with the mission to serve the community and the vision of being a leader in healthcare delivery.

3. Internal Process Perspective

Objective: Streamline and optimize internal processes to enhance efficiency, quality of care, and patient safety.

Key Performance Indicators (KPIs):

- **Patient Throughput**: Measure the time from patient admission to discharge, aiming to reduce bottlenecks and improve care flow.
- **Clinical Error Rate**: Track and reduce the incidence of medical errors, enhancing patient safety.
- **Process Improvement Implementation Rate**: Monitor the adoption of Lean, Six Sigma, or other process improvement initiatives.
- **EHR Utilization and Data Accuracy**: Ensure that electronic health records (EHRs) are used effectively, with high data accuracy and completeness.

Alignment with Mission and Vision:

- By optimizing internal processes, the healthcare system can provide efficient, safe, and high-quality care, supporting its mission of improving community health. The focus on reducing errors and improving throughput aligns with the vision of leading innovative healthcare delivery.

4. Learning and Growth Perspective

Objective: Foster a culture of continuous learning, innovation, and professional development to support staff and advance medical research.

Key Performance Indicators (KPIs):

- **Staff Training and Certification Rates**: Track the percentage of staff who complete ongoing education, certifications, and specialized training programs.
- **Employee Engagement and Satisfaction Scores**: Measure staff satisfaction and engagement levels to ensure a motivated and committed workforce.
- **Innovation in Research and Clinical Practice**: Monitor the number of new research projects, publications, and clinical trials initiated.
- **Leadership Development Program Participation**: Track participation in programs aimed at developing future healthcare leaders within the organization.

Alignment with Mission and Vision:

- These KPIs ensure that the healthcare system supports its staff in achieving professional excellence and fosters an environment conducive to innovation and research. This directly aligns with the mission of advancing medical knowledge and the vision of continuous professional development.

Aligning Key Performance Indicators with the Organization's Mission and Vision

Mission Alignment:

- **Financial Perspective**: Financial stability enables the healthcare system to sustain its mission of providing high-quality care and supporting research.
- **Customer Perspective**: KPIs related to patient satisfaction and community health ensure that the healthcare system meets its commitment to compassionate, patient-centered care.
- **Internal Process Perspective**: Streamlined processes contribute to efficient and safe care delivery, reinforcing the mission to serve the community effectively.
- **Learning and Growth Perspective**: Continuous professional development and innovation support the mission of advancing medical knowledge and improving care quality.

Vision Alignment:

- **Financial Perspective**: Financial health allows for investment in the latest technologies and facilities, positioning the organization as a leader in healthcare delivery.
- **Customer Perspective**: High patient satisfaction and improved health outcomes support the vision of exceptional service and leadership in community health.

- **Internal Process Perspective**: Efficient, innovative processes position the healthcare system as a leader in cutting-edge care delivery.
- **Learning and Growth Perspective**: A focus on staff development and research advances the healthcare system's vision of fostering innovation and continuous improvement in healthcare.

By carefully selecting and aligning KPIs with the organization's mission and vision, the Balanced Scorecard not only drives performance but also ensures that every aspect of the healthcare system is working towards the same strategic goals.

Scenario 1: Technological Transformation and Personalized Care
Overview:
In this scenario, healthcare delivery is revolutionized by rapid advancements in technology, particularly in artificial intelligence (AI), genomics, and telemedicine. These technologies enable highly personalized care, where treatments are tailored to individual genetic profiles, and AI-driven diagnostics and decision support systems enhance clinical accuracy. Telemedicine becomes the norm, supported by widespread adoption of 5G networks and advanced health monitoring devices.

Key Features:

AI and Machine Learning: AI tools are integrated into all levels of care, from diagnostics to treatment planning and patient monitoring. Machine learning algorithms predict patient outcomes, optimize resource allocation, and support personalized treatment plans.
Genomic Medicine: Widespread use of genetic testing allows for personalized medicine, where treatments are customized based on individual genetic profiles. Preventive care is enhanced by early identification of genetic predispositions to diseases.
Telemedicine and Remote Monitoring: Telehealth services expand significantly, with patients receiving care at home through virtual consultations, remote monitoring devices, and home-based diagnostic tools. The integration of wearable health tech allows continuous monitoring of vital signs and health metrics, feeding real-time data to healthcare providers.
Strategic Implications for a Multi-Hospital System:

Invest in AI and Data Analytics: To stay competitive, the system must invest in AI and data analytics capabilities. This includes training staff to work with AI tools and integrating these technologies into clinical workflows.
Expand Telehealth Infrastructure: Strengthen and expand telemedicine platforms, ensuring that all hospitals within the system can provide consistent, high-quality remote care. Consider forming partnerships with tech companies to stay at the forefront of telehealth advancements.
Develop Genomic Medicine Programs: Establish or expand genomic medicine departments, offering personalized care plans and preventive services. This could involve partnering with academic institutions for research and development in genomics.
Redesign Care Delivery Models: With more care happening remotely, the system might need to rethink physical infrastructure needs, potentially downsizing some facilities or repurposing spaces to focus on high-tech diagnostic and treatment centers.
Scenario 2: Aging Population and Chronic Disease Management
Overview:
This scenario anticipates significant demographic shifts, with an aging population leading to a dramatic increase in the prevalence of chronic diseases such as diabetes, heart disease, and dementia. Healthcare systems are increasingly focused on managing these chronic conditions, with an emphasis on integrated care models, preventive health, and community-based services.

Key Features:

Integrated Care Models: Care delivery shifts to a model that emphasizes coordination across multiple care settings, including primary care, specialists, home care, and community services. Patient-centered medical homes (PCMHs) and accountable care organizations (ACOs) become more prevalent.

Preventive Health Programs: There is a strong focus on preventive care, with widespread community health initiatives aimed at reducing the incidence of chronic diseases through lifestyle interventions, regular screenings, and early detection programs.

Geriatric Care and Long-Term Services: Demand for geriatric care, long-term care facilities, and in-home support services surges. Healthcare systems must adapt to meet the complex needs of older adults, including managing multiple comorbidities and providing end-of-life care.

Strategic Implications for a Multi-Hospital System:

Enhance Chronic Disease Management: Develop or expand chronic disease management programs, including specialized clinics, care coordination services, and remote monitoring for patients with long-term conditions. This may involve integrating more community-based services and outpatient care.

Invest in Geriatric Care: Expand geriatric services, including creating centers of excellence in geriatric medicine, training staff in geriatrics, and collaborating with long-term care providers. Consider building or acquiring facilities dedicated to elderly care.

Focus on Preventive Health: Implement community health initiatives that target chronic disease prevention, working closely with local governments, non-profits, and public health organizations. These initiatives could include health education campaigns, free screening events, and partnerships with local businesses to promote healthy lifestyles.

Adapt Infrastructure for Integrated Care: Redesign care delivery models to support integrated care, potentially establishing more PCMHs or ACOs within the hospital system. This would require creating a seamless flow of information and coordination between different care providers.

Scenario 3: Regulatory and Policy Overhaul

Overview:

In this scenario, significant policy changes occur at the national and state levels, driven by a push for universal healthcare coverage and cost containment. New regulations mandate value-based care, increased transparency in pricing, and stricter oversight of healthcare providers. These changes force healthcare systems to adapt quickly to new payment models and compliance requirements.

Key Features:

Value-Based Care: Payment models shift from fee-for-service to value-based care, where providers are reimbursed based on patient outcomes and cost-efficiency. Bundled payments, accountable care, and performance incentives become the norm.

Price Transparency and Consumer Empowerment: Regulations enforce greater transparency in healthcare pricing, making it easier for patients to compare costs and quality across providers. This leads to increased competition and pressure on hospitals to improve efficiency and patient satisfaction.

Expanded Government Healthcare Programs: Universal coverage is implemented or expanded, leading to increased patient volumes, particularly among previously uninsured or underinsured populations. Hospitals must navigate complex reimbursement structures and ensure compliance with new standards.

Strategic Implications for a Multi-Hospital System:

Shift to Value-Based Care: Invest in data analytics and care management systems that support value-based care. This includes tracking patient outcomes, managing care coordination, and optimizing resource use to meet the requirements of new payment models.

Enhance Cost Efficiency: Focus on reducing operational costs while maintaining or improving quality. This might involve streamlining administrative processes, renegotiating supplier contracts, or investing in technologies that reduce waste and improve efficiency.

Improve Patient Experience: With increased transparency and consumer choice, the hospital system must prioritize patient experience. This includes improving communication, reducing wait times, and enhancing the overall patient journey from admission to discharge.

Navigate Regulatory Compliance: Strengthen compliance programs to ensure the hospital system meets new regulatory requirements. This could involve regular audits, staff training, and investing in compliance management software.

Strategic Planning Based on Scenarios

For a multi-hospital system, strategic planning should be flexible and adaptive, accounting for the potential impacts of these scenarios. A few key strategies might include:

Scenario Planning: Develop detailed contingency plans for each scenario, ensuring the system can pivot quickly as external conditions change. This includes financial planning, resource allocation, and staff training tailored to each possible future.

Invest in Versatile Infrastructure: Build or upgrade facilities with versatility in mind, allowing them to adapt to different care delivery models, whether technology-driven or focused on chronic disease management.

Foster Strategic Partnerships: Form alliances with technology firms, government bodies, and community organizations to strengthen the system's capacity to respond to technological, demographic, or policy changes.

Focus on Workforce Development: Regardless of the scenario, a well-trained, adaptable workforce will be crucial. Invest in continuous education and skills development to prepare staff for new technologies, care models, and regulatory requirements.

By preparing for these diverse scenarios, a multi-hospital system can ensure resilience and remain well-positioned to provide high-quality care in the evolving healthcare landscape. **Scenario 1: Technological Transformation and Personalized Care**

Overview:

In this scenario, healthcare delivery is revolutionized by rapid advancements in technology, particularly in artificial intelligence (AI), genomics, and telemedicine. These technologies enable highly personalized care, where treatments are tailored to individual genetic profiles, and AI-driven diagnostics and decision support systems enhance clinical accuracy. Telemedicine becomes the norm, supported by widespread adoption of 5G networks and advanced health monitoring devices.

Key Features:

- **AI and Machine Learning:** AI tools are integrated into all levels of care, from diagnostics to treatment planning and patient monitoring. Machine learning algorithms predict patient outcomes, optimize resource allocation, and support personalized treatment plans.
- **Genomic Medicine:** Widespread use of genetic testing allows for personalized medicine, where treatments are customized based on individual genetic profiles. Preventive care is enhanced by early identification of genetic predispositions to diseases.
- **Telemedicine and Remote Monitoring:** Telehealth services expand significantly, with patients receiving care at home through virtual consultations, remote monitoring devices, and home-based diagnostic tools. The integration of wearable health tech allows continuous monitoring of vital signs and health metrics, feeding real-time data to healthcare providers.

Strategic Implications for a Multi-Hospital System:

- **Invest in AI and Data Analytics:** To stay competitive, the system must invest in AI and data analytics capabilities. This includes training staff to work with AI tools and integrating these technologies into clinical workflows.
- **Expand Telehealth Infrastructure:** Strengthen and expand telemedicine platforms, ensuring that all hospitals within the system can provide consistent, high-quality remote care. Consider forming partnerships with tech companies to stay at the forefront of telehealth advancements.
- **Develop Genomic Medicine Programs:** Establish or expand genomic medicine departments, offering personalized care plans and preventive services. This could involve partnering with academic institutions for research and development in genomics.
- **Redesign Care Delivery Models:** With more care happening remotely, the system might need to rethink physical infrastructure needs, potentially downsizing some facilities or repurposing spaces to focus on high-tech diagnostic and treatment centers.

Scenario 2: Aging Population and Chronic Disease Management

Overview:

This scenario anticipates significant demographic shifts, with an aging population leading to a dramatic increase in the prevalence of chronic diseases such as diabetes, heart disease, and dementia. Healthcare systems are increasingly focused on managing these chronic conditions, with an emphasis on integrated care models, preventive health, and community-based services.

Key Features:

- **Integrated Care Models:** Care delivery shifts to a model that emphasizes coordination across multiple care settings, including primary care, specialists, home care, and community services. Patient-centered medical homes (PCMHs) and accountable care organizations (ACOs) become more prevalent.
- **Preventive Health Programs:** There is a strong focus on preventive care, with widespread community health initiatives aimed at reducing the incidence of chronic diseases through lifestyle interventions, regular screenings, and early detection programs.
- **Geriatric Care and Long-Term Services:** Demand for geriatric care, long-term care facilities, and in-home support services surges. Healthcare systems must adapt to meet the complex needs of older adults, including managing multiple comorbidities and providing end-of-life care.

Strategic Implications for a Multi-Hospital System:

- **Enhance Chronic Disease Management:** Develop or expand chronic disease management programs, including specialized clinics, care coordination services, and remote monitoring for patients with long-term conditions. This may involve integrating more community-based services and outpatient care.
- **Invest in Geriatric Care:** Expand geriatric services, including creating centers of excellence in geriatric medicine, training staff in geriatrics, and collaborating with long-term care providers. Consider building or acquiring facilities dedicated to elderly care.
- **Focus on Preventive Health:** Implement community health initiatives that target chronic disease prevention, working closely with local governments, non-profits, and public health organizations. These initiatives could include health education campaigns, free screening events, and partnerships with local businesses to promote healthy lifestyles.
- **Adapt Infrastructure for Integrated Care:** Redesign care delivery models to support integrated care, potentially establishing more PCMHs or ACOs within the hospital system. This would require creating a seamless flow of information and coordination between different care providers.

Scenario 3: Regulatory and Policy Overhaul

Overview:

In this scenario, significant policy changes occur at the national and state levels, driven by a push for universal healthcare coverage and cost containment. New regulations mandate value-based care, increased transparency in pricing, and stricter oversight of healthcare providers. These changes force healthcare systems to adapt quickly to new payment models and compliance requirements.

Key Features:

- **Value-Based Care:** Payment models shift from fee-for-service to value-based care, where providers are reimbursed based on patient outcomes and cost-efficiency. Bundled payments, accountable care, and performance incentives become the norm.
- **Price Transparency and Consumer Empowerment:** Regulations enforce greater transparency in healthcare pricing, making it easier for patients to compare costs and quality across providers. This leads to increased competition and pressure on hospitals to improve efficiency and patient satisfaction.
- **Expanded Government Healthcare Programs:** Universal coverage is implemented or expanded, leading to increased patient volumes, particularly among previously uninsured or underinsured populations. Hospitals must navigate complex reimbursement structures and ensure compliance with new standards.

Strategic Implications for a Multi-Hospital System:

- **Shift to Value-Based Care:** Invest in data analytics and care management systems that support value-based care. This includes tracking patient outcomes, managing care coordination, and optimizing resource use to meet the requirements of new payment models.

- **Enhance Cost Efficiency:** Focus on reducing operational costs while maintaining or improving quality. This might involve streamlining administrative processes, renegotiating supplier contracts, or investing in technologies that reduce waste and improve efficiency.
- **Improve Patient Experience:** With increased transparency and consumer choice, the hospital system must prioritize patient experience. This includes improving communication, reducing wait times, and enhancing the overall patient journey from admission to discharge.
- **Navigate Regulatory Compliance:** Strengthen compliance programs to ensure the hospital system meets new regulatory requirements. This could involve regular audits, staff training, and investing in compliance management software.

Strategic Planning Based on Scenarios

For a multi-hospital system, strategic planning should be flexible and adaptive, accounting for the potential impacts of these scenarios. A few key strategies might include:

1. **Scenario Planning:** Develop detailed contingency plans for each scenario, ensuring the system can pivot quickly as external conditions change. This includes financial planning, resource allocation, and staff training tailored to each possible future.
2. **Invest in Versatile Infrastructure:** Build or upgrade facilities with versatility in mind, allowing them to adapt to different care delivery models, whether technology-driven or focused on chronic disease management.
3. **Foster Strategic Partnerships:** Form alliances with technology firms, government bodies, and community organizations to strengthen the system's capacity to respond to technological, demographic, or policy changes.
4. **Focus on Workforce Development:** Regardless of the scenario, a well-trained, adaptable workforce will be crucial. Invest in continuous education and skills development to prepare staff for new technologies, care models, and regulatory requirements.

By preparing for these diverse scenarios, a multi-hospital system can ensure resilience and remain well-positioned to provide high-quality care in the evolving healthcare landscape.

Long-term strategic planning and **agile strategic management** are two distinct approaches to guiding an organization's direction, particularly relevant in the dynamic field of healthcare. Both have unique strengths and challenges, and understanding how they differ can help nurse executives balance stability and adaptability in their organizations.

Long-Term Strategic Planning in Healthcare

Characteristics:

- **Time Horizon:** Typically involves planning over 3 to 10 years, focusing on long-term goals and objectives.
- **Predictability:** Assumes a relatively stable environment where future trends can be forecasted with some certainty.
- **Structure:** Highly structured, with detailed plans that outline specific initiatives, resource allocation, and timelines.
- **Commitment:** Significant investments in resources, including time and finances, are committed based on long-term goals.
- **Implementation:** Follows a linear approach—plan, implement, monitor, and adjust as needed based on periodic reviews.

Advantages:

- **Stability:** Provides a clear, stable framework for decision-making, helping align resources and efforts toward achieving the organization's mission and vision.
- **Comprehensive Planning:** Allows for in-depth analysis of trends, risks, and opportunities, enabling a thorough approach to resource allocation, infrastructure development, and workforce planning.
- **Long-Term Focus:** Encourages the development of sustainable initiatives, such as long-term partnerships, capital investments in new facilities, or major technology upgrades.

Challenges:

- **Rigidity**: Can be inflexible, making it difficult to adapt quickly to unexpected changes, such as new regulations, technological advancements, or public health crises.
- **Risk of Obsolescence**: Long-term plans may become outdated as healthcare environments change rapidly, potentially leading to the pursuit of goals that are no longer relevant or optimal.

Agile Strategic Management in Healthcare

Characteristics:

- **Time Horizon**: Focuses on short-term cycles, often ranging from 3 to 12 months, with continuous reassessment and adaptation.
- **Adaptability**: Designed to respond quickly to changes in the external environment, including shifts in patient needs, regulatory changes, and technological advancements.
- **Flexibility**: Emphasizes flexible, iterative processes that allow for ongoing adjustments based on feedback and evolving conditions.
- **Empowerment**: Encourages decentralized decision-making, where teams at different levels have the autonomy to make decisions and pivot as needed.
- **Implementation**: Involves iterative cycles of planning, implementing, assessing, and adjusting, often using methodologies like Lean or Scrum.

Advantages:

- **Adaptability**: Allows healthcare organizations to respond quickly to changes, such as a sudden increase in patient volume or the emergence of new healthcare technologies.
- **Innovation**: Fosters a culture of continuous improvement, where teams are encouraged to experiment with new ideas and rapidly implement successful innovations.
- **Patient-Centered Care**: Enhances the ability to meet changing patient needs, as care models and practices can be adjusted in real-time based on patient feedback and outcomes.

Challenges:

- **Potential for Disruption**: Frequent changes and adjustments can lead to confusion and burnout among staff if not managed carefully.
- **Short-Term Focus**: Risk of neglecting long-term goals in favor of short-term gains, potentially undermining the organization's strategic direction.
- **Resource Allocation**: Requires careful management to avoid overcommitting resources to initiatives that may change or be abandoned quickly.

Balancing Stability with Adaptability in Healthcare

Nurse executives must navigate the tension between the need for long-term stability and the necessity of being agile in response to rapid changes. Here's how they can balance these approaches:

1. **Hybrid Strategic Framework**:
   - **Strategy with Flexibility**: Nurse executives can develop a long-term strategic plan that includes flexible components designed for agile adjustment. For example, a 5-year plan might outline overarching goals and vision, while shorter-term objectives are set in more adaptable 6- to 12-month increments.
   - **Scenario Planning**: Incorporate scenario planning within long-term strategies to prepare for multiple potential futures. This allows the organization to pivot quickly if certain scenarios begin to unfold, combining stability with preparedness.

2. **Dynamic Resource Allocation**:
   - **Core vs. Discretionary Resources**: Allocate core resources to initiatives that require stability, such as essential services and infrastructure, while keeping discretionary resources available for agile projects. This ensures that the organization can maintain its baseline operations while still being able to invest in new opportunities as they arise.
   - **Rapid Response Teams**: Establish teams dedicated to agile management who can quickly address emerging issues, such as a public health crisis or a new regulatory requirement. These teams can operate within the framework of the long-term strategy but are empowered to act swiftly when needed.

3. **Continuous Feedback Loops:**
   - **Real-Time Data Utilization**: Implement systems that provide real-time data on patient outcomes, staff performance, and operational efficiency. Nurse executives can use this data to make informed decisions and adjust strategies as needed without waiting for annual reviews.
   - **Employee and Patient Feedback**: Regularly collect and act on feedback from both patients and staff. This helps ensure that the healthcare system remains responsive to needs as they evolve, fostering an environment of continuous improvement.
4. **Leadership and Communication:**
   - **Clear Vision with Open Communication**: Communicate the long-term vision clearly while also explaining the need for agile adjustments. Nurse executives should articulate how short-term changes align with the long-term goals, helping staff understand and buy into both stability and adaptability.
   - **Empowerment and Support**: Empower leaders at all levels to make decisions that align with the organization's agile strategies. Provide the necessary training and resources to support them in making quick, effective decisions.
5. **Cultivating a Culture of Innovation:**
   - **Encourage Experimentation**: Create an organizational culture that encourages experimentation and learning from failures. This can be done through pilot projects or innovation labs where new ideas can be tested and scaled up if successful.
   - **Balance Innovation with Tradition**: While fostering innovation, also celebrate and maintain the core values and practices that provide stability. This dual focus ensures that the organization remains grounded while also evolving.

By integrating elements of both long-term strategic planning and agile strategic management, nurse executives can create a healthcare environment that is both stable in its mission and vision yet adaptable to the rapid changes characteristic of the healthcare industry. This balance enables the organization to meet immediate challenges while staying on course for long-term success.

Implementing a new electronic health record (EHR) system across a healthcare network is a complex undertaking that requires careful planning, effective leadership, and proactive management of resistance. Kotter's 8-Step Change Model provides a structured approach to guide this significant organizational change, helping to ensure a smooth transition and widespread adoption.

Step 1: Create a Sense of Urgency

To initiate the change, it's crucial to build a sense of urgency around the need for a new EHR system. This can be done by highlighting the limitations of the current system, such as inefficiencies, data inaccuracies, and the potential risks to patient safety. Presenting data that demonstrates how the new system will improve clinical outcomes, streamline workflows, and enhance regulatory compliance can help make the case.

Addressing Resistance:

- **Communication:** Clearly communicate the risks of not adopting the new EHR, such as falling behind in technology, increasing operational costs, and potential negative impacts on patient care.
- **Engagement:** Involve frontline staff early in discussions, gathering their input on the current system's pain points to make the urgency feel more personal and relevant.

Step 2: Build a Guiding Coalition

Assemble a coalition of influential stakeholders who are committed to leading the change. This should include leaders from various departments such as IT, nursing, finance, and physicians, as well as respected frontline staff who can champion the new EHR system.

Addressing Resistance:

- **Diverse Representation:** Ensure the coalition includes representatives from different roles and departments to address concerns from all areas of the organization.
- **Visible Leadership:** Coalition members should be visible advocates for the change, demonstrating their commitment to the project and addressing concerns in real time.

Step 3: Form a Strategic Vision and Initiatives

Develop a clear vision for what the successful implementation of the new EHR system will look like and how it will benefit the healthcare network. This vision should be concise, compelling, and easily understood by all stakeholders.

Addressing Resistance:

- **Clarity:** Clearly articulate how the new system aligns with the organization's broader goals, such as improving patient care, operational efficiency, and regulatory compliance.
- **Relevance:** Tailor the vision to address specific concerns from different departments. For example, emphasize how the system will reduce administrative burdens for nurses or improve data accessibility for physicians.

Step 4: Enlist a Volunteer Army

Empower a large group of employees to take ownership of the change by involving them in the implementation process. Encourage staff to volunteer as "super users" or part of the pilot groups to test and provide feedback on the system.

Addressing Resistance:

- **Involvement:** By involving a broad base of employees, you can reduce resistance by giving staff a sense of ownership and influence over the change.
- **Support:** Provide these volunteers with the necessary training and resources to become advocates for the system, helping to address skepticism and build confidence among their peers.

Step 5: Enable Action by Removing Barriers

Identify and remove obstacles that could impede the successful implementation of the EHR system. This might include outdated workflows, inadequate training programs, or lack of resources.

Addressing Resistance:

- **Barrier Identification:** Conduct surveys or focus groups to identify potential barriers to adoption and address them proactively.
- **Flexibility:** Be prepared to modify workflows and processes to better align with the capabilities of the new system, and ensure that adequate technical support is available during the transition.

Step 6: Generate Short-Term Wins

To build momentum, create and celebrate short-term wins that demonstrate the benefits of the new EHR system. These wins might include successful pilot programs, positive feedback from users, or early improvements in data management.

Addressing Resistance:

- **Visibility:** Make these wins highly visible across the organization to build confidence in the new system.
- **Reward and Recognition:** Recognize and reward individuals and teams who contribute to these early successes, reinforcing positive behavior and encouraging continued support.

Step 7: Sustain Acceleration

After achieving early successes, maintain momentum by continuing to address challenges, expanding the implementation, and refining processes. This might involve scaling up the system across more departments or facilities within the network.

Addressing Resistance:

- **Continuous Improvement:** Regularly gather feedback from users to identify areas for improvement and demonstrate a commitment to refining the system based on their input.
- **Ongoing Training:** Offer continuous training and support to ensure that staff remain confident and competent in using the new system as it evolves.

Step 8: Institute Change

Finally, ensure that the changes become embedded in the organization's culture. This means making the new EHR system an integral part of daily operations, with policies, procedures, and performance metrics aligned to support its use.

Addressing Resistance:

- **Cultural Integration:** Reinforce the importance of the new system through regular communication, highlighting its role in achieving the organization's strategic objectives.

- **Policy Alignment:** Update organizational policies and job descriptions to reflect the use of the new EHR system, ensuring that it becomes a non-negotiable part of daily operations.

By following Kotter's 8-Step Change Model, nurse executives and healthcare leaders can effectively guide the implementation of a new EHR system, addressing resistance at each stage and ensuring a smooth transition. The focus on building a coalition, empowering employees, removing barriers, and embedding the change into the organizational culture are all critical to achieving long-term success and realizing the full benefits of the new technology.

Lewin's Change Management Model is a foundational approach to managing change in organizations, particularly effective in situations requiring cultural transformation. The model's three stages—Unfreeze, Change, and Refreeze—provide a structured framework for guiding organizations through significant transitions. When applied to a merged healthcare organization, this model can help navigate the complex process of blending different cultures, practices, and values.

Unfreeze: Preparing for Change

The **Unfreeze** stage is crucial for breaking down the status quo and creating readiness for change. In a merged healthcare organization, this involves addressing the deeply ingrained practices, beliefs, and cultural norms from both legacy organizations. The goal is to create awareness of the need for change and reduce resistance.

Strategies to Unfreeze Existing Practices:

1. **Assess Organizational Cultures:**
   o Conduct a comprehensive cultural audit to understand the distinct values, norms, and practices of each legacy organization. Identify areas of alignment and divergence.
   o Use surveys, focus groups, and interviews to gather insights from staff at all levels about their perceptions of the existing culture and the merger.

2. **Communicate the Need for Change:**
   o Develop a clear and compelling narrative that explains why cultural change is necessary. Highlight the benefits of a unified culture, such as improved patient care, streamlined processes, and enhanced collaboration.
   o Engage leadership and frontline staff in open discussions about the merger's goals, addressing concerns and uncertainties transparently.

3. **Create a Sense of Urgency:**
   o Identify specific challenges that the merger aims to address, such as inconsistent patient care standards or operational inefficiencies. Present data and case studies that illustrate the potential risks of maintaining the status quo.
   o Foster a sense of urgency by emphasizing the competitive and regulatory pressures that require a unified and adaptive culture.

4. **Build a Coalition of Change Agents:**
   o Assemble a cross-functional team of influential leaders, managers, and frontline staff from both legacy organizations to champion the change. This coalition should reflect the diversity of the merged entity, ensuring that all perspectives are represented.
   o Empower these change agents to lead by example, modeling the desired cultural behaviors and supporting their peers through the transition.

Change: Implementing New Practices

The **Change** stage involves the actual transition from old behaviors and practices to new ones. This stage is where the new, unified culture begins to take shape, and it requires careful planning and execution to ensure that the changes are accepted and internalized by all staff.

Strategies to Implement Changes:

1. **Develop and Communicate a Clear Vision:**
   o Craft a vision statement that encapsulates the desired culture of the merged organization. This vision should be specific, actionable, and aligned with the organization's mission and strategic goals.
   o Ensure that the vision is communicated consistently across all levels of the organization, using multiple channels such as town hall meetings, newsletters, and digital platforms.

2. **Align Policies and Procedures**:
   o Review and harmonize policies, procedures, and protocols from both legacy organizations. This includes clinical guidelines, administrative processes, and HR practices.
   o Introduce new policies that reinforce the desired cultural behaviors, such as those promoting interdisciplinary collaboration, patient-centered care, and continuous learning.
3. **Provide Training and Support**:
   o Offer targeted training programs that help staff develop the skills and knowledge necessary to thrive in the new cultural environment. This might include workshops on cultural competency, communication, teamwork, and change management.
   o Provide ongoing support through mentoring, coaching, and peer networks, ensuring that staff have access to resources that help them adapt to the new culture.
4. **Facilitate Open Communication and Feedback**:
   o Create platforms for ongoing dialogue where staff can share their experiences, voice concerns, and provide feedback on the change process. This could include regular town hall meetings, suggestion boxes, and anonymous surveys.
   o Actively respond to feedback and adjust the change process as needed. Demonstrating responsiveness to staff concerns helps build trust and buy-in for the new culture.
5. **Celebrate Early Wins**:
   o Identify and celebrate quick wins—early successes that demonstrate the benefits of the new culture. These could include improved patient satisfaction scores, successful cross-departmental projects, or enhanced employee engagement.
   o Publicly recognize individuals and teams who exemplify the desired cultural behaviors, reinforcing the importance of the change and motivating others to follow suit.

Refreeze: Solidifying New Behaviors

The **Refreeze** stage is about embedding the new cultural practices and behaviors into the organization's fabric so that they become the new norm. This stage ensures that the changes are sustained over time and that the organization does not revert to old habits.

Strategies to Refreeze New Behaviors:
1. **Integrate New Cultural Norms into Organizational Structures**:
   o Embed the new cultural values into organizational structures, such as performance appraisal systems, reward and recognition programs, and career development paths.
   o Ensure that recruitment and onboarding processes reflect the desired culture, selecting candidates who align with the new values and providing new hires with a comprehensive orientation to the unified culture.
2. **Reinforce Through Leadership**:
   o Encourage leaders at all levels to consistently model and reinforce the new cultural behaviors. This includes setting expectations, providing feedback, and holding staff accountable for adhering to the new norms.
   o Establish regular check-ins with leaders to assess how well the new culture is being maintained and to address any emerging challenges.
3. **Monitor and Measure Cultural Integration**:
   o Develop metrics to monitor the integration of the new culture, such as employee engagement surveys, patient satisfaction scores, and cultural alignment assessments.
   o Use these metrics to identify areas where the new culture is thriving and where additional support may be needed. Regularly review and adjust strategies to ensure continued progress.
4. **Sustain Change Through Continuous Improvement**:
   o Foster a culture of continuous improvement where feedback is regularly solicited, and adjustments are made as needed to sustain the new culture.
   o Encourage ongoing learning and development initiatives that keep the organization adaptable and responsive to future changes.
5. **Celebrate and Institutionalize the New Culture**:

- ○ Continue to celebrate milestones and achievements that exemplify the new culture. These celebrations should be integrated into the organization's routine, becoming part of the institutional memory.
- ○ Document the change process, capturing best practices and lessons learned to inform future cultural initiatives.

Lewin's Change Management Model is highly effective in addressing cultural changes within a merged healthcare organization, provided that each stage is thoughtfully managed. By carefully unfreezing existing practices, implementing well-planned changes, and refreezing new behaviors, nurse executives can guide their organizations through the complexities of cultural integration, ultimately creating a unified and resilient healthcare entity.

The ADKAR model, which stands for Awareness, Desire, Knowledge, Ability, and Reinforcement, provides a structured framework for managing change effectively, including the implementation of a new patient safety protocol. By addressing each element of the ADKAR model, healthcare leaders can guide staff through the transition, ensuring both the successful adoption and long-term sustainability of the new practices.

1. Awareness: Building Understanding of the Need for Change
Objective: Ensure that all staff understand why the new patient safety protocol is necessary and the risks of maintaining the status quo.
Actions:
- **Communicate the Rationale:** Clearly articulate the reasons for the new protocol, such as reducing medical errors, improving patient outcomes, or meeting updated regulatory standards. Use data to highlight the impact of current safety gaps and how the new protocol addresses these issues.
- **Engage Stakeholders Early:** Involve key staff members, including clinical leaders, frontline workers, and patient advocates, in discussions about the need for change. Their early buy-in will help spread awareness and understanding throughout the organization.
- **Use Multiple Channels:** Disseminate information through various channels—meetings, emails, posters, and internal newsletters—to reach all staff effectively.

Addressing Potential Challenges:
- **Overcoming Apathy:** Some staff might not see the need for change, especially if they believe current practices are sufficient. Address this by presenting compelling evidence of the risks associated with not adopting the new protocol.
- **Tailoring Messages:** Customize the message for different groups (e.g., nurses, physicians, administrative staff) to make it relevant to their roles and responsibilities.

2. Desire: Fostering the Motivation to Support and Participate in the Change
Objective: Create a sense of ownership and personal motivation among staff to adopt and support the new patient safety protocol.
Actions:
- **Highlight Benefits:** Clearly communicate the benefits of the new protocol for both patients and staff, such as reducing liability, improving patient satisfaction, and creating a safer work environment.
- **Involve Staff in the Process:** Allow staff to provide input on the protocol's implementation, which can increase their sense of ownership. For example, conduct focus groups or pilot the protocol in specific departments and gather feedback for adjustments.
- **Address Concerns:** Openly address any fears or concerns staff may have about the protocol, such as increased workload or fear of reprimand for mistakes. Reassure them that the goal is to improve safety, not to assign blame.

Addressing Potential Challenges:
- **Resistance to Change:** Some staff may resist the new protocol due to comfort with existing practices. Combat this by sharing success stories from early adopters within the organization or from similar institutions.
- **Incentivizing Adoption:** Consider offering incentives, such as recognition programs or small rewards, to encourage early adoption and active participation.

3. Knowledge: Providing the Information and Training Needed to Make the Change

Objective: Equip all staff with the knowledge they need to understand the new protocol and how to implement it effectively.

Actions:

- **Develop Comprehensive Training Programs:** Create training sessions that cover all aspects of the new protocol, including the rationale behind it, step-by-step instructions, and role-specific responsibilities.
- **Use Varied Training Methods:** Utilize a mix of training formats such as in-person workshops, e-learning modules, and hands-on simulations to cater to different learning styles.
- **Provide Clear Documentation:** Ensure that detailed, accessible documentation is available, including quick-reference guides, checklists, and FAQs.

Addressing Potential Challenges:

- **Overcoming Knowledge Gaps:** Regularly assess understanding through quizzes, scenario-based assessments, or peer reviews. Address any gaps immediately with additional training or clarification.
- **Ensuring Consistency:** Standardize training across the organization to ensure that all staff receive the same level of instruction and information.

4. Ability: Facilitating the Capability to Implement the Change

Objective: Ensure that staff not only know what to do but are also capable of applying the new protocol in their daily work.

Actions:

- **Practice and Simulation:** Incorporate simulation exercises that allow staff to practice the new protocol in a controlled environment before full implementation. This builds confidence and competence.
- **Provide Ongoing Support:** Establish support systems, such as a helpdesk or designated "super users" who can assist with questions or challenges as staff begin to use the new protocol.
- **Monitor and Adjust:** During the initial implementation phase, monitor compliance and effectiveness. Be prepared to make adjustments to the protocol or provide additional support where needed.

Addressing Potential Challenges:

- **Addressing Skill Gaps:** If some staff members struggle with certain aspects of the protocol, offer additional targeted training or one-on-one coaching.
- **Maintaining Momentum:** Keep the momentum going by regularly checking in with staff and providing encouragement and support as they transition to the new protocol.

5. Reinforcement: Ensuring the Change is Sustained Over Time

Objective: Make the new patient safety protocol a permanent part of the organizational culture by reinforcing its importance and ensuring ongoing compliance.

Actions:

- **Regular Audits and Feedback:** Conduct regular audits to ensure the protocol is being followed correctly. Provide feedback to staff based on these audits, highlighting areas of success and opportunities for improvement.
- **Celebrate Successes:** Publicly recognize departments or individuals who have successfully implemented the protocol, sharing their achievements with the entire organization to reinforce positive behavior.
- **Continuous Education:** Incorporate the protocol into ongoing training programs and new employee orientation to ensure it remains a focus for all staff, both current and incoming.
- **Policy Integration:** Embed the protocol into the hospital's official policies and procedures, making it a non-negotiable standard of care.

Addressing Potential Challenges:

- **Preventing Backsliding:** To prevent staff from reverting to old practices, continuously emphasize the importance of the protocol through leadership communications, reminders, and integration into performance evaluations.
- **Sustaining Engagement:** Keep staff engaged by periodically refreshing training, updating the protocol as needed, and involving them in any revisions or improvements to the process.

Ensuring Sustained Adoption

Sustained adoption of the new patient safety protocol hinges on a well-rounded approach that addresses both the practical and psychological aspects of change. By following the ADKAR model, healthcare leaders can guide staff through each stage of the transition, ensuring they are not only equipped with the necessary skills and knowledge but are also motivated and supported to maintain these new practices over time. Reinforcement through continuous feedback, recognition, and integration into daily routines and policies will help solidify the protocol as a permanent and effective part of patient care.

Change management plays a crucial role in promoting the adoption of evidence-based practice (EBP) within clinical settings. EBP involves integrating the best available research with clinical expertise and patient preferences to improve outcomes. Despite its proven benefits, adopting EBP can be challenging due to various barriers in healthcare environments. Effective change management strategies can facilitate this adoption by addressing these barriers and fostering a culture that embraces continuous improvement.

Role of Change Management in Promoting Evidence-Based Practice Adoption

1. **Creating Awareness and Understanding**
   - **Education and Training**: Change management begins with educating healthcare professionals about the value of EBP. This involves providing comprehensive training on how to access, appraise, and apply research findings in clinical practice. Nurse executives can organize workshops, seminars, and online courses to equip staff with the necessary skills and knowledge.
   - **Communication**: Clear and consistent communication is essential for explaining the importance of EBP. Nurse executives should articulate how EBP can enhance patient outcomes, reduce variations in care, and align with the organization's goals. Regular updates and success stories can be shared through newsletters, meetings, and digital platforms to keep the staff informed and motivated.

2. **Building a Supportive Infrastructure**
   - **Resource Allocation**: Adopting EBP requires access to resources such as databases, journals, and decision-support tools. Nurse executives must ensure that these resources are readily available and that staff are trained to use them effectively.
   - **Leadership Support**: Strong leadership support is critical for overcoming resistance to change. Nurse executives can demonstrate their commitment to EBP by actively participating in EBP initiatives, allocating time for staff to engage in EBP activities, and recognizing efforts to implement EBP.

3. **Facilitating Collaboration and Teamwork**
   - **Interdisciplinary Collaboration**: EBP often involves input from various disciplines. Change management strategies should promote collaboration among nurses, physicians, pharmacists, and other healthcare professionals. This can be achieved through interdisciplinary committees, regular meetings, and collaborative projects focused on EBP.
   - **Mentorship and Coaching**: Experienced clinicians who are already skilled in EBP can mentor others, providing guidance and support. Nurse executives can establish formal mentorship programs to help disseminate EBP skills across the organization.

4. **Empowering Staff through Participation**
   - **Involvement in Decision-Making**: Involving staff in the decision-making process regarding EBP initiatives increases their ownership and commitment. Nurse executives should create opportunities for nurses to contribute to policy development, guideline creation, and the selection of EBP projects.
   - **Feedback Mechanisms**: Implementing feedback loops allows staff to voice concerns and suggest improvements. This not only enhances the EBP process but also fosters a sense of empowerment and inclusion.

5. **Sustaining Change through Continuous Improvement**
   - **Monitoring and Evaluation**: Regularly evaluating the impact of EBP initiatives is vital to sustaining change. Nurse executives should establish metrics to assess the adoption and outcomes of EBP, such as patient outcomes, adherence rates, and staff satisfaction. These metrics can be used to make data-driven adjustments to the implementation strategy.

- o **Celebrating Successes**: Recognizing and celebrating successes in EBP adoption reinforces positive behavior. Nurse executives can highlight successful case studies, reward teams that achieve significant improvements, and share these successes across the organization to motivate others.

Overcoming Barriers to Change in Clinical Settings

Despite the clear benefits of EBP, several barriers can hinder its adoption. Nurse executives must be proactive in identifying and addressing these barriers to ensure successful implementation.

1. **Resistance to Change**
   - o **Barrier**: Clinicians may resist adopting EBP due to comfort with existing practices, skepticism about new methods, or fear of increased workload.
   - o **Strategy**: To overcome resistance, nurse executives should engage in open dialogue with staff to understand their concerns. Providing evidence of EBP's effectiveness, offering training to ease the transition, and involving staff in the change process can help reduce resistance.

2. **Lack of Time**
   - o **Barrier**: Time constraints are a significant barrier, as clinicians often struggle to find time to search for and evaluate research evidence while managing their workload.
   - o **Strategy**: Nurse executives can address this by integrating EBP into the workflow. This might include scheduling dedicated time for EBP activities, using clinical decision-support tools that provide quick access to research, or assigning specific staff to EBP roles.

3. **Limited Access to Resources**
   - o **Barrier**: Inadequate access to research databases, journals, and EBP tools can prevent clinicians from engaging with EBP.
   - o **Strategy**: Nurse executives should ensure that all staff have access to the necessary resources. This might involve investing in institutional subscriptions to medical databases, providing training on how to use these resources, and ensuring that EBP tools are user-friendly and easily accessible at the point of care.

4. **Inadequate EBP Skills**
   - o **Barrier**: Some clinicians may lack the skills to critically appraise research or apply it in clinical practice.
   - o **Strategy**: Ongoing education and training are essential. Nurse executives can implement workshops, webinars, and mentorship programs focused on developing these skills. Additionally, integrating EBP training into the orientation program for new hires can build competency from the start.

5. **Cultural Barriers**
   - o **Barrier**: The existing culture within a healthcare organization may not support EBP, particularly if there is a strong reliance on traditional practices or hierarchical decision-making.
   - o **Strategy**: Changing the organizational culture to support EBP requires a top-down and bottom-up approach. Nurse executives should lead by example, promoting a culture of inquiry and continuous learning. Encouraging open communication, collaboration, and shared decision-making can also shift the culture towards one that values and practices EBP.

Change management is essential in promoting the adoption of evidence-based practice in clinical settings. By creating a supportive infrastructure, fostering collaboration, empowering staff, and addressing barriers head-on, nurse executives can lead their organizations toward more effective, evidence-based care. This approach not only improves patient outcomes but also aligns the organization with best practices, ensuring it remains at the forefront of healthcare innovation.

Coaching and mentoring are both essential strategies in healthcare leadership development, each serving distinct but complementary purposes. Understanding the differences between these approaches allows nurse executives to use them effectively to support the growth of high-potential staff members.

Coaching in Healthcare Leadership Development

Coaching is a structured, goal-oriented process focused on developing specific skills or improving performance within a relatively short timeframe. It is typically more directive, with the coach providing targeted feedback, setting clear expectations, and guiding the coachee through specific challenges. In healthcare, coaching might involve working with a nurse on developing competencies in areas such as communication, time management, or clinical decision-making. A nurse executive can employ coaching by identifying high-potential staff who are ready to take on new responsibilities or who need to refine certain skills to progress in their careers. For example, if a nurse is being prepared for a leadership role, the executive might coach them on how to lead team meetings effectively or manage conflict. The process is often highly interactive, with regular check-ins, measurable objectives, and a focus on immediate application.

Mentoring in Healthcare Leadership Development

Mentoring, on the other hand, is a longer-term relationship focused on broader professional and personal development. Unlike coaching, which is often task-oriented, mentoring involves sharing experiences, offering guidance on career progression, and providing support as the mentee navigates their professional journey. A mentor serves as a role model, offering wisdom, advice, and encouragement, often drawing from their own experiences in similar roles.

In the context of a nurse executive, mentoring might involve helping a high-potential nurse leader think through their career path, understand the complexities of healthcare leadership, and develop the resilience needed to thrive in challenging environments. The mentor might discuss the intricacies of balancing administrative duties with patient care, or how to build a strong professional network within the organization. Mentoring is typically less formal than coaching, with meetings occurring as needed, based on the mentee's evolving needs and goals.

Employing Both Strategies for High-Potential Staff Members

A nurse executive can effectively combine coaching and mentoring to support the comprehensive development of high-potential staff. Initially, coaching might be used to address immediate skill gaps or prepare the individual for a specific role or project. For instance, a nurse identified as a future department head might receive coaching on leadership skills, such as team management or budgeting.

Once the foundational skills are developed through coaching, mentoring can be introduced to guide the nurse's long-term career growth. The nurse executive might serve as a mentor, helping the nurse navigate the broader challenges of healthcare leadership, such as strategic thinking, navigating organizational politics, and maintaining work-life balance.

By integrating both approaches, the nurse executive can ensure that high-potential staff members not only develop the specific skills needed for their current roles but also receive the broader, ongoing support necessary for long-term success and leadership within the organization.

Designing an effective coaching program for charge nurses transitioning to nurse manager roles requires a targeted approach that focuses on developing key competencies essential for leadership in a management position. The program should be structured to provide both theoretical knowledge and practical skills, while also offering personalized support to address the unique challenges of the transition.

Key Competencies for Nurse Managers

1. **Leadership and Decision-Making**
   - **Competency**: Moving from charge nurse to nurse manager involves a shift from overseeing daily operations to making strategic decisions that impact entire units or departments.
   - **Focus Areas**: Leadership styles, strategic thinking, prioritization, and ethical decision-making.
   - **Activities**: Role-playing scenarios where the nurse must navigate complex decisions, such as resource allocation or conflict resolution, and discussing the implications of different leadership styles.

2. **Financial Management**
   - **Competency**: Nurse managers are often responsible for budgeting, financial planning, and managing unit resources effectively.
   - **Focus Areas**: Budget development, cost control, financial analysis, and return on investment (ROI) for new initiatives.
   - **Activities**: Case studies on budget management, creating mock budgets, and exercises in cost-benefit analysis of nursing interventions.

3. **Human Resource Management**

- Competency: Nurse managers need to be adept at staff recruitment, retention, performance evaluation, and conflict resolution.
- Focus Areas: Talent management, workforce planning, performance appraisal, and labor law compliance.
- Activities: Workshops on conducting effective performance reviews, simulations of difficult conversations (e.g., addressing underperformance), and exercises in creating staff development plans.

4. **Communication and Interpersonal Skills**
    - Competency: Effective communication is crucial for nurse managers in dealing with staff, patients, and interdisciplinary teams.
    - Focus Areas: Active listening, conflict resolution, negotiation, and building a positive team culture.
    - Activities: Communication workshops that include practice in active listening and feedback techniques, and role-playing conflict scenarios to enhance negotiation skills.

5. **Quality Improvement and Patient Safety**
    - Competency: Nurse managers must lead initiatives that improve patient care quality and safety.
    - Focus Areas: Risk management, quality improvement (QI) methodologies, root cause analysis, and safety protocols.
    - Activities: Leading a mock QI project from problem identification to solution implementation, analyzing case studies of past QI initiatives, and conducting root cause analysis of simulated adverse events.

6. **Change Management**
    - Competency: As change agents, nurse managers need to effectively guide their teams through transitions and innovations in practice.
    - Focus Areas: Change theories, resistance management, and leading through innovation.
    - Activities: Developing a change management plan for a hypothetical unit-wide change, discussing strategies to overcome resistance, and exploring successful change initiatives in healthcare.

Structuring the Coaching Sessions

1. **Initial Assessment and Goal Setting**
    - Session Focus: Begin by assessing each charge nurse's current competencies, strengths, and areas for development. Use self-assessments, peer reviews, and direct observations to gather insights.
    - Goal: Set clear, personalized goals for the coaching program, aligned with both the individual's career aspirations and the organization's needs.

2. **Competency-Focused Modules**
    - Session Structure: Organize the coaching program into modules, each dedicated to one of the key competencies. Each module would include:
        - **Educational Component**: Brief lectures, readings, or video materials that provide foundational knowledge.
        - **Interactive Workshops**: Hands-on activities like role-playing, case studies, and group discussions to practice skills.
        - **Reflection and Feedback**: Opportunities for self-reflection on the lessons learned, followed by feedback from the coach.

3. **Real-World Application and Case Studies**
    - Session Structure: Integrate real-world scenarios into each session where participants apply what they've learned in a controlled, supportive environment. For example, a module on financial management might include reviewing a real unit's budget and proposing adjustments.
    - Goal: Ensure that participants can translate theoretical knowledge into practical, actionable strategies.

4. **Mentorship and Peer Support**
    - Session Structure: Pair each charge nurse with an experienced nurse manager who serves as a mentor throughout the program. Encourage peer support groups where participants can share experiences, challenges, and solutions.

- o **Goal**: Foster a supportive network that continues beyond the coaching sessions, providing ongoing guidance and encouragement.
5. **Feedback and Continuous Improvement**
   - o **Session Focus**: After completing each module, gather feedback from participants to adjust and refine the program. Additionally, provide regular, constructive feedback to participants on their progress.
   - o **Goal**: Adapt the program based on participant needs and ensure continuous improvement.
6. **Capstone Project**
   - o **Session Structure**: Conclude the program with a capstone project where participants demonstrate their newly acquired skills. This could involve leading a small-scale initiative within their unit, such as a quality improvement project or a new staff development program.
   - o **Goal**: Validate the charge nurses' readiness to transition into the nurse manager role and apply their skills in real-world settings.

This coaching program equips charge nurses with the competencies needed to excel as nurse managers while providing a structured yet flexible approach that supports their professional growth. The focus on practical, hands-on learning ensures that they are prepared to handle the complexities of their new roles with confidence.

Comprehensive Mentorship Program for New Graduate Nurses
Program Overview
The mentorship program for new graduate nurses is designed to support their transition from academic training to professional practice, focusing on both clinical skill enhancement and leadership development. The program pairs new graduates with experienced nurses who provide guidance, support, and knowledge sharing, ensuring that the mentees build confidence in their clinical abilities while also developing the foundational leadership skills necessary for future growth.

Program Structure
1. **Duration:** The mentorship program lasts 12 months, with formal check-ins every month and more frequent, informal interactions as needed. The first six months focus intensively on clinical skills, while the latter half gradually integrates leadership development components.
2. **Phases of Mentorship:**
   - o **Phase 1: Onboarding and Orientation (Month 1)**
     - ▪ Mentees undergo a comprehensive orientation that includes an introduction to the hospital's policies, procedures, and culture. Mentors participate in these sessions to start building rapport.
     - ▪ Mentees complete an initial self-assessment of their clinical skills and leadership interests to identify focus areas for the mentorship.
   - o **Phase 2: Clinical Skill Development (Months 2-6)**
     - ▪ Focused on refining clinical competencies, with mentors providing hands-on training, case reviews, and feedback.
     - ▪ Simulation labs and shadowing opportunities are scheduled to help mentees apply theoretical knowledge to real-world scenarios.
     - ▪ Mentors guide mentees in developing critical thinking and decision-making skills in clinical settings.
   - o **Phase 3: Leadership Development (Months 7-12)**
     - ▪ Gradual shift towards leadership skills, including team communication, time management, and conflict resolution.
     - ▪ Mentees are encouraged to take on small leadership roles within their teams, such as leading huddles or participating in committees.
     - ▪ Mentors provide coaching on professional development topics, such as career planning, networking, and continuing education.
3. **Matching Mentors and Mentees**

- o **Skill and Specialty Alignment:** Mentors are matched with mentees based on their clinical specialty to ensure relevant and effective guidance. For example, a new graduate nurse entering critical care would be paired with a seasoned critical care nurse.
- o **Personality and Communication Style:** A preliminary meeting or survey is used to assess compatibility based on personality traits, communication styles, and preferred learning methods. This helps create a more harmonious and productive mentor-mentee relationship.
- o **Leadership Aspirations:** Mentors are also chosen based on their ability to nurture leadership qualities, aligning with the mentee's long-term career goals. For instance, a nurse with aspirations in nurse management would be paired with a mentor who has experience in leadership roles.

4. **Training for Mentors**
   - o Mentors undergo training that covers effective mentoring techniques, communication strategies, and how to balance clinical teaching with leadership development. This ensures that mentors are equipped to provide comprehensive support.

Evaluation and Metrics for Program Success

To assess the effectiveness of the mentorship program, a combination of qualitative and quantitative metrics will be used:

1. **Clinical Competency Improvement**
   - o **Skills Assessments:** Regular evaluations of the mentees' clinical skills through simulations, direct observation, and feedback from supervisors. Improvement in key competencies over time is tracked.
   - o **Error Rates and Patient Outcomes:** Monitoring the mentees' involvement in clinical incidents or errors, with the goal of seeing a reduction in these rates as mentees gain proficiency.

2. **Leadership Skill Development**
   - o **360-Degree Feedback:** Collect feedback from peers, mentors, and supervisors on the mentee's leadership skills, such as communication, teamwork, and problem-solving.
   - o **Leadership Role Participation:** Track the mentee's involvement in leadership activities, such as leading projects, participating in committees, or initiating improvements in their units.

3. **Mentee Satisfaction and Retention**
   - o **Surveys and Interviews:** Conduct regular satisfaction surveys and exit interviews to gather the mentees' perceptions of the program's impact on their confidence, skills, and professional development.
   - o **Retention Rates:** Measure the retention of mentees within the organization after completing the program, with the aim of reducing turnover among new graduate nurses.

4. **Mentor Feedback and Engagement**
   - o **Mentor Surveys:** Gather feedback from mentors on the program structure, their relationships with mentees, and suggestions for improvement.
   - o **Mentor Retention:** Monitor the retention and engagement of mentors to ensure they find the program rewarding and are motivated to continue participating.

5. **Overall Program Impact**
   - o **Patient Satisfaction Scores:** Track patient satisfaction scores in areas where mentees are practicing to identify any correlation between the mentorship program and patient care quality.
   - o **Career Advancement:** Follow the career progression of mentees over several years to assess how the program contributes to their leadership development and career growth.

Continuous Improvement

The mentorship program will be reviewed annually, using the collected data to make necessary adjustments. This includes refining mentor-mentee matching criteria, updating mentor training, and evolving the focus areas based on changes in healthcare practices and organizational needs. The goal is to create a dynamic, responsive program that consistently supports the professional growth of new graduate nurses, equipping them with the skills and confidence to excel in their careers.

The Thomas-Kilmann Conflict Mode Instrument (TKI) identifies five conflict-handling styles: competing, collaborating, compromising, avoiding, and accommodating. Each style has its strengths and can be strategically applied depending on the context of the dispute. In resolving a dispute between nursing and physician teams regarding patient care protocols, it's essential to assess the situation and apply the most effective conflict resolution style or combination of styles to achieve the best outcome for patient care.

Scenario Overview

Imagine a situation where the nursing team advocates for a standardized protocol to manage post-operative care, emphasizing consistency and adherence to evidence-based practices. The physician team, however, prefers a more flexible approach, allowing individual judgment and customization based on patient-specific factors. This disagreement creates tension between the two teams, potentially affecting patient care.

1. Competing (Assertive and Uncooperative)

Application: The competing style is appropriate when a quick, decisive action is necessary, particularly when patient safety is at risk or when adherence to critical protocols is non-negotiable.

Example: If the dispute involves a critical aspect of care that has been proven through evidence to significantly reduce complications, such as infection control procedures, the nurse executive might assert the need to follow the standardized protocol. In this case, the executive would take a firm stance, explaining that while physician judgment is respected, the protocol must be followed to ensure patient safety. The decision to compete may not foster collaboration but ensures that patient safety is not compromised.

2. Collaborating (Assertive and Cooperative)

Application: Collaborating is ideal when the goal is to find a solution that satisfies both teams' concerns, especially when the issue is complex and requires the input of multiple perspectives.

Example: The nurse executive could bring both teams together in a collaborative workshop to discuss the benefits and drawbacks of each approach. The goal would be to combine the standardized protocols with the flexibility physicians seek. For instance, they might develop a core protocol with built-in flexibility for physicians to exercise their judgment in specific scenarios. This collaboration ensures that the final solution is comprehensive and acceptable to both teams, enhancing interprofessional respect and teamwork.

3. Compromising (Moderately Assertive and Cooperative)

Application: The compromising style is useful when both sides need to give up something to reach an agreement, especially when time is of the essence or the stakes are not critical.

Example: If the dispute involves a less critical aspect of patient care, such as the timing of certain non-urgent interventions, the nurse executive might propose a compromise. For example, the nursing team might agree to allow physician discretion in certain cases if the physician team agrees to adhere to the standardized protocol in the majority of situations. This approach acknowledges the importance of both perspectives while ensuring that a workable solution is implemented quickly.

4. Avoiding (Unassertive and Uncooperative)

Application: Avoiding is appropriate when the issue is minor, when emotions are too high to engage productively, or when there's a need for more time to gather information before making a decision.

Example: If the conflict is currently escalating and emotions are running high, the nurse executive might choose to avoid immediate confrontation by postponing the discussion until a later time. This allows time for tempers to cool and for both teams to reflect on the importance of the issue. The executive might then revisit the conflict in a more controlled environment, where a more productive conversation can occur.

5. Accommodating (Unassertive and Cooperative)

Application: Accommodating is effective when maintaining harmony is more important than winning the argument, or when the issue is more important to one side than the other.

Example: Suppose the dispute involves a minor aspect of the patient care protocol that the nursing team feels strongly about, but the physician team is less concerned. The nurse executive might decide to accommodate the physicians' preferences to preserve goodwill and focus on more critical issues. By allowing the physician team to have their way in this instance, the nurse executive builds trust and fosters a collaborative spirit for future, more significant discussions.

Combining Styles for Effective Resolution

In many real-world situations, a combination of conflict resolution styles might be necessary. For example, the nurse executive might begin by avoiding the issue temporarily to allow for reflection, then move to a collaborative approach to design a protocol that satisfies both teams. If collaboration fails, they might resort to compromising to reach a quick solution, using competing only when patient safety demands a non-negotiable stance.

By applying the Thomas-Kilmann Conflict Mode Instrument thoughtfully, nurse executives can effectively navigate disputes between nursing and physician teams, ensuring that patient care remains the top priority while maintaining professional relationships and a positive work environment.

To successfully implement a major organizational restructuring, it's essential to develop a consensus-building strategy that incorporates diverse perspectives and addresses potential power imbalances. This approach ensures that all stakeholders feel heard and valued, leading to greater buy-in and smoother implementation. The following strategy outlines key steps for achieving consensus in a complex healthcare environment.

1. Establish a Clear Vision and Objectives

Begin by articulating a clear, compelling vision for the restructuring, outlining the specific objectives and benefits for the organization as a whole. This vision should address how the restructuring will improve patient care, enhance operational efficiency, or position the organization for future growth. The vision should be communicated transparently across all levels of the organization to provide a shared understanding of the need for change.

2. Form an Inclusive Steering Committee

Create a steering committee responsible for guiding the restructuring process. This committee should be diverse, including representatives from various departments, levels of leadership, and frontline staff. Ensure that the committee includes voices from different professional backgrounds, genders, ethnicities, and other demographic factors to capture a broad range of perspectives. The committee should also have a balance of experienced leaders and emerging voices to reflect both institutional knowledge and fresh insights.

Addressing Power Imbalances:

- **Rotate Leadership Roles:** Rotate the chairperson role within the steering committee to prevent dominance by a single individual or group. This approach encourages shared leadership and helps balance power dynamics.
- **Facilitate Equal Participation:** Employ skilled facilitators who can manage discussions, ensuring that all committee members have the opportunity to contribute and that quieter voices are not overshadowed by more dominant personalities.

3. Conduct Stakeholder Engagement Sessions

Organize engagement sessions with various stakeholder groups, including doctors, nurses, administrative staff, patients, and community representatives. These sessions should be designed to gather input, identify concerns, and explore potential impacts of the restructuring on different parts of the organization.

Incorporating Diverse Perspectives:

- **Focus Groups and Town Halls:** Hold focus groups and town hall meetings where stakeholders can express their views in a more informal setting. These forums should encourage open dialogue and provide safe spaces for candid feedback.
- **Surveys and Feedback Tools:** Use anonymous surveys and digital feedback tools to collect input from those who may be uncomfortable speaking out in public forums. Analyze this data to identify common themes and unique concerns.

4. Develop Multiple Scenarios

Based on the feedback collected, develop several restructuring scenarios that reflect the diverse perspectives and address key concerns. Present these scenarios to the steering committee and stakeholders, highlighting the pros and cons of each option. This approach allows stakeholders to see that their input has been considered and provides a platform for further discussion and refinement.

Addressing Potential Power Imbalances:

- **Scenario Evaluation Criteria:** Develop a set of criteria for evaluating the scenarios that include considerations of equity, impact on different stakeholder groups, and alignment with the organization's mission. This helps ensure that decisions are not solely based on the interests of the most powerful groups but are balanced and fair.
- **Consensus-Building Workshops:** Hold workshops where stakeholders can collaboratively refine the scenarios, fostering a sense of shared ownership in the final decision. Use techniques like multi-voting or ranking to ensure that the final choice reflects a broad consensus rather than the preferences of a few.

5. Transparent Decision-Making Process

Ensure that the decision-making process is transparent and that all stakeholders understand how their input is being used. Regularly update the organization on the progress of the restructuring, including how feedback has influenced decisions. Make the criteria for final decisions clear and openly discuss any trade-offs that need to be made.

Incorporating Diverse Perspectives:

- **Open Access to Information:** Provide access to all relevant data, analysis, and meeting summaries so that stakeholders can see the basis for decisions. Transparency helps build trust and demonstrates that the process is fair.
- **Ongoing Dialogue:** Maintain open channels of communication throughout the process, encouraging continuous feedback and addressing new concerns as they arise.

6. Address Resistance and Power Dynamics

Anticipate resistance from groups or individuals who may feel threatened by the restructuring, particularly those in positions of power. Engage directly with these stakeholders to understand their concerns and explore ways to mitigate perceived losses or risks. Emphasize the long-term benefits of the restructuring for the entire organization, and consider compromise solutions where appropriate.

Addressing Power Imbalances:

- **Engagement of Power Holders:** Involve influential stakeholders early in the process, giving them a role in shaping the restructuring. This can help reduce opposition by making them part of the solution.
- **Empowerment of Marginalized Groups:** Actively seek out and amplify the voices of less powerful groups within the organization. This might involve providing platforms for these groups to express their views or assigning them formal roles in the restructuring process.

7. Implementation and Monitoring

Once a consensus is reached on the restructuring plan, focus on the implementation phase with the same inclusive and transparent approach. Monitor the effects of the restructuring closely, using metrics to assess its impact on different parts of the organization and adjusting as necessary.

Metrics for Evaluation:

- **Employee Satisfaction and Morale:** Regularly survey staff to gauge morale and satisfaction during and after the restructuring. Look for signs of increased engagement or persistent dissatisfaction.
- **Operational Efficiency:** Track key performance indicators related to efficiency, such as patient throughput, resource utilization, and financial performance.
- **Equity and Inclusion:** Assess whether the restructuring has achieved its goals in an equitable manner, particularly in terms of impacts on traditionally marginalized groups within the organization.
- **Patient Outcomes:** Evaluate the impact of restructuring on patient care quality, safety, and satisfaction.

Through this comprehensive consensus-building strategy, a nurse executive can successfully lead a major organizational restructuring that aligns with the organization's goals, reflects the diverse needs of its stakeholders, and fosters a more inclusive and collaborative culture.

Principled negotiation, as outlined in the Harvard Negotiation Project's book *"Getting to Yes,"* emphasizes finding mutually beneficial solutions by focusing on interests rather than positions. This approach is particularly effective in contract discussions with major insurance providers, where multiple stakeholders—patients, healthcare providers, the organization, and the insurance company—have differing needs and priorities. Nurse executives can leverage principled negotiation to achieve agreements that balance these needs while ensuring the organization's goals are met.

Key Principles of Principled Negotiation

1. **Separate the People from the Problem**
   - ○ **Application:** In contract negotiations with an insurance provider, emotions and personal biases can cloud judgment. Nurse executives should focus on the issues at hand—reimbursement rates, coverage policies, quality metrics—rather than allowing interpersonal dynamics to influence the discussions. This requires maintaining a professional tone, actively listening to the insurance provider's representatives, and addressing any concerns objectively.
   - ○ **Example:** If the insurance provider insists on lower reimbursement rates, rather than viewing this as an adversarial stance, the nurse executive could explore the reasons behind this position.

Perhaps the insurer is under pressure to control costs. Understanding this can help in framing a solution that meets both parties' needs.

2. **Focus on Interests, Not Positions**
   - **Application:** Positions are what each party wants (e.g., higher reimbursement rates, broader coverage), while interests are the underlying reasons why they want it (e.g., financial sustainability, access to care). By focusing on interests, nurse executives can uncover shared goals that can lead to creative solutions.
   - **Example:** If the insurance provider is pushing for lower rates, the nurse executive might uncover that their primary interest is in controlling healthcare costs. The nurse executive could propose alternative solutions, such as value-based payment models or bundled payments, that align with cost control while also providing fair compensation to the healthcare organization.

3. **Generate Options for Mutual Gain**
   - **Application:** Once interests are identified, the next step is to brainstorm options that can satisfy both parties. Nurse executives should collaborate with the insurance provider to explore innovative solutions that go beyond traditional fee-for-service models.
   - **Example:** Proposing a pilot program where reimbursement is tied to specific quality metrics or patient outcomes could meet the insurance provider's interest in cost control and the healthcare organization's interest in maintaining revenue and quality care. This approach encourages a partnership mentality rather than an adversarial one.

4. **Use Objective Criteria**
   - **Application:** Relying on objective, data-driven criteria can help resolve disagreements about what is fair or reasonable. Nurse executives should prepare by gathering relevant data, such as industry benchmarks, cost analyses, and outcomes data, to support their proposals.
   - **Example:** If the negotiation stalls on reimbursement rates, the nurse executive could present data on regional average rates for similar services or the costs associated with delivering those services. This objective evidence can provide a solid foundation for negotiations, making it easier to reach an agreement that both parties see as fair.

Balancing the Needs of the Organization with Other Stakeholders

1. **Patient Care and Access**
   - **Balance:** Nurse executives must ensure that negotiations with insurance providers do not compromise patient care or access to services. This might mean prioritizing certain aspects of the contract, such as coverage for essential services or minimizing patient out-of-pocket costs, even if it means accepting slightly lower reimbursement rates.
   - **Strategy:** Engage with patient advocacy groups or conduct surveys to understand patient priorities. Use this information to advocate for contract terms that align with patient needs while also addressing the organization's financial sustainability.

2. **Financial Sustainability**
   - **Balance:** While securing favorable reimbursement rates is crucial for the organization's financial health, nurse executives must also consider the insurance provider's need to control costs. A balanced approach might involve agreeing to more competitive rates for high-volume services while negotiating better terms for more complex, resource-intensive care.
   - **Strategy:** Conduct a thorough financial analysis to identify services where the organization can afford to be more flexible and those where higher reimbursement is essential. Use this analysis to guide negotiations and propose compromises that protect both the organization's and the insurer's financial interests.

3. **Staffing and Resources**
   - **Balance:** Adequate staffing and resources are essential for maintaining quality care. Negotiations should therefore include considerations for how contract terms will impact the organization's ability to invest in staffing, training, and infrastructure.
   - **Strategy:** Highlight the relationship between reimbursement rates and the organization's capacity to maintain safe staffing levels and provide high-quality care. Present data on how cuts could

negatively affect patient outcomes, using this to advocate for terms that support the organization's operational needs.

4. **Regulatory Compliance and Ethical Standards**
   o **Balance**: Contracts must comply with healthcare regulations and ethical standards, such as providing care to underserved populations. Nurse executives should ensure that any agreements uphold these standards and do not incentivize practices that could compromise care.
   o **Strategy**: Use objective criteria, such as legal and regulatory requirements, to justify the need for certain contract terms. This might include provisions that ensure equitable access to care or protect against practices that could lead to ethical dilemmas.

Implementing the Negotiated Agreement

After reaching an agreement, the nurse executive must ensure that the terms are implemented effectively. This involves:

- **Clear Communication**: Explaining the new contract terms to all relevant stakeholders within the organization, including finance, billing, and clinical teams, to ensure a smooth transition.
- **Monitoring and Evaluation**: Regularly reviewing the contract's impact on the organization's finances, patient care, and stakeholder satisfaction. This helps identify any issues early and provides data for future negotiations.
- **Maintaining Relationships**: Continuing to build a positive relationship with the insurance provider, which can facilitate smoother negotiations in the future and help resolve any issues that arise during the contract period.

By using principled negotiation techniques, nurse executives can craft agreements that balance the needs of their organization with those of patients, staff, and the insurance provider, ultimately leading to sustainable and effective healthcare delivery.

Comprehensive Budget for a New Community Health Initiative

1. Overview of the Initiative

The proposed community health initiative aims to improve access to preventive healthcare services in an underserved rural area. The program will focus on providing free health screenings, health education workshops, and immunization drives over a one-year period. The initiative will also include outreach to connect residents with local healthcare providers for ongoing care.

2. Budget Components

A. Fixed Costs

These are costs that remain constant regardless of the scale of the initiative.

1. **Personnel Salaries**
   o **Project Manager:** $75,000 annually (full-time)
   o **Community Outreach Coordinator:** $50,000 annually (full-time)
   o **Health Educators (2 positions):** $40,000 each annually (full-time)
   o **Administrative Support:** $35,000 annually (part-time)

Total Personnel Salaries: $240,000

2. **Office Space and Utilities**
   o **Rent:** $18,000 annually (based on $1,500/month)
   o **Utilities (electricity, water, internet):** $6,000 annually (estimated at $500/month)

Total Office Space and Utilities: $24,000

3. **Technology and Equipment**
   o **Computers (4 units):** $6,000 (one-time purchase)
   o **Office Furniture:** $4,000 (one-time purchase)
   o **Medical Equipment for Screenings (e.g., blood pressure monitors, scales, glucometers):** $15,000 (one-time purchase)
   o **Software for Data Management and Scheduling:** $5,000 (annual license)

Total Technology and Equipment: $30,000

4. **Marketing and Outreach Materials**
   o **Brochures, Posters, and Flyers:** $5,000 (one-time design and print)

- Website Development and Maintenance: $3,000 (initial setup and first year maintenance)
- Social Media and Digital Marketing Campaign: $7,000 (annual)

Total Marketing and Outreach Materials: $15,000

5. Insurance and Legal Fees
- Liability Insurance: $5,000 annually
- Legal Fees for Contract Reviews and Compliance: $3,000 annually

Total Insurance and Legal Fees: $8,000

6. Training and Development
- Staff Training Programs: $5,000 (one-time)
- Ongoing Professional Development: $3,000 annually

Total Training and Development: $8,000

Total Fixed Costs: $325,000

B. Variable Costs

These costs fluctuate based on the scale and reach of the initiative.

1. Medical Supplies and Consumables
- Screening Kits (e.g., glucose test strips, cholesterol kits): $10 per kit, estimated 2,000 screenings = $20,000
- Vaccines for Immunization Drives: $15 per dose, estimated 1,000 doses = $15,000
- Educational Materials (booklets, pamphlets): $2 per set, estimated 5,000 sets = $10,000

Total Medical Supplies and Consumables: $45,000

2. Travel and Transportation
- Staff Travel (mileage reimbursement for outreach): $0.56 per mile, estimated 10,000 miles = $5,600
- Mobile Clinic Rental for Outreach Events: $500 per day, estimated 50 days = $25,000
- Fuel and Maintenance for Mobile Clinic: $7,500 annually

Total Travel and Transportation: $38,100

3. Event Costs
- Venue Rentals for Workshops: $500 per event, estimated 10 events = $5,000
- Refreshments for Workshops and Screenings: $200 per event, estimated 20 events = $4,000
- Incentives for Participants (e.g., gift cards): $10 per participant, estimated 2,000 participants = $20,000

Total Event Costs: $29,000

Total Variable Costs: $112,100

3. Total Budget

- Fixed Costs: $325,000
- Variable Costs: $112,100

Grand Total: $437,100

4. Accounting for Potential Funding Uncertainties and Resource Constraints

A. Contingency Planning

1. Contingency Fund: Set aside a 10% contingency fund to cover unexpected costs or shortfalls. This would amount to $43,710.
2. Prioritization of Expenses: Identify critical components of the initiative that must be funded regardless of financial constraints, such as essential personnel, medical supplies, and basic outreach efforts. Non-essential items like additional marketing materials or higher-cost event venues can be scaled back if necessary.

B. Phased Implementation

1. Phase 1 (First 6 Months): Focus on building infrastructure, hiring key personnel, and launching initial outreach and screening programs. This phase would require the majority of the fixed costs and some variable costs related to early outreach.
2. Phase 2 (Next 6 Months): Expand services based on initial success, adjusting the scale of workshops, screenings, and immunization drives according to the available budget. If funding is uncertain, Phase 2 activities can be adjusted or delayed.

C. Diversified Funding Sources

1. **Grants and Donations:** Apply for multiple grants, including federal, state, and private foundation funding. Engage with local businesses and philanthropists for donations, emphasizing the initiative's impact on community health.
2. **Partnerships:** Collaborate with local healthcare providers, nonprofits, and educational institutions to share resources and reduce costs. For example, a local university might offer free venues for workshops or donate educational materials.
3. **Sliding Scale Services:** If applicable, introduce a sliding scale payment system for certain services (like vaccinations) to partially offset costs while still making care accessible to low-income residents.

D. Resource Reallocation

1. **In-Kind Contributions:** Seek in-kind donations from businesses or partners, such as medical supplies, printing services, or marketing support, to reduce direct costs.
2. **Staff Time Allocation:** If financial constraints tighten, consider reallocating staff time to focus on the highest-impact activities. For example, if event costs need to be reduced, more staff time could be dedicated to one-on-one outreach or small group sessions instead of large events.

E. Continuous Monitoring and Adjustment

1. **Regular Budget Reviews:** Conduct quarterly budget reviews to assess spending against projections. Adjust allocations as needed to stay within budget while maximizing impact.
2. **Performance Metrics:** Monitor key performance indicators (KPIs) such as the number of participants reached, health outcomes improved, and cost per participant. Use this data to refine the initiative and justify continued funding to stakeholders.

Through careful planning, prioritization, and proactive management of resources and potential uncertainties, this comprehensive budget and strategy will help ensure the successful implementation of the community health initiative, maximizing its impact even in the face of financial challenges.

Forecasting patient volumes and staffing needs for the upcoming fiscal year requires a systematic approach that combines historical data analysis, recognition of seasonal trends, and consideration of potential disruptive events. By applying these forecasting techniques, nurse executives can ensure that the organization is prepared to meet patient demand while optimizing staffing levels for efficiency and quality care.

Step 1: Analyzing Historical Data

1. **Data Collection and Cleaning**
   o **Collect Historical Data:** Gather data from the past three to five years on patient volumes, broken down by department, time of year, day of the week, and even time of day if possible. This should include data on inpatient admissions, outpatient visits, emergency department (ED) visits, surgeries, and other key services.
   o **Data Cleaning:** Ensure the data is clean and accurate by checking for inconsistencies, missing entries, and outliers. Adjust or exclude any data points that are anomalies due to specific, one-time events (e.g., a natural disaster or a temporary facility closure).

2. **Trend Analysis**
   o **Identify Overall Trends:** Use statistical methods to identify long-term trends in patient volumes. For example, applying linear regression could help determine if there is a steady increase or decrease in patient numbers over time.
   o **Breakdown by Department:** Analyze trends separately for each department or service line. This helps in identifying specific areas that may be growing or declining differently from the overall trend.
   o **Staffing Correlation:** Compare historical patient volumes with staffing levels during the same periods to determine how staffing needs correlate with patient demand. This can help identify periods of overstaffing or understaffing.

Step 2: Incorporating Seasonal Trends

1. **Seasonal Pattern Identification**
   o **Seasonal Decomposition:** Use techniques such as Seasonal Decomposition of Time Series (STL) to break down the data into its trend, seasonal, and residual components. This allows for the

identification of predictable seasonal patterns—such as higher patient volumes during flu season or lower volumes in summer months.

- ○ **Compare Year-over-Year**: Look at patient volumes across the same months or quarters in previous years to identify consistent seasonal peaks and troughs. This comparison helps in fine-tuning predictions for specific times of the year.

2. **Adjusting Forecasts for Seasonality**
    - ○ **Seasonal Indexing**: Develop a seasonal index based on the historical data that adjusts the baseline forecast to account for expected seasonal variations. For instance, if patient volumes consistently rise by 20% in the winter, apply this index to your baseline forecast for those months.
    - ○ **Staffing Adjustments**: Based on the seasonal trends, adjust staffing levels proactively to ensure adequate coverage during high-demand periods and avoid overstaffing during low-demand times.

Step 3: Accounting for Potential Disruptive Events

1. **Identify Potential Disruptors**
    - ○ **Historical Disruptions**: Review past years for events that significantly impacted patient volumes, such as pandemics, economic downturns, natural disasters, or public health emergencies. Understanding their impact helps prepare for similar events in the future.
    - ○ **Upcoming Events**: Consider known future events that could disrupt patient volumes, such as major policy changes (e.g., healthcare reform), local events (e.g., large public gatherings), or global events (e.g., a predicted influenza outbreak).

2. **Scenario Planning**
    - ○ **Best-Case, Worst-Case, and Most Likely Scenarios**: Develop multiple scenarios based on different assumptions about the future. For example, the worst-case scenario might involve a resurgence of a pandemic, leading to increased patient volumes and higher staffing needs, while the best-case scenario might involve steady patient volumes with no major disruptions.
    - ○ **Sensitivity Analysis**: Use sensitivity analysis to understand how changes in key variables (e.g., infection rates, economic conditions) affect patient volumes. This analysis helps in understanding the range of possible outcomes and preparing flexible staffing plans.

3. **Contingency Planning**
    - ○ **Flexible Staffing Models**: Develop staffing models that can be quickly scaled up or down in response to sudden changes in patient volume. This could include cross-training staff to work in multiple departments or having a pool of part-time or per diem staff who can be called in during peak periods.
    - ○ **Emergency Protocols**: Ensure that emergency staffing protocols are in place for rapid deployment during disruptive events. This might include agreements with staffing agencies, clear communication channels, and predefined roles for staff during a crisis.

Step 4: Implementing and Monitoring the Forecast

1. **Implementing the Forecast**
    - ○ **Budget Alignment**: Align the staffing forecast with the organization's budget for the upcoming fiscal year. Ensure that financial resources are allocated appropriately to meet predicted staffing needs.
    - ○ **Scheduling**: Use the forecast to inform the creation of staffing schedules, ensuring that shifts are adequately covered during predicted peak times and adjusted for anticipated lower demand periods.

2. **Continuous Monitoring and Adjustment**
    - ○ **Real-Time Data**: Use real-time data tracking to monitor actual patient volumes and staffing levels throughout the year. This allows for immediate adjustments to the forecast if trends deviate from expectations.
    - ○ **Regular Reviews**: Conduct quarterly reviews of the forecast versus actual data to refine predictions and adjust staffing plans as needed. This ongoing process ensures that the organization remains responsive to changes and maintains optimal staffing levels.

Integration of Historical Data, Seasonal Trends, and Disruptive Events

By integrating historical data analysis, seasonal trends, and potential disruptive events, nurse executives can create a robust and flexible forecast for patient volumes and staffing needs. This approach not only helps in managing day-to-day operations efficiently but also ensures that the organization is well-prepared to handle unexpected challenges. This proactive strategy ultimately contributes to maintaining high-quality patient care and optimizing resource utilization throughout the fiscal year.

Business Plan for the Implementation of a New Telehealth Program
Executive Summary
The proposed telehealth program aims to expand access to healthcare services for underserved populations in rural and urban areas by offering virtual consultations, remote monitoring, and digital health education. This initiative aligns with the growing demand for convenient, cost-effective healthcare solutions and leverages advancements in technology to provide high-quality care. The business plan outlines the market opportunity, strategic approach, financial projections, and risk management strategies to ensure the program's success.

1. Market Analysis
A. Industry Overview
The global telehealth market has been experiencing rapid growth, driven by increasing healthcare costs, a rising demand for remote healthcare services, and advances in technology. In the U.S., the telehealth market was valued at approximately $10.3 billion in 2020 and is expected to reach $70 billion by 2026, with a compound annual growth rate (CAGR) of around 30%. The COVID-19 pandemic has significantly accelerated the adoption of telehealth, with regulatory changes making it easier to offer and reimburse virtual care services.

B. Target Market
- **Rural Populations:** Focus on areas where access to healthcare providers is limited. Approximately 20% of the U.S. population lives in rural areas, where there are often shortages of healthcare professionals.
- **Chronic Disease Management:** Target patients with chronic conditions such as diabetes, hypertension, and heart disease. These patients require regular monitoring and follow-up, which can be efficiently managed through telehealth.
- **Elderly Population:** With the aging population growing, telehealth offers a convenient way for seniors to access care without the challenges of transportation.

C. Competitive Landscape
- **Direct Competitors:** Current providers include established telehealth companies like Teladoc, Amwell, and Doctor on Demand. These companies offer a range of services, but there is still room for specialization, particularly in underserved markets.
- **Indirect Competitors:** Traditional healthcare providers offering in-person services. However, many are now incorporating telehealth as part of their service offerings.
- **Differentiation Strategy:** The program will differentiate itself by focusing on personalized care, integrating with local healthcare systems, and offering specialized services tailored to the needs of rural and elderly populations.

D. Market Needs
- **Convenience:** Patients increasingly seek healthcare services that are easily accessible from home.
- **Cost-Efficiency:** Telehealth reduces the cost of care by minimizing the need for physical infrastructure and in-person visits.
- **Accessibility:** Telehealth can overcome geographical barriers, making it possible for patients in remote areas to receive timely care.

2. Business Model
A. Revenue Streams
- **Direct Patient Billing:** Patients will be billed for virtual consultations, remote monitoring, and other telehealth services, either directly or through insurance reimbursement.
- **Partnerships with Healthcare Providers:** Revenue will also come from partnerships with local healthcare systems, where the telehealth platform will be integrated into their service offerings.

- **Subscription Model:** Introduce a subscription model for chronic disease management, where patients pay a monthly fee for continuous monitoring and virtual consultations.

B. Service Offerings

- **Virtual Consultations:** Offer general and specialist consultations through video conferencing.
- **Remote Monitoring:** Provide devices and software for continuous monitoring of chronic conditions, with data transmitted to healthcare providers for real-time intervention.
- **Digital Health Education:** Offer educational webinars and digital resources to help patients manage their health.

C. Technology Infrastructure

- **Platform Development:** Develop a user-friendly telehealth platform compatible with multiple devices (smartphones, tablets, computers) and integrated with electronic health records (EHR).
- **Data Security:** Implement robust cybersecurity measures to protect patient data and comply with HIPAA regulations.
- **Technical Support:** Provide 24/7 technical support to ensure smooth operation and customer satisfaction.

3. Financial Projections

A. Initial Investment

- **Technology Development:** $1.5 million (platform development, integration with EHR, cybersecurity)
- **Marketing and Customer Acquisition:** $500,000 (initial marketing campaigns, partnerships, and patient outreach)
- **Personnel:** $800,000 (hiring healthcare professionals, IT support, and administrative staff)
- **Licensing and Compliance:** $200,000 (state licenses, legal fees, and compliance audits)

Total Initial Investment: $3 million

B. Revenue Projections (First 5 Years)

- **Year 1:** $2 million (modest uptake, focus on establishing the service and building partnerships)
- **Year 2:** $5 million (expanded service offerings, increased patient adoption)
- **Year 3:** $10 million (full rollout, subscription model gains traction)
- **Year 4:** $15 million (additional services introduced, strong market presence)
- **Year 5:** $20 million (mature operations, broad patient base, steady growth)

C. Operating Expenses

- **Ongoing Technology Maintenance:** $500,000 annually
- **Personnel Costs:** $1 million annually (expanding team to meet growing demand)
- **Marketing and Sales:** $600,000 annually (continuous patient acquisition and retention efforts)
- **General and Administrative:** $300,000 annually (office space, utilities, legal fees)

Total Annual Operating Expenses: $2.4 million

D. Profitability Timeline

- **Break-Even Point:** Expected in Year 3 as the program scales and subscription revenue grows.
- **Net Profit:** Anticipated to reach $7.6 million by Year 5.

4. Risk Assessment and Mitigation

A. Regulatory Risks

- **Potential Changes in Telehealth Reimbursement:** Changes in state or federal regulations could impact reimbursement rates for telehealth services.
  - **Mitigation:** Diversify revenue streams by offering subscription services and exploring direct-to-consumer models that are less dependent on insurance reimbursement.

B. Technology Risks

- **Data Breach or System Failures:** A cybersecurity breach or major technical issue could compromise patient data and disrupt services.
  - **Mitigation:** Invest in top-tier cybersecurity measures, regular audits, and have a crisis response plan in place.

C. Market Adoption Risks

- **Slow Patient Adoption:** Patients, particularly in older demographics, may be hesitant to adopt telehealth services.
  - ○ **Mitigation:** Develop targeted educational campaigns to demonstrate the benefits of telehealth and offer technical support to ease the transition.

D. Competition Risks

- **Market Saturation:** Increased competition from existing telehealth providers could limit market share.
  - ○ **Mitigation:** Focus on niche markets (rural, elderly, chronic disease management) and build strong relationships with local healthcare providers to create barriers to entry for competitors.

5. Presentation to Investors or Board Members

A. Introduction

- **Brief Overview:** Begin with a concise summary of the telehealth program, emphasizing its alignment with market trends and the growing demand for remote healthcare services.
- **Vision and Goals:** Highlight the program's potential to transform healthcare delivery, improve patient outcomes, and generate sustainable revenue.

B. Market Opportunity

- **Data-Driven Insights:** Present data from the market analysis, including growth projections and unmet needs, to demonstrate the lucrative opportunity in the telehealth space.
- **Competitive Advantage:** Explain how the program's focus on underserved markets, personalized care, and integration with local healthcare systems differentiates it from competitors.

C. Financial Projections

- **Clear Projections:** Use visuals like charts and graphs to illustrate the financial trajectory, including revenue growth, operating expenses, and profitability timelines.
- **Investment Ask:** Clearly state the investment required and what it will be used for, along with expected returns.

D. Risk Management

- **Transparency:** Acknowledge the risks associated with the telehealth program and present well-thought-out mitigation strategies.
- **Confidence in Success:** Emphasize the team's ability to navigate challenges, backed by a robust risk management plan.

E. Call to Action

- **Engage the Audience:** Invite questions, solicit feedback, and encourage board members or investors to see this as a pivotal opportunity to be part of a transformative healthcare initiative.
- **Next Steps:** Outline the timeline for securing funding, launching the program, and achieving key milestones.

This business plan provides a comprehensive roadmap for launching a successful telehealth program, demonstrating the potential for both financial returns and significant social impact. By addressing market needs, planning for risks, and presenting a solid financial strategy, this plan is designed to inspire confidence and secure the necessary support from investors or board members.

Calculating the return on investment (ROI) for a proposed nurse residency program involves quantifying both tangible benefits, such as cost savings from reduced turnover, and intangible benefits, such as improved patient outcomes and staff satisfaction. This comprehensive approach helps justify the initial costs of the program by demonstrating its long-term value to the organization.

Step 1: Calculate Tangible Benefits

1. **Reduction in Nurse Turnover**
   - ○ **Current Turnover Rate:** Start by determining the current turnover rate among new nurses (e.g., nurses with less than one year of experience).
   - ○ **Turnover Costs:** Calculate the cost of turnover, including recruitment, hiring, orientation, and lost productivity. The average cost of nurse turnover is estimated to be around $44,000 to $88,000 per nurse, depending on the organization and region.

- Projected Turnover Reduction: Research indicates that nurse residency programs can reduce turnover by 20% to 30%. Apply this percentage to the current turnover rate to estimate the number of nurses who will be retained due to the residency program.
- Cost Savings from Reduced Turnover: Multiply the projected number of retained nurses by the cost of turnover to estimate the total cost savings.

Example:

- Current Turnover Rate: 25% for new nurses.
- Number of New Nurses: 100.
- Turnover Cost per Nurse: $60,000.
- Projected Turnover Reduction: 25% reduction (from 25% to 18.75%).
- Nurses Retained Due to Program: (25% - 18.75%) * 100 = 6.25 nurses.
- Cost Savings: 6.25 nurses * $60,000 = **$375,000**.

2. **Improved Productivity**
   - Faster Time to Competency: Nurse residency programs accelerate the time it takes for new nurses to become fully competent, which improves productivity.
   - Productivity Gains: Estimate the value of increased productivity, considering factors such as reduced errors, faster patient care delivery, and increased capacity to handle patient loads.

Example:

- Estimated Productivity Gain: $10,000 per nurse.
- Total Productivity Gain: 100 nurses * $10,000 = **$1,000,000**.

3. **Enhanced Patient Care and Safety**
   - Reduction in Adverse Events: Improved training leads to fewer adverse events, such as medication errors and patient falls, which can be costly for the organization.
   - Cost Savings from Reduced Adverse Events: Estimate the reduction in adverse events and calculate the associated cost savings.

Example:

- Reduction in Adverse Events: 5 fewer events per year.
- Cost per Adverse Event: $25,000.
- Cost Savings: 5 events * $25,000 = **$125,000**.

Step 2: Estimate Intangible Benefits

1. **Improved Patient Satisfaction**
   - Impact on Reputation and Revenue: Higher patient satisfaction can lead to better patient retention, more referrals, and potentially higher reimbursements in value-based care models.
   - Qualitative Impact: While difficult to quantify, the reputation of the organization as a high-quality care provider can attract more patients and skilled staff.

2. **Increased Staff Satisfaction and Engagement**
   - Better Retention of Experienced Nurses: A supportive environment that includes a residency program can lead to higher job satisfaction among experienced nurses, reducing their turnover as well.
   - Impact on Workplace Culture: Enhanced morale and a positive work environment contribute to a culture of excellence, which can improve overall organizational performance.

3. **Leadership Development**
   - Building Future Leaders: Nurse residency programs often include leadership development components, preparing nurses for future leadership roles within the organization.
   - Long-Term Organizational Stability: Developing internal talent for leadership positions ensures organizational continuity and reduces the costs associated with external recruitment for these roles.

Step 3: Calculate the Total ROI

1. **Total Tangible Benefits**
   - Add up all tangible benefits from turnover reduction, improved productivity, and enhanced patient care.

Example:

- Turnover Reduction Savings: $375,000.
- Productivity Gains: $1,000,000.
- Patient Care Improvements: $125,000.
- **Total Tangible Benefits: $1,500,000**.

2. **Total Costs of the Nurse Residency Program**
   - **Program Development Costs**: Include costs for curriculum development, faculty, and resources.
   - **Operational Costs**: Include costs for program administration, ongoing training, and materials.
   - **Opportunity Costs**: Consider the time nurses spend in the program instead of providing direct care, though this is offset by the long-term benefits.

Example:
   - Program Development: $200,000.
   - Operational Costs: $150,000.
   - Opportunity Costs: $150,000.
   - **Total Program Costs: $500,000**.

3. **ROI Calculation**
   - ROI = (Total Tangible Benefits - Total Program Costs) / Total Program Costs * 100.
   - **Example:**
     - ROI = ($1,500,000 - $500,000) / $500,000 * 100 = **200%**.

Justifying the Initial Costs

1. **Long-Term Financial Benefits**
   - A 200% ROI demonstrates that the program not only pays for itself but also generates significant savings for the organization. These savings can be reinvested into further improving patient care, expanding services, or enhancing facilities.

2. **Sustainable Workforce Development**
   - The residency program contributes to a more stable and satisfied nursing workforce, which is crucial for maintaining high standards of patient care. By reducing turnover and fostering professional development, the program ensures that the organization remains competitive in a challenging healthcare market.

3. **Enhanced Patient Outcomes and Safety**
   - Improved patient care and safety reduce the likelihood of costly adverse events and enhance the organization's reputation. This not only improves patient satisfaction but can also lead to better outcomes in value-based care models, where reimbursement is linked to quality metrics.

4. **Strategic Alignment with Organizational Goals**
   - Investing in a nurse residency program aligns with the organization's mission to provide high-quality, patient-centered care. It also supports long-term strategic goals, such as becoming a preferred employer, improving clinical outcomes, and positioning the organization as a leader in healthcare excellence.

The initial costs of the nurse residency program are justified by the substantial ROI and the long-term benefits to both the organization and its stakeholders. This investment supports the organization's growth, stability, and commitment to quality care.

Quality and Safety

The Joint Commission's National Patient Safety Goals (NPSGs) for 2024 are designed to address critical areas of patient safety in response to evolving healthcare challenges. These goals focus on preventing common but serious issues, enhancing communication, and improving the overall quality of care across various clinical settings. Nurse executives play a crucial role in ensuring that these goals are implemented effectively, requiring targeted strategies tailored to the unique needs of different healthcare environments.

Overview of the 2024 National Patient Safety Goals

1. **Improve the Accuracy of Patient Identification**
   o **Goal:** Ensure that each patient receives the correct treatment by verifying their identity using at least two patient identifiers (e.g., name and date of birth).
   o **Emerging Challenge:** Increased use of telehealth and remote services can complicate patient identification, especially in virtual consultations where traditional verification methods might be less effective.

2. **Enhance Communication Among Caregivers**
   o **Goal:** Improve the effectiveness of communication among caregivers, particularly regarding critical test results and patient handoffs.
   o **Emerging Challenge:** The complexity of care transitions, particularly in settings where multiple providers are involved, increases the risk of miscommunication and errors.

3. **Medication Safety**
   o **Goal:** Reduce the harm associated with the use of anticoagulants, identify and resolve discrepancies in patient medications during care transitions, and ensure accurate medication labeling.
   o **Emerging Challenge:** The rise in polypharmacy, especially among elderly patients and those with chronic conditions, makes medication reconciliation more challenging and critical.

4. **Reduce Healthcare-Associated Infections (HAIs)**
   o **Goal:** Implement evidence-based practices to prevent common HAIs, including catheter-associated urinary tract infections (CAUTIs), central line-associated bloodstream infections (CLABSIs), and surgical site infections (SSIs).
   o **Emerging Challenge:** The ongoing threat of antimicrobial resistance and the impact of new and emerging infectious diseases necessitate continuous vigilance and adaptation of infection control practices.

5. **Preventing Patient Falls**
   o **Goal:** Assess and address the risk of patient falls, particularly in high-risk populations such as the elderly or those with mobility impairments.
   o **Emerging Challenge:** The increasing prevalence of frailty and cognitive decline among the aging population heightens the need for effective fall prevention strategies.

6. **Improve Surgical Safety**
   o **Goal:** Ensure that the correct surgery is performed on the correct patient and at the correct site, often using a surgical safety checklist.
   o **Emerging Challenge:** The growing complexity of surgical procedures and the use of advanced technologies such as robotics require meticulous planning and verification processes.

7. **Preventing Pressure Injuries**
   o **Goal:** Reduce the incidence of pressure injuries through regular assessment, early intervention, and evidence-based preventive measures.
   o **Emerging Challenge:** Patients with limited mobility, especially in long-term care or rehabilitation settings, are increasingly at risk as populations age.

Strategies for Nurse Executives to Ensure Compliance

1. **Tailored Education and Training Programs**
   o **Approach:** Develop and implement ongoing education and training programs that are customized to the specific needs of different clinical settings (e.g., acute care, long-term care, outpatient

facilities). Use simulation-based training to reinforce best practices, particularly for goals related to surgical safety, infection control, and fall prevention.
- o **Example:** Implement a competency-based training module on patient identification that includes scenarios relevant to telehealth and remote care environments.

2. **Implementation of Standardized Protocols and Checklists**
   - o **Approach:** Standardize protocols and checklists across all units to ensure consistency in critical areas such as patient identification, medication reconciliation, and surgical safety. These should be tailored to the workflow of each department and updated regularly based on the latest guidelines and evidence.
   - o **Example:** Introduce a digital handoff tool that ensures all relevant patient information is communicated clearly during care transitions, reducing the risk of miscommunication.

3. **Enhanced Communication and Collaboration**
   - o **Approach:** Foster a culture of open communication and teamwork, particularly during patient handoffs and interdisciplinary care planning. Regular interdisciplinary meetings and huddles can be effective in aligning teams on patient safety priorities.
   - o **Example:** Establish a "safety champion" role within each department, tasked with facilitating communication and ensuring that safety protocols are followed consistently.

4. **Leverage Technology and Data Analytics**
   - o **Approach:** Utilize electronic health records (EHRs) and data analytics to track compliance with safety goals, identify trends, and address potential gaps. Technology can also support real-time monitoring of patient conditions and automated alerts for high-risk situations.
   - o **Example:** Implement an EHR-integrated medication reconciliation tool that prompts clinicians to verify and update medication lists during each patient encounter, particularly during care transitions.

5. **Engage Patients and Families in Safety Practices**
   - o **Approach:** Involve patients and their families in safety initiatives by educating them on their role in the care process, such as verifying their identity before procedures and understanding their medication regimens. Providing clear, accessible information can empower them to participate actively in their care.
   - o **Example:** Develop a patient safety guide that explains the importance of patient identification and what patients can do to help ensure their information is accurate during telehealth appointments.

6. **Monitor and Adjust for Continuous Improvement**
   - o **Approach:** Establish a continuous quality improvement (CQI) process that regularly reviews compliance with the NPSGs, assesses the effectiveness of implemented strategies, and makes necessary adjustments. This should include regular audits, feedback loops, and action plans for addressing identified issues.
   - o **Example:** Conduct quarterly safety audits in all departments to review adherence to infection control protocols, with immediate corrective actions taken for any lapses identified.

Addressing Emerging Challenges

- **Adapting to Remote Care Settings:** As telehealth becomes more prevalent, nurse executives should focus on adapting traditional safety protocols to remote care environments. This includes revising patient identification procedures for virtual consultations and ensuring that communication tools are optimized for digital platforms.

- **Managing Complex Care Transitions:** With the increasing complexity of care transitions, particularly in multi-provider scenarios, implementing robust communication systems that ensure all relevant information is transferred accurately and comprehensively is crucial.

- **Preventing Polypharmacy Risks:** To address the challenge of polypharmacy, especially among elderly patients, nurse executives should implement rigorous medication reconciliation processes that are integrated into every point of care, supported by both technology and clinical oversight.

By implementing these strategies, nurse executives can ensure that the 2024 National Patient Safety Goals are met consistently across diverse clinical settings, ultimately leading to improved patient outcomes and enhanced overall safety.

The Joint Commission's New Leadership Standards are designed to enhance the leadership practices within healthcare organizations, directly impacting the culture of safety and quality improvement. These standards emphasize the importance of effective leadership in creating an environment where patient safety and continuous quality improvement are central to organizational operations. Nurse executives, as key leaders, play a crucial role in ensuring compliance with these standards and fostering a culture that prioritizes safety and quality.

Impact of The Joint Commission's New Leadership Standards

1. **Strengthening Governance and Accountability**
   - **Impact**: The standards require healthcare organizations to establish clear governance structures that define roles, responsibilities, and accountability for safety and quality. This ensures that leaders at all levels are aligned in their commitment to these priorities.
   - **Promotion of Safety and Quality**: By holding leaders accountable, these standards help ensure that safety and quality are not just delegated tasks but are integrated into the organization's strategic goals and day-to-day operations. Leaders are expected to set the tone for a culture where safety is prioritized, and quality improvement initiatives are actively pursued.

2. **Promoting Effective Communication**
   - **Impact**: Effective communication is critical for identifying and addressing safety concerns and quality issues. The standards emphasize the need for open, transparent communication channels across all levels of the organization.
   - **Promotion of Safety and Quality**: Open communication encourages the reporting of errors, near misses, and safety hazards without fear of retribution, which is essential for a culture of safety. Regular communication about quality improvement initiatives and progress helps to engage all staff in these efforts.

3. **Fostering a Culture of Continuous Improvement**
   - **Impact**: The standards mandate that leadership actively supports and participates in continuous quality improvement efforts. This includes the implementation of evidence-based practices and the use of data to drive improvements.
   - **Promotion of Safety and Quality**: Continuous improvement efforts ensure that the organization is always looking for ways to enhance patient care, reduce errors, and increase efficiency. By embedding these practices into the organizational culture, leaders ensure that quality improvement is a perpetual process.

4. **Emphasizing Staff Competence and Professional Development**
   - **Impact**: The standards require that healthcare organizations invest in the ongoing education and professional development of their staff. This ensures that all team members are equipped with the latest knowledge and skills to provide safe, high-quality care.
   - **Promotion of Safety and Quality**: Competent, well-trained staff are less likely to make errors and more likely to contribute positively to quality improvement initiatives. Continuous professional development also keeps the workforce engaged and aligned with the organization's safety and quality goals.

Examples of Compliance with Specific Leadership Standards

1. **Standard LD.03.01.01: The governing body is ultimately accountable for the safety and quality of care, treatment, and services.**
   - **Demonstrating Compliance**: Nurse executives can ensure that safety and quality metrics are regularly reported to the governing body. For example, they might present quarterly reports that detail the outcomes of safety initiatives, patient satisfaction surveys, and quality improvement projects. They can also establish committees or task forces that include members of the governing body to oversee these areas and make strategic decisions based on the data provided.

2. **Standard LD.03.04.01: Leaders develop and implement policies and procedures that support safety and quality.**
   - **Demonstrating Compliance**: Nurse executives can lead the development of policies that are directly aligned with safety and quality goals, such as a standardized process for incident reporting or protocols for infection control. These policies should be evidence-based and regularly reviewed

to ensure they are effective. Nurse executives can also ensure that these policies are communicated effectively to all staff through training sessions and regular updates.

3. **Standard LD.03.05.01: Leaders create and maintain a culture of safety and quality throughout the organization.**
   - ○ **Demonstrating Compliance**: Nurse executives can demonstrate a commitment to a culture of safety by establishing a non-punitive reporting system for errors and near misses. This system encourages staff to report safety concerns without fear of blame, enabling the organization to learn from these events and implement preventive measures. Additionally, nurse executives can conduct regular safety rounds where they engage directly with staff to discuss safety issues and gather feedback on potential improvements.

4. **Standard LD.03.06.01: Leaders regularly evaluate the culture of safety and quality using valid and reliable tools.**
   - ○ **Demonstrating Compliance**: Nurse executives can lead the administration of safety culture surveys, such as the Agency for Healthcare Research and Quality's (AHRQ) Hospital Survey on Patient Safety Culture, to assess the organization's safety climate. The results of these surveys should be analyzed and used to inform quality improvement initiatives. Nurse executives can also benchmark their organization's performance against industry standards to identify areas for improvement and track progress over time.

5. **Standard LD.04.04.01: Leaders establish priorities for performance improvement.**
   - ○ **Demonstrating Compliance**: Nurse executives can use data from incident reports, patient outcomes, and staff feedback to identify priority areas for improvement. For instance, if the data shows a rising trend in medication errors, the nurse executive might prioritize the implementation of a new electronic medication administration record (eMAR) system. They can then monitor the impact of this intervention and adjust strategies as needed to ensure continuous improvement.

Promoting a Culture of Safety and Quality Improvement

The Joint Commission's Leadership Standards are instrumental in promoting a culture where safety and quality are ingrained in every aspect of healthcare delivery. Nurse executives, as leaders, are pivotal in driving compliance with these standards by setting clear expectations, providing the necessary resources, and leading by example. By doing so, they not only meet regulatory requirements but also foster an environment where continuous improvement thrives, ultimately leading to better patient outcomes and a safer healthcare environment.

The Centers for Medicare & Medicaid Services (CMS) Conditions of Participation (CoPs) and the Joint Commission standards are both critical frameworks that healthcare organizations must adhere to in order to ensure safe, effective, and compliant operations. While both sets of requirements aim to improve patient care and organizational quality, they differ in scope, focus, and specificity. Understanding these differences and similarities is essential for nurse executives tasked with integrating these requirements into daily operations.

Comparison of CMS Conditions of Participation and Joint Commission Standards

Scope and Purpose

- **CMS Conditions of Participation (CoPs):**
  - ○ **Scope:** CMS CoPs are federally mandated regulations that apply to all healthcare organizations participating in Medicare and Medicaid programs. These conditions are the baseline requirements for hospitals and other healthcare entities to receive reimbursement from CMS.
  - ○ **Purpose:** The primary purpose of the CoPs is to ensure that healthcare providers meet minimum safety and quality standards. These regulations cover a broad range of operational areas, including patient rights, infection control, medical record services, and emergency preparedness.

- **Joint Commission Standards:**
  - ○ **Scope:** The Joint Commission's standards are voluntary, though widely adopted, and apply to healthcare organizations seeking accreditation. These standards are more comprehensive and often go beyond the minimum requirements set by CMS, addressing specific aspects of patient care, safety, and organizational management.
  - ○ **Purpose:** The Joint Commission's standards focus on continuous improvement in patient care quality and safety. They provide a framework for healthcare organizations to achieve higher levels

of performance and patient outcomes, often using evidence-based practices and performance improvement methodologies.

Focus Areas

- **CMS Conditions of Participation:**
  - The CoPs are highly prescriptive, focusing on compliance with federal laws and regulations. Key areas include:
    - **Patient Rights:** Ensuring patient privacy, informed consent, and access to care.
    - **Infection Control:** Mandates for infection prevention programs and protocols.
    - **Emergency Preparedness:** Requirements for emergency plans and disaster preparedness.
    - **Medical Record Services:** Standards for the maintenance, confidentiality, and completeness of patient records.

- **Joint Commission Standards:**
  - The Joint Commission's standards are more flexible and comprehensive, focusing on specific practices that enhance patient safety and care quality. Key areas include:
    - **Leadership and Governance:** Emphasizes the role of leadership in driving quality improvement and ensuring compliance.
    - **Environment of Care:** Standards for the physical environment, including safety, security, and infection control.
    - **Medication Management:** Detailed guidelines for the safe prescribing, dispensing, and administration of medications.
    - **Performance Improvement:** Encourages continuous improvement through data-driven analysis and the implementation of best practices.

Compliance and Accreditation

- **CMS Conditions of Participation:**
  - Compliance with CoPs is mandatory for Medicare and Medicaid reimbursement. CMS conducts surveys (often through state agencies) to ensure compliance, and failure to meet these conditions can result in penalties, loss of reimbursement, or exclusion from the Medicare and Medicaid programs.

- **Joint Commission Standards:**
  - Joint Commission accreditation is voluntary but highly regarded. It involves rigorous on-site evaluations and surveys. Accreditation can enhance a healthcare organization's reputation and may lead to preferred status with payers and other stakeholders. While Joint Commission accreditation often implies compliance with CMS CoPs, it is not a substitute for federal compliance.

Strategies for Nurse Executives to Integrate Requirements and Avoid Redundancy

1. **Develop a Unified Compliance Framework**
   - **Approach:** Create a single, comprehensive compliance framework that integrates both CMS CoPs and Joint Commission standards. This framework should map out where the two sets of requirements overlap and where they diverge, ensuring that all regulatory and accreditation standards are met without duplication of effort.
   - **Example:** Implement a centralized compliance tracking system that flags specific standards and conditions that apply across both CMS and Joint Commission frameworks. This allows staff to address multiple requirements simultaneously during audits, training, and daily operations.

2. **Standardize Policies and Procedures**
   - **Approach:** Align organizational policies and procedures with both CMS and Joint Commission requirements. Where standards overlap, develop standardized procedures that meet both sets of requirements, reducing the need for separate documentation or processes.
   - **Example:** A single policy on patient rights can be crafted to comply with both CMS CoPs (e.g., privacy, informed consent) and Joint Commission standards (e.g., communication of care plans, patient involvement in decision-making).

3. **Leverage Technology for Integrated Compliance**
   - o **Approach:** Utilize electronic health record (EHR) systems and compliance management software to automate documentation and ensure adherence to both CMS and Joint Commission requirements. These systems can help manage workflows, track compliance metrics, and generate reports that satisfy both regulatory and accreditation needs.
   - o **Example:** Use EHR prompts and checklists to ensure that staff complete required documentation (e.g., medication reconciliation) that meets both CMS and Joint Commission standards, thus streamlining the compliance process.
4. **Focus on Education and Training**
   - o **Approach:** Design training programs that cover both CMS CoPs and Joint Commission standards, emphasizing their integration into daily practice. Educate staff on the importance of compliance with both frameworks and how they contribute to overall patient safety and quality improvement.
   - o **Example:** Develop a comprehensive training module on infection control that addresses both CMS requirements for infection prevention and Joint Commission guidelines on best practices for reducing healthcare-associated infections (HAIs).
5. **Establish Cross-Functional Compliance Committees**
   - o **Approach:** Form cross-functional committees that include representatives from nursing, administration, legal, and quality improvement to oversee compliance efforts. These committees can monitor changes in CMS and Joint Commission standards, ensuring that the organization stays current and avoids redundancy.
   - o **Example:** A compliance committee might review and update the organization's emergency preparedness plan annually, ensuring it meets both CMS CoPs and Joint Commission standards for disaster readiness and response.
6. **Continuous Monitoring and Improvement**
   - o **Approach:** Implement a continuous monitoring process that tracks compliance with both CMS CoPs and Joint Commission standards. Use regular audits, surveys, and performance metrics to identify areas of overlap, potential gaps, and opportunities for improvement.
   - o **Example:** Conduct quarterly compliance audits that include both CMS and Joint Commission requirements, allowing for real-time adjustments to policies and procedures based on audit findings.

By integrating CMS Conditions of Participation with Joint Commission standards into a cohesive operational framework, nurse executives can ensure comprehensive compliance while minimizing redundancy. This approach not only simplifies regulatory adherence but also enhances the overall quality of care, driving continuous improvement across the organization.

The Centers for Medicare & Medicaid Services (CMS) Hospital Value-Based Purchasing (VBP) Program significantly impacts healthcare quality and financial performance by linking a portion of hospital payments to the quality of care they provide. Under this program, hospitals are incentivized to improve clinical outcomes, patient satisfaction, safety, and efficiency, as performance in these domains directly affects their reimbursement rates. Nurse executives play a crucial role in optimizing performance across these domains, ensuring that the hospital not only delivers high-quality care but also maintains financial stability.

Impact of the CMS Hospital Value-Based Purchasing Program
1. **Improvement in Healthcare Quality**
   - o The VBP program encourages hospitals to enhance the quality of care by tying reimbursement to performance in key areas. This has led to increased focus on evidence-based practices, better patient outcomes, and greater accountability in healthcare delivery.
   - o Hospitals must meet or exceed performance benchmarks in Clinical Outcomes, Person and Community Engagement, Safety, and Efficiency and Cost Reduction to receive higher payments. Poor performance can result in reduced payments, which incentivizes continuous quality improvement.
2. **Financial Implications**

- The program adjusts hospital payments based on their performance in the VBP domains, meaning that hospitals performing well can earn back their withheld payments and potentially receive additional bonuses, while poor performers may see a reduction in payments.
- For hospitals, this creates a direct financial incentive to invest in quality improvement initiatives. However, it also presents a financial risk if performance does not meet CMS benchmarks, potentially leading to significant revenue losses.

Optimizing Performance Across the VBP Program's Domains

1. **Clinical Outcomes**
   - **Focus on Evidence-Based Practices**: Nurse executives can drive the implementation of evidence-based protocols and guidelines to improve clinical outcomes. For example, standardizing care processes for conditions like heart failure, pneumonia, and acute myocardial infarction can reduce variability in care and improve patient outcomes.
   - **Data-Driven Decision-Making**: Utilize data analytics to monitor clinical performance metrics in real-time, identify trends, and implement targeted interventions. For instance, if data shows a rise in hospital readmissions, nurse executives can lead initiatives to improve discharge planning, patient education, and follow-up care to address the underlying causes.
   - **Interdisciplinary Collaboration**: Foster collaboration among nursing, physician, and allied health teams to ensure comprehensive care management, particularly for high-risk patients. Regular multidisciplinary rounds can help address complex cases more effectively, reducing complications and improving outcomes.

2. **Person and Community Engagement**
   - **Enhance Patient Experience**: Patient satisfaction scores, particularly from the Hospital Consumer Assessment of Healthcare Providers and Systems (HCAHPS) survey, are a key component of the VBP program. Nurse executives can lead efforts to improve communication, responsiveness, and patient-centered care. Initiatives such as nurse leader rounding, bedside shift reports, and personalized discharge instructions can improve the patient experience.
   - **Community Outreach and Education**: Engaging with the community through education programs, health fairs, and support groups can enhance public perception and trust in the hospital. This engagement not only improves HCAHPS scores but also promotes preventive care, leading to better health outcomes and reduced hospitalizations.
   - **Patient and Family Involvement**: Encouraging active patient and family participation in care decisions can improve satisfaction and outcomes. Implementing shared decision-making models and ensuring that patients have access to the information they need to make informed choices can positively impact person and community engagement metrics.

3. **Safety**
   - **Reduce Hospital-Acquired Conditions (HACs)**: HACs, such as infections, falls, and pressure ulcers, negatively impact safety scores. Nurse executives can champion initiatives to prevent these conditions by enforcing strict adherence to infection control practices, implementing fall prevention protocols, and ensuring that pressure ulcer prevention strategies are in place.
   - **Promote a Culture of Safety**: Creating an environment where staff feel comfortable reporting errors and near misses is essential for identifying and addressing safety issues. Nurse executives can lead efforts to establish a non-punitive reporting system, conduct regular safety huddles, and provide ongoing education on safety practices.
   - **Standardize Care Protocols**: Implementing standardized care protocols for high-risk procedures and patient populations can reduce variability and improve safety outcomes. For example, standardizing the use of checklists in surgical procedures and central line insertions can significantly reduce the risk of complications.

4. **Efficiency and Cost Reduction**
   - **Streamline Care Processes**: Nurse executives can lead efforts to eliminate inefficiencies in care delivery by streamlining processes, reducing redundancies, and optimizing resource utilization. For example, implementing Lean or Six Sigma methodologies can identify waste and improve workflow efficiency, leading to cost savings and better patient care.

- o **Focus on Preventive Care**: Emphasizing preventive care and early intervention can reduce the need for more expensive, acute care services. Nurse executives can advocate for increased investment in preventive services, such as vaccinations, screenings, and chronic disease management programs, which can help reduce overall healthcare costs while improving patient outcomes.
- o **Monitor and Manage Resource Utilization**: Regularly review resource utilization data, including length of stay, medication use, and supply costs, to identify opportunities for cost reduction. Nurse executives can implement strategies to optimize resource use, such as standardizing orders for high-cost medications or reducing unnecessary diagnostic testing, while maintaining high-quality care.

Integrating Strategies for Optimal Performance

To optimize performance across the VBP program's domains, nurse executives should take an integrated approach that aligns organizational priorities with the program's goals. This involves:

- **Cross-Functional Collaboration**: Engage all departments—nursing, physicians, administration, finance, and quality improvement—in regular discussions about VBP performance. Collaborative efforts are necessary to ensure that initiatives are well-coordinated and that all staff understand their role in meeting VBP goals.
- **Continuous Monitoring and Feedback**: Establish a robust system for continuous monitoring of performance metrics in each VBP domain. Regular feedback sessions should be held to assess progress, identify challenges, and adjust strategies as needed to stay on track.
- **Staff Education and Engagement**: Provide ongoing education and training for staff on the importance of the VBP program and how their daily work impacts these metrics. Engaging staff at all levels creates a shared commitment to achieving the organization's quality and financial goals.

By strategically addressing each domain of the VBP program, nurse executives can improve both healthcare quality and the organization's financial performance, ensuring that their hospital not only meets CMS requirements but also excels in delivering high-quality, patient-centered care.

The Magnet Recognition Program®, developed by the American Nurses Credentialing Center (ANCC), is a prestigious designation that recognizes healthcare organizations for excellence in nursing practice and patient care. The program has a significant impact on nursing excellence and patient outcomes, fostering an environment where high-quality care is not only prioritized but also continuously improved. The five components of the Magnet Model—Transformational Leadership, Structural Empowerment, Exemplary Professional Practice, New Knowledge, Innovations & Improvements, and Empirical Outcomes—each play a critical role in driving organizational success.

Impact of the Magnet Recognition Program® on Nursing Excellence and Patient Outcomes

1. **Enhanced Patient Outcomes:** Research consistently shows that Magnet-recognized hospitals have lower patient mortality rates, fewer complications, and higher patient satisfaction compared to non-Magnet hospitals. These outcomes are attributed to the program's emphasis on nursing excellence, evidence-based practice, and a supportive work environment.
2. **Increased Nurse Satisfaction and Retention:** Magnet recognition is associated with higher job satisfaction among nurses, leading to lower turnover rates. Nurses in Magnet hospitals report feeling more empowered, supported, and engaged in their work, which directly contributes to better patient care.
3. **Improved Professional Development:** The Magnet program fosters a culture of continuous learning and professional development. Nurses in Magnet-recognized organizations have greater opportunities for career advancement, ongoing education, and participation in research and innovation.
4. **Organizational Reputation and Financial Performance:** Achieving Magnet recognition enhances a hospital's reputation, making it a preferred choice for patients, nurses, and other healthcare professionals. This can lead to better financial performance through increased patient volumes and the ability to attract and retain top talent.

Contribution of the Five Magnet Model Components to Organizational Success

1. **Transformational Leadership**
   - o **Overview:** Transformational leadership in the Magnet Model involves visionary leaders who inspire and motivate their teams to achieve excellence in patient care. These leaders are forward-thinking, innovative, and committed to fostering a culture of continuous improvement.

- o **Contribution to Success:** Transformational leaders play a pivotal role in setting the strategic direction of the organization, aligning nursing goals with broader organizational objectives, and creating an environment where nurses are empowered to take initiative and lead change. This leadership style promotes a sense of ownership among nurses, leading to higher levels of engagement and accountability, which ultimately enhances patient care and outcomes.

2. **Structural Empowerment**
   - o **Overview:** Structural empowerment refers to the organization's infrastructure and resources that enable nurses to contribute meaningfully to decision-making processes, professional development, and community outreach. This component emphasizes decentralized decision-making and shared governance.
   - o **Contribution to Success:** By providing nurses with the autonomy and resources to participate in decision-making, Magnet hospitals ensure that frontline staff can influence policies and practices directly related to patient care. This empowerment leads to more responsive, patient-centered care and fosters a culture of collaboration and respect. Additionally, opportunities for professional growth and community engagement enhance job satisfaction and retention, further contributing to organizational stability and success.

3. **Exemplary Professional Practice**
   - o **Overview:** Exemplary professional practice is the foundation of the Magnet Model, focusing on the delivery of high-quality care through evidence-based practice, interdisciplinary collaboration, and a strong professional identity among nurses.
   - o **Contribution to Success:** By promoting the highest standards of nursing practice, Magnet hospitals achieve better patient outcomes, including lower infection rates, reduced readmissions, and higher patient satisfaction. The emphasis on evidence-based practice ensures that care is grounded in the latest research and best practices, leading to more effective and efficient patient care. The collaborative environment also strengthens teamwork across disciplines, enhancing the overall quality of care delivered.

4. **New Knowledge, Innovations & Improvements**
   - o **Overview:** This component encourages continuous learning and the integration of new knowledge, research, and innovations into nursing practice. It involves fostering a culture of inquiry where nurses are encouraged to engage in research, pilot new practices, and contribute to the advancement of the nursing profession.
   - o **Contribution to Success:** The focus on innovation ensures that Magnet hospitals are at the forefront of healthcare delivery, continuously adapting to new challenges and opportunities. By supporting nursing research and the implementation of innovative practices, these organizations improve patient care processes, reduce errors, and enhance outcomes. Furthermore, this commitment to innovation attracts top nursing talent who are eager to work in an environment that values and promotes cutting-edge practice.

5. **Empirical Outcomes**
   - o **Overview:** Empirical outcomes refer to the measurable results that demonstrate the impact of nursing practices on patient care, workforce satisfaction, and organizational performance. This component emphasizes the use of data to assess and improve clinical outcomes, patient satisfaction, and operational efficiency.
   - o **Contribution to Success:** By rigorously tracking and analyzing outcomes, Magnet hospitals can identify areas for improvement and implement targeted interventions to enhance performance. The focus on empirical data ensures that decision-making is evidence-based and aligned with the organization's goals. This results-driven approach leads to sustained improvements in patient care quality, nurse engagement, and organizational efficiency, contributing to the overall success and sustainability of the hospital.

Integrating the Magnet Model into Daily Operations

To effectively integrate the Magnet Model components into daily operations, nurse executives should:

- **Align Leadership Development Programs:** Develop and support leadership training programs that cultivate transformational leadership skills among nurse leaders at all levels. Encourage leaders to engage staff in setting goals and implementing changes that improve patient care.
- **Foster a Culture of Empowerment:** Implement shared governance structures that give nurses a voice in decision-making. Ensure that nurses have access to professional development opportunities and are encouraged to pursue certifications and advanced degrees.
- **Promote Evidence-Based Practice:** Support the adoption of evidence-based protocols and encourage nurses to participate in quality improvement projects. Provide access to the latest research and facilitate collaboration between clinical staff and researchers.
- **Support Innovation and Research:** Create dedicated time and resources for nurses to engage in research and innovation. Recognize and reward innovative practices that lead to improved patient outcomes.
- **Measure and Report Outcomes:** Establish robust data collection and reporting systems to track key performance indicators related to patient outcomes, nurse satisfaction, and operational efficiency. Use this data to inform strategic planning and continuous improvement efforts.

By focusing on these areas, nurse executives can ensure that their organizations not only achieve Magnet recognition but also maintain the high standards of nursing excellence and patient care that the Magnet Model represents.

Achieving and maintaining Magnet® designation, awarded by the American Nurses Credentialing Center (ANCC), is a prestigious recognition that signifies nursing excellence and high standards of patient care. The journey toward Magnet® designation requires a comprehensive strategy that involves all levels of the organization, from nurse executives to frontline staff. The process not only focuses on meeting the rigorous criteria set by the ANCC but also on fostering a culture of continuous improvement, professional development, and shared governance.

Comprehensive Strategy for Achieving and Maintaining Magnet® Designation

1. Leadership Commitment and Vision

- **Establish a Clear Vision**: Nurse executives should articulate a clear and compelling vision for Magnet® designation, linking it to the organization's mission and goals. This vision should emphasize the importance of nursing excellence, patient-centered care, and a supportive work environment.
- **Resource Allocation**: Ensure that sufficient resources—financial, human, and material—are allocated to support the journey. This includes investing in education, professional development, and the necessary infrastructure to meet Magnet® standards.
- **Magnet® Steering Committee**: Form a dedicated steering committee led by nurse executives and including representatives from various nursing roles. This committee should oversee the Magnet® application process, coordinate activities, and monitor progress.

2. Fostering a Culture of Excellence and Shared Governance

- **Promote Shared Governance**: Establish a shared governance model where nurses at all levels have a voice in decision-making processes related to nursing practice, policies, and patient care. This empowers nurses, fosters accountability, and ensures that practice changes are driven by those who are directly involved in patient care.
- **Professional Development**: Create opportunities for continuous learning and professional development. This includes supporting advanced degrees, certifications, and participation in professional organizations. Provide access to educational resources, workshops, and conferences to enhance clinical skills and leadership capabilities.
- **Evidence-Based Practice (EBP)**: Integrate EBP into the nursing culture by offering training on how to critically appraise research, apply evidence to practice, and lead EBP projects. Encourage nurses to engage in research activities, quality improvement initiatives, and the dissemination of findings through publications and presentations.

3. Engaging Staff at All Levels

- **Communication and Transparency**: Maintain open lines of communication throughout the Magnet® journey. Regularly update staff on progress, celebrate milestones, and clearly explain the significance of

Magnet® designation. Use multiple channels—town hall meetings, newsletters, intranet portals, and unit meetings—to ensure that all staff are informed and engaged.

- **Involvement in Magnet® Preparation**: Actively involve staff in preparing for the Magnet® site visit. This can include participating in mock interviews, gathering and organizing evidence of practice excellence, and contributing to the Magnet® document submission. Engaging staff in these activities ensures they understand the criteria and can confidently demonstrate how they meet the standards.
- **Recognition and Reward Programs**: Develop recognition programs that celebrate nursing excellence, such as Nurse of the Month awards, DAISY Awards, and public recognition of certifications and advanced degrees. Recognizing and rewarding excellence motivates staff and reinforces the behaviors and practices that align with Magnet® standards.

4. Quality Improvement and Patient Outcomes

- **Focus on Quality Indicators**: Track and improve key nursing-sensitive quality indicators, such as patient falls, pressure ulcers, infection rates, and patient satisfaction scores. Use data-driven approaches to identify areas for improvement and implement evidence-based interventions.
- **Patient and Family Involvement**: Promote a culture of patient- and family-centered care by involving them in care decisions, seeking feedback through surveys, and implementing changes based on their input. High levels of patient satisfaction are critical to Magnet® recognition.
- **Continuous Improvement Cycles**: Implement Plan-Do-Study-Act (PDSA) cycles to continuously monitor and improve nursing practices. Engage staff in identifying problems, testing solutions, and scaling successful interventions.

5. Sustaining Magnet® Culture

- **Ongoing Evaluation and Feedback**: After achieving Magnet® designation, sustain momentum by regularly evaluating nursing practices, quality indicators, and staff engagement. Conduct annual surveys, focus groups, and feedback sessions to assess the effectiveness of Magnet® initiatives and identify areas for improvement.
- **Leadership Development**: Invest in the ongoing development of nurse leaders to ensure they are equipped to maintain Magnet® standards. This includes mentorship programs, leadership training, and opportunities for emerging leaders to take on new challenges.
- **Continuous Learning and Innovation**: Encourage a culture of innovation where nurses are supported in exploring new ideas, implementing pilot projects, and sharing best practices. This ensures that the organization remains at the forefront of nursing excellence and continues to meet the evolving standards of Magnet® designation.

Engaging Staff at All Levels

1. **Nurse Executives**:
   - **Role**: Provide strategic direction, allocate resources, and serve as champions of the Magnet® journey. Nurse executives should be visible leaders who actively participate in Magnet® activities, model the behaviors expected of all staff, and communicate the importance of the designation.
   - **Engagement Strategies**: Lead by example, participate in shared governance, and ensure that executive decisions align with the goals of Magnet® designation.
2. **Nurse Managers and Unit Leaders**:
   - **Role**: Translate the organization's Magnet® vision into actionable goals at the unit level. Nurse managers are responsible for fostering a supportive work environment, mentoring staff, and leading quality improvement initiatives.
   - **Engagement Strategies**: Hold regular meetings to discuss Magnet® progress, involve staff in decision-making, and recognize contributions to Magnet® goals.
3. **Frontline Nurses**:
   - **Role**: Deliver high-quality, patient-centered care that aligns with Magnet® standards. Frontline nurses are the backbone of the Magnet® journey, and their daily practices must reflect the principles of excellence, safety, and innovation.
   - **Engagement Strategies**: Provide opportunities for professional growth, involve nurses in EBP and quality improvement projects, and ensure their voices are heard through shared governance.

4. **Support Staff and Interdisciplinary Teams**:
    - ○ **Role**: Collaborate with nursing teams to ensure holistic, patient-centered care. Support staff and interdisciplinary team members, including physicians, therapists, and technicians, play a crucial role in achieving the outcomes required for Magnet® designation.
    - ○ **Engagement Strategies**: Foster interdisciplinary collaboration, include support staff in Magnet® activities, and recognize their contributions to the overall success of the organization.

By implementing this comprehensive strategy and actively engaging staff at all levels, nurse executives can lead their organizations to achieve and maintain Magnet® designation. This commitment to nursing excellence not only enhances patient outcomes but also strengthens the organization's reputation, attracts top talent, and ensures long-term success in the ever-evolving healthcare landscape.

Designing a Hospital Incident Command System (HICS) structure for a large urban medical center involves establishing a clear and organized chain of command that can efficiently manage and coordinate the hospital's response to various types of emergencies. The HICS structure mirrors the Incident Command System (ICS) used by emergency services, adapted to the hospital environment to ensure a cohesive response that integrates clinical, operational, and logistical aspects of emergency management.

Hospital Incident Command System (HICS) Structure

1. Incident Commander

- **Role:** The Incident Commander (IC) is responsible for the overall management of the hospital's emergency response. This individual has ultimate authority and makes key decisions related to resource allocation, strategy, and communication.
- **Responsibilities:**
    - ○ Initiates the HICS activation and oversees the entire emergency response.
    - ○ Coordinates with external agencies, such as local emergency services and public health authorities.
    - ○ Ensures that all HICS positions are staffed and that roles are clearly understood.
- **Assignment:** Typically, the hospital CEO or another senior executive with extensive experience in hospital operations and emergency management assumes this role.

2. Command Staff

A. Public Information Officer (PIO)

- **Role:** Manages all communication between the hospital and the public, including the media, patients' families, and the community.
- **Responsibilities:**
    - ○ Develops and disseminates accurate and timely information.
    - ○ Coordinates media briefings and manages the hospital's social media channels.
    - ○ Works with the IC to ensure messaging aligns with overall strategy.
- **Assignment:** A senior communications officer or the hospital's public relations director typically fills this role.

B. Safety Officer

- **Role:** Ensures the safety of hospital staff, patients, and visitors during the emergency response.
- **Responsibilities:**
    - ○ Monitors and mitigates safety hazards throughout the hospital.
    - ○ Enforces safety protocols, including the use of personal protective equipment (PPE).
    - ○ Advises the IC on safety issues and potential risks.
- **Assignment:** This role is best suited for a senior occupational health and safety officer or someone with a strong background in hospital safety management.

C. Liaison Officer

- **Role:** Acts as the primary point of contact between the hospital and external agencies, such as emergency services, public health departments, and other healthcare facilities.
- **Responsibilities:**

- o Coordinates with local, state, and federal agencies to ensure a unified response.
- o Facilitates communication and resource sharing between the hospital and external partners.
- o Reports external developments to the IC and other command staff.
- **Assignment:** A senior administrator or external affairs officer with established relationships with external agencies would be ideal for this position.

3. General Staff

A. Operations Section Chief

- **Role:** Directs all tactical operations during the emergency, including patient care, triage, and medical services.
- **Responsibilities:**
  - o Manages clinical and non-clinical operations, ensuring that patient care continues while addressing the emergency.
  - o Coordinates with department heads to allocate resources and staff.
  - o Implements and monitors the incident action plan (IAP) developed by the Planning Section.
- **Assignment:** Typically, the Chief Nursing Officer (CNO) or a senior clinical operations director assumes this role.

B. Planning Section Chief

- **Role:** Oversees all planning activities, including the development of the IAP, resource tracking, and documentation of the incident.
- **Responsibilities:**
  - o Develops and updates the IAP based on the evolving situation.
  - o Maintains situational awareness and ensures accurate documentation of all actions taken.
  - o Coordinates with the Logistics and Operations Sections to ensure resource needs are anticipated and met.
- **Assignment:** This position is often filled by the Director of Emergency Management or a senior planning officer.

C. Logistics Section Chief

- **Role:** Responsible for acquiring, managing, and distributing resources and services needed for the hospital's emergency response.
- **Responsibilities:**
  - o Ensures the availability of supplies, equipment, and personnel.
  - o Manages transportation, IT, and communication systems.
  - o Coordinates the procurement of additional resources as needed.
- **Assignment:** The Chief Supply Chain Officer or Director of Support Services typically assumes this role.

D. Finance/Administration Section Chief

- **Role:** Manages all financial and administrative aspects of the incident, including cost tracking, reimbursement, and documentation.
- **Responsibilities:**
  - o Tracks all expenses related to the emergency response.
  - o Manages contracts, procurement, and payroll issues that arise during the incident.
  - o Prepares documentation required for insurance claims, reimbursements, and audits.
- **Assignment:** The Chief Financial Officer (CFO) or Director of Finance is best suited for this role.

4. Branches, Units, and Divisions (As Needed)

Depending on the complexity of the incident, the HICS structure may be expanded to include additional branches, units, and divisions under the Operations, Planning, Logistics, and Finance/Administration Sections. These subdivisions allow for more specialized management of specific aspects of the response.

Examples:

- **Medical Care Branch:** Oversees all patient care activities, including triage, treatment, and discharge planning. May include specific units for inpatient care, outpatient services, and specialized treatment areas.
- **Service Branch:** Manages essential services such as food, water, sanitation, and security.

- **Resource Unit:** Tracks all resources, including personnel, equipment, and supplies, ensuring they are used efficiently.
- **Cost Unit:** Monitors and records all costs associated with the incident for accurate financial reporting and reimbursement.

Implementation and Integration into Daily Operations

1. **Training and Drills:**
   - Regular training sessions and drills are essential to familiarize all staff with the HICS structure and their roles within it. Scenario-based drills should cover a range of potential emergencies, such as natural disasters, mass casualty events, and cyber-attacks.

2. **Clear Communication Protocols:**
   - Establish clear communication channels and protocols to ensure that information flows smoothly across all sections of the HICS structure. This includes setting up redundant communication systems to maintain connectivity during disruptions.

3. **Resource Allocation and Preparedness:**
   - Ensure that all necessary resources, including equipment, supplies, and personnel, are readily available and can be mobilized quickly. Regular inventory checks and maintenance schedules should be in place to keep resources in optimal condition.

4. **Regular Review and Updates:**
   - Periodically review and update the HICS structure to reflect changes in the hospital's operations, staffing, or the external threat landscape. Lessons learned from drills and real incidents should be used to refine the command system.

By assigning these roles and responsibilities and ensuring that the HICS structure is well-integrated into daily operations, the hospital can effectively respond to various types of emergencies with agility and precision. This structured approach not only ensures that all aspects of the response are covered but also fosters coordination and communication across the organization, leading to more efficient and effective emergency management.

The Hospital Incident Command System (HICS) is a standardized, flexible framework designed to assist hospitals in managing emergencies and disasters by providing a clear chain of command and structured response processes. HICS has been utilized during several real-world disaster responses, including Hurricane Katrina and the COVID-19 pandemic. By analyzing its effectiveness during these events, we can identify key lessons that can enhance future emergency preparedness efforts.

Effectiveness of HICS During Real-World Disasters

1. Hurricane Katrina (2005)

Hurricane Katrina was one of the most devastating natural disasters in U.S. history, causing widespread destruction and overwhelming healthcare systems across the Gulf Coast. The HICS model was activated in many hospitals to manage the chaos that ensued.

Effectiveness:

- **Structured Response:** HICS provided a clear organizational structure that helped hospitals manage the influx of patients, coordinate with external agencies, and allocate resources under extreme conditions. The incident command roles defined by HICS allowed for quick decision-making and delegation of tasks, which was crucial in the rapidly evolving crisis.
- **Communication and Coordination:** HICS facilitated communication within hospitals and between hospitals and external agencies, such as FEMA and the National Guard. This coordination was vital for the evacuation of patients, the distribution of medical supplies, and the deployment of additional staff.

Challenges:

- **Infrastructure Damage:** The widespread infrastructure damage, including power outages and flooding, severely hindered hospital operations, even with HICS in place. Some hospitals struggled to maintain effective communication and coordination due to damaged systems and overwhelmed resources.
- **Resource Scarcity:** Despite the structured approach provided by HICS, many hospitals faced critical shortages of supplies, staff, and functional space. The scale of the disaster overwhelmed the capabilities of many facilities, revealing gaps in preparedness for such large-scale events.

Lessons Learned:

- **Infrastructure Resilience**: Future preparedness efforts should focus on enhancing the resilience of hospital infrastructure, including backup power systems, flood protection, and redundant communication channels. Hospitals must be equipped to maintain operations even when primary systems fail.
- **Pre-Positioning Resources**: Pre-disaster planning should include the pre-positioning of critical supplies and equipment in strategic locations to ensure rapid deployment when disaster strikes. Hospitals should also establish mutual aid agreements with other facilities and suppliers.

2. COVID-19 Pandemic (2020-Present)

The COVID-19 pandemic presented an unprecedented global health crisis, testing the limits of healthcare systems worldwide. The HICS model was widely implemented to manage the response to the ongoing surge of COVID-19 patients.

Effectiveness:

- **Scalable and Flexible Response**: HICS was instrumental in providing a scalable response framework that could be adapted as the pandemic evolved. Hospitals were able to expand capacity, reallocate resources, and establish new workflows (e.g., triage areas, COVID-19 units) to meet the surge in patient demand.
- **Role Clarity and Decision-Making**: The clear delineation of roles and responsibilities within HICS facilitated efficient decision-making and task delegation, which was critical in managing the sustained pressure on healthcare facilities. Incident commanders were able to quickly implement new protocols, coordinate the acquisition of PPE, and manage staff reassignments.

Challenges:

- **Prolonged Crisis**: Unlike typical disasters, the COVID-19 pandemic was a prolonged crisis, stretching over months and years. The extended nature of the pandemic strained the HICS framework, particularly in terms of maintaining staff morale, preventing burnout, and ensuring continuous resource availability.
- **Supply Chain Disruptions**: The global nature of the pandemic caused widespread supply chain disruptions, making it difficult for hospitals to procure essential supplies, such as ventilators, PPE, and medications. This revealed vulnerabilities in the supply chain that were not fully addressed by the HICS model.

Lessons Learned:

- **Sustained Incident Command**: The prolonged nature of the COVID-19 crisis highlighted the need for a sustained incident command structure that can adapt to long-term emergencies. Hospitals should develop strategies for rotating leadership roles, providing mental health support for staff, and ensuring that the incident command structure remains effective over extended periods.
- **Supply Chain Resilience**: The pandemic underscored the importance of having diversified and resilient supply chains. Hospitals should establish multiple sources for critical supplies, build strategic reserves, and work with suppliers to ensure rapid scaling of production during emergencies.

Improving Future Emergency Preparedness

1. **Enhanced Training and Drills**
   - **Realistic Drills**: Regular, realistic drills that simulate a wide range of disaster scenarios (including prolonged crises) are essential for ensuring that hospital staff are well-prepared. These drills should involve not only hospital personnel but also external partners, such as emergency services, public health departments, and other hospitals.
   - **Cross-Training Staff**: Training staff to perform multiple roles within the HICS framework can provide greater flexibility during emergencies, allowing hospitals to adapt to unexpected challenges, such as staff shortages.
2. **Inter-Agency Coordination**
   - **Unified Command Systems**: Strengthening coordination between hospitals and other emergency response agencies is critical. Hospitals should actively participate in local and regional emergency planning efforts and establish clear communication protocols with government agencies, non-profits, and other healthcare providers.
   - **Joint Planning Exercises**: Conduct joint planning exercises with external agencies to improve interoperability and ensure that all parties understand their roles and responsibilities in a crisis.
3. **Infrastructure and Resource Resilience**

- Hardened Infrastructure: Investing in infrastructure that can withstand disasters—such as flood-resistant buildings, redundant power systems, and secure communication networks—is crucial for maintaining hospital operations during emergencies.
- Strategic Stockpiling: Hospitals should establish and maintain strategic stockpiles of essential supplies, including PPE, medications, and equipment, to mitigate the impact of supply chain disruptions during emergencies.

4. **Adaptive Incident Command Structures**
   - Dynamic Command Structures: Develop flexible incident command structures that can evolve as the situation changes. This includes planning for long-term emergencies where the traditional short-term command structure might not be sustainable.
   - Resilience Building for Staff: Implement programs to support the physical and mental well-being of staff during prolonged crises, including rotation systems, mental health services, and wellness initiatives.

5. **Data-Driven Decision-Making**
   - Real-Time Data Analytics: Invest in data analytics tools that provide real-time insights into patient volumes, resource utilization, and emerging threats. This allows incident commanders to make informed decisions quickly and adjust strategies as needed.
   - Learning from Past Events: Continuously analyze past disaster responses to identify strengths and weaknesses in the HICS implementation. Use this analysis to refine protocols and improve future responses.

By integrating these lessons and strategies, hospitals can enhance their emergency preparedness efforts, ensuring that they are better equipped to handle both short-term and prolonged crises in the future.

Creating a comprehensive disaster planning and response protocol for a rural critical access hospital involves addressing the unique challenges associated with limited resources, geographical isolation, and potential communication disruptions. The plan must be adaptable, resource-efficient, and capable of maintaining operations under difficult conditions to ensure patient safety and continuity of care.

Disaster Planning and Response Protocol

1. Risk Assessment and Hazard Vulnerability Analysis (HVA)

- **Objective:** Identify and assess potential hazards specific to the hospital's location, such as natural disasters (e.g., floods, wildfires, earthquakes), human-made events (e.g., chemical spills, mass casualty incidents), and pandemics.
- **Actions:**
  - Conduct a thorough Hazard Vulnerability Analysis (HVA) to prioritize risks based on likelihood and impact.
  - Engage local authorities, public health agencies, and community leaders in the assessment process.
  - Update the HVA annually or after significant changes in the hospital's environment or operations.

2. Establish an Incident Command Structure

- **Objective:** Implement a Hospital Incident Command System (HICS) tailored to the hospital's size and capacity.
- **Key Roles:**
  - **Incident Commander (IC):** Typically the hospital CEO or another senior administrator. Responsible for overall decision-making and coordination.
  - **Operations Chief:** Manages the hospital's operational response, including patient care, triage, and clinical support services.
  - **Logistics Chief:** Secures and manages resources, including medical supplies, equipment, and personnel.
  - **Planning Chief:** Develops and updates the Incident Action Plan (IAP) based on evolving conditions.
  - **Finance/Administration Chief:** Tracks expenditures, manages contracts, and oversees documentation and reimbursement processes.

3. Communication Plan

- **Objective:** Ensure reliable communication within the hospital and with external partners during a disaster.
- **Strategies:**
    - **Redundant Communication Systems:** Implement multiple communication channels (e.g., landlines, cell phones, two-way radios, satellite phones) to reduce reliance on any single system.
    - **Backup Communication Protocols:** Establish protocols for when primary systems fail, including the use of runners for internal communication or predetermined radio frequencies for external communication.
    - **Communication Drills:** Regularly conduct drills to test and refine communication systems, ensuring all staff are familiar with backup options.
    - **Liaison Officer:** Assign a liaison officer to maintain communication with external agencies such as emergency services, public health departments, and regional healthcare coalitions.

4. Resource Management

- **Objective:** Efficiently manage limited resources to sustain operations during a disaster.
- **Inventory and Stockpiling:**
    - Maintain an updated inventory of essential supplies (e.g., medications, PPE, food, water) with enough stock to last at least 72 hours.
    - Establish agreements with local suppliers and regional partners for rapid resupply in emergencies.
- **Mutual Aid Agreements:** Develop and maintain mutual aid agreements with neighboring hospitals, clinics, and community organizations to share resources, personnel, and equipment during disasters.
- **Triage Protocols:** Implement strict triage protocols to prioritize resource allocation based on patient needs and available resources.

5. Staffing and Surge Capacity

- **Objective:** Ensure adequate staffing and the ability to handle a surge in patient volume.
- **Staffing Contingencies:**
    - Create a staffing plan that includes on-call rotations and cross-training to allow staff to cover multiple roles.
    - Develop a volunteer pool from retired healthcare professionals or community members with medical training.
- **Surge Capacity Planning:**
    - Identify additional patient care areas within the hospital (e.g., conference rooms, hallways) and establish criteria for when to activate these areas.
    - Plan for the rapid expansion of critical care services, including the use of portable medical equipment and temporary shelters if needed.

6. Patient Care and Evacuation Plans

- **Objective:** Ensure continuous, high-quality patient care and safe evacuation if necessary.
- **Patient Tracking System:**
    - Implement a patient tracking system to monitor patient locations, conditions, and needs during a disaster.
    - Use wristbands, electronic records, and manual logs as part of a redundant tracking system.
- **Evacuation Plan:**
    - Develop a detailed evacuation plan that includes criteria for evacuation, transportation options, and coordination with receiving facilities.
    - Conduct regular evacuation drills, including scenarios that involve transporting critically ill patients.
- **Shelter-in-Place Protocol:**
    - Establish shelter-in-place protocols for scenarios where evacuation is not possible. Ensure that areas designated for sheltering are equipped with essential supplies and that staff are trained in shelter-in-place procedures.

7. Collaboration with External Agencies and Community Partners

- **Objective:** Strengthen relationships with external agencies and community partners to ensure a coordinated response.
- **Partnerships:**
  - Work closely with local emergency management, fire, police, and EMS to align disaster plans and ensure mutual support.
  - Engage with public health departments and regional healthcare coalitions for planning, resource sharing, and coordinated response efforts.
  - Collaborate with community organizations, such as churches and schools, to develop auxiliary support systems, such as additional shelter space or community volunteer coordination.
- **Joint Training and Exercises:**
  - Participate in joint training exercises with external agencies and community partners to test coordination, communication, and resource-sharing capabilities.

8. Continuous Training and Drills

- **Objective:** Ensure that all staff are prepared to execute the disaster plan effectively.
- **Regular Drills:**
  - Conduct regular drills, including full-scale exercises that simulate different disaster scenarios (e.g., mass casualty, natural disaster, hazardous material incident).
  - Include community partners in drills to test coordination and communication.
- **Staff Training:**
  - Provide ongoing training on disaster response roles, use of emergency equipment, and specific protocols (e.g., triage, evacuation).
  - Use online platforms, workshops, and hands-on training to ensure staff are well-prepared.

9. Post-Incident Recovery and Debriefing

- **Objective:** Facilitate the hospital's recovery after a disaster and ensure continuous improvement of the disaster plan.
- **Debriefing Sessions:**
  - Hold debriefing sessions with staff immediately after an incident to capture lessons learned and identify areas for improvement.
  - Involve external partners in debriefing to gain a comprehensive view of the response efforts.
- **Recovery Planning:**
  - Develop a recovery plan that outlines steps for restoring normal operations, including assessing damage, managing finances, and providing psychological support to staff.
  - Address long-term recovery needs, such as rebuilding infrastructure, restocking supplies, and reviewing financial impacts.

10. Evaluation and Plan Updates

- **Objective:** Continuously evaluate and update the disaster plan to reflect new information, technologies, and best practices.
- **Regular Review:**
  - Schedule regular reviews of the disaster plan, particularly after drills, real incidents, or changes in the hospital's operations or external environment.
- **Stakeholder Feedback:**
  - Gather feedback from staff, patients, and external partners to inform updates to the plan.
- **Adaptation to New Threats:**
  - Stay informed of emerging threats and integrate new preparedness strategies (e.g., cybersecurity, climate-related disasters) into the plan.

Addressing Unique Challenges

Limited Resources:

- **Prioritization:** Prioritize critical supplies and services, ensuring that the most essential needs are met first.
- **Resource Pooling:** Leverage mutual aid agreements to pool resources with nearby hospitals and clinics.

- **Flexible Staffing:** Cross-train staff to perform multiple roles, maximizing the hospital's human resource capacity during a crisis.

Geographical Isolation:

- **Transportation Planning:** Develop partnerships with local transportation providers and emergency services to ensure the ability to transport patients, staff, and supplies despite the hospital's remote location.
- **Telehealth Integration:** Utilize telehealth services to extend the reach of care and provide support from specialists located in urban centers during emergencies.

Communication Disruptions:

- **Redundant Systems:** Invest in satellite phones, two-way radios, and other communication technologies that are less reliant on conventional infrastructure.
- **Local Networks:** Establish a local emergency communication network that includes neighboring facilities, emergency responders, and community leaders.

By addressing these challenges with targeted strategies and maintaining a flexible, well-coordinated response structure, the rural critical access hospital can effectively manage disasters, ensuring the safety and well-being of both patients and staff.

Creating a Continuity of Operations Plan (COOP) for a multi-hospital health system facing a prolonged power outage involves careful planning to ensure that essential services are maintained, resources are allocated efficiently, and patient care quality is preserved. The plan must account for the unique challenges of a power outage, including disruptions to medical equipment, IT systems, communication networks, and supply chains. Below is a comprehensive COOP tailored to this scenario.

1. Establish the Incident Command Structure (ICS)

- **Activate the Hospital Incident Command System (HICS):** Immediately activate the HICS across the entire health system, designating an Incident Commander at the central command center to oversee the response. Each hospital within the system should have its own command post that reports to the central command.
- **Assign Roles and Responsibilities:** Clearly define roles within the ICS, including operations, logistics, planning, and finance sections. Assign a specific team to focus on power management and another on patient care continuity.

2. Prioritize Essential Services

- **Triage and Prioritization:** Identify and prioritize essential services that must remain operational during the power outage. These include:
  - **Life-Sustaining Equipment:** Critical medical equipment such as ventilators, dialysis machines, and cardiac monitors.
  - **Emergency Departments (EDs):** Ensure that EDs at each hospital remain fully functional, as they are the first point of care for incoming patients.
  - **Intensive Care Units (ICUs):** Maintain operations in ICUs to support critically ill patients.
  - **Operating Rooms (ORs):** Prioritize ORs based on the urgency of surgeries. Elective surgeries may be postponed, while emergency surgeries must be prioritized.
  - **Pharmacy Services:** Ensure that pharmacies can dispense medications, particularly for critical and time-sensitive treatments.
- **Non-Essential Services:** Temporarily suspend or scale back non-essential services, such as elective procedures, outpatient clinics, and administrative functions, to conserve power and resources.

3. Resource Allocation and Management

- **Power Management**
  - **Backup Generators:** Ensure that all backup generators are fully operational and capable of sustaining essential services. Perform an immediate check on fuel levels and arrange for additional fuel deliveries if necessary.
  - **Power Distribution:** Implement a power distribution strategy that prioritizes critical areas (e.g., ICUs, EDs) and systematically reduces power to non-critical areas.

- - Load Shedding: Instruct staff to disconnect or turn off non-essential electrical devices to reduce the load on backup generators.
  - **Human Resources**
    - Staffing Prioritization: Prioritize staffing for essential services, ensuring that enough qualified personnel are available to maintain critical functions. Consider implementing extended shifts or redeploying staff from non-essential areas to support critical care units.
    - Support and Relief: Establish rest areas and support services for staff working extended hours, including food, hydration, and mental health resources.
  - **Supplies and Equipment**
    - Critical Supplies: Inventory critical supplies such as medications, IV fluids, and medical gases. Prioritize their distribution based on patient acuity and need.
    - Resource Sharing: Coordinate resource sharing across hospitals within the system to address shortages. Implement a system to track and distribute resources efficiently.
    - Vendor Coordination: Maintain communication with key suppliers to expedite deliveries of essential items. Arrange for emergency resupply of critical items, if necessary.

4. Maintain Patient Care Quality

- **Patient Safety**
  - Monitoring and Documentation: Ensure that all patients, especially those in critical care, are continuously monitored. Establish manual documentation processes for patient care activities if electronic health records (EHRs) are unavailable.
  - Medication Management: Prioritize the administration of critical medications. Establish protocols for managing limited supplies and consider alternative therapies if necessary.
- **Patient Transfers**
  - Inter-Hospital Transfers: If a particular hospital is unable to sustain critical operations, arrange for the transfer of patients to other hospitals within the system or to external facilities. Ensure that all transfers are coordinated through the central command center.
  - EMS Coordination: Work closely with emergency medical services (EMS) to prioritize and manage patient transfers. Ensure that transport vehicles are equipped with necessary power support, such as battery-powered ventilators.
- **Communication**
  - Internal Communication: Establish reliable communication channels between the central command and individual hospitals. Use radios, satellite phones, or other backup communication methods if traditional systems fail.
  - External Communication: Keep patients, families, and the public informed through regular updates. Utilize social media, hospital websites, and local media to communicate operational status, available services, and safety instructions.

5. Long-Term Contingency Planning

- **Extended Power Outage Protocols**: Develop and implement protocols for managing a power outage lasting several days or more. This includes ensuring a steady supply of fuel for generators, maintaining a backup inventory of critical supplies, and arranging for temporary power solutions such as portable generators or solar-powered systems.
- **Partnerships and Mutual Aid Agreements**: Activate mutual aid agreements with other healthcare facilities, local government agencies, and utility companies to secure additional resources and support. Collaborate with regional partners to ensure a coordinated response.
- **Staff Well-Being and Morale**: Implement measures to support staff morale and well-being during the prolonged outage. This could include providing regular updates, offering mental health support, and recognizing the efforts of staff working under difficult conditions.

6. Post-Incident Recovery and Evaluation

- **System Restoration**: Once power is restored, prioritize the restoration of full services in a phased approach. Ensure that all systems are checked for functionality and that any critical equipment damaged during the outage is repaired or replaced.

- **After-Action Review (AAR)**: Conduct an AAR with all key stakeholders to evaluate the effectiveness of the COOP, identify strengths and weaknesses, and gather feedback from staff. Use the findings to update and improve the COOP for future incidents.
- **Documentation and Reporting**: Document the incident, the response, and any lessons learned. Submit reports to regulatory bodies as required and use the information to enhance future preparedness.

By following this COOP, the multi-hospital health system can effectively prioritize essential services, allocate resources, and maintain patient care quality during a prolonged power outage. The plan ensures that the organization remains resilient, capable of sustaining operations under challenging conditions, and prepared for future emergencies.

Community partnerships play a crucial role in enhancing healthcare emergency preparedness by fostering collaboration, resource sharing, and coordinated responses to disasters. These partnerships enable healthcare organizations to better anticipate, prepare for, and respond to emergencies by leveraging the strengths and expertise of various community stakeholders. For nurse executives, fostering these collaborations is essential to ensuring comprehensive and resilient emergency preparedness strategies.

Role of Community Partnerships in Healthcare Emergency Preparedness

1. **Resource Sharing and Optimization**
   - **Benefit:** Community partnerships allow healthcare facilities to pool resources with other organizations, such as local emergency management agencies, law enforcement, and other healthcare providers. This is particularly important during large-scale emergencies when resources such as medical supplies, personnel, and equipment may be scarce.
   - **Example:** A rural hospital might partner with nearby clinics and pharmacies to ensure a steady supply of medications and medical equipment during a disaster, or with local food suppliers to provide sustenance for patients and staff during extended emergencies.

2. **Enhanced Communication and Coordination**
   - **Benefit:** Effective communication and coordination are critical during emergencies. Partnerships with local emergency management agencies and law enforcement ensure that hospitals are integrated into broader community response efforts, facilitating timely and accurate information exchange.
   - **Example:** During a natural disaster, such as a hurricane, a hospital that has established communication protocols with local emergency services can more effectively coordinate evacuations, share real-time updates, and receive support from first responders.

3. **Expanded Surge Capacity**
   - **Benefit:** Community partnerships can help healthcare organizations manage surge capacity during emergencies, such as pandemics or mass casualty events. Collaborating with other healthcare providers, including nursing homes and outpatient clinics, allows for the distribution of patient load and the extension of care beyond the hospital setting.
   - **Example:** During the COVID-19 pandemic, many hospitals partnered with community health centers and temporary care facilities to manage the influx of patients, ensuring that critical care resources were reserved for those in most need.

4. **Comprehensive Training and Drills**
   - **Benefit:** Partnering with community organizations enables healthcare facilities to conduct more comprehensive and realistic training exercises and drills, improving preparedness across all levels of staff. Joint exercises that include local emergency management, fire departments, and law enforcement simulate real-world scenarios, enhancing the hospital's readiness.
   - **Example:** A hospital might participate in a city-wide disaster drill that involves multiple agencies, testing the facility's response to a chemical spill or active shooter scenario, and identifying areas for improvement in a coordinated response.

5. **Improved Community Trust and Engagement**
   - **Benefit:** Building strong relationships with community organizations fosters trust and engagement, which is crucial during emergencies. When healthcare providers actively collaborate

with community leaders and organizations, it reinforces the public's confidence in the healthcare system's ability to manage crises.

- o **Example:** A hospital that regularly collaborates with community health organizations for outreach and education initiatives will find that the community is more likely to comply with emergency directives and trust the hospital's guidance during an actual emergency.

Strategies for Nurse Executives to Foster Collaboration

1. **Establish Regular Communication Channels**
   - o **Approach:** Develop and maintain regular communication with local emergency management agencies, law enforcement, and other healthcare providers. This could include monthly or quarterly meetings, joint training sessions, and participation in community emergency planning committees.
   - o **Implementation:** Nurse executives can initiate regular interagency meetings to discuss emergency preparedness plans, share updates on resources, and identify potential collaboration opportunities. This ongoing dialogue helps build strong relationships and ensures that all parties are on the same page when an emergency occurs.

2. **Participate in Joint Training and Drills**
   - o **Approach:** Engage in joint emergency drills and training exercises with community partners. These drills should simulate real-world scenarios and include all relevant stakeholders, from first responders to public health officials.
   - o **Implementation:** Nurse executives can work with local emergency management agencies to design and conduct joint exercises that reflect the most likely and most dangerous threats to the community. After-action reviews should be conducted to assess performance and refine emergency plans.

3. **Develop Mutual Aid Agreements**
   - o **Approach:** Establish mutual aid agreements with other healthcare providers, including neighboring hospitals, clinics, and long-term care facilities. These agreements should outline how resources such as staff, equipment, and supplies will be shared during emergencies.
   - o **Implementation:** Nurse executives should collaborate with legal and administrative teams to draft mutual aid agreements that clearly define roles, responsibilities, and processes for resource sharing during emergencies. These agreements should be reviewed and updated regularly to ensure they remain relevant and actionable.

4. **Engage in Community Outreach and Education**
   - o **Approach:** Foster relationships with community organizations, schools, and local businesses to enhance community-wide emergency preparedness. This includes participating in public health campaigns, offering educational workshops, and supporting community resilience initiatives.
   - o **Implementation:** Nurse executives can lead or support initiatives that educate the public on emergency preparedness, such as flu vaccination drives, CPR training, or disaster preparedness workshops. By engaging with the community in non-emergency times, the hospital strengthens its role as a trusted partner in public health.

5. **Integrate Emergency Plans with Community Response Frameworks**
   - o **Approach:** Ensure that the hospital's emergency preparedness plans are aligned with local, regional, and state emergency response frameworks. This integration facilitates a cohesive response during a disaster.
   - o **Implementation:** Nurse executives should collaborate with local emergency management to align the hospital's incident command structure and response plans with those of the broader community. This may involve participating in regional planning initiatives and ensuring that hospital plans are consistent with state and federal guidelines.

6. **Advocate for Funding and Support**
   - o **Approach:** Advocate for funding and resources that support community-wide emergency preparedness initiatives. This could include grants for training, equipment, or joint projects that enhance resilience.

- - **Implementation:** Nurse executives can work with hospital leadership to apply for grants and engage with local government officials to secure funding for emergency preparedness programs. Building a coalition of community partners can strengthen the case for investment in public health infrastructure.

Overcoming Potential Challenges

- **Resource Constraints:** Rural hospitals may face limited resources, making it difficult to engage fully in community partnerships. Nurse executives can address this by prioritizing high-impact partnerships and seeking external funding or grants specifically for emergency preparedness initiatives.
- **Geographical Barriers:** For hospitals in geographically isolated areas, partnerships with distant organizations may require creative solutions, such as telecommunication tools for virtual collaboration or regional coalitions that pool resources across a wider area.
- **Coordination Complexities:** Managing partnerships with multiple organizations can be complex. Nurse executives should assign dedicated staff to oversee community partnerships and ensure that coordination efforts are streamlined and efficient.

By effectively fostering collaboration with local emergency management agencies, law enforcement, and other healthcare providers, nurse executives can enhance the hospital's emergency preparedness, improve patient outcomes during crises, and contribute to the overall resilience of the community.

Root Cause Analysis (RCA) for a Medication Error Using the "5 Whys" Technique

Scenario: A patient was administered the wrong dosage of a medication, resulting in significant harm. The error was identified after the patient developed severe side effects, leading to an extended hospital stay and additional treatments.

Step 1: Gather the Facts

- **Date and Time of Event:** October 12, 2024, at 2:30 PM
- **Location:** Inpatient Unit, Room 304
- **Patient Information:** 68-year-old male with a history of hypertension, admitted for cardiac monitoring.
- **Medication Involved:** Beta-blocker (Metoprolol) - incorrect dosage of 100 mg instead of the prescribed 50 mg.
- **Outcome:** Patient experienced bradycardia, hypotension, and required emergency intervention.

Step 2: Conduct the "5 Whys" Analysis

1. **Why was the patient given the wrong dosage of Metoprolol?**
   - The nurse administered 100 mg instead of the prescribed 50 mg.
2. **Why did the nurse administer 100 mg instead of 50 mg?**
   - The nurse misread the dosage on the electronic health record (EHR) system.
3. **Why did the nurse misread the dosage on the EHR system?**
   - The nurse was in a hurry due to a high patient load and multiple interruptions during the medication administration process.
4. **Why was the nurse in a hurry and experiencing interruptions?**
   - The unit was short-staffed, and there was no dedicated "quiet time" or protocol in place to minimize interruptions during medication administration.
5. **Why was the unit short-staffed and lacking protocols to minimize interruptions?**
   - The hospital has been experiencing staffing shortages due to increased patient admissions and has not yet implemented effective strategies to manage workload or standardized protocols to protect the medication administration process.

Step 3: Identify Root Causes

Based on the "5 Whys" analysis, the root causes of the medication error are:

- **Inadequate Staffing:** The unit was short-staffed, leading to increased workloads and hurried processes.
- **Lack of Protocols for Medication Administration:** There were no standardized protocols to minimize interruptions and ensure focused attention during medication administration.

- **Systemic Issues in EHR Design**: The EHR interface may not have been user-friendly, contributing to the risk of misreading medication orders under stress.

Step 4: Develop a Comprehensive Action Plan

1. Improve Staffing Levels and Workload Management

- **Action**: Conduct a staffing needs assessment and adjust nurse-to-patient ratios to ensure adequate coverage. Implement a float pool or on-call staff system to address short-term staffing shortages.
- **Responsible Party**: Nurse Manager and Human Resources.
- **Timeline**: Complete staffing assessment within 30 days and implement changes within 60 days.
- **Outcome Measure**: Reduction in nurse-reported workload stress and patient care errors.

2. Implement "No Interruption" Zones and Protocols

- **Action**: Establish "No Interruption" zones or times specifically for medication administration. Train staff on the importance of uninterrupted medication rounds and establish clear signage and communication protocols to support this.
- **Responsible Party**: Nursing Education Department and Unit Leaders.
- **Timeline**: Develop and implement the protocol within 45 days.
- **Outcome Measure**: Decrease in reported medication administration errors.

3. EHR System Optimization

- **Action**: Review and optimize the EHR interface to reduce the risk of dosage errors. This may include clearer font sizes, enhanced alert systems, and user-friendly design elements that highlight critical information such as dosage amounts.
- **Responsible Party**: IT Department and Clinical Informatics Team.
- **Timeline**: Conduct a review within 60 days and implement changes within 90 days.
- **Outcome Measure**: Decrease in medication order entry errors reported by nursing staff.

4. Regular Medication Administration Audits and Education

- **Action**: Implement regular audits of medication administration practices to identify and correct potential issues. Provide ongoing education and training for nursing staff on best practices in medication administration, focusing on attention to detail and error prevention.
- **Responsible Party**: Quality Improvement (QI) Team and Nursing Education Department.
- **Timeline**: Begin audits within 30 days and continue quarterly. Initiate ongoing education sessions within 45 days.
- **Outcome Measure**: Reduction in medication errors identified in audits.

5. Strengthen Communication and Reporting Culture

- **Action**: Foster a culture of open communication and non-punitive reporting of errors and near-misses. Encourage staff to report any safety concerns, including interruptions during critical tasks like medication administration.
- **Responsible Party**: Nurse Executives and Quality Improvement (QI) Team.
- **Timeline**: Launch communication campaigns and establish reporting protocols within 30 days.
- **Outcome Measure**: Increase in safety concerns and near-miss reports, leading to proactive prevention measures.

Step 5: Monitor and Evaluate the Effectiveness of the Action Plan

- **Monthly Review**: The QI team will conduct monthly reviews of medication error reports and audit findings to assess the effectiveness of the implemented actions.
- **Staff Feedback**: Collect ongoing feedback from nursing staff on the impact of the new protocols and any additional support needed.
- **Continuous Improvement**: Adjust the action plan as necessary based on monitoring data and staff input to ensure continuous improvement and sustainment of safe medication practices.

By addressing the root causes identified in the RCA through targeted interventions, the hospital can significantly reduce the likelihood of similar medication errors in the future, thereby enhancing patient safety and care quality.

Implementing a Failure Mode and Effects Analysis (FMEA) for Patient Handoffs Between Units

Failure Mode and Effects Analysis (FMEA) is a proactive tool used to identify, prioritize, and mitigate potential failures in high-risk processes. For a high-risk process like patient handoffs between units, FMEA can be particularly effective in enhancing patient safety by systematically identifying where and how the process might fail and developing strategies to prevent these failures.

1. Define the Process and Scope

- **Objective:** Clearly outline the patient handoff process between units, including the steps involved, the personnel responsible, and the tools or systems used.
- **Process Steps:**
    1. **Preparation:** The transferring unit prepares the patient's information, including medical records, medication lists, and care plans.
    2. **Communication:** The nurse or physician from the transferring unit communicates the patient's status, care needs, and any critical issues to the receiving unit.
    3. **Verification:** The receiving unit verifies the information received and asks questions if clarification is needed.
    4. **Documentation:** The handoff is documented in the patient's medical record, including the time of transfer and the names of the personnel involved.
    5. **Handoff Completion:** The patient is physically transferred to the receiving unit, and care is assumed by the receiving team.

2. Identify Potential Failure Modes

- **Objective:** Brainstorm and list all possible ways each step in the handoff process could fail.
- **Examples of Failure Modes:**
    1. **Incomplete Information Transfer:** Critical patient information (e.g., medication allergies, recent changes in condition) is omitted during the handoff.
    2. **Miscommunication:** The transferring and receiving units misunderstand each other due to unclear communication, jargon, or language barriers.
    3. **Delayed Handoff:** The handoff process is delayed, leading to a lapse in patient care or continuity.
    4. **Documentation Errors:** The handoff is not accurately documented, leading to discrepancies in the patient's medical record.
    5. **Patient Misidentification:** The wrong patient is transferred or incorrect patient information is communicated.

3. Assess the Severity, Occurrence, and Detection (Risk Priority Number - RPN)

- **Objective:** For each failure mode, assess the severity (impact on patient care), occurrence (likelihood of happening), and detection (likelihood of being detected before causing harm). Assign each a score from 1 (low) to 10 (high).
- **Example Scoring:**
    1. **Incomplete Information Transfer:**
        - **Severity:** 9 (Could result in serious harm if critical information is missed)
        - **Occurrence:** 7 (Likely to occur given the complexity of patient cases)
        - **Detection:** 4 (Moderately likely to be detected by the receiving unit)
        - **RPN = 9 × 7 × 4 = 252**
    2. **Miscommunication:**
        - **Severity:** 8 (Can cause significant treatment errors)
        - **Occurrence:** 6 (Communication breakdowns are common in high-stress environments)
        - **Detection:** 5 (Can be caught during clarification, but not always)
        - **RPN = 8 × 6 × 5 = 240**
    3. **Delayed Handoff:**
        - **Severity:** 6 (Potential to delay critical interventions)
        - **Occurrence:** 5 (Moderately common due to workflow issues)
        - **Detection:** 6 (Usually detected, but often too late to prevent delay)
        - **RPN = 6 × 5 × 6 = 180**

4. **Documentation Errors:**
   - **Severity:** 7 (Can lead to long-term errors in patient records)
   - **Occurrence:** 5 (Moderate frequency)
   - **Detection:** 7 (Often not detected until it causes an issue)
   - **RPN = 7 × 5 × 7 = 245**
5. **Patient Misidentification:**
   - **Severity:** 10 (Critical risk of harm)
   - **Occurrence:** 3 (Rare due to existing safety protocols)
   - **Detection:** 9 (Usually detected through double-checks)
   - **RPN = 10 × 3 × 9 = 270**

4. Prioritize Failure Modes

- **Objective:** Rank the failure modes based on their RPN scores, focusing first on those with the highest scores.
- **Priority Order:**
  1. **Patient Misidentification (RPN = 270)**
  2. **Incomplete Information Transfer (RPN = 252)**
  3. **Documentation Errors (RPN = 245)**
  4. **Miscommunication (RPN = 240)**
  5. **Delayed Handoff (RPN = 180)**

5. Develop Risk Mitigation Strategies

- **Objective:** Create strategies to reduce the risk of high-priority failure modes by lowering their severity, occurrence, or improving detection.

1. **Patient Misidentification:**
   - ○ **Strategy:** Implement a standardized patient identification protocol during handoffs, requiring dual-verification of patient identity using at least two identifiers (e.g., name, date of birth).
   - ○ **Action:** Train all staff on the importance of using the dual-verification system and conduct random audits to ensure compliance.
2. **Incomplete Information Transfer:**
   - ○ **Strategy:** Use standardized handoff checklists that include all critical patient information, such as allergies, current medications, and recent clinical changes.
   - ○ **Action:** Integrate the checklist into the electronic health record (EHR) system, making it mandatory for completion before handoff.
3. **Documentation Errors:**
   - ○ **Strategy:** Implement real-time documentation practices where the transferring nurse or physician documents the handoff in the patient's EHR during the communication.
   - ○ **Action:** Conduct regular training on accurate and timely documentation and use peer review processes to catch errors.
4. **Miscommunication:**
   - ○ **Strategy:** Employ the SBAR (Situation, Background, Assessment, Recommendation) communication framework to standardize verbal handoffs.
   - ○ **Action:** Provide communication skills training focused on the SBAR technique, and monitor handoffs to ensure consistency.
5. **Delayed Handoff:**
   - ○ **Strategy:** Establish clear handoff times and ensure that both units are aware of these schedules to minimize delays.
   - ○ **Action:** Use EHR alerts to notify staff when a handoff is due, and track compliance with these timelines.

6. Implement and Monitor Mitigation Strategies

- **Objective:** Roll out the mitigation strategies across the hospital and establish mechanisms to monitor their effectiveness.
- **Implementation:**

- ○ **Training:** Conduct staff training sessions on the new protocols and ensure that all team members understand their roles in mitigating risks.
- ○ **Pilot Testing:** Before full-scale implementation, pilot the new handoff process in a single unit to identify any practical challenges and make necessary adjustments.
- ○ **Communication:** Regularly communicate the importance of these strategies to staff and update them on any changes or improvements.
- **Monitoring:**
    - ○ **Audits and Reviews:** Conduct regular audits to assess compliance with the new handoff procedures and identify any areas for improvement.
    - ○ **Feedback Mechanism:** Establish a feedback loop where staff can report any issues or suggestions for further improvements in the handoff process.
    - ○ **RPN Reassessment:** Periodically reassess the RPN scores to measure the effectiveness of the mitigation strategies and adjust them as needed.

7. Continuous Improvement

- **Objective:** Ensure that the FMEA process is dynamic and responsive to changes in the clinical environment.
- **Actions:**
    - ○ **Regular Updates:** Update the FMEA as new risks emerge or as changes in the hospital environment affect the handoff process.
    - ○ **Ongoing Education:** Provide continuous education and training to staff on the importance of patient handoff safety and the role they play in mitigating risks.
    - ○ **Benchmarking:** Compare your hospital's handoff safety data with industry benchmarks to identify best practices and areas for improvement.

By carefully identifying, prioritizing, and mitigating potential failure modes in the patient handoff process using FMEA, nurse executives can significantly reduce the risk of errors, enhance patient safety, and improve the overall quality of care within the hospital.

Designing a proactive risk assessment program for a newly opened ambulatory surgery center (ASC) involves creating a comprehensive framework that identifies, evaluates, and mitigates potential risks before they lead to adverse events. This program should integrate multiple risk assessment methodologies, fostering a culture of safety that permeates every aspect of the ASC's operations. Here's how you can develop and implement this program:

1. Establish the Foundation of a Safety Culture

- **Leadership Commitment:** Ensure that leadership is visibly committed to creating and maintaining a culture of safety. This includes allocating resources for risk assessment activities, supporting staff education, and integrating safety into the center's mission and values.
- **Staff Engagement:** Involve staff at all levels in safety initiatives. Create a non-punitive environment where staff feel comfortable reporting near misses, errors, and safety concerns without fear of retribution.

2. Integrate Risk Assessment Methodologies

To build a robust risk assessment program, incorporate multiple methodologies that complement each other, providing a comprehensive view of potential risks.

A. Failure Mode and Effects Analysis (FMEA)

- **Purpose:** FMEA is a proactive method used to identify potential failures in processes and their effects on patient safety. By examining each step of a process, FMEA helps prioritize risks based on their severity, occurrence, and detectability.
- **Implementation:**
    1. **Select Critical Processes:** Identify high-risk processes such as surgical procedures, anesthesia administration, and sterilization practices.
    2. **Conduct FMEA Sessions:** Assemble multidisciplinary teams to conduct FMEA sessions. For example, analyze the surgical instrument sterilization process, identifying potential failure modes (e.g., improper cleaning) and their effects (e.g., infection risk).
    3. **Prioritize and Mitigate Risks:** Use the FMEA to prioritize risks and develop mitigation strategies, such as enhancing staff training or introducing double-check systems.

B. Root Cause Analysis (RCA)

- **Purpose**: RCA is a retrospective analysis used after an adverse event or near miss to identify the underlying causes and prevent recurrence. It focuses on understanding what went wrong and why.
- **Implementation**:
    1. **Event Investigation**: When an adverse event occurs, promptly initiate an RCA. For example, if a medication error occurs, assemble a team to investigate the incident.
    2. **Apply the "5 Whys" Technique**: Use the "5 Whys" technique to drill down to the root causes. If a wrong medication was administered, ask why each contributing factor occurred until the root cause is identified (e.g., a labeling issue or workflow interruption).
    3. **Develop Corrective Actions**: Based on the RCA findings, implement corrective actions such as process redesign, additional training, or system improvements. Monitor these changes to ensure their effectiveness.

C. Safety Audits and Checklists

- **Purpose**: Regular safety audits and the use of checklists ensure that standard procedures are consistently followed, reducing the likelihood of errors and enhancing overall safety.
- **Implementation**:
    1. **Develop and Implement Checklists**: Create checklists for critical activities, such as pre-operative verification, anesthesia safety checks, and post-operative care. These checklists should be used systematically by the surgical teams.
    2. **Conduct Regular Audits**: Perform routine safety audits to evaluate compliance with established protocols. For example, audit the adherence to hand hygiene protocols, proper use of personal protective equipment (PPE), and sterilization practices.
    3. **Feedback and Improvement**: Provide feedback from audits to staff and use the findings to make continuous improvements. Recognize teams that consistently adhere to safety practices, reinforcing positive behavior.

D. Incident Reporting and Analysis

- **Purpose**: An effective incident reporting system allows for the collection and analysis of data on near misses, errors, and adverse events, enabling the identification of trends and areas for improvement.
- **Implementation**:
    1. **Establish a Reporting System**: Set up an easy-to-use, confidential incident reporting system. Encourage all staff to report incidents without fear of blame.
    2. **Analyze Data**: Regularly analyze the data collected from reports to identify patterns and recurring issues. For instance, a trend of wrong-site surgeries might indicate a need to reinforce the surgical time-out procedure.
    3. **Implement Preventive Measures**: Use the analysis to implement preventive measures, such as updating procedures, revising training programs, or modifying the environment (e.g., improving signage or labeling).

3. Build a Comprehensive Safety Culture

- **Education and Training**: Conduct ongoing education and training programs on risk management, safety protocols, and the importance of a safety culture. All new employees should receive comprehensive safety training during onboarding.
- **Team-Based Approach**: Promote a team-based approach to safety, where every staff member understands their role in maintaining a safe environment. Regularly hold safety huddles to discuss potential risks, share lessons learned, and plan for upcoming procedures.
- **Continuous Monitoring and Improvement**: Establish a continuous monitoring system where risk assessments are regularly updated based on new information, changing conditions, or lessons learned from incidents. Encourage staff to participate in identifying risks and suggesting improvements.

4. Develop and Implement the COOP

- **Continuity of Operations Plan (COOP)**: Create a COOP specifically for the ASC that outlines procedures for maintaining critical operations during emergencies, such as power outages, natural disasters, or cyberattacks. The COOP should include:

1. **Essential Services**: Identify and prioritize essential services that must be maintained during a disruption, such as surgical procedures in progress, patient monitoring, and life-sustaining equipment.
2. **Backup Systems**: Ensure the availability of backup systems, such as generators for power and manual processes for critical documentation.
3. **Staff Roles and Responsibilities**: Clearly define staff roles and responsibilities during an emergency, ensuring that all employees know their duties and the chain of command.
4. **Communication Plan**: Develop a communication plan that includes methods for internal communication among staff and external communication with patients, families, and emergency services.

5. Monitor, Review, and Adjust the Program

- **Regular Reviews**: Schedule regular reviews of the risk assessment program to ensure its effectiveness and relevance. Update methodologies and protocols based on new risks, regulatory changes, or advancements in healthcare practices.
- **Performance Metrics**: Track performance metrics such as the number of incidents reported, the frequency of adverse events, and the results of safety audits. Use these metrics to measure the program's success and identify areas for further improvement.
- **Staff Involvement and Feedback**: Continuously involve staff in the risk assessment process, encouraging feedback and suggestions for improvement. Foster a culture where safety is a shared responsibility and where continuous improvement is part of the daily routine.

By integrating these risk assessment methodologies into a proactive, comprehensive safety program, the ambulatory surgery center can foster a robust safety culture. This approach not only mitigates potential risks but also promotes continuous improvement, ensuring high-quality patient care and operational excellence.

Technology has transformed healthcare risk assessment by enabling more precise, data-driven approaches to identifying and mitigating potential risks. Nurse executives can leverage various technological tools such as data analytics, artificial intelligence (AI), and predictive modeling to enhance patient safety, optimize operational efficiency, and improve overall care quality.

The Role of Technology in Modern Healthcare Risk Assessment

1. **Data Analytics**
   - **Overview:** Data analytics involves the systematic analysis of healthcare data to identify patterns, trends, and outliers that may indicate potential risks. This technology allows for the aggregation and analysis of vast amounts of data from electronic health records (EHRs), patient monitoring systems, and other sources.
   - **Application in Risk Assessment:**
     - **Trend Analysis:** Nurse executives can use data analytics to track trends in patient outcomes, such as infection rates, medication errors, or readmission rates. By identifying areas with increasing adverse events, targeted interventions can be implemented.
     - **Real-Time Monitoring:** Analytics can provide real-time alerts for critical conditions, such as early signs of sepsis or deteriorating patient vitals. This proactive monitoring helps in early intervention and prevention of adverse outcomes.
     - **Operational Efficiency:** Analyzing data on hospital operations, such as bed occupancy rates, staffing levels, and workflow bottlenecks, can help nurse executives identify inefficiencies and potential risks related to resource management.

2. **Artificial Intelligence (AI)**
   - **Overview:** AI involves the use of machine learning algorithms and other intelligent systems to analyze complex datasets and make predictions or decisions. AI can process data at a scale and speed beyond human capability, uncovering insights that might otherwise go unnoticed.
   - **Application in Risk Assessment:**

- **Predictive Analytics:** AI can predict patient outcomes based on historical data, such as identifying patients at high risk for complications, readmissions, or falls. For example, AI algorithms can analyze EHR data to predict which patients are most likely to develop pressure ulcers, allowing for early preventive measures.
- **Natural Language Processing (NLP):** AI-driven NLP tools can analyze unstructured data, such as physician notes and patient narratives, to identify potential risks that may not be captured in structured data fields. For example, NLP can detect mentions of symptoms or conditions in patient records that suggest a heightened risk for certain complications.
- **Decision Support:** AI-powered decision support systems can assist healthcare providers in making more accurate and timely decisions. For instance, AI can help in selecting the most appropriate treatment protocols by analyzing patient data against vast medical knowledge databases.

3. **Predictive Modeling**
   - **Overview:** Predictive modeling uses statistical techniques to create models that predict future outcomes based on historical data. In healthcare, these models can be used to assess the likelihood of various risks and guide preventive strategies.
   - **Application in Risk Assessment:**
     - **Risk Stratification:** Predictive models can stratify patients by risk levels, enabling nurse executives to allocate resources more effectively. For instance, patients identified as high-risk for readmission can receive more intensive follow-up care.
     - **Population Health Management:** Predictive models can be applied at the population level to identify communities or groups at higher risk for specific health issues, such as chronic diseases or outbreaks of infectious diseases. This allows for targeted public health interventions.
     - **Scenario Planning:** Predictive modeling can simulate different scenarios, such as the impact of a flu outbreak on hospital capacity, helping nurse executives plan and prepare for potential challenges.

Leveraging Technology to Identify and Mitigate Risks
1. **Integrating EHRs with Advanced Analytics Tools**
   - **Strategy:** Nurse executives can integrate EHR systems with advanced data analytics platforms to continuously monitor patient data for potential risks. This integration allows for the real-time analysis of patient records, identifying trends and generating alerts for immediate attention.
   - **Example:** An analytics platform could monitor vital signs, lab results, and medication administration in real-time, alerting clinicians to potential adverse drug reactions or signs of patient deterioration.

2. **Implementing AI-Driven Predictive Tools**
   - **Strategy:** Deploy AI-driven predictive tools that use machine learning algorithms to analyze patient data and predict risks such as hospital-acquired infections, falls, or readmissions. These tools can be integrated into clinical workflows to provide real-time decision support.
   - **Example:** A predictive tool could analyze patient mobility, history of falls, and current medications to predict the likelihood of a fall, prompting the care team to implement fall prevention measures.

3. **Using Predictive Modeling for Resource Allocation**
   - **Strategy:** Utilize predictive modeling to anticipate patient volumes, staff requirements, and resource needs during different periods or in response to specific events (e.g., flu season, natural disasters). This approach ensures that resources are allocated efficiently, reducing the risk of overburdened staff and compromised patient care.
   - **Example:** Predictive models could forecast an increase in ICU admissions during a flu outbreak, allowing nurse executives to preemptively allocate additional staff and resources to the ICU.

4. **Enhancing Clinical Decision-Making with AI and Predictive Analytics**

- **Strategy:** Implement AI-driven clinical decision support systems that provide evidence-based recommendations based on patient-specific data. These systems can reduce the risk of errors and ensure that patients receive the most appropriate care based on the latest clinical guidelines.
- **Example:** An AI-driven system could analyze a patient's genetic data, medical history, and current symptoms to recommend personalized treatment plans that minimize risks and optimize outcomes.

5. **Building a Data-Driven Culture**
   - **Strategy:** Foster a culture of data-driven decision-making within the organization, where staff at all levels understand the importance of using data and technology to identify and mitigate risks. This involves regular training on data interpretation, the use of predictive tools, and the integration of technology into daily workflows.
   - **Example:** Nurse executives can lead initiatives to train nurses and clinicians on how to use AI tools and predictive models, ensuring they are comfortable and confident in applying these technologies to improve patient care.

6. **Collaborating with IT and Data Science Teams**
   - **Strategy:** Nurse executives should work closely with IT and data science teams to ensure that the right technological tools are in place and that they are tailored to the specific needs of the healthcare environment. Collaboration is key to developing and refining predictive models and AI tools that are accurate, reliable, and user-friendly.
   - **Example:** Regular meetings between nurse leaders and data scientists can help ensure that predictive models are continuously updated and validated against new data, improving their accuracy and relevance.

Challenges and Considerations

1. **Data Quality and Integration:**
   - **Challenge:** The effectiveness of data analytics and AI depends on the quality and completeness of the data. Inconsistent or incomplete data can lead to inaccurate predictions and risk assessments.
   - **Solution:** Nurse executives should prioritize data quality initiatives, such as standardizing data entry procedures and ensuring that EHR systems are fully integrated across departments.

2. **Ethical Considerations:**
   - **Challenge:** The use of AI and predictive models in healthcare raises ethical questions, particularly regarding patient privacy, data security, and the potential for bias in algorithms.
   - **Solution:** Implement strict data governance policies, ensure transparency in how predictive models are developed and used, and regularly audit AI systems to identify and mitigate potential biases.

3. **Staff Training and Acceptance:**
   - **Challenge:** The successful implementation of technology in risk assessment requires that staff are well-trained and confident in using new tools. Resistance to change can hinder the adoption of these technologies.
   - **Solution:** Invest in comprehensive training programs and engage staff early in the process of implementing new technologies, emphasizing the benefits for patient care and safety.

By strategically leveraging data analytics, AI, and predictive modeling, nurse executives can transform healthcare risk assessment, enabling more proactive and effective identification and mitigation of potential risks. This not only enhances patient safety and care quality but also supports more efficient and resilient healthcare operations.

Benchmarking in healthcare quality improvement involves comparing an organization's processes, performance metrics, and outcomes against those of other organizations (external benchmarking) or different units or departments within the same organization (internal benchmarking). Both internal and external benchmarking have distinct advantages and limitations. Nurse executives can leverage both approaches to enhance organizational performance by identifying best practices, setting realistic goals, and fostering a culture of continuous improvement.

Internal Benchmarking

Advantages

1. **Relevance to Organizational Context**

o Internal benchmarking involves comparing similar units or departments within the same organization, ensuring that the comparisons are directly relevant and tailored to the specific operational environment. This makes it easier to identify actionable improvements that are feasible within the organizational culture and resource constraints.

2. **Ease of Access to Data**
   o Data for internal benchmarking is typically more accessible and readily available since it is within the same organization. This allows for more frequent and detailed comparisons, making it possible to track performance trends over time and respond quickly to emerging issues.

3. **Enhanced Staff Engagement**
   o Engaging staff in internal benchmarking fosters a sense of ownership and healthy competition. It can motivate departments or units to improve performance by learning from high-performing peers within the organization.

4. **Customizable Comparisons**
   o Internal benchmarking allows for highly customizable comparisons based on specific organizational goals. For example, nurse executives can compare patient satisfaction scores between units that serve different patient populations but have similar staffing levels or resources.

Limitations

1. **Limited Scope of Comparison**
   o Internal benchmarking is constrained by the size and diversity of the organization. Smaller organizations or those with fewer specialized units may have limited opportunities for meaningful comparisons, reducing the potential for identifying best practices or innovative solutions.

2. **Potential for Complacency**
   o Relying solely on internal comparisons can lead to complacency if all units perform at a similar level. Without external benchmarks, there's a risk of missing out on more innovative practices or higher standards being set by other organizations.

3. **Inconsistencies in Data Collection**
   o Variations in how data is collected and reported across different departments or units can complicate internal benchmarking efforts. Inconsistent data can lead to inaccurate comparisons and hinder the identification of genuine performance gaps.

External Benchmarking

Advantages

1. **Broader Perspective and Best Practices**
   o External benchmarking provides a broader perspective by comparing performance against industry standards or best practices from other organizations. This can reveal new approaches, technologies, or processes that might not be present within the organization but could significantly enhance performance.

2. **Setting Ambitious Goals**
   o By comparing against top-performing organizations, external benchmarking can help set more ambitious performance targets. This can drive innovation and push the organization to achieve higher levels of quality and efficiency.

3. **Competitive Advantage**
   o Understanding how the organization stacks up against competitors or industry leaders can be a powerful motivator for improvement. External benchmarking helps identify areas where the organization can differentiate itself and gain a competitive advantage, particularly in patient satisfaction, clinical outcomes, or operational efficiency.

4. **Objective Assessment**
   o External benchmarking provides an objective assessment of the organization's performance, free from internal biases. This can help validate internal performance assessments and identify areas where internal perceptions of performance may not align with external realities.

Limitations

1. **Data Availability and Comparability**

- Accessing reliable and comparable external data can be challenging. Differences in how data is collected, reported, or categorized across organizations can complicate comparisons. Additionally, data from other organizations might not be publicly available or may come with restrictions.

2. **Contextual Differences**
   - External benchmarking doesn't always account for the unique context of different organizations, such as variations in patient demographics, resource availability, or regulatory environments. These differences can make it difficult to apply external benchmarks directly to the organization's context.

3. **Implementation Challenges**
   - Adopting best practices from external benchmarks may require significant changes to existing processes, systems, or culture, which can be challenging and resource-intensive. The organization may also encounter resistance to change if staff feel that external comparisons are not fully applicable to their situation.

4. **Cost and Time Investment**
   - Conducting external benchmarking can be time-consuming and costly, particularly if it involves engaging external consultants, purchasing benchmarking reports, or participating in industry benchmarking groups.

Effectively Utilizing Both Approaches

Nurse executives can maximize the benefits of both internal and external benchmarking by integrating these approaches into a comprehensive quality improvement strategy.

1. **Start with Internal Benchmarking**
   - Begin with internal benchmarking to establish a baseline understanding of performance within the organization. This involves identifying internal best practices, addressing immediate performance gaps, and ensuring consistent data collection and reporting across units. For example, if one department has significantly lower infection rates, investigate the practices contributing to this success and consider implementing them across the organization.

2. **Incorporate External Benchmarking for Broader Goals**
   - Use external benchmarking to set strategic goals that align with industry standards or best practices. Identify top-performing organizations in key areas such as patient safety, clinical outcomes, or operational efficiency, and explore how their practices can be adapted to your organization. For instance, if a leading hospital has achieved outstanding patient satisfaction scores through a specific patient engagement strategy, consider piloting this strategy within your organization.

3. **Balance Ambition with Feasibility**
   - While external benchmarks can inspire ambitious goals, it's important to balance these with the feasibility of implementation within the organization's context. Nurse executives should assess the resources, time, and potential barriers involved in adopting external best practices and set realistic, phased goals that allow for gradual improvement.

4. **Foster a Continuous Improvement Culture**
   - Use both internal and external benchmarks to foster a culture of continuous improvement. Regularly share benchmarking results with staff, celebrate successes, and involve them in developing and implementing improvement plans. Encourage departments to strive for excellence by learning from both internal peers and external leaders.

5. **Monitor and Adjust**
   - Continuously monitor the impact of benchmarking activities on organizational performance. Adjust strategies as needed based on the latest internal and external data, and ensure that benchmarking remains a dynamic process that evolves with changing industry standards and organizational goals.

By effectively utilizing both internal and external benchmarking, nurse executives can drive continuous improvement, enhance patient care, and position their organization as a leader in healthcare quality.

Selecting appropriate benchmarks for a healthcare organization is crucial for evaluating performance, identifying areas for improvement, and driving strategic initiatives. The benchmarks chosen must align with the organization's unique characteristics and goals to ensure meaningful comparisons and actionable insights. Here's a set of criteria to guide the selection process:

1. Relevance to Organizational Size and Type

- **Criterion:** Select benchmarks that are relevant to the size and type of the healthcare organization (e.g., a large urban hospital, rural critical access hospital, outpatient clinic).
- **Application:**
  - A large urban medical center might benchmark against other large academic medical centers or tertiary care facilities with similar patient volumes and service offerings.
  - A small rural hospital should compare itself to other critical access hospitals with similar staffing levels and resource constraints, rather than larger institutions with vastly different capabilities.

2. Alignment with Patient Population Demographics

- **Criterion:** Choose benchmarks that reflect the demographics of the organization's patient population, including age, socioeconomic status, and prevalent health conditions.
- **Application:**
  - If the organization serves a predominantly elderly population, benchmarks should focus on metrics related to geriatric care, chronic disease management, and fall prevention.
  - An organization in a low-income area might prioritize benchmarks related to access to care, preventive services, and outcomes in underserved populations.

3. Relevance to Service Lines and Specialties

- **Criterion:** Ensure that benchmarks align with the key service lines and specialties offered by the organization.
- **Application:**
  - A hospital with a robust cardiovascular program should benchmark against institutions known for excellence in cardiac care, focusing on metrics such as readmission rates, surgical outcomes, and patient satisfaction in cardiology.
  - A healthcare system with an extensive oncology department might select benchmarks related to cancer survival rates, time-to-treatment metrics, and patient-reported outcomes specific to oncology.

4. Consistency with Strategic Goals and Objectives

- **Criterion:** Select benchmarks that support the organization's strategic goals, such as improving patient safety, enhancing care quality, reducing costs, or expanding service offerings.
- **Application:**
  - If the strategic goal is to reduce hospital-acquired infections (HAIs), benchmarks should focus on infection rates, adherence to infection prevention protocols, and outcomes of infection control initiatives.
  - For an organization aiming to improve patient satisfaction, relevant benchmarks might include patient experience scores, wait times, and the effectiveness of communication between healthcare providers and patients.

5. Comparability with Peer Organizations

- **Criterion:** Choose benchmarks that allow for direct comparison with peer organizations of similar size, scope, and complexity.
- **Application:**
  - A regional healthcare system should benchmark against other regional systems or institutions within the same geographic area to account for regional variations in healthcare delivery.
  - If benchmarking against national standards, ensure that the organization is comparing itself to institutions with similar characteristics, such as academic affiliation, teaching status, or trauma center designation.

6. Data Availability and Quality

- **Criterion:** Ensure that the benchmarks are based on reliable, accurate, and up-to-date data that the organization can access and analyze effectively.
- **Application:**
  - Use benchmarks derived from reputable sources, such as the Centers for Medicare & Medicaid Services (CMS), The Joint Commission, or industry-specific databases like Vizient or the National Database of Nursing Quality Indicators (NDNQI).
  - Consider the organization's ability to consistently collect and report the necessary data to measure against these benchmarks, ensuring that internal data systems are robust enough to support benchmarking efforts.

7. Sensitivity to Organizational Changes
- **Criterion:** Select benchmarks that can reflect the impact of organizational changes, such as the implementation of new technologies, care models, or quality improvement initiatives.
- **Application:**
  - After introducing an electronic health record (EHR) system, benchmarks should include metrics related to documentation accuracy, clinical decision support usage, and impact on patient outcomes.
  - If the organization has implemented a new care coordination program, benchmarks might include reduced readmission rates, improved care transitions, and enhanced patient satisfaction scores.

8. Relevance to Regulatory and Accreditation Requirements
- **Criterion:** Align benchmarks with the regulatory and accreditation standards the organization is required to meet, such as those set by CMS, The Joint Commission, or state health departments.
- **Application:**
  - If the organization is focused on maintaining or achieving Magnet Recognition, benchmarks should include nursing-sensitive indicators such as nurse turnover rates, patient falls, and pressure ulcer incidence.
  - For organizations participating in value-based purchasing programs, relevant benchmarks might include patient outcomes tied to financial incentives, such as mortality rates, patient experience scores, and efficiency of care delivery.

9. Feasibility of Implementation and Monitoring
- **Criterion:** Choose benchmarks that the organization has the capability to monitor and act upon, considering the availability of resources, expertise, and technology.
- **Application:**
  - If the organization has limited analytical capacity, it should focus on a few high-impact benchmarks that can be effectively tracked and managed rather than attempting to monitor a broad range of metrics.
  - Ensure that there is a clear plan for how benchmarking data will be collected, analyzed, and used to inform decision-making and performance improvement efforts.

10. Potential for Actionable Insights
- **Criterion:** Select benchmarks that will provide actionable insights, enabling the organization to identify specific areas for improvement and develop targeted interventions.
- **Application:**
  - Benchmarks related to patient safety, such as adverse event rates or compliance with safety protocols, can lead to specific, actionable changes in clinical practice.
  - Financial benchmarks, such as cost per case or length of stay, can inform efforts to optimize resource utilization and improve operational efficiency.

By carefully considering factors such as organizational size, patient population, service lines, strategic goals, and the availability of quality data, nurse executives and healthcare leaders can select benchmarks that are not only relevant but also actionable. These benchmarks will enable the organization to effectively measure performance, drive continuous improvement, and ultimately enhance the quality of care provided to patients.

Analyzing Benchmarking Data for Hospital-Acquired Infections (HAIs)

Scenario: You are tasked with analyzing benchmarking data for hospital-acquired infections (HAIs) across a multi-hospital system. The goal is to identify top-performing hospitals, investigate their best practices, and develop an action plan to improve HAI rates in lower-performing facilities.

Step 1: Analyze the Benchmarking Data

1. **Collect and Review Data**
   - Gather HAI data from each hospital in the system, focusing on key infection types such as central line-associated bloodstream infections (CLABSIs), catheter-associated urinary tract infections (CAUTIs), surgical site infections (SSIs), and ventilator-associated pneumonia (VAP).
   - Calculate HAI rates for each hospital, expressed as the number of infections per 1,000 patient days or procedures.

2. **Identify Top Performers and Lower Performers**
   - Rank the hospitals based on their HAI rates. Identify the top-performing hospitals with the lowest HAI rates and the lower-performing hospitals with higher rates.
   - For example:
     - **Hospital A**: 0.5 CLABSIs per 1,000 central line days (Top Performer)
     - **Hospital B**: 0.7 CAUTIs per 1,000 catheter days (Top Performer)
     - **Hospital C**: 1.2 SSIs per 100 surgeries (Lower Performer)
     - **Hospital D**: 2.0 VAPs per 1,000 ventilator days (Lower Performer)

Step 2: Investigate Best Practices in Top-Performing Hospitals

1. **Conduct Site Visits and Interviews**
   - Visit the top-performing hospitals (e.g., Hospitals A and B) to observe their infection prevention practices firsthand.
   - Interview key staff members, including infection preventionists, nursing leaders, and frontline staff, to understand the strategies they employ to prevent HAIs.
   - Ask questions such as:
     - How do they ensure compliance with infection prevention protocols?
     - What specific interventions have been most effective in reducing HAIs?
     - How do they educate and engage staff in infection prevention efforts?

2. **Review Policies and Protocols**
   - Obtain copies of the infection control policies and protocols used in the top-performing hospitals. Compare these with the policies in place at the lower-performing hospitals.
   - Pay attention to specific practices, such as hand hygiene enforcement, catheter insertion and maintenance procedures, environmental cleaning protocols, and the use of checklists.

3. **Analyze Data Management and Reporting Practices**
   - Investigate how top performers track and report HAI data. Do they use real-time monitoring systems? How frequently do they review infection data with clinical teams?
   - Examine how data transparency and feedback loops are integrated into their infection prevention strategies.

Step 3: Develop an Action Plan for Improvement in Lower-Performing Facilities

1. **Set Clear Goals**
   - Establish specific, measurable goals for reducing HAI rates in the lower-performing hospitals. For example:
     - **Hospital C**: Reduce SSIs by 30% within 12 months.
     - **Hospital D**: Reduce VAPs by 40% within 12 months.

2. **Implement Best Practices**
   - **Adopt Proven Interventions**: Implement the best practices identified in top-performing hospitals across the lower-performing facilities. For example:
     - **Hand Hygiene**: Ensure strict adherence to hand hygiene protocols by installing hand sanitizer dispensers at all points of care and conducting regular hand hygiene audits.
     - **Bundles of Care**: Introduce care bundles for CLABSIs, CAUTIs, SSIs, and VAPs that include a set of evidence-based practices. For instance, Hospital D could implement a VAP

prevention bundle that includes elevation of the head of the bed, daily sedation vacations, and oral care with chlorhexidine.
- **Checklists and Protocols**: Implement standardized checklists for procedures such as central line insertion and catheter maintenance to ensure consistency and reduce the risk of infection.

3. **Enhance Education and Training**
   - **Staff Education**: Provide comprehensive training for staff on infection prevention practices, focusing on areas where gaps have been identified. Use simulation-based training for high-risk procedures.
   - **Ongoing Competency Assessments**: Conduct regular competency assessments to ensure that all staff are proficient in infection prevention techniques, especially in critical areas like surgical site care and ventilator management.

4. **Improve Data Monitoring and Feedback**
   - **Real-Time Data Tracking**: Implement or enhance real-time HAI data tracking systems to allow for immediate identification of infection trends and timely interventions.
   - **Regular Feedback**: Establish a routine for sharing HAI data with clinical teams, including weekly or monthly reports. Use these sessions to discuss trends, address challenges, and reinforce accountability.

5. **Foster a Culture of Safety and Accountability**
   - **Leadership Engagement**: Engage hospital leadership in infection prevention efforts by including HAI reduction as a key performance indicator in their goals. Regularly update leadership on progress and challenges.
   - **Empower Frontline Staff**: Encourage frontline staff to take ownership of infection prevention by involving them in decision-making processes and recognizing their contributions to reducing HAIs.
   - **Non-Punitive Reporting**: Promote a culture of non-punitive reporting where staff feel safe to report near misses and breaches in infection control practices. Use this information to identify areas for improvement.

6. **Monitor Progress and Adjust Interventions**
   - **Monthly Reviews**: Conduct monthly reviews of HAI data in lower-performing hospitals to assess progress toward the established goals. Use these reviews to identify any emerging issues and adjust interventions as needed.
   - **Continuous Improvement**: Foster a mindset of continuous improvement by regularly updating protocols based on the latest evidence and feedback from staff. Encourage innovation and the adoption of new technologies or practices that could further reduce HAIs.

Step 4: Evaluate the Impact of the Action Plan

1. **Assess Outcomes**
   - After 6 to 12 months, evaluate the impact of the action plan by comparing current HAI rates with baseline data. Determine whether the targeted reductions in SSIs, VAPs, or other infections have been achieved.
   - Analyze any improvements in patient outcomes, such as reduced length of stay or lower readmission rates, as a result of the decreased infection rates.

2. **Share Successes and Lessons Learned**
   - Share the results of the improvement efforts with all hospitals in the system, highlighting successful strategies and lessons learned. This can motivate other facilities to adopt similar practices and reinforce a culture of safety and quality across the system.

3. **Sustain and Spread Best Practices**
   - Ensure that successful interventions are sustained over the long term by embedding them into standard operating procedures and training programs.
   - Consider spreading the best practices to other areas of the hospitals or other facilities within the system to drive continuous improvement in patient safety.

By systematically analyzing benchmarking data, identifying best practices, and implementing a targeted action plan, nurse executives can effectively reduce HAIs across a multi-hospital system, thereby improving patient safety and quality of care.

Risk-adjusted outcome measures are essential tools in healthcare benchmarking, particularly when comparing performance across organizations that serve different patient populations. These measures account for variations in patient demographics, comorbidities, and other factors that can influence outcomes, thereby enabling more accurate and fair comparisons between healthcare providers.

Understanding Risk-Adjusted Outcome Measures

1. **Definition and Purpose:**
   - **Risk-adjusted outcome measures** adjust for differences in patient characteristics that could affect health outcomes. This adjustment allows organizations to compare performance on a more level playing field by accounting for factors outside their control.
   - **Purpose:** The primary goal is to ensure that outcome comparisons reflect the quality of care provided rather than differences in patient populations. For example, a hospital serving a higher proportion of elderly or chronically ill patients might have worse unadjusted outcomes, but after risk adjustment, these outcomes might align more closely with those of other hospitals.

2. **Commonly Used Risk-Adjusted Measures:**
   - **Mortality Rates:** Adjusted for factors such as age, severity of illness, and comorbid conditions.
   - **Readmission Rates:** Adjusted based on patient demographics, primary diagnosis, and comorbidities.
   - **Length of Stay:** Adjusted for clinical complexity and severity of the patient's condition.
   - **Complication Rates:** Adjusted for patient risk factors that might predispose certain populations to higher complication rates.

Benefits of Using Risk-Adjusted Outcome Measures

1. **Fair Comparisons:**
   - Risk adjustment allows healthcare organizations to compare outcomes fairly, accounting for the inherent risks associated with their specific patient populations. This ensures that organizations treating more complex or high-risk patients are not unfairly penalized.

2. **Improved Benchmarking Accuracy:**
   - By accounting for patient differences, risk-adjusted measures provide a more accurate reflection of an organization's performance. This accuracy is crucial for identifying areas of improvement and making informed decisions about resource allocation and quality improvement initiatives.

3. **Enhanced Credibility:**
   - Using risk-adjusted outcomes enhances the credibility of benchmarking data. It reassures stakeholders, such as patients, payers, and regulatory bodies, that comparisons between organizations are valid and based on a thorough analysis of relevant factors.

4. **Focus on Quality Improvement:**
   - Risk-adjusted outcomes help organizations focus on areas where they can genuinely improve care quality, rather than being distracted by outcomes influenced by patient factors beyond their control. This focus promotes more meaningful quality improvement efforts.

Challenges in Using Risk-Adjusted Outcome Measures

1. **Complexity of Risk Adjustment Models:**
   - Risk adjustment models can be complex and require sophisticated statistical techniques and a deep understanding of the factors that influence patient outcomes. Developing and validating these models demands significant expertise and resources.

2. **Data Quality and Availability:**
   - The accuracy of risk-adjusted measures depends on the quality and completeness of the data used in the models. Inaccurate or missing data can lead to incorrect adjustments and misleading results.

3. **Potential for Over-Adjustment:**

- There is a risk of over-adjusting outcomes, where adjustments might mask variations in care quality. It's important to strike a balance between adjusting for legitimate patient differences and maintaining sensitivity to differences in care practices.

Strategies for Nurse Executives to Ensure Fair Comparisons

1. **Select Appropriate Benchmarking Peers:**
   - **Strategy:** Nurse executives should carefully select peer organizations for benchmarking, focusing on those with similar patient populations and care settings. This ensures that comparisons are as relevant as possible, even after risk adjustment.
   - **Implementation:** Identify hospitals or healthcare systems that serve similar demographic groups, have comparable service lines, and operate in similar environments (e.g., urban vs. rural settings). Use this peer group as the primary comparison set for benchmarking.

2. **Ensure High-Quality Data Collection:**
   - **Strategy:** Invest in robust data collection and management systems to ensure the accuracy and completeness of the data used in risk adjustment models. This includes training staff on accurate data entry and regular audits to verify data integrity.
   - **Implementation:** Implement standardized protocols for data entry, particularly for key variables used in risk adjustment (e.g., coding of comorbidities, severity of illness). Use electronic health records (EHRs) with built-in data validation checks to minimize errors.

3. **Understand and Apply the Appropriate Risk Adjustment Models:**
   - **Strategy:** Nurse executives should work with data scientists, statisticians, and quality improvement experts to understand and apply the most appropriate risk adjustment models for their organization's benchmarking efforts.
   - **Implementation:** Collaborate with external experts or use established risk adjustment tools (e.g., CMS's Hospital Compare, Vizient's Clinical Data Base) that have been validated for specific conditions and populations. Regularly review and update these models to reflect changes in patient populations and clinical practices.

4. **Regularly Review and Update Risk Adjustment Practices:**
   - **Strategy:** Continuously review and refine the organization's risk adjustment practices to ensure they remain relevant and accurate as patient populations and healthcare practices evolve.
   - **Implementation:** Establish a review committee that includes clinical leaders, data analysts, and quality improvement staff to regularly assess the effectiveness of current risk adjustment models. Make adjustments as needed based on new research, changes in patient demographics, or feedback from benchmarking results.

5. **Transparency in Reporting and Interpretation:**
   - **Strategy:** Ensure that the results of risk-adjusted benchmarking are reported transparently, with clear explanations of how adjustments were made and what they mean for the organization's performance.
   - **Implementation:** Provide clear documentation of the risk adjustment methodologies used in reports, including explanations of the variables considered and the rationale for their inclusion. Offer training sessions for staff on interpreting risk-adjusted data correctly.

6. **Focus on Actionable Insights:**
   - **Strategy:** Use risk-adjusted outcomes to identify specific areas for quality improvement, rather than solely for comparison purposes. Focus on actionable insights that can drive real improvements in patient care.
   - **Implementation:** After identifying areas where the organization underperforms compared to benchmarks, develop targeted quality improvement initiatives that address the root causes of these performance gaps. Monitor the impact of these initiatives using the same risk-adjusted measures to gauge progress.

7. **Benchmark Multiple Metrics:**
   - **Strategy:** Benchmark across a range of risk-adjusted metrics rather than relying on a single measure to get a comprehensive view of performance. This approach provides a fuller picture of where improvements are needed and where the organization excels.

- ○ **Implementation:** Track metrics such as mortality rates, readmission rates, complication rates, patient satisfaction, and length of stay, all adjusted for risk, to develop a well-rounded understanding of organizational performance.

Risk-adjusted outcome measures are indispensable in ensuring fair and accurate benchmarking in healthcare, especially when comparing organizations with different patient populations. By carefully selecting benchmarks, ensuring data quality, and applying the right risk adjustment models, nurse executives can make meaningful comparisons that truly reflect the quality of care provided. This approach not only facilitates fair comparisons but also drives targeted improvements that enhance patient outcomes and organizational performance.

Applying Lean methodology to streamline patient flow in an emergency department (ED) involves identifying and eliminating waste, optimizing processes, and continuously improving through small, incremental changes. Lean focuses on creating value for patients by ensuring that every step in the process is efficient and necessary. Here's how you can apply Lean principles to achieve these goals.

Step 1: Identify Waste in the Emergency Department
The first step in applying Lean methodology is to identify waste, which is anything that does not add value to the patient experience. In an ED, common types of waste include:

1. **Waiting:** Long wait times for patients to be seen by a healthcare provider, receive tests, or be admitted to the hospital.
2. **Overprocessing:** Redundant documentation or excessive diagnostic tests that do not contribute to better patient outcomes.
3. **Motion:** Unnecessary movement of staff, patients, or materials within the ED, leading to inefficiencies and delays.
4. **Inventory:** Overstocking or understocking of supplies, leading to clutter or delays in patient care.
5. **Transportation:** Moving patients or materials over long distances within the hospital, contributing to delays.
6. **Defects:** Errors in patient care or documentation that require rework, such as incorrect patient information or lost test results.
7. **Overproduction:** Performing tasks or procedures that are not immediately needed, leading to bottlenecks and inefficiencies.

Step 2: Develop Value Stream Maps
Value stream mapping (VSM) is a Lean tool that helps visualize the entire patient flow process from start to finish, identifying value-added and non-value-added steps. Here's how to develop value stream maps for the ED:

1. **Map the Current State**
   - ○ **Patient Arrival to Triage:** Start by mapping the steps a patient goes through from the moment they arrive at the ED to the point they are triaged. Identify the time spent at each step and any delays or bottlenecks.
   - ○ **Triage to Treatment:** Next, map the process from triage to when the patient is seen by a physician or nurse practitioner. Include steps such as waiting for an available bed, nurse assessment, and initial diagnostics.
   - ○ **Treatment to Discharge or Admission:** Finally, map the steps from treatment to discharge or admission. This includes diagnostic testing, consultations, treatments, and the discharge or admission process.
2. **Identify Bottlenecks and Waste**
   - ○ Use the value stream maps to identify where delays, redundancies, or inefficiencies occur. For example, you might find that patients wait an excessive amount of time in the triage area due to staffing shortages or that lab results take too long to be processed.
3. **Determine Value-Added vs. Non-Value-Added Steps**
   - ○ Analyze each step in the value stream map to determine whether it adds value to the patient experience. For example, direct patient care is value-added, while waiting for test results is non-value-added. The goal is to reduce or eliminate non-value-added steps.

Step 3: Implement Kaizen Events
Kaizen events are focused, short-term projects that aim to improve specific processes by eliminating waste and enhancing efficiency. Here's how to organize and execute Kaizen events in the ED:

1. **Select a Target Area**
   ○ Choose an area with significant waste or bottlenecks identified in the value stream maps. For instance, if long wait times in triage are a major issue, focus the Kaizen event on streamlining the triage process.
2. **Assemble a Cross-Functional Team**
   ○ Form a team that includes frontline staff (e.g., nurses, physicians, clerks), management, and support staff (e.g., lab technicians, transport personnel). Ensure the team is diverse and includes individuals who are directly involved in the target process.
3. **Conduct the Kaizen Event**
   ○ **Day 1: Process Mapping and Analysis**
     ▪ Re-map the current process in detail, involving the team to ensure all perspectives are considered. Identify specific waste elements within the process.
     ▪ Brainstorm potential solutions to reduce waste and improve the process.
   ○ **Day 2: Develop and Test Solutions**
     ▪ Implement small-scale tests of the proposed solutions in the ED. For example, if the problem is long wait times in triage, you might test a new fast-track process for low-acuity patients.
   ○ **Day 3: Review and Adjust**
     ▪ Evaluate the results of the tests. Collect feedback from staff and patients to determine whether the changes have improved efficiency and satisfaction.
     ▪ Refine the solutions based on feedback and prepare for full implementation.
4. **Measure Results**
   ○ Track key performance indicators (KPIs) to assess the impact of the Kaizen event. KPIs might include patient wait times, length of stay in the ED, patient satisfaction scores, and staff satisfaction.
   ○ Compare these metrics before and after the Kaizen event to determine its effectiveness.
5. **Standardize and Scale**
   ○ Once the improvements have been validated, standardize the new processes across the ED. Develop standard operating procedures (SOPs) and provide training to ensure consistent implementation.
   ○ Consider scaling successful Kaizen events to other areas of the hospital or system, applying the lessons learned to improve processes elsewhere.

Step 4: Foster a Culture of Continuous Improvement
1. **Engage and Empower Staff**
   ○ Encourage staff at all levels to identify areas for improvement and participate in ongoing Kaizen events. Create an environment where continuous improvement is part of the daily routine.
   ○ Recognize and reward staff who contribute to Lean initiatives, reinforcing the importance of their role in driving improvements.
2. **Regularly Review and Update Processes**
   ○ Schedule regular reviews of ED processes to ensure they remain efficient and aligned with patient needs. Continuously monitor KPIs and be prepared to adjust processes as necessary.
   ○ Use the Plan-Do-Study-Act (PDSA) cycle to iteratively test and refine improvements, ensuring that the ED adapts to changing circumstances and maintains high standards of care.
3. **Promote Transparency and Communication**
   ○ Share the results of Lean initiatives with the entire ED team, as well as hospital leadership. Transparency fosters trust and helps build momentum for future improvement efforts.
   ○ Establish clear communication channels to keep everyone informed about ongoing projects, changes in procedures, and the impact of Lean initiatives.

Expected Outcomes

By applying Lean methodology in the ED, you can expect several key outcomes:

- **Reduced Patient Wait Times**: Streamlining processes will reduce unnecessary delays, leading to faster triage, treatment, and discharge.

- **Improved Patient Flow**: Eliminating bottlenecks and optimizing resource allocation will enhance the overall flow of patients through the ED.
- **Increased Patient Satisfaction**: Faster service and a more efficient care process contribute to higher patient satisfaction scores.
- **Enhanced Staff Satisfaction**: Streamlined processes reduce stress and workload on staff, improving morale and job satisfaction.
- **Better Resource Utilization**: Lean initiatives help ensure that staff, equipment, and space are used more efficiently, reducing waste and costs.

By integrating Lean principles into the ED's operations, nurse executives can drive significant improvements in efficiency, patient care quality, and overall organizational performance.

Implementing a Six Sigma DMAIC (Define, Measure, Analyze, Improve, Control) project to reduce surgical site infections (SSIs) is a structured approach that ensures systematic improvement in healthcare quality. Each phase of DMAIC focuses on specific activities designed to identify the problem, analyze the root causes, implement effective solutions, and ensure long-term sustainability. Below is a detailed outline of how this project could be executed:

1. Define Phase

Objective: Clearly define the problem, scope, goals, and stakeholders involved in the project.

- **Problem Statement:**
  - The hospital has identified that the rate of surgical site infections (SSIs) is above the national average, leading to increased patient morbidity, extended hospital stays, and higher healthcare costs. This project aims to reduce SSIs by 30% within 12 months.
- **Project Scope:**
  - The scope includes all surgical departments, focusing primarily on high-risk surgeries such as orthopedic and colorectal procedures. The project will assess preoperative, intraoperative, and postoperative processes to identify improvement opportunities.
- **Goals and Objectives:**
  - Reduce the SSI rate by 30% within 12 months.
  - Improve adherence to infection prevention protocols.
  - Enhance patient outcomes and reduce length of hospital stays.
- **Key Stakeholders:**
  - Surgeons, operating room (OR) nurses, infection control specialists, anesthesiologists, hospital administration, and patients.

2. Measure Phase

Objective: Collect data to establish a baseline of current performance and identify key metrics for monitoring progress.

- **Data Collection:**
  - Gather historical data on SSI rates, categorized by procedure type, patient demographics, and surgical teams.
  - Collect data on compliance with existing infection control protocols, such as preoperative antibiotic administration, sterile technique adherence, and postoperative wound care practices.
- **Key Metrics:**
  - **Baseline SSI Rate:** Calculate the current SSI rate per 100 surgical procedures.
  - **Compliance Rates:** Measure compliance with infection control protocols, including:
    - Preoperative antibiotic timing.
    - Proper hand hygiene practices.
    - Use of sterile barriers.
    - Postoperative wound care adherence.
- **Tools and Techniques:**
  - Use control charts to monitor SSI rates over time.

- Develop process maps to visualize current surgical workflows and identify potential gaps in infection control practices.

3. Analyze Phase

Objective: Identify and analyze the root causes of SSIs to determine areas for improvement.

- **Root Cause Analysis:**
  - **Fishbone Diagram (Cause-and-Effect):** Create a fishbone diagram to categorize potential causes of SSIs into categories such as personnel, procedures, equipment, environment, and patient factors.
  - **5 Whys Analysis:** For each category, apply the "5 Whys" technique to drill down to the root cause of specific issues. For example:
    - **Problem:** High SSI rate in orthopedic surgeries.
    - **Why 1:** Improper timing of prophylactic antibiotics.
    - **Why 2:** Lack of standardized timing protocol.
    - **Why 3:** Variability in surgeon practices.
    - **Why 4:** Inconsistent communication between OR staff and pharmacy.
    - **Why 5:** Lack of automated alerts for antibiotic administration timing.
- **Data Analysis:**
  - Perform statistical analysis to identify significant correlations between infection rates and specific variables, such as patient comorbidities, type of surgery, and compliance with infection control protocols.
  - Use Pareto charts to prioritize the most common and impactful causes of SSIs.

4. Improve Phase

Objective: Develop and implement targeted solutions to address the identified root causes and improve processes to reduce SSIs.

- **Improvement Strategies:**
  - **Standardization of Protocols:** Develop and implement standardized protocols for preoperative, intraoperative, and postoperative infection prevention practices, including:
    - **Preoperative:** Ensure consistent timing of prophylactic antibiotics using standardized checklists and automated alerts integrated into the EHR system.
    - **Intraoperative:** Reinforce sterile technique through regular training and competency assessments for all OR staff. Introduce a surgical safety checklist to ensure all infection control steps are followed.
    - **Postoperative:** Implement standardized wound care protocols and ensure thorough documentation in the patient's medical record.
- **Pilot Testing:**
  - Test the new protocols in a specific surgical unit (e.g., orthopedic surgeries) to evaluate their effectiveness before full implementation. Monitor SSI rates and compliance with the new protocols during the pilot phase.
- **Staff Training and Engagement:**
  - Conduct training sessions for all surgical staff on the new protocols, emphasizing the importance of adherence to reduce SSIs. Engage staff through regular feedback sessions and involve them in the refinement of the protocols.

5. Control Phase

Objective: Ensure that the improvements are sustained over time and that the SSI rate continues to decrease.

- **Monitoring and Control Plans:**
  - **Ongoing Data Monitoring:** Continue to track SSI rates, compliance with infection prevention protocols, and other relevant metrics using control charts and regular audits.
  - **Control Charts:** Use control charts to monitor the SSI rate after the implementation of improvements, identifying any variations that may require further action.
  - **Audits and Feedback:** Conduct regular audits of the new protocols and provide feedback to surgical teams on their performance. Address any deviations from the protocols immediately to prevent regression.

- **Sustainability Strategies:**
  - ○ **Continuous Education:** Establish ongoing education and refresher courses for all surgical staff to maintain high levels of compliance with infection prevention protocols.
  - ○ **Process Ownership:** Assign process owners (e.g., infection control nurse, OR manager) to oversee the adherence to protocols and report on performance regularly.
  - ○ **Periodic Reviews:** Schedule periodic reviews of the protocols and outcomes to ensure they remain relevant and effective. Make necessary adjustments based on new evidence or changes in the surgical environment.
- **Documenting and Sharing Success:**
  - ○ Document the process improvements and share the results with all stakeholders, including surgical teams, hospital administration, and patients. Highlight the positive impact on patient outcomes and hospital performance.
  - ○ Consider publishing the findings in a professional journal or presenting them at a healthcare conference to contribute to broader knowledge and improvement in surgical infection prevention.

By following the DMAIC methodology, the hospital can systematically reduce the rate of surgical site infections. This approach not only targets the root causes of SSIs but also ensures that improvements are sustained over time, ultimately leading to better patient outcomes, enhanced staff performance, and overall organizational success.

Improving medication reconciliation processes across care transitions is critical for ensuring patient safety and continuity of care. The Plan-Do-Study-Act (PDSA) cycle is an iterative, four-step method used to test changes on a small scale before implementing them organization-wide. Here's how you can design a series of PDSA cycles to improve medication reconciliation and scale successful interventions from pilot units to the entire organization.

PDSA Cycle 1: Improve Medication Reconciliation at Admission in a Pilot Unit
Plan
- **Objective**: Reduce discrepancies in medication lists at admission by implementing a standardized medication reconciliation process in a pilot unit (e.g., medical-surgical unit).
- **Plan Details**:
  - ○ **Current State Analysis**: Assess the current medication reconciliation process, identify common discrepancies, and understand the root causes.
  - ○ **Intervention**: Introduce a standardized medication reconciliation form and a checklist for nurses and pharmacists to use during the admission process.
  - ○ **Team**: Involve frontline staff (nurses, pharmacists), unit managers, and IT support for electronic health record (EHR) updates.
  - ○ **Metrics**: Track the number of medication discrepancies identified at admission and the time required to complete medication reconciliation.

Do
- **Implement**: Roll out the standardized medication reconciliation form and checklist in the selected pilot unit. Provide training sessions for staff on the new process.
- **Monitor**: Observe the use of the new tools during the first week and collect feedback from staff on ease of use and potential challenges.

Study
- **Analyze Data**: Compare the number of medication discrepancies before and after the implementation of the new process. Evaluate staff compliance with the new tools and gather qualitative feedback on the process.
- **Key Findings**:
  - ○ Reduction in medication discrepancies by 30%.
  - ○ Staff report that the checklist is helpful but time-consuming.

Act
- **Adjust**: Refine the checklist based on staff feedback to streamline the process without compromising accuracy. Simplify the form by integrating it into the EHR system for easier access.
- **Plan Next Cycle**: Prepare to test the refined process on a larger scale by expanding to another unit.

PDSA Cycle 2: Expand Medication Reconciliation to Discharge Process
Plan

- **Objective**: Extend the improved medication reconciliation process to include discharge in the same pilot unit.
- **Plan Details**:
  - **Intervention**: Introduce a discharge medication reconciliation process that includes patient education and a review of the discharge medication list by both nurses and pharmacists.
  - **Metrics**: Track the number of medication discrepancies identified at discharge and monitor patient understanding of their discharge medications.

Do

- **Implement**: Launch the new discharge medication reconciliation process. Conduct staff training focused on patient education and communication during discharge.
- **Monitor**: Observe the implementation during the first two weeks and collect patient feedback on their understanding of their discharge medications.

Study

- **Analyze Data**: Evaluate the impact of the new process on discharge medication discrepancies and patient comprehension. Review feedback from staff and patients to assess the effectiveness of the intervention.
- **Key Findings**:
  - Discharge medication discrepancies reduced by 25%.
  - Patients report better understanding of their medications, but some confusion remains regarding changes made during hospitalization.

Act

- **Adjust**: Incorporate more patient-friendly language and visual aids into the discharge medication reconciliation process to enhance patient comprehension.
- **Plan Next Cycle**: Test the improved discharge process in a second unit and assess scalability.

PDSA Cycle 3: Integrate Medication Reconciliation into Care Transitions Across Units
Plan

- **Objective**: Integrate the improved medication reconciliation process into all care transitions (admission, transfer, discharge) across multiple units.
- **Plan Details**:
  - **Intervention**: Implement a comprehensive medication reconciliation process that covers all care transitions. This includes continuous staff training and ongoing patient education throughout their stay.
  - **Metrics**: Monitor the consistency of the medication reconciliation process across units, the number of discrepancies at each transition point, and patient outcomes such as readmission rates.

Do

- **Implement**: Roll out the comprehensive medication reconciliation process in three additional units, including surgical and critical care units.
- **Monitor**: Collect data on medication discrepancies, staff compliance, and patient outcomes over a four-week period.

Study

- **Analyze Data**: Assess the consistency of the process across different units and its impact on reducing medication discrepancies and improving patient outcomes.
- **Key Findings**:
  - Significant reduction in medication discrepancies across all transition points.
  - Positive feedback from staff on the process's consistency and effectiveness.
  - A slight reduction in 30-day readmission rates for patients whose medications were reconciled during all transitions.

Act

- **Adjust**: Make minor adjustments based on unit-specific feedback (e.g., adapting the process for the fast-paced environment of critical care). Develop unit-specific training modules.
- **Plan for Scaling**: Prepare to scale the process across the entire organization.

Scaling Successful Interventions Across the Organization

1. **Standardize Processes**
   - **Develop Standard Operating Procedures (SOPs)**: Create SOPs based on the successful PDSA cycles that outline the medication reconciliation process for all care transitions. Ensure that these SOPs are adaptable to different units while maintaining core elements.
   - **Integrate into EHR**: Work with the IT department to fully integrate the standardized medication reconciliation process into the EHR system, making it easily accessible and trackable across all units.

2. **Training and Education**
   - **Organization-Wide Training**: Develop a comprehensive training program for all clinical staff, including nurses, pharmacists, and physicians. Use simulation-based training and real-life case studies to emphasize the importance of accurate medication reconciliation.
   - **Continuous Education**: Implement ongoing education sessions to reinforce the process and update staff on any changes or improvements. Use feedback from early adopters to refine training materials.

3. **Monitor and Support Implementation**
   - **Data-Driven Monitoring**: Establish a centralized monitoring system to track the performance of the medication reconciliation process across all units. Use dashboards to visualize key metrics such as medication discrepancies, staff compliance, and patient outcomes.
   - **Regular Audits and Feedback**: Conduct regular audits to ensure compliance with the standardized process and identify areas for further improvement. Provide timely feedback to units and celebrate successes to maintain momentum.

4. **Foster a Culture of Continuous Improvement**
   - **Encourage Local Ownership**: Empower each unit to take ownership of the medication reconciliation process by involving them in ongoing PDSA cycles to refine and improve the process.
   - **Share Best Practices**: Create forums or communities of practice where staff from different units can share their experiences, challenges, and best practices. Use these insights to drive continuous improvement.
   - **Leadership Support**: Ensure ongoing support from leadership to sustain the initiative, allocate necessary resources, and emphasize the importance of medication reconciliation in improving patient safety and care quality.

By systematically applying PDSA cycles and scaling successful interventions, nurse executives can significantly improve medication reconciliation processes across care transitions, enhancing patient safety, reducing medication errors, and improving overall organizational performance.

Integrating Lean, Six Sigma, and Plan-Do-Study-Act (PDSA) methodologies in a comprehensive quality improvement (QI) program offers a powerful approach to enhancing healthcare quality, efficiency, and patient outcomes. Each methodology has unique strengths that, when combined, provide a holistic framework for addressing complex challenges in healthcare settings. Nurse executives play a critical role in fostering a culture of continuous improvement that effectively leverages these multiple approaches.

Integration of Lean, Six Sigma, and PDSA Methodologies

1. **Lean Methodology**
   - **Overview:** Lean focuses on maximizing value by eliminating waste and improving workflow efficiency. It emphasizes respect for people, continuous improvement, and the streamlining of processes to enhance patient care.
   - **Key Principles:**
     - Identify and eliminate non-value-added activities (waste).
     - Optimize processes to improve flow and reduce delays.

- Engage frontline staff in problem-solving and process improvements.
2. **Six Sigma Methodology**
   - **Overview:** Six Sigma aims to reduce variation and improve process quality by using data-driven decision-making and statistical analysis. It focuses on identifying and eliminating defects in processes to achieve near-perfect quality.
   - **Key Principles:**
     - Define, Measure, Analyze, Improve, and Control (DMAIC) framework.
     - Use of statistical tools to identify root causes of defects and variability.
     - Emphasis on achieving measurable and sustainable improvements.
3. **Plan-Do-Study-Act (PDSA) Cycle**
   - **Overview:** The PDSA cycle is a systematic series of steps for gaining knowledge and improving a process. It is iterative, allowing teams to test changes on a small scale before full implementation.
   - **Key Principles:**
     - **Plan:** Identify a goal or a problem and develop a plan to address it.
     - **Do:** Implement the plan on a small scale to test its effectiveness.
     - **Study:** Analyze the results of the test and determine what was learned.
     - **Act:** Based on the analysis, refine the plan and implement it on a larger scale if successful.

Advantages of Integrating the Methodologies
1. **Comprehensive Problem-Solving:**
   - **Integration:** Lean's focus on waste elimination and workflow efficiency can be complemented by Six Sigma's data-driven approach to reducing variability and defects. The PDSA cycle adds an iterative testing approach, allowing teams to refine solutions incrementally.
   - **Example:** A hospital might use Lean techniques to streamline the patient discharge process, apply Six Sigma to reduce variability in discharge times, and use the PDSA cycle to test changes in discharge protocols before full-scale implementation.
2. **Flexibility and Adaptability:**
   - **Integration:** The combined methodologies offer flexibility in addressing both complex and straightforward problems. Lean is effective for quick wins and process flow improvements, while Six Sigma is ideal for addressing complex quality issues. PDSA is useful for testing and refining solutions in real-world settings.
   - **Example:** When addressing a high rate of medication errors, Lean can be used to simplify the medication administration process, Six Sigma to analyze and reduce error rates, and PDSA to test the effectiveness of new safety protocols.
3. **Engagement and Empowerment of Staff:**
   - **Integration:** All three methodologies emphasize the involvement of frontline staff in the improvement process. Lean promotes staff-driven problem-solving, Six Sigma encourages data-informed decision-making, and PDSA allows for iterative feedback and refinement.
   - **Example:** Nurses and other healthcare providers can be involved in identifying inefficiencies (Lean), analyzing error patterns (Six Sigma), and testing new care delivery methods (PDSA), fostering a sense of ownership and engagement.
4. **Sustainable Improvements:**
   - **Integration:** By using Lean to create efficient processes, Six Sigma to ensure quality and consistency, and PDSA to refine and sustain improvements, organizations can achieve long-lasting results that continuously evolve.
   - **Example:** A hospital that reduces surgical site infections (SSI) might use Lean to streamline surgical prep processes, Six Sigma to standardize infection prevention protocols, and PDSA to monitor and adjust these protocols as new best practices emerge.

Fostering a Culture of Continuous Improvement
1. **Leadership Commitment and Vision**

- o **Strategy:** Nurse executives must demonstrate a strong commitment to quality improvement by integrating Lean, Six Sigma, and PDSA into the organization's strategic vision. This includes setting clear goals, allocating resources, and recognizing achievements.
- o **Implementation:** Communicate the importance of continuous improvement through regular town hall meetings, newsletters, and one-on-one interactions with staff. Highlight how these methodologies align with the organization's mission to provide high-quality patient care.

2. **Education and Training**
   - o **Strategy:** Provide comprehensive education and training to staff at all levels on the principles and tools of Lean, Six Sigma, and PDSA. This ensures that staff have the knowledge and skills to participate effectively in improvement initiatives.
   - o **Implementation:** Develop a tiered training program that includes introductory courses for all staff, in-depth training for team leaders, and advanced certification for Six Sigma (e.g., Green Belt, Black Belt) practitioners. Encourage continuous learning through workshops, simulations, and real-world project involvement.

3. **Empowerment of Frontline Staff**
   - o **Strategy:** Empower frontline staff to identify problems, propose solutions, and lead improvement projects using Lean, Six Sigma, and PDSA methodologies. Foster a culture where continuous improvement is everyone's responsibility.
   - o **Implementation:** Create cross-functional improvement teams that include nurses, physicians, and administrative staff. Provide these teams with the autonomy and resources to implement changes, and recognize their contributions to patient care improvements.

4. **Data-Driven Decision-Making**
   - o **Strategy:** Encourage the use of data and evidence in all quality improvement initiatives. Integrate data analytics into the daily operations of the organization to identify trends, measure outcomes, and guide decision-making.
   - o **Implementation:** Invest in data analytics tools that provide real-time feedback on key performance indicators (KPIs) related to patient care, safety, and efficiency. Train staff on how to interpret and act on data insights, making data transparency a priority in all QI activities.

5. **Iterative Improvement and Feedback Loops**
   - o **Strategy:** Utilize the PDSA cycle to continuously test, refine, and scale improvements. This iterative approach ensures that changes are effective and sustainable.
   - o **Implementation:** Incorporate PDSA cycles into all improvement projects, allowing teams to pilot new processes on a small scale before full implementation. Establish regular review meetings where teams present their findings, discuss challenges, and plan next steps.

6. **Recognition and Reward Systems**
   - o **Strategy:** Establish recognition and reward systems that celebrate successful quality improvement initiatives. Recognizing contributions fosters motivation and reinforces the importance of continuous improvement.
   - o **Implementation:** Create an award program that recognizes teams and individuals who achieve significant improvements in patient care or operational efficiency. Share success stories through internal communications and celebrate milestones in staff meetings.

7. **Sustaining and Spreading Improvements**
   - o **Strategy:** Ensure that successful improvements are standardized and spread across the organization. Use control plans to maintain gains and prevent regression.
   - o **Implementation:** After successful projects, develop standard operating procedures (SOPs) that incorporate the new practices. Assign process owners to monitor adherence and outcomes, and use control charts to track ongoing performance. Share best practices with other departments to replicate success across the organization.

By integrating Lean, Six Sigma, and PDSA methodologies, nurse executives can create a comprehensive quality improvement program that addresses the multifaceted challenges of healthcare delivery. This integration fosters a culture of continuous improvement, where staff are empowered to drive positive change, processes are optimized, and patient outcomes are consistently enhanced. Through leadership commitment, education, data-driven decision-making, and a focus on sustainability, nurse executives can ensure that their organization remains at the forefront of healthcare excellence.

Front-line staff engagement is critical to the success of process improvement initiatives in healthcare. These employees—nurses, technicians, aides, and others who interact directly with patients—have firsthand knowledge of daily operations, making them invaluable in identifying inefficiencies, safety risks, and opportunities for enhancement. When engaged effectively, front-line staff can drive meaningful and sustainable changes that improve patient care and operational efficiency.

The Role of Front-Line Staff Engagement in Process Improvement

1. **Informed Insight into Operational Realities**
   o   Front-line staff understand the intricacies of workflows, patient needs, and potential barriers to care because they experience them daily. Their insights are often more nuanced than those of higher-level management, making their contributions crucial for identifying practical, context-specific solutions.

2. **Early Identification of Issues**
   o   Because they are on the front lines, these employees are often the first to notice emerging problems, such as bottlenecks in patient flow, equipment malfunctions, or deviations from best practices. Engaging them in process improvement efforts allows the organization to address issues proactively rather than reactively.

3. **Increased Buy-In and Ownership**
   o   When front-line staff are involved in the design and implementation of process improvements, they are more likely to feel a sense of ownership over the changes. This buy-in is essential for the successful adoption and sustainability of new processes, as staff are more likely to support and adhere to improvements they helped create.

4. **Enhanced Innovation and Creativity**
   o   Front-line employees can contribute innovative ideas that may not have been considered by management. Their direct experience with processes enables them to think creatively about how to streamline workflows, reduce waste, and improve patient care.

5. **Improved Morale and Job Satisfaction**
   o   Empowering front-line staff to participate in process improvement fosters a sense of value and respect. This can lead to higher job satisfaction, reduced turnover, and a more positive work environment, all of which contribute to better overall performance.

Strategies for Nurse Executives to Empower Employees at All Levels

1. **Create a Culture of Continuous Improvement**
   o   **Lead by Example**: Nurse executives should model a commitment to continuous improvement, showing that quality enhancement is a priority for the organization. This involves actively participating in improvement initiatives, celebrating successes, and openly discussing areas for growth.
   o   **Embed Improvement into Daily Practice**: Encourage a mindset where every staff member views process improvement as part of their daily responsibilities. This can be achieved by integrating improvement discussions into routine meetings, such as daily huddles or shift handovers.

2. **Establish Clear Channels for Feedback and Ideas**
   o   **Suggestion Systems**: Implement formal mechanisms for staff to submit improvement ideas, such as suggestion boxes, online portals, or dedicated email addresses. Ensure that all suggestions are reviewed, acknowledged, and considered.
   o   **Open Forums and Focus Groups**: Regularly hold open forums or focus groups where front-line staff can voice their concerns and propose solutions. These sessions should be facilitated in a way that encourages candid dialogue and ensures that all voices are heard.

3. **Provide Training and Resources**
   o   **Quality Improvement Training**: Offer training programs on quality improvement methodologies, such as Lean, Six Sigma, or Plan-Do-Study-Act (PDSA) cycles. Equip staff with the tools and knowledge they need to contribute effectively to process improvement initiatives.

- o **Access to Resources**: Ensure that front-line staff have access to the resources they need to implement changes, including time, materials, and support from leadership. This might involve reallocating resources or adjusting workloads to free up time for improvement activities.

4. **Empower Teams with Autonomy**
   - o **Team-Based Improvement Projects**: Encourage front-line teams to take ownership of specific improvement projects. Allow them the autonomy to test changes, gather data, and make adjustments as needed, with the support of management.
   - o **Small Tests of Change**: Encourage staff to use small tests of change to trial new processes on a limited scale before wider implementation. This approach minimizes risk and allows for adjustments based on real-world feedback.

5. **Recognize and Reward Contributions**
   - o **Public Recognition**: Regularly acknowledge the contributions of front-line staff to process improvement efforts. This could be done through newsletters, staff meetings, or recognition programs. Highlighting specific examples of successful initiatives can inspire others to get involved.
   - o **Incentive Programs**: Consider implementing incentive programs that reward staff for identifying and implementing successful improvements. Rewards could include bonuses, extra time off, or professional development opportunities.

6. **Foster Collaboration Across Roles**
   - o **Interdisciplinary Teams**: Promote collaboration between different roles within the organization by forming interdisciplinary improvement teams. This encourages the sharing of diverse perspectives and fosters a sense of collective responsibility for quality improvement.
   - o **Peer Mentorship**: Pair experienced staff members with those who are newer to quality improvement. This mentorship can help build confidence and competence in participating in improvement initiatives.

7. **Track and Communicate Progress**
   - o **Transparent Metrics**: Make performance data transparent and accessible to all staff. This includes tracking key performance indicators (KPIs) related to quality improvement and sharing progress regularly.
   - o **Regular Updates**: Provide regular updates on the status of improvement projects, including successes, challenges, and next steps. This communication helps maintain momentum and keeps everyone informed and engaged.

8. **Support a Non-Punitive Reporting Culture**
   - o **Encourage Reporting of Issues**: Create a culture where staff feel safe reporting errors, near misses, and potential safety concerns without fear of punishment. Use these reports as opportunities for learning and improvement rather than blame.
   - o **Analyze and Act on Data**: Use the data from reports to identify trends and areas for improvement. Involve front-line staff in analyzing this data and developing action plans to address identified issues.

Engaging front-line staff in process improvement initiatives is essential for achieving meaningful and sustainable change in healthcare settings. Nurse executives play a crucial role in creating an environment where employees at all levels feel empowered to identify problems, propose solutions, and implement improvements. By fostering a culture of continuous improvement, providing the necessary training and resources, and recognizing contributions, nurse executives can harness the full potential of front-line staff to drive organizational excellence.

Human Capital Management

The Americans with Disabilities Act (ADA) is a critical piece of legislation that prohibits discrimination against individuals with disabilities and requires employers, including those in healthcare settings, to provide reasonable accommodations. These accommodations ensure that employees with disabilities can perform their job functions effectively without compromising patient safety or the quality of care.

Key Provisions of the ADA in Healthcare Settings

1. **Non-Discrimination in Employment:**
   - Healthcare organizations must ensure that all employment practices, including hiring, promotion, training, and termination, are free from discrimination based on disability. This includes both physical and mental disabilities, whether permanent or temporary.

2. **Reasonable Accommodations:**
   - Employers are required to provide reasonable accommodations to qualified employees with disabilities, enabling them to perform the essential functions of their jobs. Accommodations may include modifications to work schedules, physical changes to the workplace, or providing assistive technologies.
   - The accommodations must be "reasonable," meaning they should not impose an undue hardship on the employer or pose a direct threat to patient safety or care quality.

3. **Accessibility Standards:**
   - Healthcare facilities must ensure that their buildings, services, and programs are accessible to both employees and patients with disabilities. This includes physical accessibility, such as ramps and elevators, as well as access to communication tools for individuals with sensory impairments.

4. **Confidentiality:**
   - The ADA mandates that employers maintain the confidentiality of any medical information obtained about an employee as part of the accommodation process.

Ensuring Reasonable Accommodations While Maintaining Patient Safety and Quality of Care

1. **Individualized Assessment of Accommodation Requests:**
   - Nurse executives should assess accommodation requests on a case-by-case basis, considering the specific needs of the employee, the essential functions of the job, and the potential impact on patient care.
   - For example, if a nurse with a mobility impairment requests a modification to their work environment, the executive must evaluate how the accommodation can be provided without compromising the nurse's ability to respond quickly in emergencies.

2. **Collaboration with Occupational Health and Legal Teams:**
   - Working closely with occupational health professionals, legal advisors, and human resources, nurse executives can ensure that accommodations are legally compliant and do not negatively affect patient safety. This multidisciplinary approach helps balance the needs of employees with the organization's duty to provide high-quality care.
   - For instance, occupational health might recommend specific assistive devices that allow an employee to perform their duties safely, while legal ensures compliance with ADA requirements.

3. **Training and Education:**
   - Educating staff about the ADA and the importance of reasonable accommodations fosters an inclusive workplace culture. Training should emphasize recognizing and respecting the diverse needs of colleagues with disabilities and understanding the legal obligations under the ADA.
   - Nurse executives can implement ongoing training sessions that cover scenarios involving reasonable accommodations, equipping managers and staff with the knowledge to handle such requests appropriately.

Impact of Recent ADA Amendments on Healthcare Workforce Management

The ADA Amendments Act of 2008 (ADAAA) broadened the definition of disability, making it easier for employees to qualify for protections under the ADA. This expansion has increased the range of conditions that employers must consider when making accommodations, including episodic conditions and those that may not be immediately visible, such as mental health disorders.

1. **Increased Complexity of Accommodation Requests:**
   - With the expanded definition of disability, healthcare organizations now encounter more complex accommodation requests, particularly for conditions like mental health issues or pregnancy-related limitations. These requests may require creative solutions that accommodate the employee's needs while ensuring that patient care remains uninterrupted.
   - For example, an employee with anxiety might request a quiet workspace or flexible scheduling to attend therapy appointments. Nurse executives must balance these needs with the operational demands of the unit.
2. **Proactive Policy Development:**
   - In response to the ADAAA, nurse executives should develop clear policies that address common accommodation scenarios, particularly those related to mental health and pregnancy. These policies should outline the process for requesting accommodations, the criteria for determining reasonableness, and the steps for implementation.
   - Policies might include provisions for temporary job modifications, such as light-duty assignments for pregnant employees or telehealth options for those managing mental health conditions.
3. **Supportive Work Environment:**
   - Creating a supportive environment that encourages open communication about disabilities and accommodations is essential. Nurse executives can foster this by promoting a culture of inclusivity where employees feel comfortable discussing their needs without fear of stigma or retaliation.
   - Regularly reviewing and updating policies in light of new ADA guidance and best practices ensures that the organization remains compliant and supportive of all employees.
4. **Balancing Accommodations with Patient Care Needs:**
   - Nurse executives must ensure that accommodations do not adversely affect patient safety or care quality. This involves ongoing monitoring and, if necessary, adjusting accommodations to better align with the dynamic nature of healthcare work.
   - In situations where an accommodation might conflict with patient safety, alternative solutions should be explored. For example, if an accommodation might slow a nurse's ability to respond to emergencies, the executive might consider adjusting team workflows or reallocating responsibilities.

Integrating these strategies into workforce management allows nurse executives to meet the ADA's requirements while maintaining a high standard of care. By proactively addressing the challenges posed by the ADA and its amendments, healthcare organizations can create an inclusive environment that supports both employee well-being and patient safety.

Comprehensive OSHA Compliance Program for a Large Hospital System

Designing a comprehensive OSHA compliance program for a large hospital system requires addressing key areas such as bloodborne pathogens, hazardous materials handling, and ergonomics while integrating these requirements with existing quality and safety initiatives.

1. Bloodborne Pathogens

- **Exposure Control Plan (ECP)**: Develop and implement an ECP that meets OSHA's Bloodborne Pathogens Standard (29 CFR 1910.1030). The plan should detail measures to minimize exposure, such as universal precautions, engineering controls (e.g., sharps disposal containers), and personal protective equipment (PPE).
- **Training and Education**: Ensure that all employees, particularly those in clinical settings, receive initial and annual training on bloodborne pathogens, proper use of PPE, and procedures for handling exposure incidents.
- **Hepatitis B Vaccination**: Provide the hepatitis B vaccine to all at-risk employees at no cost and maintain records of vaccinations or signed declinations.
- **Post-Exposure Evaluation and Follow-Up**: Establish protocols for immediate response to exposure incidents, including confidential medical evaluation, counseling, and follow-up. Ensure that exposure incidents are documented and investigated to prevent recurrence.

- **Integration with Quality and Safety Initiatives**: Align bloodborne pathogen protocols with infection control programs and patient safety initiatives. Regularly review exposure incidents in safety committee meetings and incorporate lessons learned into ongoing staff training.

2. Hazardous Materials Handling

- **Hazard Communication Program (HCP)**: Implement an HCP that complies with OSHA's Hazard Communication Standard (29 CFR 1910.1200). This includes maintaining an up-to-date inventory of hazardous chemicals, ensuring that all containers are labeled, and providing Safety Data Sheets (SDS) for each chemical.
- **Training and Labeling**: Conduct training on the safe handling, storage, and disposal of hazardous materials. Emphasize the importance of proper labeling and the use of PPE when dealing with hazardous substances.
- **Spill Response Plan**: Develop a spill response plan that outlines procedures for containing and cleaning up chemical spills safely. Equip each department with appropriate spill kits and train staff on their use.
- **Waste Management**: Ensure compliance with federal, state, and local regulations for hazardous waste disposal, including biomedical waste, pharmaceuticals, and chemicals. Collaborate with environmental services and pharmacy teams to manage hazardous waste effectively.
- **Integration with Quality and Safety Initiatives**: Incorporate hazardous materials handling into broader safety initiatives, such as environmental safety rounds and routine safety audits. Engage staff in continuous improvement efforts to minimize hazardous exposures.

3. Ergonomics

- **Ergonomics Program**: Develop an ergonomics program that identifies and addresses risks related to musculoskeletal disorders (MSDs) in healthcare workers. Focus on high-risk tasks such as patient handling, repetitive movements, and prolonged standing.
- **Engineering Controls**: Invest in assistive devices such as patient lifts, adjustable workstations, and anti-fatigue mats to reduce ergonomic stressors. Ensure that these tools are readily available and properly maintained.
- **Training and Best Practices**: Train staff on safe patient handling techniques, proper body mechanics, and ergonomic principles. Regularly update training materials based on the latest research and industry standards.
- **Ergonomic Assessments**: Conduct ergonomic assessments of workstations and tasks, particularly in departments with high rates of MSDs. Use assessment results to make modifications that reduce injury risks.
- **Integration with Quality and Safety Initiatives**: Align the ergonomics program with employee health and wellness initiatives. Track and analyze injury reports to identify trends and opportunities for improvement, and integrate findings into broader occupational health strategies.

Implications of OSHA's Workplace Violence Prevention Standard

OSHA's proposed Workplace Violence Prevention for Health Care and Social Service Workers standard addresses the growing concern of workplace violence in healthcare settings. This standard emphasizes the need for healthcare employers to proactively address risk factors and implement comprehensive violence prevention programs.

1. Risk Factors in Various Healthcare Settings

- **Emergency Departments (EDs)**:
  - **High-Risk Environment**: EDs are fast-paced, high-stress environments where staff encounter patients with acute conditions, some of whom may be under the influence of drugs or alcohol or experiencing mental health crises. The presence of weapons or the need to manage emotionally charged situations increases the risk of violence.
  - **Prevention Strategies**: Implement security measures such as metal detectors, panic buttons, and surveillance cameras. Train staff in de-escalation techniques and establish protocols for managing aggressive behavior. Provide security personnel with specialized training for ED scenarios.
- **Behavioral Health Units**:
  - **Challenging Patient Population**: Behavioral health units often treat patients with severe psychiatric disorders, some of whom may exhibit unpredictable or violent behavior. The closed

environment and the need for therapeutic interventions can complicate violence prevention efforts.
- o **Prevention Strategies**: Design the physical environment to minimize risks (e.g., ligature-resistant fixtures, secure doors). Provide staff with training in nonviolent crisis intervention and conflict resolution. Develop individualized care plans that include behavioral risk assessments and interventions to reduce the likelihood of violence.
- **Long-Term Care Facilities**:
  - o **Vulnerable Populations**: Long-term care facilities house elderly or disabled residents who may have cognitive impairments, such as dementia, leading to aggression or confusion. Staffing shortages can exacerbate risks, as fewer staff members are available to respond to incidents.
  - o **Prevention Strategies**: Ensure adequate staffing levels and staff training in managing dementia-related behaviors. Foster strong relationships with residents and their families to identify potential triggers for aggressive behavior. Implement environmental modifications, such as secure exits and calm, clutter-free spaces, to reduce stress.
- **Outpatient Clinics**:
  - o **Ambulatory Settings**: Outpatient clinics, including specialty practices and primary care, face risks associated with disgruntled patients, long wait times, or emotionally charged diagnoses. These settings often lack the security infrastructure of hospitals.
  - o **Prevention Strategies**: Train staff in verbal de-escalation and recognize warning signs of potential violence. Implement appointment scheduling practices that minimize wait times and patient frustration. Consider installing security measures, such as secure reception areas and panic alarms.

2. Developing a Comprehensive Violence Prevention Program

- **Workplace Violence Prevention Committee**: Establish a multidisciplinary committee to oversee the development and implementation of the violence prevention program. The committee should include representatives from nursing, security, behavioral health, human resources, and risk management.
- **Violence Risk Assessments**: Conduct regular risk assessments to identify potential sources of violence in different settings within the hospital system. Use these assessments to inform prevention strategies and tailor interventions to specific areas.
- **Employee Training and Education**: Provide comprehensive training for all staff on recognizing, avoiding, and responding to workplace violence. Offer specialized training for high-risk areas, such as EDs and behavioral health units, focusing on de-escalation techniques and self-defense.
- **Incident Reporting and Response**: Develop clear protocols for reporting and responding to incidents of workplace violence. Ensure that all reports are taken seriously and that staff are supported following an incident. Conduct debriefings and root cause analyses to prevent future occurrences.
- **Security Measures**: Implement security measures appropriate for each setting, such as access control, security personnel, surveillance cameras, and emergency communication systems. Regularly review and update security protocols based on emerging threats.
- **Support Systems for Staff**: Provide support services for staff who experience workplace violence, including counseling, legal support, and time off if needed. Foster a culture where staff feel safe reporting incidents without fear of retaliation.

By integrating these OSHA requirements with existing quality and safety initiatives, hospital systems can create a safer work environment, improve compliance, and enhance overall organizational performance. A comprehensive approach to OSHA compliance and workplace violence prevention not only protects staff but also contributes to better patient care and organizational resilience.

The Age Discrimination in Employment Act (ADEA) is a federal law that protects employees and job applicants aged 40 and older from discrimination based on age. In the context of an aging nursing workforce, the ADEA has significant implications for how nurse executives manage their teams, particularly when it comes to balancing the retention of experienced staff with the needs for succession planning and the adoption of new technologies.

Evaluating the ADEA in the Context of an Aging Nursing Workforce

1. **Retaining Experienced Nurses:**
   - **Value of Experience:** Experienced nurses bring invaluable clinical expertise, institutional knowledge, and mentorship abilities that are crucial for maintaining high standards of patient care and for training the next generation of nurses.
   - **ADEA Compliance:** The ADEA requires that decisions regarding hiring, promotion, training, or termination are not based on age. Nurse executives must ensure that older nurses are given the same opportunities for professional development, leadership roles, and access to new technology as their younger counterparts.
   - **Challenges:** Balancing the need to keep experienced staff engaged and productive with the natural physical and cognitive changes that may accompany aging can be challenging. However, with proper support, these challenges can be managed effectively.
2. **Succession Planning:**
   - **Strategic Succession Planning:** As the nursing workforce ages, it is essential for nurse executives to implement succession planning strategies that prepare the organization for the eventual retirement of older nurses. This planning must be done in a way that respects the contributions of older nurses while also developing younger staff for future leadership roles.
   - **Knowledge Transfer:** Structured programs can be created to facilitate the transfer of knowledge from experienced nurses to newer staff. This can include mentoring, job shadowing, and documentation of best practices.
   - **Avoiding ADEA Violations:** Nurse executives must ensure that succession planning efforts do not inadvertently lead to age discrimination, such as pushing older nurses into retirement or excluding them from leadership opportunities.
3. **Technology Adoption:**
   - **Inclusive Training Programs:** The increasing use of technology in healthcare can be a barrier for some older nurses who may not be as familiar with new systems. Nurse executives should implement inclusive training programs that ensure all staff, regardless of age, have the necessary skills to use technology effectively.
   - **Supportive Environment:** Creating a supportive learning environment where older nurses feel comfortable asking questions and seeking help with new technologies is critical. This can help prevent frustration and resistance, ensuring smoother adoption of necessary innovations.

Strategies for Ensuring Compliance with the Civil Rights Act and EEO Regulations

The Civil Rights Act and Equal Employment Opportunity (EEO) regulations prohibit discrimination in hiring, promotion, and other employment practices based on race, color, religion, sex, or national origin. Compliance with these regulations is essential for maintaining a fair and equitable workplace.

1. **Developing Fair Hiring and Promotion Practices:**
   - **Structured and Objective Criteria:** Nurse executives should ensure that hiring and promotion decisions are based on clear, objective criteria that are directly related to the job's requirements. This reduces the risk of bias and ensures that all candidates are evaluated fairly.
   - **Blind Recruitment Processes:** Implementing processes that anonymize certain aspects of applications (e.g., removing names, genders, or other identifying details) can help reduce bias in hiring.
   - **Diverse Interview Panels:** Using diverse interview panels can provide different perspectives and help ensure that no single bias dominates the decision-making process.
2. **Addressing Implicit Bias:**
   - **Training and Education:** Implement regular training on implicit bias for all staff, especially those involved in hiring and promotion decisions. This training should help individuals recognize their biases and provide strategies for minimizing their impact.
   - **Regular Audits:** Conduct regular audits of hiring and promotion decisions to identify any patterns that may suggest the presence of implicit bias. These audits should review both qualitative and quantitative data.

- Feedback Mechanisms: Establish mechanisms for employees to provide feedback or raise concerns about potential bias in the hiring or promotion process. This could include anonymous surveys or a formal complaint process.

3. **Promoting Diversity in Leadership Positions:**
   - **Mentorship and Sponsorship Programs:** Implement programs that actively mentor and sponsor diverse employees, preparing them for leadership roles. This includes providing opportunities for networking, professional development, and visibility within the organization.
   - **Leadership Development:** Create leadership development programs that are accessible to all employees, with particular outreach to underrepresented groups. These programs should focus on the skills and competencies needed for leadership positions and provide participants with opportunities to practice and demonstrate these skills.
   - **Inclusive Culture**: Foster an inclusive workplace culture where diversity is valued and supported. This involves not only recruiting diverse leaders but also ensuring they feel welcomed and respected within the organization.

4. **Monitoring and Accountability:**
   - **Data-Driven Decisions:** Use data analytics to monitor diversity and inclusion metrics within the organization. This can include tracking the demographics of applicants, hires, promotions, and leadership positions.
   - **Transparency:** Communicate the organization's diversity and inclusion goals, along with progress towards these goals, to all staff. Transparency fosters accountability and demonstrates the organization's commitment to diversity.
   - **Accountability Systems:** Establish accountability systems that hold managers and leaders responsible for meeting diversity and inclusion goals. This could involve including these goals in performance evaluations or offering incentives for achieving them.

By understanding the implications of the ADEA and ensuring compliance with the Civil Rights Act and EEO regulations, nurse executives can create a workplace that values the contributions of all employees while promoting diversity, equity, and inclusion. This approach not only helps to avoid legal risks but also strengthens the organization's ability to provide high-quality care to a diverse patient population.

Case Study: Complex Reasonable Accommodation Request Under the ADA
Scenario Overview
A nurse, "Emily," has been employed at a large hospital for over ten years and works in the intensive care unit (ICU). Emily was recently diagnosed with multiple sclerosis (MS), a chronic condition that affects her mobility and energy levels. As a result, she has difficulty standing for long periods, moving quickly between patient rooms, and performing tasks that require fine motor skills. Despite her condition, Emily wants to continue working in the ICU and requests reasonable accommodations under the Americans with Disabilities Act (ADA) to help her perform her job duties effectively.

Interactive Process Analysis
1. **Initial Request for Accommodation**
   - Emily submits a formal request to the hospital's HR department, explaining her diagnosis and the challenges she faces at work. She requests accommodations, including a reduced number of physically demanding tasks, additional rest breaks, and the use of assistive devices to help with mobility.

2. **Engaging in the Interactive Process**
   - **Initial Meeting**: The HR department, in collaboration with the nurse executive overseeing the ICU, schedules a meeting with Emily to discuss her request. During this meeting, Emily provides a detailed description of her limitations and suggests specific accommodations that could help her continue working effectively.
   - **Medical Documentation**: HR requests medical documentation from Emily's healthcare provider to better understand the nature of her condition and the specific functional limitations it imposes. This documentation is used to assess whether the requested accommodations are reasonable and necessary.

- ○ **Job Analysis**: The nurse executive and HR conduct a job analysis to identify the essential functions of Emily's role as an ICU nurse. They evaluate which tasks are critical to patient care and which may be modified or reassigned to other staff members.

3. **Exploring Potential Accommodations**
   - ○ **Reduced Physical Tasks**: One possible accommodation is to modify Emily's workload by reducing the number of physically demanding tasks she performs, such as lifting or repositioning patients. These tasks could be reassigned to other nurses or support staff.
   - ○ **Additional Rest Breaks**: Emily requests additional rest breaks throughout her shift to manage fatigue. The nurse executive considers whether this accommodation would disrupt patient care or could be easily integrated into the current shift structure.
   - ○ **Assistive Devices**: Emily suggests using a mobility aid, such as a motorized scooter or walker, to help her move between patient rooms more efficiently. The nurse executive evaluates whether these devices would be practical in the fast-paced ICU environment.
   - ○ **Reassignment**: If Emily's condition makes it impossible for her to perform the essential functions of her current role even with accommodations, the nurse executive and HR may explore the possibility of reassigning her to a different position within the hospital that better aligns with her abilities.

Decision-Making Considerations
1. **Assessing Reasonableness and Feasibility**
   - ○ **Impact on Patient Care**: The nurse executive must consider whether the requested accommodations would affect patient care in the ICU. For instance, if additional rest breaks for Emily would lead to delays in patient care, the accommodation might not be feasible. However, if other nurses can cover these periods without compromising care, the accommodation may be reasonable.
   - ○ **Essential Job Functions**: The analysis should focus on whether Emily can still perform the essential functions of her job with the proposed accommodations. For example, if lifting and moving patients are critical tasks that cannot be reassigned, the nurse executive might need to explore alternative accommodations or job reassignment.
   - ○ **Undue Hardship**: The nurse executive must evaluate whether the requested accommodations would cause undue hardship to the hospital, considering factors such as cost, impact on operations, and available resources. If an accommodation is deemed too costly or disruptive, alternative solutions should be explored.

2. **Legal and Ethical Considerations**
   - ○ **Compliance with the ADA**: The hospital must ensure compliance with the ADA by providing reasonable accommodations unless doing so would cause undue hardship. The nurse executive should consult with legal counsel to confirm that the decision-making process adheres to ADA requirements.
   - ○ **Employee Well-Being**: Beyond legal obligations, the nurse executive should consider Emily's well-being and job satisfaction. Finding a mutually agreeable solution that allows Emily to continue working in a supportive environment is key to maintaining a positive workplace culture.

3. **Final Decision**
   - ○ **Accommodations Granted**: After careful consideration, the nurse executive and HR decide to implement a combination of accommodations, including additional rest breaks, the use of a mobility aid, and the reassignment of some physically demanding tasks to other staff members.
   - ○ **Ongoing Evaluation**: The accommodations are implemented on a trial basis, with regular check-ins to assess their effectiveness and address any challenges that arise. If Emily's condition changes, the accommodations may be adjusted accordingly.

Designing an Internal Audit Process for Labor Law Compliance

1. Identifying Key Areas for Compliance
- **Wage and Hour Laws**: Ensure compliance with the Fair Labor Standards Act (FLSA) and state wage and hour laws, focusing on overtime pay, minimum wage, and proper classification of employees (exempt vs. non-exempt).

- **Family and Medical Leave Act (FMLA):** Assess adherence to FMLA requirements, including employee eligibility, leave entitlements, job protection, and proper documentation.
- **Occupational Safety and Health Administration (OSHA):** Evaluate compliance with OSHA standards, particularly those related to workplace safety, injury reporting, and hazardous materials handling.
- **Equal Employment Opportunity (EEO) Laws:** Review policies and practices to ensure compliance with anti-discrimination laws, including Title VII, the ADA, and the Age Discrimination in Employment Act (ADEA).

2. Developing the Audit Process

1. **Audit Planning**
   - **Audit Scope:** Define the scope of the audit by selecting specific areas of labor law compliance to focus on. For example, an audit might prioritize wage and hour compliance and OSHA standards due to recent changes in regulations or a history of non-compliance.
   - **Audit Team:** Assemble a multidisciplinary audit team that includes HR professionals, legal advisors, compliance officers, and department managers. Ensure that team members have the necessary expertise in labor laws and regulations.

2. **Data Collection**
   - **Document Review:** Gather relevant documents, such as employee handbooks, payroll records, timesheets, leave requests, safety protocols, and training records. Review these documents to ensure they align with legal requirements and internal policies.
   - **Interviews and Surveys:** Conduct interviews with employees and managers to gain insights into daily practices and identify any gaps in compliance. Consider using anonymous surveys to gather candid feedback on compliance-related issues.

3. **Compliance Assessment**
   - **Benchmarking:** Compare the hospital's policies and practices against legal requirements and industry best practices. Identify areas where the hospital meets or exceeds standards, as well as areas where improvements are needed.
   - **Risk Identification:** Highlight areas of potential non-compliance and assess the associated risks. For example, if timekeeping practices are inconsistent, there may be a risk of wage and hour violations.

4. **Prioritizing Areas for Improvement**
   - **Risk-Based Prioritization:** Prioritize areas for improvement based on the severity of the risk and the potential impact on the organization. For instance, issues related to wage and hour compliance may be prioritized due to the financial and legal risks involved.
   - **Resource Allocation:** Allocate resources to address high-priority areas first. This may involve revising policies, implementing new training programs, or investing in technology to improve compliance.

5. **Developing and Implementing Corrective Actions**
   - **Action Plan:** Develop a detailed action plan to address identified compliance gaps. The plan should include specific steps, responsible parties, deadlines, and measures for success.
   - **Employee Training:** Implement targeted training programs to ensure that all employees understand the legal requirements and the importance of compliance. For example, provide training on proper timekeeping practices for all non-exempt employees and their supervisors.
   - **Policy Updates:** Revise and update policies and procedures as needed to ensure compliance with labor laws. Communicate these changes clearly to all employees and managers.
   - **Monitoring and Follow-Up:** Establish a system for ongoing monitoring and follow-up to ensure that corrective actions are effective. This might include regular audits, spot checks, and feedback loops to continuously improve compliance.

6. **Reporting and Continuous Improvement**
   - **Audit Report:** Prepare a comprehensive audit report summarizing findings, corrective actions taken, and recommendations for further improvement. Share the report with senior leadership and relevant stakeholders.

- o **Continuous Improvement**: Use the audit findings to inform future compliance efforts and drive continuous improvement. Regularly review and update the audit process to adapt to changes in labor laws and organizational needs.

Comprehensive Competency Assessment Framework for Nursing Staff

A comprehensive competency assessment framework for nursing staff should be tailored to accommodate various specialties and experience levels, ensuring that both clinical and leadership competencies are addressed. This framework should facilitate ongoing evaluation and improvement, fostering professional growth and maintaining high standards of patient care.

1. Components of the Competency Assessment Framework

1. **Clinical Competencies**
   - o **Core Clinical Skills:**
     - **Basic Competencies:** Include fundamental nursing skills such as patient assessment, medication administration, wound care, and infection control.
     - **Specialty-Specific Competencies:** Tailored to specific areas such as ICU, emergency, pediatrics, oncology, or surgical nursing. These might include advanced cardiac life support (ACLS) for ICU nurses or chemotherapy administration for oncology nurses.
     - **Advanced Practice Competencies:** For nurse practitioners and clinical nurse specialists, including diagnostic reasoning, prescribing medications, and performing specific procedures.
   - o **Patient Safety and Quality of Care:**
     - Emphasize adherence to evidence-based practices, patient-centered care, and safety protocols, including fall prevention, pressure ulcer prevention, and accurate documentation.

2. **Leadership Competencies**
   - o **Management Skills:**
     - Competencies in staffing, resource management, budgeting, and scheduling, particularly for charge nurses or nurse managers.
   - o **Interpersonal and Communication Skills:**
     - Conflict resolution, team leadership, and effective communication with multidisciplinary teams, patients, and families.
   - o **Change Management:**
     - Leading quality improvement initiatives, implementing evidence-based practices, and adapting to changes in healthcare policies and technologies.
   - o **Ethical Decision-Making:**
     - Upholding professional ethics, handling difficult situations with integrity, and advocating for patients and staff.

2. Methods for Ongoing Evaluation and Improvement

1. **Self-Assessment Tools**
   - o **Frequency:** Conducted annually or semi-annually.
   - o **Content:** Nurses reflect on their skills and identify areas for improvement using standardized self-assessment forms that align with clinical and leadership competencies.
   - o **Outcome:** Used to develop personalized professional development plans.

2. **Peer Review and 360-Degree Feedback**
   - o **Frequency:** At least annually, integrated with performance reviews.
   - o **Content:** Peer reviews and 360-degree feedback tools gather input from colleagues, supervisors, and subordinates, offering a comprehensive view of a nurse's performance.
   - o **Outcome:** Identifies strengths and areas for improvement, facilitating targeted training and mentorship.

3. **Direct Observation and Skills Demonstration**
   - o **Frequency:** Regular intervals, particularly for new hires or when adopting new procedures.

- o **Content:** Direct observation by supervisors or clinical educators, focusing on critical clinical skills and adherence to protocols.
- o **Outcome:** Provides real-time feedback and ensures competence in essential skills.

4. **Simulation-Based Assessments**
   - o **Frequency:** As needed, particularly for high-risk or infrequent procedures.
   - o **Content:** Use of simulation labs to assess competencies in a controlled environment, such as emergency response or complex patient scenarios.
   - o **Outcome:** Ensures readiness for real-world situations, with opportunities for debriefing and reflective learning.

5. **Ongoing Education and Certification Requirements**
   - o **Frequency:** As required by the organization or certifying bodies (e.g., annual CEUs, specialty certifications).
   - o **Content:** Continuing education courses, certification renewals, and mandatory training sessions.
   - o **Outcome:** Maintains current knowledge and skills, ensuring compliance with industry standards.

6. **Performance Improvement Plans (PIPs)**
   - o **Frequency:** Initiated when performance issues are identified.
   - o **Content:** Structured plans that outline specific goals, resources, and timelines for improvement, with regular check-ins.
   - o **Outcome:** Supports nurses in meeting competency expectations and achieving professional growth.

Multi-Modal Continuing Education Program

To address diverse learning styles and scheduling constraints, a multi-modal continuing education program should incorporate various learning methods and emerging technologies. This approach ensures that all nursing staff have access to the education they need, regardless of their learning preferences or time availability.

1. Core Components of the Continuing Education Program

1. **In-Person Workshops and Seminars**
   - o **Content:** Focus on hands-on skills training, interactive discussions, and networking opportunities. Topics might include new clinical guidelines, leadership development, or interdisciplinary collaboration.
   - o **Schedule:** Offered during different shifts or repeated to accommodate varying schedules.
   - o **Outcome:** Provides opportunities for practical skill development and peer interaction.

2. **E-Learning Modules**
   - o **Content:** Online courses covering clinical updates, regulatory changes, and leadership topics. Modules should be interactive, with quizzes and case studies to reinforce learning.
   - o **Flexibility:** Available on-demand to accommodate busy schedules.
   - o **Outcome:** Facilitates self-paced learning and allows nurses to complete mandatory training at their convenience.

3. **Microlearning Modules**
   - o **Content:** Short, focused lessons (5-10 minutes) on specific topics, such as a new medication protocol, a leadership tip, or an infection control update.
   - o **Delivery:** Accessible via mobile devices, allowing nurses to learn during breaks or on the go.
   - o **Outcome:** Supports continuous learning and knowledge retention without requiring extensive time commitment.

4. **Virtual Reality (VR) Simulations**
   - o **Content:** Immersive VR scenarios that simulate complex clinical situations, such as emergency response, surgical procedures, or patient interactions.
   - o **Access:** Available in dedicated simulation labs or via portable VR headsets.
   - o **Outcome:** Enhances experiential learning, allowing nurses to practice skills in a realistic, risk-free environment.

5. **Webinars and Live Online Discussions**
   - o **Content:** Live presentations on current topics, followed by Q&A sessions. Can include expert panels, case studies, and interactive polling.

- o **Flexibility:** Recorded for later viewing, providing options for those unable to attend live sessions.
- o **Outcome:** Keeps nurses informed about the latest developments and fosters engagement with subject matter experts.

6. **Podcasts and Audio Content**
   - o **Content:** Educational podcasts on various topics, from clinical best practices to leadership strategies.
   - o **Convenience:** Can be listened to during commutes, workouts, or other activities.
   - o **Outcome:** Supports auditory learners and provides a flexible way to stay updated on relevant topics.

2. Incorporating Emerging Technologies

1. **Adaptive Learning Platforms**
   - o **Technology:** Use AI-driven platforms that adapt content based on the learner's progress, providing additional resources or challenges as needed.
   - o **Personalization:** Tailors learning experiences to individual needs, ensuring that all nurses receive the most relevant education.
   - o **Outcome:** Maximizes learning efficiency and supports personalized professional development.

2. **Gamification**
   - o **Technology:** Integrate gamified elements into e-learning and microlearning modules, such as quizzes, leaderboards, and badges for completing courses.
   - o **Engagement:** Increases motivation and participation by making learning interactive and rewarding.
   - o **Outcome:** Encourages completion of educational requirements and fosters a culture of continuous improvement.

3. **AI-Based Analytics for Tracking Progress**
   - o **Technology:** Utilize AI to track learning progress, competency achievement, and engagement with educational content. Analytics can identify knowledge gaps and recommend additional training.
   - o **Data-Driven Insights:** Provide nurse executives with real-time data on staff development, enabling targeted interventions and resource allocation.
   - o **Outcome:** Ensures that educational programs meet the evolving needs of the workforce and supports continuous improvement in skills and knowledge.

Ongoing Evaluation and Improvement of the Program

1. **Feedback and Surveys**
   - o **Method:** Regularly gather feedback from participants through surveys and focus groups to assess the effectiveness and relevance of educational content.
   - o **Outcome:** Use feedback to refine and improve the program, ensuring it meets the needs of diverse learners.

2. **Tracking and Reporting**
   - o **Method:** Monitor participation rates, competency achievements, and performance improvements using digital platforms and AI analytics.
   - o **Outcome:** Provides insights into the program's impact and identifies areas for further development.

3. **Continuous Content Update**
   - o **Method:** Regularly review and update educational content to reflect the latest clinical guidelines, technological advancements, and healthcare trends.
   - o **Outcome:** Keeps the program current and aligned with industry standards, ensuring that nursing staff remain at the forefront of best practices.

By integrating a comprehensive competency assessment framework with a multi-modal continuing education program, nurse executives can ensure that nursing staff across all specialties and experience levels are continuously developing their clinical and leadership skills. This approach not only supports individual professional growth but also enhances the overall quality of care within the organization.

Leadership Development Initiative for High-Potential Nurse Managers

Designing a leadership development initiative for high-potential nurse managers involves creating a multifaceted program that nurtures their growth through mentorship, stretch assignments, and executive coaching. The goal is to prepare these nurse managers for higher leadership roles by enhancing their skills, broadening their experience, and fostering a leadership mindset.

1. Program Components

A. Mentorship

- **Structured Mentorship Program**: Pair each high-potential nurse manager with a seasoned nurse executive or senior leader. The mentor provides guidance, shares experiences, and offers advice on navigating leadership challenges.
- **Mentorship Goals**: Set specific goals for the mentorship relationship, such as developing strategic thinking skills, improving decision-making abilities, and building a professional network.
- **Regular Meetings**: Encourage regular meetings between mentors and mentees, ideally monthly, to discuss progress, challenges, and opportunities for growth.

B. Stretch Assignments

- **Project Leadership**: Assign nurse managers to lead critical projects that stretch their current capabilities, such as leading a quality improvement initiative, managing a departmental budget, or spearheading a new patient care program.
- **Cross-Departmental Experience**: Rotate nurse managers through different departments or service lines to broaden their understanding of hospital operations and enhance their adaptability.
- **Outcome Accountability**: Hold participants accountable for the outcomes of their stretch assignments, encouraging them to take ownership of results and learn from successes and setbacks.

C. Executive Coaching

- **One-on-One Coaching**: Provide personalized executive coaching sessions focused on leadership development, emotional intelligence, conflict resolution, and strategic thinking. Coaches help nurse managers set and achieve professional goals.
- **360-Degree Feedback Integration**: Use 360-degree feedback as part of the coaching process to identify strengths and areas for improvement. Coaches can then tailor their guidance to address specific developmental needs.
- **Leadership Style Assessment**: Incorporate leadership style assessments (e.g., DISC, Myers-Briggs) into coaching to help nurse managers understand their leadership tendencies and how to adapt them to different situations.

D. Formal Leadership Training

- **Leadership Workshops**: Offer workshops on essential leadership skills, such as change management, effective communication, and team-building. These workshops can be facilitated by internal or external experts.
- **Case Studies and Simulations**: Use healthcare-related case studies and leadership simulations to provide practical, hands-on experience in problem-solving and decision-making.
- **Networking Opportunities**: Create opportunities for nurse managers to network with senior leaders and peers within and outside the organization, fostering relationships that can support their leadership journey.

2. Measuring Program Impact on Organizational Performance

A. Key Performance Indicators (KPIs)

- **Leadership Competency Development**: Use pre- and post-program assessments to measure improvements in leadership competencies, such as strategic thinking, communication, and decision-making. These assessments can include self-assessments, 360-degree feedback, and peer evaluations.
- **Retention Rates**: Track the retention rates of high-potential nurse managers who participate in the program compared to those who do not. Higher retention rates among participants can indicate the program's effectiveness in engaging and developing leadership talent.
- **Promotion Rates**: Monitor the promotion rates of program participants to higher leadership roles. A higher rate of promotions suggests that the program successfully prepares nurse managers for advanced positions.

- **Operational Performance Metrics**: Evaluate the impact of leadership development on key operational metrics, such as patient satisfaction, staff engagement, and departmental efficiency. Improvements in these areas can reflect the positive influence of enhanced leadership.

B. Qualitative Feedback

- **Participant Feedback**: Gather qualitative feedback from program participants through surveys and focus groups to assess their satisfaction with the program, perceived value, and areas for improvement.
- **Mentor and Coach Feedback**: Collect feedback from mentors and coaches to understand how participants are progressing and how the program could be enhanced to better meet their developmental needs.
- **Organizational Feedback**: Seek input from senior leaders and colleagues on the observed changes in the leadership behaviors of participants, and how these changes are impacting team dynamics and overall performance.

C. Long-Term Impact

- **Career Progression Tracking**: Track the long-term career progression of program graduates, including their movement into senior leadership roles within the organization or industry. Success in these areas indicates sustained program impact.
- **Cultural Impact**: Assess how the program influences the organization's leadership culture, particularly in terms of fostering a more collaborative, innovative, and resilient leadership pipeline.

Analyzing the Effectiveness of Competency Assessment Tools

Competency assessment tools are essential for evaluating and developing healthcare professionals' skills, knowledge, and behaviors. Each tool offers unique strengths, and integrating them into a comprehensive professional development strategy can enhance the overall effectiveness of leadership and clinical development programs.

1. Objective Structured Clinical Examinations (OSCEs)

Effectiveness

- **Realistic Clinical Scenarios**: OSCEs simulate real-world clinical situations, allowing healthcare professionals to demonstrate their competencies in a controlled, yet realistic environment. This method is particularly effective for assessing clinical skills, critical thinking, and decision-making under pressure.
- **Standardized Assessment**: OSCEs provide a standardized approach to competency assessment, ensuring that all participants are evaluated consistently based on clear criteria. This objectivity helps to reduce bias in assessments.

Limitations

- **Resource Intensive**: OSCEs require significant resources, including time, facilities, and trained evaluators. They can be logistically challenging to organize, especially in large healthcare systems.
- **Limited Scope**: While OSCEs are excellent for assessing clinical skills, they may not fully capture non-technical competencies such as leadership, teamwork, or communication skills.

Integration into Professional Development

- **Use for Clinical Competency Certification**: Incorporate OSCEs as part of the certification or recertification process for clinical roles. Regularly update OSCE scenarios to reflect current best practices and emerging healthcare challenges.
- **Combine with Other Tools**: Complement OSCEs with other assessment tools to provide a holistic evaluation of both clinical and non-clinical competencies.

2. 360-Degree Feedback

Effectiveness

- **Comprehensive Perspective**: 360-degree feedback gathers input from a range of sources, including peers, subordinates, supervisors, and sometimes patients. This comprehensive view provides a well-rounded assessment of an individual's competencies, particularly in areas such as leadership, communication, and interpersonal skills.
- **Encourages Self-Reflection**: The feedback encourages self-reflection and promotes personal and professional growth by highlighting strengths and areas for development from multiple perspectives.

Limitations

- **Potential for Bias**: The effectiveness of 360-degree feedback depends on the honesty and objectivity of the respondents. There is potential for bias, especially if the feedback process is not conducted anonymously.
- **Resource Intensive**: Collecting and analyzing 360-degree feedback can be time-consuming and requires careful management to ensure that feedback is constructive and actionable.

Integration into Professional Development
- **Use in Leadership Development Programs**: Integrate 360-degree feedback into leadership development initiatives to assess and develop leadership behaviors. Use the feedback to tailor individual development plans and coaching sessions.
- **Follow-Up and Action Plans**: Ensure that participants receive guidance on how to interpret their feedback and create action plans to address identified areas for improvement. Offer follow-up assessments to track progress.

3. Portfolio Assessments
Effectiveness
- **Demonstrates Continuous Learning**: Portfolios allow healthcare professionals to document and reflect on their learning and development over time. This method is effective for assessing ongoing professional growth, particularly in areas such as continuing education, quality improvement projects, and self-directed learning.
- **Customizable and Flexible**: Portfolios can be customized to reflect individual goals and career paths. They are versatile tools that can include a wide range of evidence, such as case studies, research, certifications, and reflective essays.

Limitations
- **Subjectivity**: Assessing portfolios can be subjective, as they often include qualitative evidence of competency. Clear evaluation criteria and training for assessors are essential to ensure consistency.
- **Time-Consuming**: Developing and maintaining a portfolio requires a significant time commitment from the individual. Additionally, assessing portfolios can be labor-intensive for evaluators.

Integration into Professional Development
- **Use for Career Advancement**: Incorporate portfolio assessments into career advancement processes, such as applications for promotions or specialized certifications. Encourage healthcare professionals to use portfolios to demonstrate their achievements and readiness for higher-level roles.
- **Mentorship and Guidance**: Pair portfolio development with mentorship, where mentors can provide feedback and guidance on the content and structure of the portfolio. This helps ensure that portfolios accurately reflect competencies and career goals.

Integrating Competency Assessment Tools into a Comprehensive Professional Development Strategy
A. Holistic Competency Evaluation
- **Combining Tools**: Integrate OSCEs, 360-degree feedback, and portfolio assessments to create a comprehensive evaluation strategy. Use OSCEs to assess clinical competencies, 360-degree feedback for interpersonal and leadership skills, and portfolios to track continuous professional development.
- **Tailored Development Plans**: Use the results from these assessments to create tailored development plans for healthcare professionals. For example, an individual who excels in clinical skills but needs to improve leadership abilities might benefit from executive coaching combined with leadership workshops.

B. Continuous Improvement and Feedback Loops
- **Ongoing Assessment**: Implement a cyclical assessment process where professionals are regularly evaluated using different tools throughout their careers. This promotes continuous learning and adaptation to new challenges.
- **Feedback Integration**: Ensure that feedback from assessments is integrated into professional development activities, such as training programs, mentorship, and career planning. Regularly update development plans based on assessment outcomes.

C. Organizational Impact

- **Align with Organizational Goals**: Align the use of competency assessment tools with organizational goals, such as improving patient care quality, enhancing leadership capacity, and fostering a culture of continuous improvement.
- **Measure Outcomes**: Track the impact of competency assessments on key organizational metrics, such as patient satisfaction, staff engagement, and clinical outcomes. Use this data to refine the professional development strategy and ensure it meets the evolving needs of the organization.

By thoughtfully integrating these competency assessment tools into a comprehensive professional development strategy, nurse executives can support the growth and advancement of their teams, ultimately enhancing both individual performance and overall organizational success.

Succession Planning Program for Key Nursing Leadership Positions

1. Identifying Potential Successors

- **Leadership Competency Assessment:**
  - **Approach:** Begin by defining the key competencies required for nursing leadership roles, such as decision-making, communication, change management, and strategic planning. Use these competencies to assess current nursing staff, identifying those who exhibit strong potential for leadership.
  - **Tools:** Use 360-degree feedback, performance evaluations, and leadership potential assessments to create a comprehensive profile for each candidate. Consider factors such as emotional intelligence, adaptability, and a demonstrated commitment to professional growth.

- **Talent Review Meetings:**
  - **Approach:** Conduct regular talent review meetings with senior nursing leadership to discuss the performance and potential of identified candidates. During these meetings, evaluate readiness levels, identify gaps in skills, and determine appropriate development pathways.
  - **Outcome:** Develop a list of high-potential candidates and match them with potential future leadership roles based on their strengths and career aspirations.

2. Nurturing Potential Successors

- **Personalized Development Plans:**
  - **Approach:** Create individualized development plans for each identified successor, outlining specific goals, milestones, and timelines. Include opportunities for formal education (e.g., leadership courses), mentorship, and stretch assignments.
  - **Components:**
    - **Mentorship:** Pair each potential successor with a current nursing leader who can provide guidance, support, and feedback.
    - **Stretch Assignments:** Assign challenging projects or roles that push the candidate out of their comfort zone and build the competencies required for leadership.

- **Leadership Training Programs:**
  - **Approach:** Develop or leverage existing leadership training programs tailored to nursing leaders. These programs should cover topics such as financial management, strategic planning, team dynamics, and quality improvement.
  - **Delivery:** Use a mix of in-person workshops, online courses, and simulations to provide a well-rounded learning experience. Incorporate case studies and real-world scenarios relevant to nursing leadership.

- **Cross-Departmental Exposure:**
  - **Approach:** Provide opportunities for potential successors to gain experience across different departments or units. This cross-departmental exposure helps them understand the broader operations of the organization and develop a network across teams.
  - **Outcome:** By rotating through various roles, candidates gain diverse experiences that prepare them for the complex responsibilities of nursing leadership.

3. Ensuring Continuity of Operations

- **Interim Leadership Roles:**

- Approach: Prepare potential successors by offering them interim leadership roles when vacancies arise or when current leaders are on leave. This allows them to experience the responsibilities of the position while being supported by the existing leadership.
- Outcome: Interim roles provide real-time experience and help the organization assess the readiness of potential successors while ensuring that operations continue smoothly.

- **Succession Planning Database:**
  - Approach: Maintain a centralized database that tracks the development and readiness of potential successors. This database should include profiles, development plans, and performance reviews.
  - Outcome: Having a clear and up-to-date overview of succession planning helps ensure that transitions are smooth, even in the event of unexpected departures.

- **Regular Succession Plan Reviews:**
  - Approach: Review the succession plan at least annually to assess progress, make adjustments, and update the list of potential successors based on performance and organizational needs.
  - Outcome: Regular reviews ensure that the succession plan remains aligned with the organization's evolving needs and leadership requirements.

Case Study: Successful Professional Development Program

Organization: Midwest General Hospital

Objective: Improve patient outcomes and staff retention by enhancing nursing leadership and clinical skills through a comprehensive professional development program.

Program Overview: Midwest General Hospital implemented a professional development program focused on leadership training, clinical skills enhancement, and mentorship. The program targeted nurses at various stages of their careers, from new graduates to seasoned professionals aiming for leadership roles.

Key Components:

1. **Leadership Training:**
   - **Content:** The hospital partnered with a local university to offer a leadership certification program that included courses on healthcare management, strategic decision-making, and team leadership.
   - **Delivery:** The program was delivered through a combination of online modules, in-person workshops, and leadership simulations.

2. **Clinical Skills Enhancement:**
   - **Content:** Focused on evidence-based practice, the program offered advanced training in areas such as wound care, pain management, and critical care. Nurses participated in workshops, simulation labs, and on-the-job training.
   - **Delivery:** Training was tailored to each nurse's specialty, with opportunities to earn certifications in specific clinical areas.

3. **Mentorship Program:**
   - **Structure:** Each nurse was paired with a senior nurse mentor who provided guidance, support, and feedback. The mentorship program focused on both clinical and leadership development, with regular meetings and goal-setting sessions.
   - **Outcome:** The mentorship program helped nurses navigate their career paths, build confidence, and develop essential leadership skills.

Results:

- **Improved Patient Outcomes:** Within two years, the hospital saw a significant reduction in patient readmission rates and an improvement in patient satisfaction scores, attributed to better clinical decision-making and enhanced leadership at the bedside.
- **Increased Staff Retention:** Staff turnover decreased by 15%, with nurses citing the professional development opportunities as a key factor in their decision to stay with the hospital.

Key Success Factors:

1. **Tailored Development Plans:** The program's success was largely due to its customization, ensuring that each nurse's professional development plan aligned with their career goals and the hospital's needs.

2. **Leadership Buy-In:** Strong support from hospital leadership ensured that the program was adequately funded and prioritized within the organization.
3. **Ongoing Support:** The mentorship program provided continuous support and encouragement, helping nurses overcome challenges and stay motivated.

Replication in Other Organizations:

- **Customization:** Other organizations can replicate this program by tailoring it to their specific workforce and clinical needs, ensuring that the development plans are relevant and impactful.
- **Partnerships:** Collaborating with educational institutions or professional organizations can enhance the quality and credibility of the training programs offered.
- **Mentorship:** Implementing a structured mentorship program that pairs less experienced staff with seasoned professionals can foster a culture of continuous learning and support.

Cross-Training Initiative for Workforce Flexibility

Objective: Enhance workforce flexibility and career advancement opportunities while maintaining the necessary level of specialization within nursing teams.

Program Design:

1. **Needs Assessment:**
   - **Approach:** Conduct a thorough assessment of current staffing needs, identifying areas where cross-training could alleviate staffing shortages, enhance patient care, or improve operational efficiency.
   - **Outcome:** This assessment helps determine the most critical areas for cross-training, such as ICU nurses learning emergency department protocols or med-surg nurses gaining experience in telemetry.
2. **Core Cross-Training Curriculum:**
   - **Content:** Develop a core curriculum that covers essential skills across multiple specialties. The curriculum should focus on foundational knowledge and skills that are transferable across units, such as basic life support (BLS), infection control, and patient assessment.
   - **Delivery:** Use a combination of classroom instruction, online modules, and hands-on training to ensure comprehensive learning. Simulation labs can be used to practice scenarios specific to different specialties.
3. **Specialty-Specific Cross-Training Tracks:**
   - **Content:** Create specialized tracks for nurses interested in cross-training into specific areas, such as critical care, emergency nursing, or maternal-child health. These tracks should include advanced training and certifications relevant to the specialty.
   - **Outcome:** Provides nurses with the opportunity to gain in-depth knowledge and skills in another specialty, enhancing their versatility and career advancement prospects.
4. **Flexible Scheduling for Cross-Training:**
   - **Approach:** Design the cross-training program to accommodate nurses' schedules, offering flexible options such as weekend workshops, night shifts, or on-the-job training during slower periods.
   - **Outcome:** Ensures that nurses can participate in cross-training without disrupting patient care or their work-life balance.
5. **Evaluation and Certification:**
   - **Approach:** Upon completion of cross-training, nurses should undergo evaluations to assess their competency in the new specialty. This could include skills assessments, written exams, and simulations.
   - **Certification:** Offer formal certification for nurses who successfully complete cross-training, recognizing their expanded skill set and making them eligible for additional roles or responsibilities.

Balancing Specialization with Versatility:

1. **Maintaining Core Specialization:**
   - **Approach:** Ensure that cross-training complements rather than replaces a nurse's primary specialization. Nurses should maintain their proficiency in their core area while gaining additional skills.

119

- o **Outcome:** This balance allows nurses to remain experts in their specialty while providing the flexibility to support other units when needed.
2. **Rotational Assignments:**
   - o **Approach:** Implement rotational assignments where cross-trained nurses spend a certain percentage of their time in their primary unit and the remainder in other units. This rotation helps them maintain skills in both areas.
   - o **Outcome:** Rotations prevent skill atrophy in the nurse's primary specialty while fostering adaptability.
3. **Incentives and Career Advancement:**
   - o **Approach:** Offer incentives such as bonuses, career advancement opportunities, or additional certifications for nurses who participate in cross-training. Recognize and reward their expanded capabilities.
   - o **Outcome:** Incentives encourage participation in cross-training and signal the organization's commitment to workforce development.
4. **Continuous Learning and Support:**
   - o **Approach:** Provide ongoing education and support to ensure that cross-trained nurses continue to develop their skills in all relevant areas. This could include refresher courses, mentorship, and access to continuing education resources.
   - o **Outcome:** Continuous learning ensures that nurses remain competent and confident in their expanded roles, contributing to high-quality patient care across units.

By implementing these strategies, nurse executives can create a well-rounded nursing workforce that is both specialized and versatile. This approach not only enhances operational flexibility but also supports nurses' career development and satisfaction, ultimately leading to improved patient outcomes and a more resilient healthcare organization.

Analyzing the Relationship Between Employee Satisfaction and Patient Outcomes in Healthcare Settings
Employee satisfaction in healthcare settings is closely linked to patient outcomes. Satisfied employees are more likely to be engaged in their work, which leads to better patient care, fewer errors, and higher patient satisfaction. Conversely, dissatisfaction can lead to burnout, higher turnover rates, and lower quality of care. Understanding and improving employee satisfaction is essential for healthcare organizations aiming to deliver high-quality care and achieve positive patient outcomes.

Key Points of the Relationship:
1. **Engagement and Performance:**
   - o **Higher Engagement:** Employees who are satisfied with their jobs are more likely to be engaged, showing greater commitment to their roles and the organization. This engagement translates into better patient care, as engaged employees are more attentive, empathetic, and willing to go the extra mile.
   - o **Lower Error Rates:** Satisfied employees tend to experience lower levels of stress and fatigue, reducing the likelihood of errors. In healthcare, where mistakes can have serious consequences, this is a critical factor in maintaining patient safety.
2. **Retention and Continuity of Care:**
   - o **Reduced Turnover:** High employee satisfaction leads to lower turnover rates, which is crucial in maintaining continuity of care. Consistent staffing allows for stronger patient-provider relationships, better communication, and more coordinated care, all of which contribute to improved patient outcomes.
   - o **Institutional Knowledge:** Long-term employees develop deep institutional knowledge and familiarity with patients, protocols, and systems. This expertise enhances the quality of care and reduces the likelihood of errors.
3. **Patient Satisfaction:**
   - o **Positive Interactions:** Satisfied employees are more likely to create a positive, welcoming environment for patients. This directly impacts patient satisfaction scores, as patients value interactions with compassionate, responsive, and attentive healthcare providers.

- Patient Loyalty: When patients have positive experiences, they are more likely to return to the same healthcare provider for future care and recommend the provider to others, contributing to the organization's reputation and success.

Developing a Comprehensive Employee Satisfaction Survey and Action Planning Process

1. Employee Satisfaction Survey Design

A. Survey Structure and Content

- **Core Areas of Inquiry**:
    - **Work Environment**: Assess the physical and emotional work environment, including safety, resources, and facilities.
    - **Job Role and Responsibilities**: Evaluate satisfaction with job duties, workload, and autonomy.
    - **Compensation and Benefits**: Measure satisfaction with salary, benefits, and opportunities for advancement.
    - **Leadership and Management**: Gather feedback on leadership effectiveness, communication, and support from management.
    - **Professional Development**: Explore opportunities for training, career growth, and continuing education.
    - **Work-Life Balance**: Assess the organization's support for work-life balance, including flexible scheduling and wellness programs.
    - **Teamwork and Collaboration**: Evaluate the quality of teamwork, collaboration, and peer support.
    - **Recognition and Reward**: Measure satisfaction with recognition programs and reward systems.

B. Question Types

- **Likert Scale Questions**: Use a 5-point Likert scale to measure levels of agreement with statements related to the core areas. Example: "I feel supported by my immediate supervisor in my professional development."
- **Open-Ended Questions**: Include open-ended questions to capture detailed feedback and suggestions for improvement. Example: "What changes would improve your job satisfaction?"
- **Demographic Questions**: Collect demographic information (e.g., age, department, tenure) to analyze satisfaction across different employee segments.

C. Survey Distribution and Confidentiality

- **Distribution**: Use a mix of digital and paper formats to reach all employees. Ensure the survey is accessible to those with varying levels of tech literacy.
- **Confidentiality Assurance**: Clearly communicate that responses are confidential and that the data will be used to improve the workplace. Anonymous surveys can encourage more honest feedback.

2. Action Planning Process

A. Data Analysis and Reporting

- **Aggregate and Segment Data**: Analyze the survey results, focusing on overall trends as well as differences between departments, job roles, and demographic groups.
- **Identify Key Areas for Improvement**: Highlight areas where satisfaction is low and prioritize these for action. For example, if multiple departments report dissatisfaction with workload, this becomes a key area to address.
- **Benchmarking**: Compare the results with industry benchmarks or past surveys to assess progress and identify areas where the organization may be lagging.

B. Collaborative Action Planning

- **Engage Leadership and Staff**: Involve leaders, managers, and frontline staff in developing action plans. This collaboration ensures that plans are realistic, relevant, and supported by those who will implement them.
- **Set SMART Goals**: Establish Specific, Measurable, Achievable, Relevant, and Time-bound (SMART) goals for each area identified for improvement. For example, "Reduce staff turnover in the emergency department by 15% within 12 months."
- **Allocate Resources**: Ensure that the necessary resources—time, budget, personnel—are allocated to implement the action plans effectively.

C. Implementation and Monitoring

- **Pilot Programs**: Consider piloting changes in specific departments before rolling them out organization-wide. This allows for adjustments based on initial feedback.
- **Regular Check-Ins**: Monitor progress through regular check-ins and status updates. Adjust action plans as needed based on feedback and changing circumstances.
- **Communicate Progress**: Keep staff informed about the progress of action plans. Transparency builds trust and demonstrates the organization's commitment to improving employee satisfaction.

D. Continuous Improvement

- **Ongoing Feedback Loops**: Establish ongoing feedback loops, such as quarterly pulse surveys or focus groups, to monitor the impact of changes and gather additional insights.
- **Annual Review and Adjustment**: Conduct an annual review of employee satisfaction and adjust action plans as necessary. Use this review to celebrate successes and identify new challenges.

Creating a Multi-Faceted Recognition and Reward System

A well-designed recognition and reward system is essential for motivating healthcare professionals and aligning their efforts with organizational goals. The system should address both intrinsic and extrinsic motivators and be tailored to the diverse needs of different generational cohorts and cultural backgrounds.

1. Elements of the Recognition and Reward System

A. Intrinsic Motivators

- **Peer Recognition Programs**: Implement programs where employees can recognize each other's contributions. This could include "Shout Out" boards or digital platforms where staff can post positive feedback about colleagues.
- **Professional Development Opportunities**: Offer opportunities for continuous learning, such as certifications, conferences, and specialized training. These opportunities allow employees to pursue their passions and advance their careers.
- **Autonomy and Empowerment**: Encourage a culture of autonomy by involving staff in decision-making processes, such as participating in committees or quality improvement projects. Empowering employees to influence their work environment can lead to greater job satisfaction.

B. Extrinsic Motivators

- **Monetary Rewards**: Include bonuses, salary increases, and financial incentives tied to performance metrics, such as patient satisfaction scores or efficiency improvements.
- **Non-Monetary Rewards**: Offer tangible rewards like additional paid time off, gift cards, or wellness program memberships. These rewards can be given for meeting performance goals, years of service, or exceptional contributions.
- **Formal Recognition Events**: Host annual or quarterly recognition events where outstanding employees are publicly acknowledged. These events can include awards such as "Employee of the Month" or special commendations for exceptional teamwork or patient care.

C. Tailoring to Generational Cohorts

- **Baby Boomers**: Focus on recognition of experience and contributions over time. Offer opportunities for mentoring roles, formal recognition of years of service, and retirement planning support.
- **Generation X**: Emphasize work-life balance and professional growth. Offer flexible work arrangements, leadership development programs, and recognition for innovation and efficiency.
- **Millennials**: Prioritize professional development and meaningful work. Provide opportunities for skill-building, feedback, and projects that align with personal values. Recognize efforts with digital badges, public acknowledgment on social media, or opportunities for career advancement.
- **Generation Z**: Focus on technology-driven recognition and instant feedback. Implement digital platforms for recognition, provide mentorship opportunities, and offer rewards that align with their preference for flexible and dynamic work environments.

D. Cultural Sensitivity

- **Culturally Relevant Rewards**: Ensure that rewards and recognition are culturally appropriate and meaningful. For example, some employees may value public recognition, while others might prefer private acknowledgment or non-monetary rewards.

- **Inclusive Recognition Programs**: Design programs that are inclusive of diverse cultural practices and beliefs. For instance, consider dietary restrictions when offering meal-based rewards, or provide time off for culturally significant holidays.
- **Cultural Competence Training**: Include cultural competence as part of leadership training to ensure that managers understand how to recognize and reward employees in a way that respects their cultural backgrounds.

2. Measuring the Impact of the Recognition and Reward System

A. Employee Engagement and Satisfaction Metrics

- **Surveys**: Regularly survey employees to assess their satisfaction with the recognition and reward system. Include questions about how valued they feel, the fairness of rewards, and the impact on their motivation.
- **Focus Groups**: Conduct focus groups with representatives from different departments, generational cohorts, and cultural backgrounds to gather in-depth feedback on the program's effectiveness.

B. Performance Metrics

- **Employee Retention Rates**: Track retention rates before and after implementing the recognition and reward system to determine if the program is reducing turnover.
- **Productivity and Quality Metrics**: Monitor productivity, quality of care, and patient outcomes to assess whether the recognition program is leading to improved performance. Higher motivation typically translates into better patient care and more efficient operations.

C. Program Participation and Feedback

- **Participation Rates**: Measure the participation rates in various aspects of the program, such as peer recognition, development opportunities, and formal recognition events. Low participation may indicate a need for program adjustments.
- **Feedback Loops**: Establish ongoing feedback mechanisms, such as suggestion boxes or digital forums, where employees can provide input on the recognition program. Use this feedback to make continuous improvements.

By aligning the recognition and reward system with the diverse needs of healthcare professionals and continuously measuring its impact, organizations can create a motivating environment that supports both employee satisfaction and organizational success.

Designing a Shared Governance Model for a Large Academic Medical Center

A shared governance model empowers healthcare professionals, particularly nurses, to participate in decision-making processes related to clinical practice, quality improvement, and organizational policies. For a large academic medical center, this model needs to accommodate multidisciplinary collaboration, balance clinical and administrative priorities, and include mechanisms to measure its impact on organizational performance.

1. Structure of the Shared Governance Model

1. **Council-Based Framework:**
   - **Unit-Based Councils:** Each clinical unit or department has its own council, focusing on issues specific to that area, such as patient care standards, workflow efficiency, and professional development.
   - **Interdisciplinary Councils:** These councils include representatives from nursing, medicine, allied health, administration, and support services. They address broader issues that require cross-departmental collaboration, such as patient safety initiatives, interdisciplinary care coordination, and policy development.
   - **Executive Council:** Comprised of leaders from each unit-based and interdisciplinary council, along with senior leadership (e.g., CNO, CMO, COO). This council aligns the work of the other councils with the organization's strategic goals and ensures that decisions are consistent with the academic medical center's mission.

2. **Roles and Responsibilities:**
   - **Chairperson:** Each council elects a chairperson responsible for leading meetings, setting agendas, and ensuring that decisions are made collaboratively.

- o **Council Members:** Staff from various disciplines who participate in meetings, contribute to discussions, and represent their departments or units.
- o **Advisory Roles:** Senior leaders, including nurse executives and department heads, serve as advisors, providing guidance and ensuring alignment with organizational priorities.

3. **Decision-Making Process:**
   - o **Consensus-Building:** Councils use a consensus-based decision-making process, ensuring that all voices are heard and considered. For critical decisions, a two-thirds majority vote may be required.
   - o **Escalation Pathways:** Issues that cannot be resolved within a council are escalated to the Executive Council for further discussion and resolution.

2. Addressing Key Challenges

1. **Multi-Disciplinary Collaboration:**
   - o **Challenge:** Facilitating effective collaboration among diverse disciplines with differing priorities and perspectives.
   - o **Strategy:** Encourage cross-disciplinary representation in all councils and provide training in collaborative decision-making and conflict resolution. Regular interdisciplinary workshops can help break down silos and build a culture of mutual respect and understanding.

2. **Balancing Clinical and Administrative Priorities:**
   - o **Challenge:** Ensuring that clinical concerns are adequately addressed while also meeting administrative goals, such as budgetary constraints and regulatory compliance.
   - o **Strategy:** Establish clear guidelines that align clinical practice improvements with organizational objectives. Include both clinical and administrative leaders in the Executive Council to maintain a balanced perspective. Regularly review the alignment of council decisions with strategic priorities.

3. **Measuring Impact on Organizational Performance:**
   - o **Challenge:** Demonstrating the value of shared governance in improving patient outcomes, staff satisfaction, and operational efficiency.
   - o **Strategy:** Implement a robust performance measurement system that tracks key metrics, such as patient satisfaction scores, staff turnover rates, clinical outcomes, and financial performance. Use dashboards and scorecards to present data to the councils, enabling data-driven decision-making. Conduct regular evaluations of the shared governance process itself, using feedback from council members and staff to identify areas for improvement.

3. Implementation and Sustaining the Model

1. **Pilot Program:**
   - o **Approach:** Start with a pilot in a few departments or units to test the shared governance model, refine processes, and gather initial data on its effectiveness.
   - o **Outcome:** Use lessons learned from the pilot to make necessary adjustments before rolling out the model across the entire academic medical center.

2. **Training and Education:**
   - o **Approach:** Provide comprehensive training for council members on their roles, the decision-making process, and tools for effective collaboration. Offer ongoing education to adapt to new challenges and changes in the healthcare environment.
   - o **Outcome:** Ensure that all participants are well-equipped to contribute effectively to shared governance, fostering a culture of continuous learning and improvement.

3. **Communication and Engagement:**
   - o **Approach:** Maintain open lines of communication between the councils and the broader organization. Regularly update all staff on council activities, decisions, and impacts through newsletters, meetings, and intranet postings.
   - o **Outcome:** Promote transparency and engagement, ensuring that staff feel connected to the shared governance process and its outcomes.

Evaluating the Effectiveness of Employee Retention Strategies in Healthcare

Employee retention is a critical issue in healthcare, impacting the quality of patient care, organizational stability, and financial performance. A data-driven approach to evaluating and enhancing retention strategies, such as career ladders, tuition reimbursement, and flexible scheduling, can help address key drivers of turnover.

1. Evaluating Retention Strategies

1. **Career Ladders:**
   - **Overview:** Career ladders provide clear pathways for professional growth, offering nurses opportunities to advance based on experience, education, and performance.
   - **Effectiveness:**
     - **Data Points:** Track promotion rates, job satisfaction, and turnover among nurses participating in career ladder programs.
     - **Analysis:** Compare retention rates between those engaged in career ladder programs and those who are not. Evaluate how career ladders impact job satisfaction and employee engagement.

2. **Tuition Reimbursement:**
   - **Overview:** Tuition reimbursement supports employees in pursuing further education, which can lead to higher qualifications and career advancement.
   - **Effectiveness:**
     - **Data Points:** Monitor participation rates in tuition reimbursement programs, retention rates among participants, and subsequent promotions or role changes.
     - **Analysis:** Assess whether tuition reimbursement correlates with longer tenure, increased job satisfaction, and improved patient outcomes. Determine the return on investment by comparing costs with retention benefits and staff development.

3. **Flexible Scheduling:**
   - **Overview:** Flexible scheduling offers employees greater control over their work hours, which can improve work-life balance and reduce burnout.
   - **Effectiveness:**
     - **Data Points:** Measure the impact of flexible scheduling on turnover rates, absenteeism, job satisfaction, and patient care metrics.
     - **Analysis:** Evaluate whether flexible scheduling reduces burnout and turnover. Analyze differences in retention between staff with flexible schedules and those with traditional schedules, considering factors like department needs and patient care requirements.

2. Data-Driven Approach to Identifying and Addressing Turnover Drivers

1. **Collecting and Analyzing Data:**
   - **Employee Surveys:**
     - **Approach:** Regularly administer surveys to gather data on employee satisfaction, engagement, and perceived support. Include questions about the effectiveness of retention strategies, work environment, and opportunities for advancement.
     - **Outcome:** Use survey results to identify common themes and areas of concern that may be driving turnover.
   - **Exit Interviews:**
     - **Approach:** Conduct thorough exit interviews to understand why employees are leaving and whether retention strategies could have influenced their decision to stay.
     - **Outcome:** Analyze exit interview data to identify patterns in turnover and opportunities for improving retention strategies.
   - **HR Metrics:**
     - **Approach:** Track HR metrics such as turnover rates, length of service, promotion rates, and participation in retention programs. Cross-reference these metrics with patient outcomes and organizational performance data.
     - **Outcome:** Develop a comprehensive picture of retention drivers and the effectiveness of existing strategies.

2. **Identifying Key Drivers of Turnover:**

- o **Data Segmentation:**
  - **Approach:** Segment data by demographics (e.g., age, gender, role, tenure) to identify specific groups at higher risk of turnover.
  - **Outcome:** Tailor retention strategies to address the unique needs of different employee segments, such as offering targeted development programs for early-career nurses or leadership opportunities for mid-career professionals.
- o **Predictive Analytics:**
  - **Approach:** Use predictive analytics to identify employees at risk of leaving based on factors like job satisfaction scores, participation in development programs, and work-life balance metrics.
  - **Outcome:** Implement preemptive retention strategies for at-risk employees, such as career development discussions or adjustments to workload.

3. **Developing and Implementing Targeted Retention Strategies:**
   - o **Customized Development Programs:**
     - **Approach:** Based on the data, design development programs that address the specific needs of different employee groups. For example, offer leadership training for mid-career nurses or mentorship programs for new graduates.
     - **Outcome:** Enhance job satisfaction and engagement by aligning development opportunities with employees' career aspirations.
   - o **Enhanced Work-Life Balance Initiatives:**
     - **Approach:** Expand flexible scheduling options, offer wellness programs, and promote a supportive work environment. Tailor these initiatives to the needs of different departments and roles.
     - **Outcome:** Reduce burnout and improve retention by supporting employees' well-being and work-life balance.
   - o **Continuous Feedback and Adjustment:**
     - **Approach:** Regularly solicit feedback from employees on the effectiveness of retention strategies and make adjustments based on their input.
     - **Outcome:** Ensure that retention strategies remain relevant and effective in a dynamic healthcare environment.

By integrating a shared governance model into the organizational structure and using data-driven strategies to enhance employee retention, nurse executives can create a more engaged, satisfied, and stable workforce. This approach not only improves organizational performance but also enhances patient care and outcomes.

Impact of Workplace Culture on Employee Engagement and Retention

Workplace culture significantly influences employee engagement and retention, particularly in healthcare settings where the demands of the job are high, and the stakes are often life-and-death. A positive culture that fosters belonging, psychological safety, and continuous improvement can enhance job satisfaction, reduce turnover, and improve patient outcomes. Conversely, a toxic or disengaging culture can lead to burnout, high turnover rates, and suboptimal patient care.

1. Culture of Belonging

- **Impact on Engagement**: When employees feel a strong sense of belonging, they are more likely to be engaged in their work. Belonging involves feeling valued, included, and connected to colleagues and the organization. This sense of community fosters loyalty and motivation, driving employees to contribute their best efforts.
- **Impact on Retention**: A culture of belonging encourages employees to stay with the organization longer. They are less likely to seek employment elsewhere if they feel a deep connection to their team and the organization's mission. This reduces turnover rates, which can be costly and disruptive in healthcare settings.

2. Psychological Safety

- **Impact on Engagement**: Psychological safety is the belief that one can speak up, share ideas, and take risks without fear of negative consequences. In a psychologically safe environment, employees are more engaged because they feel empowered to contribute creatively and honestly. This leads to greater innovation and problem-solving, which are critical in healthcare.
- **Impact on Retention**: Employees who feel psychologically safe are more likely to stay with an organization. They feel respected and supported, which enhances job satisfaction. In contrast, a lack of psychological safety can lead to fear, stress, and ultimately, burnout and attrition.

3. Continuous Improvement

- **Impact on Engagement**: A culture of continuous improvement engages employees by involving them in the process of making their work environment and practices better. This participatory approach gives employees a sense of ownership and purpose, as they can see the direct impact of their contributions on patient care and organizational success.
- **Impact on Retention**: When employees are part of a culture that values continuous learning and improvement, they are more likely to stay with the organization. They appreciate the opportunity for growth and development, which contributes to their long-term career satisfaction.

Fostering a Positive Workplace Culture

1. Fostering a Culture of Belonging

- **Inclusive Leadership**: Nurse executives should model inclusive behavior by actively seeking input from diverse voices, acknowledging contributions from all team members, and addressing any behaviors that undermine inclusion.
- **Team Building Activities**: Facilitate regular team-building activities that allow employees to connect on a personal level, fostering stronger relationships and a sense of community.
- **Recognition Programs**: Implement recognition programs that celebrate the contributions of individuals and teams, particularly those that reinforce the values of inclusion and collaboration.

2. Promoting Psychological Safety

- **Open Communication Channels**: Establish and maintain open channels for communication, where employees can voice concerns, share ideas, and provide feedback without fear of retribution.
- **Training for Leaders**: Provide training for nurse managers and leaders on how to foster psychological safety in their teams. This includes active listening, constructive feedback, and handling conflicts with empathy.
- **Non-Punitive Error Reporting**: Create a non-punitive system for reporting errors and near-misses. Encourage staff to learn from mistakes rather than fear punishment, which enhances overall safety and trust within the team.

3. Encouraging Continuous Improvement

- **Lean and Six Sigma**: Implement Lean or Six Sigma methodologies to involve staff in process improvement projects. Encourage employees to identify inefficiencies and participate in finding solutions.
- **Ongoing Education**: Offer continuous learning opportunities through workshops, seminars, and certifications that allow employees to develop new skills and stay current with industry best practices.
- **Feedback Loops**: Establish regular feedback loops where employees can discuss what's working well and what needs improvement. Use this feedback to make iterative changes that keep the organization evolving.

Developing a Comprehensive Workforce Engagement Strategy

A comprehensive workforce engagement strategy integrates professional development, work-life balance, and alignment with the organizational mission to enhance employee satisfaction, productivity, and retention.

1. Professional Development

- **Career Pathways**: Create clear career pathways that allow employees to see their potential for growth within the organization. Offer mentorship programs, leadership development tracks, and access to continuing education.
- **Skill Development Programs**: Provide ongoing opportunities for skill development through in-house training, external courses, and certifications. Focus on both clinical skills and soft skills such as communication, leadership, and emotional intelligence.

- **Recognition of Learning Achievements**: Recognize and reward employees who pursue professional development, such as through salary increases, promotions, or public acknowledgment of their new qualifications.

2. Work-Life Balance

- **Flexible Scheduling**: Offer flexible scheduling options, such as shift swapping, part-time opportunities, or telehealth roles for certain positions, to help employees manage their personal and professional lives.
- **Wellness Programs**: Implement wellness programs that address physical, mental, and emotional health. These might include gym memberships, stress management workshops, mental health days, or access to counseling services.
- **Time Off Policies**: Ensure that time off policies are generous and flexible, allowing employees to take the necessary breaks to recharge and avoid burnout. Encourage the use of vacation days and offer paid parental leave.

3. Organizational Mission Alignment

- **Mission-Driven Culture**: Clearly communicate the organization's mission and values, and demonstrate how each employee's role contributes to the overall goals. Regularly share success stories that highlight the impact of their work on patients and the community.
- **Engagement in Strategic Planning**: Involve employees in the strategic planning process, allowing them to contribute ideas and see how their input shapes the organization's direction. This fosters a sense of ownership and alignment with the mission.
- **Community Involvement**: Encourage participation in community service or outreach programs that align with the organization's mission. This not only strengthens the connection to the mission but also enhances team cohesion and morale.

Measuring the Return on Investment (ROI) for Engagement Initiatives

1. Employee Satisfaction and Engagement Metrics

- **Surveys**: Conduct regular employee engagement and satisfaction surveys to measure the impact of the engagement strategy. Look for improvements in key areas such as job satisfaction, work-life balance, and alignment with organizational values.
- **Focus Groups**: Hold focus groups to gather qualitative data on the effectiveness of the engagement initiatives. Use this feedback to refine programs and address any issues.

2. Retention and Turnover Rates

- **Retention Rates**: Track retention rates before and after implementing engagement initiatives. A decrease in turnover indicates that the strategies are effective in keeping employees satisfied and committed to the organization.
- **Exit Interviews**: Conduct exit interviews to understand why employees are leaving and whether the engagement initiatives could have influenced their decision to stay. Use this data to make adjustments to the strategy.

3. Productivity and Performance Metrics

- **Patient Outcomes**: Monitor patient outcomes, such as satisfaction scores, quality of care, and safety metrics. Engaged employees are more likely to deliver higher-quality care, which should be reflected in these outcomes.
- **Efficiency Metrics**: Track efficiency metrics such as reduced absenteeism, lower error rates, and improved time management. These metrics can indicate higher engagement levels and better work-life balance.

4. Financial Metrics

- **Cost of Turnover**: Calculate the cost of turnover, including recruitment, training, and lost productivity. Compare these costs before and after implementing the engagement strategy to assess the financial ROI.
- **Healthcare Costs**: Evaluate the impact of wellness programs on healthcare costs, including reduced claims and lower rates of absenteeism due to illness. Cost savings here contribute to the overall ROI.

By integrating these elements into a comprehensive workforce engagement strategy and measuring the impact through a combination of qualitative and quantitative metrics, nurse executives can create a more engaged, satisfied, and productive workforce that aligns with the organization's strategic goals.

Case Study: Successful Implementation of a Shared Governance Model in a Community Hospital
Background

Community Hospital, a 200-bed facility serving a diverse suburban population, recognized the need to enhance nurse engagement, improve patient outcomes, and align nursing practice with the hospital's strategic goals. To achieve these objectives, the hospital leadership decided to implement a shared governance model, empowering nurses to participate in decision-making processes related to clinical practice, quality improvement, and professional development.

Implementation of the Shared Governance Model

1. **Initial Assessment and Planning:**
   - **Challenge:** The hospital faced low staff morale, high turnover rates, and a lack of nurse involvement in decision-making. Many nurses felt disconnected from the leadership team and believed their insights were undervalued.
   - **Strategy:** The leadership team conducted a comprehensive assessment involving surveys, focus groups, and one-on-one interviews with nursing staff. This assessment identified key areas of concern, such as the desire for greater autonomy, improved communication, and opportunities for professional growth. Based on these findings, the hospital leadership collaborated with nursing staff to design a shared governance structure tailored to the hospital's unique needs.

2. **Designing the Shared Governance Structure:**
   - **Council Structure:** The shared governance model included the formation of several councils:
     - **Unit-Based Councils:** Each clinical unit established its own council to address specific concerns and initiatives related to patient care, workflow, and staff development within that unit.
     - **Interdisciplinary Councils:** Councils composed of representatives from nursing, medicine, allied health, and support services were created to tackle broader issues such as patient safety, interdisciplinary collaboration, and hospital-wide policy development.
     - **Nursing Practice Council:** This council was responsible for reviewing and updating clinical policies and procedures, ensuring they aligned with evidence-based practices.
     - **Executive Council:** Comprised of representatives from all councils, along with senior leadership, this council provided strategic oversight and ensured that council decisions were consistent with the hospital's overall goals.

3. **Overcoming Resistance to Change:**
   - **Challenge:** Some staff members were initially resistant to the shared governance model, fearing additional workload or doubting its effectiveness. There was also concern about the potential for conflict between clinical priorities and administrative directives.
   - **Strategy:**
     - **Education and Communication:** The leadership team organized educational sessions to explain the benefits of shared governance, including how it would improve patient care, empower nurses, and enhance professional satisfaction. They also shared success stories from other hospitals that had implemented similar models.
     - **Pilot Program:** A pilot program was launched in a few units, allowing staff to experience shared governance in a controlled environment. This pilot helped address concerns and provided tangible examples of the model's positive impact.
     - **Incentives:** Participation in the shared governance councils was incentivized through professional development opportunities, recognition programs, and potential career advancement.

4. **Measurable Outcomes Achieved:**
   - **Improved Nurse Engagement:** Within the first year of implementation, nurse engagement scores, as measured by annual surveys, increased by 25%. Nurses reported feeling more valued and empowered in their roles, with greater input into decisions affecting their practice.

- o **Enhanced Patient Outcomes:** The hospital saw a 15% reduction in hospital-acquired infections and a 10% increase in patient satisfaction scores. These improvements were attributed to more consistent adherence to evidence-based practices and better interdisciplinary collaboration.
- o **Decreased Turnover:** Nurse turnover rates dropped by 20%, with exit interviews indicating that the shared governance model contributed to greater job satisfaction and a stronger sense of community among staff.
- o **Policy Improvements:** The Nursing Practice Council successfully updated several outdated clinical policies, aligning them with the latest research and best practices. This led to more standardized care and improved patient outcomes.

Conclusion

The implementation of a shared governance model at Community Hospital transformed the culture of the organization, leading to significant improvements in nurse engagement, patient outcomes, and staff retention. The success of the model was largely due to effective communication, education, and the involvement of nurses in the planning and decision-making processes. By addressing initial resistance through a pilot program and providing ongoing support, the hospital was able to create a sustainable governance structure that aligned with its strategic goals.

Designing a Mentorship Program for Nurses

Program Overview

The mentorship program is designed to pair experienced nurses with new graduates or newly hired staff, focusing on promoting both clinical excellence and leadership development. The program is structured to support the transition of new nurses into the clinical environment while fostering professional growth and leadership skills.

1. Structure of the Mentorship Program

1. **Program Goals:**
   - o **Clinical Excellence:** Ensure that new nurses develop strong clinical skills, adhere to evidence-based practices, and integrate seamlessly into the care team.
   - o **Leadership Development:** Cultivate leadership qualities in both mentees and mentors, preparing nurses for future leadership roles within the organization.

2. **Mentor Selection and Training:**
   - o **Criteria for Mentors:**
     - Minimum of 5 years of clinical experience.
     - Demonstrated expertise in their specialty area.
     - Strong communication and interpersonal skills.
     - Commitment to professional development and mentorship.
   - o **Training for Mentors:**
     - Provide mentors with training in coaching techniques, feedback delivery, and conflict resolution. Training sessions should also cover the goals of the mentorship program and the expectations for mentors.

3. **Mentorship Pairing Process:**
   - o **Matching Criteria:**
     - Pairing based on clinical specialty, career goals, and personal preferences. Consideration is given to matching mentors and mentees with compatible communication styles and personalities.
   - o **Initial Meeting:**
     - The mentorship relationship begins with a structured initial meeting where both parties discuss their goals, expectations, and preferred communication methods. A mentorship agreement is created to formalize the partnership.

4. **Program Components:**
   - o **Clinical Skill Development:**
     - Mentors guide mentees through clinical skills development, including hands-on training, case discussions, and shadowing opportunities. Regular competency assessments are conducted to track progress.
   - o **Leadership Skill Building:**

- Leadership development activities include joint participation in quality improvement projects, committee involvement, and attendance at leadership workshops. Mentors model leadership behaviors and involve mentees in decision-making processes.
  - **Regular Check-Ins:**
    - Monthly check-ins are scheduled to review progress, discuss challenges, and set new goals. These meetings also serve as opportunities to adjust the mentorship plan as needed.
5. **Evaluation and Feedback:**
   - **Ongoing Evaluation:**
     - Both mentors and mentees provide regular feedback on the program through surveys and one-on-one meetings with program coordinators. This feedback is used to make improvements to the program.
   - **End-of-Program Review:**
     - At the conclusion of the mentorship period (typically one year), a formal review is conducted to assess the achievements of the mentee, the effectiveness of the mentor, and the overall success of the program.

2. Promoting Clinical Excellence and Leadership Development
1. **Clinical Excellence:**
   - **Hands-On Training:**
     - Mentors provide hands-on training in key clinical areas, guiding mentees through complex procedures and patient care scenarios. This includes simulation training and real-time feedback during clinical practice.
   - **Case Study Discussions:**
     - Regular case study discussions allow mentees to apply theoretical knowledge to real-world situations, enhancing their clinical reasoning and decision-making skills.
2. **Leadership Development:**
   - **Involvement in Projects:**
     - Mentees are encouraged to participate in hospital-wide initiatives or quality improvement projects. Mentors guide them through the project lifecycle, from planning to implementation and evaluation, instilling project management and leadership skills.
   - **Shadowing Leadership Roles:**
     - Mentees have opportunities to shadow their mentors in leadership roles, such as charge nurse or committee chair. This exposure helps them understand the responsibilities and challenges of leadership positions.
   - **Leadership Workshops:**
     - The program includes access to leadership workshops focused on topics such as team dynamics, conflict resolution, and change management, helping mentees develop a foundation in nursing leadership.

3. Ensuring Program Success
1. **Continuous Support and Resources:**
   - **Dedicated Program Coordinator:**
     - A program coordinator is responsible for overseeing the mentorship program, providing support to mentors and mentees, and addressing any issues that arise.
   - **Resource Library:**
     - A library of resources, including articles, books, and online modules on clinical practice and leadership, is available to both mentors and mentees. This library supports ongoing learning and development.
2. **Recognition and Incentives:**
   - **Recognition of Mentors:**
     - Mentors are recognized for their contributions through awards, public acknowledgment in hospital communications, and opportunities for professional development.

- o **Mentee Graduation:**
  - ▪ Mentees who successfully complete the program receive a certificate of completion and are recognized in a graduation ceremony. This event highlights their achievements and encourages continued professional growth.
3. **Sustaining the Program:**
   - o **Alumni Network:**
     - ▪ Graduates of the mentorship program are invited to join an alumni network, where they can continue to receive support, share experiences, and potentially become mentors themselves.
   - o **Ongoing Program Evaluation:**
     - ▪ The program is regularly evaluated and updated based on feedback from participants and evolving organizational needs. This ensures that it remains relevant and effective in promoting clinical excellence and leadership development.

By structuring the mentorship program to address both clinical excellence and leadership development, the hospital can ensure that new nurses are well-prepared for their roles and that experienced nurses continue to grow professionally. This dual focus not only enhances patient care but also supports the long-term success and stability of the nursing workforce.

Evaluating the Use of Technology in Enhancing Workforce Engagement

Technology has become a powerful tool in enhancing workforce engagement in healthcare, offering solutions such as mobile apps for shift scheduling, digital platforms for communication, and gamification of learning and development activities. These tools can streamline operations, improve communication, and create more engaging work environments. However, they also present challenges, including maintaining work-life boundaries and managing digital fatigue.

1. Benefits of Technology in Workforce Engagement

A. Mobile Apps for Shift Scheduling

- **Flexibility and Convenience**: Mobile apps allow employees to view and manage their schedules from anywhere, giving them greater control over their work hours. This flexibility can improve work-life balance and job satisfaction, particularly for nurses with complex personal schedules.
- **Real-Time Updates**: Apps can provide real-time updates on schedule changes, shift availability, and staffing needs, reducing miscommunication and helping to fill shifts more efficiently. This leads to improved staffing levels and reduced burnout.
- **Ease of Communication**: Apps often include communication features, enabling quick, direct communication between staff and management. This can lead to faster decision-making and a more responsive work environment.

B. Gamification of Learning and Development

- **Increased Engagement**: Gamification introduces elements such as points, badges, leaderboards, and challenges into learning activities, making them more interactive and motivating. Employees are more likely to engage with training modules that are fun and rewarding.
- **Enhanced Learning Outcomes**: Gamified learning can improve knowledge retention and application by making training more immersive and personalized. Employees can progress at their own pace and receive immediate feedback, which enhances the learning experience.
- **Recognition and Rewards**: Gamification can be tied to recognition programs, where employees earn rewards or recognition for completing training modules or achieving high scores. This creates a positive reinforcement loop that encourages continuous learning.

2. Challenges and Considerations

A. Work-Life Boundaries

- **Blurred Lines**: The convenience of mobile apps can sometimes blur the lines between work and personal life. Employees might feel compelled to check work-related notifications outside of their scheduled hours, leading to work-life imbalance.

- **Setting Boundaries**: Nurse executives need to establish clear guidelines for the use of technology, such as when it is appropriate to send and respond to messages or check schedules. Encouraging employees to disconnect during off-hours can help maintain healthy boundaries.

B. Digital Fatigue
- **Overload of Technology**: Continuous exposure to digital tools, especially during and after work hours, can lead to digital fatigue. This can manifest as decreased productivity, frustration, and disengagement from both work and personal activities.
- **Balancing Digital Use**: It's important to balance the use of technology with traditional methods of communication and learning. For instance, in-person training sessions, face-to-face meetings, and printed materials can provide a break from digital screens and help reduce fatigue.

C. Inclusivity and Accessibility
- **Technology Adoption**: Different age groups and individuals may have varying levels of comfort with technology. While younger employees might embrace digital tools, older employees might find them challenging or less intuitive.
- **Training and Support**: Providing comprehensive training and ongoing support is crucial to ensure all employees can effectively use the technology. Offering alternative methods for those less comfortable with digital tools ensures inclusivity.

Strategy for Engaging and Retaining a Multigenerational Workforce
In healthcare, engaging and retaining a multigenerational workforce requires understanding the unique needs and preferences of different age groups while fostering intergenerational collaboration and knowledge transfer. This strategy must be flexible enough to accommodate varying work styles and career goals while promoting a cohesive, collaborative work environment.

1. Understanding the Generational Cohorts

A. Baby Boomers (Born 1946-1964)
- **Needs and Preferences**:
  - Value job security, stability, and recognition of their experience.
  - Prefer traditional learning methods and may appreciate mentoring roles.
  - Often motivated by opportunities for legacy building and contributing to the organization's mission.
- **Engagement Strategies**:
  - Provide opportunities for mentorship, allowing Boomers to share their knowledge with younger employees.
  - Recognize their contributions through service awards and public acknowledgment of their expertise.
  - Offer flexible retirement planning and phased retirement options to retain their skills and knowledge.

B. Generation X (Born 1965-1980)
- **Needs and Preferences**:
  - Value work-life balance, independence, and opportunities for professional development.
  - Prefer efficient, results-oriented work environments and are comfortable with technology.
  - Appreciate leadership roles that offer autonomy and the ability to make impactful decisions.
- **Engagement Strategies**:
  - Offer flexible work schedules and remote work options to support work-life balance.
  - Provide leadership development programs and opportunities for career advancement.
  - Encourage participation in strategic decision-making processes, such as quality improvement initiatives.

C. Millennials (Born 1981-1996)
- **Needs and Preferences**:
  - Value meaningful work, continuous learning, and feedback.
  - Prefer collaborative work environments and are highly comfortable with technology.
  - Seek opportunities for growth, innovation, and work that aligns with their personal values.

- **Engagement Strategies:**
  - ○ Implement robust professional development programs, including certifications, workshops, and gamified learning.
  - ○ Foster a culture of continuous feedback, where Millennials receive regular, constructive input on their performance.
  - ○ Align work assignments with the organization's mission and social impact initiatives, emphasizing the meaningfulness of their roles.

D. Generation Z (Born 1997-2012)

- **Needs and Preferences:**
  - ○ Value diversity, innovation, and the use of cutting-edge technology.
  - ○ Prefer clear communication, immediate feedback, and opportunities for rapid advancement.
  - ○ Highly adaptable and entrepreneurial, seeking roles that offer variety and challenge.

- **Engagement Strategies:**
  - ○ Utilize technology-driven tools for communication, learning, and performance tracking.
  - ○ Offer micro-learning opportunities and career paths that allow for quick advancement based on merit.
  - ○ Promote a diverse and inclusive work environment that values different perspectives and ideas.

2. Fostering Intergenerational Collaboration and Knowledge Transfer

A. Mentorship and Reverse Mentorship Programs

- **Mentorship:** Pair experienced employees (often Baby Boomers and Generation X) with younger employees (Millennials and Generation Z) in formal mentorship programs. This allows for the transfer of institutional knowledge, best practices, and professional wisdom.
- **Reverse Mentorship:** Implement reverse mentorship programs where younger employees mentor older colleagues on technology, social media, and new healthcare trends. This fosters mutual respect and learning across generations.

B. Cross-Generational Teams

- **Diverse Teams:** Create cross-generational teams for projects and committees. This diversity in perspectives can lead to innovative solutions and a deeper understanding of different work styles and strengths.
- **Intergenerational Training:** Develop training programs that encourage collaboration between generations. For example, workshops on communication styles, conflict resolution, and teamwork can help bridge generational gaps.

C. Knowledge Management Systems

- **Knowledge Repositories:** Develop digital repositories where employees can document and share knowledge, such as clinical guidelines, best practices, and case studies. This ensures that valuable knowledge is preserved and accessible to all generations.
- **Communities of Practice:** Establish communities of practice where employees across generations can share insights, discuss challenges, and collaborate on improving patient care. These forums can be both in-person and online, accommodating different preferences.

3. Measuring the Success of Engagement and Retention Strategies

A. Employee Satisfaction and Engagement Surveys

- **Regular Surveys:** Conduct regular employee satisfaction and engagement surveys segmented by generation to assess the effectiveness of engagement strategies. Look for trends in satisfaction, retention, and perceived value of programs.
- **Focus Groups:** Hold focus groups with representatives from each generation to gather deeper insights into their experiences and needs. Use this information to tailor engagement initiatives further.

B. Retention Rates and Turnover Analysis

- **Generational Retention Rates:** Track retention rates by generation to see if specific strategies are effectively retaining employees. A reduction in turnover, particularly in younger cohorts, indicates successful engagement.

- **Exit Interviews**: Use exit interviews to understand why employees are leaving and whether generational needs are being met. This feedback is invaluable for adjusting strategies.

C. Performance and Productivity Metrics

- **Team Performance**: Evaluate the performance of cross-generational teams on key projects to determine the impact of intergenerational collaboration. Look for improvements in innovation, problem-solving, and project outcomes.
- **Learning and Development Outcomes**: Measure participation and success rates in professional development programs, particularly those that incorporate technology and gamification. High participation and positive outcomes indicate effective engagement.

D. Organizational Culture and Mission Alignment

- **Cultural Assessments**: Conduct cultural assessments to gauge how well the organization's culture supports intergenerational collaboration and aligns with the mission. This includes evaluating diversity, inclusion, and the sense of belonging across generations.
- **Mission-Driven Engagement**: Monitor the alignment of work assignments and organizational initiatives with the overall mission. Employees who see their work as meaningful and aligned with the mission are more likely to be engaged and committed to the organization.

By thoughtfully integrating technology into workforce engagement strategies and creating a comprehensive plan that addresses the needs of a multigenerational workforce, nurse executives can foster a more cohesive, motivated, and productive healthcare team. Balancing the benefits of technology with the potential challenges, while promoting intergenerational collaboration and continuous learning, will lead to a more resilient and adaptive organization.

Health Care Delivery

Patient-Centered Medical Homes (PCMH) and Their Impact on Primary Care Delivery

The Patient-Centered Medical Home (PCMH) is a model of primary care that emphasizes comprehensive, coordinated, and accessible care that is focused on the patient's needs and preferences. This model is designed to improve the quality of care, enhance the patient experience, and reduce healthcare costs by fostering strong patient-provider relationships and utilizing a team-based approach to care.

Core Components of PCMH

1. **Comprehensive Care:**
   o **Description:** PCMHs provide comprehensive care by addressing the majority of each patient's physical and mental healthcare needs, including preventive, acute, and chronic care. A team of healthcare providers, including physicians, nurses, pharmacists, and social workers, collaborate to deliver this broad range of services.
   o **Impact:** By offering a full spectrum of care services within one model, PCMHs ensure continuity and reduce the need for patients to seek care outside the primary care setting, which can lead to better management of chronic conditions and reduced hospital admissions.

2. **Patient-Centered Care:**
   o **Description:** The PCMH model emphasizes care that is respectful of and responsive to individual patient preferences, needs, and values. Patients are treated as active participants in their care, with an emphasis on shared decision-making and personalized care plans.
   o **Impact:** This focus on patient-centered care improves patient satisfaction and engagement, leading to better adherence to treatment plans and more positive health outcomes.

3. **Coordinated Care:**
   o **Description:** PCMHs ensure that care is coordinated across all elements of the healthcare system, including specialty care, hospitals, home health care, and community services. This is achieved through effective communication, shared electronic health records (EHRs), and care coordination efforts.
   o **Impact:** Coordinated care reduces redundancies, avoids unnecessary tests and procedures, and ensures that patients receive the right care at the right time, contributing to improved health outcomes and lower costs.

4. **Accessible Services:**
   o **Description:** PCMHs strive to make healthcare services more accessible by offering extended hours, short waiting times, and around-the-clock access to care teams through phone or electronic communication. Telehealth services may also be included to enhance accessibility.
   o **Impact:** Improved access to care increases patient satisfaction, reduces emergency department visits, and supports timely interventions that prevent complications from worsening.

5. **Quality and Safety:**
   o **Description:** PCMHs are committed to continuous quality improvement through the use of evidence-based medicine, performance measurement, and a focus on patient safety. This includes regularly monitoring and improving clinical outcomes and patient experiences.
   o **Impact:** The emphasis on quality and safety helps to improve population health outcomes and reduces the likelihood of medical errors, which in turn lowers overall healthcare costs.

Addressing the Quadruple Aim of Healthcare

1. **Improving Patient Experience:**
   o PCMHs enhance the patient experience by prioritizing patient-centered care, ensuring that care is respectful, personalized, and responsive to individual needs. The emphasis on accessibility and coordinated care further improves patient satisfaction and trust in the healthcare system.

2. **Improving Population Health:**
   o By focusing on comprehensive and preventive care, PCMHs contribute to better management of chronic conditions, higher rates of preventive screenings, and more effective population health management. This proactive approach helps to reduce the incidence of disease and improve overall health outcomes across the population.

3. **Reducing Costs:**
   - The PCMH model reduces healthcare costs by decreasing the need for hospitalizations, emergency department visits, and specialty care through effective management of chronic conditions and coordinated care. The use of evidence-based practices and quality improvement initiatives also helps to eliminate unnecessary tests and procedures.
4. **Improving the Work Life of Healthcare Providers:**
   - PCMHs support healthcare providers by fostering a team-based approach to care, which helps to distribute the workload more evenly and reduce burnout. The model also emphasizes the use of technology, such as EHRs, to streamline administrative tasks and improve communication among care teams, allowing providers to focus more on patient care.

Effectiveness of Accountable Care Organizations (ACOs) in Improving Healthcare Quality and Reducing Costs

Accountable Care Organizations (ACOs) are groups of healthcare providers who voluntarily come together to provide coordinated, high-quality care to their Medicare patients. The goal of ACOs is to improve healthcare quality while reducing costs through better coordination and prevention of unnecessary services.

Evaluating the Effectiveness of ACOs

1. **Improving Healthcare Quality:**
   - ACOs focus on improving care coordination, which leads to better management of chronic conditions, reduced hospital readmissions, and higher patient satisfaction. ACOs also emphasize preventive care and the use of evidence-based practices, which contribute to improved health outcomes.
2. **Reducing Healthcare Costs:**
   - ACOs are designed to reduce costs by minimizing unnecessary tests, procedures, and hospitalizations. Through shared savings programs, ACOs are incentivized to reduce spending while maintaining or improving the quality of care. Successful ACOs have demonstrated the ability to lower overall Medicare spending while delivering high-quality care.

Comparing Different ACO Models

1. **Medicare Shared Savings Program (MSSP) ACOs:**
   - **Overview:** The MSSP is one of the most common ACO models, offering providers a share of any savings they achieve for Medicare by meeting specified quality benchmarks while keeping costs down. There are different tracks within the MSSP, ranging from upside-only risk (where providers share in savings but not losses) to two-sided risk (where providers can share in both savings and losses).
   - **Impact:** MSSP ACOs have shown moderate success in reducing costs and improving care quality. Upside-only models have been popular due to their lower financial risk, but they may not incentivize cost reduction as strongly as two-sided risk models.
2. **Next Generation ACOs:**
   - **Overview:** The Next Generation ACO model is an advanced version of the MSSP, designed for organizations experienced in coordinating care for populations. This model allows for greater financial risk and reward, including capitation payment models, which provide more predictable revenue streams for providers.
   - **Impact:** Next Generation ACOs have demonstrated significant success in reducing costs while maintaining or improving care quality. The model's flexibility in payment options and greater emphasis on financial risk has driven more aggressive cost-saving measures and innovations in care delivery.
3. **Key Differences:**
   - **Risk and Reward:** Next Generation ACOs take on greater financial risk compared to MSSP ACOs, which can lead to higher savings but also higher potential losses. This increased risk is balanced by the opportunity for greater rewards, making the model more attractive to organizations with experience in managing large populations.
   - **Flexibility:** Next Generation ACOs offer more flexibility in payment models, including the option for full capitation, which is not available in MSSP. This flexibility allows providers to tailor the financial arrangements to their specific needs and capabilities.

Both PCMHs and ACOs are transformative models that align with the goals of the quadruple aim in healthcare. PCMHs enhance primary care delivery by focusing on patient-centered, coordinated, and accessible care, which improves patient experience, population health, and provider satisfaction while reducing costs. ACOs, particularly through models like MSSP and Next Generation ACOs, have shown effectiveness in improving healthcare quality and reducing costs by incentivizing coordinated care and the elimination of unnecessary services. While both models face challenges, their continued evolution and implementation across healthcare systems offer promising pathways to achieving high-value care for patients.

Implementing a Patient-Centered Medical Home (PCMH) Model in a Large Urban Health System
The Patient-Centered Medical Home (PCMH) model is a care delivery framework that emphasizes coordinated, patient-centered care through a team-based approach. Implementing this model in a large urban health system requires careful planning, addressing challenges like care coordination, health information technology (HIT) integration, and securing provider buy-in.
1. Strategy for Implementing the PCMH Model
A. Building a Foundation for Care Coordination

- **Team-Based Care Approach**: Establish multidisciplinary care teams that include primary care physicians, nurses, care coordinators, social workers, and other allied health professionals. Each team should be responsible for managing a panel of patients, ensuring comprehensive care across the continuum.
- **Care Coordination Roles**: Clearly define roles and responsibilities for care coordinators who will serve as the primary point of contact for patients. They will manage referrals, follow-ups, and care transitions to ensure that care is seamless and patient-centered.
- **Patient Engagement**: Implement patient engagement strategies that include regular communication, education on self-management, and shared decision-making. Encourage patients to take an active role in their care plans, fostering a partnership between the patient and the care team.

B. Health Information Technology (HIT) Integration

- **Electronic Health Records (EHR) Optimization**: Enhance the EHR system to support PCMH requirements, such as care planning, coordination, and population health management. The EHR should facilitate easy sharing of patient information among care team members and support real-time data access.
- **Interoperability**: Ensure that the EHR system is interoperable with other systems used by specialists, hospitals, and external care providers. This enables the seamless exchange of patient data, which is critical for coordinated care.
- **Data Analytics**: Implement data analytics tools to track patient outcomes, identify high-risk patients, and manage population health. Use this data to inform care strategies and measure the impact of the PCMH model on patient outcomes.

C. Securing Provider Buy-In

- **Education and Training**: Provide comprehensive education and training on the PCMH model, focusing on the benefits for patients, providers, and the health system. Training should cover team-based care, care coordination, and the use of HIT in managing patient care.
- **Incentives for Providers**: Offer incentives for providers to participate in the PCMH model, such as bonuses tied to quality metrics, patient satisfaction, or efficiency improvements. Highlight how the model can reduce workload through better team collaboration and support.
- **Leadership Support**: Engage organizational leadership to champion the PCMH model. Leadership should communicate the importance of the transition, support providers during the change, and allocate the necessary resources for successful implementation.

D. Addressing Specific Urban Health Challenges

- **Social Determinants of Health (SDOH)**: Integrate strategies to address SDOH, such as transportation, housing, and food security, into the PCMH model. Care coordinators should connect patients with community resources and services that address these broader health factors.

- **Cultural Competency**: Provide cultural competency training for all staff to ensure that care is respectful of and responsive to the diverse cultural needs of the urban population. Tailor communication, education, and care plans to meet the unique needs of different cultural groups.

2. Overcoming Challenges

A. Care Coordination Challenges

- **Fragmented Care**: Address the fragmentation of care by enhancing communication and collaboration across different care settings. Establish clear protocols for information sharing and care transitions.
- **Patient Navigation**: Implement patient navigation services to help patients understand and access the complex healthcare system, ensuring they receive timely and appropriate care.

B. HIT Integration Challenges

- **EHR Adoption and Usage**: Provide ongoing support for EHR adoption, ensuring that all providers are comfortable with the technology. Offer training sessions and on-site support to address issues as they arise.
- **Security and Privacy**: Strengthen data security measures to protect patient information. Ensure compliance with HIPAA and other regulations, and educate staff on best practices for data privacy.

C. Provider Buy-In Challenges

- **Resistance to Change**: Address resistance by involving providers in the planning and implementation process. Use pilot projects to demonstrate the effectiveness of the PCMH model and gather feedback for improvement.
- **Time Constraints**: Mitigate concerns about time constraints by streamlining administrative tasks through the EHR system and optimizing workflows. Highlight how the model can ultimately save time through better care coordination and reduced duplication of services.

The Role of Telehealth in Expanding Access to Care and Improving Health Outcomes

Telehealth has become a critical component in expanding access to healthcare services, particularly for underserved populations, and improving health outcomes by offering timely, convenient, and effective care. However, the adoption of telehealth presents challenges, such as reimbursement issues and technology infrastructure, which nurse executives must address.

1. Expanding Access to Care

A. Reaching Underserved Populations

- **Rural and Remote Areas**: Telehealth can bridge the gap for patients in rural or remote areas who have limited access to healthcare providers. Through virtual consultations, patients can access specialty care without the need to travel long distances.
- **Chronic Disease Management**: Telehealth enables continuous monitoring and management of chronic conditions, allowing patients to receive regular check-ins and adjustments to their care plans without frequent in-person visits.

B. Enhancing Convenience and Efficiency

- **Flexible Scheduling**: Telehealth offers flexibility in scheduling appointments, making it easier for patients to fit healthcare into their busy lives. This can reduce no-show rates and improve adherence to treatment plans.
- **Timely Care**: Virtual consultations can reduce wait times for appointments, allowing patients to receive care more quickly. This timely intervention can prevent conditions from worsening and reduce the need for emergency care.

C. Reducing Healthcare Costs

- **Lower Overhead Costs**: Telehealth can reduce overhead costs associated with maintaining physical facilities, allowing providers to allocate resources more efficiently.
- **Preventing Hospitalizations**: By enabling early intervention and continuous monitoring, telehealth can help prevent hospitalizations, reducing healthcare costs for both patients and the system.

2. Overcoming Barriers to Telehealth Adoption

A. Reimbursement Challenges

- **Advocacy for Policy Changes**: Nurse executives should advocate for policy changes at the state and federal levels to ensure that telehealth services are reimbursed at parity with in-person visits. This includes lobbying for the expansion of telehealth coverage under Medicare, Medicaid, and private insurance.
- **Flexible Payment Models**: Explore flexible payment models that support telehealth, such as bundled payments or value-based care arrangements. These models can incentivize providers to offer telehealth services as part of comprehensive care packages.
- **Negotiating with Payers**: Engage in negotiations with private payers to secure fair reimbursement rates for telehealth services. Highlight the cost-effectiveness and improved outcomes associated with telehealth to strengthen the case for reimbursement.

B. Technology Infrastructure Challenges

- **Improving Access to Technology**: Work with community organizations and government programs to improve access to the necessary technology for telehealth, such as internet access and devices. Consider providing low-cost devices or partnering with technology companies to support patients in need.
- **Training for Providers and Patients**: Provide training and support for both providers and patients to ensure they can effectively use telehealth platforms. This includes technical support, tutorials, and user-friendly interfaces that accommodate varying levels of digital literacy.
- **Investing in Secure Platforms**: Ensure that telehealth platforms are secure and compliant with privacy regulations. Invest in technology that offers robust data protection and is easy to integrate with existing EHR systems.

C. Addressing Digital Divide and Equity

- **Equity in Telehealth**: Address the digital divide by ensuring that telehealth services are accessible to all patients, including those from low-income or technologically disadvantaged backgrounds. This may involve providing telehealth access points in community centers or clinics.
- **Cultural Competency in Telehealth**: Ensure that telehealth services are culturally competent and accessible to non-English speaking patients. This includes offering language translation services and culturally appropriate care through virtual platforms.

3. Measuring the Impact of Telehealth

A. Patient Satisfaction and Access Metrics

- **Patient Satisfaction Surveys**: Regularly survey patients who use telehealth services to assess their satisfaction with the technology, the care received, and the overall experience.
- **Access Metrics**: Track metrics such as the number of patients served via telehealth, the geographic reach of telehealth services, and reductions in wait times for appointments.

B. Health Outcomes and Cost Savings

- **Clinical Outcomes**: Monitor the impact of telehealth on clinical outcomes, such as disease management, hospitalization rates, and adherence to treatment plans.
- **Cost Analysis**: Conduct a cost-benefit analysis to determine the financial impact of telehealth, including savings from reduced hospitalizations, lower overhead costs, and improved care efficiency.

C. Provider Adoption and Utilization

- **Provider Feedback**: Collect feedback from providers on the effectiveness of telehealth in their practice, including ease of use, integration with workflows, and patient engagement.
- **Utilization Rates**: Track the utilization rates of telehealth services among providers and identify any barriers to adoption. Use this data to inform training and support initiatives.

By implementing a comprehensive strategy for the PCMH model and leveraging telehealth to expand access to care, nurse executives can improve care coordination, enhance patient outcomes, and increase operational efficiency. Addressing the challenges associated with both initiatives—such as care coordination, technology integration, provider buy-in, and reimbursement—will be crucial for their successful implementation and long-term sustainability.

Comprehensive Digital Health Strategy for a Multi-Hospital System

Objective: To create a cohesive digital health strategy that enhances patient care, improves operational efficiency, and supports the multi-hospital system's strategic goals. The strategy integrates remote patient monitoring, mobile health apps, and artificial intelligence (AI)-driven clinical decision support tools to optimize patient outcomes and streamline healthcare delivery.

1. Remote Patient Monitoring (RPM)

1. **Overview:**
   - **Technology:** Deploy RPM systems to monitor patients' vital signs, chronic disease markers, and other health metrics from their homes or long-term care facilities. Devices may include wearable sensors, connected scales, blood pressure monitors, and glucose meters.
   - **Integration:** Ensure that RPM data integrates seamlessly with the hospitals' electronic health records (EHRs), enabling real-time data access for healthcare providers.

2. **Implementation:**
   - **Target Populations:** Focus initially on high-risk populations, such as patients with chronic conditions (e.g., diabetes, heart failure) or those recently discharged from the hospital who require close follow-up.
   - **Patient Engagement:** Use patient education materials and training sessions to ensure that patients and caregivers understand how to use RPM devices effectively. Incorporate telehealth consultations to enhance engagement and adherence.
   - **Data Management:** Develop a centralized data management system to collect and analyze RPM data. Use predictive analytics to identify trends and potential issues, allowing for proactive intervention.

3. **Impact:**
   - **Reduced Readmissions:** RPM helps prevent complications by allowing early detection of health issues, thereby reducing hospital readmissions.
   - **Enhanced Chronic Disease Management:** Continuous monitoring leads to better management of chronic conditions, improving patient outcomes and quality of life.

2. Mobile Health Apps

1. **Overview:**
   - **Patient-Facing Apps:** Develop or partner with existing mobile health apps that allow patients to manage their health, access their medical records, schedule appointments, receive medication reminders, and communicate with their care teams.
   - **Provider-Facing Apps:** Implement mobile apps for healthcare providers that facilitate quick access to patient information, secure messaging, and clinical decision support tools on the go.

2. **Implementation:**
   - **Patient Portal Integration:** Integrate mobile health apps with the hospitals' patient portal to create a seamless user experience. This integration allows patients to view lab results, imaging reports, and visit summaries, enhancing their engagement and satisfaction.
   - **Customization and Accessibility:** Ensure apps are customizable to meet individual patient needs, and design them to be user-friendly and accessible for patients of all ages and tech-savviness levels.
   - **Behavioral Health Integration:** Include features for mental health support, such as mood tracking, cognitive behavioral therapy exercises, and access to virtual counseling services.

3. **Impact:**
   - **Increased Patient Engagement:** Mobile apps empower patients to take an active role in their health management, leading to better adherence to treatment plans and improved health outcomes.
   - **Operational Efficiency:** Provider-facing apps streamline workflow, reduce administrative burdens, and enable quicker decision-making, ultimately enhancing care delivery.

3. Artificial Intelligence (AI)-Driven Clinical Decision Support Tools

1. **Overview:**
   - **AI Algorithms:** Implement AI-driven tools that assist clinicians in diagnosing conditions, predicting patient outcomes, and recommending treatment options. These tools analyze vast amounts of patient data to identify patterns that might not be apparent to human providers.

- o **Use Cases:** Focus on areas such as early detection of sepsis, risk stratification for cardiovascular events, and personalized treatment recommendations for cancer patients.

2. **Implementation:**
   - o **EHR Integration:** Integrate AI tools directly into the EHR system, ensuring that they are part of the clinicians' existing workflows. This integration is crucial for maximizing the utility and adoption of AI in clinical settings.
   - o **Training and Support:** Provide training sessions for clinicians on how to effectively use AI tools in their decision-making processes. Ensure that there is ongoing support and troubleshooting available.
   - o **Ethical Considerations:** Develop guidelines for the use of AI in clinical practice, addressing issues such as transparency, bias, and patient consent.

3. **Impact:**
   - o **Improved Diagnostic Accuracy:** AI tools can enhance diagnostic accuracy by providing evidence-based recommendations and reducing the likelihood of human error.
   - o **Personalized Care:** AI-driven insights allow for more personalized care plans, improving patient outcomes and satisfaction.

4. Data Security and Privacy

1. **Overview:**
   - o **Compliance:** Ensure that all digital health tools comply with relevant regulations such as HIPAA to protect patient data. Implement robust cybersecurity measures to prevent breaches and unauthorized access.
   - o **Patient Consent:** Obtain explicit patient consent for the use of RPM devices, mobile health apps, and AI tools, ensuring they understand how their data will be used.

2. **Implementation:**
   - o **Encryption:** Use end-to-end encryption for all data transmitted between devices, apps, and hospital systems.
   - o **Regular Audits:** Conduct regular security audits to identify and address potential vulnerabilities in the digital health infrastructure.

3. **Impact:**
   - o **Patient Trust:** Strong data security measures build patient trust in digital health tools, increasing their willingness to use these technologies.

5. Measuring Success

1. **Key Performance Indicators (KPIs):**
   - o **Patient Outcomes:** Track improvements in patient outcomes, such as reduced readmission rates, better chronic disease management, and increased patient satisfaction scores.
   - o **Operational Efficiency:** Measure reductions in administrative time, improvements in clinical decision-making speed, and overall cost savings.
   - o **Adoption Rates:** Monitor the adoption and usage rates of RPM devices, mobile apps, and AI tools among both patients and providers.

2. **Continuous Improvement:**
   - o **Feedback Loops:** Establish feedback loops with patients and providers to gather insights on their experiences with the digital health tools. Use this feedback to make iterative improvements to the strategy.
   - o **Ongoing Training:** Provide ongoing training and support to ensure that staff remain proficient in using digital health tools and are aware of any updates or new features.

Ethical Principles in Healthcare Leadership: Autonomy, Beneficence, Non-Maleficence, and Justice

Healthcare leadership is deeply rooted in ethical principles that guide decision-making in complex scenarios. The four key principles—autonomy, beneficence, non-maleficence, and justice—serve as foundational elements in the ethical framework for leaders.

1. Autonomy

- **Definition:** Autonomy refers to respecting the right of individuals to make decisions about their own lives and medical care. In healthcare, this means respecting patients' rights to make informed decisions about their treatment options.
- **Application in Leadership:**
    - ○ **Patient-Centered Care:** Leaders must ensure that policies and practices uphold patient autonomy by promoting informed consent, respecting advance directives, and providing accurate and comprehensive information to patients.
    - ○ **Staff Autonomy:** Beyond patient care, healthcare leaders must also respect the autonomy of healthcare providers by involving them in decision-making processes and supporting their professional judgment.
- **Complex Scenarios:**
    - ○ **End-of-Life Decisions:** In cases where patients face end-of-life decisions, leaders must navigate the tension between respecting patient autonomy and ensuring that patients have all the information they need to make informed choices.

2. Beneficence

- **Definition:** Beneficence involves acting in the best interest of the patient by promoting good and preventing harm. This principle requires healthcare providers and leaders to prioritize actions that benefit patients and improve their health and well-being.
- **Application in Leadership:**
    - ○ **Quality Improvement Initiatives:** Leaders must champion initiatives that enhance patient care, such as implementing evidence-based practices, investing in staff education, and improving healthcare infrastructure.
    - ○ **Holistic Care Models:** Leaders can promote holistic care models that address not only physical health but also emotional, social, and psychological well-being, thus fulfilling the principle of beneficence.
- **Complex Scenarios:**
    - ○ **Resource Allocation:** Leaders often face decisions where they must balance the benefits of certain treatments or technologies with their costs and availability, ensuring that the resources used indeed lead to a significant net benefit.

3. Non-Maleficence

- **Definition:** Non-maleficence means "do no harm." It obliges healthcare providers and leaders to avoid actions that could cause unnecessary harm or suffering to patients.
- **Application in Leadership:**
    - ○ **Risk Management:** Leaders must implement robust risk management strategies to minimize harm, including strict adherence to safety protocols, infection control measures, and regular training for staff.
    - ○ **Ethical Decision-Making:** In decision-making, leaders must carefully consider the potential risks of proposed actions, ensuring that any harm is minimized and outweighed by the benefits.
- **Complex Scenarios:**
    - ○ **Invasive Procedures:** When considering the introduction of new, potentially risky procedures or treatments, leaders must weigh the potential harms against the anticipated benefits, ensuring that patient safety is the foremost concern.

4. Justice

- **Definition:** Justice in healthcare refers to fairness in the distribution of resources, treatments, and opportunities. It requires that all patients are treated equally and that disparities in care are addressed.
- **Application in Leadership:**
    - ○ **Equitable Access to Care:** Leaders are responsible for ensuring that healthcare services are distributed fairly, with particular attention to underserved populations. This includes advocating for policies that reduce health disparities and improve access to care for all patients.

- o **Fair Employment Practices:** Justice also applies to the fair treatment of healthcare workers, ensuring that hiring, promotion, and compensation practices are equitable and free from discrimination.
- **Complex Scenarios:**
  - o **Resource Scarcity:** In situations of limited resources, such as during a pandemic, leaders must make difficult decisions about how to allocate resources fairly and justly, ensuring that all patients receive appropriate care based on need.

Integrating Ethical Principles into Leadership Decision-Making

1. **Ethical Committees:**
   - o Establishing ethics committees that include a diverse group of stakeholders can help leaders navigate complex decisions, ensuring that all ethical principles are considered.
2. **Training and Education:**
   - o Regular training on ethical principles and their application in healthcare leadership can equip leaders with the tools to make informed and balanced decisions.
3. **Transparency and Accountability:**
   - o Leaders should ensure transparency in decision-making processes, providing clear rationales for their decisions, particularly when ethical dilemmas arise. This builds trust and accountability within the organization.
4. **Stakeholder Engagement:**
   - o Engaging patients, staff, and community members in decision-making processes ensures that diverse perspectives are considered, promoting justice and respecting autonomy.

By integrating these ethical principles into their decision-making processes, healthcare leaders can navigate the complexities of the healthcare environment while upholding the highest standards of patient care and organizational integrity.

Analyzing the ANA Code of Ethics for Nurses with Interpretive Statements

The American Nurses Association (ANA) Code of Ethics for Nurses with Interpretive Statements serves as a foundational document guiding the ethical practice of nursing. It provides a framework for making ethical decisions and outlines the duties and obligations of nurses to patients, the public, and the profession. For nurse executives, integrating these ethical standards into organizational policies and practices is essential for fostering a culture of ethical practice and ensuring that patient care is delivered with integrity and compassion.

1. Overview of the ANA Code of Ethics

The ANA Code of Ethics consists of nine provisions, each accompanied by interpretive statements that provide further guidance. These provisions cover a wide range of ethical responsibilities, including respect for human dignity, patient advocacy, accountability, and commitment to personal and professional growth. Key themes include:

- **Provision 1: Respect for Human Dignity:** Nurses must practice with compassion and respect for the inherent dignity, worth, and unique attributes of every person.
- **Provision 2: Commitment to the Patient:** The nurse's primary commitment is to the patient, whether an individual, family, group, community, or population.
- **Provision 3: Advocacy for Patient Rights:** Nurses must advocate for the rights, health, and safety of patients.
- **Provision 4: Accountability and Responsibility:** Nurses are responsible and accountable for their own practice and must take action to ensure patient safety and quality of care.
- **Provision 5: Duty to Self and Others:** Nurses owe the same duties to themselves as to others, including the responsibility to preserve integrity and safety, maintain competence, and continue personal and professional growth.
- **Provision 6: Environment and Ethical Obligation:** Nurses must establish, maintain, and improve the ethical environment of the work setting and conditions of employment.
- **Provision 7: Contributions to the Profession:** Nurses should contribute to the advancement of the profession through practice, education, administration, and knowledge development.

- **Provision 8: Collaboration for Public Health**: Nurses must collaborate with other health professionals and the public to protect human rights, promote health diplomacy, and reduce health disparities.
- **Provision 9: Social Justice**: Nurses must articulate nursing values, maintain the integrity of the profession, and integrate principles of social justice into nursing and health policy.

2. Integrating the ANA Code of Ethics into Organizational Policies and Practices

A. Policy Development

- **Ethical Guidelines and Protocols**: Develop and implement organizational policies that explicitly reflect the provisions of the ANA Code of Ethics. For example, policies on patient consent, privacy, and advocacy should align with the ethical standards outlined in the Code.
- **Ethics Committees**: Establish or strengthen ethics committees within the organization to provide oversight and guidance on complex ethical issues. These committees should include representatives from nursing, medical, legal, and administrative backgrounds.
- **Inclusive Policy-Making**: Involve nursing staff at all levels in the development and review of policies to ensure that they reflect the values and ethical principles of the nursing profession. This promotes a sense of ownership and accountability among nurses.

B. Education and Training

- **Ethics Education**: Incorporate the ANA Code of Ethics into the orientation program for new hires and ongoing education for all nursing staff. This ensures that nurses understand their ethical obligations and how to apply them in practice.
- **Case Studies and Simulations**: Use case studies and simulations to help nurses and other healthcare providers apply the Code of Ethics in real-world scenarios. These exercises can be particularly effective in discussing difficult issues such as end-of-life care or patient advocacy.
- **Continuing Education**: Offer continuing education courses focused on ethical decision-making and the application of the ANA Code of Ethics. Encourage nurses to pursue certifications in ethics or related fields.

C. Promoting an Ethical Culture

- **Ethical Leadership**: Nurse executives must model ethical behavior and decision-making, demonstrating a commitment to the principles outlined in the ANA Code of Ethics. This includes transparency, integrity, and a focus on patient-centered care.
- **Open Communication**: Foster an environment where nurses feel comfortable discussing ethical concerns without fear of retaliation. Encourage open dialogue about ethical challenges and provide support for nurses facing difficult decisions.
- **Recognition and Accountability**: Recognize and reward ethical behavior in nursing practice. At the same time, hold staff accountable for actions that violate ethical standards, ensuring that there are clear consequences for unethical behavior.

D. Monitoring and Evaluation

- **Ethics Audits**: Regularly conduct ethics audits to assess how well the organization's policies and practices align with the ANA Code of Ethics. Use the findings to make improvements and address any gaps in ethical compliance.
- **Feedback Mechanisms**: Implement mechanisms for nurses to provide feedback on ethical issues they encounter in their practice. Use this feedback to refine policies and provide additional support where needed.
- **Outcome Measurement**: Measure the impact of ethical practices on patient outcomes, staff satisfaction, and overall organizational performance. Use these metrics to demonstrate the value of integrating ethical standards into organizational operations.

Applying Ethical Decision-Making Frameworks to Resolve a Complex Ethical Dilemma

Scenario: Resource Allocation During a Pandemic

Situation: A large urban hospital is facing a severe shortage of ventilators during a pandemic. The demand for ventilators far exceeds the available supply, forcing the healthcare team to make difficult decisions about which patients will receive this life-saving treatment. The ethical dilemma centers on how to allocate limited resources fairly and justly while maximizing the number of lives saved.

Ethical Decision-Making Framework: The Four-Box Method

The Four-Box Method, developed by Jonsen, Siegler, and Winslade, is a widely used framework for analyzing ethical dilemmas in clinical practice. It divides the decision-making process into four categories: Medical Indications, Patient Preferences, Quality of Life, and Contextual Features.

A. Medical Indications

- **Patient Condition**: Assess the medical condition of each patient requiring a ventilator. Consider factors such as the severity of illness, likelihood of recovery, and the potential benefits and burdens of ventilator support.
- **Prognosis**: Evaluate the prognosis for each patient if they receive ventilator support versus if they do not. Patients with a higher likelihood of survival and recovery with ventilator support might be prioritized.

B. Patient Preferences

- **Advance Directives**: Review advance directives and other documentation of patient preferences regarding life-sustaining treatment. Patients who have expressed a desire not to receive aggressive interventions may be deprioritized for ventilator allocation.
- **Capacity for Decision-Making**: Consider the capacity of patients to participate in decision-making. For patients who are unable to communicate their preferences, surrogates or legal representatives should be consulted.

C. Quality of Life

- **Expected Quality of Life**: Consider the expected quality of life for each patient after recovery. This includes assessing both physical and cognitive outcomes. Patients with a reasonable expectation of returning to a good quality of life may be given priority.
- **Potential for Suffering**: Evaluate the potential for prolonged suffering or a significant decline in quality of life even with the use of a ventilator. In some cases, it may be more ethical to prioritize patients with a better overall prognosis.

D. Contextual Features

- **Justice and Fairness**: Ensure that the allocation process is fair and equitable, avoiding discrimination based on age, disability, socioeconomic status, or other non-clinical factors. Consider implementing a random allocation system (e.g., lottery) if patients have similar medical indications.
- **Resource Availability**: Factor in the overall availability of resources, including ventilators, staff, and supportive care. Ensure that decisions are consistent across the organization and that clear guidelines are followed.
- **Legal and Policy Considerations**: Adhere to legal requirements and organizational policies regarding resource allocation. Ensure that the decision-making process is transparent and that all stakeholders are informed.

Resolution: Using the Four-Box Method, the hospital creates a transparent, consistent, and ethically sound process for allocating ventilators. The process includes a multidisciplinary committee that reviews each case based on medical indications, patient preferences, quality of life, and contextual factors. This committee ensures that decisions are made fairly and in alignment with both ethical standards and legal obligations.

Applying the MORAL Model

Scenario: Genetic Testing and Privacy

Situation: A patient undergoing genetic testing at a large healthcare facility discovers they carry a gene associated with a high risk for a serious hereditary condition. The patient's family members could also be at risk, but the patient is reluctant to share this information with them due to concerns about privacy and potential discrimination.

Ethical Decision-Making Framework: The MORAL Model

The MORAL Model is a structured approach to ethical decision-making in healthcare. It stands for Massage the dilemma, Outline the options, Resolve the dilemma, Act by applying the chosen option, and Look back and evaluate the process.

A. Massage the Dilemma

- **Identify the Ethical Conflict**: The ethical conflict involves the patient's right to privacy versus the potential harm to family members who are unaware of their genetic risk. The dilemma is whether to respect the patient's wishes or to disclose the information to at-risk relatives.

- **Gather Relevant Information**: Collect information on the patient's concerns, the implications of genetic testing for the patient and their family, and the potential legal and ethical implications of disclosing genetic information without consent.

B. Outline the Options

- **Option 1: Respect Patient Privacy**: Respect the patient's decision not to disclose their genetic information to family members, upholding their right to privacy and autonomy.
- **Option 2: Encourage Voluntary Disclosure**: Counsel the patient on the importance of sharing the information with at-risk relatives, providing support and resources to facilitate this process.
- **Option 3: Disclose Without Consent**: Disclose the genetic information to at-risk relatives without the patient's consent, prioritizing the principle of nonmaleficence (preventing harm).

C. Resolve the Dilemma

- **Ethical Principles**: Weigh the ethical principles of autonomy, beneficence, nonmaleficence, and justice. Autonomy supports the patient's right to privacy, while beneficence and nonmaleficence support the protection of family members from harm.
- **Decision**: The recommended resolution is to prioritize voluntary disclosure by the patient, with the healthcare team providing strong encouragement and resources. If the patient refuses, the decision to disclose without consent should be carefully considered in consultation with legal and ethical experts, weighing the potential harm to family members.

D. Act by Applying the Chosen Option

- **Implement the Decision**: The healthcare provider will have a candid conversation with the patient, emphasizing the potential benefits of informing family members and offering support throughout the process. If the patient remains adamant, further steps will be taken in consultation with the ethics committee and legal advisors.

E. Look Back and Evaluate the Process

- **Review the Outcome**: Evaluate the outcome of the decision, including whether the patient disclosed the information and how the family responded. Assess the ethical process used to make the decision and identify any areas for improvement.
- **Document the Decision**: Ensure that the decision-making process and the outcome are well-documented, including the ethical considerations that informed the final decision.

By integrating the ANA Code of Ethics into organizational practices and applying ethical decision-making frameworks like the Four-Box Method and the MORAL model, nurse executives can navigate complex ethical dilemmas while upholding the highest standards of patient care and professional integrity.

Evaluating the Ethical Implications of Emerging Healthcare Technologies

Emerging healthcare technologies such as CRISPR gene editing and AI-driven diagnostics hold tremendous potential to revolutionize medicine, offering new ways to treat diseases, improve patient outcomes, and enhance healthcare delivery. However, these technologies also raise significant ethical concerns that must be carefully considered by healthcare leaders, including nurse executives.

1. CRISPR Gene Editing

Ethical Implications:

1. **Autonomy and Consent:**
    - **Issue:** CRISPR technology allows for the editing of genes to prevent or treat genetic disorders. However, obtaining informed consent becomes complex when dealing with germline modifications (changes that are heritable). Patients may not fully understand the long-term implications of such edits, and future generations affected by these changes cannot consent.
    - **Consideration:** Nurse executives must ensure that patients receive comprehensive information about the risks, benefits, and uncertainties associated with gene editing. In cases involving potential future generations, ethical committees should be consulted to weigh the broader implications.
2. **Beneficence vs. Non-Maleficence:**

- o **Issue:** While CRISPR offers the possibility of curing genetic diseases, there are concerns about off-target effects (unintended genetic modifications) that could cause harm. The balance between beneficence (doing good) and non-maleficence (avoiding harm) is delicate.
- o **Consideration:** Before implementing CRISPR-based treatments, nurse executives must ensure rigorous testing and validation of the technology to minimize risks. Clinical trials should be carefully monitored, and patients should be informed about potential uncertainties.

3. **Equity and Justice:**
- o **Issue:** Access to CRISPR technology could be limited by cost, leading to disparities in who benefits from these advances. There is also the risk of "designer babies," where genetic modifications are used for non-medical enhancements, further exacerbating social inequalities.
- o **Consideration:** Nurse executives should advocate for equitable access to emerging technologies and work with policymakers to ensure that CRISPR is used ethically, focusing on therapeutic applications rather than enhancements.

2. AI-Driven Diagnostics
Ethical Implications:

1. **Accuracy and Accountability:**
- o **Issue:** AI-driven diagnostics rely on algorithms to analyze medical data and provide diagnostic recommendations. While AI can enhance diagnostic accuracy, there is a risk of errors, bias in algorithms, and over-reliance on technology.
- o **Consideration:** Nurse executives must ensure that AI tools are thoroughly validated and that healthcare providers are trained to interpret AI recommendations critically. There should also be clear protocols for accountability when AI-generated diagnoses lead to errors.

2. **Patient Privacy:**
- o **Issue:** AI systems require large datasets to function effectively, raising concerns about patient privacy and data security. There is also the potential for misuse of data if not properly governed.
- o **Consideration:** Nurse executives must prioritize robust data protection measures and ensure compliance with privacy regulations such as HIPAA. Patients should be informed about how their data will be used and have the option to opt out.

3. **Transparency and Trust:**
- o **Issue:** The "black box" nature of some AI algorithms, where the decision-making process is not fully transparent, can lead to distrust among patients and providers.
- o **Consideration:** Nurse executives should advocate for the use of explainable AI models where possible and ensure that providers can clearly communicate how AI tools contribute to clinical decisions. Building trust requires transparency and open communication about the role of AI in patient care.

Balancing Innovation with Patient Safety and Ethical Considerations

1. **Ethics Committees and Oversight:**
- o Establish or strengthen ethics committees within the organization to review the implementation of emerging technologies. These committees should include diverse stakeholders, including ethicists, clinicians, patients, and community representatives, to provide balanced perspectives on the ethical implications of new technologies.

2. **Pilot Programs and Phased Implementation:**
- o Before fully integrating emerging technologies, consider running pilot programs to evaluate their impact on patient care, safety, and ethical concerns. Collect data on outcomes, patient satisfaction, and ethical challenges, using this information to refine the implementation strategy.

3. **Ongoing Education and Training:**
- o Provide continuous education and training for healthcare providers on the ethical implications of emerging technologies. This training should cover both the technical aspects of the technology and the broader ethical considerations, ensuring that staff are well-equipped to make informed decisions.

4. **Patient and Public Engagement:**

- Engage patients and the public in discussions about the use of emerging technologies. This can be done through public forums, patient advisory boards, and informed consent processes that fully explain the potential risks and benefits of new technologies.

5. **Regulatory Compliance and Advocacy:**
   - Ensure that the adoption of new technologies complies with all relevant regulatory requirements. Nurse executives should also advocate for policies that promote the ethical use of emerging technologies and address concerns such as access, equity, and patient safety.

Developing an Ethics Education Program for Healthcare Staff

An effective ethics education program is crucial for equipping healthcare staff with the knowledge and skills to navigate common ethical dilemmas in various clinical settings. The program should be comprehensive, practical, and tailored to the specific needs of the organization.

1. Program Structure and Content
1. **Core Modules:**
   - **Introduction to Ethical Principles:**
     - Overview of the foundational ethical principles in healthcare: autonomy, beneficence, non-maleficence, and justice.
   - **Ethical Decision-Making Frameworks:**
     - Training on using ethical decision-making models, such as the Four-Box Method or the Ethics of Care approach, to analyze and resolve dilemmas.
   - **Informed Consent and Patient Autonomy:**
     - Emphasis on the importance of informed consent, strategies for ensuring patient understanding, and respecting patient autonomy, even in complex cases.
   - **Confidentiality and Privacy:**
     - Detailed exploration of confidentiality and privacy concerns, including HIPAA compliance and managing sensitive patient information in the digital age.
2. **Specialized Modules:**
   - **End-of-Life Care:**
     - Ethical considerations in palliative care, advance directives, and decisions regarding life-sustaining treatments.
   - **Emerging Technologies:**
     - Ethical implications of new technologies such as AI, telemedicine, and genetic testing. Case studies illustrating potential benefits and risks.
   - **Cultural Competence and Health Equity:**
     - Addressing disparities in care, understanding cultural differences, and promoting equitable treatment for all patients.
   - **Resource Allocation:**
     - Ethical challenges in resource allocation, particularly during crises such as pandemics, including triage protocols and the distribution of scarce resources.
3. **Interactive Components:**
   - **Case Studies and Role-Playing:**
     - Engage staff in analyzing real-world case studies and participating in role-playing exercises to practice ethical decision-making in a safe, controlled environment.
   - **Ethics Rounds:**
     - Regular ethics rounds where staff can discuss current ethical challenges they are facing in their practice, guided by ethics committee members or trained facilitators.
   - **Discussion Groups:**
     - Small group discussions that allow for deep dives into specific ethical issues, fostering peer learning and the exchange of diverse perspectives.

2. Measuring Program Effectiveness
1. **Pre- and Post-Training Assessments:**
   - **Knowledge and Attitudes:**

- Administer assessments before and after the training to measure changes in knowledge, understanding of ethical principles, and attitudes toward ethical decision-making.
  - o **Scenario-Based Testing:**
    - Use scenario-based questions to evaluate how participants would apply ethical principles in real-life situations, comparing responses before and after the training.
2. **Ethics Consultations and Incidents:**
   - o **Tracking Requests:**
     - Monitor the number and nature of ethics consultations requested before and after the program. A decrease in the need for consultations on routine issues may indicate improved staff confidence and competence.
   - o **Incident Reports:**
     - Analyze reports of ethical issues or breaches, looking for trends or improvements in how such situations are handled following the training.
3. **Participant Feedback:**
   - o **Surveys:**
     - Collect feedback from participants through surveys, focusing on the relevance, clarity, and applicability of the training content.
   - o **Focus Groups:**
     - Conduct focus groups with participants to gather qualitative insights into how the training has impacted their daily practice and decision-making.
4. **Patient Outcomes and Satisfaction:**
   - o **Correlating Ethical Decisions with Outcomes:**
     - Examine patient outcomes in cases where significant ethical decisions were made, assessing whether the outcomes align with ethical standards and patient satisfaction.
   - o **Patient Feedback:**
     - Include questions in patient satisfaction surveys about their perceptions of the ethical conduct of staff, particularly in situations involving informed consent, communication, and respect for patient autonomy.
5. **Ongoing Monitoring and Improvement:**
   - o **Continuous Evaluation:**
     - Implement a system for ongoing evaluation of the ethics education program, with periodic reviews and updates based on new developments in healthcare ethics, participant feedback, and emerging challenges.
   - o **Ethics Champion Program:**
     - Identify and train "ethics champions" within each department who can provide ongoing support, lead discussions, and serve as resources for their colleagues, ensuring that ethical considerations remain a central part of daily practice.

By carefully designing the ethics education program and employing a robust evaluation strategy, healthcare organizations can foster a culture of ethical awareness and decision-making, ultimately leading to improved patient care and staff satisfaction.

Designing a Comprehensive Cybersecurity Strategy for a Large Healthcare Organization

Healthcare organizations are prime targets for cyberattacks due to the sensitive nature of the data they handle. A comprehensive cybersecurity strategy must address various threats, including ransomware attacks, insider threats, and vulnerabilities in medical devices. The strategy should focus on prevention, detection, response, and recovery, ensuring that patient data remains secure while maintaining the integrity and availability of critical healthcare systems.

1. Threats and Corresponding Security Measures

A. Ransomware Attacks

- **Threat Overview**: Ransomware is a type of malware that encrypts data, rendering it inaccessible until a ransom is paid. Healthcare organizations are particularly vulnerable because of the critical need for continuous access to patient records and other essential data.
- **Preventive Measures**:
    - **Regular Backups**: Implement a robust backup strategy that includes regular, encrypted backups stored offsite or in the cloud. Ensure that backups are tested regularly to confirm they can be restored quickly in the event of an attack.
    - **Email Security**: Deploy advanced email filtering systems to detect and block phishing attempts, a common vector for ransomware. Train staff to recognize phishing emails and report suspicious activity.
    - **Patch Management**: Ensure that all systems, including operating systems, applications, and medical devices, are regularly updated with the latest security patches to protect against vulnerabilities that could be exploited by ransomware.
- **Detection and Response**:
    - **Intrusion Detection Systems (IDS)**: Implement IDS to monitor network traffic for signs of ransomware activity. Early detection can prevent the spread of ransomware across the network.
    - **Incident Response Plan**: Develop and regularly update an incident response plan specific to ransomware attacks. This plan should include steps for isolating affected systems, communicating with stakeholders, and restoring data from backups.

B. Insider Threats

- **Threat Overview**: Insider threats can come from employees, contractors, or business associates who have legitimate access to systems but misuse that access intentionally or unintentionally, leading to data breaches or other security incidents.
- **Preventive Measures**:
    - **Access Controls**: Implement strict access controls based on the principle of least privilege, ensuring that employees only have access to the data and systems necessary for their job functions. Regularly review and update access permissions.
    - **User Monitoring**: Use user activity monitoring tools to detect unusual or unauthorized access to sensitive data. Set up alerts for activities such as large data downloads, access to restricted areas, or off-hours access.
    - **Security Awareness Training**: Conduct regular training sessions for all employees on cybersecurity best practices, including how to recognize and report suspicious activity. Emphasize the importance of protecting patient data and the consequences of insider threats.
- **Detection and Response**:
    - **Behavioral Analytics**: Implement behavioral analytics software to identify patterns of behavior that may indicate an insider threat. For example, sudden changes in login patterns or access to data outside of normal job duties can trigger an investigation.
    - **Incident Reporting**: Establish a clear and anonymous reporting process for employees to report potential insider threats without fear of retaliation.

C. Medical Device Vulnerabilities

- **Threat Overview**: Medical devices, such as infusion pumps, imaging machines, and monitoring systems, often have vulnerabilities due to outdated software or lack of encryption. These devices can be targeted by cybercriminals to disrupt patient care or access sensitive data.
- **Preventive Measures**:
    - **Device Inventory and Risk Assessment**: Maintain an up-to-date inventory of all connected medical devices and conduct regular risk assessments to identify vulnerabilities. Prioritize devices based on their criticality to patient care and the potential impact of a breach.
    - **Segmentation and Isolation**: Segregate medical devices on a separate, secure network to limit the potential spread of malware or unauthorized access. Implement network segmentation to isolate devices in the event of a security breach.

- Vendor Management: Work closely with medical device manufacturers to ensure that devices are regularly updated with security patches. Establish clear expectations for cybersecurity in contracts with vendors and require compliance with industry standards.
- **Detection and Response**:
  - Continuous Monitoring: Deploy continuous monitoring tools to detect abnormal behavior or unauthorized access to medical devices. Ensure that alerts are investigated promptly by the cybersecurity team.
  - Emergency Procedures: Develop and practice emergency procedures for isolating and mitigating threats to medical devices, including protocols for maintaining patient care during a device-related cybersecurity incident.

2. Additional Security Measures

A. Data Encryption

- At Rest and In Transit: Ensure that all sensitive data, including patient records and financial information, is encrypted both at rest and in transit. Use strong encryption protocols to protect data from unauthorized access or interception.
- Secure Communication Channels: Implement secure communication channels, such as encrypted email and secure messaging platforms, for transmitting sensitive information within and outside the organization.

B. Multi-Factor Authentication (MFA)

- User Authentication: Require multi-factor authentication for access to all critical systems, including the EHR, financial systems, and administrative platforms. MFA adds an extra layer of security, making it more difficult for unauthorized users to gain access even if login credentials are compromised.
- Privileged Accounts: Apply additional security measures, such as hardware tokens or biometric authentication, for privileged accounts with access to highly sensitive data or systems.

C. Incident Response and Recovery

- Comprehensive Incident Response Plan: Develop a comprehensive incident response plan that covers all types of cyber threats, including ransomware, insider threats, and medical device vulnerabilities. Regularly test the plan through drills and tabletop exercises.
- Business Continuity and Disaster Recovery (BCDR): Integrate cybersecurity into the organization's BCDR plan to ensure that critical operations can continue in the event of a cyberattack. This includes maintaining access to patient records, ensuring the availability of medical devices, and restoring systems from backups.

D. Regular Security Audits and Assessments

- Vulnerability Assessments: Conduct regular vulnerability assessments and penetration testing to identify weaknesses in the organization's cybersecurity defenses. Address identified vulnerabilities promptly to minimize risk.
- Compliance Audits: Ensure compliance with healthcare cybersecurity regulations, such as HIPAA and HITECH, by conducting regular audits and addressing any gaps in compliance.

Challenges and Opportunities of Health Information Exchange (HIE) and Interoperability

Health Information Exchange (HIE) and interoperability are critical components of modern healthcare, enabling the seamless sharing of patient information across different healthcare providers and systems. While HIE and interoperability offer significant opportunities to improve care coordination and patient outcomes, they also present challenges related to data security, privacy, and standardization.

1. Challenges of HIE and Interoperability

A. Data Security and Privacy

- Sensitive Data Exposure: The exchange of health information across multiple platforms increases the risk of data breaches, exposing sensitive patient data to unauthorized access. Ensuring robust security measures are in place across all participating entities is crucial.
- Patient Consent Management: Managing patient consent for data sharing across different providers and systems can be complex, particularly in cases where patients receive care from multiple providers. Clear and consistent consent management practices are necessary to ensure patient privacy is respected.

B. Standardization and Compatibility

- **Lack of Standardization**: Different EHR systems and HIE platforms may use varying data standards and formats, leading to compatibility issues. This lack of standardization can result in incomplete or inaccurate data sharing, compromising the quality of care.
- **Interoperability Challenges**: Achieving true interoperability requires that systems can not only share data but also interpret and use the data meaningfully. This requires adherence to common standards, such as HL7 FHIR (Fast Healthcare Interoperability Resources), and ongoing collaboration among vendors and healthcare organizations.

C. Financial and Technical Barriers

- **Cost of Implementation**: Implementing and maintaining HIE and interoperable systems can be costly, particularly for smaller healthcare organizations. Costs include not only the technology itself but also training, ongoing maintenance, and compliance with regulations.
- **Technical Complexity**: Integrating disparate systems and ensuring seamless data exchange is technically complex. It requires significant IT resources and expertise, which may be challenging for organizations with limited IT staff.

2. Opportunities of HIE and Interoperability

A. Improved Care Coordination and Patient Outcomes

- **Seamless Data Sharing**: HIE and interoperability enable the seamless sharing of patient information across different healthcare providers, leading to more coordinated and efficient care. Providers can access complete and up-to-date patient records, reducing the risk of errors and duplicative tests.
- **Enhanced Continuity of Care**: With interoperable systems, patients can move between different healthcare providers without the need for redundant data entry or manual transfer of records. This enhances the continuity of care, particularly for patients with chronic conditions or complex care needs.

B. Population Health Management

- **Data Aggregation for Analytics**: HIE enables the aggregation of data from multiple sources, allowing for comprehensive population health analytics. This data can be used to identify trends, track outcomes, and inform public health interventions.
- **Targeted Interventions**: With access to comprehensive patient data, healthcare organizations can implement targeted interventions for at-risk populations, improving overall health outcomes and reducing healthcare costs.

C. Patient Empowerment

- **Patient Access to Health Information**: Interoperability and HIE give patients greater access to their own health information, empowering them to take an active role in managing their health. Patients can access their records through patient portals and share their data with providers as needed.
- **Informed Decision-Making**: With comprehensive and accurate health information, patients are better equipped to make informed decisions about their care, leading to better engagement and satisfaction.

3. Promoting Data Sharing While Ensuring Patient Privacy and Data Security

A. Establishing Clear Data Governance Policies

- **Data Access and Sharing Policies**: Develop and enforce clear policies on who can access and share patient data within the organization and with external entities. Ensure that these policies comply with legal and regulatory requirements, such as HIPAA.
- **Role-Based Access Controls**: Implement role-based access controls to ensure that only authorized personnel can access specific types of patient data. Regularly review access permissions to ensure they align with job responsibilities.

B. Implementing Advanced Data Security Measures

- **Encryption and Tokenization**: Use encryption to protect patient data both at rest and in transit. Tokenization can be used to replace sensitive data with non-sensitive equivalents, reducing the risk of data breaches.
- **Regular Security Audits**: Conduct regular security audits of HIE systems and interoperable platforms to identify vulnerabilities and ensure compliance with security standards. Address any identified issues promptly to maintain a high level of data security.

C. Enhancing Patient Consent and Privacy Management

- **Transparent Consent Processes**: Develop transparent processes for obtaining and managing patient consent for data sharing. Ensure that patients understand how their data will be used and have the ability to control their data sharing preferences.
- **Patient Education**: Educate patients about their rights regarding health information exchange and how they can protect their privacy. Provide clear information on how to access and manage their health data through patient portals.

D. Collaborating with Stakeholders

- **Vendor Collaboration**: Work closely with EHR vendors and HIE providers to ensure that systems are interoperable, secure, and user-friendly. Participate in industry initiatives aimed at improving interoperability standards.
- **Stakeholder Engagement**: Engage with other healthcare organizations, public health agencies, and policymakers to promote data sharing while ensuring privacy and security. Advocate for common standards and best practices across the healthcare ecosystem.

E. Monitoring and Continuous Improvement

- **Real-Time Monitoring**: Implement real-time monitoring tools to detect and respond to unauthorized access or data breaches. Ensure that the organization has a robust incident response plan in place to address security incidents.
- **Continuous Improvement**: Regularly review and update cybersecurity and data governance policies to adapt to emerging threats and changes in technology. Foster a culture of continuous improvement in data security and privacy practices.

By designing a comprehensive cybersecurity strategy and addressing the challenges and opportunities of HIE and interoperability, nurse executives can protect patient data while promoting the seamless exchange of health information. This dual focus on security and interoperability is essential for delivering high-quality, coordinated care in the modern healthcare landscape.

Impact of Meaningful Use and Subsequent Regulations on Health IT Adoption and Utilization

1. Overview of Meaningful Use and Subsequent Regulations:

- **Meaningful Use (MU) Program:** Launched under the Health Information Technology for Economic and Clinical Health (HITECH) Act of 2009, the Meaningful Use program aimed to incentivize healthcare providers to adopt and effectively use Electronic Health Records (EHRs). The program was structured in three stages:
    - **Stage 1:** Focused on data capture and sharing, requiring providers to adopt EHRs and start collecting and sharing basic patient information.
    - **Stage 2:** Emphasized advanced clinical processes, including the use of health information exchange (HIE) and patient engagement.
    - **Stage 3:** Concentrated on improved outcomes, requiring providers to demonstrate measurable improvements in care quality and efficiency through the use of EHRs.

- **Subsequent Regulations:**
    - **MACRA (Medicare Access and CHIP Reauthorization Act of 2015):** Introduced the Quality Payment Program (QPP), which replaced Meaningful Use with the Merit-based Incentive Payment System (MIPS) and Advanced Alternative Payment Models (APMs). These programs continue to emphasize the use of health IT to improve quality, cost efficiency, and patient outcomes.
    - **21st Century Cures Act:** Focuses on promoting interoperability, reducing information blocking, and making EHRs more accessible to patients.

2. Impact on Health IT Adoption and Utilization:

1. **Widespread EHR Adoption:**
    - **Pre-MU Landscape:** Prior to Meaningful Use, EHR adoption was limited, with only a small percentage of healthcare providers using electronic records. MU provided financial incentives and penalties that significantly accelerated adoption.

- o **Current State:** As of today, EHR adoption is nearly universal across hospitals and large physician practices. The program has laid the foundation for digital transformation in healthcare by establishing EHRs as the standard for patient record-keeping.

2. **Enhanced Data Exchange and Interoperability:**
   - o **Initial Focus on Data Capture:** Early stages of MU emphasized the importance of capturing patient data in a structured format, which was critical for future data sharing efforts.
   - o **Interoperability:** Subsequent regulations have pushed for greater interoperability, enabling more seamless data exchange between different EHR systems, providers, and even patients. The 21st Century Cures Act has furthered this goal by prohibiting information blocking and promoting the use of standardized APIs to improve data sharing.

3. **Increased Focus on Quality and Outcomes:**
   - o **Quality Reporting:** The MU program established the foundation for quality reporting, requiring providers to track and report on specific clinical quality measures (CQMs). This focus has evolved under MACRA, where health IT is now integral to the value-based care model.
   - o **Outcome-Driven Care:** By integrating EHR data with quality metrics, providers can now more accurately measure and improve patient outcomes, which is a significant shift from volume-based care to value-based care.

4. **Patient Engagement:**
   - o **Patient Portals:** Meaningful Use incentivized the development and adoption of patient portals, allowing patients to access their health records, communicate with providers, and manage their care online. This has increased patient engagement and involvement in their own healthcare.
   - o **Access to Data:** Regulations like the 21st Century Cures Act have furthered this trend by ensuring that patients have easier access to their medical records through interoperable systems.

5. **Challenges and Unintended Consequences:**
   - o **Usability Issues:** While MU spurred EHR adoption, it also highlighted significant usability issues. Many providers reported frustration with cumbersome EHR interfaces and documentation requirements, which sometimes detracted from patient care.
   - o **Burnout:** The increased documentation burden associated with EHRs has been linked to clinician burnout, leading to ongoing efforts to optimize EHR systems and reduce administrative tasks.

3. Future Trends and Anticipated Developments:

1. **Advancements in Interoperability:**
   - o **Continued Focus:** With the groundwork laid by Meaningful Use and the 21st Century Cures Act, the push for interoperability will continue. Future trends include more widespread use of standardized APIs, real-time data exchange, and greater integration of health IT systems across the care continuum.
   - o **Patient-Controlled Health Data:** There will be a growing emphasis on patient-controlled health data, where patients can easily share their health records across different providers and settings, leading to more coordinated care.

2. **AI and Predictive Analytics:**
   - o **Integration with EHRs:** AI-driven tools and predictive analytics will become more integrated into EHR systems, providing clinicians with decision support, risk stratification, and predictive insights that can improve care delivery.
   - o **Focus on Outcomes:** These technologies will enhance the ability of providers to focus on preventive care and personalized medicine, ultimately improving patient outcomes.

3. **Telehealth and Remote Monitoring:**
   - o **Expansion of Digital Health:** The integration of telehealth and remote patient monitoring into EHR systems will continue to grow, particularly in the post-pandemic era. This trend will enable more comprehensive care management, particularly for chronic conditions and rural populations.
   - o **EHR Optimization:** EHRs will need to evolve to better support these modalities, incorporating telehealth documentation, billing, and remote monitoring data into the standard workflows.

4. **Regulatory Evolution:**

- Focus on Usability and Safety: Future regulations may focus more on EHR usability, safety, and the reduction of clinician burden. This could include requirements for EHR vendors to meet specific usability standards and reduce the cognitive load on providers.
- Data Privacy and Security: As health IT systems become more interconnected, there will be increased emphasis on data privacy and cybersecurity, with regulations likely evolving to address emerging threats and ensure patient data protection.

Strategy for Implementing a New Electronic Health Record (EHR) System Across a Multi-Hospital Network

Implementing a new EHR system across a multi-hospital network is a complex, multi-faceted project that requires careful planning and execution. Below is a comprehensive strategy that addresses key challenges such as data migration, staff training, and workflow optimization.

1. Planning and Preparation

1. **Stakeholder Engagement:**
   - **Form a Steering Committee:** Establish a steering committee composed of key stakeholders from across the hospital network, including clinical, IT, administrative, and financial representatives. This committee will oversee the project, make critical decisions, and ensure alignment with organizational goals.
   - **Involve End-Users Early:** Engage clinicians, nurses, and other end-users early in the process to gather input on system requirements, workflows, and potential pain points. Their involvement is crucial for ensuring that the system meets the needs of all users.

2. **Vendor Selection:**
   - **Conduct a Needs Assessment:** Assess the specific needs of the hospital network, including clinical workflows, interoperability requirements, and regulatory compliance. Use this assessment to inform the selection of an EHR vendor.
   - **Evaluate Vendors:** Evaluate potential vendors based on criteria such as system functionality, user experience, scalability, support services, and cost. Consider conducting site visits or demos with current users of the EHR systems under consideration.
   - **Contract Negotiation:** Negotiate terms that include not only the software but also implementation support, training, ongoing maintenance, and future upgrades.

3. **Project Management:**
   - **Develop a Detailed Project Plan:** Create a comprehensive project plan that outlines key milestones, timelines, resource allocation, and risk management strategies. Assign a dedicated project manager to oversee the implementation process.
   - **Budgeting:** Develop a detailed budget that accounts for all costs, including software, hardware, training, data migration, and potential downtime during the transition.

2. Data Migration and Integration

1. **Data Mapping and Cleansing:**
   - **Data Inventory:** Conduct a thorough inventory of existing data in the current EHR systems across all hospitals. Identify data that needs to be migrated, including patient records, lab results, imaging, billing information, and clinical notes.
   - **Data Mapping:** Map data fields from the old system to the new EHR system, ensuring compatibility and consistency. This step is crucial to ensure that data is accurately transferred without loss or corruption.
   - **Data Cleansing:** Perform data cleansing to eliminate duplicates, correct errors, and standardize formats. This ensures that only high-quality data is migrated to the new system.

2. **Migration Process:**
   - **Phased Approach:** Consider a phased approach to data migration, starting with less critical data and gradually moving to more critical records. This allows for testing and troubleshooting before full-scale migration.
   - **Parallel Systems:** During the migration period, consider running the old and new systems in parallel to ensure that data is being accurately transferred and that there are no disruptions to patient care.

- Testing and Validation: After migration, conduct extensive testing to validate the accuracy and completeness of the data. Engage clinicians in this process to verify that patient records are intact and accessible.

3. Interoperability and Integration:
   - System Integration: Ensure that the new EHR system is fully integrated with other existing systems, such as lab information systems (LIS), radiology information systems (RIS), pharmacy systems, and financial management systems.
   - Interoperability Standards: Implement interoperability standards such as HL7, FHIR, and DICOM to facilitate seamless data exchange between the new EHR system and external systems, including other healthcare providers, payers, and public health agencies.

3. Staff Training and Change Management

1. Comprehensive Training Program:
   - Role-Based Training: Develop a role-based training program that addresses the specific needs of different user groups, such as physicians, nurses, administrative staff, and IT personnel. Training should focus on both the technical aspects of the system and how it integrates into daily workflows.
   - Training Formats: Use a variety of training formats, including in-person workshops, online tutorials, simulation labs, and job aids. Consider creating a training environment that mirrors the live system, allowing users to practice in a risk-free setting.

2. Change Management:
   - Communication Strategy: Develop a communication strategy to keep all stakeholders informed about the progress of the EHR implementation, key milestones, and what to expect during the transition. Transparent communication helps build trust and reduces anxiety.
   - Champions and Super Users: Identify EHR champions and super users within each department who can provide on-the-ground support, troubleshoot issues, and encourage their peers to embrace the new system.
   - Feedback Loops: Establish feedback loops to gather input from users throughout the implementation process. Use this feedback to make adjustments to training, workflows, and system configuration as needed.

4. Workflow Optimization

1. Workflow Analysis:
   - Current State Mapping: Conduct a thorough analysis of current clinical and administrative workflows to understand how they are affected by the existing EHR system. Identify inefficiencies, bottlenecks, and areas for improvement.
   - Future State Design: Design future-state workflows that leverage the capabilities of the new EHR system to improve efficiency, reduce redundancy, and enhance patient care. Engage frontline staff in this process to ensure that the new workflows are practical and effective.

2. Workflow Integration:
   - Customization: Customize the EHR system to align with the optimized workflows, ensuring that the system supports rather than hinders clinical and administrative processes. This may involve configuring order sets, clinical pathways, documentation templates, and decision support tools.
   - Testing and Refinement: Pilot the new workflows in select departments to identify any issues and make necessary adjustments. Continuously refine workflows based on user feedback and performance data.

3. Monitoring and Continuous Improvement:
   - Performance Metrics: Establish key performance indicators (KPIs) to monitor the impact of the new EHR system on workflow efficiency, patient outcomes, and user satisfaction. Examples of KPIs include time to complete clinical documentation, order turnaround times, and staff satisfaction scores.
   - Ongoing Optimization: Use the data collected to identify areas for ongoing optimization. Regularly review and update workflows, training, and system configurations to ensure that the EHR system continues to meet the needs of the organization.

5. Go-Live and Post-Implementation Support

1. **Go-Live Strategy:**
    - o **Staggered Go-Live:** Consider a staggered go-live approach, where the EHR system is rolled out gradually across different hospitals or departments. This allows for focused support and minimizes the risk of widespread disruptions.
    - o **On-Site Support:** Provide on-site support during the go-live period, with IT specialists, trainers, and super users available to assist with any issues that arise.

2. **Post-Implementation Support:**
    - o **Help Desk and Troubleshooting:** Establish a dedicated help desk to provide ongoing support and troubleshoot any issues that users encounter after go-live. Ensure that the help desk is staffed with knowledgeable personnel who can provide quick and effective solutions.
    - o **Continuous Training:** Offer ongoing training and refresher courses to help staff stay up-to-date with the EHR system's features and functionalities. This is particularly important as the system is updated or new modules are introduced.
    - o **User Feedback and System Enhancements:** Continue to gather feedback from users and use this information to prioritize system enhancements and updates. Engage users in the process of identifying and testing new features.

By following this comprehensive strategy, a multi-hospital network can successfully implement a new EHR system that enhances patient care, improves operational efficiency, and supports the organization's long-term goals.

Analyzing the Potential of Emerging Technologies in Healthcare

Emerging technologies like blockchain and the Internet of Things (IoT) have the potential to revolutionize healthcare delivery and data management. These technologies can address several current challenges, including data security, interoperability, patient engagement, and real-time health monitoring.

1. Blockchain in Healthcare

A. Potential Applications

- • **Data Security and Integrity**: Blockchain technology provides a decentralized and immutable ledger system, making it highly secure for storing sensitive healthcare data. Each transaction is recorded on a block and linked to the previous one, ensuring that data cannot be altered without detection.
- • **Interoperability**: Blockchain can facilitate secure and seamless data exchange across different healthcare systems, addressing the challenge of interoperability. By creating a unified and standardized platform for health data exchange, blockchain can ensure that patient information is accessible to authorized healthcare providers across different settings.
- • **Patient-Centered Care**: Blockchain empowers patients by giving them control over their health data. Patients can grant or revoke access to their data in real-time, ensuring privacy and fostering trust between patients and healthcare providers.
- • **Supply Chain Management**: Blockchain can improve transparency and traceability in the healthcare supply chain. It can be used to track the movement of pharmaceuticals and medical devices from manufacturers to end-users, reducing the risk of counterfeit products entering the market.

B. Addressing Current Challenges

- • **Data Breaches:** Blockchain's secure and decentralized nature significantly reduces the risk of data breaches, ensuring that sensitive patient information remains protected.
- • **Lack of Data Interoperability:** Blockchain can bridge the gap between different healthcare systems by enabling secure data exchange, thus improving care coordination and reducing redundancies.
- • **Inefficiencies in Medical Records Management:** Blockchain can streamline the management of medical records by providing a single, comprehensive view of a patient's health history, accessible to all authorized parties.

2. Internet of Things (IoT) in Healthcare

A. Potential Applications

- **Remote Patient Monitoring**: IoT devices, such as wearable sensors and connected medical devices, enable continuous monitoring of patients' vital signs and health conditions. This real-time data can be transmitted to healthcare providers, allowing for timely interventions and personalized care.
- **Smart Hospitals**: IoT can enhance hospital operations by connecting various systems and devices. For example, IoT can optimize patient flow, manage inventory, and ensure the timely maintenance of medical equipment, leading to improved efficiency and patient outcomes.
- **Medication Adherence**: IoT-enabled pill dispensers and reminders can help ensure that patients take their medications as prescribed, reducing the risk of adverse outcomes due to non-adherence.
- **Chronic Disease Management**: IoT devices can play a critical role in managing chronic conditions such as diabetes, hypertension, and heart disease. By continuously monitoring health parameters, IoT can help patients and providers manage these conditions more effectively.

B. Addressing Current Challenges
- **Access to Care**: IoT can expand access to care, particularly in remote or underserved areas. By enabling remote monitoring and telehealth services, IoT can reduce the need for in-person visits, making healthcare more accessible.
- **Patient Engagement**: IoT devices can enhance patient engagement by providing real-time feedback on health status and encouraging proactive management of health conditions.
- **Data Overload**: While IoT generates vast amounts of data, advanced analytics and AI can be integrated to filter and analyze this data, providing actionable insights for healthcare providers.

3. Challenges and Considerations for Adoption
A. Data Security and Privacy
- **Blockchain**: While blockchain offers enhanced security, there are concerns about the scalability of the technology and the privacy of data stored on a decentralized network. Healthcare organizations must carefully consider how to implement blockchain while ensuring compliance with regulations like HIPAA.
- **IoT**: The proliferation of IoT devices introduces new vulnerabilities, as each connected device can be a potential entry point for cyberattacks. Ensuring the security of IoT networks and devices is critical to protecting patient data.

B. Integration with Existing Systems
- **Blockchain**: Integrating blockchain with existing healthcare systems can be challenging due to the technology's relatively new and complex nature. Interoperability with legacy systems and standardization across platforms are key hurdles.
- **IoT**: For IoT to be effective, it must seamlessly integrate with existing EHRs and other healthcare systems. This requires robust infrastructure and compatibility between devices and platforms.

C. Cost and ROI
- **Blockchain**: Implementing blockchain technology can be costly, particularly for smaller healthcare organizations. The return on investment (ROI) will depend on the extent to which blockchain can improve efficiencies and reduce costs related to data management and security.
- **IoT**: While IoT can improve patient outcomes and operational efficiency, the initial investment in devices, infrastructure, and analytics platforms can be significant. Organizations must weigh these costs against the potential benefits.

Comparing Quantitative and Qualitative Research Methodologies in Healthcare

Research in healthcare often employs either quantitative or qualitative methodologies, depending on the research question and objectives. Each approach has distinct advantages and is suited to different types of research inquiries. Mixed-methods research, which combines both, can offer a more comprehensive understanding of complex healthcare issues.

1. Quantitative Research Methodologies
A. Overview
- Quantitative research focuses on quantifying relationships, behaviors, or phenomena through statistical, mathematical, or computational techniques. It is often used to test hypotheses, establish causality, or measure the prevalence of certain conditions.

B. Examples of Research Questions
- **Prevalence Studies**: What is the prevalence of hypertension among adults aged 40-60 in an urban population?
- **Clinical Trials**: Does a new medication reduce blood pressure more effectively than the current standard treatment in patients with hypertension?
- **Epidemiological Studies**: What are the risk factors associated with the development of type 2 diabetes in middle-aged adults?

C. Methods and Data Collection
- **Surveys and Questionnaires**: Structured instruments used to collect data from large samples.
- **Clinical Trials**: Controlled experiments that test the effectiveness of interventions.
- **Observational Studies**: Studies that observe outcomes without manipulating variables, such as cohort or case-control studies.
- **Statistical Analysis**: Data is analyzed using statistical techniques to identify patterns, correlations, or differences between groups.

D. Advantages
- **Objectivity**: Quantitative research provides objective, measurable data that can be statistically analyzed.
- **Generalizability**: Results from large, randomized samples can often be generalized to broader populations.
- **Precision**: Quantitative methods allow for precise measurement of variables and the ability to test specific hypotheses.

E. Limitations
- **Contextual Understanding**: Quantitative research may not fully capture the context or nuances of the phenomena being studied.
- **Limited Flexibility**: Predefined hypotheses and structured data collection methods can limit the exploration of new or unexpected findings.

2. Qualitative Research Methodologies

A. Overview
- Qualitative research focuses on exploring and understanding complex phenomena, behaviors, or experiences through in-depth data collection and analysis. It is often used to generate new theories, explore meanings, and understand the context of healthcare experiences.

B. Examples of Research Questions
- **Patient Experiences**: How do patients with chronic pain perceive and manage their condition in their daily lives?
- **Healthcare Provider Perspectives**: What are the challenges faced by healthcare providers in delivering end-of-life care in a hospital setting?
- **Cultural Beliefs and Health**: How do cultural beliefs influence the healthcare decisions of immigrant populations in urban areas?

C. Methods and Data Collection
- **Interviews**: In-depth, open-ended interviews with individuals to explore their experiences and perspectives.
- **Focus Groups**: Group discussions facilitated to explore collective views or shared experiences.
- **Ethnography**: Immersive observation and participation in a specific community or setting to understand behaviors and practices.
- **Thematic Analysis**: Data is analyzed to identify patterns, themes, and meanings within the qualitative data.

D. Advantages
- **Depth of Understanding**: Qualitative research provides a deep, contextualized understanding of complex issues, capturing the richness of human experiences.
- **Flexibility**: Researchers can explore new areas or adjust focus based on emerging findings during the study.
- **Participant-Centered**: Qualitative methods allow participants to express themselves in their own words, providing insights that structured surveys might miss.

E. Limitations

- **Subjectivity**: The findings of qualitative research can be influenced by the researcher's interpretations, making them less objective.
- **Limited Generalizability**: Results are often specific to the context or population studied and may not be generalizable to other settings.
- **Time-Intensive**: Data collection and analysis in qualitative research can be time-consuming and resource-intensive.

3. Mixed-Methods Research Designs

A. Overview

- Mixed-methods research combines both quantitative and qualitative approaches to provide a more comprehensive understanding of a research problem. This approach allows researchers to explore both the breadth and depth of an issue.

B. Examples of Research Questions

- **Patient Outcomes and Experiences**: How effective is a new diabetes management program in improving clinical outcomes (quantitative) and how do patients experience the program in their daily lives (qualitative)?
- **Health Policy Impact**: What is the impact of a new healthcare policy on patient access to care (quantitative), and how do healthcare providers perceive the policy's implementation (qualitative)?

C. Types of Mixed-Methods Designs

- **Convergent Design**: Quantitative and qualitative data are collected and analyzed separately but then compared or combined to draw conclusions.
- **Explanatory Sequential Design**: Quantitative data is collected and analyzed first, followed by qualitative data to explain or expand on the quantitative findings.
- **Exploratory Sequential Design**: Qualitative data is collected first to explore a topic, followed by quantitative data to measure or test the findings on a larger scale.

D. Advantages

- **Comprehensive Insight**: Mixed-methods research provides a fuller understanding of research questions by integrating numerical data with rich, contextual insights.
- **Validation**: The use of both quantitative and qualitative data can help validate findings, providing more robust conclusions.
- **Flexibility**: Researchers can adapt the study design to address complex questions that require both statistical analysis and deep exploration.

E. Limitations

- **Complexity**: Mixed-methods research can be complex to design, execute, and analyze, requiring expertise in both quantitative and qualitative methods.
- **Resource-Intensive**: This approach often requires more time, funding, and resources than using a single methodology.
- **Integration Challenges**: Combining data from different methods can be challenging, particularly when the results are conflicting or require different types of interpretation.

In healthcare research, the choice between quantitative, qualitative, or mixed-methods approaches depends on the research question, the nature of the phenomena being studied, and the goals of the research. Each methodology offers unique strengths and, when used appropriately, can significantly contribute to the advancement of healthcare knowledge and practice.

Analysis of Evidence-Based Practice Models

Evidence-based practice (EBP) models provide structured approaches for integrating research evidence into clinical practice to improve patient outcomes. Different models cater to various organizational needs, processes, and contexts. Three prominent EBP models include the Iowa Model, the ACE Star Model, and the PARIHS (Promoting Action on Research Implementation in Health Services) Framework. Nurse executives play a crucial role in selecting and adapting these models to align with their organization's goals, culture, and resources.

1. The Iowa Model of Evidence-Based Practice

Overview:

- **Purpose:** The Iowa Model focuses on promoting the systematic use of research findings and other evidence to improve nursing practice. It is particularly suited for organizations that are already familiar with quality improvement processes.
- **Process:** The model involves identifying triggers (either problem-focused or knowledge-focused) that highlight the need for change, forming a team, selecting and critiquing relevant research, piloting the change in practice, evaluating outcomes, and implementing the change broadly if successful.

Strengths:

- **Adaptability:** The Iowa Model is highly adaptable to various clinical settings and is particularly effective in organizations that prioritize quality improvement and patient safety.
- **Focus on Piloting:** The model emphasizes piloting changes before widespread implementation, which allows for testing and refinement of new practices.

Limitations:

- **Complexity:** The model can be complex to implement, particularly in settings where staff are not familiar with research processes.

Application:

- **Best Fit:** The Iowa Model is best suited for organizations that have a culture of continuous quality improvement and a structure that supports collaborative efforts. Nurse executives can use this model when the goal is to address specific clinical problems with evidence-based interventions.

2. ACE Star Model of Knowledge Transformation

Overview:

- **Purpose:** The ACE Star Model provides a framework for translating research knowledge into practice. It emphasizes the transformation of knowledge from discovery to integration and application.
- **Process:** The model includes five stages: Knowledge Discovery, Evidence Summary, Translation into Practice Recommendations, Integration into Practice, and Evaluation of Outcomes.

Strengths:

- **Comprehensive Framework:** The ACE Star Model provides a clear, step-by-step process that bridges the gap between research evidence and clinical practice.
- **Focus on Knowledge Transformation:** The model emphasizes not just the use of research, but the transformation of that research into practical, actionable knowledge.

Limitations:

- **Resource-Intensive:** The model can be resource-intensive, requiring dedicated personnel and time for each stage of the knowledge transformation process.

Application:

- **Best Fit:** The ACE Star Model is ideal for organizations that are focused on large-scale implementation of evidence-based practices across multiple settings or specialties. Nurse executives can use this model to guide systematic, organization-wide changes in practice, particularly when integrating complex or new knowledge.

3. PARIHS Framework

Overview:

- **Purpose:** The PARIHS Framework emphasizes the interplay between evidence, context, and facilitation in the successful implementation of evidence-based practices.
- **Process:** The framework is structured around three key elements: Evidence (quality and type of evidence), Context (the environment or setting where change is being implemented), and Facilitation (the process of enabling change).

Strengths:

- **Contextual Focus:** The PARIHS Framework recognizes the importance of the organizational context and the role of facilitation in successful implementation, making it highly adaptable to different settings.
- **Holistic Approach:** By considering evidence, context, and facilitation together, the framework offers a more holistic approach to implementing EBP.

Limitations:

- **Complexity in Application:** The framework's focus on multiple interacting factors can make it challenging to apply, especially in environments where context and facilitation are not well understood or supported.

Application:

- **Best Fit:** The PARIHS Framework is most effective in organizations that are undergoing significant changes or where the context plays a crucial role in the success of EBP initiatives. Nurse executives can use this model when working in diverse or complex settings, where understanding and modifying the context is key to implementing change.

Selecting and Adapting EBP Models

1. **Assess Organizational Readiness:**
   - **Evaluate Culture and Infrastructure:** Nurse executives should assess the organization's culture, existing infrastructure, and staff readiness for EBP. Organizations with a strong quality improvement culture might be more aligned with the Iowa Model, while those focused on broad knowledge transformation may benefit from the ACE Star Model.

2. **Align with Strategic Goals:**
   - **Link to Strategic Objectives:** The chosen EBP model should align with the organization's strategic goals, such as improving patient safety, reducing variability in care, or enhancing staff engagement. The PARIHS Framework, for example, might be ideal for an organization prioritizing cultural change and leadership development.

3. **Resource Availability:**
   - **Consider Resources and Support:** The selection of an EBP model should take into account the availability of resources, including time, personnel, and financial investment. The ACE Star Model might require more substantial resources due to its comprehensive approach, while the Iowa Model might be more feasible in resource-constrained environments.

4. **Customization and Flexibility:**
   - **Adaptation to Local Context:** Nurse executives should be prepared to adapt the chosen model to fit the specific context of their organization. This might involve modifying the steps of the Iowa Model to align with existing quality improvement processes or tailoring the facilitation strategies in the PARIHS Framework to better suit the organization's leadership structure.

Strategy for Promoting a Culture of Inquiry and Research

To foster a culture of inquiry and research within a healthcare organization, nurse executives must create an environment that encourages curiosity, supports research activities, and values the application of evidence to improve patient care.

1. Building the Foundation

1. **Leadership Commitment:**
   - **Demonstrate Support:** Nurse executives must visibly support and prioritize research and inquiry, integrating these values into the organization's mission and strategic goals. This can include making research a key performance indicator for departments and leaders.
   - **Allocate Resources:** Ensure that adequate resources, including time, funding, and access to research tools, are available for staff to engage in inquiry and research activities.

2. **Education and Training:**
   - **Provide Research Education:** Offer regular educational sessions on research methodologies, critical appraisal of evidence, and the principles of EBP. This can include workshops, seminars, and online courses tailored to different levels of staff expertise.
   - **Mentorship Programs:** Establish mentorship programs where experienced researchers and nurse scientists mentor less experienced staff, guiding them through the research process and helping them develop their skills.

3. **Access to Resources:**
   - **Library and Database Access:** Ensure that staff have access to a well-stocked medical library, online databases, and other research tools that enable them to conduct literature reviews and stay current with the latest evidence.

- Research Committees: Create or strengthen research committees that can provide guidance, review proposals, and assist with securing funding for research projects.

2. Encouraging Participation and Engagement

1. **Incentivize Research Participation:**
   - **Recognition and Rewards:** Develop recognition programs that reward staff for their contributions to research and inquiry. This can include awards, public recognition, and opportunities for professional development.
   - **Career Advancement:** Link research participation to career advancement opportunities, such as promotions, leadership roles, or academic appointments. This encourages staff to engage in research as a pathway to career growth.

2. **Facilitate Collaborative Research:**
   - **Interdisciplinary Teams:** Promote the formation of interdisciplinary research teams that bring together nurses, physicians, pharmacists, and other healthcare professionals. This collaborative approach enriches the research process and broadens its impact.
   - **Partnerships with Academic Institutions:** Establish partnerships with local universities and research institutions to provide additional support, expertise, and opportunities for staff to engage in research activities.

3. **Integrate Research into Clinical Practice:**
   - **EBP Rounds and Journal Clubs:** Regularly hold evidence-based practice (EBP) rounds and journal clubs where staff can discuss recent research findings, share insights, and explore how to apply new evidence in their practice.
   - **Pilot Research Projects:** Encourage departments to pilot small-scale research projects focused on specific clinical questions or challenges. Successful pilots can lead to larger studies and broader implementation of findings.

3. Measuring and Sustaining Success

1. **Evaluation Metrics:**
   - **Research Output:** Track the number of research projects initiated, completed, and published within the organization. Monitor the participation rates of staff in research activities and educational programs.
   - **Application of Research:** Measure the extent to which research findings are implemented in clinical practice, assessing their impact on patient outcomes, care quality, and operational efficiency.

2. **Continuous Feedback and Improvement:**
   - **Feedback Loops:** Establish feedback mechanisms where staff can provide input on the research culture, available resources, and support systems. Use this feedback to make continuous improvements to the research infrastructure.
   - **Celebrate Success:** Regularly celebrate research successes within the organization, highlighting impactful projects and sharing stories of how research has led to improved patient care.

3. **Sustaining the Culture:**
   - **Ongoing Education:** Provide continuous learning opportunities to keep staff engaged with the latest research methods and findings. This helps maintain momentum and ensures that the culture of inquiry remains vibrant.
   - **Adaptation to Changing Needs:** Stay attuned to the evolving needs of the organization and the healthcare environment. Adapt the research strategy as necessary to address emerging challenges, new technologies, and shifts in patient care priorities.

By implementing these strategies, nurse executives can create a robust culture of inquiry and research within their organization, leading to continuous improvements in patient care, staff engagement, and overall healthcare outcomes.

Evaluating the Strengths and Limitations of Various Research Designs

Understanding the strengths and limitations of different research designs is crucial for interpreting and applying research findings in healthcare. Different designs are suited to different types of research questions and can impact the validity, generalizability, and applicability of the results.

1. Randomized Controlled Trials (RCTs)

Strengths

- **Causal Inference**: RCTs are considered the gold standard for determining causal relationships between interventions and outcomes. The random assignment of participants to treatment and control groups helps minimize selection bias and confounding variables.
- **Control Over Variables**: By controlling for extraneous variables, RCTs provide high internal validity, making it easier to attribute observed effects to the intervention itself.
- **Blinding**: The use of blinding (e.g., double-blinding where both participants and researchers are unaware of group assignments) reduces bias in outcome assessment, enhancing the credibility of the results.

Limitations

- **Generalizability**: The strict inclusion criteria and controlled environment of RCTs can limit the generalizability of the findings to real-world settings. The participants may not be representative of the broader population.
- **Ethical Concerns**: In some cases, RCTs may raise ethical issues, particularly if withholding the intervention from the control group could result in harm or if participants are exposed to potential risks.
- **Cost and Complexity**: RCTs are resource-intensive, often requiring significant time, funding, and logistical coordination. This can limit their feasibility, especially for large-scale or long-term studies.

Impact on Interpretation and Application

- RCTs provide strong evidence for the efficacy of interventions, making them highly valuable for clinical decision-making and guideline development. However, their findings should be interpreted with caution when applied to diverse populations or real-world settings that differ from the study conditions.

2. Cohort Studies

Strengths

- **Observational Realism**: Cohort studies follow groups of individuals over time, observing outcomes as they occur naturally. This design offers high external validity, as it reflects real-world conditions.
- **Exposure-Outcomes Relationship**: Cohort studies are particularly useful for studying the relationship between risk factors (exposures) and the development of diseases or outcomes over time. They can establish temporal sequences, helping to infer causality.
- **Longitudinal Data**: By collecting data over extended periods, cohort studies can identify long-term effects and trends that might not be observable in shorter studies.

Limitations

- **Confounding Variables**: Since cohort studies are observational, they are more susceptible to confounding factors that can bias the results. Researchers must use statistical techniques to control for these confounders.
- **Time and Resource Intensive**: Long-term cohort studies require significant time and resources to follow participants, which can lead to high attrition rates and loss to follow-up, potentially biasing the results.
- **Causality**: While cohort studies can suggest associations and potential causal relationships, they cannot definitively establish causality as RCTs can.

Impact on Interpretation and Application

- Cohort studies provide valuable insights into risk factors and disease progression, which can inform public health policies and preventive strategies. However, results should be interpreted with an understanding of potential confounders and the observational nature of the data.

3. Qualitative Case Studies

Strengths

- **In-Depth Understanding**: Qualitative case studies provide a deep, contextualized understanding of complex phenomena, often focusing on a single case or a small number of cases. This approach is ideal for exploring new or poorly understood issues.

- **Rich Data**: The use of interviews, observations, and document analysis allows for the collection of rich, detailed data that captures the experiences, perspectives, and motivations of participants.
- **Flexibility**: Qualitative case studies are flexible, allowing researchers to explore emerging themes and adjust the study focus based on new insights.

Limitations

- **Generalizability**: The findings from qualitative case studies are often specific to the particular cases studied and may not be generalizable to other settings or populations.
- **Subjectivity**: The interpretive nature of qualitative research can introduce subjectivity, as findings are influenced by the researcher's perspectives and the context in which the study is conducted.
- **Time-Consuming**: Collecting and analyzing qualitative data is labor-intensive and time-consuming, often requiring significant resources for a small-scale study.

Impact on Interpretation and Application

- Qualitative case studies are valuable for generating hypotheses, exploring complex issues, and providing context to quantitative findings. They are best applied when the goal is to understand the intricacies of a particular case or phenomenon, rather than to generalize findings broadly.

Guide for Critically Appraising Research Articles

Critical appraisal is a systematic process used to assess the trustworthiness, relevance, and value of research evidence. This guide provides a framework for critically appraising research articles, focusing on key elements such as study design, sample selection, data collection methods, and statistical analysis.

1. Study Design

Questions to Consider

- **Appropriateness of the Design**: Is the study design (e.g., RCT, cohort study, qualitative case study) appropriate for answering the research question? Does the design align with the study objectives?
- **Strengths and Limitations**: What are the strengths and limitations of the chosen design? How might these impact the validity and reliability of the findings?

Exercise

- **Case Study**: Compare two research articles on a similar topic, one using an RCT design and the other using a cohort study design. Evaluate which design is more appropriate for the research question and why.

2. Sample Selection

Questions to Consider

- **Sampling Method**: How were participants selected for the study? Was the sampling method (e.g., random sampling, convenience sampling) appropriate for the research question and design?
- **Sample Size**: Is the sample size adequate to detect a meaningful effect (in quantitative studies) or to provide in-depth insights (in qualitative studies)?
- **Bias and Representation**: Are there potential sources of bias in the sample selection? Is the sample representative of the population being studied?

Exercise

- **Critical Appraisal**: Review the sampling methods of a quantitative study and a qualitative study. Identify potential sources of bias and discuss how these might affect the study's conclusions.

3. Data Collection Methods

Questions to Consider

- **Validity of Instruments**: Were the data collection instruments (e.g., surveys, interviews, observations) valid and reliable? Were they pre-tested or validated in previous studies?
- **Data Collection Process**: Was the data collection process clearly described? Were steps taken to minimize bias during data collection (e.g., blinding, standardized procedures)?
- **Ethical Considerations**: Were ethical considerations, such as informed consent and confidentiality, adequately addressed?

Exercise

- **Data Collection Critique**: Select an article and evaluate the data collection methods used. Consider the validity and reliability of the instruments and any potential sources of bias introduced during data collection.

4. Statistical Analysis (for Quantitative Studies)

Questions to Consider

- **Appropriateness of Statistical Tests**: Were the statistical tests used appropriate for the type of data and research question? Were assumptions for these tests met?
- **Effect Size and Significance**: Were effect sizes reported along with p-values? Do the results have practical as well as statistical significance?
- **Confounding Variables**: Were confounding variables controlled for in the analysis? How might unaccounted-for confounders affect the results?

Exercise

- **Statistical Analysis Review**: Review the statistical analysis section of a quantitative research article. Identify the statistical tests used and assess whether they were appropriate. Discuss how the results should be interpreted in light of the analysis.

5. Data Analysis Methods (for Qualitative Studies)

Questions to Consider

- **Data Analysis Approach**: Was the data analysis approach (e.g., thematic analysis, grounded theory) appropriate for the research question and data collected?
- **Transparency of Analysis**: Was the process of data analysis clearly described? Were steps taken to ensure the credibility and trustworthiness of the findings (e.g., triangulation, member checking)?
- **Interpretation of Findings**: Were the findings interpreted in the context of the existing literature and the study's theoretical framework?

Exercise

- **Qualitative Analysis Critique**: Examine the data analysis section of a qualitative study. Evaluate the transparency and rigor of the analysis process. Discuss whether the findings are well-supported by the data.

6. Interpretation of Results

Questions to Consider

- **Consistency with Hypotheses**: Do the results support the study's hypotheses or research questions? Are alternative explanations for the findings considered?
- **Generalizability and Applicability**: Are the study findings generalizable to other settings or populations? How applicable are the results to clinical practice or policy-making?
- **Limitations and Biases**: Does the discussion section acknowledge the study's limitations? How might these limitations affect the interpretation and application of the findings?

Exercise

- **Interpretation Discussion**: Review the discussion section of a research article. Critique how the authors have interpreted the results, considering the study's design, sample, and analysis. Identify any potential biases or limitations that could affect the conclusions.

Practice Exercises for Critical Appraisal Skills

1. **Appraise an RCT**: Select a published RCT and critically appraise it using the questions outlined in this guide. Focus on study design, sample selection, data collection, and statistical analysis. Summarize the strengths and limitations of the study.
2. **Appraise a Cohort Study**: Choose a cohort study and evaluate its methodology, including sample selection, data collection methods, and the handling of confounders. Discuss how the study's design impacts the validity and generalizability of the findings.
3. **Appraise a Qualitative Case Study**: Find a qualitative case study and appraise its approach to data collection, analysis, and interpretation. Reflect on how the qualitative methodology provides depth and context to the findings.

4. **Compare and Contrast**: Compare two research articles on the same topic, one using a quantitative approach and the other a qualitative approach. Critically appraise each article and discuss how the different methodologies lead to different insights and implications for practice.
5. **Mock Critical Appraisal Session**: Organize a group exercise where participants critically appraise a research article together, discussing each element outlined in this guide. This collaborative approach can enhance critical thinking and expose participants to different perspectives.

By mastering the skills of critical appraisal, healthcare professionals can more effectively evaluate research evidence, leading to better-informed decisions in clinical practice, policy development, and healthcare management.

Analyzing the Hierarchy of Evidence in Healthcare Research

In healthcare research, the hierarchy of evidence is a framework used to rank the strength and reliability of evidence derived from different types of studies. This hierarchy guides clinicians, researchers, and policymakers in making informed decisions by assessing the quality and validity of research findings.

1. The Hierarchy of Evidence

1. **Expert Opinion and Background Information:**
    o   **Description:** This level includes opinions from clinical experts, textbook information, and non-systematic observations. It is the lowest level of evidence due to its subjective nature and lack of rigorous testing.
    o   **Use in Practice:** While expert opinions are valuable, they are often based on experience rather than empirical data. Therefore, they are typically used as a starting point for further investigation rather than a basis for clinical decisions.

2. **Case Reports and Case Series:**
    o   **Description:** These are detailed reports of individual cases or a series of cases, often used to describe novel conditions or responses to treatment. They lack control groups and are more descriptive than analytical.
    o   **Use in Practice:** Case reports can provide insight into rare conditions or unusual presentations but are not sufficient to establish cause-effect relationships. They are often used to generate hypotheses for further research.

3. **Cross-Sectional Studies:**
    o   **Description:** Cross-sectional studies examine the relationship between variables at a single point in time within a specific population. They can identify associations but cannot determine causality.
    o   **Use in Practice:** These studies are useful for assessing the prevalence of conditions or risk factors but are limited in their ability to inform clinical interventions.

4. **Case-Control Studies:**
    o   **Description:** Case-control studies compare patients with a condition (cases) to those without it (controls), looking retrospectively for exposure to risk factors. They are useful for studying rare diseases or conditions.
    o   **Use in Practice:** While these studies can suggest associations, they are prone to recall bias and cannot definitively establish causality. They are often used to identify potential risk factors that can be tested in more rigorous studies.

5. **Cohort Studies:**
    o   **Description:** Cohort studies follow a group of individuals over time to assess the impact of different exposures on outcomes. They can be prospective (following participants forward in time) or retrospective.
    o   **Use in Practice:** Cohort studies are valuable for establishing temporal relationships between risk factors and outcomes, providing stronger evidence than case-control studies. However, they require more time and resources.

6. **Randomized Controlled Trials (RCTs):**
    o   **Description:** RCTs are considered the gold standard for determining the effectiveness of interventions. Participants are randomly assigned to either the intervention or control group, minimizing bias and allowing for causal inferences.

- o **Use in Practice:** RCTs provide high-quality evidence for clinical decision-making and are often used to inform treatment guidelines and protocols. However, they can be expensive and may not always be feasible for all research questions.
7. **Systematic Reviews and Meta-Analyses:**
     - o **Description:** Systematic reviews synthesize evidence from multiple studies on a specific topic, while meta-analyses use statistical methods to combine data from several RCTs or other studies. These approaches provide a comprehensive assessment of the available evidence.
     - o **Use in Practice:** Systematic reviews and meta-analyses represent the highest level of evidence and are critical for developing clinical guidelines and informing policy decisions. They provide a broad overview of the evidence and help to resolve inconsistencies among individual studies.

2. Impact of the Level of Evidence on Clinical Decision-Making and Policy Development
1. **Clinical Decision-Making:**
     - o **Evidence-Based Practice:** The strength of the evidence significantly influences clinical decision-making. Higher levels of evidence, such as those from RCTs and systematic reviews, are more likely to be integrated into clinical practice guidelines and protocols. Clinicians rely on these robust sources to make informed decisions that maximize patient outcomes and minimize risks.
     - o **Risk-Benefit Analysis:** When high-level evidence is available, it allows for a clearer assessment of the benefits and potential harms of an intervention, leading to more precise and effective treatment choices. In contrast, lower-level evidence might be used with caution, often supplemented by clinical judgment and patient preferences.
2. **Policy Development:**
     - o **Guideline Formation:** Policymakers and professional organizations, such as the American Heart Association or the National Institute for Health and Care Excellence (NICE), prioritize high-level evidence when developing clinical guidelines and health policies. Systematic reviews and meta-analyses, in particular, are often used to create evidence-based recommendations that influence practice standards and reimbursement policies.
     - o **Resource Allocation:** High-quality evidence helps policymakers determine where to allocate resources effectively, whether in public health interventions, funding research, or supporting healthcare infrastructure. Strong evidence can justify investments in specific treatments or prevention strategies that demonstrate significant benefits.
3. **Challenges in Interpretation:**
     - o **Complexity of Evidence:** Despite the hierarchy, not all high-level evidence is straightforward to interpret. Systematic reviews and meta-analyses may include studies with varying methodologies and quality, leading to conflicting conclusions. Clinicians and policymakers must critically appraise the evidence, considering the quality, applicability, and potential biases of the included studies.
     - o **Practical Application:** In some cases, high-level evidence may not be available for specific clinical scenarios, necessitating reliance on lower levels of evidence or expert consensus. This requires a careful balance between available data, clinical judgment, and patient-centered care.

Strategy for Implementing an Evidence-Based Practice (EBP) Initiative Across a Healthcare System
Implementing an EBP initiative across a healthcare system involves a strategic approach that addresses potential barriers, engages stakeholders, and ensures sustainability. The goal is to integrate research evidence into clinical practice systematically to improve patient outcomes and care quality.

1. Establish a Clear Vision and Goals
1. **Define the EBP Objectives:**
     - o **Clinical Improvement:** Identify specific clinical areas where evidence-based interventions can lead to significant improvements, such as reducing hospital-acquired infections, enhancing chronic disease management, or improving surgical outcomes.
     - o **System-Wide Consistency:** Aim for uniformity in care practices across the healthcare system by standardizing evidence-based protocols and reducing variability in care delivery.
2. **Align with Organizational Priorities:**

- Strategic Alignment: Ensure that the EBP initiative aligns with the healthcare system's broader strategic goals, such as enhancing patient safety, improving quality metrics, or achieving accreditation requirements.
- Leadership Support: Secure commitment from top leadership, including the CEO, CNO, and medical directors, to champion the EBP initiative and allocate the necessary resources.

2. Engage and Educate Stakeholders

1. **Engage Clinical Leaders:**
   - Form EBP Champions: Identify and train EBP champions within each department who can lead the initiative, advocate for its benefits, and support their peers in adopting evidence-based practices.
   - Interdisciplinary Collaboration: Promote collaboration among nurses, physicians, pharmacists, and other healthcare professionals to create a multidisciplinary approach to EBP. This ensures buy-in across different levels of the organization.

2. **Education and Training:**
   - EBP Training Programs: Develop comprehensive training programs that educate staff on the principles of EBP, how to critically appraise research, and how to integrate evidence into clinical practice. Use workshops, online modules, and simulation-based learning.
   - Ongoing Professional Development: Offer continuing education credits for EBP-related training, encouraging staff to maintain and enhance their EBP skills over time.

3. Address Barriers to Implementation

1. **Resistance to Change:**
   - Identify Sources of Resistance: Understand the reasons behind resistance, which may include fear of increased workload, skepticism about new practices, or discomfort with changing established routines.
   - Change Management Strategies: Implement change management strategies that include transparent communication, involvement of staff in decision-making, and addressing concerns through open forums and Q&A sessions.

2. **Resource Constraints:**
   - Allocate Resources: Ensure that sufficient resources are allocated to support the EBP initiative, including access to research databases, time for staff to participate in training and EBP activities, and IT support for data collection and analysis.
   - Leverage Technology: Use technology to streamline the implementation process, such as integrating evidence-based guidelines into the EHR system, which can prompt clinicians at the point of care and reduce the manual workload.

3. **Time Constraints:**
   - Protected Time for EBP Activities: Designate protected time for staff to engage in EBP activities, such as attending training sessions, participating in journal clubs, or conducting research. This demonstrates the organization's commitment to EBP and alleviates concerns about workload.
   - Efficient Workflow Integration: Work with department leaders to integrate EBP activities into existing workflows, minimizing disruption to patient care and daily operations.

4. Implement and Sustain the EBP Initiative

1. **Pilot Projects:**
   - Start Small: Begin with pilot projects in select departments or units to test the implementation process, identify challenges, and gather data on outcomes. Choose projects that are likely to demonstrate quick wins, which can build momentum and support for broader implementation.
   - Evaluate and Scale: Evaluate the outcomes of pilot projects, including patient outcomes, staff satisfaction, and process efficiency. Use the lessons learned to refine the implementation strategy and scale up the initiative across the healthcare system.

2. **Monitor and Measure Outcomes:**
   - Data-Driven Decision Making: Establish key performance indicators (KPIs) to monitor the impact of the EBP initiative, such as reduced readmission rates, improved patient satisfaction scores, and adherence to clinical guidelines.

- Continuous Feedback: Create feedback mechanisms where staff can report on their experiences with EBP implementation, identify challenges, and suggest improvements. Use this feedback to make iterative changes to the initiative.

3. **Sustainability:**
    - **Embed EBP into Organizational Culture:** Foster a culture of inquiry where evidence-based practice is embedded into the daily routines of healthcare providers. Celebrate successes and recognize contributions to EBP in staff evaluations and awards.
    - **Ongoing Support and Resources:** Continue to provide resources, training, and leadership support to sustain the EBP initiative. Regularly update staff on new evidence, guidelines, and best practices to keep the initiative dynamic and responsive to changes in healthcare.

By following this comprehensive strategy, nurse executives can successfully implement an evidence-based practice initiative across a healthcare system, overcoming barriers, and ensuring that evidence-based care becomes a standard part of clinical practice, ultimately leading to improved patient outcomes and organizational performance.

Framework for Measuring the Outcomes of Evidence-Based Practice Initiatives

Implementing evidence-based practice (EBP) initiatives in healthcare is essential for improving patient outcomes and enhancing the quality of care. To effectively measure the success of these initiatives, a comprehensive framework that includes both process measures and patient outcome measures is necessary. This framework should also incorporate strategies for continuous quality improvement (CQI) to ensure sustained progress.

1. Process Measures

A. Definition and Purpose

- **Process measures** assess the implementation and adherence to specific practices or interventions. These measures help to determine whether the EBP initiatives are being executed as planned and can identify areas where adjustments are needed.

B. Key Process Measures

- **Adherence to Clinical Guidelines**: Evaluate the extent to which healthcare providers follow evidence-based clinical guidelines and protocols. This could include adherence to specific procedures, such as hand hygiene compliance or the timely administration of antibiotics.
- **Education and Training**: Measure the percentage of staff who have completed training on the EBP initiative. This could include workshops, online modules, or in-service training sessions related to the new practice.
- **Intervention Implementation Rate**: Track the rate at which the evidence-based intervention is implemented in eligible cases. For example, in an initiative to reduce catheter-associated urinary tract infections (CAUTIs), measure the proportion of patients who receive proper catheter care.
- **Documentation Compliance**: Monitor the completeness and accuracy of documentation related to the EBP initiative. Proper documentation is essential for tracking progress and identifying areas for improvement.

C. Strategies for Continuous Quality Improvement

- **Regular Audits and Feedback**: Conduct regular audits of process measures and provide feedback to healthcare teams. Use this feedback to highlight areas of success and opportunities for improvement.
- **PDSA Cycles**: Utilize Plan-Do-Study-Act (PDSA) cycles to test small changes in the implementation process and assess their impact. This iterative approach allows for continuous refinement of the intervention.
- **Collaborative Learning Sessions**: Organize collaborative learning sessions where healthcare teams can share best practices, challenges, and solutions related to the EBP initiative. These sessions can foster a culture of continuous learning and improvement.

2. Patient Outcome Measures

A. Definition and Purpose

- **Patient outcome measures** assess the impact of the EBP initiative on patient health and well-being. These measures are directly linked to the ultimate goal of improving patient outcomes through the implementation of evidence-based practices.

B. Key Patient Outcome Measures

- **Clinical Outcomes**: Measure specific clinical outcomes related to the EBP initiative. For example, in a CAUTI reduction initiative, track the incidence of CAUTIs per 1,000 catheter days.

- **Patient Safety Indicators**: Monitor indicators of patient safety, such as the rate of adverse events, hospital-acquired infections, or medication errors. These measures help assess the effectiveness of the EBP initiative in enhancing patient safety.
- **Patient Satisfaction and Experience**: Assess patient satisfaction and experience through surveys and feedback mechanisms. Patient-reported outcomes can provide valuable insights into the perceived quality of care and areas for improvement.
- **Length of Stay and Readmission Rates**: Track changes in the average length of hospital stays and readmission rates. Successful EBP initiatives should lead to reduced lengths of stay and lower readmission rates, reflecting better patient outcomes.

C. Strategies for Continuous Quality Improvement

- **Outcome Data Analysis**: Regularly analyze patient outcome data to identify trends and variations in performance. Use this analysis to pinpoint areas where further improvements are needed.
- **Benchmarking**: Compare patient outcome measures with industry benchmarks or peer organizations. Benchmarking helps set performance goals and provides a reference point for evaluating progress.
- **Patient Involvement in Improvement**: Engage patients and their families in the continuous improvement process. Collect their input on care processes and outcomes to ensure that the EBP initiative is aligned with patient needs and preferences.

The Role of Clinical Practice Guidelines in Promoting Evidence-Based Practice

Clinical practice guidelines are essential tools for promoting evidence-based practice (EBP) in healthcare. They provide standardized recommendations based on the best available evidence, helping healthcare providers make informed decisions about patient care. However, the use of these guidelines must be balanced with the need for individualized patient care, as not all patients fit neatly into the parameters of standardized protocols.

1. Strengths of Clinical Practice Guidelines

A. Standardization of Care

- Clinical practice guidelines standardize care across different settings and providers, ensuring that patients receive consistent and evidence-based treatment regardless of where they are treated. This standardization helps reduce variations in care, which can lead to improved patient outcomes.

B. Informed Decision-Making

- Guidelines synthesize the latest research and expert consensus, providing healthcare providers with a reliable source of information for making clinical decisions. By following guidelines, providers can be confident that their care practices are aligned with the best available evidence.

C. Quality Improvement

- Guidelines serve as a foundation for quality improvement initiatives. They establish benchmarks for care, which can be used to measure performance and identify areas for improvement. Adherence to guidelines is often linked to improved patient outcomes and reduced healthcare costs.

2. Limitations of Clinical Practice Guidelines

A. Lack of Flexibility

- While guidelines provide standardized recommendations, they may not account for the unique circumstances of individual patients. Strict adherence to guidelines without considering patient preferences, comorbidities, or specific clinical situations can lead to suboptimal care.

B. Rapidly Evolving Evidence

- The pace of medical research means that guidelines can quickly become outdated. It can take time to update guidelines in response to new evidence, potentially leading to the continued use of practices that are no longer considered best practice.

C. Overreliance on Guidelines

- An overreliance on guidelines can stifle clinical judgment and creativity. Healthcare providers may feel constrained by guidelines, even when their clinical experience suggests that a different approach might be more appropriate for a particular patient.

3. Balancing Guidelines with Individualized Care

A. Clinical Judgment and Flexibility

- Nurse executives should encourage providers to use clinical guidelines as a foundation for care but not as a rigid rulebook. Providers should be trained to apply guidelines flexibly, taking into account the individual needs and preferences of each patient.

B. Shared Decision-Making

- Incorporate shared decision-making into the care process, where patients are actively involved in discussing treatment options based on the guidelines and their own values and preferences. This approach ensures that care is both evidence-based and patient-centered.

C. Continuous Education and Updates

- Implement continuous education programs to keep providers informed about updates to clinical guidelines and the underlying evidence. This ongoing education helps ensure that care practices remain current and relevant.

D. Use of Decision Support Tools

- Integrate clinical decision support tools within electronic health records (EHRs) to help providers apply guidelines appropriately. These tools can provide real-time guidance while allowing providers to adjust recommendations based on individual patient factors.

Case Study: Successful Implementation of Evidence-Based Practice – Reducing Catheter-Associated Urinary Tract Infections (CAUTIs)

1. Background and Objectives

A. Problem Identification

- Catheter-associated urinary tract infections (CAUTIs) are one of the most common healthcare-associated infections (HAIs) in hospitals. They are associated with increased morbidity, extended hospital stays, and higher healthcare costs. A large urban hospital identified a high rate of CAUTIs as a significant issue requiring immediate attention.

B. Objectives

- The primary objective of the initiative was to reduce the incidence of CAUTIs by implementing evidence-based practices related to catheter use, insertion, and maintenance.

2. Key Success Factors

A. Strong Leadership and Commitment

- The success of the initiative was driven by strong leadership from nurse executives and infection control teams. Hospital leadership demonstrated a clear commitment to reducing CAUTIs by allocating resources, setting clear goals, and holding staff accountable for outcomes.

B. Multidisciplinary Collaboration

- The initiative involved a multidisciplinary team, including nurses, physicians, infection control specialists, and quality improvement personnel. This collaboration ensured that all aspects of catheter care were addressed, from insertion to maintenance and removal.

C. Evidence-Based Protocols

- The hospital implemented evidence-based protocols for catheter use, emphasizing the following key practices:
  - **Avoiding Unnecessary Catheterization**: Strict criteria were established for catheter use, reducing the number of unnecessary catheterizations.
  - **Aseptic Insertion Technique**: All staff were trained in aseptic techniques for catheter insertion, minimizing the risk of introducing pathogens.
  - **Daily Review and Early Removal**: Catheters were reviewed daily, and those no longer necessary were removed promptly to reduce the duration of catheter use.
  - **Maintenance and Hygiene**: Staff followed standardized protocols for catheter maintenance, including regular hygiene and monitoring for signs of infection.

D. Continuous Education and Training

- Ongoing education and training were provided to all staff involved in catheter care. This included in-service training sessions, competency assessments, and the use of simulation exercises to reinforce best practices.

E. Monitoring and Feedback

- Continuous monitoring of CAUTI rates was conducted, with real-time data provided to clinical teams. Feedback loops were established so that staff could see the impact of their efforts and make adjustments as needed.

F. Patient and Family Engagement

- Patients and their families were educated about the risks associated with catheters and the importance of hygiene. This engagement helped ensure that patients were informed and involved in their care, which contributed to the overall success of the initiative.

3. Outcomes and Lessons Learned

A. Outcomes

- The initiative led to a significant reduction in CAUTI rates, with a decrease of over 50% within the first year. This improvement was sustained over time, leading to better patient outcomes, shorter hospital stays, and reduced healthcare costs.

B. Lessons Learned

- **Leadership Commitment**: Strong leadership is essential for the success of EBP initiatives. Leaders must be actively involved in setting goals, allocating resources, and holding teams accountable.
- **Team Collaboration**: Multidisciplinary collaboration is crucial for addressing complex healthcare issues. Involving all relevant stakeholders ensures that all aspects of care are considered.
- **Education and Training**: Continuous education and training are necessary to ensure that evidence-based practices are consistently followed. Competency assessments and simulations can help reinforce learning.
- **Data-Driven Improvement**: Continuous monitoring and feedback allow teams to track progress and make data-driven adjustments. Transparency in reporting outcomes helps maintain momentum and accountability.

4. Application to Other Clinical Areas

The success factors identified in the CAUTI reduction initiative can be applied to other clinical areas by following a similar approach:

- **Identifying a Clear Problem**: Start by identifying a specific clinical issue that requires improvement, such as reducing surgical site infections or improving medication reconciliation.
- **Leadership and Commitment**: Ensure that leadership is fully committed to the initiative and provides the necessary support and resources.
- **Multidisciplinary Collaboration**: Form a multidisciplinary team that includes all relevant stakeholders, from clinicians to quality improvement specialists.
- **Evidence-Based Protocols**: Develop and implement protocols based on the best available evidence, ensuring that they are tailored to the specific clinical area.
- **Continuous Education**: Provide ongoing education and training to staff, using competency assessments and simulations to reinforce best practices.
- **Monitoring and Feedback**: Implement a robust system for monitoring outcomes and providing feedback to the team, ensuring that the initiative remains on track and that improvements are sustained over time.

By applying these principles, healthcare organizations can successfully implement EBP initiatives across various clinical areas, leading to improved patient outcomes and overall healthcare quality.

Analysis of the HCAHPS Survey Components and Their Impact on Hospital Reimbursement and Reputation

The Hospital Consumer Assessment of Healthcare Providers and Systems (HCAHPS) survey is a standardized tool used to measure patients' perceptions of their hospital experience. It is the first national, publicly reported survey of patients' perspectives of hospital care, and its results have significant implications for hospital reimbursement and reputation.

1. Components of the HCAHPS Survey

The HCAHPS survey consists of 29 questions that encompass multiple domains of patient experience. The key domains include:

1. **Communication with Nurses:**

- Focus: Measures how often nurses communicated well with patients, including listening carefully, explaining things clearly, and treating patients with courtesy and respect.
- Impact: Effective communication with nurses is critical for patient satisfaction, as it directly influences patients' understanding of their care and their overall experience.

2. **Communication with Doctors:**
   - Focus: Evaluates how often doctors communicated well with patients, including listening, explaining, and showing respect.
   - Impact: Like nurse communication, doctor-patient interactions play a vital role in how patients perceive the quality of care they receive.

3. **Responsiveness of Hospital Staff:**
   - Focus: Assesses how quickly hospital staff responded to patients' needs, such as assistance with bathroom needs and response to call buttons.
   - Impact: Responsiveness affects patients' comfort and safety during their stay, influencing their overall satisfaction.

4. **Cleanliness and Quietness of the Hospital Environment:**
   - Focus: Measures patients' perceptions of the cleanliness of their room and bathroom, as well as how quiet the area around their room was at night.
   - Impact: A clean and quiet environment is essential for patient recovery and comfort, directly affecting patient satisfaction and perceptions of care quality.

5. **Pain Management:**
   - Focus: Evaluates how well hospital staff helped patients manage their pain, including how often their pain was well controlled and how often the staff did everything they could to help with pain.
   - Impact: Effective pain management is a critical component of patient care and satisfaction, influencing patients' comfort and experience.

6. **Communication about Medications:**
   - Focus: Assesses whether hospital staff explained the purpose of new medications and described potential side effects in an understandable way.
   - Impact: Proper communication about medications is essential for patient safety and satisfaction, as it helps patients understand their treatment and reduces the risk of medication errors.

7. **Discharge Information:**
   - Focus: Measures how well patients were informed about what to do during their recovery at home, including understanding their discharge instructions.
   - Impact: Clear discharge instructions are crucial for a safe transition from hospital to home and can significantly impact patient outcomes and satisfaction.

8. **Overall Hospital Rating:**
   - Focus: Patients are asked to rate the hospital on a scale from 0 to 10, with 0 being the worst and 10 being the best.
   - Impact: The overall rating provides a summary measure of patient satisfaction and influences public perceptions of the hospital's quality.

9. **Willingness to Recommend:**
   - Focus: Patients are asked whether they would recommend the hospital to friends and family.
   - Impact: This metric reflects overall patient satisfaction and trust in the hospital's services, impacting the hospital's reputation.

2. Impact on Hospital Reimbursement and Reputation

1. **Hospital Reimbursement:**
   - **Value-Based Purchasing (VBP) Program:** The Centers for Medicare & Medicaid Services (CMS) uses HCAHPS scores as a key component of its VBP program. Hospitals' reimbursement rates are adjusted based on their performance on HCAHPS and other quality measures. High HCAHPS scores can lead to financial rewards, while low scores may result in penalties, making patient satisfaction a direct driver of financial outcomes.

2. **Hospital Reputation:**

- o **Public Reporting:** HCAHPS results are publicly reported on the CMS Hospital Compare website, where they are accessible to patients, insurers, and the general public. Hospitals with high HCAHPS scores can attract more patients and gain a competitive advantage in the healthcare market. Conversely, poor scores can damage a hospital's reputation, leading to lower patient volumes and decreased market share.

Strategies for Improving Performance Across HCAHPS Domains

To enhance performance across the HCAHPS domains, hospitals can implement the following strategies:

1. **Enhance Communication with Nurses and Doctors:**
   - o **Training Programs:** Implement regular training programs focused on communication skills for nurses and doctors. Role-playing, simulation, and patient feedback can be used to reinforce these skills.
   - o **Hourly Rounding:** Establish hourly rounding protocols where nurses proactively check on patients, addressing needs before they arise. This improves communication and responsiveness.

2. **Improve Responsiveness of Hospital Staff:**
   - o **Call Light Response Teams:** Create dedicated teams responsible for responding to patient call lights within a specified timeframe. Use technology to track response times and identify areas for improvement.
   - o **Lean Process Improvement:** Apply Lean principles to streamline workflows, ensuring that staff can respond quickly to patient needs without unnecessary delays.

3. **Maintain a Clean and Quiet Hospital Environment:**
   - o **Environmental Services Training:** Provide ongoing training for environmental services staff on the importance of cleanliness in patient rooms and bathrooms. Implement daily room checks and a cleanliness checklist.
   - o **Noise Reduction Initiatives:** Implement noise reduction strategies such as quiet hours, sound-absorbing materials, and white noise machines. Educate staff on the importance of minimizing noise, especially at night.

4. **Enhance Pain Management Practices:**
   - o **Multimodal Pain Management:** Adopt a multimodal approach to pain management that includes both pharmacological and non-pharmacological interventions. Involve pain specialists when necessary.
   - o **Pain Rounds:** Implement regular pain rounds where interdisciplinary teams assess and address patients' pain levels, ensuring that pain is managed effectively and promptly.

5. **Improve Communication about Medications:**
   - o **Medication Education Tools:** Develop easy-to-understand medication education materials that include the purpose of each medication and potential side effects. Use teach-back methods to ensure patient understanding.
   - o **Pharmacist Involvement:** Involve pharmacists in patient education, particularly for patients with complex medication regimens. Pharmacists can provide detailed explanations and answer patient questions.

6. **Strengthen Discharge Planning and Information:**
   - o **Discharge Checklists:** Develop standardized discharge checklists that ensure all necessary information is communicated to the patient. Include written instructions and follow-up appointments.
   - o **Post-Discharge Follow-Up:** Implement a post-discharge follow-up program where nurses or care coordinators contact patients within 48 hours of discharge to address any concerns and reinforce discharge instructions.

7. **Improve Overall Hospital Rating and Willingness to Recommend:**
   - o **Patient Experience Teams:** Create dedicated patient experience teams responsible for monitoring HCAHPS scores, identifying areas for improvement, and implementing targeted interventions.
   - o **Patient and Family Advisory Councils (PFACs):** Establish PFACs to gather direct feedback from patients and families about their experiences. Use this feedback to guide quality improvement initiatives.

Designing a Comprehensive Patient and Family Engagement Program for a Pediatric Hospital

A comprehensive patient and family engagement program in a pediatric hospital is essential for improving care quality, enhancing patient and family satisfaction, and fostering a collaborative care environment. The following elements can be integrated into the program:

1. Family Advisory Councils

1. **Establish a Family Advisory Council (FAC):**
   - **Composition:** Include parents, guardians, caregivers, and former patients, as well as hospital staff such as nurses, doctors, social workers, and administrators.
   - **Purpose:** The FAC will serve as a forum for families to provide input on hospital policies, programs, and services. Their perspectives will guide decisions on care delivery, patient safety, and facility improvements.
   - **Meetings:** Hold regular meetings (e.g., monthly or quarterly) where council members discuss issues, review proposed changes, and share experiences. Ensure that council members feel heard and valued.

2. **Incorporate Family Feedback into Hospital Operations:**
   - **Feedback Mechanisms:** Develop structured feedback mechanisms, such as surveys, suggestion boxes, and online forums, where families can share their thoughts on hospital services and care processes.
   - **Implementation:** Use feedback from the FAC to implement changes that enhance the patient and family experience. Provide regular updates to the council on how their input is being used to drive improvements.

2. Bedside Rounding

1. **Implement Family-Centered Bedside Rounding:**
   - **Inclusion of Families:** During daily rounds, encourage the active participation of patients (when age-appropriate) and their families. Allow them to ask questions, share observations, and participate in decision-making about the patient's care.
   - **Structured Communication:** Develop a structured approach to bedside rounding that includes introductions, discussion of the patient's current status, review of the care plan, and solicitation of family input. Use plain language and avoid medical jargon to ensure understanding.

2. **Training for Healthcare Providers:**
   - **Communication Skills:** Provide training for healthcare providers on how to effectively engage with families during bedside rounding. Focus on listening skills, empathy, and collaborative decision-making.
   - **Cultural Sensitivity:** Train staff to recognize and respect cultural differences that may influence family dynamics and communication preferences during rounds.

3. Shared Decision-Making Tools

1. **Develop Age-Appropriate Decision Aids:**
   - **Visual and Interactive Tools:** Create decision aids that are appropriate for different age groups, including visual aids, storyboards, and interactive tools that help children and families understand treatment options.
   - **Customizable Plans:** Develop tools that allow families to customize care plans based on their values, preferences, and the child's specific medical condition. Ensure that these tools are accessible in multiple languages.

2. **Integrate Shared Decision-Making into Care Planning:**
   - **Interdisciplinary Approach:** Encourage an interdisciplinary approach to shared decision-making, involving doctors, nurses, social workers, and child life specialists. This ensures that families receive comprehensive information and support.
   - **Empower Families:** Empower families to be active participants in the care planning process by providing them with the necessary information, support, and time to make informed decisions. Use the shared decision-making tools as a foundation for these discussions.

4. Support Services for Families

1. **Family Resource Center:**

- o **Services Offered:** Establish a Family Resource Center within the hospital that provides families with access to educational materials, support groups, counseling services, and wellness programs. Offer resources on coping with illness, navigating the healthcare system, and managing stress.
- o **Accessibility:** Ensure that the center is easily accessible and staffed by knowledgeable professionals who can assist families in finding the information and support they need.

  2. **24/7 Family Support Line:**
     - o **Purpose:** Create a 24/7 support line that families can call to ask questions, seek advice, or express concerns. The support line should be staffed by trained nurses or social workers who can provide immediate assistance or direct families to appropriate resources.
     - o **Integration with Care Teams:** Ensure that the support line is integrated with the hospital's care teams, allowing for seamless communication between the family and the healthcare providers.

5. Education and Empowerment Programs

1. **Family Education Workshops:**
   - o **Content:** Offer workshops on a variety of topics, such as understanding a child's diagnosis, navigating the healthcare system, and preparing for surgery or discharge. Tailor content to the needs and concerns of families.
   - o **Delivery Methods:** Provide these workshops in-person and online to accommodate different learning styles and schedules. Use interactive methods, such as Q&A sessions, role-playing, and hands-on demonstrations.

2. **Peer Support Programs:**
   - o **Peer Mentors:** Develop a peer support program where experienced families mentor those who are new to the hospital or dealing with a challenging diagnosis. This provides emotional support and practical advice from others who have gone through similar experiences.
   - o **Support Groups:** Organize support groups where families can connect with others in similar situations, share their experiences, and receive support. Facilitate these groups with trained counselors or social workers.

6. Evaluating and Sustaining the Program

1. **Continuous Evaluation:**
   - o **Surveys and Feedback:** Regularly survey families to assess their satisfaction with the engagement program and identify areas for improvement. Collect both quantitative and qualitative data to guide program enhancements.
   - o **Metrics for Success:** Develop key performance indicators (KPIs) to measure the impact of the engagement program, such as patient satisfaction scores, readmission rates, and family participation in decision-making.

2. **Sustaining the Program:**
   - o **Leadership Support:** Ensure ongoing support from hospital leadership, including funding and resources, to maintain and grow the patient and family engagement program.
   - o **Adaptation to Feedback:** Continuously adapt the program based on feedback from families, staff, and the advisory council. Keep the program dynamic and responsive to the changing needs of the patient population.

By implementing these strategies, a pediatric hospital can create a comprehensive patient and family engagement program that enhances the quality of care, improves patient and family satisfaction, and fosters a collaborative care environment.

Evaluating the Effectiveness of Service Excellence Initiatives in Healthcare

Service excellence initiatives like AIDET (Acknowledge, Introduce, Duration, Explanation, Thank You) and the Studer Group's Evidence-Based LeadershipSM model are designed to enhance patient experiences, improve communication, and foster a culture of high-quality care. Their effectiveness depends on how well they are implemented and tailored to the specific needs of different healthcare settings.

1. AIDET (Acknowledge, Introduce, Duration, Explanation, Thank You)
A. Overview

- **AIDET** is a communication framework used by healthcare providers to enhance patient interactions. It helps structure conversations with patients to ensure clarity, build trust, and reduce anxiety.

B. Effectiveness

- **Improved Patient Satisfaction**: AIDET has been shown to improve patient satisfaction by ensuring that patients feel acknowledged, informed, and respected during their interactions with healthcare providers. Patients who understand their care plan and know what to expect are generally more satisfied with their experience.
- **Enhanced Communication**: By structuring communication, AIDET reduces misunderstandings and improves the clarity of information conveyed to patients. This leads to better patient compliance and engagement.
- **Consistency in Care Delivery**: AIDET promotes consistency across the organization by providing a standard approach to patient interactions, ensuring that all staff members communicate in a way that supports the organization's commitment to service excellence.

C. Tailoring to Different Healthcare Settings

- **Emergency Departments**: In fast-paced environments like emergency departments, AIDET can be adapted to ensure that even brief interactions are meaningful. For example, the "Duration" component might focus on setting expectations for waiting times or the steps of the care process.
- **Outpatient Clinics**: In outpatient settings, AIDET can be tailored to address the specific needs of patients who may have more frequent and varied interactions with different providers. Customizing the "Explanation" component to address individual treatment plans can enhance patient understanding and satisfaction.
- **Long-Term Care Facilities**: In long-term care settings, where patients may have ongoing relationships with caregivers, AIDET can be adapted to reinforce continuity of care and build deeper trust. The "Thank You" component can be emphasized to express gratitude for the patient's trust and cooperation over time.

2. Studer Group's Evidence-Based LeadershipSM Model

A. Overview

- The **Evidence-Based LeadershipSM (EBL) model** by the Studer Group focuses on aligning leadership behaviors with the organization's goals to drive performance improvement. It emphasizes clear communication, accountability, and the use of evidence-based practices to achieve measurable outcomes.

B. Effectiveness

- **Leadership Alignment**: The EBL model helps align the behaviors and goals of leaders at all levels with the organization's mission and strategic objectives. This alignment ensures that everyone is working toward the same outcomes, leading to more cohesive and focused efforts.
- **Performance Improvement**: By focusing on evidence-based practices, the EBL model drives continuous improvement in both clinical and operational performance. It encourages leaders to use data to guide decision-making and hold themselves and their teams accountable for results.
- **Employee Engagement**: The model emphasizes the importance of recognizing and rewarding staff for their contributions, which can lead to higher levels of employee engagement and job satisfaction. Engaged employees are more likely to provide high-quality care and enhance the patient experience.

C. Tailoring to Different Healthcare Settings

- **Hospitals**: In large hospital settings, the EBL model can be used to drive system-wide improvements by aligning leadership across departments and ensuring that all initiatives are grounded in evidence-based practices. The model's focus on accountability and data-driven decision-making is particularly relevant in complex, multidisciplinary environments.
- **Ambulatory Care Centers**: In ambulatory care centers, the EBL model can be adapted to focus on the specific challenges of outpatient care, such as patient flow, appointment scheduling, and coordination of care across multiple providers. Leadership behaviors that emphasize efficiency and patient-centered care are critical in these settings.
- **Home Health and Hospice**: In home health and hospice settings, the EBL model can be tailored to address the unique needs of patients receiving care in their homes. Leadership behaviors that prioritize compassion,

communication, and personalized care planning are essential to delivering high-quality care in these environments.

Strategy for Leveraging Patient-Reported Outcome Measures (PROMs) to Improve Clinical Care and Patient Satisfaction

Patient-reported outcome measures (PROMs) provide valuable insights into patients' perceptions of their health, quality of life, and the effectiveness of their treatments. Leveraging PROMs can lead to more personalized care, improved clinical outcomes, and higher patient satisfaction.

1. Key Components of the Strategy

A. Data Collection

- **Selecting PROMs**: Choose PROMs that are relevant to the patient population and aligned with clinical goals. Consider factors such as the condition being treated, the patient's demographic characteristics, and the outcomes that matter most to patients.
- **Timing and Frequency**: Determine the optimal timing and frequency for administering PROMs to capture meaningful data. For example, PROMs may be collected at baseline, during treatment, and at follow-up visits to monitor changes over time.
- **Technology Integration**: Use digital platforms, such as patient portals or mobile apps, to facilitate the collection of PROMs. These tools can streamline data collection, improve response rates, and reduce the burden on both patients and providers.

B. Data Interpretation

- **Clinical Relevance**: Train clinicians to interpret PROMs in the context of clinical care. This includes understanding what constitutes a meaningful change in PROM scores and how these changes relate to clinical outcomes.
- **Benchmarking and Comparison**: Compare PROM data across different patient groups, treatment protocols, or time periods to identify trends, disparities, or areas for improvement. Benchmarking against national or regional data can also provide insights into the organization's performance relative to peers.
- **Patient-Centered Analysis**: Focus on individual patient scores to tailor treatment plans to each patient's unique needs and preferences. For example, if a patient reports ongoing pain despite treatment, the care plan may be adjusted to address this issue more effectively.

C. Integration into Clinical Workflows

- **Incorporating PROMs into EHRs**: Integrate PROMs into electronic health records (EHRs) so that they are readily accessible to clinicians during patient visits. This integration allows PROMs to be used as part of routine clinical assessments and decision-making.
- **Team-Based Care**: Involve the entire care team, including physicians, nurses, and allied health professionals, in reviewing and acting on PROM data. Collaborative discussions about PROMs can lead to more comprehensive and coordinated care plans.
- **Patient Engagement**: Share PROM results with patients to engage them in their care. Discussing PROMs during visits can help patients better understand their health status and the impact of their treatment, leading to more informed decision-making.

2. Addressing Challenges

A. Data Collection Challenges

- **Patient Participation**: Encourage patient participation in PROMs by explaining the importance of their input and how it contributes to their care. Simplifying the process and offering multiple options for completing PROMs (e.g., online, in-clinic, by phone) can increase response rates.
- **Cultural Sensitivity**: Ensure that PROMs are culturally sensitive and available in multiple languages to accommodate diverse patient populations. This approach helps capture accurate and meaningful data from all patients.

B. Data Interpretation Challenges

- **Training and Education**: Provide training for clinicians on how to interpret PROM data and integrate it into clinical decision-making. Ongoing education and support are essential to ensure that PROMs are used effectively and consistently.

- **Overcoming Variability**: Address the variability in PROM responses by considering the context of each patient's situation. For example, differences in literacy, health beliefs, and socioeconomic status can influence how patients respond to PROMs.

C. Integration Challenges

- **Workflow Integration**: Collaborate with clinical teams to integrate PROMs into existing workflows without disrupting care delivery. Identify points in the care process where PROMs can be reviewed and discussed with minimal impact on time and resources.
- **Technological Barriers**: Address technological barriers by providing adequate IT support and ensuring that EHR systems are compatible with PROM data collection and analysis tools.

Impact of Organizational Culture on Patient Experience and Satisfaction

Organizational culture plays a critical role in shaping patient experience and satisfaction. A patient-centered culture that aligns with the organization's mission and values can lead to improved patient outcomes, higher satisfaction rates, and a stronger reputation in the community.

1. Influence of Organizational Culture on Patient Experience

A. Core Values and Mission Alignment

- **Mission-Driven Care**: When an organization's culture is aligned with its mission, employees are more likely to internalize and act upon the core values that prioritize patient-centered care. This alignment fosters a sense of purpose and commitment among staff, which translates into better patient experiences.
- **Consistency in Care Delivery**: A strong organizational culture promotes consistency in care delivery, ensuring that all employees, from frontline staff to executives, work toward the same goals. Patients benefit from a cohesive approach to care that reflects the organization's commitment to quality and compassion.

B. Employee Engagement and Morale

- **Engaged Employees**: A positive organizational culture that values and supports employees leads to higher levels of engagement and morale. Engaged employees are more likely to go above and beyond in their interactions with patients, contributing to a positive patient experience.
- **Empowerment and Autonomy**: When employees feel empowered to make decisions and take ownership of their work, they are more likely to deliver personalized, patient-centered care. Empowered employees can respond more effectively to patient needs and preferences.

C. Communication and Teamwork

- **Collaborative Culture**: A culture that promotes collaboration and open communication among staff members enhances teamwork and coordination of care. Patients benefit from a seamless care experience when their providers work together effectively and share information transparently.
- **Effective Communication with Patients**: A culture that values clear and compassionate communication with patients improves patient understanding, satisfaction, and engagement. Patients who feel heard and respected are more likely to trust their providers and adhere to treatment plans.

2. Strategies for Fostering a Patient-Centered Culture

A. Leadership Commitment

- **Modeling Behavior**: Nurse executives and other leaders must model patient-centered behaviors and attitudes. By demonstrating a commitment to patient care in their actions and decisions, leaders set the tone for the entire organization.
- **Vision and Goals**: Clearly communicate the organization's vision and goals related to patient care. Ensure that these goals are reflected in strategic planning, performance evaluations, and reward systems.

B. Employee Engagement

- **Involvement in Decision-Making**: Involve employees at all levels in decision-making processes that impact patient care. This inclusion fosters a sense of ownership and accountability, motivating staff to contribute to a positive patient experience.
- **Recognition and Rewards**: Recognize and reward employees who exemplify patient-centered care. Public recognition, awards, and incentives can reinforce the behaviors and attitudes that support the organization's mission.

C. Continuous Improvement and Learning

- **Feedback Loops**: Establish feedback loops that allow patients and staff to provide input on care processes and outcomes. Use this feedback to identify areas for improvement and to make data-driven decisions that enhance patient care.
- **Ongoing Education**: Provide ongoing education and training focused on patient-centered care, communication skills, and teamwork. Ensure that all employees understand the importance of their role in shaping the patient experience.

D. Creating a Healing Environment
- **Physical Environment**: Design the physical environment of the healthcare facility to promote healing and comfort. This includes creating welcoming spaces, reducing noise levels, and ensuring privacy for patients and families.
- **Emotional and Spiritual Support**: Offer emotional and spiritual support services to patients and their families. Integrating these services into the care process reflects the organization's commitment to holistic, patient-centered care.

Conclusion: Tailoring Service Excellence Initiatives to Healthcare Settings

Service excellence initiatives like AIDET and the Evidence-Based LeadershipSM model can significantly enhance patient experiences and satisfaction when tailored to the specific needs of different healthcare settings. By leveraging patient-reported outcome measures (PROMs) and fostering a patient-centered organizational culture, nurse executives can drive continuous improvement in clinical care and patient satisfaction, ultimately aligning with the organization's mission and values.

Practice Test Questions

Welcome to the Practice Test section of the ANCC Nurse Executive Advanced Exam Prep Study Guide. This section is designed to help you reinforce your knowledge, assess your understanding of key concepts, and build the confidence needed to excel on the exam.

Why Answers and Explanations are Included Right After Each Question:

1. **Instant Feedback:** By providing the answer and explanation immediately after each question, you can quickly assess your understanding of the material. If you answer correctly, the explanation will reinforce your knowledge. If you answer incorrectly, you'll have the opportunity to learn from your mistake and clarify any misunderstandings on the spot.
2. **Efficient Learning:** We've eliminated the need to flip back and forth between questions and an answer key. This streamlined approach allows you to maintain your focus and momentum as you work through the practice test, making your study sessions more productive.
3. **Enhanced Retention:** Research has demonstrated that receiving immediate feedback on your responses significantly improves learning and retention. Reviewing the answer and explanation right after answering helps solidify the information in your memory, increasing the likelihood that you'll recall and apply it during the actual exam.

How to Use This Section Effectively:

- **Cover the Answers:** We encourage you to take a piece of paper or another object to cover the answers while you work through each question. This will simulate a true testing environment and allow you to test your knowledge without any hints.

- **Repetition of Key Topics:** You may notice that some important topics are covered multiple times in different ways throughout the practice questions. This repetition is intentional and designed to reinforce critical concepts and ensure that you're well-prepared for the exam.

As you progress through these practice questions, take your time to understand each answer and the reasoning behind it. This approach will not only prepare you for the types of questions you'll encounter on the exam but also deepen your understanding of the content areas that are most critical to your success as a Nurse Executive.

Let's begin—each question brings you one step closer to mastering the material and achieving your certification goals.

1. A nurse executive is implementing a new care delivery model aimed at improving patient outcomes and reducing costs. Which of the following metrics would be most appropriate to evaluate the long-term success of this initiative?
a. Patient satisfaction scores
b. Staff turnover rates
c. Risk-adjusted mortality index
d. Return on investment (ROI)

Answer: c. Risk-adjusted mortality index. Explanation: While all options are important metrics, the risk-adjusted mortality index is the most comprehensive measure for evaluating long-term success of a care delivery model. It accounts for patient acuity and provides a standardized comparison of outcomes across different patient populations. Patient satisfaction (a) is important but doesn't necessarily correlate with clinical outcomes. Staff turnover (b) may indicate organizational health but doesn't directly measure patient outcomes. ROI (d) is crucial for financial viability but doesn't capture the quality of care. The risk-adjusted mortality index balances both quality and efficiency, aligning with the dual goals of improving outcomes and reducing costs.

2. A Chief Nursing Officer is leading a major organizational restructuring. Which leadership approach from the Full Range Leadership Model would be most effective in inspiring staff to embrace the change and exceed performance expectations?
a. Management-by-exception (active)
b. Contingent reward
c. Transformational leadership
d. Laissez-faire leadership

Answer: c. Transformational leadership. Explanation: Transformational leadership is the most effective approach for inspiring staff during major organizational changes. It focuses on motivating followers to transcend self-interests for the good of the organization, fostering innovation, and challenging the status quo. Unlike management-by-exception (active) or contingent reward, which are transactional approaches, transformational leadership creates a compelling vision and inspires intrinsic motivation. Laissez-faire leadership, characterized by a hands-off approach, would be ineffective in guiding staff through significant changes.

3. In a critical care unit struggling with high turnover rates, the nurse manager decides to implement a Servant Leadership approach. Which action best exemplifies this leadership style?
a. Instituting a strict performance review system
b. Delegating all decision-making to team leaders
c. Prioritizing the personal and professional growth of staff nurses
d. Focusing solely on improving patient satisfaction scores

Answer: c. Prioritizing the personal and professional growth of staff nurses. Explanation: Servant Leadership in healthcare emphasizes the leader's role in serving and developing their followers. By prioritizing the growth of staff nurses, the manager embodies the core principle of Servant Leadership: putting the needs of others first. This approach can lead to increased job satisfaction, improved retention, and ultimately better patient care. Option (a) aligns more with transactional leadership, (b) with laissez-faire, and (d) focuses on outcomes rather than staff development, which is central to Servant Leadership.

4. A newly appointed Nurse Executive is tasked with improving collaboration between nursing and physician teams. Using the Situational Leadership II model, which leadership style would be most appropriate if the teams have high commitment but low competence in interprofessional collaboration?
a. Delegating
b. Supporting
c. Coaching
d. Directing

Answer: c. Coaching. Explanation: In the Situational Leadership II model, the Coaching style is most appropriate when followers have high commitment but low competence. This style combines high directive behavior with high supportive behavior. The teams' high commitment indicates they're motivated to improve collaboration, but their low competence suggests they need guidance and instruction. The leader would provide specific instructions and closely monitor performance while offering encouragement and soliciting input. Delegating (a) is for high competence and commitment, Supporting (b) for high competence but variable commitment, and Directing (d) for low competence and commitment.

5. A healthcare organization is experiencing rapid technological changes and increased competition. Which leadership theory would be most effective in fostering innovation and adaptability among nursing staff?
a. Great Man Theory
b. Trait Theory
c. Transformational Leadership Theory
d. Path-Goal Theory

Answer: c. Transformational Leadership Theory. Explanation: Transformational Leadership Theory is most suitable for fostering innovation and adaptability in rapidly changing environments. This theory emphasizes inspiring and motivating followers to exceed expectations, challenge assumptions, and create innovative solutions. Unlike the Great Man Theory (a) or Trait Theory (b), which focus on innate leadership characteristics, Transformational Leadership can be learned and applied. Path-Goal Theory (d), while useful for clarifying goals, doesn't emphasize innovation and change to the same degree as Transformational Leadership.

6. A nurse manager notices that her unit's patient satisfaction scores have been consistently high, but staff members are showing signs of burnout. Which component of Authentic Leadership should she prioritize to address this issue?
a. Self-awareness
b. Balanced processing
c. Internalized moral perspective
d. Relational transparency

Answer: a. Self-awareness. Explanation: In Authentic Leadership, self-awareness is crucial for understanding one's impact on others and recognizing discrepancies between desired outcomes and current realities. By prioritizing self-awareness, the nurse manager can better understand the disconnect between high patient satisfaction and staff burnout, leading to more effective interventions. Balanced processing (b) involves objectively analyzing data before making decisions. Internalized moral perspective (c) refers to self-regulation guided by internal moral standards. Relational transparency (d) involves openly sharing information and feelings. While all components are important, self-awareness is the foundation for recognizing and addressing complex leadership challenges.

7. A nurse executive is implementing a new electronic health record system. Using the Full Range Leadership Model, which leadership behavior would be most effective in ensuring staff compliance with the new system?
a. Idealized influence
b. Individualized consideration
c. Contingent reward
d. Management-by-exception (passive)

Answer: c. Contingent reward. Explanation: While transformational leadership components like idealized influence (a) and individualized consideration (b) are generally beneficial, in this specific situation where ensuring compliance is the primary goal, contingent reward (a transactional leadership behavior) would be most effective. Contingent reward involves setting clear expectations and providing rewards for meeting those expectations, which can be particularly useful when implementing new systems or processes. Management-by-exception (passive) (d) involves waiting for problems to arise before taking action and would not be effective in ensuring proactive compliance with a new system.

8. In applying the Situational Leadership II model to a nurse residency program, which leadership style would be most appropriate for new graduate nurses in their first month of practice?
a. Supporting
b. Coaching
c. Delegating
d. Directing

Answer: d. Directing. Explanation: The Directing style in the Situational Leadership II model is most appropriate for followers with low competence and high commitment, which typically describes new graduate nurses in their first month of practice. This style involves high directive behavior and low supportive behavior, providing clear instructions and closely supervising performance. New graduates require specific guidance and structure as they develop their clinical skills. As they gain competence over time, the leader would shift to Coaching (b), then Supporting (a), and eventually Delegating (c) styles to match their developmental progress.

9. A healthcare organization is struggling with nurse retention. The Chief Nursing Officer believes that implementing Authentic Leadership principles could help. Which of the following strategies would be most aligned with Authentic Leadership to improve retention?
a. Implementing a robust reward and recognition program
b. Increasing salaries and benefits across the board
c. Fostering an environment of open communication and shared decision-making
d. Instituting a stricter performance management system

Answer: c. Fostering an environment of open communication and shared decision-making. Explanation: Authentic Leadership emphasizes transparency, ethical behavior, and balanced processing of information. By fostering open communication and shared decision-making, the CNO aligns with key principles of Authentic Leadership, promoting trust, engagement, and a sense of value among staff. This approach addresses intrinsic motivators, which are more effective for long-term retention than extrinsic rewards (a, b). While recognition and compensation are important, they don't directly reflect Authentic Leadership principles. Option (d) could potentially undermine the trust and openness central to Authentic Leadership.

10. A nurse leader is working to improve interdepartmental collaboration in a hospital. Which leadership style from the Full Range Leadership Model would be most effective in building long-term, sustainable partnerships across departments?
a. Laissez-faire leadership
b. Transactional leadership
c. Transformational leadership
d. Management-by-exception (active)

Answer: c. Transformational leadership. Explanation: Transformational leadership is the most effective style for building long-term, sustainable partnerships across departments. This style focuses on inspiring and motivating followers to work towards a shared vision, fostering innovation, and encouraging collaboration. Transformational leaders can articulate a compelling future state of interdepartmental cooperation and inspire others to transcend their immediate self-interests for the greater good of the organization. Laissez-faire leadership (a) is too hands-off for this task. Transactional leadership (b) and management-by-exception (active) (d) are more focused on short-term goals and compliance, rather than the long-term cultural change needed for sustainable collaboration.

11. In a Magnet-designated hospital, the Chief Nursing Officer is mentoring unit managers on Servant Leadership principles. Which of the following behaviors would best exemplify Servant Leadership in practice?
a. Making all decisions unilaterally to protect staff from added stress
b. Focusing primarily on achieving departmental goals and metrics
c. Prioritizing the professional development and well-being of staff members
d. Delegating all problem-solving to team leaders to empower them

Answer: c. Prioritizing the professional development and well-being of staff members. Explanation: Servant Leadership emphasizes putting the needs of followers first and helping them develop and perform as highly as possible. By prioritizing the professional development and well-being of staff members, the leader embodies the core principle of Servant Leadership. This approach can lead to increased job satisfaction, improved patient outcomes, and stronger organizational commitment. Option (a) contradicts the empowerment aspect of Servant Leadership. Option (b) focuses too narrowly on outcomes rather than people. While option (d) involves empowerment, Servant Leadership doesn't mean abdicating leadership responsibilities entirely.

12. A nurse executive is tasked with improving collaboration between the emergency department and inpatient units. Which emotional intelligence component would be most crucial in addressing interdepartmental conflicts and fostering a collaborative environment?
a. Self-awareness
b. Self-regulation
c. Social awareness
d. Relationship management

Answer: d. Relationship management. Explanation: While all components of emotional intelligence are important, relationship management is most crucial for improving interdepartmental collaboration. This component involves the ability to inspire, influence, and develop others while managing conflict. It enables the nurse executive to navigate complex interpersonal dynamics, mediate conflicts, and build strong, collaborative relationships across departments. Self-awareness (a) and self-regulation (b) are more internally focused, while social awareness (c), although important, doesn't directly address the active management of relationships required in this scenario.

13. In implementing a new patient safety initiative, a Chief Nursing Officer notices resistance from senior physicians. Which trust-building strategy would be most effective in gaining their support?
a. Mandating participation through executive orders
b. Offering financial incentives for compliance
c. Engaging physicians in the initiative's design and implementation
d. Presenting comprehensive data on patient outcomes

Answer: c. Engaging physicians in the initiative's design and implementation. Explanation: Engaging physicians in the initiative's design and implementation is the most effective trust-building strategy in this scenario. This approach demonstrates respect for their expertise, fosters ownership, and builds trust through collaboration. Mandating participation (a) can increase resistance and damage trust. Financial incentives (b) may be seen as manipulative and don't address underlying concerns. While presenting data (d) is important, it alone doesn't build trust as effectively as active engagement in the process.

14. A healthcare system is planning a major expansion. Which stakeholder mapping technique would be most effective in identifying and prioritizing key stakeholders for engagement?
a. PESTLE analysis
b. Power/Interest grid
c. SWOT analysis
d. Stakeholder salience model

Answer: b. Power/Interest grid. Explanation: The Power/Interest grid is the most effective stakeholder mapping technique for this scenario. It allows for the visualization and categorization of stakeholders based on their level of power (ability to influence the project) and interest (level of concern about the project). This helps in prioritizing engagement strategies, focusing resources on high-power, high-interest stakeholders while monitoring others. PESTLE analysis (a) is for macro-environmental factors. SWOT analysis (c) is for organizational strategic planning. The stakeholder salience model (d), while useful, doesn't provide as clear a prioritization method as the Power/Interest grid for engagement purposes.

15. A nurse leader is implementing a new collaborative practice model in a critical care unit. Which of the following outcomes would be the strongest indicator of successful implementation?
a. Increased patient satisfaction scores
b. Decreased length of stay for patients
c. Improved interdisciplinary team communication
d. Reduced medication errors

Answer: c. Improved interdisciplinary team communication. Explanation: While all outcomes are important, improved interdisciplinary team communication is the strongest indicator of successful implementation of a collaborative practice model. This outcome directly reflects enhanced collaboration and teamwork, which are core elements of such models. Increased patient satisfaction (a) and decreased length of stay (b), while desirable, could result from various factors. Reduced medication errors (d) is a potential consequence of improved collaboration but doesn't directly indicate successful model implementation as clearly as improved communication does.

16. A newly appointed nurse executive is struggling to connect with and influence various departments within the hospital. Which emotional intelligence skill should they prioritize developing to address this challenge?
a. Empathy
b. Self-confidence
c. Adaptability
d. Achievement orientation

Answer: a. Empathy. Explanation: Empathy, a key component of emotional intelligence, is crucial for a nurse executive to connect with and influence various departments. It involves understanding others' perspectives, concerns, and motivations, which is essential for building rapport and trust across diverse groups. While self-confidence (b) is important for leadership, it doesn't directly address the connection challenge. Adaptability (c) is valuable but doesn't specifically target relationship-building. Achievement orientation (d) focuses more on personal drive than on understanding and connecting with others.

17. In developing a stakeholder engagement plan for a hospital merger, which approach would be most effective in managing stakeholders with high influence but low interest?
a. Regularly inform them of project progress
b. Consult them on all major decisions
c. Empower them to make key project decisions
d. Monitor their position with minimal communication

Answer: a. Regularly inform them of project progress. Explanation: For stakeholders with high influence but low interest, the most effective approach is to keep them informed. This strategy ensures they remain aware of the project's progress without overwhelming them with details or responsibilities they may not desire. Consulting them on all decisions (b) or empowering them to make key decisions (c) would be more appropriate for high-influence, high-interest stakeholders. Minimal communication (d) risks alienating these influential stakeholders and potentially turning them into opponents if they feel overlooked.

18. A healthcare organization is implementing a new electronic health record system. Which collaborative practice model would be most effective in ensuring smooth integration across all departments?
a. Multidisciplinary model
b. Interdisciplinary model
c. Transdisciplinary model
d. Interprofessional collaborative practice model

Answer: d. Interprofessional collaborative practice model. Explanation: The interprofessional collaborative practice model is most effective for this scenario as it emphasizes seamless integration of various healthcare professions, fostering shared decision-making and collective ownership of outcomes. This model goes beyond the multidisciplinary model (a), which involves parallel work, and the interdisciplinary model (b), which involves more coordination but less integration. The transdisciplinary model (c), while highly integrated, often blurs professional boundaries, which may not be appropriate for EHR implementation where specific professional expertise is crucial.

19. A nurse manager notices increasing tension between nursing staff and respiratory therapists. Which trust-building strategy would be most effective in improving this interdisciplinary relationship?
a. Implementing a formal grievance process
b. Organizing social events for both teams
c. Establishing joint training and simulation exercises
d. Rotating staff between departments

Answer: c. Establishing joint training and simulation exercises. Explanation: Joint training and simulation exercises are the most effective trust-building strategy in this scenario. This approach fosters mutual understanding of roles, builds shared experiences, and improves communication in a controlled, professional setting. A formal grievance process (a) may address symptoms but not underlying trust issues. Social events (b) can help but may not directly address professional interactions. Rotating staff (d) could potentially exacerbate tensions and may not be practical or safe in specialized areas.

20. In applying emotional intelligence to leadership, a Chief Nursing Officer is working on improving their ability to recognize and understand their own emotional reactions. Which EI component are they focusing on?
a. Self-management
b. Social awareness
c. Self-awareness
d. Relationship management

Answer: c. Self-awareness. Explanation: The Chief Nursing Officer is focusing on self-awareness, a fundamental component of emotional intelligence. Self-awareness involves recognizing one's own emotions, strengths, weaknesses, values, and impact on others. This is distinct from self-management (a), which involves controlling one's emotions and impulses. Social awareness (b) relates to understanding others' emotions and organizational dynamics. Relationship management (d) involves influencing and developing others and managing conflict.

21. A healthcare system is implementing a major change in care delivery models. Which stakeholder engagement technique would be most effective in building support among front-line staff who are skeptical of the change?
a. Town hall meetings to announce the changes
b. One-on-one meetings with department heads
c. Participatory workshops involving staff in the change process
d. Regular email updates on the change initiative

Answer: c. Participatory workshops involving staff in the change process. Explanation: Participatory workshops are the most effective technique for engaging skeptical front-line staff. This approach allows staff to actively contribute to the change process, voice concerns, and feel ownership over the outcomes. It addresses the psychological need for autonomy and competence, crucial for overcoming resistance to change. Town hall meetings (a) and email updates (d) are more passive forms of communication that don't actively involve staff. One-on-one meetings with department heads (b) may be useful but don't directly engage front-line staff in the process.

22. A large urban hospital is conducting a strategic planning session. Which component of a SWOT analysis would be most appropriate for categorizing a projected nursing shortage in the next five years?
a. Strength
b. Weakness
c. Opportunity
d. Threat

Answer: d. Threat. Explanation: A projected nursing shortage would be categorized as a Threat in a SWOT analysis. Threats are external factors that could negatively impact the organization's performance. The nursing shortage is an external labor market condition that the hospital doesn't directly control but could significantly affect its operations. It's not a Strength (a) or Weakness (b) as these are internal factors. While some might view it as an Opportunity (c) to innovate in staffing models, the primary impact of a shortage is negative, making it a Threat in the SWOT framework.

23. In implementing a Balanced Scorecard approach, a Chief Nursing Officer wants to improve patient satisfaction scores. Which perspective of the Balanced Scorecard would this goal primarily fall under?
a. Financial Perspective
b. Internal Business Process Perspective
c. Learning and Growth Perspective
d. Customer Perspective

Answer: d. Customer Perspective. Explanation: Patient satisfaction scores primarily align with the Customer Perspective in the Balanced Scorecard framework. In healthcare, patients are considered customers, and their satisfaction is a key measure of how the organization is perceived by its primary stakeholders. While improving satisfaction may impact financial outcomes (a) or require changes in internal processes (b) and staff development (c), the direct measure of patient satisfaction is fundamentally a customer-centric metric, fitting squarely within the Customer Perspective.

24. A healthcare system is using scenario planning to prepare for future pandemics. Which of the following would be the most critical factor to consider in developing these scenarios?
a. Current hospital bed capacity
b. Potential variations in pathogen transmission rates
c. Staff vaccination rates
d. Available personal protective equipment (PPE) inventory

Answer: b. Potential variations in pathogen transmission rates. Explanation: In scenario planning for pandemics, potential variations in pathogen transmission rates are the most critical factor to consider. This factor can dramatically affect the scale and speed of a pandemic's spread, influencing all other planning aspects. While hospital capacity (a), staff vaccination rates (c), and PPE inventory (d) are important considerations, they are more responsive elements that would be adjusted based on the transmission scenarios. The transmission rate drives the fundamental dynamics of a pandemic and would be the cornerstone of different scenario projections.

25. A nurse executive is using Porter's Five Forces to assess the competitive landscape for a new ambulatory surgery center. Which force would best capture the potential for patients to choose alternative treatment options, such as non-surgical interventions?
a. Threat of new entrants
b. Bargaining power of suppliers
c. Threat of substitute products or services
d. Rivalry among existing competitors

Answer: c. Threat of substitute products or services. Explanation: In Porter's Five Forces model, the potential for patients to choose alternative treatment options, like non-surgical interventions, falls under the "Threat of substitute products or services." This force assesses how easily customers (patients) can switch to alternatives that fulfill the same need. It's not about new entrants (a) which would be new surgery centers, or supplier power (b) which relates to input providers like medical equipment manufacturers. While these alternatives might influence rivalry (d), the core concept of patients opting for different treatment modalities is best captured by the substitutes force.

26. During a Balanced Scorecard implementation, a hospital is struggling to align departmental goals with overall organizational objectives. Which of the following strategies would be most effective in addressing this challenge?
a. Implementing a new performance management system
b. Creating a strategy map to visualize cause-and-effect relationships
c. Increasing the frequency of performance reviews
d. Standardizing key performance indicators across all departments

Answer: b. Creating a strategy map to visualize cause-and-effect relationships. Explanation: Creating a strategy map is the most effective approach to align departmental goals with organizational objectives in a Balanced Scorecard implementation. Strategy maps visually represent how different objectives across the four perspectives of the Balanced Scorecard interact and contribute to overall strategy, helping staff understand how their work connects to broader goals. While a new performance management system (a) or standardized KPIs (d) might help, they don't directly address the alignment issue. Increasing review frequency (c) might improve monitoring but doesn't inherently improve strategic alignment.

27. A healthcare organization is conducting a SWOT analysis and identifies its strong brand reputation in the community. However, the executive team is debating whether this should be classified as a Strength or an Opportunity. Which classification is most appropriate, and why?
a. Strength, because it's an internal factor the organization controls
b. Opportunity, because it can be leveraged for future growth
c. Strength, but it should also be listed as an Opportunity
d. Opportunity, because public perception is an external factor

Answer: a. Strength, because it's an internal factor the organization controls. Explanation: In a SWOT analysis, a strong brand reputation should be classified as a Strength. Strengths are internal factors that give the organization an advantage. While a strong reputation can certainly be leveraged for future opportunities (b), its classification in SWOT is based on its nature as an internal, controllable factor rather than its potential use. It shouldn't be double-listed (c) as this would confuse the analysis. Although public perception involves external stakeholders, the brand reputation itself is built and maintained by the organization, making it an internal factor rather than an external Opportunity (d).

28. In scenario planning for pandemic preparedness, a hospital system has developed four distinct scenarios. Which of the following approaches would be most effective in enhancing the organization's resilience across these scenarios?
a. Selecting the most likely scenario and optimizing preparations for it
b. Averaging the requirements across all scenarios for a balanced approach
c. Identifying common elements across scenarios and prioritizing these in preparation
d. Preparing fully for the worst-case scenario to ensure maximum readiness

Answer: c. Identifying common elements across scenarios and prioritizing these in preparation. Explanation: Identifying and prioritizing common elements across scenarios is the most effective approach for enhancing organizational resilience. This strategy allows for flexible preparation that can be beneficial regardless of which scenario unfolds, optimizing resource allocation and adaptability. Selecting the most likely scenario (a) risks being unprepared if another scenario occurs. Averaging requirements (b) may result in inadequate preparation for any specific scenario. Preparing fully for the worst-case scenario (d) could lead to overallocation of resources to unlikely events, potentially compromising overall preparedness.

29. A nurse executive is using the Balanced Scorecard to improve operational efficiency in the emergency department. Which of the following metrics would best fit under the Internal Business Process perspective?
a. Patient satisfaction scores
b. Door-to-doctor time
c. Staff turnover rate
d. Cost per patient visit

Answer: b. Door-to-doctor time. Explanation: Door-to-doctor time is the most appropriate metric for the Internal Business Process perspective of the Balanced Scorecard in this context. This perspective focuses on key internal operational processes that impact customer satisfaction and financial outcomes. Door-to-doctor time directly reflects the efficiency of ED operations. Patient satisfaction scores (a) belong to the Customer perspective. Staff turnover rate (c) would typically fall under the Learning and Growth perspective. Cost per patient visit (d) is a Financial perspective metric. The Internal Business Process perspective captures how well the organization is performing in key operational areas.

30. In applying Porter's Five Forces analysis to a rural hospital, which force would most appropriately capture the challenge of attracting and retaining specialized medical staff?
a. Bargaining power of suppliers
b. Threat of new entrants
c. Bargaining power of buyers
d. Rivalry among existing competitors

Answer: a. Bargaining power of suppliers. Explanation: In Porter's Five Forces model, the challenge of attracting and retaining specialized medical staff is best captured by the "Bargaining power of suppliers." In this context, healthcare professionals can be considered suppliers of specialized labor. Their scarcity in rural areas increases their bargaining power, affecting the hospital's ability to negotiate terms and potentially impacting costs and service quality. This doesn't relate to new entrants (b) or buyers (patients) (c). While staff shortages might influence rivalry (d), the core issue is the power dynamic between the hospital and the specialized workforce, making it a supplier power issue.

31. During a SWOT analysis, a healthcare organization identifies increasing local demand for mental health services. There's disagreement about whether this should be classified as an Opportunity or a Threat. Which is the most appropriate classification and why?
a. Opportunity, because it represents potential for service expansion
b. Threat, because it indicates a growing health problem in the community
c. Both Opportunity and Threat, as it has dual implications
d. Neither, as it's a neutral market condition

Answer: a. Opportunity, because it represents potential for service expansion. Explanation: Increasing local demand for mental health services should be classified as an Opportunity in a SWOT analysis. Opportunities are external factors that the organization could potentially leverage for its benefit. The growing demand represents a chance for the healthcare organization to expand services, increase market share, or develop new programs to meet community needs. While it does indicate a health issue (b), from a strategic planning perspective, this demand growth is primarily an opportunity for the organization to fulfill its mission and potentially grow. It shouldn't be classified as both (c) as this would muddy the analysis. Market conditions that directly affect potential organizational growth are not considered neutral (d) in SWOT analysis.

32. A large healthcare system is implementing a new Electronic Health Record (EHR) system. Using Kotter's 8-Step Change Model, which step should the nurse executive prioritize to address widespread anxiety among staff about the new system?
a. Establishing a sense of urgency
b. Creating a guiding coalition
c. Developing a vision and strategy
d. Communicating the change vision

Answer: d. Communicating the change vision. Explanation: In this scenario, communicating the change vision is crucial. While establishing urgency (a) is important early on, and a guiding coalition (b) and vision development (c) are necessary, the widespread anxiety indicates a need for clear, consistent communication about the change. This step in Kotter's model involves using every vehicle possible to constantly communicate the new vision and strategies, teaching new behaviors by the example of the guiding coalition. It directly addresses staff concerns by providing clarity, purpose, and direction, which can alleviate anxiety and build support for the EHR implementation.

33. A hospital is undergoing a major culture shift towards a more patient-centered care model. Applying Lewin's Change Management Model, which phase would involve actively modifying existing care delivery processes and staff behaviors?
a. Unfreezing
b. Moving
c. Refreezing
d. Analyzing

Answer: b. Moving. Explanation: In Lewin's Change Management Model, the "Moving" phase is where active changes to processes and behaviors occur. This phase involves making the actual changes to transition from the old state to the desired new state. "Unfreezing" (a) is the preparatory phase where the need for change is established. "Refreezing" (c) occurs after changes are made to stabilize the new state. "Analyzing" (d) is not a specific phase in Lewin's model, though analysis occurs throughout the process.

34. Two healthcare organizations are merging, and the nurse executive is using the ADKAR model to manage the transition. Staff members are expressing doubts about the necessity of the merger. Which element of ADKAR should the executive focus on addressing first?
a. Ability
b. Desire

c. Awareness
d. Knowledge

Answer: c. Awareness. Explanation: In the ADKAR model, Awareness of the need for change is the first element and foundational to the change process. The staff's doubts about the necessity of the merger indicate a lack of awareness about why the change is happening. Before addressing Desire (b) to support the change, Ability (a) to implement skills and behaviors, or providing Knowledge (d) about how to change, it's crucial to establish a clear understanding of why the change is necessary. This awareness can help overcome initial resistance and set the stage for subsequent elements of the ADKAR model.

35. A healthcare organization is implementing a new patient safety protocol, but is encountering resistance from long-standing staff members. Which resistance management strategy would be most effective in this situation?
a. Mandating compliance through policy changes
b. Offering financial incentives for adoption
c. Engaging resistors in the implementation process
d. Providing additional training sessions

Answer: c. Engaging resistors in the implementation process. Explanation: Engaging resistors in the implementation process is often the most effective strategy for managing resistance, especially from experienced staff. This approach acknowledges their expertise, addresses their concerns directly, and can turn resistors into advocates for the change. Mandating compliance (a) may increase resistance and resentment. Financial incentives (b) can be effective short-term but don't address underlying concerns. While additional training (d) can be helpful, it assumes the resistance is due to lack of knowledge rather than other factors like loss of status or disagreement with the change.

36. In applying Kotter's 8-Step Change Model to an EHR implementation, a nurse executive notices that initial enthusiasm for the project is waning. Which step should be revisited to reinvigorate the change effort?
a. Empowering employees for broad-based action
b. Generating short-term wins
c. Consolidating gains and producing more change
d. Anchoring new approaches in the culture

Answer: b. Generating short-term wins. Explanation: When enthusiasm wanes during a change process, generating and celebrating short-term wins can reinvigorate the effort. This step in Kotter's model involves planning for visible improvements, creating those wins, and visibly recognizing and rewarding people who made the wins possible. It provides evidence that sacrifices are worth it, rewards change agents, helps fine-tune vision and strategies, undermines cynics, keeps bosses on board, and builds momentum. While the other steps are important, short-term wins are crucial for maintaining momentum in long-term change projects like EHR implementation.

37. A healthcare system is using Lewin's Change Management Model to shift towards value-based care. Which of the following actions would be most appropriate during the "Unfreezing" phase?
a. Implementing new care coordination protocols
b. Highlighting the limitations of the current fee-for-service model
c. Stabilizing new reimbursement structures

d. Evaluating the success of the new care model

Answer: b. Highlighting the limitations of the current fee-for-service model. Explanation: During the "Unfreezing" phase of Lewin's model, the focus is on creating motivation for change by destabilizing the current state. Highlighting the limitations of the current fee-for-service model creates dissatisfaction with the status quo, which is crucial for unfreezing. Implementing new protocols (a) would occur in the "Moving" phase. Stabilizing new structures (c) and evaluating success (d) would happen during the "Refreezing" phase. The unfreezing phase is about preparing the organization for change, not implementing or solidifying it.

38. In a merger between two healthcare organizations, the ADKAR model is being used to guide change management. Staff from both organizations are unsure how to operate in the new, combined entity. Which element of ADKAR should the leadership team prioritize at this stage?
a. Awareness
b. Desire
c. Knowledge
d. Ability

Answer: c. Knowledge. Explanation: Given that staff are unsure how to operate in the new entity, the priority should be on the Knowledge element of ADKAR. This stage involves providing information, training, and education on how to change. While Awareness (a) of the need for change and Desire (b) to participate are important, the scenario indicates these may already be in place. The uncertainty about operations suggests a knowledge gap. Ability (d) to implement new skills comes after the necessary knowledge has been acquired. Focusing on Knowledge will provide staff with the information they need to function effectively in the merged organization.

39. A nurse executive is leading a major healthcare reform initiative and encountering significant resistance. Which of the following resistance management strategies aligns best with transformational leadership principles?
a. Clearly communicating consequences for non-compliance
b. Providing detailed step-by-step instructions for new procedures
c. Inspiring staff by connecting the change to a higher purpose
d. Offering bonuses for early adopters of the new system

Answer: c. Inspiring staff by connecting the change to a higher purpose. Explanation: Inspiring staff by connecting the change to a higher purpose aligns best with transformational leadership principles. This approach focuses on motivating followers by appealing to higher ideals and moral values, which is a key aspect of transformational leadership. It can help overcome resistance by shifting the focus from personal inconvenience to the broader positive impact of the change. Communicating consequences (a) is more aligned with transactional leadership. Providing detailed instructions (b) is important but doesn't address the inspirational aspect of overcoming resistance. Offering bonuses (d) is an extrinsic motivator, which is less effective for long-term change than intrinsic motivation fostered by transformational leadership.

40. During an EHR implementation using Kotter's 8-Step Change Model, the nurse executive realizes that middle managers are not actively supporting the change. Which step should be revisited to address this issue?
a. Creating a sense of urgency

b. Forming a powerful guiding coalition
c. Creating short-term wins
d. Anchoring new approaches in the culture

Answer: b. Forming a powerful guiding coalition. Explanation: The lack of active support from middle managers indicates a need to revisit the step of forming a powerful guiding coalition. This step involves putting together a group with enough power to lead the change effort and getting the group to work together as a team. Middle managers are crucial members of this coalition as they bridge top leadership with front-line staff. Their active support is essential for driving change throughout the organization. While other steps like creating urgency (a) or short-term wins (c) are important, the specific issue of middle management buy-in is best addressed by strengthening the guiding coalition. Anchoring new approaches (d) comes later in the process.

41. A healthcare organization is transitioning to a new care delivery model. Using the ADKAR change management model, which of the following would be the most appropriate action to address the "Reinforcement" element?
a. Conducting pre-implementation training sessions
b. Sharing success stories from early adopters
c. Explaining the rationale behind the new model
d. Providing hands-on practice with new procedures

Answer: b. Sharing success stories from early adopters. Explanation: Sharing success stories from early adopters is the most appropriate action for the "Reinforcement" element of ADKAR. Reinforcement involves actions that sustain the change and prevent people from reverting to old behaviors. Success stories serve as positive reinforcement, demonstrating the benefits of the new model and encouraging continued adherence. Conducting pre-implementation training (a) aligns with the Knowledge element. Explaining the rationale (c) relates to the Awareness element. Providing hands-on practice (d) is part of building Ability. Reinforcement is about maintaining the change after it has been implemented, which is best achieved through sharing positive outcomes and successes.

42. A nurse executive is implementing a coaching program for emerging nurse leaders using the GROW model. Which sequence of questions best aligns with the GROW model's structure?
a. What do you want to achieve? What's happening now? What options do you have? What will you do?
b. What's happening now? What do you want to achieve? What options do you have? What will you do?
c. What options do you have? What do you want to achieve? What's happening now? What will you do?
d. What will you do? What do you want to achieve? What's happening now? What options do you have?

Answer: a. What do you want to achieve? What's happening now? What options do you have? What will you do? Explanation: The GROW model follows the sequence: Goal, Reality, Options, Will (or Way Forward). This sequence helps coachees set clear goals, assess their current situation, explore possible actions, and commit to specific steps. Option (a) correctly follows this sequence, starting with goal-setting, then assessing the current reality, exploring options, and finally determining actions. The other options scramble this logical progression, which is crucial for effective coaching conversations using the GROW model.

43. A healthcare organization is implementing a reverse mentoring program to improve EHR adoption among senior nursing staff. Which of the following would be the most appropriate pairing for this program?

a. A seasoned nurse manager mentoring a new graduate nurse
b. An IT specialist mentoring a Chief Nursing Officer
c. A tech-savvy staff nurse mentoring an experienced nurse practitioner
d. Two nurse managers from different departments mentoring each other

Answer: c. A tech-savvy staff nurse mentoring an experienced nurse practitioner. Explanation: Reverse mentoring involves younger or less senior employees mentoring older or more senior colleagues, typically in areas where the younger employee has more expertise, such as technology. In this scenario, a tech-savvy staff nurse mentoring an experienced nurse practitioner is the most appropriate pairing. This arrangement allows for the transfer of technological knowledge from a likely younger, more tech-fluent nurse to a more experienced clinician who may be less familiar with EHR systems. Options (a) and (b) represent traditional mentoring relationships, while (d) describes peer mentoring, not reverse mentoring.

44. A nurse executive is implementing a 360-degree feedback process for nurse managers. Which of the following is the most critical factor for ensuring the effectiveness of this process?
a. Ensuring anonymity of feedback providers
b. Linking feedback directly to compensation decisions
c. Limiting feedback to positive comments only
d. Conducting the process annually without fail

Answer: a. Ensuring anonymity of feedback providers. Explanation: Ensuring anonymity of feedback providers is critical for the effectiveness of 360-degree feedback. Anonymity encourages honest, unbiased feedback by reducing fear of repercussions, especially when feedback comes from subordinates or peers. Linking feedback directly to compensation (b) can lead to inflated or overly negative feedback and is generally not recommended. Limiting feedback to positive comments only (c) defeats the purpose of comprehensive feedback. While consistent timing is important, conducting the process annually without fail (d) is less critical than ensuring the quality and honesty of the feedback through anonymity.

45. In developing a succession planning strategy for key leadership positions, a Chief Nursing Officer is considering various approaches. Which of the following strategies would be most effective in creating a robust leadership pipeline?
a. Focusing exclusively on external recruitment for fresh perspectives
b. Implementing a formal mentorship program paired with stretch assignments
c. Relying solely on performance reviews to identify potential successors
d. Limiting succession planning to C-suite positions only

Answer: b. Implementing a formal mentorship program paired with stretch assignments. Explanation: Implementing a formal mentorship program paired with stretch assignments is the most effective strategy for creating a robust leadership pipeline. This approach combines guided development (mentorship) with practical leadership experience (stretch assignments), allowing potential successors to grow their skills and demonstrate their capabilities. Focusing exclusively on external recruitment (a) neglects internal talent development. Relying solely on performance reviews (c) is too narrow and may miss leadership potential. Limiting succession planning to C-suite positions (d) is too restrictive and doesn't create a comprehensive leadership pipeline throughout the organization.

46. A nurse manager is using the GROW model in a coaching session with a charge nurse who is struggling with conflict resolution. Which of the following questions would be most appropriate for the 'Options' stage of the GROW model?
a. "What specific outcome do you want to achieve in managing team conflicts?"
b. "How have you handled similar situations in the past?"
c. "What are three different approaches you could take to address this conflict?"
d. "Which approach will you commit to trying in the next week?"

Answer: c. "What are three different approaches you could take to address this conflict?" Explanation: The 'Options' stage of the GROW model focuses on exploring possible solutions or actions. Asking about different approaches directly addresses this stage by encouraging the coachee to brainstorm multiple solutions. Question (a) relates to the 'Goal' stage, (b) to the 'Reality' stage, and (d) to the 'Will' or 'Way Forward' stage. By exploring multiple options, the charge nurse can consider a range of possible actions before deciding on the best course forward.

47. In implementing a reverse mentoring program for EHR adoption, several senior nurses express skepticism about being mentored by junior staff. Which of the following strategies would be most effective in addressing this resistance?
a. Mandating participation in the program for all senior staff
b. Offering financial incentives for participation
c. Emphasizing the mutual learning benefits for both mentors and mentees
d. Allowing senior staff to choose their own mentors from the IT department

Answer: c. Emphasizing the mutual learning benefits for both mentors and mentees. Explanation: Emphasizing the mutual learning benefits is the most effective strategy to address resistance to reverse mentoring. This approach highlights that both parties gain valuable insights: senior staff improve their tech skills while junior staff gain leadership experience and organizational knowledge. It reframes the relationship as a collaborative learning opportunity rather than a hierarchical reversal. Mandating participation (a) could increase resistance. Financial incentives (b) don't address the underlying skepticism. Allowing choice of mentors from IT (d) misses the point of reverse mentoring with clinical staff and doesn't address the core resistance.

48. A healthcare organization is implementing 360-degree feedback for nurse managers. One year after implementation, participation rates are low. Which of the following is the most likely reason for this issue?
a. Lack of clarity on how the feedback will be used
b. Too frequent feedback cycles
c. Overly complex feedback forms
d. Insufficient anonymity in the feedback process

Answer: a. Lack of clarity on how the feedback will be used. Explanation: Lack of clarity on how feedback will be used is the most likely reason for low participation rates in 360-degree feedback. When participants (both givers and receivers of feedback) are uncertain about the purpose and consequences of the feedback, they may be hesitant to engage fully in the process. This uncertainty can lead to fear of negative repercussions or skepticism about the value of participation. Too frequent cycles (b) typically lead to feedback fatigue rather than low participation. Overly complex forms (c) might reduce the quality of feedback but are less likely to significantly impact participation rates. Insufficient anonymity (d) would more likely result in biased feedback rather than low participation.

49. A Chief Nursing Officer is developing a succession planning strategy and wants to ensure a diverse leadership pipeline. Which of the following approaches would be most effective in achieving this goal?
a. Implementing blind review processes for all internal promotions
b. Establishing diversity quotas for leadership positions
c. Creating mentorship programs specifically for underrepresented groups
d. Outsourcing recruitment for all leadership positions to ensure objectivity

Answer: c. Creating mentorship programs specifically for underrepresented groups. Explanation: Creating mentorship programs specifically for underrepresented groups is the most effective approach for ensuring a diverse leadership pipeline. This strategy addresses systemic barriers that may prevent certain groups from advancing to leadership positions by providing targeted support, networking opportunities, and skill development. Blind review processes (a) may help reduce bias in selection but don't actively develop a diverse pipeline. Establishing quotas (b) can be controversial and may not address underlying issues of preparation and support. Outsourcing recruitment (d) doesn't necessarily ensure diversity and neglects internal talent development.

50. In a coaching session using the GROW model, a nurse leader is working with a unit manager on improving staff engagement. The manager has identified low morale as a key issue. Which of the following questions best represents the 'Reality' stage of the GROW model?
a. "What does high staff engagement look like to you?"
b. "What factors do you think are contributing to the low morale?"
c. "What strategies have you considered to improve staff morale?"
d. "What specific actions will you take this week to address the issue?"

Answer: b. "What factors do you think are contributing to the low morale?" Explanation: The 'Reality' stage of the GROW model focuses on exploring the current situation in depth. Asking about factors contributing to low morale helps the manager assess the current reality of the situation. This question encourages a detailed examination of present circumstances, which is crucial before moving on to exploring options. Question (a) relates more to the 'Goal' stage, (c) to the 'Options' stage, and (d) to the 'Will' or 'Way Forward' stage. Understanding the current reality is essential for developing effective solutions in the coaching process.

51. A healthcare organization is implementing a comprehensive leadership development program that includes 360-degree feedback, coaching, and succession planning. Which of the following metrics would be most effective in evaluating the long-term success of this program?
a. Number of internal promotions to leadership positions
b. Participant satisfaction scores with the program
c. Reduction in external hiring costs for leadership roles
d. Improvement in organizational performance indicators

Answer: d. Improvement in organizational performance indicators. Explanation: Improvement in organizational performance indicators is the most effective metric for evaluating the long-term success of a comprehensive leadership development program. This metric directly links leadership development to organizational outcomes, demonstrating the program's impact on the organization's overall performance. While internal promotions (a) and reduced external hiring costs (c) are relevant, they don't necessarily indicate improved leadership quality or organizational performance. Participant satisfaction (b) is important but doesn't measure the program's impact on the organization. Organizational performance indicators (e.g., patient outcomes, financial performance, employee engagement) provide a more holistic view of the program's effectiveness in developing leaders who positively impact the organization.

52. A nurse manager needs to quickly communicate a critical patient safety issue to the attending physician. Which communication technique is most appropriate for this situation?
a. Open-ended questioning
b. SBAR (Situation, Background, Assessment, Recommendation)
c. Teach-back method
d. Reflective listening

Answer: b. SBAR (Situation, Background, Assessment, Recommendation). Explanation: SBAR is the most appropriate technique for quickly and effectively communicating critical patient information. It provides a structured format that ensures all essential information is conveyed concisely. The Situation presents the current status, Background gives relevant history, Assessment offers the communicator's evaluation, and Recommendation suggests the next steps. This format is particularly useful in time-sensitive, high-stakes situations like patient safety concerns. Open-ended questioning (a) is more suitable for gathering information. The teach-back method (c) is used to confirm patient understanding. Reflective listening (d) is beneficial for counseling but not for rapid information transfer in critical situations.

53. During a crucial conversation about a nurse's declining performance, the nurse becomes defensive and starts blaming others. Using the Crucial Conversations model, which skill should the nurse leader employ next?
a. Make the content safe
b. Master my stories
c. STATE my path
d. Explore others' paths

Answer: a. Make the content safe. Explanation: When defensiveness arises in a crucial conversation, making the content safe is the most appropriate next step. This involves stepping out of the content of the conversation to address the safety concern. By ensuring psychological safety, the leader can reduce defensiveness and re-establish dialogue. "Master my stories" (b) is about managing one's own interpretations before the conversation. "STATE my path" (c) is used to share one's views safely. "Explore others' paths" (d) is important but can only happen effectively after safety is restored. Safety must be addressed before productive dialogue can continue.

54. A Chief Nursing Officer is preparing for union contract negotiations. Which negotiation strategy would be most effective in fostering a collaborative approach while still achieving organizational goals?
a. Distributive bargaining
b. Integrative bargaining
c. Positional bargaining
d. Concession bargaining

Answer: b. Integrative bargaining. Explanation: Integrative bargaining, also known as interest-based bargaining, is the most effective strategy for fostering collaboration while achieving organizational goals. This approach focuses on identifying mutual interests and creating solutions that benefit both parties. It encourages creativity and can lead to more sustainable agreements. Distributive bargaining (a) is a win-lose approach that can damage relationships. Positional bargaining (c) often leads to impasses as parties stick to fixed positions. Concession bargaining (d) involves one party yielding to the other's demands, which doesn't align with achieving organizational goals. Integrative bargaining allows for maintaining positive relationships with the union while still addressing the organization's needs.

55. A heated argument erupts between a physician and a nurse in the emergency department. As the nurse leader, which de-escalation technique should you employ first?
a. Physical stance: Maintain a non-threatening posture
b. Empathy: Acknowledge the emotions of both parties
c. Tone and volume: Lower your voice and speak calmly
d. Distraction: Introduce an unrelated topic to divert attention

Answer: a. Physical stance: Maintain a non-threatening posture. Explanation: In a heated conflict situation, the first and most immediate action should be to adopt a non-threatening physical stance. This non-verbal cue can immediately begin to defuse tension without requiring verbal engagement, which might initially escalate the situation. A non-threatening posture signals safety and can help calm agitated individuals. While empathy (b), calm tone (c), and distraction (d) are all valid de-escalation techniques, they are most effective after establishing a non-threatening presence. The physical stance sets the stage for further de-escalation efforts and can have an immediate impact on the emotional temperature of the situation.

56. A nurse executive is implementing the SBAR technique hospital-wide to improve communication. Which of the following metrics would be most indicative of successful adoption?
a. Increased patient satisfaction scores
b. Reduction in communication-related sentinel events
c. Decreased length of stay for patients
d. Improved staff satisfaction survey results

Answer: b. Reduction in communication-related sentinel events. Explanation: A reduction in communication-related sentinel events is the most direct indicator of successful SBAR adoption. SBAR is primarily implemented to improve critical communication and patient safety. While increased patient satisfaction (a), decreased length of stay (c), and improved staff satisfaction (d) are positive outcomes, they are influenced by many factors beyond communication techniques. The reduction in communication-related sentinel events directly reflects improved information transfer and understanding in critical situations, which is the primary goal of SBAR implementation.

57. Using the Crucial Conversations model, a nurse manager is addressing a conflict between two staff members. Which step should the manager take to "Make it Safe" if mutual purpose is at risk?
a. Apologize for any misunderstandings
b. Contrast to fix misunderstandings
c. Create a mutual purpose
d. Use CRIB to get to mutual purpose

Answer: d. Use CRIB to get to mutual purpose. Explanation: When mutual purpose is at risk in a crucial conversation, using CRIB (Commit to seek mutual purpose, Recognize the purpose behind the strategy, Invent a mutual purpose, Brainstorm new strategies) is the most effective approach. This technique helps parties find common ground and align their goals. Apologizing (a) may be necessary but doesn't address the lack of mutual purpose. Contrasting (b) is used to address intent, not purpose. Creating a mutual purpose (c) is the goal, but CRIB provides a structured method to achieve this. CRIB offers a comprehensive strategy to re-establish mutual purpose and move the conversation forward productively.

58. During union contract negotiations, the hospital administration and union representatives reach an impasse over nurse-to-patient ratios. Which negotiation tactic would be most appropriate for the Chief Nursing Officer to employ?
a. Ultimatum: Set a non-negotiable final offer
b. Logrolling: Trade concessions on different issues
c. Reframing: Restructure the issue to find common ground
d. Flinching: Express shock at the union's proposal

Answer: c. Reframing: Restructure the issue to find common ground. Explanation: Reframing the issue is the most appropriate tactic in this situation. By restructuring the discussion around shared interests (e.g., patient safety, quality care) rather than positions (specific ratios), the CNO can potentially break the impasse and find a mutually acceptable solution. This approach aligns with integrative bargaining principles. An ultimatum (a) can escalate conflict and damage relationships. Logrolling (b) might be useful but doesn't address the core issue. Flinching (d) is a manipulative tactic that doesn't contribute to collaborative problem-solving. Reframing can lead to creative solutions that address both parties' underlying concerns.

59. A patient's family member becomes verbally aggressive towards a nurse, accusing them of negligence. As the nurse leader, which de-escalation technique should you prioritize?
a. Set clear boundaries for acceptable behavior
b. Validate the family member's concerns
c. Offer choices to give a sense of control
d. Use silence to allow for emotional release

Answer: b. Validate the family member's concerns. Explanation: Validating the family member's concerns is the priority in this situation. This technique acknowledges their emotions without agreeing with accusations, which can help de-escalate the situation by making the person feel heard and understood. Setting boundaries (a), while important, may escalate tension if done before validation. Offering choices (c) is useful but premature if the person doesn't feel their concerns are recognized. Using silence (d) can be effective but may be interpreted as dismissive without first acknowledging the person's distress. Validation opens the door for further communication and problem-solving.

60. A nurse executive is training department leaders on using the SBAR technique. Which of the following would be the most effective method to reinforce adoption of this communication tool?
a. Distribute laminated SBAR pocket cards to all staff
b. Incorporate SBAR into daily huddles and handoffs

c. Offer financial incentives for documented SBAR usage

d. Mandate completion of an online SBAR training module

Answer: b. Incorporate SBAR into daily huddles and handoffs. Explanation: Incorporating SBAR into daily huddles and handoffs is the most effective method to reinforce its adoption. This approach integrates the technique into routine practice, making it a habitual part of communication rather than an additional task. It provides regular opportunities for practice and feedback in real-world contexts. Distributing pocket cards (a) can be helpful but doesn't ensure active use. Financial incentives (c) may lead to superficial compliance without true skill development. Mandatory online training (d) provides knowledge but doesn't reinforce practical application. By making SBAR a part of daily operations, leaders can model its use and create a culture of structured communication.

61. A hospital is considering expanding its outpatient surgery service line. Which financial metric would be most appropriate for evaluating the profitability of this expansion?

a. Return on Investment (ROI)

b. Contribution Margin Ratio

c. Operating Margin

d. Earnings Before Interest, Taxes, Depreciation, and Amortization (EBITDA)

Answer: b. Contribution Margin Ratio. Explanation: The Contribution Margin Ratio is the most appropriate metric for evaluating the profitability of a service line expansion. It measures the percentage of revenue available to cover fixed costs and contribute to profit after variable costs are paid. This ratio is particularly useful for decision-making about service expansions because it focuses on the incremental profit potential of the new service. ROI (a) is a broader measure that doesn't specifically address service line profitability. Operating Margin (c) includes fixed costs, which may not change with the expansion. EBITDA (d) is more relevant for overall organizational financial health rather than specific service line analysis.

62. A Chief Financial Officer presents a capital budgeting analysis for a new MRI machine, showing a positive Net Present Value (NPV) but a negative Internal Rate of Return (IRR). Which of the following is the most likely explanation for this discrepancy?

a. The discount rate used is higher than the IRR

b. The project has non-conventional cash flows

c. The NPV calculation is incorrect

d. The IRR method is always more accurate than NPV

Answer: b. The project has non-conventional cash flows. Explanation: A positive NPV with a negative IRR most likely indicates non-conventional cash flows, where there are multiple sign changes in the cash flow stream over the project's life. This can occur in healthcare projects with high initial investments, varying cash flows, and potential reinvestment costs. In such cases, the NPV method is generally more reliable. The discount rate being higher than IRR (a) would result in a negative NPV. An incorrect NPV calculation (c) is possible but less likely given the scenario. The IRR method is not always more accurate than NPV (d), especially with non-conventional cash flows.

63. A nurse executive is implementing Activity-Based Costing (ABC) in the emergency department. Which of the following would be the most appropriate cost driver for nurse staffing expenses?

a. Number of patient visits
b. Patient acuity levels
c. Length of stay
d. Number of procedures performed

Answer: b. Patient acuity levels. Explanation: In Activity-Based Costing, patient acuity levels are the most appropriate cost driver for nurse staffing expenses in the emergency department. Acuity levels directly influence the amount of nursing care required, making it a more accurate reflection of resource consumption than simple patient volume. Number of patient visits (a) doesn't account for the varying intensity of care needed. Length of stay (c) may not correlate directly with nursing care intensity in an ED setting. Number of procedures (d) is relevant but doesn't fully capture the ongoing nursing care required. Using acuity as a cost driver allows for more precise allocation of nursing costs to patients based on their care needs.

64. A healthcare organization is evaluating two capital investment options using the payback period method. Project A has a payback period of 3 years, and Project B has a payback period of 4 years. Both projects have a useful life of 10 years. Which of the following statements is most accurate?
a. Project A is always the better choice because it has a shorter payback period
b. Project B is likely the better choice because it has a longer useful life relative to its payback period
c. The payback period method is insufficient for making this decision
d. Both projects should be rejected because their payback periods exceed 2 years

Answer: c. The payback period method is insufficient for making this decision. Explanation: The payback period method is insufficient for making this decision because it doesn't account for the time value of money or cash flows beyond the payback period. While Project A has a shorter payback period (a), this doesn't necessarily make it the better choice, as it ignores potential higher returns from Project B in later years. The statement about Project B (b) is not supported by the given information. Rejecting both projects based solely on an arbitrary 2-year threshold (d) is not a sound financial practice. A more comprehensive analysis using methods like NPV or IRR would be necessary to make an informed decision between these projects.

65. A hospital is using contribution margin analysis to evaluate its service lines. The orthopedic surgery service has a high contribution margin but is operating at a loss. What is the most likely explanation for this situation?
a. Variable costs are too high
b. Fixed costs are too high
c. Reimbursement rates are too low
d. Patient volume is insufficient

Answer: b. Fixed costs are too high. Explanation: If a service line has a high contribution margin but is operating at a loss, the most likely explanation is that fixed costs are too high. The contribution margin represents the revenue available to cover fixed costs and generate profit after variable costs are paid. A high contribution margin indicates that variable costs are well-managed relative to revenue. However, if this margin is insufficient to cover fixed costs, the service line will operate at a loss. High variable costs (a) would result in a low contribution margin. Low reimbursement rates (c) would affect the contribution margin. Insufficient patient volume (d) could be a factor, but with a high contribution margin, it's more likely that fixed costs are the primary issue.

66. A nurse executive is analyzing the revenue cycle management process. Which of the following metrics would be most indicative of front-end revenue cycle efficiency?
a. Days in Accounts Receivable
b. Clean Claim Rate
c. Collection Rate
d. Denial Rate

Answer: b. Clean Claim Rate. Explanation: The Clean Claim Rate is the most indicative metric of front-end revenue cycle efficiency. It measures the percentage of claims that are submitted without errors and are processed without additional information or corrections needed. A high clean claim rate reflects effective front-end processes such as accurate patient registration, insurance verification, and coding. Days in Accounts Receivable (a) is more reflective of overall revenue cycle performance. Collection Rate (c) and Denial Rate (d) are important metrics but are more indicative of back-end revenue cycle processes. Improving the clean claim rate can significantly enhance overall revenue cycle efficiency by reducing delays and rework.

67. A healthcare organization is considering implementing a new electronic health record (EHR) system. Using the Net Present Value (NPV) method, which of the following factors would have the greatest impact on the project's NPV?
a. The initial investment cost
b. The projected annual cost savings
c. The discount rate used
d. The project's expected lifespan

Answer: c. The discount rate used. Explanation: The discount rate used in NPV calculations typically has the greatest impact on a project's NPV, especially for long-term projects like EHR implementation. The discount rate reflects the time value of money and the project's risk. A small change in the discount rate can significantly alter the NPV, potentially changing a positive NPV to a negative one or vice versa. While the initial investment cost (a), projected annual cost savings (b), and project lifespan (d) are all important factors, they generally have a more linear impact on NPV. The discount rate's compound effect over time makes it particularly influential, especially in healthcare IT projects with long lifespans and uncertain future benefits.

68. An outpatient clinic is using Activity-Based Costing to analyze its costs. Which of the following activities would be most appropriate to consider as a batch-level activity?
a. Scheduling patient appointments
b. Performing individual patient examinations
c. Maintaining clinic equipment
d. Processing insurance claims

Answer: a. Scheduling patient appointments. Explanation: In Activity-Based Costing, scheduling patient appointments is most appropriately considered a batch-level activity. Batch-level activities are performed for a group of units (in this case, patients) rather than for each individual unit. Appointment scheduling often involves processing multiple patients at once, making it a batch activity. Performing individual patient examinations (b) is a unit-level activity as it's done for each patient. Maintaining clinic equipment (c) is typically a facility-level activity as it supports the entire operation. Processing insurance claims (d) could be considered either unit-level or batch-level, depending on the specific process, but is less clearly a batch activity than appointment scheduling.

69. A hospital is evaluating the purchase of a new surgical robot using the Internal Rate of Return (IRR) method. The project has an IRR of 12%, and the hospital's cost of capital is 10%. However, the Chief Financial Officer is hesitant to approve the project. What is the most likely reason for this hesitation?
a. The IRR is lower than the cost of capital
b. The IRR method doesn't account for project size
c. The project likely has a negative NPV
d. The IRR method assumes reinvestment at the IRR

Answer: b. The IRR method doesn't account for project size. Explanation: The most likely reason for the CFO's hesitation is that the IRR method doesn't account for project size. While the IRR (12%) exceeds the cost of capital (10%), suggesting the project is profitable, IRR is a relative measure and doesn't indicate the absolute value added to the organization. A small project with a high IRR might add less value than a larger project with a lower IRR. The IRR isn't lower than the cost of capital (a). A positive IRR above the cost of capital typically indicates a positive NPV, not negative (c). While the IRR method does assume reinvestment at the IRR (d), this is not likely the primary concern given the information provided.

70. A nurse executive is optimizing the revenue cycle management process and notices a high rate of claim denials due to medical necessity issues. Which of the following strategies would be most effective in addressing this problem?
a. Implement automated coding software
b. Increase staffing in the billing department
c. Enhance clinical documentation improvement programs
d. Outsource the entire revenue cycle management process

Answer: c. Enhance clinical documentation improvement programs. Explanation: Enhancing clinical documentation improvement (CDI) programs would be the most effective strategy for addressing high denial rates due to medical necessity issues. CDI programs focus on ensuring that the clinical documentation accurately reflects the care provided and supports the medical necessity of treatments and procedures. This improved documentation directly addresses the root cause of medical necessity denials. Automated coding software (a) might improve coding accuracy but doesn't address the underlying documentation issues. Increasing billing staff (b) doesn't solve the problem of inadequate clinical documentation. Outsourcing the entire revenue cycle (d) is an extreme measure that doesn't specifically target the medical necessity documentation issue and may not be cost-effective.

71. A hospital is preparing for its Joint Commission survey and is focusing on the National Patient Safety Goal (NPSG) related to medication safety. Which of the following interventions would be most effective in addressing the NPSG requirement to "use medicines safely"?
a. Implementing a barcode medication administration system
b. Conducting monthly medication error reporting meetings
c. Requiring all nurses to complete an annual medication safety course
d. Posting a list of high-alert medications in medication rooms

Answer: a. Implementing a barcode medication administration system. Explanation: Implementing a barcode medication administration system is the most effective intervention for addressing the NPSG requirement to "use medicines safely." This technology significantly reduces medication errors by ensuring the right patient receives the right medication, in the right dose, via the right route, at the right time. It provides a real-time check against the medication order and patient information. While the other options contribute to medication safety, they don't provide the same level of direct error prevention at the point of care. Monthly error meetings (b) are reactive. Annual courses (c) may not impact daily practice as effectively. Posting high-alert medication lists (d) is helpful but relies on manual checks, which are less reliable than automated systems.

72. A Chief Nursing Officer is reviewing the hospital's compliance with CMS Conditions of Participation (CoP) for nursing services. Which of the following would be the most critical area to address to ensure compliance?
a. Implementing a shared governance model
b. Ensuring 24-hour nursing services are provided by or under the supervision of an RN
c. Maintaining a 4:1 patient-to-nurse ratio in all units
d. Requiring BSN degrees for all nursing leadership positions

Answer: b. Ensuring 24-hour nursing services are provided by or under the supervision of an RN. Explanation: Ensuring 24-hour nursing services are provided by or under the supervision of an RN is the most critical area for compliance with CMS Conditions of Participation for nursing services. This is a fundamental requirement in the CoP and directly impacts patient safety and care quality. While shared governance (a) is beneficial, it's not a specific CoP requirement. A 4:1 patient-to-nurse ratio (c) is not mandated by CMS CoP for all units. Requiring BSN degrees for leadership (d) may be a good practice but is not a specific CoP requirement. The 24-hour RN supervision is a non-negotiable standard that must be met for Medicare/Medicaid participation.

73. A healthcare organization experiences a breach of unsecured protected health information (PHI) affecting 600 patients. According to HIPAA Breach Notification Rule, within what timeframe must the organization notify the affected individuals?
a. 30 days
b. 60 days
c. 90 days
d. 180 days

Answer: b. 60 days. Explanation: Under the HIPAA Breach Notification Rule, covered entities must notify affected individuals of a breach of unsecured protected health information without unreasonable delay and no later than 60 days following the discovery of the breach. This timeframe applies to breaches affecting 500 or more individuals. The 60-day period is the maximum allowed; notifications should be sent as soon as reasonably possible. The 30-day option (a) is too short, while 90 days (c) and 180 days (d) exceed the maximum allowed time. This rule ensures timely notification to affected individuals, allowing them to take steps to protect themselves from potential harm resulting from the breach.

74. A hospital is applying for Magnet Recognition® and is focusing on the "New Knowledge, Innovations & Improvements" component. Which of the following best exemplifies this Magnet component?
a. Implementing a shared governance structure
b. Achieving high patient satisfaction scores

c. Conducting and applying nursing research to practice
d. Maintaining competitive nurse salaries and benefits

Answer: c. Conducting and applying nursing research to practice. Explanation: Conducting and applying nursing research to practice best exemplifies the Magnet Recognition Program's "New Knowledge, Innovations & Improvements" component. This component emphasizes the importance of research, evidence-based practice, and innovation in nursing. It requires organizations to demonstrate how they integrate new knowledge into nursing practice to improve patient outcomes. Implementing shared governance (a) aligns more with the "Structural Empowerment" component. High patient satisfaction scores (b) relate to "Exemplary Professional Practice" but don't specifically demonstrate new knowledge generation. Maintaining competitive salaries (d) is important for recruitment and retention but doesn't directly contribute to new knowledge or innovation as required by this Magnet component.

75. A nurse executive is reviewing the organization's HIPAA Security Rule compliance. Which of the following is NOT a required implementation specification under the Security Rule's Administrative Safeguards?
a. Security awareness and training program
b. Information system activity review
c. Annual external security audits
d. Security incident procedures

Answer: c. Annual external security audits. Explanation: Annual external security audits are not a specific required implementation specification under the HIPAA Security Rule's Administrative Safeguards. While external audits can be beneficial, they are not mandated by the Security Rule. The other options are required specifications: Security awareness and training programs (a) are necessary to ensure staff understand security policies and procedures. Information system activity review (b) is required to regularly review records of information system activity. Security incident procedures (d) are necessary for identifying, responding to, and documenting security incidents. The Security Rule allows flexibility in how organizations implement these safeguards, but it does specify certain required and addressable implementation specifications.

76. A hospital is working to meet the Joint Commission's National Patient Safety Goal of improving staff communication. Which of the following interventions would be most effective in addressing this goal?
a. Implementing a no-interruption zone during medication administration
b. Standardizing handoff communication using a structured tool like I-PASS
c. Requiring all staff to wear identification badges
d. Installing whiteboards in patient rooms for care plan documentation

Answer: b. Standardizing handoff communication using a structured tool like I-PASS. Explanation: Standardizing handoff communication using a structured tool like I-PASS (Illness severity, Patient summary, Action list, Situation awareness and contingency plans, Synthesis by receiver) would be most effective in addressing the Joint Commission's goal of improving staff communication. This directly targets a critical point of communication in patient care, reducing errors and improving continuity of care. While a no-interruption zone (a) can improve medication safety, it doesn't broadly address staff communication. Requiring ID badges (c) aids in identification but doesn't improve communication quality. Whiteboards (d) can enhance patient communication but don't significantly impact staff-to-staff communication, which is the focus of this safety goal.

77. In preparing for CMS Conditions of Participation compliance, a hospital is focusing on patient rights. Which of the following is NOT a specific requirement under the CMS CoP regarding patient rights?
a. Informing patients of their right to make decisions regarding medical care
b. Providing patients with a list of all charges within 24 hours of admission
c. Ensuring patients' right to personal privacy
d. Protecting patients from all forms of abuse or harassment

Answer: b. Providing patients with a list of all charges within 24 hours of admission. Explanation: Providing patients with a list of all charges within 24 hours of admission is not a specific requirement under the CMS Conditions of Participation regarding patient rights. While transparency in healthcare costs is increasingly important, this specific timeframe for charge disclosure is not mandated in the CoP. The other options are required: Informing patients of their right to make decisions about their care (a), ensuring patients' right to personal privacy (c), and protecting patients from abuse or harassment (d) are all explicitly stated in the CoP. The CMS CoP focus on fundamental patient rights and protections rather than specific administrative procedures like charge disclosure timing.

78. A healthcare organization is implementing a new electronic health record (EHR) system. To comply with the HIPAA Security Rule, which of the following should be the FIRST step in ensuring the security of electronic protected health information (ePHI) in the new system?
a. Conducting a risk analysis
b. Implementing access controls
c. Establishing a disaster recovery plan
d. Training staff on the new system's security features

Answer: a. Conducting a risk analysis. Explanation: Conducting a risk analysis should be the first step in ensuring HIPAA Security Rule compliance when implementing a new EHR system. A risk analysis helps identify potential risks and vulnerabilities to the confidentiality, integrity, and availability of ePHI. This analysis informs all subsequent security measures and is a fundamental requirement of the Security Rule. While implementing access controls (b), establishing a disaster recovery plan (c), and training staff (d) are all important aspects of HIPAA compliance, they should be informed by the results of a comprehensive risk analysis. The risk analysis provides the foundation for a tailored, risk-based approach to securing ePHI in the new system.

79. As part of the Magnet Recognition Program® application process, a hospital is focusing on the "Structural Empowerment" component. Which of the following best demonstrates this Magnet component?
a. Implementing evidence-based practice projects
b. Achieving high nurse satisfaction scores
c. Establishing a clinical ladder program for nurses
d. Maintaining low nurse-to-patient ratios

Answer: c. Establishing a clinical ladder program for nurses. Explanation: Establishing a clinical ladder program for nurses best demonstrates the Magnet Recognition Program's "Structural Empowerment" component. This component focuses on the development and involvement of nurses at all levels of the organization. A clinical ladder program provides a structured pathway for professional growth and advancement, empowering nurses to develop their skills and take on greater responsibilities. Implementing evidence-based practice projects (a) aligns more with the "New Knowledge, Innovations & Improvements" component. High nurse satisfaction (b), while important, is an outcome rather than a structural element. Maintaining low nurse-to-patient ratios (d) is more related to "Exemplary Professional Practice." The clinical ladder directly addresses the structural aspect of empowerment by creating opportunities for nurses to advance within the organization.

80. A Joint Commission surveyor identifies a patient safety concern related to medication reconciliation during transitions of care. Which of the following actions would be most appropriate for the nurse executive to take IMMEDIATELY following this observation?
a. Implement a new electronic medication reconciliation tool
b. Provide additional training to all staff on medication reconciliation
c. Develop a corrective action plan with specific, measurable goals
d. Conduct a root cause analysis of medication reconciliation errors

Answer: c. Develop a corrective action plan with specific, measurable goals. Explanation: Developing a corrective action plan with specific, measurable goals is the most appropriate immediate action following a Joint Commission surveyor's observation of a patient safety concern. This demonstrates a commitment to addressing the issue promptly and systematically. The plan should outline concrete steps to improve the medication reconciliation process, timelines for implementation, and metrics to measure improvement. While implementing a new tool (a) or providing additional training (b) might be part of the solution, these actions are premature without a comprehensive plan. Conducting a root cause analysis (d) is valuable but may take time and doesn't immediately address the surveyor's concerns. The corrective action plan shows leadership's immediate response and strategic approach to resolving the identified safety issue.

81. A mass casualty incident occurs in the community, and the hospital activates its Hospital Incident Command System (HICS). Which HICS role is primarily responsible for coordinating patient care operations during the incident?
a. Incident Commander
b. Operations Section Chief
c. Planning Section Chief
d. Logistics Section Chief

Answer: b. Operations Section Chief. Explanation: The Operations Section Chief is primarily responsible for coordinating patient care operations during a mass casualty incident under the HICS structure. This role manages all tactical operations directly applicable to the primary mission, including overseeing medical care, patient tracking, and other clinical services. The Incident Commander (a) provides overall strategic direction but doesn't directly manage operations. The Planning Section Chief (c) focuses on collecting and evaluating information for planning purposes. The Logistics Section Chief (d) is responsible for providing facilities, services, and materials to support the incident response, not direct patient care operations.

82. A hospital is developing its surge capacity plan for mass casualty incidents. Which of the following strategies would be LEAST effective in rapidly increasing bed capacity?
a. Implementing reverse triage protocols
b. Converting non-clinical areas to patient care spaces
c. Canceling all elective procedures
d. Constructing a new hospital wing

Answer: d. Constructing a new hospital wing. Explanation: Constructing a new hospital wing would be the least effective strategy for rapidly increasing bed capacity during a mass casualty incident. Surge capacity planning focuses on quickly adaptable solutions that can be implemented in hours or days, not long-term construction projects. Reverse triage protocols (a) help identify patients who can be safely discharged or transferred, freeing up beds. Converting non-clinical areas (b) provides immediate additional space for patient care. Canceling elective procedures (c) quickly frees up beds and staff. These strategies align with the immediate needs of surge capacity, while construction projects are too time-consuming and resource-intensive for emergency response.

83. During a regional disaster, a hospital's Incident Commander is considering partial evacuation. Which of the following factors would be the MOST critical in making this decision?
a. The hospital's current occupancy rate
b. The projected financial impact of evacuation
c. The immediate threat to life safety within the facility
d. The availability of transportation resources

Answer: c. The immediate threat to life safety within the facility. Explanation: The immediate threat to life safety within the facility is the most critical factor in deciding whether to evacuate during a disaster. This factor directly relates to the primary responsibility of protecting patients, staff, and visitors from harm. While the current occupancy rate (a), financial impact (b), and availability of transportation (d) are important considerations, they are secondary to the immediate safety threat. If there's a direct, imminent danger to life safety (e.g., structural damage, loss of critical systems), evacuation becomes necessary regardless of other factors. The decision to evacuate is primarily based on the assessment of risk to human life and safety within the facility.

84. A nurse executive is reviewing the hospital's Continuity of Operations Plan (COOP). Which of the following elements is MOST essential for ensuring continued functionality during a prolonged power outage?
a. A communication plan for notifying staff and patients
b. Procedures for accessing and protecting vital records
c. Identification of alternate care sites
d. A strategy for maintaining critical healthcare services

Answer: d. A strategy for maintaining critical healthcare services. Explanation: In a Continuity of Operations Plan, a strategy for maintaining critical healthcare services is the most essential element for ensuring continued functionality during a prolonged power outage. This strategy would include plans for backup power systems, prioritization of essential services, and procedures for operating with limited resources. While a communication plan (a), procedures for vital records (b), and identification of alternate sites (c) are important components of a COOP, the ability to maintain critical healthcare services is fundamental to the hospital's core mission and directly impacts patient safety and care continuity during a crisis.

85. In preparing for a potential influenza pandemic, a hospital is focusing on surge capacity planning. Which of the following metrics would be MOST useful in determining the hospital's maximum surge capacity?
a. Average daily census
b. Number of negative pressure rooms
c. Staff-to-patient ratios by unit

d. Total licensed bed capacity

Answer: c. Staff-to-patient ratios by unit. Explanation: Staff-to-patient ratios by unit would be the most useful metric in determining a hospital's maximum surge capacity during an influenza pandemic. While physical space is important, the limiting factor in surge capacity is often staffing. Understanding current ratios allows planners to calculate how many additional patients can be safely cared for with existing staff, or how much staff augmentation is needed. Average daily census (a) doesn't account for potential space conversions. The number of negative pressure rooms (b) is relevant but too specific for overall capacity planning. Total licensed bed capacity (d) doesn't reflect staffing limitations or the reality of current operations.

86. A hospital is conducting a tabletop exercise to test its evacuation procedures. Which of the following should be the FIRST priority in the evacuation sequence?
a. Patients in the intensive care unit
b. Patients in the emergency department
c. Ambulatory patients
d. Patients in labor and delivery

Answer: c. Ambulatory patients. Explanation: In a hospital evacuation, ambulatory patients should typically be the first priority in the evacuation sequence. This "walk, wheel, carry" approach prioritizes those who can move with minimal assistance, allowing for the quickest reduction in the facility's census and freeing up resources for more complex evacuations. While patients in the ICU (a), emergency department (b), and labor and delivery (d) often require more complex care, starting with ambulatory patients allows for a more efficient use of resources and reduces the overall evacuation time. This approach also allows staff to focus more intensively on higher-acuity patients as the evacuation progresses.

87. During a major earthquake, a hospital loses primary and backup power. The Incident Commander must decide whether to shelter in place or evacuate. Which of the following factors would be LEAST relevant in making this immediate decision?
a. The structural integrity of the building
b. The estimated time for power restoration
c. The availability of patient transport vehicles
d. The hospital's insurance coverage for natural disasters

Answer: d. The hospital's insurance coverage for natural disasters. Explanation: The hospital's insurance coverage for natural disasters would be the least relevant factor in making an immediate decision to shelter in place or evacuate during a power loss following an earthquake. This decision must prioritize immediate safety concerns and patient care capabilities. The structural integrity of the building (a) directly impacts safety. The estimated time for power restoration (b) affects the ability to provide care. The availability of transport vehicles (c) is crucial for evacuation feasibility. Insurance coverage, while important for long-term recovery, does not impact the immediate safety and care concerns that drive urgent evacuation decisions.

88. A nurse executive is developing the hospital's Hospital Incident Command System (HICS) structure. Which of the following positions should report directly to the Incident Commander?

a. Medical Care Branch Director
b. Public Information Officer
c. Resources Unit Leader
d. Security Branch Director

Answer: b. Public Information Officer. Explanation: In the HICS structure, the Public Information Officer (PIO) reports directly to the Incident Commander. The PIO is responsible for interfacing with the public and media and with other agencies with incident-related information requirements. This direct reporting line ensures that all external communications are aligned with the Incident Commander's strategy and priorities. The Medical Care Branch Director (a) typically reports to the Operations Section Chief. The Resources Unit Leader (c) is usually under the Planning Section. The Security Branch Director (d) generally reports to the Operations Section Chief. Direct access to the Incident Commander allows the PIO to quickly disseminate accurate, approved information during a crisis.

89. A hospital is updating its Continuity of Operations Plan (COOP). Which of the following should be the HIGHEST priority in ensuring continuity of essential functions during a disaster?
a. Establishing mutual aid agreements with nearby facilities
b. Identifying and protecting vital records and databases
c. Designating alternate care sites for service relocation
d. Ensuring redundancy in critical infrastructure systems

Answer: d. Ensuring redundancy in critical infrastructure systems. Explanation: Ensuring redundancy in critical infrastructure systems should be the highest priority in a Continuity of Operations Plan. This includes backup systems for power, water, communications, and other essential utilities. Without these systems, a healthcare facility cannot maintain its core functions, regardless of other preparations. While mutual aid agreements (a), protecting vital records (b), and designating alternate sites (c) are important components of a COOP, they become less relevant if the facility cannot maintain basic operations due to infrastructure failures. Redundant systems provide the foundation for continuing essential healthcare services during a disaster.

90. A mass casualty incident occurs, overwhelming local hospitals. As part of the regional response, your facility must rapidly increase its capacity. Which surge capacity strategy would provide the MOST immediate impact on patient care capabilities?
a. Implementing crisis standards of care
b. Canceling all non-emergency outpatient services
c. Discharging all clinically appropriate inpatients
d. Converting post-anesthesia care units to ICU beds

Answer: c. Discharging all clinically appropriate inpatients. Explanation: Discharging all clinically appropriate inpatients would provide the most immediate impact on patient care capabilities in a mass casualty situation. This strategy, often called "reverse triage," quickly frees up beds, staff, and resources to accommodate incoming casualties. Implementing crisis standards of care (a) changes practice protocols but doesn't immediately create capacity. Canceling outpatient services (b) frees up some resources but doesn't directly impact inpatient capacity. Converting PACU to ICU beds (d) increases critical care capacity but takes more time and may not be as broadly applicable as general discharges. Rapid discharge of appropriate patients provides an immediate increase in capacity across multiple units and levels of care.

91. A hospital experiences a wrong-site surgery, a sentinel event. As the Chief Nursing Officer, you're leading the Root Cause Analysis (RCA). Which of the following questions is MOST crucial to ask first in the RCA process?
a. "Who was responsible for marking the surgical site?"
b. "What factors contributed to the event occurring?"
c. "How can we prevent this from happening again?"
d. "When was the last time staff were trained on site verification?"

Answer: b. "What factors contributed to the event occurring?" Explanation: In Root Cause Analysis, the most crucial initial question focuses on identifying contributing factors rather than assigning blame or jumping to solutions. This question encourages a comprehensive examination of all potential causes, including system issues, human factors, and environmental conditions. Asking about responsibility (a) may lead to blame and hinder open discussion. Considering prevention (c) is important but premature at the start of RCA. Focusing on training timing (d) narrows the scope too quickly. The broad exploration of contributing factors sets the foundation for a thorough and effective RCA, leading to more robust corrective actions.

92. A nurse executive is conducting a Failure Mode and Effects Analysis (FMEA) on the hospital's medication administration process. Which step in the FMEA process is MOST critical for prioritizing improvement efforts?
a. Identifying potential failure modes
b. Calculating the Risk Priority Number (RPN)
c. Determining current process controls
d. Brainstorming potential effects of each failure

Answer: b. Calculating the Risk Priority Number (RPN). Explanation: Calculating the Risk Priority Number (RPN) is the most critical step for prioritizing improvement efforts in FMEA. The RPN, derived from multiplying severity, occurrence, and detection scores, provides a quantitative measure to rank failure modes. This allows the team to focus resources on the highest-risk areas first. While identifying failure modes (a), determining controls (c), and brainstorming effects (d) are all important FMEA steps, the RPN calculation synthesizes this information into an actionable prioritization tool, guiding where to allocate limited improvement resources for maximum impact on patient safety.

93. Using the Swiss Cheese Model to analyze a medication error that reached a patient, which layer of defense would BEST represent the role of barcode medication administration technology?
a. Organizational influences
b. Unsafe supervision
c. Preconditions for unsafe acts
d. Technological defenses

Answer: d. Technological defenses. Explanation: In the Swiss Cheese Model, barcode medication administration technology best represents a technological defense layer. This model illustrates how multiple layers of defense (each represented by a slice of cheese) can have weaknesses (holes) that, when aligned, allow errors to occur. Barcode technology serves as a specific, direct barrier to medication errors at the point of administration. Organizational influences (a) typically refer to high-level policies or culture. Unsafe supervision (b) relates to management practices.

Preconditions for unsafe acts (c) might include factors like fatigue or poor communication. The technological defense layer is the most appropriate categorization for a specific tool like barcode medication administration.

94. A hospital is using the SAFER (Scope, Approach, Focus, Evaluate, Results) matrix for proactive risk assessment. Which quadrant of the matrix would include risks that require the MOST urgent attention?
a. High likelihood, low impact
b. Low likelihood, high impact
c. High likelihood, high impact
d. Low likelihood, low impact

Answer: c. High likelihood, high impact. Explanation: In the SAFER matrix, risks categorized as high likelihood and high impact require the most urgent attention. These risks represent the greatest threat to patient safety and organizational performance due to their frequency and potential severity. High likelihood, low impact risks (a) may be frequent but less critical. Low likelihood, high impact risks (b) are serious but occur less often, often addressed through contingency planning. Low likelihood, low impact risks (d) typically receive the least priority. The SAFER matrix helps prioritize risk mitigation efforts, with the high likelihood, high impact quadrant demanding immediate action and resource allocation to prevent potentially frequent and severe adverse events.

95. During a Root Cause Analysis (RCA) for a patient fall resulting in injury, the team identifies multiple contributing factors. Which of the following is the BEST example of a root cause rather than a contributing factor?
a. The patient was on multiple medications known to increase fall risk
b. The call light was out of the patient's reach
c. The unit was short-staffed on the night of the incident
d. There was no standardized fall risk assessment protocol in place

Answer: d. There was no standardized fall risk assessment protocol in place. Explanation: The lack of a standardized fall risk assessment protocol is the best example of a root cause in this scenario. A root cause is a fundamental, systemic issue that, if corrected, would prevent similar events from occurring. The absence of a standardized protocol represents a systemic gap in patient safety processes. The other options, while important, are more immediate contributing factors: medication effects (a) vary by patient, call light placement (b) is a situational factor, and staffing issues (c) may fluctuate. Addressing the root cause of lacking a standardized protocol would create a consistent, system-wide approach to fall prevention, potentially mitigating various contributing factors.

96. In conducting a Failure Mode and Effects Analysis (FMEA) on the hospital's discharge process, which of the following failure modes would likely have the HIGHEST severity rating?
a. Discharge instructions printed in the wrong language
b. Medication reconciliation errors
c. Incorrect follow-up appointment date provided
d. Patient belongings left behind in the room

Answer: b. Medication reconciliation errors. Explanation: Medication reconciliation errors would likely have the highest severity rating in an FMEA of the discharge process. Severity in FMEA relates to the potential impact of a failure mode on patient safety or quality of care. Medication errors can lead to serious adverse events, including readmissions or even fatalities. While discharge instructions in the wrong language (a) could cause problems, it's less likely to directly result in severe harm. An incorrect follow-up date (c) might delay care but is generally less immediately dangerous. Leaving belongings behind (d) is inconvenient but unlikely to cause severe patient harm. The potential for direct, severe patient harm makes medication reconciliation errors the most critical from a severity perspective.

97. A nurse executive is applying the Swiss Cheese Model to analyze a series of near-misses in the OR. Which of the following represents the MOST effective way to strengthen the system according to this model?
a. Implementing stricter disciplinary measures for staff errors
b. Increasing the number and diversity of defensive layers
c. Focusing solely on improving technological safeguards
d. Eliminating all potential for human error in the process

Answer: b. Increasing the number and diversity of defensive layers. Explanation: According to the Swiss Cheese Model, increasing the number and diversity of defensive layers is the most effective way to strengthen the system. This approach acknowledges that no single layer of defense is perfect (each has "holes"), but multiple diverse layers make it less likely for all holes to align and allow an error to pass through. Stricter discipline (a) doesn't address systemic issues and can hinder reporting. Focusing solely on technology (c) neglects other important aspects like human factors and processes. Eliminating all human error (d) is unrealistic and ignores the value of human judgment in complex situations. Diverse defensive layers (e.g., protocols, training, technology, culture) provide comprehensive protection against errors.

98. A hospital is using Failure Mode and Effects Analysis (FMEA) to improve its blood transfusion process. Which of the following metrics would be MOST useful in determining the detection rating for a potential failure mode?
a. Frequency of near-miss reports related to blood transfusions
b. Number of staff trained in blood transfusion procedures
c. Time elapsed between error occurrence and detection
d. Percentage of blood transfusions double-checked by two nurses

Answer: c. Time elapsed between error occurrence and detection. Explanation: The time elapsed between error occurrence and detection would be the most useful metric for determining the detection rating in FMEA. The detection rating assesses how quickly and reliably a failure can be identified before affecting the patient. A shorter time to detection indicates a higher likelihood of catching errors before harm occurs. Near-miss reports (a) are valuable but don't directly measure detection capability. Staff training numbers (b) may influence detection but don't measure it directly. While double-checking (d) is a good practice, it doesn't necessarily reflect how quickly errors are caught. The time-to-detection metric provides a clear, quantifiable measure of the system's ability to identify failures promptly.

99. In applying the SAFER matrix for proactive risk assessment, a hospital identifies several high-impact, low-likelihood events. Which of the following is the MOST appropriate risk management strategy for these events?
a. Implement daily monitoring and rapid response protocols
b. Develop comprehensive contingency plans and conduct regular drills
c. Reallocate resources to focus on more frequent, lower-impact events
d. Transfer the risk through insurance or contractual agreements

Answer: b. Develop comprehensive contingency plans and conduct regular drills. Explanation: For high-impact, low-likelihood events identified in the SAFER matrix, developing comprehensive contingency plans and conducting regular drills is the most appropriate strategy. These events, often called "black swan" events, are rare but potentially catastrophic, making preparation crucial. Contingency planning ensures readiness, while drills maintain staff competency and reveal plan weaknesses. Daily monitoring (a) is resource-intensive and less effective for rare events. Focusing on more frequent, lower-impact events (c) neglects the potential severity of these rare occurrences. While risk transfer (d) may be part of the strategy, it doesn't prepare the organization to handle the event if it occurs. Comprehensive planning and drilling balance resource use with preparedness for these critical, if infrequent, scenarios.

100. A Root Cause Analysis (RCA) team is investigating a series of central line-associated bloodstream infections (CLABSIs). Which of the following findings would be considered the STRONGEST root cause, as opposed to a contributing factor?
a. Inconsistent adherence to hand hygiene protocols among staff
b. Recent shortage of preferred central line kits
c. Lack of a standardized insertion checklist and monitoring process
d. High patient-to-nurse ratios on affected units

Answer: c. Lack of a standardized insertion checklist and monitoring process. Explanation: The lack of a standardized insertion checklist and monitoring process represents the strongest root cause in this scenario. A root cause is a fundamental, correctable issue that, if addressed, would prevent the problem from recurring across various situations. The absence of standardized processes indicates a systemic gap in safety protocols. Inconsistent hand hygiene (a), while important, is more a symptom of underlying systemic or cultural issues. Equipment shortages (b) and high patient-to-nurse ratios (d) are contributing factors that may vary over time. Implementing a standardized checklist and monitoring process would create a consistent, measurable approach to preventing CLABSIs, addressing various contributing factors and providing a framework for sustained improvement.

101. A healthcare organization is experiencing high turnover rates among its nursing staff. As a nurse executive, which of the following strategies would be most effective in addressing this issue and improving retention?
a. Increase salaries across the board to make compensation more competitive.
b. Implement a mentorship program that pairs new nurses with experienced staff.
c. Introduce mandatory overtime policies to ensure adequate staffing levels.
d. Focus on recruitment efforts to bring in a larger pool of new hires.

Answer: b. Implement a mentorship program that pairs new nurses with experienced staff. Explanation: While competitive salaries can help with retention, a mentorship program is more effective in creating a supportive work environment, which can lead to increased job satisfaction and reduced turnover. Mandatory overtime can increase burnout, and focusing solely on recruitment doesn't address the underlying issues causing turnover.

102. During a strategic planning meeting, the nurse executive proposes a shift towards a value-based care model. Which of the following should be the primary focus to successfully implement this model?
a. Increasing the volume of patients seen by each provider.
b. Enhancing the quality of care through evidence-based practices.

c. Reducing the operational costs by limiting resources.
d. Expanding the range of services offered to cover more specialties.

Answer: b. Enhancing the quality of care through evidence-based practices. Explanation: Value-based care focuses on improving patient outcomes and quality of care, not just the quantity of services provided. Implementing evidence-based practices ensures that care is effective and meets the highest standards, which is central to the success of a value-based care model.

103. A nurse executive is tasked with improving patient satisfaction scores in a large hospital. Which of the following initiatives is most likely to have a long-term positive impact on patient satisfaction?
a. Providing additional training for nurses on communication skills.
b. Redesigning the hospital's physical layout to be more patient-friendly.
c. Offering financial incentives to staff for achieving high patient satisfaction scores.
d. Implementing a faster discharge process to reduce patient wait times.

Answer: a. Providing additional training for nurses on communication skills. Explanation: Effective communication is a critical factor in patient satisfaction. By enhancing nurses' communication skills, patients are more likely to feel understood and cared for, which can lead to higher satisfaction levels. Physical layout and discharge times are important but do not have as direct an impact on the patient-nurse relationship.

104. A hospital is analyzing its NDNQI data and notices a significant increase in patient falls on a medical-surgical unit. Which of the following interventions would be MOST appropriate as an initial response to this data?
a. Implement a new fall risk assessment tool hospital-wide
b. Increase staffing ratios on all units to improve patient monitoring
c. Conduct a focused review of fall circumstances and prevention measures on the affected unit
d. Mandate fall prevention education for all nursing staff annually

Answer: c. Conduct a focused review of fall circumstances and prevention measures on the affected unit. Explanation: When NDNQI data shows a significant increase in falls on a specific unit, conducting a focused review of fall circumstances and prevention measures on that unit is the most appropriate initial response. This targeted approach allows for a detailed analysis of contributing factors unique to the unit, such as patient population, environmental issues, or staff practices. Implementing a new fall risk tool hospital-wide (a) is too broad and may not address unit-specific issues. Increasing staffing ratios across all units (b) is resource-intensive and may not be necessary or effective. Mandating annual education (d) is a long-term strategy that doesn't address the immediate issue. A focused review provides actionable insights for targeted interventions specific to the problem area.

105. In analyzing HCAHPS survey results, a hospital notes low scores in the "Communication with Nurses" domain. Which of the following strategies would be MOST effective in improving these scores?
a. Implementing hourly rounding protocols
b. Increasing the nurse-to-patient ratio
c. Providing patients with whiteboards for communication
d. Offering communication skills workshops for nurses

Answer: a. Implementing hourly rounding protocols. Explanation: Implementing hourly rounding protocols is likely to be the most effective strategy for improving HCAHPS scores in the "Communication with Nurses" domain. Hourly rounding provides regular, structured opportunities for nurse-patient interaction, addressing patient needs proactively and demonstrating attentiveness. This directly impacts patients' perceptions of nurse communication. Increasing nurse-to-patient ratios (b) may help but doesn't guarantee improved communication. Whiteboards (c) can aid communication but don't address the interpersonal aspect measured by HCAHPS. Communication skills workshops (d) can be beneficial but may not translate immediately to practice. Hourly rounding creates a systematic approach to frequent, meaningful nurse-patient interactions, directly addressing the communication aspect measured in HCAHPS.

106. A hospital is striving to improve its Leapfrog Hospital Safety Grade. Which of the following measures would have the GREATEST impact on this score?
a. Reducing central line-associated bloodstream infections (CLABSIs)
b. Improving hand hygiene compliance
c. Implementing a new electronic health record system
d. Increasing the number of board-certified physicians

Answer: a. Reducing central line-associated bloodstream infections (CLABSIs). Explanation: Reducing central line-associated bloodstream infections (CLABSIs) would have the greatest impact on improving a hospital's Leapfrog Hospital Safety Grade. CLABSIs are a key measure in the Leapfrog safety score, weighted heavily due to their significant impact on patient outcomes and their preventability. While hand hygiene compliance (b) is important and contributes to infection prevention, it's not directly measured in the Leapfrog grade. Implementing a new EHR system (c) might indirectly improve safety but isn't a specific Leapfrog measure. The number of board-certified physicians (d) is not a primary factor in the Leapfrog safety grade. Focusing on reducing CLABSIs demonstrates measurable improvement in a critical patient safety area directly assessed by Leapfrog.

107. When risk-adjusting mortality rates for benchmarking purposes, which of the following factors is MOST critical to include in the adjustment model?
a. Patient age and gender
b. Hospital teaching status
c. Patient comorbidities and severity of illness
d. Length of hospital stay

Answer: c. Patient comorbidities and severity of illness. Explanation: Patient comorbidities and severity of illness are the most critical factors to include when risk-adjusting mortality rates. These factors have the most direct impact on a patient's likelihood of mortality, independent of the quality of care provided. Including them in the risk adjustment model allows for fairer comparisons between hospitals serving different patient populations. While age and gender (a) are important, they don't capture the full complexity of a patient's condition. Hospital teaching status (b) is an institutional characteristic, not a patient-level factor for risk adjustment. Length of stay (d) can be both a cause and effect of patient condition and care quality, making it less suitable for initial risk adjustment. Comorbidities and illness severity provide the most comprehensive picture of patient risk, enabling more accurate benchmarking.

108. A Chief Nursing Officer is reviewing NDNQI data on nurse satisfaction and notices a decline in the "Autonomy" subscale. Which of the following interventions would be MOST likely to improve this metric?
a. Implementing a shared governance model
b. Increasing opportunities for continuing education
c. Improving nurse-to-patient ratios
d. Offering competitive salaries and benefits

Answer: a. Implementing a shared governance model. Explanation: Implementing a shared governance model would be most likely to improve the NDNQI "Autonomy" subscale. Shared governance structures provide nurses with opportunities to participate in decision-making processes affecting their practice, directly addressing feelings of autonomy and control over their work environment. While continuing education (b) is valuable, it doesn't directly increase workplace autonomy. Improving nurse-to-patient ratios (c) may reduce workload but doesn't necessarily increase decision-making power. Competitive compensation (d) is important for satisfaction but doesn't specifically target autonomy. Shared governance creates formal channels for nurses to influence policies and practices, directly enhancing their sense of professional autonomy.

109. In analyzing HCAHPS data, a hospital notes that its "Responsiveness of Hospital Staff" scores are below the national average. Which of the following metrics would be MOST useful in identifying the root cause of this issue?
a. Average call light response time
b. Nurse-to-patient ratios
c. Patient satisfaction with pain management
d. Staff turnover rates

Answer: a. Average call light response time. Explanation: Average call light response time would be the most useful metric for identifying the root cause of low scores in the HCAHPS "Responsiveness of Hospital Staff" domain. This metric directly measures how quickly staff respond to patient needs, which is a key component of perceived responsiveness. Nurse-to-patient ratios (b) may influence responsiveness but don't directly measure it. Patient satisfaction with pain management (c) is a separate HCAHPS domain and may not correlate directly with staff responsiveness. Staff turnover rates (d) could affect overall care quality but don't specifically measure responsiveness. Call light response time provides a quantifiable measure of staff responsiveness that closely aligns with the HCAHPS question about getting help as soon as wanted.

110. A hospital is participating in the Leapfrog Hospital Survey and wants to improve its score on the "Safe Practice #1: Leadership Structures and Systems." Which of the following actions would MOST directly address this safe practice?
a. Implementing a comprehensive hand hygiene program
b. Establishing regular patient safety rounds by leadership
c. Increasing the budget for patient safety initiatives
d. Hiring additional patient safety officers

Answer: b. Establishing regular patient safety rounds by leadership. Explanation: Establishing regular patient safety rounds by leadership would most directly address Leapfrog's "Safe Practice #1: Leadership Structures and Systems." This practice emphasizes the active involvement of senior administrative leadership and clinical leadership in patient safety initiatives. Leadership rounds demonstrate visible commitment to safety, facilitate direct communication about safety concerns, and help identify systemic issues. While a hand hygiene program (a) is important, it's not specifically a leadership structure. Increasing the safety budget (c) and hiring safety officers (d) can support safety efforts but don't directly demonstrate leadership engagement as required by this safe practice. Leadership rounds create a structured mechanism for top-down and bottom-up communication about safety, aligning closely with Leapfrog's emphasis on leadership involvement in safety culture.

111. When risk-adjusting readmission rates, which of the following factors would be LEAST appropriate to include in the adjustment model?
a. Patient's primary diagnosis
b. Presence of comorbidities
c. Hospital's average length of stay
d. Patient's socioeconomic status

Answer: c. Hospital's average length of stay. Explanation: The hospital's average length of stay would be the least appropriate factor to include when risk-adjusting readmission rates. Risk adjustment should focus on patient characteristics that influence their likelihood of readmission, independent of the quality of care provided. The hospital's average length of stay is an institutional characteristic that may reflect both patient factors and care practices, making it unsuitable for risk adjustment. Patient's primary diagnosis (a), presence of comorbidities (b), and socioeconomic status (d) are all patient-level factors that can significantly influence readmission risk independent of hospital care quality. Including the hospital's length of stay could inappropriately adjust for potential quality issues, defeating the purpose of fair benchmarking.

112. A nurse executive is analyzing NDNQI data on hospital-acquired pressure injuries (HAPIs) and notices significant variation between units. Which of the following approaches would be MOST effective in reducing this variation?
a. Implementing a standardized skin assessment tool across all units
b. Increasing staffing levels on units with higher HAPI rates
c. Conducting a root cause analysis on each reported HAPI
d. Providing financial incentives for units with lower HAPI rates

Answer: a. Implementing a standardized skin assessment tool across all units. Explanation: Implementing a standardized skin assessment tool across all units would be the most effective approach to reducing variation in hospital-acquired pressure injury (HAPI) rates. Standardization ensures consistent risk assessment and prevention strategies across the organization, addressing potential disparities in practice that could lead to unit-level variations. Increasing staffing (b) on specific units doesn't address the underlying cause of variation and may not be sustainable. Conducting root cause analyses on each HAPI (c) is reactive and resource-intensive. Financial incentives (d) may motivate improvement but don't provide the tools for consistent practice. A standardized assessment tool provides a foundation for uniform, evidence-based HAPI prevention practices, promoting consistency and reducing unwarranted variation in outcomes across units.

113. In reviewing HCAHPS scores, a hospital finds that its performance on the question "Before giving you any new medicine, how often did hospital staff tell you what the medicine was for?" is significantly below benchmark. Which of the following interventions would MOST directly address this specific issue?
a. Implementing bedside medication verification
b. Providing patients with written medication information sheets
c. Incorporating teach-back methods for medication education

d. Increasing pharmacy involvement in medication reconciliation

Answer: c. Incorporating teach-back methods for medication education. Explanation: Incorporating teach-back methods for medication education would most directly address low scores on the HCAHPS question about explaining new medications. Teach-back ensures that staff not only provide information about new medications but also verify patient understanding, directly aligning with the HCAHPS question's focus on staff communication about medication purpose. Bedside medication verification (a) improves safety but doesn't necessarily involve explaining medication purposes. Written information sheets (b) provide reference material but don't ensure verbal explanation or understanding. Increased pharmacy involvement in reconciliation (d) is valuable but doesn't directly address bedside communication about new medications. Teach-back methods create a standardized approach to medication education that ensures patients receive and comprehend information about their new medications, directly improving performance on this HCAHPS measure.

114. A nurse executive in a large healthcare facility is tasked with ensuring compliance with the ADA (Americans with Disabilities Act) in accommodating a nurse with a newly diagnosed visual impairment. Which of the following actions is most consistent with ADA requirements for reasonable accommodation?
a. Reassigning the nurse to a less demanding administrative role regardless of her preferences.
b. Providing assistive technology and modifying her workspace to enable her to continue in her current role.
c. Encouraging the nurse to take early retirement as a cost-effective solution.
d. Limiting the nurse's patient care responsibilities to only those that don't involve direct patient interaction.

Answer: b. Providing assistive technology and modifying her workspace to enable her to continue in her current role. Explanation: The ADA requires employers to make reasonable accommodations that enable employees to perform the essential functions of their job unless it causes undue hardship. Providing assistive technology and workspace modifications respects the nurse's role and abilities, supporting her continued employment in her current position.

115. During a routine OSHA compliance audit, a nurse executive discovers that several departments are not adhering to the Bloodborne Pathogens Standard, particularly in terms of proper disposal of sharps. Which of the following is the most appropriate initial action to address this issue?
a. Terminating staff members who are found to be non-compliant with disposal protocols.
b. Conducting an immediate training session on proper sharps disposal for all relevant staff.
c. Reassigning the responsibility of sharps disposal to a specialized team within the hospital.
d. Issuing a memo reminding staff of the importance of adhering to OSHA standards.

Answer: b. Conducting an immediate training session on proper sharps disposal for all relevant staff. Explanation: Education and training are key strategies for ensuring compliance with OSHA's Bloodborne Pathogens Standard. An immediate training session addresses the issue directly and helps prevent future non-compliance, while termination or reassignment may be excessive without first attempting to correct the behavior through training.

116. A nurse executive is planning succession strategies for a team where several members are nearing retirement age. Which of the following strategies would best align with the Age Discrimination in Employment Act (ADEA)?
a. Prioritizing younger employees for leadership training programs to ensure long-term leadership stability.
b. Offering early retirement packages to older employees as an incentive to create opportunities for younger staff.

c. Developing a mentorship program where experienced nurses can guide younger staff in leadership skills.
d. Limiting older employees' participation in succession planning to ensure smoother transitions.

Answer: c. Developing a mentorship program where experienced nurses can guide younger staff in leadership skills. Explanation: The ADEA prohibits age discrimination and promotes equal opportunities for older workers. A mentorship program utilizes the experience of older employees while fostering leadership skills in younger staff, without violating the principles of the ADEA.

117. A newly hired nurse raises concerns that she has been treated unfairly during the hiring process due to her ethnicity. As a nurse executive, which of the following actions best aligns with Title VII of the Civil Rights Act?
a. Offering her additional compensation as a goodwill gesture to resolve the issue quickly.
b. Conducting a thorough investigation into the hiring process to identify any potential biases.
c. Providing cultural sensitivity training for all staff involved in the hiring process.
d. Suggesting that she withdraw her complaint to maintain a harmonious work environment.

Answer: b. Conducting a thorough investigation into the hiring process to identify any potential biases. Explanation: Title VII prohibits employment discrimination based on race, color, religion, sex, or national origin. Investigating the hiring process ensures that any potential biases are identified and addressed, upholding the legal and ethical standards required by Title VII.

118. A nurse executive is reviewing the hospital's policies to ensure compliance with the OSHA Bloodborne Pathogens Standard. Which of the following changes would most effectively enhance compliance with the standard?
a. Increasing the frequency of bloodborne pathogen training from annually to bi-annually.
b. Requiring that only licensed personnel handle and dispose of sharps and biohazardous materials.
c. Installing additional sharps disposal containers in every patient room and high-traffic areas.
d. Implementing a system of random checks to monitor staff compliance with bloodborne pathogen protocols.

Answer: c. Installing additional sharps disposal containers in every patient room and high-traffic areas. Explanation: Easy access to sharps disposal containers significantly reduces the risk of improper disposal, a key component of compliance with the OSHA Bloodborne Pathogens Standard. Increasing training frequency or random checks are beneficial but less directly impactful on day-to-day compliance.

119. In response to a complaint regarding age discrimination, the nurse executive must assess the hospital's compliance with the Age Discrimination in Employment Act (ADEA). Which of the following scenarios would most likely violate ADEA?
a. An older nurse is passed over for a promotion in favor of a younger candidate with less experience but more recent training.
b. A retirement planning seminar is offered to all employees over 50.
c. An older nurse is given the option to transition to part-time work due to personal health reasons.
d. All employees are required to participate in ongoing professional development, regardless of age.

Answer: a. An older nurse is passed over for a promotion in favor of a younger candidate with less experience but more recent training. Explanation: The ADEA prohibits discrimination against employees aged 40 and older. Passing over an older employee for a promotion in favor of a less experienced younger candidate could be viewed as age discrimination, especially if the older employee is otherwise qualified for the role.

120. A nurse executive is reviewing the hospital's hiring practices to ensure they comply with Title VII of the Civil Rights Act. Which practice is most likely to be in violation of Title VII?
a. Implementing a standardized interview process to ensure fairness.
b. Requiring candidates to take a personality test as part of the hiring process.
c. Asking candidates about their marital status during the interview.
d. Ensuring that job descriptions do not specify gender preferences.

Answer: c. Asking candidates about their marital status during the interview. Explanation: Title VII prohibits employment discrimination based on factors such as sex, which can be related to questions about marital status. Asking about marital status could lead to discrimination and is generally considered inappropriate and potentially illegal under Title VII.

121. During a labor dispute, the nurse executive must ensure that the hospital complies with the National Labor Relations Act (NLRA). Which action would most likely violate the NLRA?
a. Permitting union representatives to meet with employees in non-patient care areas.
b. Requiring employees to sign a document waiving their right to join a union as a condition of employment.
c. Hosting informational sessions for staff on the potential impacts of unionization.
d. Allowing employees to discuss union matters during their breaks.

Answer: b. Requiring employees to sign a document waiving their right to join a union as a condition of employment. Explanation: The NLRA protects employees' rights to join or form unions and engage in collective bargaining. Forcing employees to waive these rights as a condition of employment is a clear violation of the NLRA.

122. A nurse executive is updating the hospital's emergency preparedness plan, focusing on OSHA's requirements for the Bloodborne Pathogens Standard. Which of the following should be a priority in the updated plan?
a. Stockpiling personal protective equipment (PPE) in designated emergency response areas.
b. Providing annual bloodborne pathogen training only for new hires.
c. Reducing the number of designated first responders to minimize potential exposure.
d. Limiting the use of PPE to situations involving confirmed bloodborne pathogens.

Answer: a. Stockpiling personal protective equipment (PPE) in designated emergency response areas. Explanation: OSHA's Bloodborne Pathogens Standard requires that PPE be readily available to protect employees from exposure. Ensuring that PPE is stockpiled and accessible in emergency areas is critical for compliance and staff safety.

123. A nurse executive is developing a succession plan and needs to ensure compliance with the Age Discrimination in Employment Act (ADEA). Which strategy would be most appropriate?
a. Offering leadership training programs exclusively to employees under 40.

b. Implementing a mentorship program that includes employees of all ages.

c. Gradually phasing out older employees to make room for younger talent.

d. Limiting the responsibilities of older employees to reduce their workload.

Answer: b. Implementing a mentorship program that includes employees of all ages. Explanation: The ADEA requires that opportunities be provided without discrimination based on age. A mentorship program that is inclusive of all ages helps in knowledge transfer and supports career development without violating ADEA provisions.

124. A large healthcare system is implementing a clinical ladder program based on Benner's Novice to Expert model. A nurse leader is tasked with ensuring that nurses at the "Proficient" level are appropriately recognized and developed. Which of the following strategies would best align with Benner's description of a "Proficient" nurse?

a. Providing structured mentorship to new graduate nurses

b. Encouraging participation in interdisciplinary research projects

c. Assigning the nurse to lead initiatives that require deep understanding of clinical situations

d. Facilitating regular skills labs to enhance technical competencies

Answer: c. Assigning the nurse to lead initiatives that require deep understanding of clinical situations. Explanation: According to Benner's model, a "Proficient" nurse has developed the ability to perceive situations holistically rather than in isolated parts. These nurses have an intuitive grasp of complex clinical situations, making them ideal candidates for leading initiatives that require advanced clinical judgment and leadership.

125. A nurse executive is developing a competency assessment framework for a specialty area, such as oncology nursing. Which element is most critical to ensure that the framework is both comprehensive and reflective of the specialty's complexities?

a. Including basic clinical skills applicable across all nursing areas

b. Focusing primarily on the latest chemotherapy administration techniques

c. Incorporating standards from professional oncology nursing organizations

d. Prioritizing the evaluation of teamwork and communication within the unit

Answer: c. Incorporating standards from professional oncology nursing organizations. Explanation: Competency frameworks for specialty areas like oncology nursing must align with standards set by professional organizations (e.g., ONS - Oncology Nursing Society) to ensure that they reflect the most current and comprehensive practices specific to the field, covering all necessary competencies beyond just clinical skills.

126. A nurse executive is leading the implementation of a Just Culture within a hospital to improve error reporting and management. Which of the following actions best supports the principles of Just Culture?

a. Instituting zero-tolerance policies for any errors made by nursing staff

b. Focusing on system failures rather than individual blame in adverse events

c. Encouraging nurses to self-report errors and accepting minimal consequences

d. Creating a mandatory annual training session on error prevention

Answer: b. Focusing on system failures rather than individual blame in adverse events. Explanation: Just Culture emphasizes accountability while encouraging an environment where errors are seen as opportunities to improve systems and processes. By focusing on system failures rather than individual blame, the organization fosters a culture of safety and continuous improvement.

127. In developing an interprofessional education (IPE) initiative aimed at enhancing collaborative practice among healthcare teams, which approach is most likely to be effective?
a. Conducting discipline-specific training sessions to strengthen individual competencies
b. Implementing simulation-based scenarios that require joint decision-making
c. Hosting lectures from experts in various healthcare fields without interactive elements
d. Organizing social events to improve relationships among different professional groups

Answer: b. Implementing simulation-based scenarios that require joint decision-making. Explanation: Simulation-based IPE allows healthcare professionals to practice collaborative decision-making in a controlled environment, which is essential for improving teamwork and communication in real clinical settings. This approach aligns with the core goals of IPE by actively engaging participants in interprofessional collaboration.

128. A nurse executive is tasked with evaluating the effectiveness of the hospital's current clinical ladder program. Which metric would be most indicative of success in aligning with Benner's Novice to Expert model?
a. Number of nurses promoted annually within the clinical ladder
b. Retention rates of nurses who have achieved higher levels in the program
c. Satisfaction scores from nurses who participate in the program
d. Frequency of participation in continuing education courses

Answer: b. Retention rates of nurses who have achieved higher levels in the program. Explanation: Retention rates are a key indicator of the success of a clinical ladder program, as they reflect the program's ability to engage and retain skilled nurses. High retention at advanced levels suggests that the program effectively supports professional growth and aligns with Benner's model by fostering expertise.

129. A hospital is planning to introduce a competency assessment framework in its critical care unit. To ensure that this framework is dynamic and evolves with the changing demands of the specialty, which strategy should the nurse executive prioritize?
a. Updating the framework annually based on new research findings
b. Including a standardized test that all nurses must pass each year
c. Consulting with critical care nurses to identify areas of needed development
d. Partnering with external experts to conduct periodic audits of nurse competencies

Answer: a. Updating the framework annually based on new research findings. Explanation: Competency frameworks in rapidly evolving specialties like critical care must be regularly updated to reflect the latest evidence-based practices. Annual updates ensure that the framework remains relevant and supports the ongoing development of critical care nurses.

130. When implementing Just Culture principles in a healthcare setting, which of the following challenges is most likely to hinder successful adoption?
a. Resistance from staff who prefer traditional punitive approaches
b. Lack of awareness among staff about the importance of patient safety
c. High turnover rates among nursing staff in the facility
d. Insufficient training resources for nurses on the Just Culture model

Answer: a. Resistance from staff who prefer traditional punitive approaches. Explanation: A significant challenge in adopting Just Culture is overcoming resistance from individuals who are accustomed to a blame-oriented culture. This resistance can impede the shift toward a more balanced approach that focuses on learning and improvement, rather than punishment.

131. A nurse executive is evaluating the outcomes of an interprofessional education (IPE) program that was recently implemented. Which outcome would most strongly indicate that the program has successfully enhanced interprofessional collaboration?
a. Increased participation rates in subsequent IPE sessions
b. Improved patient satisfaction scores related to care coordination
c. Higher scores on individual licensing exams across disciplines
d. More frequent informal consultations among team members

Answer: b. Improved patient satisfaction scores related to care coordination. Explanation: Patient satisfaction scores related to care coordination are a direct measure of how well the healthcare team collaborates in practice. Improved scores suggest that the IPE program has effectively enhanced the team's ability to work together to provide seamless, patient-centered care.

132. During the implementation of a clinical ladder program, a nurse executive observes that many experienced nurses are not progressing to higher levels. What is the most likely cause of this issue, and how should it be addressed?
a. The program's criteria are too rigorous; criteria should be revised to lower the thresholds
b. There is a lack of awareness or understanding of the program; increased communication and education are needed
c. Nurses are not interested in advancing; the program should be replaced with a different incentive
d. The program is not aligned with nurses' professional goals; goals should be reassessed and realigned

Answer: b. There is a lack of awareness or understanding of the program; increased communication and education are needed. Explanation: A common issue with clinical ladder programs is that nurses may not fully understand how to advance within them. Improving communication and education about the program can help clarify the benefits and steps required for progression, encouraging more nurses to participate.

133. A nurse executive is developing a Just Culture initiative and wants to assess its effectiveness after implementation. Which metric would be the most appropriate indicator of success in promoting a Just Culture?
a. Reduction in the total number of reported errors
b. Increase in the number of errors reported by staff
c. Improvement in staff satisfaction scores regarding safety culture

d. Decrease in the number of adverse events

Answer: b. Increase in the number of errors reported by staff. Explanation: In a Just Culture, an increase in reported errors typically indicates a more open and transparent reporting environment, where staff feel safe to report mistakes without fear of punishment. This metric suggests that the initiative is successfully fostering a culture of learning and improvement.

134. A hospital is experiencing long emergency department (ED) wait times and decides to use Lean Six Sigma DMAIC methodology to address the issue. In the "Measure" phase, which of the following metrics would be MOST useful in quantifying the problem?
a. Patient satisfaction scores for ED visits
b. Door-to-doctor time for ED patients
c. Number of patients leaving without being seen
d. ED staff overtime hours

Answer: b. Door-to-doctor time for ED patients. Explanation: Door-to-doctor time is the most useful metric for quantifying ED wait times in the "Measure" phase of DMAIC. This metric directly measures the time from patient arrival to first physician contact, providing a clear, quantifiable indicator of wait times. Patient satisfaction scores (a) are important but don't provide a specific time measurement. Patients leaving without being seen (c) is a consequence of long wait times but doesn't quantify the wait itself. Staff overtime (d) may be related to efficiency issues but doesn't directly measure patient wait times. Door-to-doctor time offers a precise, relevant measurement that can be tracked and analyzed throughout the DMAIC process to assess improvements in ED wait times.

135. A nurse manager is implementing a Plan-Do-Study-Act (PDSA) cycle to reduce pressure ulcer incidence. Which of the following actions best represents the "Study" phase of this cycle?
a. Training staff on a new turning schedule
b. Analyzing data on pressure ulcer rates before and after intervention
c. Developing a new risk assessment tool
d. Implementing skin care protocols hospital-wide

Answer: b. Analyzing data on pressure ulcer rates before and after intervention. Explanation: Analyzing data on pressure ulcer rates before and after the intervention best represents the "Study" phase of the PDSA cycle. This phase involves examining the results of the implemented change to determine its effectiveness. Comparing pre- and post-intervention data allows for objective evaluation of the improvement effort. Training staff (a) is part of the "Do" phase. Developing a new assessment tool (c) would typically occur in the "Plan" phase. Implementing protocols hospital-wide (d) might be part of the "Act" phase if the initial cycle proves successful. The "Study" phase is critical for understanding the impact of the intervention and informing decisions about next steps in the improvement process.

136. A healthcare organization wants to optimize patient flow using Value Stream Mapping. Which of the following would be the MOST appropriate first step in this process?
a. Identifying all departments involved in patient care
b. Calculating the average length of stay for patients
c. Defining the start and end points of the patient journey to be mapped

d. Interviewing staff about perceived bottlenecks in patient flow

Answer: c. Defining the start and end points of the patient journey to be mapped. Explanation: Defining the start and end points of the patient journey is the most appropriate first step in Value Stream Mapping for patient flow optimization. This step establishes the scope of the mapping process, ensuring a clear focus and boundaries for the analysis. Identifying all departments (a) is important but premature without defining the journey's scope. Calculating average length of stay (b) provides useful data but doesn't guide the mapping process. Interviewing staff about bottlenecks (d) is valuable but should occur after the scope is defined. By first establishing the specific patient journey to be examined, the organization can then effectively map the value stream, identify waste, and target improvements within a well-defined context.

137. A hospital is planning a Kaizen event to improve medication administration processes. Which of the following team compositions would be MOST effective for this event?
a. Nurses from various units and a pharmacy representative
b. Nurses, pharmacists, physicians, and a patient safety officer
c. Nursing leadership and hospital administration
d. Nurses, pharmacists, IT staff, and a lean facilitator

Answer: d. Nurses, pharmacists, IT staff, and a lean facilitator. Explanation: For a Kaizen event focused on medication administration processes, a team composition of nurses, pharmacists, IT staff, and a lean facilitator would be most effective. This multidisciplinary team covers the key aspects of medication administration: nurses as primary administrators, pharmacists for medication expertise, IT staff for technology-related issues (e.g., electronic medication records), and a lean facilitator to guide the rapid improvement process. While option (b) includes important stakeholders, it lacks IT representation, which is crucial for modern medication systems. Option (a) is too limited in scope. Option (c) lacks frontline staff crucial for identifying and implementing practical improvements. The chosen composition ensures a comprehensive view of the process with the necessary skills to implement rapid changes.

138. In applying Lean Six Sigma to reduce ED wait times, which of the following tools would be MOST useful in the "Analyze" phase of DMAIC?
a. Control chart
b. Fishbone diagram
c. Pareto chart
d. Value stream map

Answer: b. Fishbone diagram. Explanation: A fishbone diagram (also known as an Ishikawa or cause-and-effect diagram) would be most useful in the "Analyze" phase of DMAIC for reducing ED wait times. This tool helps identify and categorize potential root causes of the problem, allowing the team to explore various factors contributing to long wait times. Control charts (a) are typically used in the "Control" phase to monitor process stability. Pareto charts (c) are useful but more focused on prioritizing issues rather than exploring causes. Value stream maps (d) are valuable but more commonly used in the "Measure" phase to understand the current process flow. The fishbone diagram's ability to visually organize multiple potential causes makes it particularly suited for the in-depth analysis required in this phase of DMAIC.

139. A nurse leader is implementing a PDSA cycle to improve hand hygiene compliance. After the initial cycle shows modest improvement, what should be the NEXT step?
a. Conclude the project and report results to administration
b. Immediately implement the changes hospital-wide
c. Conduct another PDSA cycle with modifications based on learnings
d. Switch to a different quality improvement methodology

Answer: c. Conduct another PDSA cycle with modifications based on learnings. Explanation: Conducting another PDSA cycle with modifications based on learnings from the initial cycle is the most appropriate next step. PDSA is an iterative process designed for continuous improvement. The modest improvement in the first cycle provides valuable insights that can be used to refine the approach in subsequent cycles. Concluding the project (a) after one cycle would be premature, especially with only modest improvement. Implementing changes hospital-wide (b) without further testing could be risky and inefficient. Switching methodologies (d) is unnecessary when PDSA is showing progress and offering learning opportunities. Multiple PDSA cycles allow for fine-tuning interventions and building on initial successes to achieve more significant improvements over time.

140. In a Value Stream Mapping exercise for surgical patients, the team identifies a significant delay between surgery completion and inpatient bed assignment. Which Lean concept would be MOST relevant in addressing this issue?
a. 5S (Sort, Set in order, Shine, Standardize, Sustain)
b. Just-in-Time
c. Poka-Yoke
d. Takt Time

Answer: b. Just-in-Time. Explanation: The Just-in-Time concept from Lean methodology would be most relevant in addressing the delay between surgery completion and inpatient bed assignment. Just-in-Time focuses on delivering the right product (in this case, an available inpatient bed) at the right time, in the right amount, minimizing waste and waiting. This concept can guide improvements in bed management processes to ensure beds are ready when needed for post-surgical patients. 5S (a) is more relevant to workplace organization. Poka-Yoke (c) relates to error-proofing and might not directly address timing issues. Takt Time (d) is about production pacing and less applicable to this specific delay. Just-in-Time principles can help synchronize bed availability with surgical schedules, reducing delays and improving patient flow.

141. A hospital is planning a Kaizen event to reduce medication errors. Which of the following timeframes is MOST appropriate for this event?
a. One day
b. Three to five days
c. Two weeks
d. One month

Answer: b. Three to five days. Explanation: A timeframe of three to five days is most appropriate for a Kaizen event focused on reducing medication errors. Kaizen events are designed to be short, focused improvement activities that produce rapid results. Three to five days provides enough time for the team to analyze the current process, identify issues, develop and implement solutions, and begin measuring results, while maintaining the intensity and focus characteristic of Kaizen events. One day (a) is typically too short for a complex issue like medication errors. Two weeks (c) or one month (d) are too long for a Kaizen event and risk losing momentum and focus. The three to five-day timeframe balances the need for thorough analysis and implementation with the Kaizen principle of rapid, concentrated improvement efforts.

142. In using Lean Six Sigma to improve ED throughput, the team calculates a sigma level of 2.5 for the current process. What does this sigma level indicate about the process performance?
a. The process is performing at world-class levels
b. The process is meeting industry standards
c. The process has significant room for improvement
d. The process is failing and needs immediate overhaul

Answer: c. The process has significant room for improvement. Explanation: A sigma level of 2.5 indicates that the process has significant room for improvement. In Six Sigma, higher sigma levels indicate better process performance, with 6 sigma being the goal (3.4 defects per million opportunities). A 2.5 sigma level corresponds to approximately 158,700 defects per million opportunities, or about 84% accuracy. This is far from world-class performance (a) or industry standards (b) for a critical process like ED throughput. While it indicates substantial opportunity for improvement, it doesn't necessarily mean the process is failing and needs immediate overhaul (d). This sigma level suggests that targeted improvements could yield significant benefits, making it an appropriate candidate for a Lean Six Sigma project.

143. A nurse manager is leading a PDSA cycle to implement a new fall prevention protocol. Which of the following best represents an appropriate "Act" phase action if the "Study" phase shows mixed results?
a. Abandon the new protocol and return to previous practices
b. Implement the protocol hospital-wide without changes
c. Modify the protocol based on feedback and initiate another PDSA cycle
d. Extend the study phase to gather more data before making decisions

Answer: c. Modify the protocol based on feedback and initiate another PDSA cycle. Explanation: Modifying the protocol based on feedback and initiating another PDSA cycle is the most appropriate "Act" phase action when results are mixed. This approach aligns with the continuous improvement philosophy of PDSA, using learnings from the initial cycle to refine the intervention. Abandoning the protocol (a) is premature, especially if some positive results were observed. Implementing hospital-wide without changes (b) ignores the opportunity to improve based on initial findings. Extending the study phase (d) may delay potential improvements and doesn't utilize the valuable feedback already obtained. By modifying the protocol and initiating another cycle, the team can address identified issues, build on successes, and continue the improvement process iteratively.

144. A nurse executive is considering implementing the Gallup Q12 survey to improve workforce engagement within a large healthcare facility. Which of the following steps should be prioritized after the survey results are collected to ensure the most effective action planning?
a. Immediately sharing all raw data with the entire staff to promote transparency.
b. Analyzing the results to identify key areas of concern and developing targeted action plans with leadership.
c. Focusing on departments with the lowest engagement scores and implementing mandatory training sessions.
d. Using the results to create a one-size-fits-all engagement program for all departments.

Answer: b. Analyzing the results to identify key areas of concern and developing targeted action plans with leadership. Explanation: Effective action planning requires a focused approach, where leadership analyzes the survey data to pinpoint specific areas of concern. This allows for targeted interventions that address the unique needs of different departments, rather than a blanket approach that may not be effective across all areas.

145. A Magnet®-designated hospital is revising its shared governance model to enhance nursing engagement and decision-making. Which of the following changes would most effectively strengthen the shared governance structure?
a. Limiting the number of shared governance councils to streamline decision-making.
b. Ensuring that only senior nurses with over 10 years of experience can chair the councils.
c. Encouraging participation from all levels of nursing staff in council activities and decision-making processes.
d. Rotating council membership on a bi-annual basis to maintain fresh perspectives.

Answer: c. Encouraging participation from all levels of nursing staff in council activities and decision-making processes. Explanation: Shared governance thrives on inclusivity and collaboration. Encouraging participation from all levels of nursing staff ensures diverse perspectives and enhances engagement, which is crucial in a Magnet® environment. Limiting participation or excluding less experienced nurses can undermine the goals of shared governance.

146. To enhance employee recognition and satisfaction, a nurse executive is considering implementing the DAISY Award program for exceptional nursing care. Which of the following factors should be emphasized to ensure the program's success and sustainability?
a. Ensuring the selection process is exclusively driven by management to maintain consistency.
b. Making the program competitive by awarding only the top-performing nurse annually.
c. Involving patients and their families in the nomination process to recognize the impact of nurses' work.
d. Keeping the program low-key to avoid creating resentment among staff who are not recognized.

Answer: c. Involving patients and their families in the nomination process to recognize the impact of nurses' work. Explanation: The DAISY Award program is most effective when it highlights the meaningful contributions of nurses, as perceived by patients and their families. This approach ensures the recognition is heartfelt and directly tied to the patient experience, enhancing both nurse satisfaction and patient care quality.

147. A nurse executive is exploring the implementation of self-scheduling and flexible shifts as part of a work-life balance initiative. Which of the following potential outcomes should be closely monitored to evaluate the success of this initiative?
a. A decrease in overall staffing costs due to more efficient scheduling.
b. An increase in patient satisfaction scores due to improved staff morale.
c. A reduction in overtime hours as staff manage their own schedules.
d. A potential rise in conflicts among staff over preferred shift assignments.

Answer: b. An increase in patient satisfaction scores due to improved staff morale. Explanation: Improved work-life balance through self-scheduling and flexible shifts can lead to increased staff satisfaction and morale, which often translates to better patient care and higher satisfaction scores. While managing conflicts is important, the primary goal is to enhance the work environment and patient outcomes.

148. After implementing the Gallup Q12 survey, a nurse executive notices that the question "At work, my opinions seem to count" received the lowest engagement score across multiple departments. Which of the following actions would best address this issue and improve engagement?
a. Hosting a series of town hall meetings where staff can voice their concerns directly to leadership.
b. Sending out an anonymous survey to gather more detailed feedback on the specific issue.
c. Mandating departmental meetings focused solely on addressing this specific survey question.
d. Assigning team leaders to communicate survey results and encourage staff to submit their opinions in writing.

Answer: a. Hosting a series of town hall meetings where staff can voice their concerns directly to leadership.
Explanation: Town hall meetings provide an open forum for employees to express their opinions and concerns, making them feel heard and valued. This approach addresses the core issue of the low engagement score and fosters a more inclusive and communicative work environment.

149. A nurse executive in a Magnet® organization is evaluating the effectiveness of the shared governance model currently in place. Which of the following indicators would most strongly suggest that the model is functioning successfully?
a. An increase in the number of decisions made solely by nursing leadership.
b. A significant rise in staff turnover, indicating a possible issue with the current structure.
c. Higher levels of nursing staff involvement in policy development and clinical practice improvements.
d. A reduction in the frequency of shared governance council meetings due to decreased participation.

Answer: c. Higher levels of nursing staff involvement in policy development and clinical practice improvements.
Explanation: Successful shared governance models are characterized by active staff participation in decision-making processes, particularly in areas like policy development and clinical practice. This engagement indicates that nurses are empowered and invested in the governance structure.

150. In an effort to promote work-life balance, a nurse executive is considering the introduction of a compressed workweek option. Which potential challenge should be addressed first to ensure successful implementation?
a. The risk of increased fatigue among nurses working longer shifts.
b. The possibility of reduced continuity of care for patients.
c. The potential for conflicts in staff preferences regarding shift patterns.
d. The difficulty in managing time-off requests under the new schedule.

Answer: a. The risk of increased fatigue among nurses working longer shifts. Explanation: While a compressed workweek can offer benefits, longer shifts may lead to nurse fatigue, which can negatively impact both nurse well-being and patient care. Addressing this risk is crucial to ensuring the success and safety of the work-life balance initiative.

151. The nurse executive at a large hospital plans to implement an employee recognition program similar to the DAISY Award but tailored to non-nursing staff. Which of the following elements should be emphasized to ensure the program is perceived as equitable and meaningful across all departments?
a. Ensuring that only a small, select group of staff can be nominated each year.
b. Developing clear, transparent criteria for recognition that applies to all staff equally.
c. Focusing on recognizing teams rather than individual contributions to promote collaboration.
d. Limiting the recognition to departments with the highest patient satisfaction scores.

Answer: b. Developing clear, transparent criteria for recognition that applies to all staff equally. Explanation: For a recognition program to be meaningful and perceived as fair, it is essential to have clear, consistent criteria that apply across all departments. This transparency ensures that all staff members have an equal opportunity to be recognized for their contributions, fostering a positive organizational culture.

152. A nurse executive is tasked with improving employee engagement through the implementation of the Gallup Q12 survey. After completing the survey, the results indicate that the question "In the last seven days, I have received recognition or praise for doing good work" scored particularly low. Which strategy would be most effective in addressing this issue?
a. Increasing the frequency of performance reviews to provide more regular feedback.
b. Instituting a daily recognition program where managers are required to acknowledge good work.
c. Implementing a formal, quarterly award ceremony to recognize outstanding employees.
d. Creating a peer recognition system where colleagues can nominate each other for good work.

Answer: d. Creating a peer recognition system where colleagues can nominate each other for good work. Explanation: A peer recognition system allows for more frequent and meaningful recognition, as it empowers employees to acknowledge each other's contributions on a regular basis. This approach directly addresses the issue highlighted by the survey results and promotes a culture of appreciation within the organization.

153. As part of a work-life balance initiative, the nurse executive introduces a flexible shift policy allowing staff to choose their shifts. Which of the following potential outcomes should be most closely monitored to ensure the policy's effectiveness?
a. A significant increase in staff satisfaction and morale.
b. A potential imbalance in shift coverage, leading to staffing shortages during peak times.
c. A decrease in the use of agency staff due to improved scheduling flexibility.
d. An overall reduction in sick leave usage among nursing staff.

Answer: b. A potential imbalance in shift coverage, leading to staffing shortages during peak times. Explanation: While flexible shifts can improve work-life balance and staff satisfaction, there is a risk of imbalanced shift coverage if not carefully managed. Monitoring and addressing this issue is critical to maintaining adequate staffing levels and ensuring continuity of care.

154. A nurse executive is leading the effort to obtain Patient-Centered Medical Home (PCMH) recognition for the hospital's primary care clinics. Which of the following actions would most effectively support the PCMH recognition criteria related to care coordination?

a. Implementing an electronic health record (EHR) system that allows for real-time communication with specialists
b. Increasing the number of full-time primary care physicians in each clinic
c. Conducting quarterly patient satisfaction surveys to assess clinic performance
d. Offering walk-in services to improve patient access to care

Answer: a. Implementing an electronic health record (EHR) system that allows for real-time communication with specialists. Explanation: The PCMH model emphasizes care coordination, particularly in managing transitions of care between different providers. An EHR system that enables real-time communication supports this criterion by facilitating seamless care coordination across the healthcare team, ensuring that patient information is consistently shared and updated.

155. In the context of an Accountable Care Organization (ACO) shared savings model, what is the most critical factor for a nurse executive to monitor to ensure the organization meets its financial and quality targets?
a. The number of new patient referrals to the ACO
b. The percentage of patients receiving preventive care services
c. The organization's readmission rates within 30 days of discharge
d. The total length of stay for all patients within the ACO

Answer: c. The organization's readmission rates within 30 days of discharge. Explanation: In ACO shared savings models, reducing unnecessary hospital readmissions is crucial for achieving both cost savings and quality care metrics. Monitoring and managing readmission rates help ensure the organization avoids penalties and maximizes its potential for shared savings by demonstrating effective care coordination and management.

156. A hospital is participating in the Comprehensive Care for Joint Replacement (CJR) bundled payment initiative. Which strategy would be most effective for a nurse executive to implement to ensure the hospital stays within the bundled payment target?
a. Standardizing preoperative assessment protocols to reduce variability in patient outcomes
b. Increasing the number of joint replacement surgeries performed annually
c. Expanding the postoperative care team to include more physical therapists
d. Developing partnerships with skilled nursing facilities to ensure high-quality post-discharge care

Answer: d. Developing partnerships with skilled nursing facilities to ensure high-quality post-discharge care. Explanation: The CJR bundled payment initiative covers all services related to joint replacement, including post-discharge care. By partnering with skilled nursing facilities, the hospital can ensure that patients receive consistent, high-quality care after surgery, reducing the risk of complications and readmissions, which is essential for staying within the bundled payment target.

157. In designing a population health management strategy focused on risk stratification, which of the following approaches would best enable the identification of high-risk patients for targeted interventions?
a. Using a predictive analytics tool that incorporates socioeconomic data and comorbidities
b. Conducting annual wellness exams for all patients
c. Implementing a universal screening program for chronic diseases
d. Increasing the frequency of routine follow-up visits for all patients

Answer: a. Using a predictive analytics tool that incorporates socioeconomic data and comorbidities. Explanation: Risk stratification involves categorizing patients based on their likelihood of experiencing adverse health outcomes. A predictive analytics tool that considers both clinical and socioeconomic factors allows for a more precise identification of high-risk patients, enabling targeted interventions that can improve outcomes and reduce healthcare costs.

158. A nurse executive is tasked with improving care coordination within the Patient-Centered Medical Home (PCMH) model. Which of the following initiatives would be most effective in addressing social determinants of health (SDOH) that impact patient outcomes?
a. Integrating social workers into the primary care team to address SDOH needs
b. Expanding hours of operation to accommodate working patients
c. Increasing the availability of telehealth services for rural patients
d. Providing transportation vouchers to patients for medical appointments

Answer: a. Integrating social workers into the primary care team to address SDOH needs. Explanation: Addressing social determinants of health, such as housing, food security, and employment, is critical for improving patient outcomes within the PCMH model. By integrating social workers into the primary care team, the organization can more effectively identify and manage SDOH-related issues, leading to better care coordination and overall patient health.

159. When implementing an Accountable Care Organization (ACO) model, which outcome measure should a nurse executive prioritize to demonstrate value-based care?
a. Patient satisfaction scores
b. Rate of emergency department utilization
c. Number of patients enrolled in chronic disease management programs
d. Total cost of care per beneficiary

Answer: d. Total cost of care per beneficiary. Explanation: ACOs are designed to provide value-based care by improving quality while reducing costs. The total cost of care per beneficiary is a critical measure that reflects the efficiency and effectiveness of care delivered across the continuum. By prioritizing this outcome, the nurse executive can better align the organization's performance with ACO goals.

160. A healthcare organization is looking to optimize its participation in the Comprehensive Care for Joint Replacement (CJR) model. Which of the following data analytics initiatives should a nurse executive prioritize to enhance decision-making and outcomes?
a. Analyzing patient-reported outcomes to assess satisfaction with care
b. Tracking utilization rates of operating rooms for joint replacements
c. Evaluating post-discharge readmission rates and associated factors
d. Reviewing staff productivity levels during peak surgery times

Answer: c. Evaluating post-discharge readmission rates and associated factors. Explanation: In the CJR model, managing post-discharge outcomes is crucial for controlling costs and ensuring patient recovery. Analyzing readmission rates and identifying factors contributing to these outcomes enables targeted interventions that can improve patient care and reduce financial penalties under the bundled payment structure.

161. A nurse executive is developing a population health management program focused on chronic disease prevention. Which of the following strategies is most likely to be successful in reducing the incidence of chronic diseases within the community?
a. Partnering with local gyms to offer discounted memberships to patients
b. Implementing community-based education programs on healthy living
c. Providing free annual physical exams to all residents in the community
d. Increasing the number of specialists available to manage chronic conditions

Answer: b. Implementing community-based education programs on healthy living. Explanation: Prevention is a key component of population health management. Community-based education programs that promote healthy behaviors, such as proper nutrition and exercise, are effective in reducing the incidence of chronic diseases. These programs empower individuals to take proactive steps in managing their health, leading to long-term benefits.

162. To enhance the financial performance of a healthcare organization participating in an ACO, which action should a nurse executive take to improve the alignment between care delivery and cost savings?
a. Increasing the frequency of routine check-ups for all patients
b. Establishing protocols for early discharge planning and follow-up care
c. Expanding the number of services offered within primary care settings
d. Hiring additional specialty providers to manage complex cases

Answer: b. Establishing protocols for early discharge planning and follow-up care. Explanation: Effective discharge planning and follow-up care are essential for preventing readmissions and managing patient care transitions, which are key to achieving cost savings in an ACO. By focusing on these areas, the nurse executive can help reduce unnecessary hospitalizations and improve the overall efficiency of care delivery.

163. A hospital is integrating a bundled payment initiative for joint replacements into its overall financial strategy. Which of the following actions should the nurse executive prioritize to mitigate the financial risks associated with the bundled payment model?
a. Increasing the volume of joint replacement surgeries to maximize revenue
b. Negotiating lower costs with suppliers of surgical implants and devices
c. Enhancing preoperative screening to identify and optimize high-risk patients
d. Reducing the length of stay in the hospital to decrease inpatient costs

Answer: c. Enhancing preoperative screening to identify and optimize high-risk patients. Explanation: Preoperative screening and optimization are critical to reducing complications, which can lead to costly readmissions and extended care needs under a bundled payment model. By focusing on these factors, the nurse executive can improve patient outcomes and mitigate financial risks associated with the bundled payment initiative.

164. A hospital ethics committee is deliberating on whether to continue life-sustaining treatment for a patient in a persistent vegetative state. Using the Four-Box Method, which box would address the patient's previously expressed wishes?
a. Medical Indications
b. Patient Preferences
c. Quality of Life
d. Contextual Features

Answer: b. Patient Preferences. Explanation: In the Four-Box Method for ethical decision-making, the "Patient Preferences" box specifically addresses the patient's wishes, values, and any advance directives. This box focuses on respecting patient autonomy and includes consideration of previously expressed wishes, which is crucial in cases where the patient can no longer communicate. The Medical Indications box (a) deals with the clinical aspects of the case. Quality of Life (c) considers the patient's current and future quality of life. Contextual Features (d) examines broader issues like family dynamics or resource allocation. For ethical decision-making in this scenario, the patient's previously expressed wishes fall squarely within the Patient Preferences domain.

165. During a pandemic, a hospital faces a critical shortage of ventilators. Which ethical principle should guide the decision-making process for ventilator allocation?
a. First-come, first-served
b. Prioritizing healthcare workers
c. Maximizing benefits (saving the most lives)
d. Random selection

Answer: c. Maximizing benefits (saving the most lives). Explanation: In pandemic resource allocation, the ethical principle of maximizing benefits, or utilitarianism, is generally considered the most appropriate guide. This approach aims to save the most lives or life-years possible with limited resources, aligning with public health ethics. First-come, first-served (a) doesn't consider clinical factors or overall outcomes. Prioritizing healthcare workers (b), while potentially justifiable to maintain workforce capacity, isn't the primary ethical consideration for general resource allocation. Random selection (d) ensures fairness but doesn't optimize the use of limited resources to save lives. Maximizing benefits considers both the number of lives saved and the prognosis of patients, aiming for the best overall outcome in a crisis situation.

166. A nurse executive is facing a decision about implementing a new staffing model that could improve efficiency but might increase nurse workload. Which provision of the ANA Code of Ethics is MOST relevant to this decision?
a. Provision 2: Primary commitment to the patient
b. Provision 3: Advocacy for the patient
c. Provision 5: Duty to self and others
d. Provision 6: Contribution to healthcare environments

Answer: d. Provision 6: Contribution to healthcare environments. Explanation: Provision 6 of the ANA Code of Ethics, which addresses the nurse's obligation to contribute to healthcare environments that foster high standards of nursing and health care, is most relevant to this decision. This provision emphasizes the nurse's role in establishing, maintaining, and improving healthcare environments and conditions of employment conducive to safe, quality health care. The staffing model decision directly impacts the healthcare environment and working conditions. While Provision 2 (a) and Provision 3 (b) are important, they focus more on direct patient care. Provision 5 (c) relates to promoting personal health and safety, which is less directly applicable to this organizational decision. Provision 6 guides nurse executives in balancing organizational needs with the imperative to maintain a positive practice environment.

167. An ethics committee is reviewing its structure and function. Which of the following would be the MOST important characteristic for ensuring the committee's effectiveness?
a. Having a majority of physician members
b. Meeting only when ethical dilemmas arise
c. Multidisciplinary representation
d. Focusing primarily on policy development

Answer: c. Multidisciplinary representation. Explanation: Multidisciplinary representation is the most important characteristic for ensuring an ethics committee's effectiveness. A diverse committee composition, including healthcare professionals from various disciplines, ethicists, community representatives, and potentially legal counsel, ensures a broad range of perspectives and expertise in addressing complex ethical issues. Having a physician majority (a) limits the diversity of viewpoints. Meeting only when dilemmas arise (b) prevents proactive ethics work and education. While policy development is important, focusing primarily on this (d) neglects the committee's other crucial functions like case consultation and education. Multidisciplinary representation enhances the committee's ability to comprehensively analyze ethical issues, consider various stakeholder perspectives, and provide well-rounded guidance to the organization.

168. Using the Four-Box Method, a nurse executive is analyzing an ethical dilemma involving a terminally ill patient requesting experimental treatment. Which box would address the cost and potential benefit of the treatment to society?
a. Medical Indications
b. Patient Preferences
c. Quality of Life
d. Contextual Features

Answer: d. Contextual Features. Explanation: In the Four-Box Method, the "Contextual Features" box would address the cost and potential societal benefit of experimental treatment for a terminally ill patient. This box considers broader issues beyond the individual case, including social, legal, economic, and institutional factors. The cost of treatment and its potential benefit to society (e.g., advancing medical knowledge) fall within these contextual considerations. Medical Indications (a) focuses on the clinical aspects of the treatment. Patient Preferences (b) addresses the patient's wishes and values. Quality of Life (c) considers the impact on the patient's life quality. The societal implications of providing experimental treatment, including resource allocation and potential scientific advancements, are best captured in the Contextual Features box.

169. During a pandemic, a hospital must decide whether to cancel elective surgeries to conserve resources. Which ethical framework would be MOST appropriate for guiding this decision?
a. Deontological ethics
b. Virtue ethics
c. Care ethics

d. Utilitarianism

Answer: d. Utilitarianism. Explanation: Utilitarianism would be the most appropriate ethical framework for guiding the decision to cancel elective surgeries during a pandemic. This framework focuses on maximizing overall benefit and minimizing harm for the greatest number of people. In a resource-constrained pandemic situation, canceling elective surgeries to conserve resources for urgent and COVID-19-related care aligns with utilitarian principles by potentially saving more lives overall. Deontological ethics (a) emphasizes moral rules and might not flexibly address the complex trade-offs in a crisis. Virtue ethics (b) focuses on character traits and doesn't provide clear guidance for population-level decisions. Care ethics (c) emphasizes compassion and responsiveness in individual relationships, which may not scale well to systemic decisions. Utilitarianism provides a clear rationale for difficult resource allocation decisions in public health emergencies.

170. A nurse leader is applying the ANA Code of Ethics to a situation where a nurse refuses to care for a patient due to personal beliefs. Which provision of the Code is MOST relevant to address this issue?
a. Provision 1: Respect for human dignity
b. Provision 2: Commitment to the patient
c. Provision 4: Accountability and responsibility for practice
d. Provision 7: Advancement of the nursing profession

Answer: b. Provision 2: Commitment to the patient. Explanation: Provision 2 of the ANA Code of Ethics, which addresses the nurse's primary commitment to the patient, is most relevant to this situation. This provision states that the nurse's primary commitment is to the patient, whether an individual, family, group, community, or population. It emphasizes that personal values and beliefs must not compromise this primary commitment to the patient's health and well-being. While respect for human dignity (Provision 1, a) is important, it doesn't directly address the conflict between personal beliefs and professional duty. Accountability (Provision 4, c) is relevant but doesn't specifically focus on the commitment to patient care. Advancing the profession (Provision 7, d) is less directly applicable to this individual patient care situation. Provision 2 provides clear guidance on prioritizing patient care over personal beliefs in professional practice.

171. An ethics committee is discussing the implementation of a new organ donation policy. Which of the following approaches would BEST ensure a comprehensive ethical analysis?
a. Focusing solely on maximizing the number of organs donated
b. Prioritizing the autonomy of potential donors above all other considerations
c. Balancing principles of autonomy, beneficence, non-maleficence, and justice
d. Deferring entirely to legal counsel's recommendations

Answer: c. Balancing principles of autonomy, beneficence, non-maleficence, and justice. Explanation: Balancing the four core principles of bioethics - autonomy, beneficence, non-maleficence, and justice - would best ensure a comprehensive ethical analysis of a new organ donation policy. This approach considers multiple ethical dimensions: respecting individual choice (autonomy), promoting good outcomes (beneficence), avoiding harm (non-maleficence), and ensuring fair distribution (justice). Focusing solely on maximizing donations (a) neglects other important ethical considerations. Prioritizing autonomy above all else (b) may overlook other crucial ethical principles. Deferring entirely to legal counsel (d) addresses legal but not necessarily ethical concerns. A balanced consideration of all four principles allows for a nuanced, thorough ethical analysis that can guide policy development in this complex area.

172. A hospital is forming a new ethics committee. Which of the following should be the committee's PRIMARY function?
a. To make final decisions on all ethical dilemmas in the hospital
b. To provide a forum for discussion and guidance on ethical issues
c. To create and enforce ethical policies for the entire organization
d. To serve as a legal advisory body for the hospital administration

Answer: b. To provide a forum for discussion and guidance on ethical issues. Explanation: The primary function of a hospital ethics committee should be to provide a forum for discussion and guidance on ethical issues. This role allows the committee to serve as a resource for staff, patients, and families in navigating complex ethical situations, offering consultations and recommendations rather than making binding decisions. Making final decisions on all ethical dilemmas (a) oversteps the committee's advisory role and may infringe on clinical decision-making. While policy input is important, creating and enforcing ethical policies for the entire organization (c) is typically beyond the scope of an ethics committee and may overlap with other administrative functions. Serving as a legal advisory body (d) is not the primary purpose of an ethics committee, which focuses on ethical rather than legal guidance. The forum and guidance function allows the committee to educate, advise, and promote ethical reflection throughout the organization.

173. In applying the Four-Box Method to an ethical dilemma involving a patient refusing life-saving treatment, which box would address the patient's right to make this decision?
a. Medical Indications
b. Patient Preferences
c. Quality of Life
d. Contextual Features

Answer: b. Patient Preferences. Explanation: In the Four-Box Method, the "Patient Preferences" box would address the patient's right to refuse life-saving treatment. This box specifically deals with the principle of respect for patient autonomy, including the patient's right to make informed decisions about their care, even if those decisions go against medical advice. The Medical Indications box (a) focuses on the clinical aspects and potential benefits of treatment. Quality of Life (c) considers the impact of treatment or non-treatment on the patient's life quality. Contextual Features (d) examines broader social, legal, or economic factors. The patient's right to refuse treatment, stemming from the ethical principle of autonomy, is a core component of the Patient Preferences box in this ethical analysis framework.

174. A nurse executive is leading an initiative to ensure the hospital meets Meaningful Use criteria for Electronic Health Records (EHR) under the Medicare and Medicaid EHR Incentive Programs. Which of the following actions would best support achieving Stage 2 Meaningful Use criteria?
a. Implementing computerized provider order entry (CPOE) for medication orders only.
b. Ensuring that more than 50% of patients are provided electronic access to their health information within 36 hours of discharge.
c. Encouraging all providers to use paper charts in addition to EHRs to ensure accuracy.
d. Limiting the use of clinical decision support systems to reduce alert fatigue among providers.

Answer: b. Ensuring that more than 50% of patients are provided electronic access to their health information within 36 hours of discharge. Explanation: Stage 2 Meaningful Use criteria emphasize patient engagement, including timely electronic access to health information. Providing patients with access to their records within 36 hours of discharge directly supports this goal, whereas the other options do not align with the specific requirements of Stage 2.

175. During a cybersecurity audit, the nurse executive identifies several gaps in the hospital's current IT security measures. Which of the following NIST Cybersecurity Framework (CSF) functions should be prioritized first to strengthen the hospital's cybersecurity posture?
a. Detecting unauthorized access attempts in real-time.
b. Identifying assets, systems, and data critical to the hospital's operations.
c. Recovering from a cyberattack by restoring affected systems and data.
d. Responding to identified threats through immediate containment and mitigation actions.

Answer: b. Identifying assets, systems, and data critical to the hospital's operations. Explanation: The first function of the NIST CSF is "Identify," which involves understanding the assets and systems that need protection. Without a clear identification of critical resources, other cybersecurity efforts like detection, response, and recovery may not be effectively targeted or prioritized.

176. A nurse executive is tasked with ensuring the hospital's compliance with the HITECH Act, which aims to promote the adoption and meaningful use of health information technology. Which of the following measures would be most effective in preventing breaches of protected health information (PHI)?
a. Encrypting all electronic health records to prevent unauthorized access.
b. Conducting quarterly training sessions on the proper use of EHRs.
c. Limiting the use of mobile devices to access patient records within the hospital.
d. Implementing biometric authentication systems for accessing EHRs.

Answer: a. Encrypting all electronic health records to prevent unauthorized access. Explanation: The HITECH Act emphasizes the protection of PHI, and encryption is a critical safeguard against unauthorized access to electronic health records. While training, device limitations, and biometric authentication are important, encryption directly addresses the risk of data breaches by securing sensitive information.

177. In an effort to enhance interoperability, the nurse executive is considering the adoption of the HL7 FHIR standard for the hospital's health information exchange (HIE). Which of the following challenges is most likely to arise during the implementation of FHIR?
a. Difficulty in training staff on the technical aspects of FHIR.
b. Incompatibility with legacy systems that use older data exchange formats.
c. Increased costs associated with transitioning to a cloud-based EHR system.
d. Decreased patient engagement due to the complexity of accessing health data.

Answer: b. Incompatibility with legacy systems that use older data exchange formats. Explanation: HL7 FHIR is designed to improve interoperability, but it may face challenges integrating with older systems that use outdated data formats. Addressing this incompatibility is crucial to successful implementation. Training and cost issues are secondary to the primary challenge of ensuring that FHIR can work effectively with existing systems.

178. The hospital's IT department has proposed the integration of a new clinical decision support system (CDSS) that leverages real-time data analytics. As the nurse executive, what should be your primary consideration to ensure the system aligns with the hospital's Meaningful Use goals?
a. Whether the system will reduce the overall documentation burden on clinical staff.
b. How well the system supports the generation of patient-specific education materials.
c. The system's ability to facilitate clinical workflows and improve patient outcomes.
d. Whether the system allows for seamless integration with the hospital's financial management software.

Answer: c. The system's ability to facilitate clinical workflows and improve patient outcomes. Explanation: Meaningful Use criteria emphasize improving patient outcomes through the use of EHRs and related technologies. A CDSS that enhances clinical workflows and supports better patient care aligns directly with these goals, making it the primary consideration over other factors.

179. In response to a recent cyberattack, the nurse executive must lead efforts to improve the hospital's cybersecurity defenses. Which of the following NIST CSF functions should be prioritized to ensure a robust response to future threats?
a. Protecting sensitive data by implementing advanced encryption methods.
b. Recovering from incidents by restoring data from secure backups.
c. Responding to incidents with a comprehensive incident response plan.
d. Detecting anomalies in network traffic to identify potential breaches.

Answer: c. Responding to incidents with a comprehensive incident response plan. Explanation: The "Respond" function of the NIST CSF focuses on the ability to manage and contain security incidents. A well-developed incident response plan is crucial for minimizing the impact of cyberattacks and ensuring the hospital can quickly recover, making it a priority after experiencing a breach.

180. The nurse executive is tasked with evaluating the hospital's current EHR system to ensure compliance with the HITECH Act's requirements. Which of the following elements is most critical to assess in this evaluation?
a. The system's ability to generate comprehensive billing reports.
b. The system's compliance with the latest HIPAA security rule updates.
c. The system's ease of use for clinical staff across all departments.
d. The system's capacity for high-volume data storage.

Answer: b. The system's compliance with the latest HIPAA security rule updates. Explanation: The HITECH Act reinforces the need for strict adherence to HIPAA security standards. Ensuring that the EHR system is up-to-date with the latest HIPAA rules is critical for maintaining compliance and protecting patient information, making this the most important aspect to assess.

181. A nurse executive is considering various strategies to improve the hospital's compliance with Meaningful Use requirements. Which of the following initiatives would be most effective in meeting the Stage 3 criteria, which focus on improving patient outcomes?
a. Implementing advanced data analytics to identify trends in patient care.
b. Reducing the use of paper records to decrease administrative overhead.
c. Increasing the frequency of EHR training for all clinical staff.
d. Expanding telehealth services to reach underserved populations.

Answer: d. Expanding telehealth services to reach underserved populations. Explanation: Stage 3 Meaningful Use criteria emphasize improved patient outcomes and population health. Expanding telehealth services directly addresses these goals by increasing access to care for underserved populations, thereby enhancing overall health outcomes.

182. The nurse executive is leading a project to adopt HL7 FHIR standards for EHR interoperability across multiple healthcare facilities. Which of the following is the most significant benefit of implementing HL7 FHIR in this context?
a. Reduced costs associated with data storage and management.
b. Simplified access to comprehensive patient data from multiple sources.
c. Increased speed of processing insurance claims.
d. Enhanced ability to generate custom financial reports.

Answer: b. Simplified access to comprehensive patient data from multiple sources. Explanation: HL7 FHIR is designed to facilitate the exchange of health information across different systems, making patient data more accessible and comprehensive. This interoperability is critical in a multi-facility environment, where accessing complete patient records from various sources improves care coordination and outcomes.

183. The nurse executive is reviewing the hospital's cybersecurity protocols in light of increasing threats. Which of the following actions would best align with the "Protect" function of the NIST Cybersecurity Framework?
a. Installing advanced intrusion detection systems to monitor network traffic.
b. Developing a detailed incident response plan for potential breaches.
c. Conducting regular training sessions on secure data handling practices for all staff.
d. Implementing multi-factor authentication for all system access points.

Answer: d. Implementing multi-factor authentication for all system access points. Explanation: The "Protect" function of the NIST CSF focuses on safeguarding systems and data from cyber threats. Multi-factor authentication is a critical protective measure that significantly enhances security by requiring multiple forms of verification for system access, reducing the risk of unauthorized access.

184. A nurse executive is reviewing a study that aims to assess the impact of a new nursing intervention on patient outcomes. The study uses a randomized controlled trial (RCT) design, which is considered one of the highest levels of evidence. Why is the RCT design considered more robust than a cohort study for this type of research?
a. RCTs are typically less expensive and easier to conduct than cohort studies
b. RCTs allow for random assignment, which minimizes selection bias and confounding variables
c. Cohort studies cannot provide information about cause-and-effect relationships

d. RCTs focus more on qualitative data, making them superior in clinical settings

Answer: b. RCTs allow for random assignment, which minimizes selection bias and confounding variables. Explanation: Randomized controlled trials (RCTs) are considered the gold standard in clinical research because they allow for random assignment of participants to intervention or control groups, minimizing selection bias and confounding variables, thus providing stronger evidence for cause-and-effect relationships.

185. A nurse researcher is designing a mixed methods study to evaluate the effectiveness of a new patient education program. Which of the following best describes the advantage of using a mixed methods design in this context?
a. It allows for the collection of both qualitative and quantitative data, providing a comprehensive understanding of the program's impact
b. It reduces the overall time and resources needed to conduct the study by combining methods
c. It simplifies the data analysis process by merging qualitative and quantitative results
d. It eliminates the need for a control group, making the study more ethical

Answer: a. It allows for the collection of both qualitative and quantitative data, providing a comprehensive understanding of the program's impact. Explanation: Mixed methods research combines both qualitative and quantitative approaches, enabling the researcher to explore the depth and breadth of the research question. This approach is particularly valuable in healthcare quality improvement studies, where understanding both numerical outcomes and patient experiences is crucial.

186. A nurse executive is preparing a research proposal that involves human subjects and must undergo review by the Institutional Review Board (IRB). Which of the following elements is most important to include in the IRB submission to ensure approval?
a. A detailed budget outlining the financial costs of the study
b. A comprehensive plan for recruiting study participants
c. A clear description of how informed consent will be obtained and documented
d. A timeline showing the anticipated start and end dates of the study

Answer: c. A clear description of how informed consent will be obtained and documented. Explanation: The IRB's primary concern is the protection of human subjects. A clear and thorough informed consent process ensures that participants understand the study's risks, benefits, and procedures, which is crucial for ethical approval.

187. In a translational research project focused on reducing hospital-acquired infections (HAIs), a nurse executive is applying the "bench to bedside" model. What is the most appropriate first step in this translational research process?
a. Conducting basic laboratory research to identify potential interventions for HAIs
b. Implementing the selected interventions directly into clinical practice
c. Training nursing staff on infection control protocols derived from research
d. Disseminating research findings to stakeholders in the healthcare system

Answer: a. Conducting basic laboratory research to identify potential interventions for HAIs. Explanation: The "bench to bedside" model begins with basic research (bench) that identifies potential interventions or treatments. These findings are then translated into clinical settings (bedside) through further research, testing, and eventual implementation. Starting with basic research ensures that the interventions are grounded in solid scientific evidence.

188. A nurse researcher is conducting a systematic review to determine the best practices for managing chronic pain in older adults. What type of evidence should be prioritized in this review to ensure the highest level of reliability?
a. Case reports and expert opinions from leading pain management specialists
b. Randomized controlled trials (RCTs) and meta-analyses of RCTs
c. Cohort studies and cross-sectional surveys of pain management techniques
d. Narrative reviews and editorials published in reputable journals

Answer: b. Randomized controlled trials (RCTs) and meta-analyses of RCTs. Explanation: Systematic reviews prioritize evidence from randomized controlled trials (RCTs) and meta-analyses of RCTs because these study designs provide the most reliable and generalizable findings, minimizing bias and confounding factors.

189. A hospital's nursing research team is planning a study to explore the experiences of patients with chronic illness. The team decides to use a qualitative research design. Which of the following research methods is most appropriate for this type of study?
a. Randomized controlled trial (RCT)
b. Grounded theory
c. Cross-sectional survey
d. Case-control study

Answer: b. Grounded theory. Explanation: Grounded theory is a qualitative research method used to explore and generate theories based on participants' experiences. This method is well-suited for studying complex phenomena like the lived experiences of patients with chronic illness, as it allows for in-depth exploration of their perspectives.

190. A nurse executive is evaluating the results of a translational research project that has moved from basic science to clinical implementation. Which outcome would best indicate the success of this "bench to bedside" initiative?
a. The publication of findings in a high-impact nursing journal
b. The adoption of new clinical guidelines based on the research findings
c. An increase in grant funding for further basic research
d. The training of additional staff in the research process

Answer: b. The adoption of new clinical guidelines based on the research findings. Explanation: The ultimate goal of translational research is to apply scientific discoveries from basic research to clinical practice. The adoption of new clinical guidelines based on the research indicates that the findings have successfully influenced patient care practices, reflecting the success of the translational research effort.

191. A nursing research team is conducting a mixed methods study to improve patient adherence to medication regimens. During data analysis, the team encounters conflicting results between the qualitative and quantitative findings. What is the best approach to address this issue?
a. Disregard the conflicting qualitative data as less reliable
b. Conduct additional qualitative interviews to clarify the discrepancies
c. Combine the results into a single narrative without addressing the conflict
d. Report the conflicting results separately and discuss possible reasons in the conclusion

Answer: d. Report the conflicting results separately and discuss possible reasons in the conclusion. Explanation: In mixed methods research, it is important to acknowledge and analyze conflicting results. Reporting the findings separately allows for a nuanced discussion of how different methods may yield different insights, which can lead to a more comprehensive understanding of the research question.

192. A nurse executive is reviewing a study that uses an Institutional Review Board (IRB) exemption for quality improvement (QI) research. Under what circumstances can a QI study be exempt from full IRB review?
a. The study involves no patient interaction or data collection
b. The study is solely intended to improve internal processes within the organization
c. The study has been funded by a federal agency with its own ethical guidelines
d. The study is conducted in an academic setting with no direct patient care implications

Answer: b. The study is solely intended to improve internal processes within the organization. Explanation: Quality improvement (QI) studies that are designed to improve internal processes and do not involve research on human subjects may be exempt from full IRB review. However, it is essential to consult with the IRB to confirm that the study qualifies for exemption based on its scope and methodology.

193. A nurse executive is involved in a translational research project aimed at developing new protocols for sepsis management. At what stage of the research process should the nurse executive begin engaging clinical staff in the development and testing of these protocols?
a. After the protocols have been finalized based on preclinical research
b. During the initial stages of protocol development to incorporate clinical insights
c. Only after securing IRB approval for clinical testing
d. Once the protocols have been implemented in a pilot study

Answer: b. During the initial stages of protocol development to incorporate clinical insights. Explanation: Engaging clinical staff early in the translational research process ensures that the protocols are practical and feasible in the clinical setting. Their insights can help refine the protocols and increase the likelihood of successful implementation and adoption in practice.

194. A nurse executive is implementing a new fall prevention protocol using the Johns Hopkins Nursing Evidence-Based Practice (JHNEBP) model. Which step in the model is MOST crucial for ensuring successful integration of the protocol into daily practice?
a. Formulating the EBP question
b. Conducting the evidence review

c. Translating the evidence into practice
d. Identifying the practice problem

Answer: c. Translating the evidence into practice. Explanation: While all steps in the JHNEBP model are important, translating the evidence into practice is most crucial for ensuring successful integration of the new fall prevention protocol. This step involves creating an action plan, implementing practice change, evaluating outcomes, and disseminating results. It bridges the gap between research evidence and actual clinical practice. Formulating the EBP question (a) and identifying the practice problem (d) are initial steps that don't directly address implementation. Conducting the evidence review (b) is essential but doesn't ensure practice change. The translation step is where the evidence becomes actionable, making it the most critical for successful integration into daily nursing practice.

195. When formulating a PICOT question for an evidence-based inquiry on reducing central line-associated bloodstream infections (CLABSIs), which of the following best represents the 'I' (Intervention) component?
a. Adult ICU patients
b. Chlorhexidine skin preparation
c. Standard central line care bundles
d. CLABSI rates

Answer: b. Chlorhexidine skin preparation. Explanation: In a PICOT question, the 'I' represents the Intervention or exposure being considered. Chlorhexidine skin preparation is an intervention that could be studied to reduce CLABSIs. Adult ICU patients (a) would represent the 'P' (Population) in the PICOT framework. Standard central line care bundles (c) would likely be the 'C' (Comparison) against which the intervention is measured. CLABSI rates (d) would be the 'O' (Outcome) being measured. The intervention component is crucial in PICOT formulation as it defines the specific practice or treatment being investigated for its effectiveness in addressing the clinical question.

196. A healthcare organization is using the Consolidated Framework for Implementation Research (CFIR) to guide the implementation of a new evidence-based pressure ulcer prevention program. Which CFIR domain would be MOST relevant in addressing staff resistance to the new program?
a. Intervention Characteristics
b. Outer Setting
c. Inner Setting
d. Characteristics of Individuals

Answer: d. Characteristics of Individuals. Explanation: The CFIR domain "Characteristics of Individuals" would be most relevant in addressing staff resistance to a new evidence-based program. This domain includes constructs such as knowledge and beliefs about the intervention, self-efficacy, and individual stage of change, which directly relate to individual staff members' attitudes and behaviors towards the new program. Intervention Characteristics (a) focus on the attributes of the intervention itself. Outer Setting (b) deals with external influences. Inner Setting (c) addresses organizational culture and climate, which are important but less directly tied to individual resistance. Understanding and addressing the characteristics of individuals is crucial for overcoming resistance and facilitating successful implementation of evidence-based practices.

197. In conducting a rapid critical appraisal of a randomized controlled trial on a new pain management technique, which of the following elements is MOST important to assess for validity?
a. Sample size calculation
b. Randomization method
c. Blinding procedure
d. Statistical analysis technique

Answer: b. Randomization method. Explanation: In a rapid critical appraisal of a randomized controlled trial (RCT), the randomization method is most important to assess for validity. Proper randomization is fundamental to the integrity of an RCT as it helps ensure that any differences between groups are due to the intervention rather than selection bias. While sample size calculation (a) is important for study power, it doesn't directly affect internal validity. Blinding (c) is crucial but secondary to randomization in terms of foundational validity. The statistical analysis technique (d) is important for interpreting results but doesn't affect the basic validity of the study design. A flawed randomization process can undermine the entire study, making it the most critical element to assess in a rapid appraisal for validity.

198. A nurse leader is applying the Johns Hopkins Nursing Evidence-Based Practice (JHNEBP) model to improve pain management practices. Which of the following best represents the 'Practice' component of the PET (Practice, Evidence, Translation) process?
a. Conducting a systematic review of pain management literature
b. Identifying current pain assessment methods on the unit
c. Implementing new pain management protocols based on evidence
d. Evaluating patient satisfaction with pain control

Answer: b. Identifying current pain assessment methods on the unit. Explanation: In the JHNEBP model's PET process, the 'Practice' component involves identifying the practice question or problem. Identifying current pain assessment methods on the unit represents this initial step of recognizing current practices and potential areas for improvement. Conducting a systematic review (a) falls under the 'Evidence' component. Implementing new protocols (c) and evaluating patient satisfaction (d) are part of the 'Translation' phase. The Practice step is crucial as it sets the foundation for the entire EBP process by clearly defining the clinical issue to be addressed, making the identification of current practices a key element of this component.

199. When formulating a PICOT question to investigate the effectiveness of nurse-led discharge planning in reducing hospital readmissions, which element represents the 'C' (Comparison) component?
a. Patients discharged from medical-surgical units
b. Nurse-led discharge planning
c. Standard discharge procedures
d. 30-day readmission rates

Answer: c. Standard discharge procedures. Explanation: In a PICOT question, the 'C' represents the Comparison or Control, which is typically the current standard of care or an alternative intervention. Standard discharge procedures serve as the comparison against which nurse-led discharge planning (the intervention) would be measured. Patients discharged from medical-surgical units (a) would be the 'P' (Population). Nurse-led discharge planning (b) is the 'I' (Intervention). 30-day readmission rates (d) represent the 'O' (Outcome). The comparison component is crucial in

PICOT formulation as it provides a baseline or alternative against which the effectiveness of the intervention can be evaluated.

200. A healthcare system is using the Consolidated Framework for Implementation Research (CFIR) to implement a new evidence-based handoff communication tool. Which CFIR construct would be MOST relevant in assessing the tool's compatibility with existing workflows?
a. Intervention Source
b. Relative Advantage
c. Complexity
d. Compatibility

Answer: d. Compatibility. Explanation: The CFIR construct of Compatibility would be most relevant in assessing how well the new handoff communication tool fits with existing workflows. Compatibility refers to the degree of tangible fit between meaning and values attached to the intervention by involved individuals, how those align with individuals' own norms, values, and perceived risks and needs, and how the intervention fits with existing workflows and systems. Intervention Source (a) relates to the perception of whether the intervention is externally or internally developed. Relative Advantage (b) is the stakeholders' perception of the advantage of implementing the intervention versus an alternative solution. Complexity (c) is the perceived difficulty of implementation. Compatibility directly addresses the fit with existing practices, making it most relevant for assessing integration with current workflows.

201. In conducting a rapid critical appraisal of a qualitative study on nurses' experiences with a new electronic health record system, which of the following is MOST important to assess for trustworthiness?
a. Sample size
b. Data saturation
c. Statistical significance of findings
d. Generalizability of results

Answer: b. Data saturation. Explanation: In a rapid critical appraisal of a qualitative study, assessing for data saturation is most important for establishing trustworthiness. Data saturation occurs when no new themes or information emerge from additional data collection, indicating that the sample size was sufficient to capture the full range of experiences or perspectives. Sample size (a) alone doesn't guarantee comprehensive data in qualitative research. Statistical significance (c) is not applicable to qualitative studies. Generalizability (d) is not typically a goal of qualitative research, which often focuses on in-depth understanding of specific contexts. Data saturation provides evidence that the study has captured the depth and breadth of the phenomenon under investigation, enhancing the credibility and completeness of the findings.

202. A nurse executive is using the Johns Hopkins Nursing Evidence-Based Practice (JHNEBP) model to address high turnover rates among new graduate nurses. Which of the following best represents the 'Evidence' component of the PET process in this scenario?
a. Surveying current new graduate nurses about job satisfaction
b. Reviewing literature on effective nurse retention strategies
c. Implementing a new mentorship program for new graduates
d. Analyzing turnover data from the past five years

Answer: b. Reviewing literature on effective nurse retention strategies. Explanation: In the JHNEBP model's PET process, the 'Evidence' component involves searching, appraising, and synthesizing the best available evidence related to the practice question. Reviewing literature on effective nurse retention strategies directly aligns with this evidence-gathering step. Surveying current nurses (a) and analyzing turnover data (d) would be part of the 'Practice' component, where the problem is identified and defined. Implementing a new mentorship program (c) would fall under the 'Translation' component, where evidence-based solutions are put into practice. The systematic review of literature is crucial for identifying evidence-based strategies that have been proven effective in addressing nurse turnover, making it the core activity of the Evidence component in this scenario.

203. When applying the Consolidated Framework for Implementation Research (CFIR) to evaluate the implementation of a new fall prevention protocol, which domain would best address the hospital's readiness for change?
a. Intervention Characteristics
b. Outer Setting
c. Inner Setting
d. Process

Answer: c. Inner Setting. Explanation: The CFIR domain of Inner Setting would best address the hospital's readiness for change when implementing a new fall prevention protocol. This domain includes constructs such as structural characteristics, networks and communications, culture, and implementation climate, which all contribute to an organization's readiness for change. Intervention Characteristics (a) focus on attributes of the intervention itself. Outer Setting (b) deals with external influences like patient needs and resources. Process (d) relates to the activities of planning, engaging, executing, and reflecting on the implementation. The Inner Setting domain specifically captures the organizational context, including its capacity and willingness to undertake change, making it most relevant for assessing readiness to implement a new protocol.

204. A nurse executive is leading the implementation of the AIDET® service excellence program across the hospital. Which of the following actions would best ensure the consistent application of AIDET® principles by all staff members?
a. Mandating a one-time training session on AIDET® for all staff.
b. Integrating AIDET® practices into the annual performance review process.
c. Creating a dedicated AIDET® task force to monitor and report compliance.
d. Implementing a reward system for staff who consistently demonstrate AIDET® behaviors.

Answer: b. Integrating AIDET® practices into the annual performance review process. Explanation: By embedding AIDET® practices into the performance review process, the hospital ensures that staff are held accountable for consistently applying these principles. This approach reinforces the importance of service excellence in daily interactions, leading to sustained improvements in patient experience.

205. To improve patient-centered care, the nurse executive is establishing a Patient and Family Advisory Council (PFAC). Which of the following best practices should be prioritized to maximize the council's impact on service improvement?
a. Limiting council membership to patients who have received care within the last six months.
b. Including a diverse group of patients and family members who represent the hospital's patient population.
c. Allowing only hospital executives to set the agenda for council meetings to maintain focus.

212. To improve service excellence, the nurse executive is considering implementing the AIDET® framework in conjunction with the hospital's existing patient satisfaction initiatives. Which of the following strategies would best integrate AIDET® into current practices?
a. Training only newly hired staff on AIDET® principles to ensure consistent application.
b. Requiring all patient interactions to begin with a scripted AIDET® introduction.
c. Incorporating AIDET® into ongoing staff education and reinforcement programs.
d. Using AIDET® only for interactions with patients who have previously expressed dissatisfaction.

Answer: c. Incorporating AIDET® into ongoing staff education and reinforcement programs. Explanation: Continuous education and reinforcement are key to ensuring that AIDET® principles become a consistent part of daily practice. Integrating AIDET® into existing education programs helps sustain the framework's application across all patient interactions, enhancing overall service excellence.

213. A nurse executive is evaluating the outcomes of a recently established Patient and Family Advisory Council (PFAC). Which of the following indicators would best demonstrate the council's effectiveness in improving patient experience?
a. A decrease in the number of patient complaints received by the hospital.
b. An increase in the number of initiatives developed with input from the PFAC.
c. A higher engagement rate among PFAC members in hospital activities.
d. An improvement in patient satisfaction scores in areas targeted by the PFAC.

Answer: d. An improvement in patient satisfaction scores in areas targeted by the PFAC. Explanation: The effectiveness of the PFAC is best demonstrated by measurable improvements in patient satisfaction in areas where the council has provided input. This outcome indicates that the council's recommendations are having a positive impact on the patient experience, validating its role in hospital operations.

214. A nurse executive is leading a quality improvement initiative using the Institute for Healthcare Improvement (IHI) Model for Improvement. The team has identified a specific aim, and they are now selecting measures to determine if the changes lead to improvement. Which of the following types of measures should be prioritized to effectively monitor progress?
a. Process measures that track the steps of care delivery
b. Structural measures that assess the healthcare setting and resources
c. Outcome measures that reflect the impact on patient health
d. Balancing measures that evaluate the unintended consequences of changes

Answer: c. Outcome measures that reflect the impact on patient health. Explanation: In the IHI Model for Improvement, outcome measures are critical as they directly reflect the success of the changes in terms of patient health. While process and structural measures are also important, outcome measures provide the most direct evidence of improvement, aligning with the ultimate goal of quality improvement efforts.

215. A hospital is using Statistical Process Control (SPC) charts to monitor the rate of central line-associated bloodstream infections (CLABSI) in the intensive care unit. The nurse executive notices a series of eight consecutive points below the centerline on the SPC chart. What does this pattern suggest?

a. Normal process variation
b. A shift indicating an improvement in the process
c. A random variation that requires no action
d. An outlier event that needs investigation

Answer: b. A shift indicating an improvement in the process. Explanation: In SPC charts, a series of eight consecutive points below the centerline typically indicates a shift in the process, suggesting a significant improvement. This pattern warrants further investigation to understand the changes leading to the improvement and to ensure the process remains stable.

216. During a quality improvement project aimed at reducing surgical site infections (SSI), the nurse executive decides to use the Donabedian model to structure the evaluation. Which of the following would be considered a "process" measure within this model?
a. The rate of surgical site infections per 1,000 surgeries
b. The availability of sterile surgical instruments in the operating room
c. The adherence to preoperative antibiotic prophylaxis protocols
d. The number of operating rooms meeting standard safety regulations

Answer: c. The adherence to preoperative antibiotic prophylaxis protocols. Explanation: In the Donabedian model, process measures evaluate the actions taken during care delivery. Adherence to preoperative antibiotic prophylaxis protocols is a process measure because it assesses the specific actions healthcare providers take to prevent SSIs, directly influencing patient outcomes.

217. A nurse executive is implementing the Just Culture algorithm to address a medication error that occurred in the hospital. The error was made by a nurse who mistakenly administered the wrong dose of medication. The nurse was found to have followed all the correct procedures except for double-checking the dosage due to time pressure. According to the Just Culture algorithm, how should this situation be classified and addressed?
a. As reckless behavior requiring disciplinary action
b. As human error with a focus on system improvement
c. As at-risk behavior requiring coaching and education
d. As a criminal act requiring immediate termination

Answer: c. As at-risk behavior requiring coaching and education. Explanation: In Just Culture, at-risk behavior is when an individual makes a choice that increases risk where the risk is not recognized or is mistakenly believed to be justified. The nurse's failure to double-check the dosage due to time pressure falls into this category and should be addressed with coaching and education to reinforce the importance of following safety protocols even in stressful situations.

218. In a quality improvement project focused on reducing patient falls, the team identifies several potential changes to test. According to the IHI Model for Improvement, what is the next best step for the nurse executive to take?
a. Implement all proposed changes hospital-wide to maximize impact
b. Conduct a root cause analysis to understand why falls occur
c. Run small tests of change using Plan-Do-Study-Act (PDSA) cycles

d. Survey patients to gather feedback on their perceptions of safety

Answer: c. Run small tests of change using Plan-Do-Study-Act (PDSA) cycles. Explanation: The IHI Model for Improvement advocates for testing changes on a small scale using PDSA cycles before broader implementation. This approach allows the team to assess the impact of each change, refine the interventions, and ensure they lead to the desired improvement in reducing patient falls.

219. A nurse executive is monitoring the implementation of a new hand hygiene protocol using Statistical Process Control (SPC) charts. After several weeks, the chart shows a single data point outside the upper control limit. How should this be interpreted?
a. It indicates normal variation, and no action is required
b. It suggests a special cause variation that should be investigated
c. It represents a common cause variation, and the process is in control
d. It is an error in data collection, and the point should be disregarded

Answer: b. It suggests a special cause variation that should be investigated. Explanation: A data point outside the control limits on an SPC chart indicates special cause variation, meaning that an unusual event or factor has impacted the process. This warrants investigation to determine the cause and to address any underlying issues that may have led to the deviation.

220. The nurse executive at a large healthcare facility is applying the Donabedian model to assess the quality of care in the emergency department. Which of the following would be considered a "structure" measure in this context?
a. The frequency of timely administration of pain relief medications
b. The patient satisfaction scores regarding their overall experience
c. The number of fully equipped resuscitation carts available in the department
d. The rate of correct diagnoses made by emergency physicians

Answer: c. The number of fully equipped resuscitation carts available in the department. Explanation: Structure measures in the Donabedian model refer to the physical and organizational infrastructure within which care is provided. The availability of fully equipped resuscitation carts is a structure measure, as it pertains to the resources and equipment necessary to deliver quality care.

221. A nurse executive is utilizing the Just Culture algorithm to review a near-miss event where a nurse almost administered the wrong medication but caught the error before giving it to the patient. What is the most appropriate response based on the Just Culture principles?
a. Punish the nurse to set an example for others
b. Investigate the system factors that contributed to the near-miss
c. Ignore the event since no harm occurred to the patient
d. Implement a strict no-tolerance policy for similar mistakes

Answer: b. Investigate the system factors that contributed to the near-miss. Explanation: Just Culture focuses on understanding the systemic causes of errors and near-misses rather than blaming individuals. Investigating the system factors allows the organization to identify and address weaknesses in processes that may lead to similar events in the future, thereby improving overall safety.

222. A quality improvement team is using Statistical Process Control (SPC) charts to monitor patient wait times in the outpatient clinic. After several months, the team observes that the data points are consistently trending downward but still remain within the control limits. What does this pattern suggest about the process?
a. The process is improving, and no further changes are needed
b. The process is out of control and requires immediate intervention
c. The process is stable but may be undergoing a gradual improvement
d. The process is stable, and the changes are having no impact

Answer: c. The process is stable but may be undergoing a gradual improvement. Explanation: A consistent downward trend within the control limits on an SPC chart suggests that the process is stable but shows signs of gradual improvement. The team should continue to monitor the process to ensure that the trend continues and to identify any further opportunities for enhancement.

223. A nurse executive is tasked with implementing a new electronic health record (EHR) system to improve patient care quality. Using the Donabedian model, which aspect of this implementation should be evaluated as an "outcome" measure?
a. The number of EHR training sessions completed by staff
b. The patient mortality rate following the implementation of the EHR
c. The availability of technical support for the EHR system
d. The ease of use of the EHR system for nursing staff

Answer: b. The patient mortality rate following the implementation of the EHR. Explanation: Outcome measures in the Donabedian model assess the results of care, such as changes in patient health status. The patient mortality rate is an outcome measure that reflects the overall impact of the EHR implementation on patient care quality, making it a critical factor to evaluate in determining the success of the new system.

224. A hospital is implementing TeamSTEPPS to improve patient safety. Which of the following TeamSTEPPS tools would be MOST effective in addressing communication breakdowns during patient handoffs?
a. SBAR (Situation, Background, Assessment, Recommendation)
b. CUS (Concerned, Uncomfortable, Safety issue)
c. Two-Challenge Rule
d. Briefs

Answer: a. SBAR (Situation, Background, Assessment, Recommendation). Explanation: SBAR is the most effective TeamSTEPPS tool for addressing communication breakdowns during patient handoffs. It provides a standardized structure for communicating critical information, ensuring that all essential elements are conveyed consistently. SBAR is specifically designed for situations like handoffs where comprehensive yet concise information transfer is crucial. CUS (b) is used for speaking up about safety concerns. The Two-Challenge Rule (c) is for challenging authority in critical situations. Briefs (d) are used for planning before a procedure or shift. SBAR's structured approach directly targets the common issues in handoff communication, making it the most appropriate tool for improving this specific aspect of patient safety.

225. In applying Crew Resource Management (CRM) principles to reduce medication errors, which of the following strategies would be MOST effective in promoting a culture of safety?
a. Implementing strict punitive measures for errors
b. Encouraging anonymous error reporting
c. Focusing solely on individual accountability
d. Limiting communication to formal channels

Answer: b. Encouraging anonymous error reporting. Explanation: Encouraging anonymous error reporting is most aligned with CRM principles in promoting a culture of safety. This approach fosters open communication about errors and near-misses without fear of retribution, enabling learning and system improvement. Strict punitive measures (a) contradict CRM principles by discouraging open communication. Focusing solely on individual accountability (c) overlooks systemic factors contributing to errors. Limiting communication to formal channels (d) restricts the free flow of safety-critical information. Anonymous reporting supports a just culture where errors are viewed as opportunities for improvement rather than reasons for punishment, aligning closely with CRM's emphasis on open communication and continuous learning.

226. A surgical team is implementing the Universal Protocol to prevent wrong-site surgery. Which step in the protocol is MOST critical for ensuring patient safety?
a. Verifying patient identity and procedure
b. Marking the surgical site
c. Conducting a pre-procedure time-out
d. Obtaining informed consent

Answer: c. Conducting a pre-procedure time-out. Explanation: While all steps of the Universal Protocol are important, conducting a pre-procedure time-out is the most critical step for ensuring patient safety in preventing wrong-site surgery. The time-out serves as a final verification where all team members pause to confirm the correct patient, procedure, and site, and address any concerns. It's the last barrier against errors before incision. Verifying patient identity and procedure (a) and marking the surgical site (b) are crucial but occur earlier in the process. Obtaining informed consent (d), while necessary, doesn't directly prevent wrong-site surgery. The time-out is unique in bringing together all previous safety checks with active participation from the entire surgical team, making it the most critical step in the Universal Protocol.

227. A healthcare organization is striving to become a High-Reliability Organization (HRO). Which of the following practices BEST exemplifies the HRO principle of preoccupation with failure?
a. Implementing rigid protocols for all procedures
b. Conducting regular leadership rounds focused on safety
c. Rewarding staff for identifying potential safety risks
d. Prioritizing efficiency over redundancy in safety checks

Answer: c. Rewarding staff for identifying potential safety risks. Explanation: Rewarding staff for identifying potential safety risks best exemplifies the HRO principle of preoccupation with failure. This practice encourages vigilance and proactive identification of weak signals that could lead to errors, aligning with HROs' focus on anticipating and preventing failures before they occur. Implementing rigid protocols (a) can sometimes hinder adaptability, another key HRO principle. Leadership rounds (b) are valuable but don't specifically target preoccupation with failure. Prioritizing efficiency over redundancy (d) contradicts HRO principles, which often emphasize thoughtful redundancy in critical safety processes. By incentivizing staff to actively seek out potential risks, the organization demonstrates a cultural commitment to ongoing safety awareness and improvement.

228. In implementing TeamSTEPPS, a nurse leader notices that team members are hesitant to speak up about safety concerns. Which TeamSTEPPS strategy would be MOST effective in addressing this issue?
a. Task assistance
b. Conflict resolution
c. Assertive statement
d. Huddle

Answer: c. Assertive statement. Explanation: The assertive statement strategy from TeamSTEPPS would be most effective in addressing team members' hesitancy to speak up about safety concerns. This technique provides a structured, non-confrontational way to voice concerns, using the format: "I am concerned, I am uncomfortable, This is a safety issue." It empowers team members to assert themselves in a professional manner when they perceive a risk to patient safety. Task assistance (a) is about offering help with tasks. Conflict resolution (b) addresses interpersonal conflicts rather than safety communication. Huddles (d) are brief team meetings but don't specifically target assertive communication. The assertive statement technique directly addresses the identified problem by giving team members a tool to overcome hesitation in voicing safety concerns.

229. A hospital is applying Crew Resource Management (CRM) principles to improve teamwork in the operating room. Which of the following CRM concepts is MOST important for effective decision-making during surgical crises?
a. Situational awareness
b. Explicit coordination
c. Workload management
d. Leadership

Answer: a. Situational awareness. Explanation: Situational awareness is the most important CRM concept for effective decision-making during surgical crises. It involves maintaining a comprehensive understanding of the current situation, anticipating future events, and continuously reassessing the environment. In a surgical crisis, situational awareness enables team members to quickly identify problems, assess resources, and make informed decisions. Explicit coordination (b) is important for team communication but doesn't directly address decision-making. Workload management (c) is crucial for efficiency but less critical in acute crisis decision-making. While leadership (d) is vital, effective leadership in crises relies heavily on situational awareness. The ability to maintain a clear picture of the evolving situation is fundamental to making rapid, effective decisions in high-pressure surgical environments.

230. In implementing the Universal Protocol, a hospital notices inconsistent compliance with the site-marking process. Which of the following interventions would be MOST effective in improving adherence to this step?
a. Increasing disciplinary actions for non-compliance
b. Standardizing marking tools and procedures across all surgical areas

c. Requiring surgeons to mark sites in the preoperative area only

d. Eliminating site marking in favor of verbal verification only

Answer: b. Standardizing marking tools and procedures across all surgical areas. Explanation: Standardizing marking tools and procedures across all surgical areas would be most effective in improving adherence to the site-marking process. This approach reduces variability and confusion, making it easier for all staff to consistently follow the protocol regardless of the specific surgical area. Increasing disciplinary actions (a) may lead to underreporting of issues rather than improved compliance. Requiring marking only in the preoperative area (c) may not account for all scenarios and could introduce new risks. Eliminating site marking (d) removes a critical safety check and contradicts best practices. Standardization aligns with high-reliability principles by creating clear, consistent expectations and processes, thereby reducing the likelihood of errors in site marking.

231. A healthcare organization is adopting High-Reliability Organization (HRO) principles. Which of the following practices BEST demonstrates the HRO characteristic of reluctance to simplify?

a. Creating detailed checklists for all procedures

b. Encouraging diverse perspectives in problem-solving

c. Implementing a zero-tolerance policy for errors

d. Centralizing decision-making authority

Answer: b. Encouraging diverse perspectives in problem-solving. Explanation: Encouraging diverse perspectives in problem-solving best demonstrates the HRO characteristic of reluctance to simplify. This practice acknowledges the complexity of healthcare environments and resists the temptation to oversimplify issues. By involving diverse viewpoints, organizations can uncover nuanced understandings of problems and develop more comprehensive solutions. Creating detailed checklists (a) can be useful but may oversimplify complex processes. A zero-tolerance policy for errors (c) contradicts HRO principles of learning from mistakes. Centralizing decision-making (d) goes against HRO principles of deferring to expertise. Embracing diverse perspectives allows organizations to maintain a more complete and nuanced view of their operations and potential risks, aligning closely with the HRO reluctance to simplify.

232. In applying TeamSTEPPS principles, a nurse executive wants to improve situational monitoring in the emergency department. Which of the following strategies would be MOST effective in enhancing this skill among staff?

a. Implementing a shared mental model approach

b. Increasing the frequency of formal team meetings

c. Enhancing electronic health record documentation

d. Focusing on individual task completion efficiency

Answer: a. Implementing a shared mental model approach. Explanation: Implementing a shared mental model approach would be most effective in enhancing situational monitoring skills among emergency department staff. This strategy involves ensuring that all team members have a common understanding of the team's goals, tasks, and roles. It promotes active awareness of the evolving situation and each member's part in it. Increasing formal meetings (b) may improve communication but doesn't directly enhance real-time situational awareness. Enhancing EHR documentation (c) is important for information sharing but doesn't necessarily improve active monitoring. Focusing on individual task efficiency (d) might actually detract from overall situational awareness. The shared mental model approach aligns closely with TeamSTEPPS principles of mutual support and situational awareness, enabling staff to better monitor and understand the dynamic ED environment.

233. A surgical team is struggling with effective communication during complex procedures. Which Crew Resource Management (CRM) technique would be MOST beneficial in improving team communication in this context?
a. Closed-loop communication
b. Sterile cockpit rule
c. Debriefing
d. Cross-monitoring

Answer: a. Closed-loop communication. Explanation: Closed-loop communication would be most beneficial in improving team communication during complex surgical procedures. This technique involves the sender initiating a message, the receiver accepting the message and confirming its receipt, and the sender verifying that the message was received correctly. It ensures clear, accurate information transfer, which is crucial in complex, high-stakes environments like surgery. The sterile cockpit rule (b) limits unnecessary communication but doesn't improve the quality of essential communication. Debriefing (c) is valuable for post-procedure learning but doesn't address real-time communication issues. Cross-monitoring (d) is important for team situational awareness but doesn't directly target communication clarity. Closed-loop communication directly addresses the challenge of ensuring clear, accurate information transfer in the complex, often noisy surgical environment.

234. The nurse executive is tasked with optimizing the hospital's reimbursement under the DRG (Diagnosis-Related Group) system. Which of the following strategies would most effectively improve DRG-based reimbursement while maintaining high-quality patient care?
a. Encouraging physicians to document all relevant comorbidities and complications.
b. Reducing the length of stay for all patients to the minimum possible.
c. Limiting diagnostic testing to reduce overall patient care costs.
d. Implementing a single care pathway for each DRG to standardize treatment.

Answer: a. Encouraging physicians to document all relevant comorbidities and complications. Explanation: Accurate and comprehensive documentation of comorbidities and complications is crucial for optimizing DRG-based reimbursement, as it ensures that the hospital is appropriately compensated for the complexity of care provided. Reducing length of stay or limiting diagnostics could negatively impact patient care, while standardized pathways may not account for individual patient needs.

235. A hospital's Value-Based Purchasing (VBP) program scores have been declining, particularly in the domain of patient outcomes. As the nurse executive, which of the following actions should be prioritized to improve the hospital's VBP performance?
a. Increasing patient satisfaction by enhancing amenities and services.
b. Developing a multidisciplinary team to focus on reducing hospital-acquired infections (HAIs).
c. Introducing mandatory overtime to ensure adequate staffing levels at all times.
d. Focusing on public relations efforts to improve the hospital's image in the community.

Answer: b. Developing a multidisciplinary team to focus on reducing hospital-acquired infections (HAIs). Explanation: The VBP program ties reimbursement to performance on specific quality measures, including patient outcomes. Reducing HAIs directly impacts these outcomes, leading to better VBP scores. While patient satisfaction is important, outcomes have a more significant impact on VBP reimbursement.

236. A nurse executive is evaluating the hospital's supply chain management practices and considering the implementation of a just-in-time (JIT) inventory system. Which potential challenge is most critical to address before implementing JIT in a healthcare setting?
a. Ensuring that the hospital has sufficient storage space for inventory.
b. Developing strong relationships with reliable suppliers to avoid stockouts.
c. Training staff on how to manage larger inventory levels efficiently.
d. Increasing the frequency of inventory audits to ensure accuracy.

Answer: b. Developing strong relationships with reliable suppliers to avoid stockouts. Explanation: In a JIT inventory system, supplies are ordered and delivered just as they are needed, minimizing on-hand inventory. However, this approach requires reliable suppliers to prevent stockouts, which could compromise patient care. Addressing supplier reliability is crucial to the successful implementation of JIT in healthcare.

237. During a routine audit, the nurse executive discovers that the hospital is losing revenue due to inadequate charge capture processes. Which of the following steps would be most effective in optimizing charge capture for revenue integrity?
a. Increasing the number of staff responsible for charge entry to reduce workload.
b. Implementing a more comprehensive coding education program for clinical staff.
c. Conducting periodic audits to identify missed charges and correct documentation errors.
d. Reducing the complexity of billing codes to streamline the charge capture process.

Answer: c. Conducting periodic audits to identify missed charges and correct documentation errors. Explanation: Periodic audits can uncover patterns of missed charges and documentation errors that affect revenue. By identifying and addressing these issues, the hospital can improve charge capture and enhance revenue integrity. Education and process simplification are also important but less immediately impactful than targeted audits.

238. A nurse executive is reviewing the hospital's performance under the Value-Based Purchasing (VBP) program. The hospital's scores for the "Efficiency and Cost Reduction" domain are below the national average. Which strategy would most effectively improve performance in this domain?
a. Increasing the use of generic medications to reduce drug costs.
b. Implementing a care coordination program to reduce readmissions.
c. Enhancing staff training to improve clinical documentation accuracy.
d. Expanding marketing efforts to attract higher-paying patients.

Answer: b. Implementing a care coordination program to reduce readmissions. Explanation: The "Efficiency and Cost Reduction" domain in the VBP program often includes measures related to the cost of care, such as readmission rates. By improving care coordination, the hospital can reduce unnecessary readmissions, thereby lowering costs and improving its VBP scores. Other options, while potentially beneficial, do not directly target the cost reduction domain.

239. The nurse executive at a healthcare system with multiple facilities is tasked with standardizing supply chain management practices across all locations. Which of the following strategies would best support the efficient implementation of just-in-time (JIT) inventory across the system?
a. Centralizing procurement to achieve economies of scale and consistency in supply.
b. Allowing each facility to manage its own JIT inventory independently.
c. Reducing the variety of supplies ordered to simplify inventory management.
d. Investing in automated inventory tracking systems to monitor supply levels in real-time.

Answer: d. Investing in automated inventory tracking systems to monitor supply levels in real-time. Explanation: Real-time tracking systems are essential for the effective implementation of JIT inventory, especially across multiple facilities. These systems ensure that supply levels are continuously monitored, reducing the risk of stockouts and enabling timely reordering. Centralized procurement and inventory reduction are secondary considerations.

240. A nurse executive is analyzing the hospital's revenue cycle to identify opportunities for improvement in charge capture. Which of the following scenarios represents the most significant risk to accurate charge capture?
a. A lack of standardized processes for documenting and billing ancillary services.
b. The use of manual entry systems for patient charges, which increases the risk of data entry errors.
c. Delayed submission of charges due to a high volume of daily transactions.
d. The reliance on a single coder for all patient charges across multiple departments.

Answer: a. A lack of standardized processes for documenting and billing ancillary services. Explanation: Inconsistent or non-standardized documentation and billing processes can lead to significant revenue loss due to missed or incorrect charges. Addressing this risk by standardizing processes is crucial for accurate charge capture. While manual systems and staffing issues are also risks, they are less critical than ensuring consistent processes across the board.

241. The hospital's Value-Based Purchasing (VBP) program scores indicate a need for improvement in the "Patient Experience of Care" domain. As the nurse executive, which initiative would be most effective in boosting performance in this area?
a. Launching a campaign to improve nurse-patient communication through AIDET® training.
b. Reducing the length of patient stays to increase turnover and efficiency.
c. Implementing stricter visitation policies to maintain a quieter environment.
d. Focusing on discharge planning to ensure a smooth transition to post-acute care.

Answer: a. Launching a campaign to improve nurse-patient communication through AIDET® training. Explanation: The "Patient Experience of Care" domain heavily relies on patients' perceptions of communication and care quality. AIDET® training focuses on improving communication skills, which can directly impact patient satisfaction scores and, consequently, VBP performance. Length of stay and visitation policies are less impactful on patient experience.

242. A nurse executive is tasked with improving the hospital's revenue integrity through better charge capture practices. Which of the following technologies would be most beneficial in achieving this goal?
a. Implementing an electronic health record (EHR) system with integrated charge capture capabilities.

b. Installing a new patient portal to increase transparency in billing.
c. Using telehealth platforms to capture additional revenue streams.
d. Adopting an automated patient scheduling system to reduce no-shows.

Answer: a. Implementing an electronic health record (EHR) system with integrated charge capture capabilities.
Explanation: An EHR system with integrated charge capture ensures that all billable services are accurately documented and billed, improving revenue integrity. While patient portals, telehealth, and scheduling systems have their benefits, they do not directly address the core issue of accurate charge capture within the revenue cycle.

243. To optimize DRG-based reimbursement, a nurse executive is considering strategies to improve clinical documentation. Which of the following approaches would best support accurate and comprehensive documentation?
a. Increasing the frequency of audits to ensure compliance with documentation standards.
b. Implementing regular, targeted education sessions on DRG-related documentation for clinical staff.
c. Assigning a dedicated documentation specialist to each department to oversee record-keeping.
d. Using a standardized template for all patient records to simplify the documentation process.

Answer: b. Implementing regular, targeted education sessions on DRG-related documentation for clinical staff.
Explanation: Ongoing education tailored to DRG-related documentation helps clinical staff understand the importance of accurate and thorough record-keeping, leading to better reimbursement. While audits and specialists can be helpful, proactive education ensures that documentation is correct from the outset.

244. A nurse executive is facing a significant nursing shortage in the hospital and must develop a workforce planning model to address this challenge. Which strategy is most effective in building a sustainable workforce for the future?
a. Increasing the recruitment of international nurses to fill immediate gaps
b. Implementing a nurse residency program to support new graduates
c. Offering signing bonuses to attract experienced nurses from other facilities
d. Outsourcing nursing positions to temporary staffing agencies

Answer: b. Implementing a nurse residency program to support new graduates. Explanation: A nurse residency program helps new graduates transition into professional practice by providing them with the necessary support, mentorship, and training. This strategy not only addresses immediate staffing needs but also builds a sustainable workforce by reducing turnover and promoting long-term retention of nurses.

245. A healthcare organization is experiencing high turnover rates among its nursing staff. The nurse executive is tasked with developing a total rewards strategy to improve retention. Which component of the total rewards approach is most likely to address the primary reasons for turnover in healthcare?
a. Increasing base salaries for all nursing staff
b. Offering comprehensive wellness programs, including mental health support
c. Providing annual bonuses tied to individual performance metrics
d. Expanding professional development opportunities and career advancement paths

Answer: d. Expanding professional development opportunities and career advancement paths. Explanation: Career development and advancement opportunities are crucial for retaining nursing staff. By offering clear pathways for professional growth, the organization can increase job satisfaction, reduce turnover, and attract talent committed to long-term careers within the organization.

246. A nurse executive is transitioning the organization's performance management system from annual reviews to a continuous feedback model. What is the primary advantage of adopting a continuous feedback approach in performance management?
a. It reduces the administrative burden of preparing for annual reviews
b. It allows for real-time adjustments to performance and development plans
c. It eliminates the need for formal performance documentation
d. It increases the likelihood of positive employee ratings

Answer: b. It allows for real-time adjustments to performance and development plans. Explanation: Continuous feedback provides timely input on performance, enabling employees to make immediate improvements and align their actions with organizational goals. This approach fosters ongoing development and prevents issues from persisting until the next annual review.

247. During collective bargaining agreement negotiations, the nursing union proposes a significant increase in wages. The nurse executive recognizes the need to balance financial sustainability with fair compensation. Which negotiation strategy is most appropriate in this scenario?
a. Agree to the wage increase to avoid a potential strike
b. Reject the proposal and present a counteroffer with minimal increases
c. Propose a phased wage increase combined with other non-monetary benefits
d. Focus on reducing other benefits to offset the cost of the wage increase

Answer: c. Propose a phased wage increase combined with other non-monetary benefits. Explanation: A phased wage increase allows the organization to manage financial impact over time while addressing the union's concerns. Combining this with non-monetary benefits, such as improved working conditions or additional paid time off, creates a balanced package that meets the needs of both parties.

248. A nurse executive is evaluating the impact of a new performance management system that includes continuous feedback and 360-degree evaluations. Which metric would best assess the effectiveness of this system in improving staff performance?
a. Employee satisfaction scores related to performance reviews
b. The number of performance improvement plans initiated
c. The percentage of staff who receive high ratings in their evaluations
d. The frequency of feedback provided to each employee

Answer: a. Employee satisfaction scores related to performance reviews. Explanation: Employee satisfaction with the performance review process reflects the perceived fairness and value of the system. High satisfaction scores indicate that employees feel the system is constructive and supportive of their professional growth, suggesting its effectiveness in improving staff performance.

249. In addressing a nursing shortage, a nurse executive decides to implement a workforce planning model that incorporates predictive analytics. Which of the following is the most significant advantage of using predictive analytics in workforce planning?
a. It guarantees an immediate solution to current staffing shortages
b. It provides data-driven insights to anticipate future staffing needs
c. It simplifies the recruitment process by automating candidate selection
d. It reduces the cost of recruitment by identifying the most cost-effective strategies

Answer: b. It provides data-driven insights to anticipate future staffing needs. Explanation: Predictive analytics allows the organization to forecast staffing needs based on trends such as patient volume, staff turnover, and demographic changes. This proactive approach helps in planning for future shortages and making informed decisions to ensure a stable workforce.

250. A nurse executive is designing a total rewards strategy to attract top healthcare talent in a highly competitive market. Which of the following elements is most likely to differentiate the organization from competitors?
a. Offering competitive salaries aligned with market rates
b. Providing flexible work schedules and telehealth opportunities
c. Offering standard benefits such as health insurance and retirement plans
d. Ensuring timely payment of performance bonuses

Answer: b. Providing flexible work schedules and telehealth opportunities. Explanation: In a competitive market, offering flexible work arrangements, such as telehealth opportunities, can be a significant differentiator. These options appeal to professionals seeking work-life balance and the ability to work remotely, making the organization more attractive to top talent.

251. During negotiations of a collective bargaining agreement, the nurse executive encounters resistance from union leaders regarding proposed changes to health benefits. Which strategy is most effective in reaching a mutually agreeable solution?
a. Withdrawing the proposed changes to avoid conflict
b. Providing detailed cost analysis to demonstrate the necessity of changes
c. Offering additional wage increases in exchange for accepting benefit changes
d. Allowing union leaders to have final decision-making authority on the benefits

Answer: b. Providing detailed cost analysis to demonstrate the necessity of changes. Explanation: Offering a transparent cost analysis helps union leaders understand the financial realities and rationale behind the proposed changes. This approach builds trust and encourages a collaborative negotiation process, increasing the likelihood of reaching a mutually agreeable solution.

252. A healthcare organization has implemented a new performance management system that emphasizes goal alignment across all levels of staff. How should the nurse executive measure the success of this system in achieving organizational objectives?

a. Monitoring the percentage of employees who meet their individual goals
b. Tracking improvements in patient outcomes related to staff performance
c. Reviewing the consistency of performance ratings across departments
d. Evaluating the frequency of employee feedback sessions

Answer: b. Tracking improvements in patient outcomes related to staff performance. Explanation: The success of a performance management system is ultimately reflected in its impact on patient care. By linking staff performance with patient outcomes, the nurse executive can assess whether the system is effectively contributing to the organization's objectives and improving overall healthcare quality.

253. In an effort to mitigate nursing shortages, the nurse executive is considering various workforce planning models. Which model is most likely to provide a long-term solution by addressing both recruitment and retention challenges?
a. A short-term staffing agency contract to fill immediate vacancies
b. A mentorship program that pairs experienced nurses with new graduates
c. A financial incentive program that offers signing bonuses for new hires
d. A partnership with local nursing schools to create a pipeline of new graduates

Answer: d. A partnership with local nursing schools to create a pipeline of new graduates. Explanation: Partnering with local nursing schools helps create a steady flow of new graduates into the organization, addressing both recruitment and retention. This model ensures a continuous supply of qualified nurses while fostering long-term relationships that support the organization's workforce needs over time.

254. A healthcare system is considering expanding its orthopedic service line. Which financial metric would be MOST crucial in determining the potential profitability of this expansion?
a. Return on Investment (ROI)
b. Contribution Margin
c. Operating Margin
d. Earnings Before Interest, Taxes, Depreciation, and Amortization (EBITDA)

Answer: b. Contribution Margin. Explanation: Contribution Margin is the most crucial metric for determining the potential profitability of a service line expansion. It represents the revenue remaining after variable costs are covered, indicating how much the service contributes to covering fixed costs and generating profit. This metric is particularly useful for service line analysis as it focuses on the incremental impact of the expansion. While ROI (a) is important, it doesn't specifically address ongoing profitability. Operating Margin (c) includes fixed costs, which may not change significantly with expansion. EBITDA (d) is more relevant for overall organizational financial health. Contribution Margin provides the clearest picture of how the orthopedic service line expansion would contribute to the system's financial performance.

255. A hospital is implementing a digital marketing strategy to increase patient acquisition for its new telemedicine services. Which of the following approaches would be MOST effective in targeting potential patients?
a. Broad-based social media advertising
b. Search engine optimization for telemedicine-related keywords
c. Television commercials during prime time

d. Direct mail campaigns to local households

Answer: b. Search engine optimization for telemedicine-related keywords. Explanation: Search engine optimization (SEO) for telemedicine-related keywords would be the most effective digital marketing approach for targeting potential telemedicine patients. This strategy ensures that the hospital appears prominently in search results when potential patients are actively seeking telemedicine services, capturing them at the point of need. Broad-based social media advertising (a) may have a wide reach but less precise targeting. Television commercials (c) and direct mail campaigns (d) are traditional marketing methods that may not effectively reach the digital-savvy audience seeking telemedicine services. SEO aligns with the digital nature of telemedicine and targets patients who are already expressing interest through their search behavior, making it the most effective for this specific service.

256. A prestigious hospital faces a crisis when a surgical error leads to a patient death and negative media coverage. Which of the following should be the FIRST step in managing this reputational crisis?
a. Issue a detailed public statement explaining the incident
b. Conduct an internal investigation to determine fault
c. Develop a comprehensive media relations strategy
d. Establish a dedicated hotline for patient concerns

Answer: a. Issue a detailed public statement explaining the incident. Explanation: Issuing a detailed public statement explaining the incident should be the first step in managing this reputational crisis. In crisis management, prompt, transparent communication is crucial to maintaining trust and controlling the narrative. A detailed statement demonstrates accountability, provides accurate information to counteract speculation, and shows the organization's commitment to addressing the issue. Conducting an internal investigation (b) is necessary but shouldn't delay initial communication. Developing a media strategy (c) is important but comes after the initial response. Establishing a hotline (d) is valuable but doesn't address the immediate need for public information. The public statement sets the tone for the organization's response and forms the foundation for subsequent crisis management actions.

257. A community hospital is conducting a Community Health Needs Assessment (CHNA). Which data source would provide the MOST comprehensive information about the community's health status and needs?
a. Hospital admission data
b. Local health department statistics
c. Community surveys and focus groups
d. National health databases

Answer: c. Community surveys and focus groups. Explanation: Community surveys and focus groups would provide the most comprehensive information about the community's health status and needs for a CHNA. This primary data collection method allows for direct input from community members, capturing their perceived health needs, barriers to care, and social determinants of health that may not be reflected in secondary data sources. Hospital admission data (a) is limited to those who have accessed hospital services. Local health department statistics (b) are valuable but may not capture all community perspectives. National health databases (d) lack local specificity. Community surveys and focus groups offer rich, contextual information directly from the population served, aligning with the CHNA's goal of understanding and addressing community-specific health needs.

258. A healthcare organization is analyzing the profitability of its cardiovascular service line. Which of the following metrics would be MOST useful in assessing the service line's market position relative to competitors?
a. Patient satisfaction scores
b. Physician referral patterns
c. Market share percentage
d. Length of stay benchmarks

Answer: c. Market share percentage. Explanation: Market share percentage would be the most useful metric in assessing the cardiovascular service line's market position relative to competitors. This metric directly quantifies the organization's portion of the total cardiovascular care market in the area, providing clear insight into its competitive standing. Patient satisfaction scores (a) are important for quality but don't directly reflect market position. Physician referral patterns (b) influence market share but don't provide a comprehensive view of market position. Length of stay benchmarks (d) relate to efficiency but not market standing. Market share percentage offers a direct comparison to competitors and indicates the service line's relative strength in capturing patient volume, which is crucial for strategic positioning and growth planning.

259. In developing a digital marketing strategy for a new oncology center, which of the following approaches would be MOST effective in building patient trust and credibility?
a. Testimonial videos from celebrity cancer survivors
b. Frequent promotional emails about cancer screening offers
c. Educational content marketing focusing on cancer prevention and treatment options
d. Pay-per-click advertising for specific cancer treatments

Answer: c. Educational content marketing focusing on cancer prevention and treatment options. Explanation: Educational content marketing focusing on cancer prevention and treatment options would be the most effective approach in building patient trust and credibility for a new oncology center. This strategy positions the center as a knowledgeable, patient-focused resource, providing valuable information that helps patients make informed decisions about their health. Celebrity testimonials (a) may attract attention but don't necessarily build trust in the center's expertise. Frequent promotional emails (b) can be perceived as intrusive and may not effectively convey the center's capabilities. Pay-per-click advertising (d) can drive traffic but doesn't build deep credibility. Educational content demonstrates the center's expertise and commitment to patient education, fostering trust and establishing the center as a credible authority in oncology care.

260. A multi-hospital system is facing public criticism over its pricing practices. Which brand management strategy would be MOST effective in addressing this reputational challenge?
a. Launching a new advertising campaign highlighting quality of care
b. Implementing a transparent pricing policy and patient cost estimator tool
c. Offering discounts on popular services for a limited time
d. Expanding charity care programs without addressing pricing concerns

Answer: b. Implementing a transparent pricing policy and patient cost estimator tool. Explanation: Implementing a transparent pricing policy and patient cost estimator tool would be the most effective strategy in addressing criticism over pricing practices. This approach directly addresses the core issue by providing clarity and accessibility to pricing information, demonstrating a commitment to transparency and patient-centered care. Launching a quality-focused advertising campaign (a) doesn't address the specific concern about pricing. Offering discounts (c) is a short-term solution that doesn't address systemic pricing issues. Expanding charity care (d), while beneficial, doesn't resolve concerns about general pricing practices. Transparency in pricing aligns with growing consumer demands for healthcare cost information and can help rebuild trust by empowering patients with the information they need to make informed decisions about their care and its costs.

261. Following a Community Health Needs Assessment (CHNA), a hospital identifies diabetes as a significant health issue in its service area. Which of the following implementation strategies would have the GREATEST long-term impact on community health?
a. Offering free diabetes screening events at the hospital
b. Developing a comprehensive diabetes education and management program
c. Providing discounted insulin to community members
d. Launching a diabetes awareness media campaign

Answer: b. Developing a comprehensive diabetes education and management program. Explanation: Developing a comprehensive diabetes education and management program would have the greatest long-term impact on community health. This strategy addresses the issue holistically, providing ongoing support for prevention, early detection, and management of diabetes. It offers sustainable benefits by empowering community members with knowledge and skills for long-term health management. Free screening events (a) are valuable but offer only point-in-time intervention. Providing discounted insulin (c) addresses immediate need but doesn't promote long-term management skills. A media campaign (d) raises awareness but doesn't provide direct intervention or education. A comprehensive program can lead to lasting behavior changes and improved health outcomes, addressing the root causes and ongoing management of diabetes in the community.

262. A healthcare organization is considering entering the urgent care market. Which of the following analyses would be MOST critical in determining the viability of this new service line?
a. Competitor landscape assessment
b. Capital equipment cost analysis
c. Staffing model projections
d. Payer mix analysis of the target area

Answer: a. Competitor landscape assessment. Explanation: A competitor landscape assessment would be the most critical analysis in determining the viability of entering the urgent care market. This analysis provides crucial information about existing market saturation, unmet needs, and potential differentiation strategies. Understanding the competitive environment is essential for identifying market opportunities and positioning the new urgent care service effectively. While capital equipment costs (b), staffing models (c), and payer mix (d) are important considerations, they are secondary to understanding the competitive landscape. The competitor analysis informs whether there's a viable market opportunity and how the organization can uniquely position itself, which is fundamental to the success of a new service line in a potentially crowded market like urgent care.

263. In developing a marketing strategy for a new minimally invasive surgical program, which target audience should be the PRIMARY focus for initial marketing efforts?
a. Potential patients in the community
b. Referring primary care physicians
c. Health insurance companies

d. Hospital board members

Answer: b. Referring primary care physicians. Explanation: Referring primary care physicians should be the primary focus for initial marketing efforts of a new minimally invasive surgical program. These physicians play a crucial role in patient referrals and are often the gatekeepers for specialty care. By targeting referring physicians, the hospital can establish a steady stream of patient referrals, which is essential for the program's success. While potential patients (a) are important, they typically rely on their primary care doctors for specialty referrals. Health insurance companies (c) are stakeholders but don't directly influence patient choice for this type of service. Hospital board members (d) are internal stakeholders and not the target for external marketing efforts. Focusing on referring physicians leverages existing healthcare networks and can lead to sustained patient volume for the new program.

264. A nurse executive is preparing a report on potential nursing workforce issues to present to a state legislative committee. Which of the following actions best exemplifies the use of Kingdon's Multiple Streams framework in health policy analysis?
a. Presenting only the solutions that align with the current political climate to increase the likelihood of adoption.
b. Identifying the problem stream by gathering data on nursing shortages and proposing a solution once a policy window opens.
c. Prioritizing stakeholder opinions and political feasibility over evidence-based solutions.
d. Focusing on the economic implications of proposed policies to ensure legislative support.

Answer: b. Identifying the problem stream by gathering data on nursing shortages and proposing a solution once a policy window opens. Explanation: Kingdon's Multiple Streams framework involves identifying the problem stream, policy stream, and political stream. In this case, gathering data on nursing shortages represents the problem stream, and proposing a solution when a policy window opens reflects the integration of the three streams to influence policy-making.

265. As a nurse executive advocating for increased funding for nurse staffing, which strategy would be most effective in a grassroots advocacy campaign?
a. Organizing a meeting with high-level policymakers to discuss staffing issues.
b. Creating a social media campaign to mobilize community support for increased nurse staffing.
c. Focusing solely on direct lobbying efforts to influence legislators.
d. Publishing an academic article detailing the importance of nurse staffing ratios.

Answer: b. Creating a social media campaign to mobilize community support for increased nurse staffing. Explanation: Grassroots advocacy campaigns are most effective when they engage the public and build broad support. A social media campaign can reach a wide audience, raise awareness, and generate public pressure on policymakers to act on the issue. Direct lobbying and academic publications, while valuable, are not central to grassroots strategies.

266. During the legislative process, a nurse executive is monitoring a bill that proposes mandatory nurse-to-patient ratios. At which stage of the process should the nurse executive focus efforts on influencing the outcome?
a. When the bill is introduced in the legislature.
b. During the committee review and hearings stage.
c. After the bill passes and is awaiting the governor's signature.

d. Once the bill becomes law and regulations are being drafted.

Answer: b. During the committee review and hearings stage. Explanation: The committee review and hearings stage is critical in the legislative process, as this is when the bill is examined in detail, and amendments can be made. This stage offers the best opportunity to influence the outcome through testimony, lobbying, and presenting evidence. Once a bill passes committee, it becomes harder to alter.

267. A nurse executive is analyzing the potential impact of a proposed federal rule that would change reimbursement rates for advanced practice registered nurses (APRNs). Which of the following factors is most important to consider in a regulatory impact analysis (RIA)?
a. The political affiliations of the rule's proponents and opponents.
b. The rule's potential effects on healthcare access in underserved areas.
c. The historical precedent for similar rule changes in other healthcare fields.
d. The public opinion surrounding APRNs' scope of practice.

Answer: b. The rule's potential effects on healthcare access in underserved areas. Explanation: A regulatory impact analysis (RIA) assesses the potential effects of a proposed rule, including economic, social, and health impacts. Considering how the rule would affect healthcare access in underserved areas is crucial, as it addresses the broader implications of the policy change on population health and equity.

268. In a meeting with a state senator, the nurse executive presents a case for passing a bill that would expand the scope of practice for nurse practitioners (NPs). Which of the following approaches is most likely to persuade the senator?
a. Highlighting how the bill aligns with the senator's previous voting record on healthcare issues.
b. Emphasizing the bill's potential to reduce state healthcare spending through fewer hospitalizations.
c. Criticizing the senator's past opposition to similar bills.
d. Providing detailed case studies from other states where similar legislation has been successful.

Answer: a. Highlighting how the bill aligns with the senator's previous voting record on healthcare issues. Explanation: Tailoring the argument to align with the senator's values and voting history is an effective advocacy strategy. It shows that the proposed bill is consistent with the senator's past positions, increasing the likelihood of support. Emphasizing alignment with known priorities is more persuasive than criticism or general arguments.

269. The nurse executive is preparing a grassroots campaign to support a proposed law that addresses nurse burnout. Which of the following actions should be the first step in this campaign?
a. Launching a petition to gather public support for the proposed law.
b. Engaging local media to raise awareness about nurse burnout.
c. Educating the nursing staff about the proposed law and its potential benefits.
d. Meeting with community leaders to discuss the importance of the proposed legislation.

Answer: c. Educating the nursing staff about the proposed law and its potential benefits. Explanation: Before launching broader advocacy efforts, it is crucial to ensure that the nursing staff is informed and supportive of the proposed law. This internal education forms the foundation of the campaign, ensuring that staff can effectively advocate and engage others in the community and media.

270. A nurse executive is tasked with drafting a policy brief to support the passage of a bill related to telehealth expansion. Which element should be prioritized to effectively communicate the need for the legislation?
a. A detailed cost-benefit analysis showing the economic impact of telehealth expansion.
b. An overview of the technological advancements in telehealth over the last decade.
c. Testimonials from patients who have benefited from telehealth services.
d. A summary of the legal challenges associated with telehealth reimbursement.

Answer: a. A detailed cost-benefit analysis showing the economic impact of telehealth expansion. Explanation: Policymakers often prioritize economic data when making decisions. A cost-benefit analysis that demonstrates the financial advantages of telehealth expansion is likely to be persuasive, especially when combined with data on improved access and outcomes. While testimonials are compelling, economic analysis is more impactful in a policy brief.

271. A nurse executive is part of a coalition advocating for legislation that would fund additional nursing education programs to address workforce shortages. Which of the following tactics would be most effective in gaining legislative support for the bill?
a. Emphasizing the long-term economic benefits of a larger nursing workforce.
b. Highlighting the coalition's bipartisan support and collaboration.
c. Organizing a public demonstration to raise awareness about the bill.
d. Criticizing the current education system for failing to produce enough nurses.

Answer: a. Emphasizing the long-term economic benefits of a larger nursing workforce. Explanation: Legislators are often motivated by the economic impact of policies. Demonstrating that investing in nursing education will lead to long-term savings and economic benefits, such as reduced healthcare costs and job creation, is an effective way to gain support for the bill. Positive framing of the benefits is more persuasive than criticism.

272. As part of a regulatory impact analysis (RIA), a nurse executive is assessing a proposed rule that would require hospitals to publicly report nurse staffing levels. Which of the following considerations is most relevant to the RIA?
a. The potential cost to hospitals of implementing the reporting requirements.
b. The anticipated response of nurse unions to the proposed rule.
c. The political implications of increased transparency in healthcare.
d. The historical success of similar reporting requirements in other industries.

Answer: a. The potential cost to hospitals of implementing the reporting requirements. Explanation: A regulatory impact analysis focuses on understanding the economic implications of a proposed rule, including costs to stakeholders. Assessing the financial burden on hospitals of complying with the reporting requirements is critical to determining the feasibility and impact of the regulation. Other factors are secondary to the direct economic impact.

273. A nurse executive is engaged in advocacy efforts to pass a healthcare bill that would expand Medicaid coverage in the state. During a meeting with legislators, which strategy would be most effective in securing their support?
a. Presenting national data showing the benefits of Medicaid expansion in other states.
b. Criticizing opponents of the bill for their stance on healthcare funding.
c. Highlighting specific examples of constituents who would benefit from the expansion.
d. Offering to organize a town hall meeting to discuss the bill with the public.

Answer: c. Highlighting specific examples of constituents who would benefit from the expansion. Explanation: Personalizing the impact of Medicaid expansion by providing examples of constituents who would benefit makes the issue more relatable and compelling for legislators. This approach can be more effective in securing support than national data or criticism, as it directly connects the policy to the needs of the legislator's electorate.

274. A nurse executive is leading a team using the design thinking methodology to develop a new patient-centered care model. During the "Empathize" phase, which action is most critical to ensure that the team fully understands the needs of patients?
a. Reviewing patient satisfaction surveys from the past year
b. Conducting in-depth interviews with a diverse group of patients and their families
c. Analyzing data on hospital readmission rates and patient outcomes
d. Benchmarking against other hospitals with successful patient-centered care models

Answer: b. Conducting in-depth interviews with a diverse group of patients and their families. Explanation: The "Empathize" phase in design thinking focuses on gaining a deep understanding of the end users' experiences and needs. Conducting in-depth interviews with patients and families provides valuable qualitative insights that are essential for developing a patient-centered care model.

275. A healthcare startup is applying Lean Startup principles to develop a new telehealth service. Which of the following steps best represents the "Build-Measure-Learn" feedback loop in this context?
a. Launching a full-scale marketing campaign to attract users
b. Developing a minimum viable product (MVP) and testing it with a small group of patients
c. Creating detailed business plans and financial projections
d. Conducting a SWOT analysis to evaluate market competition

Answer: b. Developing a minimum viable product (MVP) and testing it with a small group of patients. Explanation: The Lean Startup approach emphasizes building a minimum viable product (MVP) to quickly test assumptions and gather user feedback. The "Build-Measure-Learn" loop allows the startup to iterate and refine the service based on real-world data, minimizing waste and accelerating innovation.

276. A nurse executive is developing a novel medical device intended to improve patient safety. To protect the intellectual property (IP) of this innovation, which action should be taken first?
a. Filing for a patent to secure exclusive rights to the invention
b. Publishing the device's design details in a peer-reviewed journal
c. Presenting the innovation at a healthcare industry conference

d. Registering the device name and logo as trademarks

Answer: a. Filing for a patent to secure exclusive rights to the invention. Explanation: Filing for a patent is the most effective way to protect the intellectual property of a new medical device. A patent grants the inventor exclusive rights to the design and use of the invention, preventing others from making, using, or selling it without permission.

277. A hospital is considering partnering with an innovation accelerator to develop new healthcare solutions. Which of the following is the primary benefit of engaging with an innovation accelerator for this purpose?
a. Access to venture capital funding and investment opportunities
b. Rapid prototyping and testing of new ideas in a controlled environment
c. Guaranteed commercial success of the developed products
d. Reduced risk of failure due to established market demand

Answer: b. Rapid prototyping and testing of new ideas in a controlled environment. Explanation: Innovation accelerators provide resources, mentorship, and a structured environment that facilitate the rapid development and testing of new healthcare solutions. This allows healthcare organizations to quickly refine their ideas and bring innovative products or services to market more efficiently.

278. A nurse executive is leading a team to apply design thinking principles to redesign the hospital's patient discharge process. During the "Ideate" phase, what should the team focus on?
a. Generating a wide range of creative solutions without judgment
b. Selecting the most practical solution based on available resources
c. Testing a prototype of the chosen solution with a small group of patients
d. Conducting a root cause analysis of issues in the current discharge process

Answer: a. Generating a wide range of creative solutions without judgment. Explanation: The "Ideate" phase in design thinking involves brainstorming to generate a broad range of ideas. The goal is to encourage creativity and explore multiple possibilities without prematurely evaluating or dismissing any concepts, fostering innovative thinking.

279. A healthcare entrepreneur is using Lean Startup principles to create a new mobile app for chronic disease management. The initial user feedback suggests that the app's interface is confusing. What is the most appropriate next step according to Lean Startup methodology?
a. Discontinue the project and start over with a new idea
b. Release the app to a larger audience to gather more data
c. Pivot by redesigning the interface based on user feedback
d. Increase marketing efforts to attract more users despite the feedback

Answer: c. Pivot by redesigning the interface based on user feedback. Explanation: In Lean Startup methodology, a pivot involves making a significant change to the product based on user feedback. Redesigning the interface to address user concerns aligns with the principle of iterative improvement, enhancing the product's viability in the market.

280. A nurse executive is developing a healthcare innovation that integrates AI-driven diagnostics into routine clinical workflows. To protect this innovation, which form of intellectual property protection is most relevant?
a. Copyright protection for the AI algorithms used
b. Trademark protection for the product name and branding
c. Trade secret protection for the underlying AI technology
d. Patent protection for the specific diagnostic methods developed

Answer: d. Patent protection for the specific diagnostic methods developed. Explanation: Patent protection is most relevant for new diagnostic methods that involve innovative applications of AI technology. A patent secures the exclusive rights to the invention, preventing others from using or selling the technology without authorization.

281. A hospital system is considering establishing an internal innovation incubator to foster new healthcare solutions. What is a key advantage of having an internal incubator within a healthcare organization?
a. It ensures immediate access to external venture capital funding
b. It promotes a culture of innovation and collaboration among staff
c. It guarantees the rapid commercialization of all developed solutions
d. It eliminates the need for partnerships with external innovation entities

Answer: b. It promotes a culture of innovation and collaboration among staff. Explanation: An internal innovation incubator fosters a culture of creativity and collaboration by providing a dedicated space and resources for staff to develop and test new ideas. This can lead to increased employee engagement and the development of innovative solutions that align with the organization's goals.

282. A nurse executive is participating in an innovation accelerator focused on healthcare technology. Which of the following outcomes is the most realistic expectation from this engagement?
a. Immediate large-scale adoption of the developed technology
b. Significant improvements in patient outcomes within the first month
c. Iterative refinement of the technology based on user feedback
d. Elimination of all risks associated with the new technology

Answer: c. Iterative refinement of the technology based on user feedback. Explanation: Innovation accelerators emphasize rapid development and iterative refinement. Engaging with an accelerator provides opportunities to receive user feedback and make ongoing improvements to the technology, which is crucial for successful innovation in healthcare.

283. A healthcare startup is using Lean Startup principles to develop a new wearable device for monitoring vital signs. Which metric is most important to track during the early stages of development to ensure the product meets user needs?
a. Number of devices sold in the first month
b. User engagement and feedback on the device's functionality
c. Total revenue generated from initial sales

d. Market share captured by the new device

Answer: b. User engagement and feedback on the device's functionality. Explanation: In the early stages of development, it is crucial to focus on user engagement and feedback to ensure that the product effectively meets the needs of its target audience. This information allows the startup to refine the device, improving its functionality and increasing the likelihood of success in the market.

284. A healthcare system is implementing a population health management strategy for diabetic patients. Which risk stratification approach would be MOST effective in identifying patients for targeted interventions?
a. Categorizing patients based solely on HbA1c levels
b. Using a predictive model that incorporates clinical, claims, and social determinant data
c. Stratifying patients based on the number of ED visits in the past year
d. Classifying patients according to their insurance type

Answer: b. Using a predictive model that incorporates clinical, claims, and social determinant data. Explanation: A predictive model incorporating clinical, claims, and social determinant data would be the most effective approach for risk stratification in population health management. This comprehensive model considers multiple factors that influence health outcomes and healthcare utilization. While HbA1c levels (a) are important for diabetes management, they don't capture the full complexity of a patient's risk profile. ED visit frequency (c) may indicate poor disease management but doesn't provide a complete picture. Insurance type (d) might reflect access to care but doesn't directly correlate with clinical risk. The predictive model's multifaceted approach allows for more accurate identification of high-risk patients who would benefit most from targeted interventions, enabling more effective resource allocation and personalized care strategies.

285. A community health center is developing a screening program for social determinants of health (SDOH). Which of the following screening tools would be MOST comprehensive in identifying various SDOH factors?
a. Patient Health Questionnaire-9 (PHQ-9)
b. Protocol for Responding to and Assessing Patients' Assets, Risks, and Experiences (PRAPARE)
c. Generalized Anxiety Disorder-7 (GAD-7)
d. Mini-Mental State Examination (MMSE)

Answer: b. Protocol for Responding to and Assessing Patients' Assets, Risks, and Experiences (PRAPARE). Explanation: The PRAPARE tool would be the most comprehensive in identifying various social determinants of health factors. PRAPARE is specifically designed to assess a wide range of SDOH, including housing, food security, transportation, social and emotional health, and other factors that significantly impact health outcomes. The PHQ-9 (a) and GAD-7 (c) are focused on mental health screening for depression and anxiety, respectively, and don't address broader SDOH. The MMSE (d) is used for cognitive impairment screening. PRAPARE's comprehensive approach allows healthcare providers to identify multiple social and economic factors that may affect a patient's health, enabling more holistic and effective interventions to address these determinants.

286. A health system is launching a diabetes prevention initiative as part of its chronic care management program. Which of the following outcome measures would be MOST indicative of the program's long-term success?
a. Number of participants enrolled in the program

b. Reduction in average HbA1c levels among participants
c. Percentage of participants who maintain or decrease their BMI over two years
d. Participant satisfaction scores with the program

Answer: c. Percentage of participants who maintain or decrease their BMI over two years. Explanation: The percentage of participants who maintain or decrease their BMI over two years would be the most indicative measure of long-term success for a diabetes prevention initiative. This metric reflects sustained lifestyle changes, which are crucial for preventing diabetes progression. While enrollment numbers (a) indicate program reach, they don't measure effectiveness. Reduction in HbA1c levels (b) is important but may not capture pre-diabetic participants or long-term trends. Participant satisfaction (d) is valuable for program improvement but doesn't necessarily correlate with health outcomes. BMI maintenance or reduction over an extended period demonstrates the program's effectiveness in helping participants achieve and sustain the lifestyle modifications necessary for diabetes prevention, aligning with the long-term goals of chronic disease management.

287. A community paramedicine program is being developed to reduce frequent ED utilization. Which of the following strategies would be MOST effective in identifying and engaging high-utilizer patients?
a. Implementing a universal screening protocol in the ED
b. Analyzing claims data to identify patients with multiple ED visits
c. Partnering with primary care providers to refer high-risk patients
d. Conducting community health fairs to raise awareness about the program

Answer: b. Analyzing claims data to identify patients with multiple ED visits. Explanation: Analyzing claims data to identify patients with multiple ED visits would be the most effective strategy for identifying and engaging high-utilizer patients in a community paramedicine program. This approach provides objective, comprehensive data on utilization patterns, allowing for targeted outreach to those who would benefit most from the program. A universal ED screening protocol (a) may miss patients between visits and burden ED staff. Partnering with primary care providers (c) is valuable but may miss unaffiliated patients or those without regular primary care. Community health fairs (d) are good for general awareness but less effective for targeting high utilizers. Claims data analysis offers a systematic, data-driven method to identify the specific population that the community paramedicine program aims to serve, enabling more efficient resource allocation and intervention planning.

288. In developing a population health management strategy, a healthcare organization wants to address health disparities in its diabetic population. Which intervention would be MOST effective in reducing these disparities?
a. Offering telehealth services for diabetes management
b. Providing culturally tailored diabetes education programs
c. Implementing a universal diabetes screening protocol
d. Increasing the number of endocrinologists on staff

Answer: b. Providing culturally tailored diabetes education programs. Explanation: Providing culturally tailored diabetes education programs would be most effective in reducing health disparities among the diabetic population. This approach addresses not only clinical needs but also cultural, linguistic, and socioeconomic factors that contribute to disparities in diabetes management and outcomes. Telehealth services (a) can improve access but may not address cultural barriers or health literacy issues. Universal screening (c) is important for early detection but doesn't directly address management disparities. Increasing endocrinologists (d) improves specialty care access but doesn't necessarily address the root causes of disparities. Culturally tailored education programs can improve patient engagement, understanding, and self-management skills, leading to better health outcomes and reduced disparities across diverse patient populations.

289. A nurse executive is implementing a risk stratification model for the hospital's congestive heart failure (CHF) population. Which of the following factors would be LEAST relevant in this model?
a. Number of CHF-related hospitalizations in the past year
b. Patient's zip code
c. Medication adherence history
d. Left ventricular ejection fraction

Answer: b. Patient's zip code. Explanation: While all listed factors can be relevant in a comprehensive risk stratification model, the patient's zip code would be the least directly relevant for CHF risk stratification. Although zip code can be a proxy for social determinants of health, it's less specific to CHF management compared to the other factors. The number of CHF-related hospitalizations (a) directly indicates disease severity and management. Medication adherence history (c) is crucial for understanding treatment effectiveness and patient engagement. Left ventricular ejection fraction (d) is a key clinical indicator of heart function in CHF patients. While socioeconomic factors are important, clinical and behavioral factors typically have a more direct impact on CHF outcomes and should be prioritized in the risk stratification model.

290. A population health manager is designing an intervention program for patients with multiple chronic conditions. Which of the following approaches would be MOST effective in improving outcomes for this complex patient population?
a. Implementing disease-specific care pathways for each condition
b. Assigning a care coordinator to manage care across all conditions
c. Focusing interventions on the most severe condition only
d. Increasing the frequency of specialist visits for each condition

Answer: b. Assigning a care coordinator to manage care across all conditions. Explanation: Assigning a care coordinator to manage care across all conditions would be the most effective approach for patients with multiple chronic conditions. This strategy provides holistic, patient-centered care that addresses the complexities and interactions of multiple conditions. A care coordinator can ensure comprehensive care planning, medication management, and coordination among various providers. Implementing disease-specific pathways (a) may lead to fragmented care that doesn't address condition interactions. Focusing on only the most severe condition (c) neglects the impact of comorbidities. Increasing specialist visits (d) may improve condition-specific care but doesn't ensure coordination across conditions. The care coordinator approach aligns with the principles of integrated care management, which is particularly beneficial for complex patients with multiple chronic conditions.

291. In developing a community paramedicine program, which of the following outcome measures would be MOST indicative of the program's success in reducing ED utilization?
a. Number of home visits conducted by community paramedics
b. Patient satisfaction scores with the program
c. Reduction in 30-day ED return visits for enrolled patients
d. Number of referrals to primary care providers

Answer: c. Reduction in 30-day ED return visits for enrolled patients. Explanation: A reduction in 30-day ED return visits for enrolled patients would be the most indicative measure of a community paramedicine program's success in reducing ED utilization. This metric directly assesses the program's primary goal of decreasing unnecessary ED use by providing alternative care pathways. The number of home visits (a) indicates program activity but not necessarily its impact on ED use. Patient satisfaction (b) is important for program improvement but doesn't directly measure ED utilization reduction. Referrals to primary care (d) are valuable but don't guarantee reduced ED visits. The 30-day ED return visit metric provides clear evidence of the program's effectiveness in managing patients' health needs outside the ED setting, demonstrating its impact on utilization patterns.

292. A healthcare system is implementing a social determinants of health (SDOH) screening program in its primary care clinics. Which of the following strategies would be MOST effective in ensuring that identified SDOH needs are addressed?
a. Providing patients with a list of community resources
b. Implementing an electronic referral system integrated with community-based organizations
c. Offering on-site social services consultations
d. Training physicians to counsel patients on SDOH issues

Answer: b. Implementing an electronic referral system integrated with community-based organizations. Explanation: Implementing an electronic referral system integrated with community-based organizations would be the most effective strategy for addressing identified SDOH needs. This approach creates a seamless connection between healthcare providers and community resources, facilitating timely and appropriate referrals. It also allows for tracking referral outcomes and follow-up. Providing a list of resources (a) is helpful but places the burden of action on patients. On-site social services consultations (c) are valuable but may have limited availability and scope. Training physicians to counsel on SDOH (d) is important but doesn't directly link patients to resources. The integrated electronic referral system streamlines the process of connecting patients with needed services, improving the likelihood that SDOH needs are effectively addressed.

293. A population health initiative aims to reduce cardiovascular disease risk in a community with high rates of obesity and smoking. Which intervention would likely have the GREATEST impact on long-term population health outcomes?
a. Launching a media campaign about heart-healthy lifestyles
b. Offering free cholesterol screenings at community events
c. Implementing a comprehensive workplace wellness program
d. Increasing the number of cardiology specialists in local hospitals

Answer: c. Implementing a comprehensive workplace wellness program. Explanation: Implementing a comprehensive workplace wellness program would likely have the greatest impact on long-term population health outcomes for cardiovascular disease risk reduction. This approach offers sustained engagement with a significant portion of the adult population, addressing multiple risk factors (like obesity and smoking) in an environment where people spend much of their time. It can include interventions such as smoking cessation support, healthy eating options, exercise programs, and stress management. A media campaign (a) raises awareness but may not lead to sustained behavior change. Free screenings (b) are beneficial for early detection but don't address underlying behaviors. Increasing cardiology specialists (d) improves treatment access but doesn't focus on prevention. A workplace wellness program provides ongoing support for lifestyle changes, potentially impacting a large segment of the population over an extended period, making it the most effective for long-term population health improvement.

294. A nurse executive is involved in developing a new quality measure for patient safety that will be submitted for endorsement by the National Quality Forum (NQF). Which of the following steps is most critical to ensure the measure meets NQF endorsement criteria?
a. Ensuring the measure is easy to implement across diverse healthcare settings.
b. Validating the measure with data from a single institution to demonstrate its effectiveness.
c. Aligning the measure with existing national priorities and frameworks for healthcare quality.
d. Developing the measure based on feedback from internal stakeholders only.

Answer: c. Aligning the measure with existing national priorities and frameworks for healthcare quality. Explanation: The NQF endorsement process requires that quality measures align with national priorities and frameworks, such as those set by the National Quality Strategy. This alignment ensures that the measure addresses relevant and impactful areas of healthcare quality. While implementation ease and validation are important, alignment with national priorities is crucial for endorsement.

295. A nurse executive is tasked with creating a composite measure to evaluate overall hospital quality. Which of the following is a key consideration when selecting individual quality measures to include in the composite?
a. Choosing measures that are exclusively process-oriented to simplify data collection.
b. Including only measures that have been shown to improve patient satisfaction scores.
c. Ensuring that the selected measures reflect both clinical outcomes and patient safety.
d. Selecting measures that are easily understood by the general public.

Answer: c. Ensuring that the selected measures reflect both clinical outcomes and patient safety. Explanation: A well-designed composite measure should provide a comprehensive view of hospital quality, which includes both clinical outcomes and patient safety. This balance ensures that the composite measure accurately reflects the overall quality of care provided by the hospital, rather than focusing on a single aspect such as process or satisfaction.

296. In preparing a report on hospital performance for a pay-for-performance (P4P) program, a nurse executive must consider risk adjustment to ensure fair comparisons across hospitals. Which of the following factors is most appropriate to include in a risk adjustment model?
a. The hospital's geographic location and population density.
b. The socioeconomic status of the patient population served.
c. The hospital's staffing levels and nurse-to-patient ratios.
d. The average length of stay for patients in the hospital.

Answer: b. The socioeconomic status of the patient population served. Explanation: Risk adjustment models often include factors like socioeconomic status to account for the impact of external factors on patient outcomes. This ensures that hospitals serving higher-risk populations are not unfairly penalized in comparisons. While geographic location and staffing levels might influence outcomes, they are not typically included in standard risk adjustment models.

297. A nurse executive is evaluating a pay-for-performance (P4P) program that rewards hospitals for reducing readmission rates. Which of the following strategies would be most effective in improving the hospital's performance under this program?
a. Implementing a robust discharge planning process that includes follow-up care coordination.
b. Increasing the frequency of patient education sessions on medication adherence.
c. Reducing the length of hospital stays to decrease the risk of complications.
d. Enhancing the hospital's public relations efforts to improve its reputation.

Answer: a. Implementing a robust discharge planning process that includes follow-up care coordination. Explanation: A comprehensive discharge planning process with coordinated follow-up care is critical in preventing readmissions, which directly impacts performance in a P4P program focused on reducing readmissions. Patient education and hospital stays are important, but coordinated care post-discharge is the most direct method to address readmission rates.

298. A nurse executive is part of a team developing a new quality measure for hospital-acquired infections (HAIs). Which of the following criteria should be prioritized to ensure the measure is effective and reliable?
a. The measure should be based on the latest clinical guidelines and evidence-based practices.
b. The measure should be easily adjustable to accommodate changes in hospital reporting capabilities.
c. The measure should focus on the financial impact of HAIs on hospital revenue.
d. The measure should emphasize patient satisfaction with infection prevention efforts.

Answer: a. The measure should be based on the latest clinical guidelines and evidence-based practices. Explanation: Quality measures for HAIs must be grounded in the most current clinical guidelines and evidence-based practices to ensure they effectively reduce infection rates and improve patient safety. While financial impact and patient satisfaction are important, clinical accuracy and relevance are paramount for a reliable quality measure.

299. A hospital is participating in a national pay-for-performance (P4P) program that includes a composite measure for overall hospital quality. The nurse executive is tasked with analyzing the hospital's performance. Which of the following approaches would provide the most comprehensive understanding of the hospital's standing?
a. Reviewing individual scores for each component of the composite measure to identify areas of improvement.
b. Comparing the hospital's composite score to national benchmarks without analyzing individual components.
c. Focusing solely on measures that have financial incentives attached to them.
d. Conducting a patient satisfaction survey to gather additional qualitative data.

Answer: a. Reviewing individual scores for each component of the composite measure to identify areas of improvement. Explanation: Analyzing the individual components of a composite measure allows the hospital to pinpoint specific areas needing improvement, providing a targeted approach to enhancing overall quality. Simply comparing composite scores or focusing only on financially incentivized measures does not provide the depth of understanding needed for meaningful quality improvement.

300. A nurse executive is developing a quality measure to assess patient outcomes after surgery. To ensure that the measure fairly compares outcomes across hospitals, which risk adjustment method should be used?

a. Adjusting for the type of surgery performed across different hospitals.
b. Including patient demographics such as age, gender, and comorbidities in the adjustment model.
c. Standardizing the length of stay across all surgical patients.
d. Excluding high-risk patients from the measurement to focus on typical cases.

Answer: b. Including patient demographics such as age, gender, and comorbidities in the adjustment model.
Explanation: Risk adjustment for patient demographics and comorbidities is essential to ensure that comparisons of surgical outcomes are fair and account for varying patient populations. This approach prevents hospitals serving more complex cases from being unfairly penalized. Adjusting for the type of surgery and excluding high-risk patients could introduce bias or limit the measure's applicability.

301. The nurse executive is leading a task force to evaluate the effectiveness of current pay-for-performance (P4P) programs at the hospital. Which of the following metrics would be most appropriate to assess the success of these programs?
a. The overall financial impact of the P4P programs on the hospital's revenue.
b. The improvement in patient outcomes and reduction in adverse events linked to P4P initiatives.
c. The number of new staff members hired to support P4P program implementation.
d. The hospital's reputation and public perception as influenced by P4P results.

Answer: b. The improvement in patient outcomes and reduction in adverse events linked to P4P initiatives.
Explanation: The primary goal of P4P programs is to improve patient outcomes and reduce adverse events. Assessing these metrics is the most appropriate way to measure the success of the programs. Financial impact and reputation are secondary considerations, as the focus should be on quality improvement.

302. A nurse executive is tasked with creating a new composite measure to assess hospital quality, specifically targeting post-operative complications. Which combination of metrics would best serve as components of this composite measure?
a. Patient satisfaction scores, length of stay, and surgical site infection rates.
b. Readmission rates, surgical site infection rates, and patient mortality within 30 days post-surgery.
c. Length of stay, patient satisfaction scores, and the number of surgeries performed.
d. Surgical site infection rates, number of surgeries performed, and staffing levels.

Answer: b. Readmission rates, surgical site infection rates, and patient mortality within 30 days post-surgery.
Explanation: These metrics directly reflect post-operative outcomes and complications, making them appropriate components for a composite measure of hospital quality in the surgical domain. Patient satisfaction and length of stay are important but less directly related to the specific quality outcomes being targeted.

303. A nurse executive is reviewing a proposed quality measure that seeks NQF endorsement. During the review, which of the following characteristics should be considered most critical for NQF endorsement?
a. The measure's ability to be universally implemented across all healthcare settings.
b. The measure's focus on patient-centered outcomes that reflect meaningful changes in care.
c. The measure's alignment with financial incentives for healthcare providers.
d. The measure's capacity to reduce administrative burden through automation.

Answer: b. The measure's focus on patient-centered outcomes that reflect meaningful changes in care. Explanation: The NQF prioritizes measures that are patient-centered and lead to meaningful improvements in healthcare quality. While universal implementation and alignment with financial incentives are important, the focus on outcomes that improve patient care is the most critical factor for NQF endorsement.

304. A nurse executive is leading the implementation of a Clinical Decision Support (CDS) system in a large healthcare organization. Which of the following strategies is most effective in ensuring that the CDS system supports evidence-based practice without overwhelming clinicians with alerts?
a. Implementing all possible alerts to maximize patient safety
b. Prioritizing high-impact alerts and customizing them to specific clinical workflows
c. Disabling alerts during high-volume periods to reduce clinician burden
d. Requiring clinicians to manually override each alert to ensure compliance

Answer: b. Prioritizing high-impact alerts and customizing them to specific clinical workflows. Explanation: Prioritizing and customizing alerts ensures that the CDS system is both effective and manageable, reducing alert fatigue and enhancing the integration of evidence-based practice into clinicians' workflows. This strategy focuses on delivering relevant information when it is most needed, improving decision-making without overwhelming the user.

305. A nurse executive is tasked with optimizing nursing documentation to improve both quality and efficiency. Which approach is most likely to achieve this goal?
a. Implementing mandatory documentation for every patient interaction
b. Streamlining documentation templates to reduce redundancy and focus on critical data
c. Requiring nurses to document in real-time during patient care activities
d. Expanding the documentation requirements to include all possible patient data points

Answer: b. Streamlining documentation templates to reduce redundancy and focus on critical data. Explanation: Streamlining documentation templates helps eliminate unnecessary steps and focuses on capturing essential information. This approach enhances efficiency and ensures that the quality of documentation supports patient care without burdening nurses with excessive data entry.

306. A healthcare organization is using data analytics to manage its nursing workforce more effectively. Which metric would be most useful for predicting future staffing needs?
a. Historical nurse turnover rates
b. Average patient satisfaction scores
c. Current nurse-to-patient ratios
d. Total number of nursing hours worked per shift

Answer: a. Historical nurse turnover rates. Explanation: Historical nurse turnover rates provide valuable insight into staffing trends and can be used to predict future needs. By analyzing turnover patterns, the organization can proactively plan for recruitment and retention efforts, ensuring that staffing levels remain adequate to meet patient care demands.

307. A nurse executive is overseeing the development of a telehealth program aimed at managing chronic disease in rural populations. Which of the following considerations is most critical for ensuring the success of the telehealth program?
a. Selecting telehealth technology with the most advanced features
b. Ensuring that the program is designed to be culturally sensitive and accessible to the target population
c. Limiting the scope of services to reduce the complexity of the program
d. Implementing the program across all rural areas simultaneously to maximize reach

Answer: b. Ensuring that the program is designed to be culturally sensitive and accessible to the target population. Explanation: For a telehealth program to be successful, it must be accessible and acceptable to the target population. Cultural sensitivity and accessibility ensure that the program meets the unique needs of rural populations, leading to higher engagement and better health outcomes.

308. During the rollout of a Clinical Decision Support (CDS) system, a nurse executive notices that clinicians are frequently overriding alerts. What is the most likely cause, and what action should be taken?
a. The CDS alerts are not relevant to the clinicians' practice; reassess and customize the alerts
b. The clinicians are resistant to change; increase mandatory training sessions
c. The technology is malfunctioning; contact the vendor for technical support
d. The clinicians are not aware of the importance of the alerts; implement an awareness campaign

Answer: a. The CDS alerts are not relevant to the clinicians' practice; reassess and customize the alerts. Explanation: Frequent overrides often indicate that the alerts are not appropriately tailored to clinical workflows, leading to alert fatigue. Reassessing and customizing the alerts ensures that they are relevant and useful, improving clinician compliance and patient safety.

309. A nurse executive is optimizing the documentation system to support quality improvement initiatives. Which type of documentation should be prioritized to ensure that data collected is most useful for these initiatives?
a. Detailed narrative notes documenting every aspect of patient care
b. Structured data fields that align with key quality metrics
c. Minimal documentation to reduce nurse workload
d. Free-text entries to allow nurses to provide comprehensive information

Answer: b. Structured data fields that align with key quality metrics. Explanation: Structured data fields ensure that documentation is standardized and directly supports the measurement of key quality metrics. This approach makes it easier to analyze data for quality improvement initiatives and ensures that documentation contributes to enhancing patient care outcomes.

310. A healthcare system is using predictive analytics to forecast nursing staff shortages. Which data source would provide the most accurate predictions for short-term staffing needs?

a. Real-time patient acuity levels
b. Nurse satisfaction survey results
c. Monthly staffing budgets
d. Annual performance reviews

Answer: a. Real-time patient acuity levels. Explanation: Real-time patient acuity levels offer immediate insight into the intensity of care required, making them a critical data source for predicting short-term staffing needs. This information allows for dynamic adjustments to staffing levels, ensuring that the workforce can meet the demands of patient care.

311. A nurse executive is leading the implementation of a new telehealth program in a multi-hospital system. What is the most important factor to consider when developing the training program for clinicians?
a. Ensuring that the training includes technical skills for operating telehealth equipment
b. Limiting training to essential functions to minimize time away from patient care
c. Focusing on the cost-effectiveness of telehealth services to encourage buy-in
d. Emphasizing the administrative aspects of telehealth documentation and billing

Answer: a. Ensuring that the training includes technical skills for operating telehealth equipment. Explanation: Effective telehealth training must equip clinicians with the technical skills necessary to operate the equipment confidently. Without this foundational knowledge, the program's implementation could be hindered by user errors or a lack of proficiency, negatively impacting patient care.

312. A nurse executive is evaluating the effectiveness of a CDS system that has been integrated into the electronic health record (EHR). Which outcome would best indicate that the CDS system is functioning as intended?
a. A decrease in the time clinicians spend documenting in the EHR
b. An increase in the number of alerts generated by the system
c. Improved adherence to clinical guidelines and protocols
d. A reduction in the overall number of patient visits to the hospital

Answer: c. Improved adherence to clinical guidelines and protocols. Explanation: The primary goal of a CDS system is to support clinical decision-making by aligning practice with evidence-based guidelines. An improvement in adherence to these guidelines indicates that the CDS system is effectively enhancing the quality of care.

313. A nurse executive is tasked with enhancing nursing documentation practices to support data-driven decision-making. Which strategy is most effective for ensuring that documentation supports this goal?
a. Increasing the frequency of mandatory documentation audits
b. Simplifying documentation requirements to reduce time spent on charting
c. Integrating real-time data analytics tools directly into the documentation system
d. Encouraging nurses to use free-text notes to capture detailed patient information

Answer: c. Integrating real-time data analytics tools directly into the documentation system. Explanation: Integrating data analytics tools into the documentation system allows for the immediate analysis of documentation, supporting data-driven decision-making. This approach ensures that documentation is not only accurate and efficient but also actionable in real-time, leading to better patient care and operational efficiency.

314. A nurse executive is assessing the cultural competence of the healthcare organization. Which of the following tools would best provide a comprehensive evaluation of the organization's cultural competence?
a. Patient satisfaction surveys with a focus on diversity and inclusion.
b. The Cultural Competence Assessment Tool for Hospitals (CCATH).
c. Staff focus groups discussing cultural challenges in patient care.
d. The Hospital Consumer Assessment of Healthcare Providers and Systems (HCAHPS).

Answer: b. The Cultural Competence Assessment Tool for Hospitals (CCATH). Explanation: The CCATH is specifically designed to evaluate the cultural competence of healthcare organizations, assessing factors such as leadership commitment, communication, and workforce diversity. Patient satisfaction surveys and HCAHPS provide valuable feedback but do not comprehensively assess organizational cultural competence.

315. A nurse executive notices that team members are hesitant to speak up during meetings about patient safety concerns. Which of the following strategies would be most effective in promoting psychological safety within the healthcare team?
a. Conducting anonymous surveys to gather feedback on safety concerns.
b. Introducing a strict no-blame policy for errors reported by staff.
c. Encouraging open dialogue by regularly recognizing staff who voice concerns.
d. Mandating additional training sessions on patient safety protocols.

Answer: c. Encouraging open dialogue by regularly recognizing staff who voice concerns. Explanation: Psychological safety is fostered when team members feel their input is valued and supported. Regularly recognizing and encouraging those who speak up reinforces a culture where team members feel safe to express concerns. While no-blame policies and training are important, active recognition directly supports psychological safety.

316. A nurse executive is implementing a new organizational learning framework to enhance continuous improvement. Which of the following approaches best exemplifies triple-loop learning in a healthcare setting?
a. Regularly updating clinical guidelines based on the latest research evidence.
b. Encouraging staff to question underlying assumptions and values that guide clinical practice.
c. Conducting routine audits to ensure compliance with established protocols.
d. Providing feedback on performance metrics to improve individual skills.

Answer: b. Encouraging staff to question underlying assumptions and values that guide clinical practice. Explanation: Triple-loop learning goes beyond improving actions (single-loop) and revising strategies (double-loop); it involves questioning and reshaping the underlying assumptions and values of the organization. This approach leads to deeper transformation and innovation in healthcare practices.

317. A nurse executive is leading a diversity, equity, and inclusion (DEI) initiative aimed at increasing diversity in leadership positions. Which of the following strategies would be most effective in achieving this goal?
a. Implementing a mentorship program that pairs diverse staff with senior leaders.
b. Offering financial incentives to diverse candidates for leadership roles.
c. Requiring implicit bias training for all current leaders within the organization.
d. Establishing diversity quotas for hiring into leadership positions.

Answer: a. Implementing a mentorship program that pairs diverse staff with senior leaders. Explanation: A mentorship program provides ongoing support, guidance, and opportunities for diverse staff to advance into leadership positions, creating a sustainable approach to increasing diversity. Financial incentives and quotas can be controversial, and while bias training is important, mentorship directly supports career advancement.

318. A nurse executive is tasked with integrating organizational learning into the healthcare system. Which of the following best represents the transition from single-loop to double-loop learning?
a. Revising policies after identifying gaps in compliance during routine audits.
b. Encouraging reflective practice sessions to evaluate the effectiveness of current procedures.
c. Standardizing training programs across departments to ensure consistency.
d. Implementing new technology to streamline existing workflows.

Answer: b. Encouraging reflective practice sessions to evaluate the effectiveness of current procedures. Explanation: Double-loop learning involves not just correcting errors (single-loop) but also reflecting on and altering the underlying policies, goals, or frameworks that led to those errors. Reflective practice sessions facilitate this deeper level of organizational learning and adaptation.

319. A nurse executive is assessing the current climate of psychological safety within the organization. Which of the following indicators would most strongly suggest a lack of psychological safety among staff?
a. Frequent reports of burnout and high turnover rates.
b. A high number of incident reports submitted anonymously.
c. A consistent decline in patient satisfaction scores over time.
d. Limited participation in team meetings and decision-making processes.

Answer: d. Limited participation in team meetings and decision-making processes. Explanation: A key indicator of low psychological safety is when staff are reluctant to engage in team discussions or decision-making, often due to fear of criticism or retribution. This behavior signals that team members do not feel safe to express their ideas or concerns openly.

320. A nurse executive is working to foster an inclusive culture that supports diversity within the organization. Which of the following actions would most effectively promote an inclusive environment?
a. Hosting annual cultural competence training for all staff members.
b. Creating employee resource groups (ERGs) to provide support and advocacy for diverse populations within the organization.
c. Conducting periodic diversity audits to assess representation across departments.
d. Increasing the number of diversity-focused events and celebrations throughout the year.

Answer: b. Creating employee resource groups (ERGs) to provide support and advocacy for diverse populations within the organization. Explanation: ERGs create a space for underrepresented groups to connect, share experiences, and advocate for necessary changes, thereby fostering an inclusive culture. While training and audits are important, ERGs offer ongoing support and engagement that is crucial for sustained inclusivity.

321. A nurse executive is evaluating the effectiveness of the organization's DEI initiatives. Which of the following metrics would provide the most meaningful assessment of progress in promoting diversity in leadership?
a. The percentage of leadership positions filled by individuals from diverse backgrounds.
b. The overall employee satisfaction scores from annual surveys.
c. The frequency of DEI training sessions attended by staff.
d. The number of diversity-related incidents reported within the organization.

Answer: a. The percentage of leadership positions filled by individuals from diverse backgrounds. Explanation: The proportion of diverse individuals in leadership roles is a direct measure of the success of DEI initiatives aimed at increasing representation. Other metrics, such as training attendance or incident reports, provide supplementary information but do not directly measure leadership diversity.

322. A nurse executive is introducing a cultural competence assessment tool across the organization. Which of the following strategies would best ensure the tool's effectiveness in improving cultural competence?
a. Administering the tool annually and using the results to develop targeted training programs.
b. Incorporating the tool's results into individual performance reviews to encourage accountability.
c. Focusing the tool's application on departments with the highest patient diversity.
d. Using the tool as part of the onboarding process for new hires only.

Answer: a. Administering the tool annually and using the results to develop targeted training programs. Explanation: Regular administration of the cultural competence assessment allows the organization to track progress over time and identify specific areas needing improvement. Using the results to create targeted training programs ensures that interventions are relevant and effective.

323. A nurse executive is implementing a new framework for organizational learning. Which of the following practices would best facilitate triple-loop learning within the organization?
a. Establishing regular debriefings after major initiatives to reflect on outcomes and underlying assumptions.
b. Using root cause analysis to identify and correct operational errors.
c. Conducting quarterly performance reviews focused on meeting predefined goals.
d. Standardizing best practices across departments to reduce variability in care delivery.

Answer: a. Establishing regular debriefings after major initiatives to reflect on outcomes and underlying assumptions. Explanation: Triple-loop learning involves challenging and rethinking the fundamental assumptions and values that guide organizational behavior. Regular debriefings that encourage deep reflection on these aspects help to foster an environment where triple-loop learning can occur, leading to more profound organizational transformation.

324. A nurse executive is tasked with ensuring compliance with the Stark Law in the organization. Which of the following practices would most likely result in a violation of the Stark Law?
a. A physician referring patients to a physical therapy clinic owned by their spouse
b. A hospital offering reduced rent to physicians who lease office space in a hospital-owned building
c. A physician receiving compensation for consulting services provided to a pharmaceutical company
d. A physician referring patients to a hospital where they have an ownership interest in the MRI equipment used

Answer: d. A physician referring patients to a hospital where they have an ownership interest in the MRI equipment used. Explanation: The Stark Law prohibits physicians from referring patients to entities with which they have a financial relationship, such as ownership of diagnostic equipment. This referral would violate the law unless an exception applies, as it involves a direct financial interest that could influence the physician's referral patterns.

325. A nurse executive is implementing a Corporate Integrity Agreement (CIA) as part of a settlement with the Office of Inspector General (OIG). Which of the following is a key component that must be included in the CIA to ensure compliance?
a. A commitment to reducing healthcare costs within the organization
b. The appointment of a compliance officer responsible for overseeing adherence to the CIA
c. The development of a new strategic plan focused on market expansion
d. The provision of financial incentives to employees who identify compliance issues

Answer: b. The appointment of a compliance officer responsible for overseeing adherence to the CIA. Explanation: A key component of a Corporate Integrity Agreement is the appointment of a compliance officer who is responsible for ensuring that the organization adheres to the terms of the agreement. This role is critical for monitoring compliance activities and reporting to the OIG.

326. In revising the medical staff bylaws, a nurse executive must ensure that they align with both state and federal regulations. Which of the following provisions is most likely to be legally problematic if included in the bylaws?
a. A requirement for all medical staff to complete annual continuing education
b. A clause allowing the medical executive committee to summarily suspend clinical privileges without due process
c. A policy mandating peer review for all adverse patient outcomes
d. A provision allowing the credentialing committee to grant temporary privileges in emergencies

Answer: b. A clause allowing the medical executive committee to summarily suspend clinical privileges without due process. Explanation: Due process is a fundamental legal right for medical staff. A bylaw provision that allows suspension of privileges without due process could be legally challenged and may not comply with regulatory standards, making it problematic.

327. A hospital's credentialing committee is reviewing applications for privileges from several advanced practice providers (APPs). Which of the following elements is most critical in the credentialing process to ensure compliance with regulatory standards?
a. Verifying the applicant's malpractice insurance coverage

b. Assessing the applicant's ability to generate revenue for the hospital
c. Confirming the applicant's clinical competence through primary source verification
d. Reviewing the applicant's references from previous employers

Answer: c. Confirming the applicant's clinical competence through primary source verification. Explanation: Primary source verification of an applicant's credentials and clinical competence is a critical step in the credentialing process. This ensures that the hospital meets regulatory standards and that providers granted privileges are qualified to deliver safe and effective care.

328. A nurse executive is leading an internal audit to assess compliance with the Anti-Kickback Statute. Which of the following scenarios is most likely to be flagged as a potential violation?
a. A hospital offering discounted rates on services to uninsured patients
b. A hospital providing free office space to a referring physician in exchange for patient referrals
c. A physician referring patients to a specialist within the same healthcare system
d. A hospital entering into a joint venture with a group of physicians to open a new outpatient clinic

Answer: b. A hospital providing free office space to a referring physician in exchange for patient referrals. Explanation: The Anti-Kickback Statute prohibits offering or receiving anything of value in exchange for referrals of services that are reimbursed by federal healthcare programs. Providing free office space to a physician in exchange for patient referrals is a clear violation of this statute.

329. During the development of new medical staff bylaws, the nurse executive encounters resistance from the medical staff regarding a proposed peer review process. What is the most effective strategy to address their concerns while ensuring compliance with legal and regulatory requirements?
a. Mandating the peer review process without further discussion
b. Involving legal counsel to explain the necessity of the peer review process
c. Offering financial incentives to medical staff who participate in peer reviews
d. Removing the peer review requirement from the bylaws to maintain staff morale

Answer: b. Involving legal counsel to explain the necessity of the peer review process. Explanation: Involving legal counsel can help clarify the legal and regulatory requirements for peer review, addressing concerns while ensuring compliance. Legal counsel can also provide reassurance that the process is designed to protect both patients and practitioners.

330. A nurse executive is reviewing the hospital's credentialing and privileging process to ensure alignment with The Joint Commission's standards. Which aspect of the process is most critical to review for compliance?
a. The frequency of staff meetings within the credentialing committee
b. The use of evidence-based guidelines in the privileging decisions
c. The documentation of the peer review process for initial and re-credentialing
d. The speed of the credentialing process to expedite the start of new providers

Answer: c. The documentation of the peer review process for initial and re-credentialing. Explanation: Proper documentation of the peer review process is essential for compliance with The Joint Commission's standards. This ensures that the hospital can demonstrate a thorough evaluation of providers' competencies and qualifications when granting or renewing privileges.

331. A nurse executive is developing a compliance program to prevent violations of the Stark Law and Anti-Kickback Statute. Which of the following actions is most likely to strengthen the program's effectiveness?
a. Conducting quarterly reviews of all physician contracts and financial relationships
b. Mandating annual compliance training sessions for all non-clinical staff
c. Implementing a policy that limits physician compensation to below-market rates
d. Offering bonuses to employees who report potential compliance issues

Answer: a. Conducting quarterly reviews of all physician contracts and financial relationships. Explanation: Regular reviews of physician contracts and financial relationships help identify and address potential compliance risks before they become violations. This proactive approach is crucial for maintaining compliance with the Stark Law and Anti-Kickback Statute.

332. A nurse executive is implementing new medical staff bylaws that include a detailed credentialing process for advanced practice providers (APPs). Which of the following is most important to ensure the credentialing process is fair and unbiased?
a. Involving APPs in the development of the credentialing criteria
b. Using a standardized set of criteria for all applicants
c. Allowing individual department heads to set their own credentialing standards
d. Prioritizing applicants from prestigious medical institutions

Answer: b. Using a standardized set of criteria for all applicants. Explanation: A standardized set of criteria ensures that all applicants are evaluated fairly and consistently, reducing the risk of bias in the credentialing process. This approach aligns with best practices and regulatory standards, promoting equity and transparency.

333. A nurse executive is leading the hospital's response to a regulatory audit focused on compliance with the Anti-Kickback Statute. Which documentation is most critical to provide during the audit?
a. Copies of all hospital policies and procedures
b. Records of any gifts or benefits provided to referring physicians
c. Minutes from all medical staff meetings over the past year
d. Patient satisfaction surveys related to referred services

Answer: b. Records of any gifts or benefits provided to referring physicians. Explanation: The Anti-Kickback Statute prohibits offering or receiving anything of value in exchange for patient referrals. Detailed records of gifts or benefits provided to physicians are critical during an audit to demonstrate compliance and address any potential concerns raised by regulators.

334. A hospital is planning a major renovation of its emergency department. Which evidence-based design principle would be MOST effective in reducing patient stress and improving outcomes?
a. Implementing a centralized nursing station
b. Maximizing natural light and views of nature
c. Installing high-tech medical equipment in all rooms
d. Using bright, stimulating colors throughout the department

Answer: b. Maximizing natural light and views of nature. Explanation: Maximizing natural light and views of nature is the most effective evidence-based design principle for reducing patient stress and improving outcomes in an emergency department renovation. Research has consistently shown that exposure to natural light and nature views can reduce stress, improve mood, and even reduce pain perception and length of stay. A centralized nursing station (a) may improve staff efficiency but doesn't directly address patient stress. High-tech equipment (c) is important for care but doesn't necessarily reduce stress. Bright, stimulating colors (d) may actually increase stress in an emergency setting. Natural light and nature views create a more calming environment, aligning with evidence-based design principles that focus on patient-centered care and stress reduction in healthcare settings.

335. In implementing energy efficiency initiatives, a hospital facilities manager is considering various technologies. Which of the following would likely provide the GREATEST long-term energy savings?
a. LED lighting retrofits
b. HVAC system upgrades with smart controls
c. Installation of low-flow water fixtures
d. Implementation of a recycling program

Answer: b. HVAC system upgrades with smart controls. Explanation: HVAC system upgrades with smart controls would likely provide the greatest long-term energy savings for a hospital. HVAC systems typically account for the largest portion of energy consumption in healthcare facilities. Smart controls allow for optimized performance based on occupancy, time of day, and external conditions, significantly reducing energy waste. While LED lighting retrofits (a) offer substantial savings, they generally impact a smaller portion of overall energy use compared to HVAC. Low-flow water fixtures (c) conserve water but have less impact on energy consumption. A recycling program (d) is environmentally beneficial but doesn't directly affect energy use. The combination of HVAC upgrades and smart controls addresses the most energy-intensive system in the hospital, offering the greatest potential for long-term energy savings and cost reduction.

336. A new hospital wing is being designed with a focus on infection control. Which design feature would be MOST effective in reducing healthcare-associated infections?
a. Installing copper-infused surfaces in high-touch areas
b. Implementing a 100% single-patient room model
c. Using seamless flooring materials throughout the facility
d. Installing HEPA air filtration systems in all patient rooms

Answer: b. Implementing a 100% single-patient room model. Explanation: Implementing a 100% single-patient room model would be the most effective design feature for reducing healthcare-associated infections in a new hospital wing. Single-patient rooms significantly reduce the risk of cross-contamination between patients, allow for better isolation practices, and improve cleaning and disinfection processes. While copper-infused surfaces (a) have antimicrobial properties, their effect is limited to surface contact transmission. Seamless flooring (c) can improve cleaning efficacy but doesn't address airborne or direct patient-to-patient transmission. HEPA filtration (d) is beneficial for air quality but doesn't address other transmission routes as comprehensively as single rooms. The single-patient room model provides a multifaceted approach to infection control, addressing various transmission routes and aligning with current best practices in healthcare facility design.

337. A hospital is upgrading its emergency power system. Which configuration would provide the HIGHEST level of reliability for critical care areas?
a. N+1 redundancy for generators
b. Parallel redundant UPS systems
c. Redundant utility feeds from different substations
d. Separate emergency and equipment branches

Answer: b. Parallel redundant UPS systems. Explanation: Parallel redundant UPS (Uninterruptible Power Supply) systems would provide the highest level of reliability for critical care areas in a hospital's emergency power system. This configuration ensures continuous power supply even if one UPS unit fails, offering seamless power transition and protection against both utility failures and internal system faults. N+1 generator redundancy (a) is valuable but doesn't provide the same level of immediate, uninterrupted power as UPS systems. Redundant utility feeds (c) improve reliability but don't protect against momentary interruptions. Separate emergency and equipment branches (d) are standard practice but don't inherently provide the same level of redundancy as parallel UPS systems. The parallel redundant UPS configuration offers the most robust protection against power interruptions, which is crucial for life-support equipment and other critical systems in healthcare settings.

338. In designing a new surgical suite, which infection control measure would be MOST effective in reducing the risk of surgical site infections?
a. Installing UV-C light disinfection systems
b. Implementing laminar airflow ventilation
c. Using antimicrobial curtains between surgical bays
d. Installing automatic doors with motion sensors

Answer: b. Implementing laminar airflow ventilation. Explanation: Implementing laminar airflow ventilation would be the most effective measure in reducing the risk of surgical site infections in a new surgical suite design. Laminar airflow systems create a unidirectional flow of filtered air over the surgical field, significantly reducing airborne contaminants and the risk of infection. UV-C light disinfection (a) can be effective but is typically used for surface decontamination rather than continuous protection during procedures. Antimicrobial curtains (c) may help reduce surface contamination but don't address airborne transmission as effectively. Automatic doors (d) can reduce touch contamination but have limited impact on airborne pathogens in the surgical field. Laminar airflow ventilation provides continuous protection throughout surgical procedures, aligning with best practices for infection control in high-risk surgical environments.

339. A healthcare facility is implementing a comprehensive sustainability program. Which of the following initiatives would have the GREATEST impact on reducing the facility's carbon footprint?
a. Transitioning to reusable sharps containers
b. Implementing a building automation system for energy management
c. Establishing an on-site organic waste composting program

d. Switching to environmentally friendly cleaning products

Answer: b. Implementing a building automation system for energy management. Explanation: Implementing a building automation system for energy management would have the greatest impact on reducing a healthcare facility's carbon footprint. This system can optimize energy use across the entire facility, controlling HVAC, lighting, and other energy-intensive systems based on occupancy, time of day, and other factors. Energy consumption typically accounts for the largest portion of a hospital's carbon emissions. While transitioning to reusable sharps containers (a) reduces waste, it has a smaller impact on overall emissions. On-site composting (c) is beneficial but affects a smaller portion of the facility's carbon footprint. Environmentally friendly cleaning products (d) reduce chemical use but have minimal impact on carbon emissions. The building automation system addresses the core issue of energy consumption, offering the most significant potential for reducing the facility's overall carbon footprint.

340. In designing a new pediatric unit, which evidence-based design feature would be MOST effective in promoting family-centered care?
a. Installing interactive play areas in waiting rooms
b. Providing fold-out beds in patient rooms for family members
c. Using child-friendly artwork and decor throughout the unit
d. Implementing a centralized family resource center

Answer: b. Providing fold-out beds in patient rooms for family members. Explanation: Providing fold-out beds in patient rooms for family members would be the most effective evidence-based design feature for promoting family-centered care in a pediatric unit. This feature directly supports family presence and participation in care, which is a core principle of family-centered care. It allows family members to stay comfortably with the child, enhancing emotional support and enabling more active involvement in care decisions and processes. Interactive play areas (a) are beneficial but don't directly involve families in bedside care. Child-friendly artwork (c) improves the environment but doesn't actively promote family involvement. A centralized resource center (d) is valuable but doesn't facilitate continuous family presence. The in-room accommodations for family members align most closely with evidence-based practices for family-centered care, supporting improved outcomes and patient/family satisfaction.

341. A hospital is renovating its intensive care unit with a focus on staff efficiency and patient safety. Which design feature would be MOST effective in achieving these goals?
a. Decentralized nursing stations with direct visibility to patient rooms
b. Implementation of a pneumatic tube system for medication delivery
c. Installation of ceiling-mounted patient lifts in all rooms
d. Use of antimicrobial surfaces throughout the unit

Answer: a. Decentralized nursing stations with direct visibility to patient rooms. Explanation: Decentralized nursing stations with direct visibility to patient rooms would be the most effective design feature for improving staff efficiency and patient safety in an ICU renovation. This layout reduces walking distances for nurses, increases time spent in direct patient care, and allows for continuous visual monitoring of patients. A pneumatic tube system (b) may improve medication delivery efficiency but doesn't address overall patient monitoring. Ceiling-mounted lifts (c) enhance safety during patient transfers but don't impact continuous monitoring or overall efficiency. Antimicrobial surfaces (d) can reduce infection risk but don't directly improve staff efficiency or patient monitoring. The decentralized nursing station design aligns with evidence-based practices for ICU layouts, promoting both efficient workflows and enhanced patient safety through improved visibility and reduced response times.

342. In developing an emergency power testing protocol, which of the following approaches would MOST effectively ensure system reliability?
a. Monthly full-load testing of all generators
b. Quarterly black-start tests of the entire emergency power system
c. Annual load bank testing at 100% capacity for 4 hours
d. Weekly no-load tests of generators with monthly transfer switch tests

Answer: b. Quarterly black-start tests of the entire emergency power system. Explanation: Quarterly black-start tests of the entire emergency power system would most effectively ensure system reliability. These tests simulate a complete power outage and verify the entire system's ability to start up and function as intended, including generators, transfer switches, and distribution systems. Monthly full-load testing (a) is beneficial but may not test all components together. Annual load bank testing (c) is important for verifying capacity but doesn't test the system's startup and transfer capabilities as frequently. Weekly no-load tests with monthly transfer switch tests (d) are useful for maintenance but don't comprehensively test the system under realistic conditions. The quarterly black-start tests provide the most thorough evaluation of the emergency power system's reliability under conditions closest to an actual emergency, aligning with best practices for healthcare facility emergency preparedness.

343. A hospital is implementing infection control measures in its HVAC system design. Which of the following strategies would be MOST effective in reducing airborne pathogen transmission?
a. Increasing the frequency of filter changes
b. Implementing ultraviolet germicidal irradiation (UVGI) in air handling units
c. Maintaining positive air pressure in patient care areas relative to corridors
d. Installing standalone air purifiers in high-risk areas

Answer: c. Maintaining positive air pressure in patient care areas relative to corridors. Explanation: Maintaining positive air pressure in patient care areas relative to corridors would be the most effective strategy for reducing airborne pathogen transmission in a hospital HVAC system design. This approach prevents the inflow of potentially contaminated air from common areas into patient rooms, significantly reducing the risk of airborne infections. Increasing filter change frequency (a) is beneficial but doesn't address airflow direction. UVGI in air handling units (b) can be effective but may not prevent contamination from adjacent spaces. Standalone air purifiers (d) can be useful supplements but don't provide systematic protection like proper air pressure management. Positive pressure in patient care areas is a fundamental principle in healthcare HVAC design for infection control, providing continuous protection against airborne pathogens entering from less controlled areas.

344. A nurse executive is overseeing the implementation of a new inventory management system that uses par levels and reorder points to maintain supply availability. Which of the following actions would best ensure that the system optimizes inventory without causing shortages or overstock?
a. Setting par levels based on the highest usage month to prevent stockouts.
b. Regularly reviewing and adjusting reorder points based on actual usage patterns.
c. Maintaining par levels uniformly across all departments to simplify management.
d. Ordering in bulk quantities to take advantage of discounts, regardless of usage.

Answer: b. Regularly reviewing and adjusting reorder points based on actual usage patterns. Explanation: Reorder points should be regularly adjusted according to actual usage to ensure that inventory levels remain optimal. This approach prevents both shortages and overstock by aligning reorder points with real demand rather than fixed estimates or discounts, which could lead to inefficiencies.

345. A nurse executive is evaluating the benefits of using a Group Purchasing Organization (GPO) for the hospital's procurement needs. Which of the following would be the most significant advantage of GPO utilization in healthcare procurement?
a. Increased autonomy in vendor selection.
b. Greater purchasing power leading to cost savings.
c. Enhanced control over the customization of products.
d. Faster procurement processes due to fewer contracts.

Answer: b. Greater purchasing power leading to cost savings. Explanation: GPOs leverage the collective buying power of their members to negotiate lower prices with vendors, resulting in significant cost savings. While GPOs may reduce customization and autonomy, the primary benefit lies in their ability to achieve better pricing and terms through volume purchasing.

346. During a review of the hospital's procurement process, the nurse executive identifies that strategic sourcing could enhance efficiency and cost-effectiveness. Which of the following practices best exemplifies strategic sourcing in healthcare procurement?
a. Establishing long-term partnerships with a select group of high-performing vendors.
b. Rotating suppliers frequently to ensure competitive pricing.
c. Prioritizing the purchase of products from local vendors to support the community.
d. Selecting vendors based on the lowest bid regardless of quality.

Answer: a. Establishing long-term partnerships with a select group of high-performing vendors. Explanation: Strategic sourcing focuses on developing long-term partnerships with vendors who consistently deliver high-quality products and services. This approach fosters collaboration, improves reliability, and can lead to better pricing and service levels over time, unlike rotating suppliers or prioritizing cost alone.

347. A nurse executive is tasked with optimizing the hospital's supply chain to improve vendor relationship management. Which strategy would most effectively strengthen relationships with key vendors in the healthcare supply chain?
a. Conducting annual performance reviews with vendors and providing feedback.
b. Negotiating shorter contract terms to increase flexibility in vendor selection.
c. Limiting communication with vendors to formal channels to maintain professionalism.
d. Focusing on reducing costs by frequently switching vendors to find the lowest price.

Answer: a. Conducting annual performance reviews with vendors and providing feedback. Explanation: Regular performance reviews with vendors allow for open communication about expectations, performance, and areas for improvement. This practice fosters a collaborative relationship, helping to build trust and improve service quality, which is more effective than frequently switching vendors or limiting communication.

348. A nurse executive is considering a shift to a just-in-time (JIT) inventory management system to reduce on-hand inventory. Which of the following potential risks should be most closely monitored to ensure the success of this system?
a. The possibility of increased costs due to smaller, more frequent orders.
b. The reliability and responsiveness of suppliers in delivering on time.
c. The risk of having too much inventory on hand, leading to waste.
d. The need for additional storage space to accommodate larger inventory levels.

Answer: b. The reliability and responsiveness of suppliers in delivering on time. Explanation: JIT inventory systems depend on the timely delivery of supplies to meet immediate demand, so supplier reliability is critical. Any delays or disruptions in the supply chain can lead to shortages and impact patient care. While cost and storage considerations are important, supplier reliability is the most significant risk factor in JIT systems.

349. A nurse executive is evaluating the hospital's use of Group Purchasing Organizations (GPOs) to ensure the best value in procurement. Which of the following strategies would most likely enhance the hospital's procurement outcomes through GPO utilization?
a. Consolidating all purchases through a single GPO to simplify the procurement process.
b. Using multiple GPOs to access a broader range of suppliers and product options.
c. Relying solely on GPO contracts without seeking additional competitive bids.
d. Limiting GPO participation to non-clinical supplies to maintain control over clinical products.

Answer: b. Using multiple GPOs to access a broader range of suppliers and product options. Explanation: Utilizing multiple GPOs allows the hospital to access a wider range of suppliers, products, and pricing options, enhancing procurement flexibility and value. While consolidation simplifies processes, it may limit access to diverse options that could better meet the hospital's needs.

350. A nurse executive is tasked with improving the hospital's inventory management practices by adjusting par levels for frequently used supplies. Which of the following factors should be given the highest priority when determining appropriate par levels?
a. The historical usage patterns of the supplies.
b. The shelf life and expiration dates of the supplies.
c. The cost of the supplies and available budget.
d. The storage capacity available for the supplies.

Answer: a. The historical usage patterns of the supplies. Explanation: Par levels should be primarily based on historical usage patterns to ensure that supplies are available when needed without overstocking. While cost, shelf life, and storage capacity are important, they are secondary to ensuring that par levels reflect actual demand.

351. A nurse executive is leading a team to assess the hospital's vendor relationship management practices. Which of the following would be the most effective approach to improving vendor collaboration and ensuring high-quality supply chain performance?
a. Increasing competition among vendors by frequently reopening bids.
b. Standardizing communication protocols to streamline interactions with vendors.
c. Developing joint initiatives with key vendors to drive innovation and process improvements.
d. Reducing the number of vendors to simplify the supply chain and reduce costs.

Answer: c. Developing joint initiatives with key vendors to drive innovation and process improvements. Explanation: Collaborative initiatives with vendors can lead to innovations that improve supply chain efficiency and product quality. This partnership approach fosters mutual investment in success, leading to better outcomes than simply focusing on cost reduction or competition.

352. The nurse executive is reviewing a report on the hospital's supply chain performance, particularly focusing on strategic sourcing outcomes. Which metric would best indicate the success of strategic sourcing efforts?
a. The percentage of total procurement costs reduced over the past year.
b. The number of new vendors added to the hospital's supplier list.
c. The frequency of supply stockouts experienced in clinical departments.
d. The average delivery time from vendors for critical supplies.

Answer: a. The percentage of total procurement costs reduced over the past year. Explanation: Strategic sourcing aims to optimize procurement by securing the best value for goods and services. A reduction in total procurement costs is a key indicator of the success of these efforts. While delivery time and stockouts are important, cost reduction is the primary goal of strategic sourcing.

353. A nurse executive is implementing an automated inventory management system to improve supply chain efficiency. Which feature of the system would be most critical for maintaining optimal inventory levels?
a. Real-time tracking of inventory usage and automatic reorder triggers.
b. Integration with financial systems for budgeting and cost analysis.
c. Compatibility with existing electronic health record (EHR) systems.
d. Ability to generate detailed reports on supplier performance.

Answer: a. Real-time tracking of inventory usage and automatic reorder triggers. Explanation: Real-time tracking and automatic reorder triggers ensure that inventory levels are consistently maintained, reducing the risk of shortages or overstock. While integration with financial systems and reporting are valuable, the ability to manage inventory in real-time is crucial for supply chain efficiency.

354. A nurse executive is leading the development of clinical practice guidelines (CPGs) for the management of sepsis in the hospital. Which step is most critical to ensure the successful implementation and adherence to the new guidelines by the clinical staff?
a. Developing the guidelines solely based on expert opinion
b. Incorporating feedback from all stakeholders, including frontline staff, during the development process
c. Mandating immediate adherence to the guidelines without a transition period

d. Limiting the guidelines to a brief summary to avoid overwhelming staff with details

Answer: b. Incorporating feedback from all stakeholders, including frontline staff, during the development process. Explanation: Engaging stakeholders, especially frontline staff, during the development of clinical practice guidelines ensures that the guidelines are practical, relevant, and more likely to be accepted and followed. This collaborative approach fosters ownership and adherence to the guidelines.

355. During a peer review process, a nurse executive discovers that a physician has consistently failed to follow the established clinical practice guidelines for managing hypertension. What is the most appropriate initial action to take in response to this finding?
a. Immediately suspend the physician's clinical privileges
b. Provide the physician with education and support to improve adherence to the guidelines
c. Report the physician to the state medical board for non-compliance
d. Revise the clinical practice guidelines to accommodate the physician's preferences

Answer: b. Provide the physician with education and support to improve adherence to the guidelines. Explanation: The primary goal of peer review is to improve the quality of care. Offering education and support to the physician addresses the non-compliance in a constructive manner, promoting better adherence to clinical guidelines and enhancing patient outcomes.

356. A hospital is implementing a Clinical Documentation Improvement (CDI) program to enhance the accuracy and completeness of patient records. Which strategy would most effectively support the success of this program?
a. Requiring all physicians to complete a mandatory documentation course annually
b. Hiring certified CDI specialists to collaborate with clinical staff on documentation practices
c. Implementing a financial penalty for incomplete or inaccurate documentation
d. Reducing the number of required documentation fields to simplify the process

Answer: b. Hiring certified CDI specialists to collaborate with clinical staff on documentation practices. Explanation: Certified CDI specialists play a key role in improving the quality of clinical documentation by working directly with clinical staff to ensure that records are accurate, complete, and reflective of the patient's condition. This collaboration leads to better coding, billing, and overall quality of care.

357. A nurse executive is integrating utilization review (UR) and case management (CM) functions to streamline care coordination. Which outcome would best indicate the success of this integration?
a. A decrease in the length of hospital stays without an increase in readmission rates
b. An increase in the number of patients admitted through the emergency department
c. Higher patient satisfaction scores related to discharge planning
d. A reduction in the overall number of case management staff required

Answer: a. A decrease in the length of hospital stays without an increase in readmission rates. Explanation: Successful integration of utilization review and case management should result in more efficient care coordination, leading to reduced lengths of stay while maintaining or improving patient outcomes, as evidenced by stable or reduced readmission rates.

358. In a peer review process focused on quality assurance, a nurse executive must ensure fairness and objectivity. Which of the following actions is most critical to achieving this goal?
a. Selecting reviewers who are personal friends of the provider under review
b. Using a standardized scoring system for all cases reviewed
c. Allowing the provider under review to choose their own reviewers
d. Conducting reviews only on cases where there is a patient complaint

Answer: b. Using a standardized scoring system for all cases reviewed. Explanation: A standardized scoring system ensures consistency and objectivity in the peer review process, reducing the potential for bias and ensuring that all cases are evaluated against the same criteria.

359. A nurse executive is tasked with improving clinical documentation to support accurate coding and reimbursement. Which approach is most likely to yield long-term improvements in documentation quality?
a. Implementing an electronic health record (EHR) template that includes all possible diagnosis codes
b. Providing ongoing training and feedback to clinical staff on effective documentation practices
c. Allowing physicians to delegate documentation tasks to administrative staff
d. Conducting quarterly audits to identify documentation errors and correcting them retroactively

Answer: b. Providing ongoing training and feedback to clinical staff on effective documentation practices. Explanation: Continuous education and feedback are essential for fostering long-term improvements in documentation practices. This approach ensures that clinical staff are consistently aware of best practices and can apply them to produce high-quality documentation.

360. A nurse executive is involved in the development of a new clinical practice guideline for managing diabetes in the hospital. To ensure the guideline is evidence-based, what should be the primary focus during its development?
a. Including recommendations from the most recent randomized controlled trials (RCTs) and meta-analyses
b. Consulting with only the most experienced physicians in the field
c. Adopting guidelines from other institutions without modifications
d. Simplifying the guideline to include only the most common treatment protocols

Answer: a. Including recommendations from the most recent randomized controlled trials (RCTs) and meta-analyses. Explanation: Incorporating evidence from the most recent RCTs and meta-analyses ensures that the guideline is based on the highest level of evidence, promoting the best possible outcomes for patients with diabetes.

361. A hospital is experiencing issues with the timeliness and accuracy of utilization review (UR) processes. Which strategy would best address these issues?
a. Increasing the frequency of UR meetings to address cases more promptly
b. Implementing automated software to assist with the review of patient cases
c. Reducing the criteria used for determining medical necessity

d. Delegating the UR process to a third-party vendor

Answer: b. Implementing automated software to assist with the review of patient cases. Explanation: Automated software can enhance the efficiency and accuracy of the utilization review process by providing real-time analysis of patient data, reducing the potential for human error, and ensuring that reviews are completed in a timely manner.

362. A nurse executive is evaluating the effectiveness of a Clinical Documentation Improvement (CDI) program. Which metric would be most indicative of the program's success?
a. An increase in the number of clinical documentation queries issued to physicians
b. A decrease in the number of coding errors identified during audits
c. An increase in the overall volume of documented patient encounters
d. A reduction in the time required to complete patient documentation

Answer: b. A decrease in the number of coding errors identified during audits. Explanation: A successful CDI program should lead to more accurate and complete documentation, which in turn reduces coding errors. This metric directly reflects the program's impact on improving the quality of clinical documentation.

363. A nurse executive is tasked with ensuring the effective implementation of a newly developed clinical practice guideline for stroke management. Which step is most important to monitor during the initial implementation phase?
a. The level of staff engagement with the guideline during training sessions
b. The number of patients diagnosed with stroke following guideline implementation
c. The frequency of deviations from the guideline in clinical practice
d. The cost of implementing the guideline across the organization

Answer: c. The frequency of deviations from the guideline in clinical practice. Explanation: Monitoring deviations from the guideline during the initial implementation phase is critical to identifying barriers to adherence and areas where additional support or education may be needed. This step helps ensure the guideline is followed consistently, leading to better patient outcomes.

364. A long-term care facility is implementing person-centered care planning. Which of the following approaches would be MOST effective in ensuring that care plans reflect residents' individual preferences and values?
a. Conducting standardized quality of life assessments for all residents
b. Implementing a consistent daily routine for all residents
c. Holding regular care planning meetings that include the resident and their family
d. Assigning a primary caregiver to each resident

Answer: c. Holding regular care planning meetings that include the resident and their family. Explanation: Regular care planning meetings that include the resident and their family are the most effective approach for ensuring person-centered care plans in long-term care settings. This method directly involves residents in decision-making about their care, allowing for the incorporation of individual preferences, values, and goals. Standardized assessments (a) provide useful information but may not capture individual nuances. A consistent daily routine (b) contradicts the principle of personalization in care. Assigning a primary caregiver (d) can enhance continuity but doesn't ensure resident involvement in care planning. Including residents and families in care planning meetings aligns with core principles of person-centered care, promoting autonomy and individualized care delivery.

365. A hospital is seeking Planetree certification for patient-centered care. Which of the following initiatives would be MOST aligned with Planetree's emphasis on healing environments?
a. Implementing a no-visitors policy to reduce infection risk
b. Standardizing room decor for easier maintenance
c. Integrating nature and art into the hospital design
d. Centralizing all patient services for operational efficiency

Answer: c. Integrating nature and art into the hospital design. Explanation: Integrating nature and art into the hospital design is most aligned with Planetree's emphasis on creating healing environments. Planetree certification criteria strongly emphasize the physical environment's role in promoting healing and well-being. Nature and art elements can reduce stress, promote relaxation, and create a more humanizing environment. A no-visitors policy (a) contradicts Planetree's focus on family involvement. Standardizing decor (b) neglects individual preferences and the therapeutic potential of environment. Centralizing services (d) may improve efficiency but doesn't necessarily create a healing environment. The integration of nature and art reflects Planetree's holistic approach to patient-centered care, recognizing the environment's impact on the healing process.

366. In implementing shared decision-making tools, a healthcare system is considering various approaches. Which of the following would be MOST effective in promoting patient engagement in treatment decisions?
a. Providing patients with detailed statistical data on treatment outcomes
b. Using decision aids that present balanced information on options and outcomes
c. Having physicians make recommendations based on clinical expertise
d. Offering patients a choice between two pre-selected treatment options

Answer: b. Using decision aids that present balanced information on options and outcomes. Explanation: Using decision aids that present balanced information on options and outcomes is the most effective approach for promoting patient engagement in shared decision-making. These tools provide patients with clear, unbiased information about their condition, treatment options, potential benefits, and risks, enabling informed participation in decision-making. Detailed statistical data (a) may overwhelm patients without proper context. Physician recommendations based solely on clinical expertise (c) don't fully engage patients in the decision process. Limiting choices to two pre-selected options (d) restricts patient involvement and may not cover all viable alternatives. Well-designed decision aids support patient understanding and facilitate meaningful discussions with healthcare providers, aligning with core principles of shared decision-making and patient-centered care.

367. A nurse executive is developing strategies to enhance cultural competence in patient-centered care delivery. Which of the following approaches would be MOST effective in improving staff cultural competence?
a. Providing annual online cultural diversity training
b. Hiring staff members from diverse cultural backgrounds
c. Implementing ongoing, case-based cultural competence education
d. Translating all patient education materials into multiple languages

Answer: c. Implementing ongoing, case-based cultural competence education. Explanation: Implementing ongoing, case-based cultural competence education would be most effective in improving staff cultural competence. This approach provides continuous learning opportunities grounded in real-world scenarios, allowing staff to develop practical skills in culturally sensitive care delivery. Annual online training (a) may be too infrequent and lacks practical application. Hiring diverse staff (b) can contribute to cultural competence but doesn't ensure all staff develop these skills. Translating materials (d) is important for patient communication but doesn't directly improve staff competence. Case-based, ongoing education promotes deep understanding and application of cultural competence principles, enabling staff to provide more effective, patient-centered care across diverse populations.

368. In a long-term care setting, which person-centered care approach would be MOST effective in promoting residents' autonomy and quality of life?
a. Implementing a points-based reward system for participating in activities
b. Allowing residents to choose their daily schedules, including meal times
c. Assigning residents to activities based on their past interests
d. Standardizing room layouts for all residents to ensure equity

Answer: b. Allowing residents to choose their daily schedules, including meal times. Explanation: Allowing residents to choose their daily schedules, including meal times, is the most effective person-centered approach for promoting autonomy and quality of life in long-term care. This practice respects individual preferences and routines, enhancing residents' sense of control and normalcy. A points-based reward system (a) may encourage participation but doesn't truly promote autonomy. Assigning activities based on past interests (c) makes assumptions about current preferences. Standardizing room layouts (d) contradicts personalization principles. Choice in daily schedules aligns closely with person-centered care philosophies, recognizing residents as individuals with unique preferences and supporting their right to make decisions about their daily lives.

369. A hospital is implementing Planetree certification criteria focused on family involvement. Which of the following policies would BEST support this aspect of patient-centered care?
a. Extending visiting hours to 12 hours per day
b. Allowing family presence during rounds and shift changes
c. Providing a family lounge on each unit
d. Offering monthly family education sessions

Answer: b. Allowing family presence during rounds and shift changes. Explanation: Allowing family presence during rounds and shift changes best supports the Planetree certification criteria for family involvement in patient-centered care. This policy actively integrates family members into the care process, promoting transparency, communication, and shared decision-making. Extended visiting hours (a) improve access but don't necessarily involve families in care discussions. A family lounge (c) provides comfort but doesn't directly involve families in care. Monthly education sessions (d) are beneficial but infrequent and don't address day-to-day involvement. Family presence during key clinical interactions aligns with Planetree's emphasis on partnering with families, viewing them as integral to the care team rather than just visitors.

370. In developing shared decision-making tools for cancer treatment options, which of the following elements is MOST crucial for ensuring effective patient engagement?
a. Inclusion of five-year survival statistics for each treatment option

b. Detailed explanations of the biological mechanisms of each treatment

c. Visual aids depicting potential side effects and quality of life impacts

d. Testimonials from patients who have undergone each treatment

Answer: c. Visual aids depicting potential side effects and quality of life impacts. Explanation: Visual aids depicting potential side effects and quality of life impacts are the most crucial element for ensuring effective patient engagement in shared decision-making for cancer treatment. These aids help patients understand the practical implications of different treatments on their daily lives, which is often a key factor in treatment decisions. Five-year survival statistics (a) are important but may not convey the full picture of treatment impact. Detailed biological explanations (b) may be too complex for many patients to apply to decision-making. Patient testimonials (d) can be informative but may not represent typical experiences. Visual representations of side effects and quality of life impacts provide accessible, relevant information that helps patients weigh options in the context of their personal values and lifestyle preferences.

371. A healthcare system is implementing cultural competence training for staff. Which of the following approaches would be MOST effective in developing staff's ability to provide culturally sensitive care?

a. Providing a comprehensive manual on cultural practices of various ethnic groups

b. Offering language classes for the most common non-English languages in the community

c. Implementing simulation-based training scenarios with diverse patient actors

d. Requiring staff to complete an online module on cultural diversity annually

Answer: c. Implementing simulation-based training scenarios with diverse patient actors. Explanation: Implementing simulation-based training scenarios with diverse patient actors would be the most effective approach for developing staff's ability to provide culturally sensitive care. This method allows for hands-on practice in realistic situations, promoting experiential learning and the development of practical skills in cross-cultural communication and care delivery. A comprehensive manual (a) provides information but doesn't ensure practical application. Language classes (b) are valuable but don't address broader cultural competence issues. Annual online modules (d) may increase knowledge but lack the interactive element crucial for skill development. Simulation-based training provides a safe environment for staff to practice and receive feedback on their cultural competence skills, leading to more effective translation of knowledge into practice.

372. In a long-term care facility implementing person-centered care, which approach would be MOST effective in supporting residents' spiritual needs?

a. Designating a non-denominational chapel space

b. Scheduling regular visits from local religious leaders

c. Integrating spiritual preferences into each resident's care plan

d. Offering group meditation sessions weekly

Answer: c. Integrating spiritual preferences into each resident's care plan. Explanation: Integrating spiritual preferences into each resident's care plan is the most effective approach for supporting spiritual needs in a person-centered care model. This method ensures that spiritual care is individualized, respecting the diverse beliefs and practices of residents and incorporating spirituality into overall care planning. A non-denominational chapel (a) provides space but doesn't address individual needs. Scheduled visits from religious leaders (b) may not cater to all beliefs or preferences. Weekly meditation sessions (d) offer a spiritual practice but may not suit all residents. By including spiritual preferences in care plans, the facility can provide tailored support that aligns with each resident's beliefs and values, truly embodying the principles of person-centered care.

373. A hospital is seeking to improve its cultural competence in patient-centered care delivery. Which of the following strategies would be MOST effective in addressing language barriers with limited English proficiency (LEP) patients?
a. Providing pictorial communication boards in all patient rooms
b. Implementing a professional medical interpreter service available 24/7
c. Encouraging bilingual staff to act as interpreters when available
d. Offering English language classes for LEP patients and families

Answer: b. Implementing a professional medical interpreter service available 24/7. Explanation: Implementing a professional medical interpreter service available 24/7 is the most effective strategy for addressing language barriers with LEP patients in a culturally competent, patient-centered care model. Professional interpreters are trained in medical terminology and cultural nuances, ensuring accurate and culturally appropriate communication. Pictorial boards (a) can be helpful but are limited in conveying complex medical information. Using bilingual staff as interpreters (c) may seem convenient but can lead to errors and ethical issues if staff are not trained in medical interpretation. Offering English classes (d) is beneficial long-term but doesn't address immediate communication needs in healthcare settings. A professional interpreter service ensures that LEP patients can fully participate in their care decisions and receive equitable, patient-centered care regardless of language barriers.

374. A nurse executive is tasked with developing a project charter for a new hospital-wide patient safety initiative. Which of the following elements is most critical to include in the project charter to ensure alignment with organizational goals?
a. A detailed timeline for each project task and deliverable.
b. A clear statement of the project's scope, including defined boundaries and exclusions.
c. A list of all potential risks and their corresponding mitigation strategies.
d. A breakdown of the project budget by department.

Answer: b. A clear statement of the project's scope, including defined boundaries and exclusions. Explanation: The project scope is a fundamental component of the project charter, as it defines what is included and excluded from the project. This clarity helps ensure that the project aligns with organizational goals and prevents scope creep. While timelines, risks, and budgets are important, the scope provides the foundation for all other project elements.

375. A nurse executive is overseeing a healthcare construction project using the Critical Path Method (CPM). During the project, an unforeseen delay occurs in one of the critical tasks. What is the most likely consequence of this delay?
a. The project will be delayed by the length of time equal to the duration of the delayed task.
b. Non-critical tasks will need to be accelerated to meet the original deadline.
c. The project's budget will automatically increase to accommodate the delay.
d. The delay will have no impact on the project's timeline if it does not exceed the float of non-critical tasks.

Answer: a. The project will be delayed by the length of time equal to the duration of the delayed task. Explanation: In the Critical Path Method, the critical path is the sequence of tasks that determines the overall project duration. Any delay in a critical task directly impacts the project's timeline, delaying the completion of the project by at least the duration of the delayed task. Non-critical tasks do not affect the timeline unless their delay exceeds the available float.

376. A nurse executive is implementing an Agile project management approach for a healthcare IT system upgrade. Which of the following practices is most aligned with Agile principles in managing this project?
a. Conducting detailed upfront planning to avoid changes during the project.
b. Utilizing a fixed timeline and scope to ensure the project stays within budget.
c. Holding regular sprint reviews with stakeholders to adapt to changing needs and priorities.
d. Assigning a dedicated project manager to make all key decisions independently.

Answer: c. Holding regular sprint reviews with stakeholders to adapt to changing needs and priorities. Explanation: Agile project management emphasizes flexibility and iterative progress through regular sprint reviews, allowing teams to adapt to changing needs and priorities. This approach contrasts with traditional project management, which focuses on fixed timelines, scopes, and decision-making hierarchies.

377. A nurse executive is managing a multi-disciplinary healthcare project with numerous stakeholders, including clinical staff, IT professionals, and hospital administration. Which stakeholder management strategy would be most effective in ensuring project success?
a. Involving stakeholders only during key project milestones to minimize disruptions.
b. Regularly communicating project progress and incorporating stakeholder feedback throughout the project lifecycle.
c. Assigning one stakeholder as the representative for all decision-making to streamline communication.
d. Limiting stakeholder involvement to the planning phase to prevent delays during execution.

Answer: b. Regularly communicating project progress and incorporating stakeholder feedback throughout the project lifecycle. Explanation: Effective stakeholder management involves continuous engagement and communication with stakeholders throughout the project. This ensures that their feedback is considered, reducing resistance and increasing the likelihood of project success. Involving stakeholders only at milestones or during planning may lead to misalignment and delays.

378. A nurse executive is developing a project charter for a telehealth implementation project. Which of the following components is essential to include in the charter to establish a clear direction for the project?
a. A detailed risk management plan outlining potential obstacles.
b. A summary of the project's return on investment (ROI) analysis.
c. The identification of the project sponsor and their role in decision-making.
d. A description of the technical specifications for the telehealth platform.

Answer: c. The identification of the project sponsor and their role in decision-making. Explanation: The project sponsor is a critical component of the project charter as they provide the necessary authority, resources, and support for the project. Clearly identifying the sponsor and their role helps establish a clear direction and accountability, which is essential for project success. While risk management, ROI, and technical specifications are important, the sponsor's role is fundamental in guiding the project.

379. A healthcare organization is using the Critical Path Method (CPM) to manage the construction of a new wing. Midway through the project, a non-critical task experiences a delay. What impact is this delay likely to have on the project?
a. It will delay the project by the length of the delay unless additional resources are allocated.
b. It will have no impact on the project's timeline as long as the delay does not exceed the task's float.
c. It will cause all subsequent tasks to be delayed, impacting the overall timeline.
d. It will necessitate a complete re-evaluation of the project's critical path.

Answer: b. It will have no impact on the project's timeline as long as the delay does not exceed the task's float.
Explanation: In CPM, non-critical tasks have float (or slack) time, which allows them to be delayed without affecting the overall project timeline. The delay will only impact the timeline if it exceeds the available float. Therefore, the delay in a non-critical task is unlikely to affect the project's completion unless it surpasses the float.

380. A nurse executive is introducing Agile project management for a new EHR system implementation. Which of the following challenges is most likely to arise when applying Agile principles in this healthcare context?
a. Difficulty in maintaining stakeholder engagement due to frequent changes in project scope.
b. Increased rigidity in the project timeline due to fixed sprint durations.
c. Lack of flexibility in adapting to new regulatory requirements during the project.
d. Challenges in ensuring consistent team participation throughout the project.

Answer: a. Difficulty in maintaining stakeholder engagement due to frequent changes in project scope. Explanation: Agile principles involve flexibility and iterative development, which can lead to frequent changes in project scope. This may challenge stakeholder engagement as they might find it difficult to keep up with the evolving nature of the project. Ensuring clear communication and involving stakeholders in sprint reviews can help mitigate this challenge.

381. A nurse executive is managing a healthcare project with multiple interdependent tasks. Which of the following scenarios would most likely result in a delay of the overall project timeline?
a. A task with no float time is delayed by a week.
b. A non-critical task is delayed by several days but does not exceed its float.
c. A critical task is completed ahead of schedule.
d. A resource is reassigned from a non-critical task to a critical task.

Answer: a. A task with no float time is delayed by a week. Explanation: A task with no float time is on the critical path, meaning any delay directly impacts the overall project timeline. Delays in non-critical tasks or early completion of critical tasks do not necessarily delay the project, but a delay in a critical task with no float will result in a project delay.

382. A nurse executive is tasked with managing stakeholder expectations for a new hospital-wide quality improvement project. Which approach is most likely to prevent misunderstandings and ensure stakeholder alignment throughout the project?
a. Setting expectations at the beginning of the project and avoiding changes to prevent confusion.
b. Holding regular stakeholder meetings to review progress, discuss challenges, and adjust expectations as needed.
c. Limiting the distribution of project information to reduce the risk of conflicting opinions.

d. Delegating stakeholder communication to a project manager to streamline the process.

Answer: b. Holding regular stakeholder meetings to review progress, discuss challenges, and adjust expectations as needed. Explanation: Regular stakeholder meetings allow for ongoing communication, helping to manage expectations, address concerns, and ensure alignment as the project progresses. This approach reduces the risk of misunderstandings and keeps stakeholders engaged and informed, which is essential for project success.

383. A nurse executive is developing a project charter for a new clinical workflow redesign initiative. To ensure the project's success, which of the following should be clearly defined in the charter?
a. The specific technologies to be used in the workflow redesign.
b. The roles and responsibilities of each project team member.
c. The preferred vendors for any necessary equipment purchases.
d. The project's anticipated impact on the organization's public image.

Answer: b. The roles and responsibilities of each project team member. Explanation: Clearly defining the roles and responsibilities of each team member in the project charter is critical to ensuring accountability and effective collaboration. This clarity helps avoid confusion, ensures tasks are completed on time, and aligns team efforts with the project's goals. While technology, vendors, and public image are important considerations, the clarity of team roles is fundamental to project success.

384. A nurse executive is tasked with leading the curriculum development for a new advanced practice nursing program. Which of the following considerations is most critical to ensure the curriculum meets accreditation standards?
a. Incorporating input from current nursing students on curriculum content
b. Aligning the curriculum with the latest evidence-based practice guidelines and competencies set by accrediting bodies
c. Focusing primarily on theoretical knowledge rather than clinical skills
d. Limiting the number of clinical hours to reduce the program's cost

Answer: b. Aligning the curriculum with the latest evidence-based practice guidelines and competencies set by accrediting bodies. Explanation: To ensure that the program meets accreditation standards, it is essential to align the curriculum with evidence-based practice guidelines and competencies established by accrediting bodies such as the Commission on Collegiate Nursing Education (CCNE) or the Accreditation Commission for Education in Nursing (ACEN). This alignment ensures that graduates are prepared to meet professional standards and practice requirements.

385. A nurse executive is designing a simulation-based education program to enhance clinical decision-making skills for advanced practice nursing students. What is the most important factor to consider when developing the simulation scenarios?
a. Ensuring the scenarios are identical to real-life clinical situations
b. Including a variety of low-fidelity simulations to reduce costs
c. Designing scenarios that gradually increase in complexity to match students' skill levels
d. Focusing exclusively on rare clinical events that students are unlikely to encounter in practice

Answer: c. Designing scenarios that gradually increase in complexity to match students' skill levels. Explanation: It is crucial to design simulation scenarios that align with students' current knowledge and skills while progressively increasing in complexity. This approach allows students to build confidence and competence incrementally, reinforcing learning and improving clinical decision-making abilities.

386. A nurse executive is exploring academic-practice partnerships to enhance clinical education for nursing students. Which of the following strategies would best support the success of such a partnership?
a. Establishing a shared governance model where both academic and practice partners have equal decision-making authority
b. Focusing solely on providing more clinical placement opportunities for students
c. Limiting the partnership to short-term projects to maintain flexibility
d. Ensuring that the partnership remains exclusive to one healthcare organization

Answer: a. Establishing a shared governance model where both academic and practice partners have equal decision-making authority. Explanation: A shared governance model fosters collaboration, mutual respect, and shared responsibility between academic and practice partners. This approach enhances the partnership's success by ensuring that decisions reflect the needs and expertise of both educational institutions and healthcare organizations.

387. A nursing school is facing a shortage of qualified faculty for its advanced practice nursing program. What faculty development strategy should the nurse executive prioritize to address this challenge?
a. Offering short-term contracts to attract adjunct faculty
b. Providing mentorship and leadership development programs to prepare current faculty for advanced roles
c. Increasing the workload of existing faculty to cover the shortage
d. Recruiting retired nurses as part-time faculty to fill gaps

Answer: b. Providing mentorship and leadership development programs to prepare current faculty for advanced roles. Explanation: Mentorship and leadership development programs are essential for building a sustainable faculty pipeline. By preparing current faculty for advanced roles, the nursing school can address the shortage more effectively and ensure that faculty members are equipped to meet the demands of teaching advanced practice nursing students.

388. A nurse executive is evaluating the effectiveness of a newly implemented simulation-based education program in a graduate nursing program. Which outcome measure would best indicate the program's success in improving clinical skills?
a. Students' satisfaction scores with the simulation experience
b. The number of simulation sessions completed by each student
c. Improvement in students' clinical performance during subsequent clinical rotations
d. The cost-effectiveness of the simulation program compared to traditional methods

Answer: c. Improvement in students' clinical performance during subsequent clinical rotations. Explanation: The ultimate goal of simulation-based education is to enhance students' clinical skills. Therefore, improvements in clinical performance during real-world clinical rotations are the most relevant measure of the program's success, as they demonstrate the practical application of skills learned during simulation.

389. In a new advanced practice nursing program, the curriculum emphasizes interprofessional education (IPE). What is the most effective way to integrate IPE into the program to enhance collaborative practice?
a. Requiring students to complete online modules on teamwork and communication
b. Including case-based learning sessions where students from different healthcare disciplines work together to solve clinical problems
c. Assigning group projects that involve only nursing students to strengthen their nursing identity
d. Offering elective courses on interprofessional collaboration that students can choose to take

Answer: b. Including case-based learning sessions where students from different healthcare disciplines work together to solve clinical problems. Explanation: Case-based learning sessions involving students from various healthcare disciplines foster interprofessional collaboration by allowing them to practice working together to solve real-world clinical problems. This approach enhances students' ability to collaborate effectively in team-based care settings.

390. A nurse executive is tasked with developing an evaluation tool to measure the effectiveness of faculty development programs in nursing education. Which of the following metrics should be prioritized in the evaluation tool?
a. The number of faculty members attending development programs
b. Faculty members' self-reported confidence in their teaching abilities after the program
c. Student feedback on the quality of instruction received from faculty who participated in the development programs
d. The financial cost of the faculty development programs

Answer: c. Student feedback on the quality of instruction received from faculty who participated in the development programs. Explanation: Student feedback on the quality of instruction is a critical indicator of the effectiveness of faculty development programs. It reflects whether the professional development initiatives have translated into improved teaching practices and better educational outcomes for students.

391. A nursing program is considering the introduction of virtual simulation technology as part of its curriculum. What is the most significant advantage of virtual simulation in nursing education?
a. It eliminates the need for any physical clinical placements
b. It allows for standardized, repeatable training experiences in a controlled environment
c. It reduces the overall time required for clinical education
d. It is less expensive than traditional clinical simulations using mannequins

Answer: b. It allows for standardized, repeatable training experiences in a controlled environment. Explanation: Virtual simulation offers the advantage of providing consistent, repeatable scenarios where students can practice and refine their skills in a controlled environment. This standardization is crucial for ensuring that all students receive the same high-quality learning experience, regardless of variations in clinical placement opportunities.

392. A nurse executive is designing a curriculum for a new advanced practice nursing program with a focus on evidence-based practice (EBP). Which instructional strategy would be most effective in promoting EBP among students?
a. Incorporating EBP content into every course within the curriculum
b. Requiring students to complete a single EBP-focused course during their final semester
c. Assigning EBP-related readings without mandatory assignments
d. Encouraging students to independently explore EBP resources outside of the curriculum

Answer: a. Incorporating EBP content into every course within the curriculum. Explanation: Embedding EBP content throughout the curriculum ensures that students consistently engage with evidence-based practice principles in various contexts, reinforcing the importance of EBP and preparing them to apply it in their advanced practice roles.

393. A nurse executive is planning to establish academic-practice partnerships to provide students with enhanced clinical education opportunities. Which of the following is most critical to the long-term success of these partnerships?
a. Establishing clear communication channels and regular meetings between academic and practice leaders
b. Limiting the partnerships to a single academic year to assess their effectiveness
c. Prioritizing partnerships with high-profile healthcare organizations
d. Focusing solely on increasing the number of clinical placement slots available

Answer: a. Establishing clear communication channels and regular meetings between academic and practice leaders. Explanation: Effective communication and regular collaboration between academic and practice leaders are essential for maintaining alignment, addressing challenges, and ensuring that the partnership continues to meet the needs of both educational institutions and healthcare organizations. This approach supports the sustainability and success of the partnership.

394. A healthcare organization is evaluating the effectiveness of its compliance program. Which of the following metrics would be MOST indicative of a robust culture of compliance?
a. Number of compliance training sessions conducted annually
b. Percentage of staff who can accurately describe reporting procedures
c. Frequency of leadership communications about compliance
d. Volume of calls to the compliance hotline

Answer: b. Percentage of staff who can accurately describe reporting procedures. Explanation: The percentage of staff who can accurately describe reporting procedures is the most indicative metric of a robust culture of compliance. This measure demonstrates not just awareness, but understanding and potential readiness to act on compliance issues. While the number of training sessions (a) is important, it doesn't ensure comprehension or internalization of compliance principles. Leadership communications (c) contribute to culture but don't measure staff understanding. The volume of hotline calls (d) could indicate either a strong reporting culture or numerous compliance issues. Staff ability to describe reporting procedures reflects both the effectiveness of training and the integration of compliance into organizational culture, suggesting a higher likelihood of early problem detection and reporting.

395. A nurse executive is reviewing the organization's whistleblower protection policy. Which of the following elements is MOST critical for ensuring the policy's effectiveness?
a. Guaranteeing anonymity for all whistleblowers
b. Offering financial incentives for reporting violations
c. Providing clear anti-retaliation provisions and enforcement mechanisms
d. Requiring all reports to be submitted in writing

Answer: c. Providing clear anti-retaliation provisions and enforcement mechanisms. Explanation: Clear anti-retaliation provisions and enforcement mechanisms are the most critical elements for ensuring the effectiveness of a whistleblower protection policy. These provisions create a safe environment for reporting by explicitly prohibiting retaliation and outlining consequences for violations, addressing the primary concern of potential whistleblowers. Guaranteeing anonymity (a) may not always be possible or legal in all situations. Financial incentives (b) could encourage false reports and may be viewed as unethical. Requiring written reports (d) could discourage reporting by creating barriers. Strong anti-retaliation measures directly address the fear of repercussions, which is often the main deterrent to reporting, thus fostering a culture of transparency and accountability.

396. In managing conflicts of interest for healthcare executives, which of the following approaches would be MOST effective in maintaining organizational integrity?
a. Prohibiting all outside financial interests for executives
b. Requiring annual disclosure and review of potential conflicts
c. Limiting executive involvement in vendor selection processes
d. Mandating divestment of conflicting interests upon hiring

Answer: b. Requiring annual disclosure and review of potential conflicts. Explanation: Requiring annual disclosure and review of potential conflicts is the most effective approach for managing conflicts of interest while maintaining organizational integrity. This method provides regular opportunities to identify and address conflicts, allowing for nuanced evaluation of each situation. Prohibiting all outside financial interests (a) may be overly restrictive and potentially limit valuable expertise. Limiting involvement in vendor selection (c) addresses only one type of potential conflict. Mandatory divestment upon hiring (d) doesn't account for conflicts that may arise over time. Annual disclosure and review allows for ongoing management of conflicts, promotes transparency, and enables the organization to make informed decisions about how to handle potential conflicts, balancing ethical concerns with the retention of valuable leadership talent.

397. A hospital is participating in a multi-center clinical trial. Which ethical consideration is MOST crucial when obtaining informed consent from potential participants?
a. Ensuring the consent form is written at an 8th-grade reading level
b. Providing a comprehensive list of all possible side effects
c. Clearly explaining the right to withdraw from the study at any time
d. Offering financial compensation for participation

Answer: c. Clearly explaining the right to withdraw from the study at any time. Explanation: Clearly explaining the right to withdraw from the study at any time is the most crucial ethical consideration in obtaining informed consent for clinical trial participation. This element is fundamental to respecting participant autonomy and ensuring voluntary participation throughout the study. While an appropriate reading level (a) is important for comprehension, it doesn't address the voluntary nature of participation. A comprehensive list of side effects (b) is necessary but doesn't ensure ongoing voluntariness. Financial compensation (d) can be appropriate but must be carefully managed to avoid undue influence. The right to withdraw without penalty is a cornerstone of ethical research, empowering participants to make ongoing decisions about their involvement based on their personal circumstances and experiences in the trial.

398. A compliance officer is developing metrics to evaluate the effectiveness of the organization's compliance program. Which of the following would be the MOST valuable indicator of program impact?
a. Number of compliance policies updated annually
b. Percentage decrease in substantiated compliance violations over time
c. Frequency of compliance committee meetings
d. Amount of resources allocated to compliance training

Answer: b. Percentage decrease in substantiated compliance violations over time. Explanation: The percentage decrease in substantiated compliance violations over time is the most valuable indicator of compliance program impact. This metric directly measures the program's effectiveness in preventing and addressing compliance issues, which is the ultimate goal of any compliance program. The number of policies updated (a) doesn't necessarily reflect improved compliance. The frequency of committee meetings (c) indicates activity but not outcomes. Resources allocated to training (d) are an input measure rather than an outcome. A decrease in substantiated violations over time suggests that the compliance program is effectively identifying and mitigating risks, changing behavior, and fostering a culture of compliance, providing concrete evidence of the program's positive impact on organizational practices.

399. In developing a whistleblower protection policy, which of the following elements would be MOST effective in encouraging staff to report potential violations?
a. Implementing a confidential online reporting system
b. Establishing a non-retaliation clause with specific protections
c. Offering monetary rewards for validated reports
d. Requiring mandatory reporting of all suspected violations

Answer: b. Establishing a non-retaliation clause with specific protections. Explanation: Establishing a non-retaliation clause with specific protections would be most effective in encouraging staff to report potential violations. This element directly addresses the primary concern of many potential whistleblowers: fear of reprisal. By clearly outlining protections against retaliation, the policy can help create a safe environment for reporting. A confidential online system (a) is useful but doesn't address fears of identification and retaliation. Monetary rewards (c) may incentivize reporting but can also lead to false reports and ethical concerns. Mandatory reporting (d) may increase reports but doesn't address the underlying fears preventing voluntary reporting. A strong non-retaliation clause with specific, enforceable protections provides the assurance staff need to feel safe in coming forward with concerns.

400. A healthcare executive is faced with a potential conflict of interest involving a family member's business. Which of the following actions would BEST align with ethical management of this situation?
a. Recusing oneself from all decisions related to the family member's business
b. Disclosing the relationship and following the organization's conflict of interest policy
c. Divesting any financial interests in the family member's business
d. Resigning from the executive position to avoid any appearance of conflict

Answer: b. Disclosing the relationship and following the organization's conflict of interest policy. Explanation: Disclosing the relationship and following the organization's conflict of interest policy is the best action for ethical management of this situation. This approach ensures transparency and allows the organization to make informed decisions about how to manage the potential conflict. Recusing oneself from all related decisions (a) may be part of the solution but might be overly broad without proper disclosure. Divesting financial interests (c) could be appropriate but may not be necessary in all cases and doesn't address non-financial conflicts. Resigning (d) is an extreme measure that may not be necessary if the conflict can be appropriately managed. Disclosure and adherence to established policies provide a balanced approach that maintains integrity while allowing for nuanced management of the situation based on organizational guidelines.

401. In designing a compliance training program for a large healthcare system, which approach would be MOST effective in ensuring staff understanding and retention of key compliance concepts?
a. Mandating quarterly online compliance modules for all staff
b. Conducting annual in-person compliance workshops with case studies
c. Implementing a continuous, role-specific microlearning program
d. Distributing comprehensive compliance manuals to all departments

Answer: c. Implementing a continuous, role-specific microlearning program. Explanation: Implementing a continuous, role-specific microlearning program would be most effective in ensuring staff understanding and retention of key compliance concepts. This approach provides ongoing, targeted education that is relevant to each employee's specific role and responsibilities. Microlearning, with its short, focused content, aligns with adult learning principles and can improve retention. Quarterly online modules (a) may become routine and fail to engage staff deeply. Annual workshops (b) are valuable but infrequent and may not address evolving compliance issues. Comprehensive manuals (d) are useful references but don't ensure active learning or retention. A continuous, role-specific program keeps compliance top-of-mind, addresses real-world scenarios relevant to each role, and allows for rapid dissemination of updates, fostering a culture of ongoing compliance awareness and education.

402. A hospital is reviewing its policy on physician participation in industry-sponsored clinical trials. Which of the following guidelines would BEST address potential conflicts of interest while supporting valuable research?
a. Prohibiting all industry-sponsored research to avoid conflicts
b. Allowing participation with full disclosure and institutional review
c. Permitting research involvement only for non-compensated trials
d. Limiting participation to senior physicians with established reputations

Answer: b. Allowing participation with full disclosure and institutional review. Explanation: Allowing participation in industry-sponsored clinical trials with full disclosure and institutional review best addresses potential conflicts of interest while supporting valuable research. This approach recognizes the importance of industry-sponsored research while implementing safeguards to maintain integrity. Full disclosure ensures transparency, and institutional review provides oversight to manage potential conflicts. Prohibiting all industry-sponsored research (a) would significantly limit important research opportunities. Permitting only non-compensated trials (c) could severely restrict research funding and participation. Limiting participation to senior physicians (d) doesn't necessarily address conflicts of interest and may exclude valuable contributions from other qualified researchers. The combination of disclosure and review allows for case-by-case evaluation, balancing the benefits of research with ethical considerations.

403. In evaluating the effectiveness of a healthcare organization's compliance program, which of the following metrics would provide the MOST comprehensive insight into the program's impact on organizational culture?
a. Number of compliance violations reported annually
b. Percentage of employees who believe leadership is committed to compliance
c. Frequency of compliance policy updates
d. Amount of fines or penalties incurred for compliance breaches

Answer: b. Percentage of employees who believe leadership is committed to compliance. Explanation: The percentage of employees who believe leadership is committed to compliance provides the most comprehensive insight into the compliance program's impact on organizational culture. This metric reflects the extent to which compliance values have been internalized throughout the organization and indicates employees' perception of leadership's genuine commitment to ethical practices. The number of violations reported (a) could indicate either a strong reporting culture or numerous compliance issues. Policy update frequency (c) measures activity but not cultural impact. Fines or penalties (d) reflect past failures rather than current culture. Employee perception of leadership commitment is a strong indicator of a compliance-oriented culture, suggesting that compliance principles are integrated into daily operations and decision-making at all levels of the organization.

404. A nurse executive observes power dynamics within an interprofessional healthcare team where physicians dominate decision-making, often disregarding input from nursing staff. Which strategy would be most effective in addressing these power imbalances to foster more collaborative decision-making?
a. Reinforcing the authority of the nurse leaders by establishing a formal hierarchy within the team.
b. Encouraging nurses to document their concerns and submit them through the chain of command.
c. Facilitating interprofessional team-building exercises that emphasize equal contribution from all members.
d. Allowing the existing dynamics to persist, as physicians are often more knowledgeable about clinical decisions.

Answer: c. Facilitating interprofessional team-building exercises that emphasize equal contribution from all members. Explanation: Interprofessional team-building exercises can help break down hierarchical barriers and foster a culture of mutual respect and collaboration. By promoting equal contributions from all team members, this approach directly addresses power imbalances and improves team dynamics, leading to better decision-making and patient outcomes.

405. A healthcare organization is experiencing high turnover among nursing staff, with many citing perceptions of unfair treatment as a primary reason for leaving. According to organizational justice theory, which intervention would most effectively address these concerns?
a. Implementing a transparent promotion process with clear criteria and open communication.
b. Increasing salaries across the board to demonstrate the organization's commitment to its employees.
c. Offering flexible work schedules to improve work-life balance.
d. Conducting anonymous surveys to identify specific instances of perceived unfairness.

Answer: a. Implementing a transparent promotion process with clear criteria and open communication. Explanation: Organizational justice theory suggests that perceptions of fairness in processes, such as promotions, significantly impact employee satisfaction and retention. A transparent promotion process with clear, communicated criteria addresses concerns of unfair treatment, helping to reduce turnover and improve organizational commitment. While salary increases and work-life balance improvements are important, fairness in key processes is crucial for addressing justice perceptions.

406. A nurse executive notices that staff nurses often go above and beyond their job descriptions by voluntarily mentoring new nurses and participating in quality improvement initiatives. Which concept best explains these behaviors?
a. Role ambiguity in nursing roles.
b. Psychological contract breach leading to increased effort.
c. Organizational citizenship behaviors (OCBs) enhancing team effectiveness.
d. Power distance reducing formal expectations of performance.

Answer: c. Organizational citizenship behaviors (OCBs) enhancing team effectiveness. Explanation: Organizational citizenship behaviors (OCBs) are discretionary actions by employees that go beyond their formal job descriptions, such as mentoring and participating in initiatives. These behaviors contribute to team effectiveness and overall organizational performance, reflecting a positive work environment and strong organizational commitment.

407. A nurse executive is concerned about the impact of a recent psychological contract breach, where the organization failed to deliver on promised career advancement opportunities. Which of the following outcomes is most likely to result from this breach?
a. Increased employee engagement and willingness to work overtime.
b. Enhanced trust in organizational leadership.
c. Decreased job satisfaction and organizational commitment.
d. Improvement in team collaboration and communication.

Answer: c. Decreased job satisfaction and organizational commitment. Explanation: Psychological contract breaches occur when employees perceive that the organization has failed to fulfill promised obligations, leading to decreased job satisfaction, reduced organizational commitment, and potentially higher turnover. Such breaches can erode trust and negatively impact the employee-employer relationship.

408. In an effort to promote organizational citizenship behaviors (OCBs) among staff, a nurse executive introduces a recognition program that rewards employees who demonstrate exceptional teamwork and initiative. Which of the following outcomes would be the most likely result of this program?
a. Increased competition among employees, leading to a decrease in teamwork.
b. A shift in focus from patient care to winning recognition, reducing care quality.
c. Enhanced team morale and a greater willingness to engage in discretionary efforts.
d. Higher turnover rates as employees seek organizations with similar recognition programs.

Answer: c. Enhanced team morale and a greater willingness to engage in discretionary efforts. Explanation: Recognition programs that reward OCBs are likely to enhance team morale and encourage employees to go beyond their formal roles, leading to increased discretionary efforts that benefit the organization. While potential risks exist, well-designed programs can positively reinforce the desired behaviors.

409. A nurse executive is addressing concerns about perceived inequities in workload distribution within a healthcare team. According to the principles of organizational justice, which approach would most effectively improve perceptions of fairness?
a. Reassigning tasks based on seniority to ensure experienced staff handle the most challenging duties.
b. Involving team members in the decision-making process regarding task assignments.
c. Increasing compensation for those with heavier workloads to balance the perceived inequity.
d. Rotating assignments regularly to ensure that all team members experience equal workloads over time.

Answer: b. Involving team members in the decision-making process regarding task assignments. Explanation: Involving team members in decisions about task assignments enhances perceptions of procedural justice, as employees feel their voices are heard and considered. This participatory approach fosters a sense of fairness and ownership, which is more effective than simply rotating assignments or adjusting compensation.

410. A nurse executive is evaluating the organizational culture of a hospital that is known for its hierarchical structure, where lower-level staff rarely question decisions made by senior management. What is the most likely impact of this power dynamic on the organization's overall effectiveness?
a. Improved decision-making speed due to a streamlined hierarchy.
b. Reduced innovation as lower-level staff feel discouraged from offering new ideas.
c. Increased job satisfaction among lower-level staff due to clear role definitions.
d. Enhanced communication flow, as decisions are clearly communicated from the top down.

Answer: b. Reduced innovation as lower-level staff feel discouraged from offering new ideas. Explanation: Hierarchical structures with significant power distances can stifle innovation by discouraging lower-level staff from voicing new ideas or challenging existing practices. This lack of input from frontline workers can hinder organizational adaptability and creativity, negatively impacting overall effectiveness.

411. A healthcare organization is implementing changes to improve psychological contract fulfillment among employees. Which of the following actions is most likely to strengthen the psychological contract between the organization and its nursing staff?
a. Conducting exit interviews with departing staff to understand their reasons for leaving.
b. Regularly communicating progress on organizational goals and how they align with staff expectations.
c. Increasing the frequency of mandatory staff training sessions.
d. Centralizing decision-making processes to ensure consistency in organizational policies.

Answer: b. Regularly communicating progress on organizational goals and how they align with staff expectations. Explanation: Strengthening the psychological contract involves aligning organizational actions with the expectations and perceived obligations of employees. Regular communication about how organizational goals and initiatives align with staff expectations helps build trust and ensures that employees feel their contributions are valued.

412. A nurse executive notices that organizational citizenship behaviors (OCBs) have declined following a restructuring that reduced opportunities for professional development. What is the most likely explanation for this decline in OCBs?
a. Increased job satisfaction due to reduced workload and expectations.

b. A sense of organizational commitment strengthened by fewer responsibilities.

c. Perceptions of a weakened psychological contract leading to reduced discretionary effort.

d. Greater clarity in role definitions leading to a focus on core job responsibilities.

Answer: c. Perceptions of a weakened psychological contract leading to reduced discretionary effort. Explanation: The reduction in professional development opportunities may be perceived as a breach of the psychological contract, leading to decreased organizational commitment and a reduction in OCBs. Employees may feel less inclined to engage in discretionary behaviors when they perceive that the organization is not fulfilling its obligations to them.

413. A nurse executive is tasked with addressing concerns about power dynamics that have led to conflicts within a healthcare team. Which intervention is most likely to equalize power and improve team dynamics?

a. Assigning a mediator to resolve conflicts and enforce decisions.

b. Encouraging open dialogue and shared decision-making among all team members.

c. Restricting decision-making authority to the most experienced team members.

d. Rotating leadership roles among team members to distribute power.

Answer: b. Encouraging open dialogue and shared decision-making among all team members. Explanation: Encouraging open dialogue and shared decision-making helps equalize power within the team by giving all members a voice in decisions. This approach promotes collaboration and reduces conflicts by ensuring that everyone's perspectives are considered, leading to better team dynamics and outcomes.

414. A nurse executive is implementing an Enterprise Risk Management (ERM) framework in a large healthcare organization. Which of the following actions is most critical to ensure the ERM framework effectively addresses risks across the organization?

a. Assigning the responsibility of risk management to the legal department

b. Integrating risk management into strategic planning and decision-making processes at all levels of the organization

c. Limiting risk management activities to financial risks to prioritize resource allocation

d. Focusing exclusively on external risks such as market competition and regulatory changes

Answer: b. Integrating risk management into strategic planning and decision-making processes at all levels of the organization. Explanation: An effective ERM framework requires integration into all strategic planning and decision-making processes across the organization. This approach ensures that risks are identified, assessed, and managed proactively, supporting the organization's overall goals and sustainability.

415. A healthcare organization is adopting a clinical risk stratification tool to enhance patient safety. Which of the following best describes a key advantage of using such a tool?

a. It eliminates the need for human judgment in clinical decision-making

b. It standardizes the identification of high-risk patients, enabling targeted interventions

c. It reduces the overall cost of care by minimizing the need for specialist consultations

d. It focuses solely on the financial risks associated with patient care

Answer: b. It standardizes the identification of high-risk patients, enabling targeted interventions. Explanation: Clinical risk stratification tools help standardize the process of identifying patients at high risk for adverse events. This allows for targeted interventions that can prevent complications and improve patient safety, leading to better outcomes.

416. A nurse executive is developing liability risk reduction strategies for a high-risk specialty, such as obstetrics. Which strategy is most effective in minimizing liability risk in this context?
a. Implementing a zero-tolerance policy for all clinical errors
b. Encouraging open communication and full disclosure with patients following adverse events
c. Reducing the number of high-risk procedures performed in the department
d. Focusing on reducing costs associated with malpractice insurance premiums

Answer: b. Encouraging open communication and full disclosure with patients following adverse events. Explanation: Open communication and full disclosure with patients after adverse events can reduce liability risk by fostering trust and potentially preventing litigation. This approach aligns with ethical practice and can improve patient satisfaction, even in the event of complications.

417. A nurse executive is evaluating the organization's current risk financing strategies. Which approach would best protect the organization from potential financial losses due to liability claims?
a. Self-insuring all risks to save on premium costs
b. Purchasing a comprehensive malpractice insurance policy with adequate coverage limits
c. Focusing on reducing operational costs to offset potential liability expenses
d. Relying on government programs to cover all potential liabilities

Answer: b. Purchasing a comprehensive malpractice insurance policy with adequate coverage limits. Explanation: A comprehensive malpractice insurance policy with adequate coverage limits provides essential financial protection against liability claims. This approach ensures that the organization is safeguarded against potentially significant financial losses, supporting its long-term sustainability.

418. A healthcare system is integrating an ERM framework across multiple facilities. What is the most significant challenge the nurse executive should anticipate in this process?
a. Ensuring consistent risk management practices across diverse organizational cultures
b. Aligning the ERM framework with existing financial reporting systems
c. Limiting the scope of ERM to specific departments or service lines
d. Reducing the number of personnel involved in risk management activities

Answer: a. Ensuring consistent risk management practices across diverse organizational cultures. Explanation: Implementing an ERM framework across multiple facilities requires consistency in risk management practices, which can be challenging due to variations in organizational culture. The nurse executive must focus on fostering a unified approach to risk management that aligns with the overarching goals of the healthcare system.

419. A hospital is using a clinical risk stratification tool to identify patients at risk of falls. Which data should be prioritized when using this tool to accurately stratify risk?

a. Patient age and history of falls
b. Patient satisfaction scores and length of stay
c. The number of medications the patient is currently taking
d. The patient's insurance coverage and financial status

Answer: a. Patient age and history of falls. Explanation: Age and history of falls are significant predictors of fall risk and should be prioritized in risk stratification. These factors provide critical insights into a patient's vulnerability, allowing for the implementation of targeted fall prevention strategies.

420. A nurse executive is tasked with developing a risk financing strategy that balances cost and coverage for a healthcare organization. Which of the following strategies would be most effective?
a. Opting for the highest deductible insurance plan to lower premium costs
b. Utilizing a combination of self-insurance and excess liability coverage to balance risk retention and transfer
c. Eliminating all optional insurance coverages to reduce expenses
d. Relying solely on government-backed insurance programs for risk financing

Answer: b. Utilizing a combination of self-insurance and excess liability coverage to balance risk retention and transfer. Explanation: Combining self-insurance with excess liability coverage allows the organization to retain manageable risks while transferring larger, catastrophic risks to an insurer. This balanced approach helps control costs while ensuring adequate financial protection.

421. A nurse executive is leading an initiative to reduce liability risks in a high-risk specialty such as surgery. What is the most effective strategy to achieve this goal?
a. Reducing the number of surgeries performed to minimize exposure
b. Standardizing surgical protocols and implementing checklists to ensure compliance with best practices
c. Requiring patients to sign additional liability waivers before surgery
d. Focusing on increasing the volume of surgeries to improve staff experience

Answer: b. Standardizing surgical protocols and implementing checklists to ensure compliance with best practices. Explanation: Standardizing protocols and using checklists are proven methods for reducing errors and enhancing patient safety in high-risk specialties. These strategies help ensure that best practices are consistently followed, thereby reducing liability risks.

422. A nurse executive is reviewing the hospital's insurance coverage for cyber liability in light of increased cyber threats. What should be the primary focus when selecting a cyber liability insurance policy?
a. Ensuring that the policy covers both first-party and third-party liabilities
b. Selecting a policy with the lowest possible premium to reduce costs
c. Limiting coverage to data breaches involving financial information only
d. Focusing exclusively on coverage for external hacking incidents

Answer: a. Ensuring that the policy covers both first-party and third-party liabilities. Explanation: A comprehensive cyber liability insurance policy should cover both first-party liabilities (e.g., costs associated with data recovery and breach notification) and third-party liabilities (e.g., legal claims from affected individuals). This broad coverage is essential for protecting the organization against the wide range of risks associated with cyber threats.

423. A nurse executive is tasked with implementing an ERM framework to address clinical and operational risks. Which of the following is the best method to identify and prioritize risks within the organization?
a. Conducting a comprehensive risk assessment that involves input from all levels of staff
b. Limiting the risk assessment to financial risks to streamline the process
c. Focusing exclusively on risks identified by senior leadership
d. Using a standardized risk management software without additional input

Answer: a. Conducting a comprehensive risk assessment that involves input from all levels of staff. Explanation: A comprehensive risk assessment that includes input from all levels of staff ensures that a wide range of risks are identified and prioritized based on their potential impact. This approach fosters a culture of risk awareness and ensures that the ERM framework addresses the organization's most significant risks.

424. A large urban hospital is experiencing significant ED crowding and extended wait times. Which of the following strategies would be MOST effective in improving ED throughput?
a. Implementing a fast-track system for low-acuity patients
b. Increasing ED staffing during peak hours
c. Adopting a hospital-wide patient flow initiative
d. Expanding the physical space of the ED

Answer: c. Adopting a hospital-wide patient flow initiative. Explanation: Adopting a hospital-wide patient flow initiative would be the most effective strategy for improving ED throughput in this scenario. ED crowding is often a symptom of system-wide inefficiencies rather than just an ED-specific issue. A hospital-wide approach addresses bottlenecks throughout the facility, including inpatient bed availability and discharge processes, which significantly impact ED flow. While a fast-track system (a) can help with low-acuity patients, it doesn't address the root causes of crowding. Increasing ED staffing (b) may help but doesn't solve broader hospital flow issues. Expanding ED space (d) doesn't address the underlying causes of delays. A comprehensive, hospital-wide initiative tackles the multifaceted nature of patient flow, potentially reducing ED boarding times, improving bed turnover, and optimizing discharge processes across the entire facility.

425. In implementing a bed management system, which key performance indicator (KPI) would be MOST crucial for evaluating its effectiveness in improving patient flow?
a. Average length of stay (ALOS)
b. Bed turnover time
c. Patient satisfaction scores
d. Staff overtime hours

Answer: b. Bed turnover time. Explanation: Bed turnover time is the most crucial KPI for evaluating the effectiveness of a bed management system in improving patient flow. This metric directly measures the efficiency of the process from when a patient is discharged to when the bed is ready for the next admission, encompassing cleaning, preparation, and assignment of the bed. A reduction in bed turnover time indicates improved coordination and efficiency in bed management processes. Average length of stay (a), while important, is influenced by many factors beyond bed management. Patient satisfaction scores (c) are valuable but don't directly measure operational efficiency. Staff overtime hours (d) may be impacted by bed management but aren't a direct measure of patient flow. Bed turnover time provides a clear, focused metric that reflects the core function of an effective bed management system.

426. A hospital is seeking to improve operating room (OR) scheduling efficiency. Which of the following approaches would be MOST effective in reducing delays and maximizing OR utilization?
a. Implementing a block scheduling system with performance-based allocation
b. Extending OR hours to accommodate more cases
c. Increasing the number of anesthesiologists on staff
d. Standardizing surgical equipment sets for common procedures

Answer: a. Implementing a block scheduling system with performance-based allocation. Explanation: Implementing a block scheduling system with performance-based allocation would be the most effective approach for improving OR scheduling efficiency. This system allocates OR time to surgeons or services based on their historical utilization and efficiency metrics, incentivizing efficient use of OR time. It allows for better planning and utilization of available OR slots. Extending OR hours (b) may increase capacity but doesn't address efficiency issues. Increasing anesthesiologist staffing (c) might help with coverage but doesn't directly improve scheduling efficiency. Standardizing equipment sets (d) can reduce setup time but doesn't address broader scheduling challenges. A performance-based block scheduling system aligns resource allocation with efficiency, potentially reducing delays, improving utilization, and creating a data-driven approach to OR management.

427. In developing a comprehensive discharge planning process, which of the following elements is MOST critical for reducing readmissions and improving care transitions?
a. Providing patients with written discharge instructions
b. Conducting medication reconciliation prior to discharge
c. Scheduling follow-up appointments before the patient leaves
d. Implementing a post-discharge phone call program

Answer: b. Conducting medication reconciliation prior to discharge. Explanation: Conducting medication reconciliation prior to discharge is the most critical element for reducing readmissions and improving care transitions in a comprehensive discharge planning process. Medication errors and adverse drug events are leading causes of post-discharge complications and readmissions. Thorough medication reconciliation ensures that patients have an accurate and complete medication list, understands their medications, and can adhere to their regimen post-discharge. While written instructions (a) are important, they may not be fully understood or followed. Scheduling follow-up appointments (c) is valuable but doesn't address immediate post-discharge risks. Post-discharge phone calls (d) can help but occur after the patient has left the hospital. Medication reconciliation directly addresses a major risk factor for readmissions and complications, forming a crucial foundation for safe care transitions.

428. A community hospital is experiencing frequent ED diversions due to lack of inpatient bed availability. Which of the following strategies would be MOST effective in addressing this issue?
a. Implementing a real-time bed tracking system

b. Increasing the number of ED observation units
c. Adopting a proactive discharge planning process starting at admission
d. Expanding inpatient bed capacity

Answer: c. Adopting a proactive discharge planning process starting at admission. Explanation: Adopting a proactive discharge planning process starting at admission would be the most effective strategy for addressing frequent ED diversions due to lack of inpatient bed availability. This approach focuses on improving patient flow throughout the entire hospital stay, potentially reducing length of stay and creating a more predictable and efficient discharge process. By planning for discharge from the point of admission, the hospital can better anticipate bed availability and manage patient flow. A real-time bed tracking system (a) provides information but doesn't actively improve bed turnover. Increasing ED observation units (b) may help some patients but doesn't address inpatient bed availability. Expanding bed capacity (d) is resource-intensive and doesn't address underlying flow issues. Proactive discharge planning addresses the root cause of bed shortages by optimizing the entire patient journey, potentially reducing unnecessary delays in discharges and improving overall bed availability.

429. In optimizing ED throughput, which of the following process improvements would have the GREATEST impact on reducing patient wait times?
a. Implementing bedside registration for all patients
b. Adopting a split-flow model for patient triage and treatment
c. Increasing the number of triage nurses during peak hours
d. Implementing point-of-care testing for common lab tests

Answer: b. Adopting a split-flow model for patient triage and treatment. Explanation: Adopting a split-flow model for patient triage and treatment would have the greatest impact on reducing patient wait times and optimizing ED throughput. This model separates patients based on acuity and expected disposition, allowing for more efficient use of resources and reduced bottlenecks. It can significantly decrease wait times for both high and low-acuity patients by streamlining processes and reducing unnecessary steps. Bedside registration (a) can help but doesn't fundamentally change patient flow. Increasing triage nurses (c) may speed up initial assessment but doesn't address treatment delays. Point-of-care testing (d) can reduce lab turnaround times but doesn't comprehensively improve overall patient flow. The split-flow model represents a systemic change in ED operations that can lead to more efficient use of resources and improved patient throughput across all acuity levels.

430. A surgical department is struggling with frequent delays and cancellations. Which of the following strategies would be MOST effective in improving OR scheduling efficiency?
a. Implementing a robust pre-operative assessment clinic
b. Increasing the number of available ORs
c. Extending scheduled OR hours into evenings and weekends
d. Hiring additional surgical staff

Answer: a. Implementing a robust pre-operative assessment clinic. Explanation: Implementing a robust pre-operative assessment clinic would be the most effective strategy for improving OR scheduling efficiency and reducing delays and cancellations. This approach addresses many common causes of day-of-surgery delays and cancellations, such as incomplete workups, undisclosed medical issues, or patient unreadiness for surgery. By identifying and addressing potential issues well in advance, the clinic can significantly reduce last-minute changes that disrupt OR schedules.

Increasing available ORs (b) or extending hours (c) doesn't address the root causes of inefficiencies. Hiring additional staff (d) may help with capacity but doesn't solve scheduling problems. A comprehensive pre-operative assessment clinic can improve patient preparation, reduce cancellations, and allow for more accurate scheduling, ultimately leading to better OR utilization and efficiency.

431. In managing patient flow across a healthcare system, which of the following technological solutions would be MOST effective in optimizing bed utilization?
a. An AI-powered predictive analytics system for patient discharge planning
b. A centralized bed management dashboard with real-time updates
c. RFID tracking for patient movement throughout the facility
d. Automated text messaging system for interdepartmental communication

Answer: a. An AI-powered predictive analytics system for patient discharge planning. Explanation: An AI-powered predictive analytics system for patient discharge planning would be the most effective technological solution for optimizing bed utilization across a healthcare system. This advanced tool can analyze multiple data points (e.g., patient condition, treatment progress, historical data) to predict likely discharge dates with high accuracy. This foresight allows for proactive discharge planning and better management of bed capacity. A centralized bed management dashboard (b) provides current information but doesn't offer predictive capabilities. RFID tracking (c) improves patient localization but doesn't directly impact discharge planning. An automated messaging system (d) may improve communication but doesn't provide predictive insights. The AI-powered system's ability to anticipate future bed availability enables more strategic patient flow management, potentially reducing bottlenecks and improving overall system capacity.

432. A hospital is implementing a new care transitions program to reduce readmissions. Which of the following interventions would be MOST effective in ensuring successful transitions of care?
a. Providing patients with detailed written discharge instructions
b. Conducting post-discharge follow-up calls within 48 hours
c. Implementing a transition coach program for high-risk patients
d. Sending discharge summaries to primary care providers within 24 hours

Answer: c. Implementing a transition coach program for high-risk patients. Explanation: Implementing a transition coach program for high-risk patients would be the most effective intervention for ensuring successful care transitions and reducing readmissions. Transition coaches provide personalized support to patients as they move from hospital to home, addressing individual needs, barriers to care, and ensuring understanding of and adherence to care plans. This comprehensive approach goes beyond standard discharge processes to provide ongoing support during a critical period. While detailed instructions (a) are important, they may not be fully understood or followed. Follow-up calls (b) are helpful but provide limited intervention. Timely discharge summaries (d) improve communication with PCPs but don't directly support patients. A transition coach program offers intensive, patient-centered support that can address multiple factors contributing to readmission risk, making it the most comprehensive and potentially effective approach.

433. In optimizing patient flow in a large academic medical center, which of the following strategies would have the GREATEST impact on reducing ED boarding times?
a. Implementing a "discharge by noon" initiative for inpatient units
b. Creating a centralized transfer center for accepting outside referrals

c. Establishing a hospital-wide escalation protocol for bed shortages
d. Expanding the capacity of the post-anesthesia care unit (PACU)

Answer: c. Establishing a hospital-wide escalation protocol for bed shortages. Explanation: Establishing a hospital-wide escalation protocol for bed shortages would have the greatest impact on reducing ED boarding times in a large academic medical center. This strategy creates a systematic, organization-wide response to bed capacity issues, involving leadership at all levels to take immediate action when bottlenecks occur. It allows for rapid reallocation of resources, expedited discharges, and potential repurposing of spaces to meet urgent bed needs. A "discharge by noon" initiative (a) can help with flow but may not be flexible enough for varying daily needs. A centralized transfer center (b) improves external patient flow but doesn't directly address internal bed shortages. Expanding PACU capacity (d) may help with surgical patient flow but doesn't comprehensively address hospital-wide bed management. The escalation protocol provides a dynamic, responsive approach to managing bed shortages across the entire facility, potentially preventing or quickly resolving ED boarding situations.

434. A nurse executive is part of the due diligence team evaluating a potential acquisition of a smaller healthcare facility. Which of the following factors is most critical to assess during the due diligence process to ensure a successful acquisition?
a. The reputation of the acquired facility within the local community.
b. The alignment of clinical practices and protocols between the two organizations.
c. The geographic proximity of the acquired facility to the acquiring organization's headquarters.
d. The number of years the acquired facility has been in operation.

Answer: b. The alignment of clinical practices and protocols between the two organizations. Explanation: During the due diligence process, it is crucial to assess the alignment of clinical practices and protocols to ensure a smooth integration post-acquisition. Discrepancies in these areas can lead to operational inefficiencies, quality issues, and challenges in providing cohesive patient care. While reputation and proximity are important, clinical alignment directly impacts the success of the merger.

435. Following a merger between two healthcare systems, the nurse executive is tasked with developing a cultural integration strategy. Which of the following approaches is most likely to promote successful cultural integration?
a. Implementing a uniform code of conduct across both organizations immediately after the merger.
b. Focusing on identifying and preserving the unique cultural strengths of each organization.
c. Prioritizing the culture of the acquiring organization and requiring the acquired organization to adapt.
d. Minimizing discussions about cultural differences to avoid potential conflicts.

Answer: b. Focusing on identifying and preserving the unique cultural strengths of each organization. Explanation: Successful cultural integration involves recognizing and preserving the unique strengths of each organization while blending them to create a cohesive new culture. This approach fosters mutual respect and collaboration, helping to mitigate potential resistance. A uniform code of conduct or prioritizing one culture over the other can lead to resentment and hinder integration.

436. A nurse executive is evaluating the potential synergies that could be realized from a proposed healthcare system consolidation. Which of the following synergies would most effectively improve patient care quality?

a. Consolidating administrative functions to reduce overhead costs.
b. Integrating electronic health records (EHR) systems to provide a unified patient care platform.
c. Combining purchasing departments to negotiate better prices with suppliers.
d. Reducing the number of clinical staff to eliminate redundancies.

Answer: b. Integrating electronic health records (EHR) systems to provide a unified patient care platform. Explanation: Integrating EHR systems across the consolidated healthcare entities can significantly enhance patient care quality by providing a comprehensive, unified platform for accessing patient records. This integration supports better clinical decision-making, reduces the risk of errors, and improves continuity of care. While cost savings through consolidation are important, patient care quality should be the priority.

437. During the evaluation of a proposed merger, the nurse executive raises concerns about potential antitrust issues. Which of the following scenarios would most likely trigger antitrust scrutiny in the healthcare market?
a. The merger would create the largest healthcare provider in the region, potentially limiting patient choice.
b. The merger involves two organizations with complementary services and no overlap in patient populations.
c. The merger is expected to result in significant cost savings for both organizations.
d. The merger would allow the combined entity to offer a broader range of services.

Answer: a. The merger would create the largest healthcare provider in the region, potentially limiting patient choice. Explanation: Antitrust issues arise when a merger significantly reduces competition in the market, leading to potential monopolistic behavior that limits patient choice and drives up costs. A merger that creates the largest provider in a region could trigger regulatory scrutiny if it is perceived to reduce competition. Mergers with complementary services are less likely to face such issues.

438. A nurse executive is involved in the post-merger integration of two healthcare systems. Which of the following strategies would best facilitate the realization of anticipated synergies?
a. Immediately reducing staff levels to eliminate redundancies and cut costs.
b. Establishing cross-functional integration teams to identify and implement best practices from both organizations.
c. Mandating the use of the acquiring organization's policies and procedures across the merged entity.
d. Delaying the integration of clinical services until all administrative functions have been consolidated.

Answer: b. Establishing cross-functional integration teams to identify and implement best practices from both organizations. Explanation: Cross-functional integration teams bring together expertise from both organizations to identify and implement best practices, thereby realizing synergies that improve efficiency, reduce costs, and enhance patient care. This collaborative approach ensures that the best aspects of each organization are preserved and leveraged during the integration process.

439. A nurse executive is assessing the cultural challenges that might arise during the integration of two healthcare organizations following a merger. Which of the following cultural differences is most likely to impact the success of the integration?
a. Differences in organizational size and market share.
b. Variations in leadership styles and decision-making processes.
c. Discrepancies in the geographic locations of the two organizations.

d. Differences in the types of services offered by each organization.

Answer: b. Variations in leadership styles and decision-making processes. Explanation: Differences in leadership styles and decision-making processes can significantly impact the success of a merger by affecting how decisions are made and implemented across the merged organization. These variations can lead to conflicts and resistance, making it essential to address them early in the integration process. Organizational size, market share, and service offerings are important but less directly impactful on day-to-day operations.

440. A nurse executive is tasked with evaluating the effectiveness of the due diligence process in a recent healthcare acquisition. Which of the following outcomes would best indicate that the due diligence process was successful?
a. The acquisition was completed on time and under budget.
b. No major operational disruptions occurred post-acquisition.
c. The financial performance of the acquired entity exceeded expectations.
d. The integration of clinical services and workflows was seamless.

Answer: d. The integration of clinical services and workflows was seamless. Explanation: A successful due diligence process should ensure that the acquired entity's clinical services and workflows integrate smoothly with those of the acquiring organization, minimizing disruptions to patient care and operations. While financial performance and timelines are important, seamless integration is a key indicator of effective due diligence in healthcare acquisitions.

441. In the context of a proposed healthcare merger, the nurse executive is concerned about maintaining patient satisfaction during the transition. Which of the following actions would most effectively address this concern?
a. Conducting patient satisfaction surveys before and after the merger to track changes in patient perceptions.
b. Delaying changes to patient-facing services until after the merger is fully completed.
c. Communicating regularly with patients about what to expect during the transition and how it will benefit them.
d. Reducing the number of services offered during the transition to simplify operations.

Answer: c. Communicating regularly with patients about what to expect during the transition and how it will benefit them. Explanation: Regular communication with patients about the changes they can expect during the merger, along with an emphasis on the benefits, helps manage expectations and maintain satisfaction. This approach minimizes uncertainty and reassures patients, which is crucial during a transition period. Surveys and operational changes are important, but proactive communication is key to maintaining patient trust.

442. A nurse executive is analyzing the potential financial benefits of a proposed healthcare merger. Which of the following synergies would most likely lead to long-term financial stability for the merged entity?
a. Reducing the overall number of clinical staff to decrease labor costs.
b. Streamlining supply chain operations to leverage bulk purchasing power.
c. Consolidating administrative offices to reduce overhead expenses.
d. Increasing the number of locations to expand market presence.

Answer: b. Streamlining supply chain operations to leverage bulk purchasing power. Explanation: Streamlining supply chain operations and leveraging bulk purchasing power can result in significant cost savings and operational efficiencies, leading to long-term financial stability for the merged entity. While reducing staff or consolidating offices might provide short-term savings, supply chain optimization offers sustainable financial benefits. Expanding locations might increase revenue but also adds complexity and costs.

443. A nurse executive is concerned about the regulatory implications of a proposed healthcare merger, particularly in relation to antitrust laws. Which of the following strategies would most effectively address these concerns during the planning stages of the merger?
a. Engaging legal counsel to conduct a thorough antitrust review early in the merger planning process.
b. Increasing the focus on public relations efforts to mitigate potential public backlash.
c. Expanding the services offered by the merged entity to demonstrate community benefit.
d. Reducing the scale of the merger to avoid attracting regulatory attention.

Answer: a. Engaging legal counsel to conduct a thorough antitrust review early in the merger planning process. Explanation: Engaging legal counsel early in the planning process to conduct a thorough antitrust review helps identify and address potential regulatory concerns before they become issues. This proactive approach ensures that the merger complies with antitrust laws, reducing the risk of legal challenges and delays. Public relations and service expansion are important but do not directly address regulatory compliance.

444. A nurse executive is leading a team to establish research priorities for the clinical nursing department. Which approach is most effective in ensuring that the research priorities align with both clinical practice needs and organizational goals?
a. Setting research priorities based solely on current trends in nursing literature
b. Conducting a Delphi survey with input from frontline nurses, nurse leaders, and key stakeholders
c. Selecting research topics that are easiest to study and publish
d. Focusing on research that aligns primarily with the interests of the nurse executive

Answer: b. Conducting a Delphi survey with input from frontline nurses, nurse leaders, and key stakeholders. Explanation: The Delphi method involves gathering input from a diverse group of experts and stakeholders, leading to a consensus on research priorities that reflect the practical needs of clinical practice and the strategic goals of the organization. This approach ensures that research efforts are relevant and impactful.

445. A nurse researcher is preparing a grant proposal to secure funding for a study on reducing hospital-acquired infections (HAIs). Which element of the grant proposal is most critical to increasing the likelihood of receiving funding?
a. Including a detailed timeline that outlines each phase of the research study
b. Focusing on the theoretical background of HAIs without specifying the research methodology
c. Requesting the maximum allowable budget to ensure all potential costs are covered
d. Using complex, technical language to demonstrate expertise in the subject matter

Answer: a. Including a detailed timeline that outlines each phase of the research study. Explanation: A detailed timeline is essential in a grant proposal as it demonstrates the feasibility and planning of the research project.

Funders need to see that the research can be completed within a reasonable timeframe and that the investigator has considered the logistical aspects of the study.

446. A nurse executive is developing a strategy to disseminate the findings of a recent nursing research project. Which dissemination method would be most effective for reaching both academic audiences and clinical practitioners?
a. Publishing the research in a high-impact peer-reviewed nursing journal
b. Presenting the findings at a local nursing conference attended only by clinical staff
c. Posting a summary of the findings on the hospital's internal website
d. Creating a research blog focused on the details of the study methodology

Answer: a. Publishing the research in a high-impact peer-reviewed nursing journal. Explanation: Publishing in a high-impact peer-reviewed journal ensures that the research reaches a wide audience, including both academics and clinical practitioners. This method provides credibility and facilitates the integration of research findings into evidence-based practice across various settings.

447. A nurse executive wants to build research capacity within the clinical nursing environment. Which of the following initiatives is most likely to foster a research culture among clinical nurses?
a. Mandating that all nurses participate in research activities regardless of interest or experience
b. Providing funding and protected time for clinical nurses to engage in research projects
c. Focusing research activities exclusively on senior nursing staff with advanced degrees
d. Limiting research opportunities to nurses in leadership positions to ensure control over outcomes

Answer: b. Providing funding and protected time for clinical nurses to engage in research projects. Explanation: Funding and protected time are essential to building research capacity, as they allow nurses to engage in research without compromising their clinical responsibilities. This support encourages participation and fosters a culture where research is valued as a critical component of nursing practice.

448. A nurse researcher has completed a study on the impact of nurse-patient ratios on patient outcomes. What is the most effective knowledge translation strategy to ensure the findings are implemented into clinical practice?
a. Holding a single seminar for nurse leaders to discuss the research findings
b. Developing a comprehensive implementation plan that includes staff education, policy revisions, and continuous monitoring of outcomes
c. Publishing the study in an academic journal without further action
d. Emailing the study's abstract to all nursing staff with a recommendation to read the full article

Answer: b. Developing a comprehensive implementation plan that includes staff education, policy revisions, and continuous monitoring of outcomes. Explanation: Knowledge translation involves more than just disseminating findings; it requires a strategic plan to integrate research into practice. By combining education, policy changes, and ongoing monitoring, the findings are more likely to be successfully adopted in clinical settings.

449. A nurse executive is leading a team in writing a grant proposal to fund a multi-site research project. What is the most critical factor to address when describing the project's significance in the proposal?
a. The potential for the project to generate future research opportunities
b. The alignment of the project with national health priorities and its potential to improve patient outcomes
c. The personal interest and expertise of the principal investigator in the research topic
d. The likelihood of the project receiving additional funding from other sources

Answer: b. The alignment of the project with national health priorities and its potential to improve patient outcomes. Explanation: Funders prioritize projects that address critical health issues and have the potential to significantly impact patient outcomes. Demonstrating alignment with national priorities and emphasizing the expected benefits for patients will make the proposal more compelling and likely to receive funding.

450. A healthcare organization is aiming to increase nursing participation in research. Which strategy is most effective in promoting sustained nurse engagement in research activities?
a. Requiring all nurses to conduct research as part of their annual performance evaluation
b. Establishing a mentorship program that pairs experienced nurse researchers with novice nurses interested in research
c. Offering financial incentives only to nurses who publish their research in top-tier journals
d. Limiting research activities to designated research units within the organization

Answer: b. Establishing a mentorship program that pairs experienced nurse researchers with novice nurses interested in research. Explanation: Mentorship programs help novice nurses develop research skills and build confidence. By pairing them with experienced researchers, the organization fosters a supportive environment that encourages ongoing participation in research, ultimately integrating it into the culture of nursing practice.

451. A nurse executive is preparing to submit a grant application for a project aimed at improving chronic disease management in underserved communities. What is the most important factor to emphasize in the grant application's budget justification?
a. The need for top-of-the-line equipment to ensure the success of the project
b. The alignment of the budget with the project's goals and the cost-effectiveness of the proposed activities
c. The inclusion of contingency funds to cover unexpected expenses
d. The potential for the project to generate revenue for the organization

Answer: b. The alignment of the budget with the project's goals and the cost-effectiveness of the proposed activities. Explanation: A well-justified budget demonstrates that the funds requested are directly tied to achieving the project's objectives and that the resources will be used efficiently. This alignment is crucial for convincing funders that the project is feasible and that their investment will be used effectively.

452. A nurse researcher is planning to disseminate the findings of a study on nurse burnout across multiple hospital units. Which dissemination strategy would be most effective for influencing policy changes within the organization?
a. Presenting the findings at an external nursing conference
b. Publishing the study in a specialty-focused academic journal

c. Preparing a policy brief for the hospital's leadership team that includes actionable recommendations based on the research findings

d. Sharing the findings on social media platforms to raise public awareness

Answer: c. Preparing a policy brief for the hospital's leadership team that includes actionable recommendations based on the research findings. Explanation: A policy brief tailored for the leadership team is an effective way to translate research findings into actionable steps that can influence organizational policy. This approach ensures that decision-makers are informed of the research's implications and are provided with specific recommendations for implementation.

453. A nurse executive is focused on building a robust research infrastructure within the nursing department. Which action is most likely to achieve this goal?

a. Developing a centralized research office that provides support for all nursing research activities, including grant writing, data analysis, and dissemination

b. Encouraging individual nurses to pursue research projects independently without formal organizational support

c. Prioritizing research topics that align with the executive team's interests, regardless of clinical relevance

d. Limiting research activities to the most experienced nursing staff to ensure high-quality outcomes

Answer: a. Developing a centralized research office that provides support for all nursing research activities, including grant writing, data analysis, and dissemination. Explanation: A centralized research office provides essential resources and support, facilitating the development and execution of research projects. This infrastructure promotes a systematic approach to research, enhances collaboration, and increases the likelihood of successful outcomes and sustained research activity within the organization.

454. A healthcare organization is conducting a risk analysis as required by the HIPAA Security Rule. Which of the following approaches would be MOST comprehensive in identifying potential vulnerabilities?

a. Reviewing past security incident reports

b. Conducting penetration testing of network systems

c. Analyzing the entire data lifecycle across all systems and processes

d. Surveying staff about their cybersecurity concerns

Answer: c. Analyzing the entire data lifecycle across all systems and processes. Explanation: Analyzing the entire data lifecycle across all systems and processes provides the most comprehensive approach to identifying potential vulnerabilities in a HIPAA Security Rule risk analysis. This method examines how protected health information (PHI) is created, received, maintained, and transmitted throughout the organization, covering all potential points of exposure or breach. Reviewing past incidents (a) is useful but may miss new or evolving threats. Penetration testing (b) is valuable for network security but doesn't address all aspects of data handling. Staff surveys (d) can provide insights but may miss technical vulnerabilities. The data lifecycle analysis ensures a thorough examination of all potential risks to PHI, aligning closely with HIPAA's requirement for a comprehensive risk analysis.

455. In developing an incident response plan for data breaches, which of the following elements is MOST critical for ensuring timely and effective response?

a. Detailed procedures for notifying affected individuals

b. Clear roles and responsibilities for the incident response team

c. A comprehensive list of all potential breach scenarios

d. Procedures for preserving evidence for potential legal action

Answer: b. Clear roles and responsibilities for the incident response team. Explanation: Clear roles and responsibilities for the incident response team are the most critical element for ensuring timely and effective response to data breaches. This clarity enables swift, coordinated action when a breach occurs, with each team member understanding their specific duties and authority. While notification procedures (a) are important, they come after the initial response. A list of potential scenarios (c) can be helpful but may not cover all possibilities and doesn't guide immediate action. Evidence preservation (d) is crucial but secondary to the initial response. Well-defined roles and responsibilities form the foundation of an effective incident response, allowing for rapid mobilization and decision-making in the critical early stages of breach management.

456. A hospital is implementing a mobile device management (MDM) solution for clinical environments. Which of the following features would be MOST effective in protecting patient data on mobile devices?

a. Mandatory complex passwords for all devices

b. Remote wipe capability for lost or stolen devices

c. Encryption of all data stored on the device

d. Restriction of app installations to an approved list

Answer: c. Encryption of all data stored on the device. Explanation: Encryption of all data stored on the device is the most effective feature for protecting patient data in a mobile device management solution for clinical environments. Encryption ensures that even if a device is lost, stolen, or compromised, the data remains unreadable and protected. While complex passwords (a) are important, they can be bypassed if a device is physically compromised. Remote wipe capability (b) is useful but requires timely action and may not protect data before the wipe occurs. App restriction (d) helps prevent malware but doesn't directly protect stored data. Encryption provides a constant layer of protection for all data on the device, aligning with HIPAA requirements for data security and offering the strongest safeguard against unauthorized access to patient information.

457. In designing social engineering awareness training for healthcare staff, which of the following approaches would be MOST effective in changing behavior and reducing vulnerabilities?

a. Monthly email bulletins with cybersecurity tips

b. Annual mandatory online training modules

c. Interactive simulations of common social engineering attacks

d. Posters and visual reminders in staff areas

Answer: c. Interactive simulations of common social engineering attacks. Explanation: Interactive simulations of common social engineering attacks would be the most effective approach for changing behavior and reducing vulnerabilities in healthcare staff. This method provides hands-on experience in recognizing and responding to real-world social engineering tactics, allowing staff to practice their skills in a safe environment. Monthly email bulletins (a) provide information but may not be engaging or retained. Annual online modules (b) offer comprehensive information but may not translate to daily practice. Posters and reminders (d) can reinforce concepts but don't provide active learning. Interactive simulations engage staff more deeply, creating memorable experiences that are more likely to translate into improved awareness and behavior in real-world situations, making them particularly effective for addressing the human element of cybersecurity.

458. A healthcare organization has experienced a ransomware attack. According to HIPAA breach notification rules, under what circumstances must the organization notify the Department of Health and Human Services (HHS) within 60 days?
a. If the attack affected more than 500 individuals
b. If any protected health information was encrypted
c. If the ransom was paid to recover the data
d. If the attack originated from outside the United States

Answer: a. If the attack affected more than 500 individuals. Explanation: Under HIPAA breach notification rules, a healthcare organization must notify the Department of Health and Human Services (HHS) within 60 days if a breach affects more than 500 individuals. This requirement ensures that significant breaches are promptly reported to the appropriate authorities. The encryption of PHI (b) during a ransomware attack doesn't negate the need for notification if access to the data was compromised. Whether a ransom was paid (c) or the origin of the attack (d) don't determine the notification requirement. The 500-individual threshold is a key criterion in HIPAA's tiered approach to breach notification, with larger breaches requiring more immediate and comprehensive reporting to HHS.

459. In conducting a HIPAA Security Rule risk analysis, which of the following threat sources should be given the HIGHEST priority in a healthcare setting?
a. Natural disasters affecting IT infrastructure
b. Insider threats from authorized users
c. State-sponsored cyberattacks
d. Malware and ransomware attacks

Answer: b. Insider threats from authorized users. Explanation: Insider threats from authorized users should be given the highest priority in a HIPAA Security Rule risk analysis for healthcare settings. While all listed threats are significant, insider threats pose a unique and often underestimated risk. Authorized users have legitimate access to sensitive data and systems, making their potential for causing harm, whether intentional or accidental, particularly high. Natural disasters (a) are important but often have established mitigation strategies. State-sponsored attacks (c) are serious but less common than insider threats. Malware and ransomware (d) are frequent but can often be mitigated with technical controls. Insider threats require a combination of technical, administrative, and physical safeguards, making them complex to address and critical to prioritize in risk analysis and mitigation strategies.

460. A hospital is implementing a Bring Your Own Device (BYOD) policy for clinical staff. Which of the following measures would be MOST effective in ensuring HIPAA compliance while allowing for the benefits of BYOD?
a. Requiring staff to sign a detailed acceptable use policy
b. Implementing a mobile device management (MDM) solution with containerization
c. Restricting BYOD use to non-clinical areas of the hospital
d. Mandating the use of a specific brand of devices for all staff

Answer: b. Implementing a mobile device management (MDM) solution with containerization. Explanation: Implementing a mobile device management (MDM) solution with containerization would be the most effective measure for ensuring HIPAA compliance in a BYOD environment. Containerization creates a secure, isolated environment on the device for work-related applications and data, separating it from personal use. This approach allows for strong security controls over protected health information while maintaining user privacy and device functionality. An acceptable use policy (a) is important but doesn't provide technical enforcement. Restricting BYOD to non-clinical areas (c) limits its benefits and may lead to policy violations. Mandating specific devices (d) defeats the purpose of BYOD and may be impractical. MDM with containerization offers a balanced solution that addresses security, compliance, and usability concerns in a BYOD healthcare setting.

461. In developing an incident response plan for a potential data breach, which of the following steps should be prioritized IMMEDIATELY after discovering a breach?
a. Notifying affected individuals
b. Conducting a thorough investigation to determine the cause
c. Containing and mitigating the breach to prevent further data loss
d. Preparing a public statement and media response

Answer: c. Containing and mitigating the breach to prevent further data loss. Explanation: Containing and mitigating the breach to prevent further data loss should be the immediate priority after discovering a potential data breach. This step is crucial to limit the scope and impact of the breach, potentially reducing harm to individuals and the organization. While all listed steps are important, they should follow initial containment efforts. Notifying individuals (a) is necessary but premature before understanding the breach's extent. A thorough investigation (b) is crucial but should not delay immediate containment actions. Preparing a public statement (d) is important for larger breaches but comes after initial response and assessment. The priority on containment aligns with best practices in incident response, focusing first on stopping ongoing data loss before moving to other critical steps.

462. A healthcare organization is conducting social engineering awareness training. Which of the following training scenarios would be MOST effective in preparing staff to recognize and respond to phishing attempts?
a. A lecture on the different types of phishing attacks
b. An email-based simulation of a phishing attack
c. A quiz on identifying suspicious email characteristics
d. A demonstration of how hackers create phishing emails

Answer: b. An email-based simulation of a phishing attack. Explanation: An email-based simulation of a phishing attack would be the most effective training scenario for preparing staff to recognize and respond to phishing attempts. This approach provides hands-on, realistic experience in identifying and handling phishing emails in a safe, controlled environment. It allows staff to apply their knowledge in a practical setting, reinforcing learning through active engagement. A lecture (a) provides information but lacks practical application. A quiz (c) tests knowledge but doesn't simulate real-world conditions. A demonstration of hacker techniques (d) is informative but doesn't directly practice response skills. The simulation approach combines education with practical experience, making it more likely that staff will recognize and appropriately respond to actual phishing attempts in their daily work.

463. In implementing mobile device security measures, which of the following strategies would be MOST effective in preventing unauthorized access to protected health information (PHI) on lost or stolen devices?
a. Requiring complex passcodes for all devices

b. Implementing remote tracking and location services
c. Enforcing automatic data wiping after failed login attempts
d. Using biometric authentication for device access

Answer: c. Enforcing automatic data wiping after failed login attempts. Explanation: Enforcing automatic data wiping after a specified number of failed login attempts would be the most effective strategy for preventing unauthorized access to PHI on lost or stolen mobile devices. This measure ensures that even if a device falls into the wrong hands, the sensitive data it contains becomes inaccessible after repeated failed access attempts, providing a last line of defense against data breaches. While complex passcodes (a) are important, they can potentially be bypassed. Remote tracking (b) helps locate devices but doesn't prevent data access if the device is found. Biometric authentication (d) enhances security but can be compromised in some scenarios. Automatic data wiping provides a failsafe that renders the data unrecoverable, aligning with HIPAA's requirements for protecting PHI from unauthorized access, even in worst-case scenarios of device loss or theft.

464. A nurse executive is evaluating the effectiveness of a care coordination model designed for patients with complex chronic conditions. Which of the following outcomes would best indicate the success of the model?
a. An increase in patient satisfaction scores related to communication.
b. A reduction in emergency department visits and hospital readmissions.
c. An increase in the number of care coordination meetings held monthly.
d. A decrease in the average length of stay for hospitalized patients.

Answer: b. A reduction in emergency department visits and hospital readmissions. Explanation: The success of a care coordination model for complex chronic conditions is best indicated by a reduction in emergency department visits and hospital readmissions, as these outcomes reflect improved management of patients' conditions and better coordination of care across different settings. Patient satisfaction and length of stay are important but less directly related to the effectiveness of care coordination.

465. A nurse executive is implementing a transitional care intervention aimed at reducing readmissions among elderly patients discharged from the hospital. Which of the following strategies would be most effective in achieving this goal?
a. Scheduling follow-up appointments with primary care providers before discharge.
b. Providing patients with detailed written discharge instructions.
c. Offering post-discharge home visits by a multidisciplinary team.
d. Ensuring that patients receive a follow-up phone call within 48 hours of discharge.

Answer: c. Offering post-discharge home visits by a multidisciplinary team. Explanation: Post-discharge home visits by a multidisciplinary team are highly effective in reducing readmissions, as they allow for a comprehensive assessment of the patient's environment, adherence to treatment, and early identification of potential issues. While follow-up appointments, written instructions, and phone calls are helpful, home visits provide a more thorough and proactive approach.

466. A nurse executive is concerned about the workload of case managers who are managing a large number of patients. Which strategy would best optimize case management caseloads while maintaining high-quality care?

a. Assigning caseloads based on the geographic location of patients to reduce travel time.
b. Prioritizing high-risk patients for intensive case management and reducing the caseload for those with fewer needs.
c. Increasing the number of case managers to ensure each manager has a smaller caseload.
d. Utilizing a standardized time-based model where each case manager has a similar number of hours allocated per patient.

Answer: b. Prioritizing high-risk patients for intensive case management and reducing the caseload for those with fewer needs. Explanation: Optimizing caseloads by prioritizing high-risk patients ensures that case managers focus their efforts on those who need the most intensive care, allowing for more effective management of resources. This strategy balances workload while maintaining quality care, unlike simply increasing staff or using a time-based model that may not reflect patient needs.

467. A nurse executive is overseeing the development of an interdisciplinary care planning process for patients with multiple chronic conditions. Which of the following tools would best support effective interdisciplinary care planning?
a. A standardized care pathway that all team members must follow.
b. A shared electronic health record (EHR) system that facilitates real-time communication and updates among team members.
c. A checklist to ensure all team members attend every care planning meeting.
d. A weekly report summarizing each patient's progress and care plan.

Answer: b. A shared electronic health record (EHR) system that facilitates real-time communication and updates among team members. Explanation: A shared EHR system that allows real-time communication and updates is essential for effective interdisciplinary care planning, as it ensures that all team members have access to the most current information and can coordinate care seamlessly. While standardized pathways and checklists are useful, they are less flexible and may not fully support dynamic, ongoing communication.

468. A nurse executive is tasked with reducing hospital readmissions by implementing a new transitional care model. Which of the following components is most critical to include in this model to ensure its effectiveness?
a. Assigning a single point of contact for patients post-discharge.
b. Limiting the model to patients with the highest risk of readmission.
c. Providing a financial incentive for patients who attend follow-up appointments.
d. Creating a patient portal for patients to access their discharge information online.

Answer: a. Assigning a single point of contact for patients post-discharge. Explanation: Having a single point of contact ensures continuity of care and clear communication for patients post-discharge, which is critical to preventing readmissions. This person can help coordinate follow-up care, address patient concerns, and ensure that care transitions smoothly from the hospital to the home or another care setting. Limiting the model to high-risk patients or providing financial incentives, while useful, do not address the importance of continuous, coordinated care.

469. A nurse executive is analyzing data to optimize the case management process for patients with complex needs. Which metric would be most indicative of effective case management?
a. The number of cases closed each month.
b. The average length of time each case remains open.

c. The percentage of patients who meet their care plan goals.
d. The satisfaction scores of the case management team.

Answer: c. The percentage of patients who meet their care plan goals. Explanation: The most meaningful metric for evaluating the effectiveness of case management is the percentage of patients who achieve their care plan goals, as it directly reflects the success of the case management process in improving patient outcomes. Metrics like case closure rates or satisfaction scores do not necessarily indicate the quality or effectiveness of care.

470. A nurse executive is implementing an interdisciplinary care planning process for a population with complex chronic conditions. Which of the following practices would best ensure the success of this process?
a. Holding biweekly meetings where all care team members review and update the care plans together.
b. Assigning one discipline to lead the care planning process for each patient.
c. Creating separate care plans for each discipline involved in the patient's care.
d. Implementing a rotating leadership model where a different discipline leads the care planning process each month.

Answer: a. Holding biweekly meetings where all care team members review and update the care plans together. Explanation: Regular interdisciplinary meetings where all care team members collaborate to review and update care plans ensure that all aspects of the patient's care are considered and coordinated effectively. This approach fosters communication, alignment, and a shared understanding of patient needs, leading to better outcomes than siloed or rotating leadership models.

471. A nurse executive is exploring strategies to enhance the effectiveness of care coordination for patients with multiple chronic conditions. Which of the following approaches is most likely to improve care coordination outcomes?
a. Implementing a disease-specific care coordination model for each chronic condition.
b. Utilizing a patient-centered medical home (PCMH) model that integrates all aspects of patient care.
c. Increasing the frequency of patient follow-up appointments with specialists.
d. Delegating care coordination responsibilities to individual specialty teams.

Answer: b. Utilizing a patient-centered medical home (PCMH) model that integrates all aspects of patient care. Explanation: The PCMH model is designed to provide comprehensive, coordinated care that integrates all aspects of a patient's health needs, making it an ideal approach for managing multiple chronic conditions. This model improves care coordination by ensuring that all healthcare providers work together to address the whole patient, rather than focusing on individual diseases or specialties.

472. A nurse executive is tasked with optimizing the caseloads of case managers to improve patient outcomes. Which of the following factors should be considered the most important when determining the appropriate caseload for each case manager?
a. The complexity of the patients' needs.
b. The geographic distribution of the patients.
c. The case manager's years of experience.
d. The number of hours the case manager works per week.

Answer: a. The complexity of the patients' needs. Explanation: The complexity of the patients' needs is the most critical factor in determining appropriate caseloads, as more complex cases require more time and resources to manage effectively. Balancing caseloads based on patient complexity ensures that case managers can provide the necessary attention to each patient, leading to better outcomes. Geographic distribution, experience, and hours worked are secondary considerations.

473. A nurse executive is developing a new interdisciplinary care planning tool to be used across the organization. Which feature would be most critical to include in this tool to enhance the coordination of care?
a. A standardized template for documenting patient progress.
b. A feature that allows real-time updates and notifications for all team members.
c. A checklist of tasks for each discipline involved in the patient's care.
d. An option to generate printed care plans for patient review.

Answer: b. A feature that allows real-time updates and notifications for all team members. Explanation: Real-time updates and notifications are critical for enhancing care coordination, as they ensure that all team members have immediate access to the most current information about the patient's care. This feature facilitates timely communication, reduces errors, and improves the overall effectiveness of the interdisciplinary care planning process. Standardized templates and checklists are helpful, but real-time communication is essential for effective coordination.

474. A nurse executive is conducting a service line profitability analysis to determine whether to expand the hospital's cardiology services. Which metric is most critical to include in this analysis to accurately assess profitability?
a. The total number of cardiology procedures performed annually
b. The average length of stay for cardiology patients
c. The contribution margin per cardiology procedure
d. The overall patient satisfaction scores for the cardiology department

Answer: c. The contribution margin per cardiology procedure. Explanation: The contribution margin, which is the difference between the revenue generated by each procedure and the variable costs associated with it, is a key metric in profitability analysis. It helps determine how much each procedure contributes to covering fixed costs and generating profit, making it crucial for assessing the profitability of expanding cardiology services.

475. A nurse executive is evaluating the adoption of a new electronic health record (EHR) system and conducts a cost-benefit analysis. Which factor should be prioritized in the cost-benefit analysis to ensure a comprehensive evaluation?
a. The initial purchase cost of the EHR system
b. The potential long-term savings from improved workflow efficiency and reduced errors
c. The cost of training staff to use the new system
d. The availability of customer support from the EHR vendor

Answer: b. The potential long-term savings from improved workflow efficiency and reduced errors. Explanation: While the initial purchase cost and training expenses are important, the long-term benefits of improved efficiency and reduced errors can have a significant impact on overall cost savings. Prioritizing these factors ensures that the cost-benefit analysis captures the full financial implications of adopting the EHR system.

476. A nurse executive is performing a break-even analysis for a proposed new outpatient surgical center. Which of the following is the most important variable to accurately estimate in this analysis?
a. The projected volume of surgeries performed per month
b. The total number of staff needed to operate the center
c. The cost of medical supplies for each procedure
d. The marketing expenses to promote the new center

Answer: a. The projected volume of surgeries performed per month. Explanation: The projected volume of surgeries is critical in break-even analysis, as it directly affects revenue generation. Accurately estimating this volume helps determine when the center will begin to cover its costs and start generating profit, making it a key variable in the analysis.

477. A hospital's operating budget reveals a significant variance between the budgeted and actual expenses for the emergency department. As the nurse executive, what is the most appropriate initial step to address this variance?
a. Adjust the budget to reflect the higher actual expenses
b. Investigate the underlying causes of the variance by analyzing specific cost drivers
c. Implement immediate cost-cutting measures across the emergency department
d. Reallocate funds from other departments to cover the variance

Answer: b. Investigate the underlying causes of the variance by analyzing specific cost drivers. Explanation: Before taking any corrective action, it is essential to understand the root causes of the variance. Analyzing cost drivers such as patient volume, staffing, and supply usage provides insights into why the variance occurred and helps develop targeted strategies to manage expenses more effectively.

478. A nurse executive is considering the implementation of a new telehealth program and is conducting a cost-benefit analysis. Which of the following benefits should be given the most weight in the decision-making process?
a. The ability to offer telehealth services to more rural patients
b. The initial cost of purchasing telehealth equipment
c. The potential reduction in hospital readmission rates due to better follow-up care
d. The time required to train staff on the use of telehealth technology

Answer: c. The potential reduction in hospital readmission rates due to better follow-up care. Explanation: Reducing hospital readmissions can significantly lower healthcare costs and improve patient outcomes, making it a highly valuable benefit in the cost-benefit analysis. This benefit should be prioritized when assessing the overall impact of implementing a telehealth program.

479. A nurse executive is performing a variance analysis for a new labor and delivery unit. The analysis reveals that actual labor costs are significantly higher than budgeted. Which factor is most likely to contribute to this variance?
a. Higher-than-expected patient volume leading to increased staffing needs

b. Decreased utilization of labor and delivery services

c. A reduction in the average length of stay for postpartum patients

d. An increase in the number of elective cesarean sections

Answer: a. Higher-than-expected patient volume leading to increased staffing needs. Explanation: Increased patient volume typically requires additional staffing, leading to higher labor costs. This is a common cause of variance in labor costs, as more resources are needed to accommodate the higher demand for services in the labor and delivery unit.

480. A healthcare organization is considering launching a new wellness program. The nurse executive is tasked with conducting a break-even analysis. Which of the following is the most critical fixed cost that must be included in the analysis?

a. The salaries of the wellness program coordinators

b. The variable cost of health education materials

c. The cost of hosting wellness events and activities

d. The anticipated savings from reduced employee absenteeism

Answer: a. The salaries of the wellness program coordinators. Explanation: Salaries of program coordinators are a fixed cost that will remain constant regardless of the number of participants in the wellness program. Including these fixed costs in the break-even analysis is crucial to determine the minimum level of program participation required to cover all costs.

481. A nurse executive is evaluating the profitability of the hospital's oncology service line. What is the most appropriate method to assess profitability in this context?

a. Calculating the total revenue generated by the oncology service line

b. Comparing the oncology service line's revenue to that of other service lines

c. Determining the net profit margin by subtracting total costs from total revenue

d. Analyzing patient satisfaction scores for the oncology service line

Answer: c. Determining the net profit margin by subtracting total costs from total revenue. Explanation: The net profit margin provides a clear measure of profitability by accounting for both revenue and costs. This metric allows the nurse executive to assess whether the oncology service line is financially sustainable and contributing positively to the organization's overall performance.

482. A nurse executive is performing a cost-benefit analysis for the adoption of robotic surgery technology. Which cost should be considered a sunk cost and therefore excluded from the analysis?

a. The initial research and feasibility study expenses

b. The purchase price of the robotic surgery system

c. The annual maintenance contract for the robotic system

d. The cost of training surgeons on the new technology

Answer: a. The initial research and feasibility study expenses. Explanation: Sunk costs are expenses that have already been incurred and cannot be recovered. The initial research and feasibility study costs are sunk costs and should not be included in the cost-benefit analysis, as they do not impact future financial decisions regarding the adoption of the technology.

483. A hospital's surgical department has exceeded its budget for supplies. The nurse executive conducts a variance analysis and identifies a significant increase in the use of surgical supplies. What is the most likely explanation for this variance?
a. A decrease in the number of surgical procedures performed
b. A higher-than-expected rate of surgical complications requiring additional supplies
c. An improvement in surgical outcomes leading to shorter procedures
d. A reduction in supply prices negotiated by the purchasing department

Answer: b. A higher-than-expected rate of surgical complications requiring additional supplies. Explanation: Surgical complications often require additional supplies and interventions, leading to increased costs. This is a common reason for variances in supply expenses, particularly in surgical departments where complications can have a significant financial impact.

484. A nurse executive is leading a global health initiative in a developing country. Which cross-cultural leadership competency would be MOST crucial for building trust and collaboration with local healthcare workers?
a. Proficiency in the local language
b. Extensive knowledge of local healthcare policies
c. Cultural humility and openness to learning
d. Expertise in advanced medical technologies

Answer: c. Cultural humility and openness to learning. Explanation: Cultural humility and openness to learning is the most crucial cross-cultural leadership competency for building trust and collaboration in a global health initiative. This approach acknowledges the leader's limitations in understanding the local context and demonstrates respect for local knowledge and practices. While language proficiency (a) is beneficial, it's not as fundamental as the attitude of humility. Knowledge of local policies (b) is important but can be acquired. Expertise in advanced technologies (d) may not be relevant or appropriate in all settings. Cultural humility fosters a collaborative relationship, encouraging mutual learning and respect, which is essential for the success of global health initiatives, especially in diverse cultural contexts.

485. In addressing global nursing workforce migration, which of the following strategies would MOST effectively balance the needs of source and destination countries?
a. Implementing strict quotas on nurse migration from developing countries
b. Developing bilateral agreements for ethical recruitment and skills transfer
c. Offering financial incentives for nurses to return to their home countries
d. Standardizing nursing education curricula globally

Answer: b. Developing bilateral agreements for ethical recruitment and skills transfer. Explanation: Developing bilateral agreements for ethical recruitment and skills transfer is the most effective strategy for balancing the needs of both source and destination countries in nursing workforce migration. This approach recognizes the reality of global mobility while addressing concerns of brain drain. It can include provisions for temporary migration, knowledge exchange, and capacity building in source countries. Strict quotas (a) may be overly restrictive and difficult to enforce. Financial incentives for return (c) can be helpful but don't address systemic issues. Standardizing curricula globally (d) doesn't directly address migration impacts. Bilateral agreements provide a framework for mutually beneficial arrangements that can support health system strengthening in source countries while meeting workforce needs in destination countries.

486. Which Sustainable Development Goal (SDG) most directly aligns with nursing's role in addressing global health inequities?
a. SDG 1: No Poverty
b. SDG 3: Good Health and Well-being
c. SDG 4: Quality Education
d. SDG 5: Gender Equality

Answer: b. SDG 3: Good Health and Well-being. Explanation: SDG 3: Good Health and Well-being most directly aligns with nursing's role in addressing global health inequities. This goal specifically targets health-related issues, including universal health coverage, access to quality healthcare services, and addressing global health threats. While nursing contributes to all SDGs, SDG 3 is most closely tied to the core of nursing practice and its impact on global health. SDG 1 (a) relates to nursing indirectly through social determinants of health. SDG 4 (c) is relevant to nursing education but not as directly to practice. SDG 5 (d) intersects with nursing workforce issues but is not as comprehensive in addressing health inequities. SDG 3 encompasses the breadth of nursing's impact on global health, from primary care to specialized services and public health initiatives.

487. In preparing for global health security threats, which of the following nursing roles would be MOST critical in enhancing a country's pandemic preparedness?
a. Increasing the number of ICU-trained nurses
b. Developing a cadre of nurse epidemiologists and public health nurses
c. Expanding nurse practitioner roles in primary care
d. Training more nurse educators to increase workforce capacity

Answer: b. Developing a cadre of nurse epidemiologists and public health nurses. Explanation: Developing a cadre of nurse epidemiologists and public health nurses would be most critical in enhancing a country's pandemic preparedness for global health security. These specialized nurses play crucial roles in disease surveillance, outbreak investigation, and population-level health interventions, which are fundamental to early detection and response to pandemics. While ICU-trained nurses (a) are important for severe case management, they don't address prevention and early response. Expanding nurse practitioner roles (c) improves primary care but doesn't specifically target pandemic preparedness. Increasing nurse educators (d) is valuable for long-term workforce development but doesn't directly enhance immediate preparedness. Nurse epidemiologists and public health nurses contribute to the core functions of pandemic preparedness: surveillance, prevention, and coordinated response strategies.

488. A nurse leader is developing a global health program focused on maternal and child health in resource-limited settings. Which of the following approaches would be MOST effective in ensuring sustainable impact?
a. Providing state-of-the-art medical equipment to local hospitals
b. Implementing a train-the-trainer program for local healthcare workers

c. Offering free health services through visiting medical teams
d. Developing a telemedicine program for remote consultations

Answer: b. Implementing a train-the-trainer program for local healthcare workers. Explanation: Implementing a train-the-trainer program for local healthcare workers would be most effective in ensuring sustainable impact for a maternal and child health program in resource-limited settings. This approach builds local capacity, empowering healthcare workers to continue and expand the program independently. It respects local expertise while addressing knowledge gaps, promoting long-term sustainability. Providing advanced equipment (a) may not be sustainable without ongoing support and may not align with local resources. Free services through visiting teams (c) offer temporary relief but don't build local capacity. Telemedicine (d) can be valuable but may face infrastructure challenges and doesn't directly enhance local skills. The train-the-trainer model aligns with principles of sustainable development and empowerment in global health initiatives.

489. In addressing the challenges of global nursing workforce migration, which of the following policies would MOST effectively support ethical recruitment practices?
a. Implementing a global nursing licensure system
b. Establishing mandatory service periods in source countries before migration
c. Developing compensation schemes for source countries losing nurses
d. Creating international standards for nursing education and practice

Answer: d. Creating international standards for nursing education and practice. Explanation: Creating international standards for nursing education and practice would most effectively support ethical recruitment practices in global nursing workforce migration. This approach ensures a baseline of competency across countries, facilitating fair mobility while potentially reducing the exploitation of nurses from lower-resource settings. It can help address concerns about quality of care and patient safety in both source and destination countries. A global licensure system (a) might facilitate migration but doesn't necessarily ensure ethical practices. Mandatory service periods (b) may be seen as restrictive and difficult to enforce internationally. Compensation schemes (c) acknowledge the issue but don't address underlying educational and practice disparities. International standards promote a level playing field, potentially reducing brain drain by improving practice conditions globally and ensuring that migrating nurses are adequately prepared for their roles.

490. Which of the following strategies would be MOST effective in strengthening nursing's contribution to achieving the Sustainable Development Goals (SDGs) globally?
a. Increasing the number of nurses in high-level policy-making positions
b. Expanding advanced practice nursing roles in primary care settings
c. Focusing nursing research on SDG-related health outcomes
d. Incorporating SDG-focused content into all levels of nursing education

Answer: a. Increasing the number of nurses in high-level policy-making positions. Explanation: Increasing the number of nurses in high-level policy-making positions would be most effective in strengthening nursing's contribution to achieving the SDGs globally. Nurses in these roles can influence health policy, resource allocation, and strategic planning at national and international levels, ensuring that nursing perspectives and expertise are integrated into SDG-related initiatives across all sectors. Expanding advanced practice roles (b) improves care delivery but has less direct impact on policy. Focusing nursing research on SDGs (c) is valuable but may have limited influence without corresponding policy changes. Incorporating SDG content in education (d) raises awareness but doesn't directly impact policy and implementation. Nurses in policy-making positions can advocate for and shape comprehensive approaches to achieving the SDGs, leveraging nursing's unique insights into health systems and community needs.

491. A global health initiative aims to improve access to mental health services in low- and middle-income countries. Which of the following nursing interventions would have the MOST sustainable impact?
a. Providing online mental health first aid training for community health workers
b. Establishing nurse-led mental health clinics in urban centers
c. Integrating mental health assessment and care into primary healthcare nursing roles
d. Implementing telepsychiatry services with nurses as facilitators

Answer: c. Integrating mental health assessment and care into primary healthcare nursing roles. Explanation: Integrating mental health assessment and care into primary healthcare nursing roles would have the most sustainable impact on improving access to mental health services in low- and middle-income countries. This approach leverages existing healthcare infrastructure and workforce, making mental health care more accessible and reducing stigma by integrating it with general health services. Online training for community health workers (a) is valuable but may face technological barriers and doesn't fully integrate services. Nurse-led clinics in urban centers (b) improve access but may not reach rural populations. Telepsychiatry services (d) can expand access but may face infrastructure challenges and cultural barriers. Integration into primary care aligns with WHO recommendations for mental health service delivery in resource-limited settings, offering a scalable and sustainable approach to improving mental health access.

492. In preparing nurses for global health security roles, which of the following competencies should be prioritized to enhance pandemic preparedness?
a. Advanced clinical skills in critical care management
b. Proficiency in multiple languages for international communication
c. Expertise in epidemiology and disease surveillance systems
d. Skills in managing large-scale vaccination campaigns

Answer: c. Expertise in epidemiology and disease surveillance systems. Explanation: Expertise in epidemiology and disease surveillance systems should be prioritized in preparing nurses for global health security roles to enhance pandemic preparedness. This competency is crucial for early detection, monitoring, and response to potential outbreaks, forming the foundation of effective pandemic preparedness and response. Advanced critical care skills (a) are important for managing severe cases but don't address prevention and early response. Language proficiency (b) is beneficial but not as fundamental as epidemiological skills. Vaccination campaign management (d) is valuable but narrower in scope than overall surveillance and epidemiology. Epidemiological expertise enables nurses to contribute to critical functions such as data analysis, outbreak investigation, and the development of evidence-based interventions, which are essential for preventing and mitigating pandemics.

493. A nurse leader is developing a cross-cultural training program for nurses participating in global health initiatives. Which of the following components would be MOST crucial for fostering effective cross-cultural collaboration?
a. Intensive language immersion courses
b. Detailed study of local healthcare systems and policies
c. Training in cultural self-awareness and reflexivity
d. Comprehensive overview of global health disparities

Answer: c. Training in cultural self-awareness and reflexivity. Explanation: Training in cultural self-awareness and reflexivity would be the most crucial component for fostering effective cross-cultural collaboration in global health initiatives. This approach helps nurses recognize their own cultural biases, assumptions, and worldviews, enabling them to interact more effectively and respectfully with people from different cultural backgrounds. It promotes a mindset of openness, curiosity, and continuous learning, which is essential for navigating complex cross-cultural situations. While language skills (a) are helpful, they don't ensure cultural competence. Knowledge of local systems (b) is important but secondary to self-awareness. An overview of global health disparities (d) provides context but doesn't directly improve cross-cultural skills. Cultural self-awareness and reflexivity form the foundation for developing other cross-cultural competencies, enabling nurses to adapt their approaches and build trusting relationships across diverse cultural contexts.

494. A nurse executive is leading an initiative to increase patient portal adoption and utilization within a healthcare organization. Which of the following strategies would most effectively drive patient engagement with the portal?
a. Requiring all patients to sign up for the portal during their initial visit without further follow-up.
b. Providing personalized training sessions for patients on how to use the portal effectively.
c. Limiting portal features to basic functions such as appointment scheduling to avoid overwhelming patients.
d. Offering incentives, such as discounted co-pays, for patients who use the portal regularly.

Answer: b. Providing personalized training sessions for patients on how to use the portal effectively. Explanation: Personalized training sessions help patients understand how to use the portal, addressing potential barriers such as low health literacy or unfamiliarity with technology. This strategy increases both adoption and utilization by empowering patients to navigate the portal confidently. Incentives and basic features may attract initial interest, but education is crucial for sustained engagement.

495. A healthcare organization is launching a health literacy assessment program to improve patient outcomes. Which of the following approaches would best support the success of this program?
a. Administering a one-time literacy assessment to all new patients during intake.
b. Integrating health literacy assessments into routine care visits with personalized follow-up.
c. Limiting the program to high-risk populations, such as elderly or non-English speaking patients.
d. Providing patients with generic educational materials regardless of their literacy levels.

Answer: b. Integrating health literacy assessments into routine care visits with personalized follow-up. Explanation: Integrating health literacy assessments into routine care visits ensures ongoing evaluation and allows healthcare providers to tailor communication and education to individual patient needs. This approach supports continuous improvement in patient understanding and engagement, which is more effective than one-time assessments or generic materials.

496. A nurse executive is implementing shared decision-making tools to enhance patient involvement in care decisions. Which of the following practices would most effectively support the integration of these tools into clinical workflows?
a. Training clinicians to use the tools only when patients explicitly request them.
b. Embedding the tools within the electronic health record (EHR) system to prompt their use during relevant clinical encounters.

c. Requiring patients to review the tools independently before meeting with their provider.
d. Limiting the use of shared decision-making tools to complex cases with multiple treatment options.

Answer: b. Embedding the tools within the electronic health record (EHR) system to prompt their use during relevant clinical encounters. Explanation: Embedding shared decision-making tools in the EHR system prompts clinicians to use them during appropriate encounters, ensuring that these tools become a routine part of care. This integration supports consistent use and enhances patient involvement in decision-making. Training alone or limiting tool use reduces their overall impact.

497. A nurse executive is working to integrate Patient-Reported Outcome Measures (PROMs) into the care delivery process. Which of the following steps is most critical to ensure that PROMs effectively enhance patient care?
a. Collecting PROMs data at the initial visit and storing it in the patient's chart.
b. Using PROMs data to tailor care plans and guide clinical decision-making throughout the patient's treatment.
c. Providing patients with paper forms to complete PROMs at each visit.
d. Using PROMs data solely for research purposes to identify trends in patient outcomes.

Answer: b. Using PROMs data to tailor care plans and guide clinical decision-making throughout the patient's treatment. Explanation: To effectively enhance patient care, PROMs data should be actively used to inform care plans and clinical decisions, ensuring that treatment is aligned with the patient's reported outcomes and experiences. Simply collecting data without application or using it solely for research misses the opportunity to improve real-time patient care.

498. A nurse executive is tasked with improving the usability of a patient portal to increase engagement among elderly patients. Which design feature would be most beneficial for this population?
a. Including a comprehensive FAQ section covering all possible portal functionalities.
b. Simplifying navigation with larger text, intuitive icons, and clear, step-by-step instructions.
c. Offering an extensive range of features that cater to various health management needs.
d. Requiring multi-factor authentication to enhance security for all users.

Answer: b. Simplifying navigation with larger text, intuitive icons, and clear, step-by-step instructions. Explanation: Simplified navigation with larger text, intuitive icons, and clear instructions is crucial for elderly patients, who may face challenges with vision, dexterity, or technology. This design enhances usability and accessibility, making the portal easier for them to use. While security and comprehensive features are important, ease of use is paramount for this demographic.

499. A nurse executive is reviewing the effectiveness of health literacy interventions in a multicultural patient population. Which of the following strategies would best address diverse health literacy needs?
a. Translating all educational materials into multiple languages without adjusting content complexity.
b. Developing culturally tailored health literacy programs that consider language, cultural beliefs, and health practices.
c. Using a single, standardized health literacy tool for all patients regardless of background.
d. Focusing on digital literacy training as the primary intervention for improving health literacy.

Answer: b. Developing culturally tailored health literacy programs that consider language, cultural beliefs, and health practices. Explanation: Culturally tailored programs that address language, cultural beliefs, and health practices are most effective in meeting the diverse health literacy needs of a multicultural population. This approach ensures that interventions are relevant and accessible, enhancing patient understanding and engagement. Simply translating materials or using a standardized tool may not address all cultural nuances.

500. A healthcare organization is implementing shared decision-making tools to empower patients in their treatment choices. Which outcome would best indicate that these tools are successfully integrated into patient care?
a. An increase in the number of treatment options presented to patients during consultations.
b. Higher patient satisfaction scores related to involvement in care decisions.
c. A decrease in the length of time spent on patient consultations.
d. Improved adherence to treatment plans regardless of patient preferences.

Answer: b. Higher patient satisfaction scores related to involvement in care decisions. Explanation: Higher patient satisfaction scores related to involvement in care decisions indicate that shared decision-making tools are successfully empowering patients to participate in their treatment choices. This outcome reflects that patients feel heard and involved, which is the primary goal of these tools. An increase in options or reduced consultation time does not necessarily reflect meaningful patient engagement.

501. A nurse executive is tasked with increasing the response rate for Patient-Reported Outcome Measures (PROMs) across the organization. Which strategy would be most effective in achieving this goal?
a. Sending PROMs to patients via mail with a request to return them at their convenience.
b. Integrating PROMs into routine clinical visits and discussing their importance with patients during the appointment.
c. Offering financial incentives for patients who complete and return PROMs.
d. Limiting the distribution of PROMs to high-risk patients to focus resources effectively.

Answer: b. Integrating PROMs into routine clinical visits and discussing their importance with patients during the appointment. Explanation: Integrating PROMs into routine clinical visits and discussing their importance with patients directly engages them in the process and emphasizes the relevance of their input. This strategy is more effective than mailing forms or offering incentives, as it aligns PROMs completion with the care process and encourages patient participation.

502. A nurse executive is working on a strategy to increase patient engagement with the portal, particularly in underserved populations. Which approach would be most likely to improve portal adoption in these communities?
a. Offering internet access in community centers and providing onsite assistance to sign up for the portal.
b. Sending detailed email instructions on how to use the portal to all patients.
c. Adding complex health tracking features to the portal to increase its value.
d. Requiring all new patients to register for the portal as part of the intake process.

Answer: a. Offering internet access in community centers and providing onsite assistance to sign up for the portal. Explanation: Providing internet access in community centers along with onsite assistance helps overcome barriers such as lack of technology access and unfamiliarity with digital tools, which are common in underserved populations. This approach directly addresses the challenges these communities face, promoting greater portal adoption.

503. A nurse executive is implementing a new patient portal feature that allows patients to view their lab results in real time. Which measure would best evaluate the impact of this feature on patient engagement?
a. The number of patients who log into the portal to view their lab results within 24 hours of availability.
b. The overall increase in patient portal registrations after the feature is introduced.
c. The reduction in phone calls to the lab results department requesting information.
d. The average time patients spend on the portal after the feature is implemented.

Answer: a. The number of patients who log into the portal to view their lab results within 24 hours of availability. Explanation: Tracking the number of patients who log in to view their lab results within 24 hours is a direct measure of engagement with the new portal feature. It reflects how quickly and effectively patients are using the portal to access their health information, which is the primary goal of the feature.

504. A nurse executive is designing a new graduate nurse residency program to improve retention and transition to practice. Which component is most critical to include in the program to ensure its success?
a. A series of online modules covering basic nursing skills
b. A mentorship component pairing new graduates with experienced nurses
c. Mandatory weekly written reflections on clinical experiences
d. A focus on theoretical knowledge over practical skill development

Answer: b. A mentorship component pairing new graduates with experienced nurses. Explanation: Mentorship is critical in supporting new graduate nurses as they transition from student to professional roles. Experienced nurses provide guidance, feedback, and emotional support, helping new graduates build confidence and competence, which can improve retention and job satisfaction.

505. A hospital is implementing a specialty certification support program for its nursing staff. Which strategy would most effectively encourage participation in the certification process?
a. Requiring all nurses to obtain specialty certification as a condition of employment
b. Offering financial incentives such as reimbursement for certification exam fees and bonuses for certification achievement
c. Limiting certification opportunities to senior nursing staff to maintain high standards
d. Providing mandatory certification review courses during work hours

Answer: b. Offering financial incentives such as reimbursement for certification exam fees and bonuses for certification achievement. Explanation: Financial incentives help reduce barriers to obtaining certification, making it more accessible and appealing to nursing staff. Reimbursement for exam fees and bonuses for achieving certification are strong motivators that encourage participation and demonstrate the organization's commitment to professional development.

506. A nurse executive is developing a leadership pipeline program to ensure a steady supply of qualified nursing leaders within the organization. Which approach is most effective for identifying high-potential candidates for leadership roles?

a. Selecting candidates based solely on years of experience in the organization

b. Implementing a formal talent review process that includes performance evaluations, leadership potential assessments, and succession planning

c. Choosing candidates who have expressed interest in leadership roles during annual reviews

d. Promoting staff members who have consistently met their clinical performance metrics

Answer: b. Implementing a formal talent review process that includes performance evaluations, leadership potential assessments, and succession planning. Explanation: A formal talent review process allows the organization to systematically assess leadership potential and performance. This approach ensures that high-potential candidates are identified based on objective criteria and are developed strategically for future leadership roles.

507. A nurse executive is tasked with addressing workplace violence in the healthcare setting. What is the most effective strategy to create a safer environment for staff?

a. Installing additional security cameras in high-risk areas of the facility

b. Providing de-escalation training and support resources for staff

c. Implementing a zero-tolerance policy for any form of workplace violence

d. Increasing the number of security personnel on-site during peak hours

Answer: b. Providing de-escalation training and support resources for staff. Explanation: De-escalation training equips staff with the skills needed to manage potentially violent situations before they escalate. Combined with support resources, this proactive approach helps create a safer work environment by empowering staff to handle conflicts effectively and reduce the incidence of violence.

508. A nurse executive is evaluating the effectiveness of a newly implemented nurse residency program. Which outcome measure would best indicate the program's success?

a. The number of participants who complete the program

b. The improvement in clinical competence as measured by pre- and post-program assessments

c. The overall cost of the program compared to traditional orientation

d. The number of nurse educators involved in the program

Answer: b. The improvement in clinical competence as measured by pre- and post-program assessments. Explanation: Measuring the improvement in clinical competence through assessments before and after the program provides direct evidence of the program's effectiveness. This metric shows whether the residency program is successfully enhancing the skills and confidence of new graduate nurses.

509. A nurse executive is developing a support program for nursing staff seeking specialty certification. What is the most important resource to include in the program to ensure its effectiveness?

a. Access to a library of certification study guides and textbooks

b. Monthly meetings to discuss certification goals and challenges

c. One-on-one mentoring sessions with certified nurses in the specialty area

d. An online forum for nurses to share study tips and resources

Answer: c. One-on-one mentoring sessions with certified nurses in the specialty area. Explanation: Mentorship from certified nurses provides personalized guidance, support, and encouragement throughout the certification process. This one-on-one interaction can address specific challenges and increase the likelihood of success, making it a critical resource for the program.

510. A nurse executive is leading the development of a leadership pipeline program focused on increasing diversity in nursing leadership roles. Which strategy is most likely to achieve this goal?
a. Implementing blind recruitment processes to eliminate bias in candidate selection
b. Providing targeted leadership development opportunities for underrepresented groups
c. Offering leadership roles exclusively to internal candidates to maintain consistency
d. Encouraging all nurses to apply for leadership positions regardless of their background

Answer: b. Providing targeted leadership development opportunities for underrepresented groups. Explanation: Targeted leadership development opportunities help address the barriers faced by underrepresented groups, fostering a more diverse and inclusive leadership pipeline. This approach ensures that diversity is actively promoted and supported within the organization.

511. A healthcare organization has experienced an increase in workplace violence incidents. As a nurse executive, what is the first step you should take to address this issue?
a. Develop a comprehensive workplace violence prevention program that includes staff training, incident reporting protocols, and support services
b. Implement a new policy requiring all visitors to undergo security screening
c. Increase the presence of law enforcement personnel in high-risk areas of the facility
d. Conduct a survey to gather staff feedback on their experiences with workplace violence

Answer: a. Develop a comprehensive workplace violence prevention program that includes staff training, incident reporting protocols, and support services. Explanation: A comprehensive prevention program is the most effective first step in addressing workplace violence. This program should include staff training on recognizing and de-escalating potential violence, clear reporting protocols for incidents, and access to support services for affected staff.

512. A nurse executive is tasked with evaluating the long-term impact of a new graduate nurse residency program on nurse retention. Which method would provide the most accurate assessment?
a. Comparing retention rates of program graduates to those of nurses who did not participate in the program
b. Surveying program participants about their job satisfaction immediately after program completion
c. Analyzing the cost-effectiveness of the residency program compared to traditional onboarding methods
d. Monitoring the number of nurses who seek employment outside the organization within the first year post-residency

Answer: a. Comparing retention rates of program graduates to those of nurses who did not participate in the program. Explanation: Comparing retention rates between program graduates and those who did not participate provides a clear measure of the program's impact on long-term retention. This comparison allows the nurse executive to assess whether the residency program effectively supports nurse retention.

513. A nurse executive is addressing increasing incidents of lateral violence among staff in a busy hospital unit. Which strategy is most likely to reduce lateral violence and improve the work environment?
a. Implementing a peer mediation program to resolve conflicts among staff
b. Enforcing a zero-tolerance policy with immediate termination for perpetrators
c. Rotating staff assignments to prevent prolonged exposure to stressful environments
d. Offering anonymous reporting options for staff to report incidents of lateral violence

Answer: a. Implementing a peer mediation program to resolve conflicts among staff. Explanation: A peer mediation program provides a structured, non-punitive approach to conflict resolution, helping to address the underlying causes of lateral violence. This strategy promotes open communication and collaboration among staff, contributing to a healthier and more supportive work environment.

514. A large hospital is implementing a Lean daily management system. Which of the following practices would be MOST effective in promoting continuous improvement and staff engagement?
a. Monthly quality improvement meetings with leadership
b. Daily huddles with visual management boards at unit levels
c. Quarterly performance reviews for all staff members
d. Annual Kaizen events for major process improvements

Answer: b. Daily huddles with visual management boards at unit levels. Explanation: Daily huddles with visual management boards at the unit level are the most effective practice for promoting continuous improvement and staff engagement in a Lean daily management system. This approach provides real-time performance visibility, enables quick problem identification and resolution, and involves frontline staff in improvement efforts daily. Monthly meetings (a) are too infrequent for daily management. Quarterly reviews (c) don't support daily engagement in improvement. Annual Kaizen events (d) are valuable but don't facilitate continuous, daily improvement. Daily huddles with visual boards align with Lean principles of transparency, frequent communication, and empowering frontline staff to drive improvements, making them central to an effective Lean daily management system in healthcare.

515. In applying the Theory of Constraints (TOC) to reduce emergency department (ED) wait times, which of the following would be the MOST appropriate first step?
a. Increasing staffing levels across all ED shifts
b. Implementing a fast-track system for low-acuity patients
c. Identifying the primary bottleneck in patient flow
d. Expanding the physical space of the ED

Answer: c. Identifying the primary bottleneck in patient flow. Explanation: Identifying the primary bottleneck in patient flow is the most appropriate first step in applying the Theory of Constraints to reduce ED wait times. TOC focuses on identifying and addressing the main constraint (bottleneck) that limits overall system performance. By pinpointing this constraint, efforts can be targeted where they will have the greatest impact. Increasing staffing (a) or expanding space (d) may not address the root cause of delays if they're not the primary constraint. Implementing a fast-track system (b) could be beneficial but should follow bottleneck identification. The TOC approach ensures that improvement efforts are focused on the most critical limiting factor in the ED's patient flow, potentially leading to more significant and sustainable reductions in wait times.

516. A nurse executive is using queueing theory to optimize staffing in an outpatient clinic. Which of the following metrics would be MOST useful in determining appropriate staffing levels?
a. Average patient satisfaction scores
b. Utilization rate of clinical staff
c. Number of patients seen per hour
d. Percentage of patients who leave without being seen

Answer: b. Utilization rate of clinical staff. Explanation: The utilization rate of clinical staff would be the most useful metric in determining appropriate staffing levels when applying queueing theory to an outpatient clinic. Utilization rate directly reflects the balance between service capacity (staff) and demand (patient volume), which is central to queueing theory. It helps identify whether the system is understaffed (high utilization, long waits) or overstaffed (low utilization, inefficiency). Patient satisfaction (a) is important but doesn't directly inform staffing needs. Patients seen per hour (c) doesn't account for complexity or quality of care. The percentage of patients leaving without being seen (d) is a symptom of poor queueing but doesn't provide specific staffing insights. Staff utilization rate provides the most direct input for queueing models to optimize staffing levels for efficient patient flow.

517. In implementing a Theory of Constraints (TOC) approach to improve operating room (OR) efficiency, which of the following would be the MOST effective strategy for managing the constraint?
a. Extending OR hours to increase capacity
b. Implementing a block scheduling system
c. Cross-training staff to increase flexibility
d. Optimizing turnover time between surgeries

Answer: d. Optimizing turnover time between surgeries. Explanation: Optimizing turnover time between surgeries would be the most effective strategy for managing the constraint in an OR setting using the Theory of Constraints approach. In many OR systems, the time between surgeries (for cleaning, setup, etc.) often represents a significant constraint on overall throughput. By focusing on reducing this non-value-added time, the OR can increase its capacity without extending hours or adding resources. Extending OR hours (a) adds capacity but doesn't address efficiency. Block scheduling (b) can improve utilization but doesn't necessarily address the core constraint. Cross-training staff (c) enhances flexibility but may not target the primary bottleneck. Optimizing turnover time directly addresses a common constraint in OR efficiency, aligning with TOC principles of maximizing constraint utilization and subordinating other processes to the constraint's needs.

518. A healthcare system is using demand forecasting techniques to optimize nurse staffing. Which of the following factors would be MOST crucial to include in the forecasting model?
a. Historical patient census data
b. Seasonal illness trends
c. Nurse overtime hours
d. Patient satisfaction scores

Answer: b. Seasonal illness trends. Explanation: Seasonal illness trends would be the most crucial factor to include in a demand forecasting model for nurse staffing optimization. This factor captures cyclical patterns in healthcare demand that significantly impact staffing needs, such as flu seasons or seasonal allergies. While historical census data (a) is important, it may not capture future trends or seasonal variations. Nurse overtime hours (c) reflect past staffing inadequacies rather than future needs. Patient satisfaction scores (d) are important for quality but don't directly predict staffing requirements. Incorporating seasonal illness trends allows for more accurate prediction of fluctuations in patient volume and acuity, enabling proactive staffing adjustments to meet anticipated demand. This approach aligns with advanced forecasting techniques that consider cyclical and seasonal factors in healthcare demand.

519. In applying Lean principles to improve medication administration processes, which of the following would be the MOST effective approach to identify and eliminate waste?
a. Conducting time-motion studies of nurses during medication rounds
b. Implementing an electronic medication administration record (eMAR) system
c. Creating a value stream map of the entire medication process
d. Increasing the frequency of medication safety audits

Answer: c. Creating a value stream map of the entire medication process. Explanation: Creating a value stream map of the entire medication process would be the most effective approach to identify and eliminate waste in medication administration using Lean principles. Value stream mapping provides a comprehensive view of the entire process, from ordering to administration, allowing for identification of non-value-added steps, delays, and inefficiencies across the whole system. Time-motion studies (a) can be useful but focus only on the administration phase. Implementing an eMAR (b) may improve efficiency but doesn't inherently identify waste. Increasing safety audits (d) focuses on errors rather than process efficiency. The value stream map aligns with Lean's holistic approach to process improvement, enabling a systemic view of waste and opportunities for streamlining the entire medication process.

520. A hospital is applying queueing theory to reduce wait times in its radiology department. Which of the following interventions would MOST effectively improve patient flow according to queueing theory principles?
a. Increasing the number of radiologists on staff
b. Implementing a priority system for urgent cases
c. Extending operating hours of the radiology department
d. Balancing arrival rates through scheduled appointments

Answer: d. Balancing arrival rates through scheduled appointments. Explanation: Balancing arrival rates through scheduled appointments would most effectively improve patient flow in the radiology department according to queueing theory principles. This intervention addresses one of the fundamental aspects of queueing theory: managing arrival variability. By smoothing out patient arrivals, it reduces peak congestion and idle time, leading to more consistent and efficient utilization of resources. Increasing staff (a) adds capacity but doesn't address variability. A priority system (b) may improve urgent case management but can increase wait times for non-urgent cases. Extending hours (c) spreads demand but doesn't necessarily balance it. Scheduled appointments help match capacity with demand more precisely, reducing overall wait times and improving resource utilization, which aligns closely with queueing theory's focus on optimizing service systems.

521. In implementing a Lean daily management system in a nursing unit, which of the following metrics would be MOST appropriate to display on a visual management board?
a. Monthly patient satisfaction scores
b. Daily patient falls and medication errors
c. Quarterly staff turnover rates
d. Annual budget variance

Answer: b. Daily patient falls and medication errors. Explanation: Daily patient falls and medication errors would be the most appropriate metric to display on a visual management board in a Lean daily management system for a nursing unit. These metrics provide immediate, actionable information that can drive daily improvement efforts and rapid problem-solving. They directly relate to patient safety and quality of care, core concerns for nursing units. Monthly satisfaction scores (a) are too infrequent for daily management. Quarterly turnover rates (c) and annual budget variance (d) are important but don't support daily operational improvements. The focus on daily safety events aligns with Lean principles of visual management, daily focus on key performance indicators, and continuous improvement, enabling the team to identify and address issues promptly.

522. A healthcare organization is applying the Theory of Constraints (TOC) to improve patient flow through its entire system. Which of the following would be the MOST effective method to identify the system's primary constraint?
a. Analyzing patient satisfaction survey results
b. Reviewing departmental budget allocations
c. Mapping the patient journey and identifying the longest queues
d. Conducting staff surveys on perceived bottlenecks

Answer: c. Mapping the patient journey and identifying the longest queues. Explanation: Mapping the patient journey and identifying the longest queues would be the most effective method to identify the primary constraint in a healthcare system using the Theory of Constraints. This approach provides a system-wide view of patient flow, allowing for the identification of the most significant bottleneck that limits overall throughput. Patient satisfaction surveys (a) may indicate problems but don't pinpoint specific constraints. Budget allocations (b) don't necessarily reflect operational bottlenecks. Staff perceptions (d) can be valuable but may be biased or limited to departmental views. The patient journey mapping aligns with TOC's systemic approach, focusing on the constraint that most limits the entire system's performance, which is crucial for targeted improvement efforts.

523. In using demand forecasting for nurse staffing, which of the following techniques would be MOST appropriate for capturing both long-term trends and seasonal variations in patient volume?
a. Simple moving average
b. Exponential smoothing
c. Time series decomposition
d. Linear regression

Answer: c. Time series decomposition. Explanation: Time series decomposition would be the most appropriate technique for capturing both long-term trends and seasonal variations in patient volume for nurse staffing demand forecasting. This method breaks down the time series data into its component parts: trend, seasonality, and residual (irregular) components. It allows for the identification and separate analysis of long-term patterns and recurring seasonal fluctuations, which are crucial in healthcare demand. Simple moving average (a) smooths short-term fluctuations but doesn't distinguish between trend and seasonality. Exponential smoothing (b) can account for trends but doesn't explicitly model seasonality. Linear regression (d) can identify trends but doesn't handle seasonality well. Time series decomposition provides a comprehensive understanding of the various factors influencing patient volume over time, enabling more accurate and nuanced staffing predictions.

524. A nurse executive is tasked with assessing the return on investment (ROI) for a recently implemented telehealth program. Which of the following metrics would be most critical in evaluating the financial impact of the program?
a. The number of telehealth visits conducted per month.
b. The reduction in hospital readmission rates attributed to telehealth follow-ups.
c. The patient satisfaction scores specific to telehealth services.
d. The percentage of patients who continue using telehealth after their initial visit.

Answer: b. The reduction in hospital readmission rates attributed to telehealth follow-ups. Explanation: The reduction in hospital readmission rates is a critical metric for evaluating the ROI of a telehealth program because it directly impacts healthcare costs. By reducing readmissions, the program can demonstrate its financial value through cost savings, which is more indicative of ROI than patient volume or satisfaction alone.

525. A nurse executive is designing a remote patient monitoring (RPM) program for patients with chronic heart failure. Which of the following elements is most critical to ensure the program's success?
a. Selecting RPM devices that are easy for patients to use with minimal training.
b. Ensuring that the RPM program is integrated with the hospital's financial management system.
c. Limiting enrollment to patients who have demonstrated full adherence to previous treatment plans.
d. Setting a fixed schedule for data review, regardless of patient condition or changes.

Answer: a. Selecting RPM devices that are easy for patients to use with minimal training. Explanation: Ease of use is crucial for patient adherence to an RPM program. If devices are user-friendly, patients are more likely to engage with the program consistently, leading to better monitoring outcomes. Integration with financial systems and adherence history are important but secondary to the patient's ability to effectively use the technology.

526. A nurse executive is planning to expand a telehealth program across state lines. Which licensing and credentialing issue is most likely to affect the success of this expansion?
a. The need for physicians to reapply for privileges at each participating facility.
b. Variability in state laws regarding telehealth reimbursement.
c. Differences in scope of practice regulations for nurse practitioners between states.
d. The requirement for dual licensure in the states where the telehealth services will be provided.

Answer: d. The requirement for dual licensure in the states where the telehealth services will be provided. Explanation: Interstate telehealth practice often requires healthcare providers to be licensed in each state where patients reside, which can complicate program expansion. Dual licensure ensures compliance with state regulations, which is crucial for legal and operational success. Scope of practice and reimbursement are important but are secondary to the licensing requirement.

527. A nurse executive is integrating virtual care with traditional in-person care delivery. Which strategy would best ensure seamless coordination between virtual and traditional care models?
a. Using separate electronic health record (EHR) systems for virtual and in-person visits to maintain clear distinctions.
b. Developing standardized protocols for when patients should be transitioned from virtual to in-person care.
c. Prioritizing virtual visits over in-person visits to maximize the use of telehealth resources.
d. Assigning different care teams to manage virtual and in-person patients to avoid overlap.

Answer: b. Developing standardized protocols for when patients should be transitioned from virtual to in-person care. Explanation: Standardized protocols help ensure that patients receive the appropriate level of care, whether virtual or in-person, and facilitate smooth transitions when necessary. This approach maintains care continuity and quality. Using separate EHRs or different teams could fragment care and reduce coordination effectiveness.

528. A nurse executive is evaluating the impact of a remote patient monitoring (RPM) program for patients with diabetes. Which of the following outcomes would most effectively demonstrate the program's success?
a. An increase in the number of enrolled patients using RPM devices.
b. A reduction in the average HbA1c levels among monitored patients.
c. Higher patient satisfaction scores related to convenience.
d. A decrease in the number of in-person visits required for these patients.

Answer: b. A reduction in the average HbA1c levels among monitored patients. Explanation: A reduction in HbA1c levels directly indicates improved diabetes management, which is a key goal of an RPM program. This outcome reflects the program's clinical effectiveness, which is more meaningful than simply increasing enrollment or reducing visits, which may not necessarily correlate with better health outcomes.

529. A nurse executive is leading the implementation of a telehealth program aimed at improving access to mental health services in rural areas. Which of the following challenges is most likely to impact the program's success?
a. The initial cost of purchasing telehealth equipment for providers.
b. Ensuring patient privacy and confidentiality during virtual sessions.
c. The need for specialized training for providers on using telehealth technology.
d. Scheduling conflicts between virtual appointments and in-person consultations.

Answer: b. Ensuring patient privacy and confidentiality during virtual sessions. Explanation: Protecting patient privacy and confidentiality is critical in mental health services, where sensitive information is often discussed. Failure to ensure secure virtual sessions could lead to breaches of trust and legal issues, significantly impacting the program's success. While costs, training, and scheduling are important, privacy concerns are paramount in this context.

530. A nurse executive is exploring telehealth ROI assessment methodologies for a new chronic care management program. Which approach would provide the most comprehensive evaluation of the program's financial impact?
a. Comparing the program's operational costs to those of similar in-person services.
b. Analyzing the reduction in emergency department visits and hospitalizations among program participants.
c. Tracking patient satisfaction and engagement levels over time.
d. Measuring the number of telehealth visits conducted annually.

Answer: b. Analyzing the reduction in emergency department visits and hospitalizations among program participants.
Explanation: By analyzing the reduction in costly emergency visits and hospitalizations, the ROI of a telehealth program can be assessed in terms of direct cost savings and improved patient outcomes. This approach provides a comprehensive understanding of the program's financial impact, beyond operational costs or visit counts.

531. A nurse executive is implementing a virtual care integration strategy for a healthcare system. Which of the following actions is most critical to ensure that virtual care complements traditional care delivery?
a. Training all clinical staff on telehealth technology and patient interaction protocols.
b. Establishing clear guidelines for when virtual care is appropriate versus when in-person care is required.
c. Offering incentives to patients who choose virtual care over traditional care.
d. Developing separate care pathways for virtual and in-person services to maintain clear boundaries.

Answer: b. Establishing clear guidelines for when virtual care is appropriate versus when in-person care is required.
Explanation: Clear guidelines help ensure that virtual care is used appropriately and complements traditional care, rather than replacing it indiscriminately. This approach maintains the quality and continuity of care. Training and incentives are important but secondary to ensuring proper care delivery decisions.

532. A nurse executive is responsible for addressing licensing and credentialing challenges as part of a multi-state telehealth expansion. Which of the following strategies would be most effective in overcoming these challenges?
a. Establishing a telehealth-specific credentialing committee within the organization.
b. Advocating for participation in the Interstate Medical Licensure Compact (IMLC) to simplify licensing.
c. Creating a separate credentialing process for telehealth providers to expedite approvals.
d. Limiting telehealth services to states where the organization already holds licenses.

Answer: b. Advocating for participation in the Interstate Medical Licensure Compact (IMLC) to simplify licensing.
Explanation: The IMLC allows for streamlined licensing across participating states, making it easier for healthcare providers to offer telehealth services across state lines. This strategy reduces the complexity and delays associated with obtaining multiple state licenses, which is more effective than internal committees or separate processes.

533. A nurse executive is planning to implement a telehealth program for managing chronic conditions in an underserved population. Which strategy would best ensure the program's accessibility and effectiveness?
a. Partnering with local community organizations to provide telehealth education and support.
b. Requiring all patients to have high-speed internet access to participate in the program.
c. Offering telehealth services exclusively during traditional business hours.
d. Focusing the program on a single chronic condition to simplify management.

Answer: a. Partnering with local community organizations to provide telehealth education and support. Explanation: Partnering with local organizations ensures that patients receive the education and support they need to effectively use telehealth services, addressing potential barriers such as technology access and health literacy. This strategy enhances program accessibility and effectiveness, particularly in underserved populations.

534. A nurse executive at an academic medical center is exploring an affiliation with a community hospital to expand specialized services. Which factor is most critical to ensure the success of this strategic partnership?
a. Aligning the mission and values of both institutions to create a unified vision
b. Centralizing all administrative functions to streamline operations
c. Limiting the affiliation to shared financial resources
d. Ensuring that the academic medical center maintains full control over clinical decisions

Answer: a. Aligning the mission and values of both institutions to create a unified vision. Explanation: Successful strategic partnerships require alignment of mission and values to ensure both institutions work towards a common goal. This alignment fosters collaboration and trust, which are essential for the partnership's long-term success and for delivering high-quality patient care.

535. A nurse executive is leading the formation of a public-private partnership (PPP) aimed at improving access to healthcare services in an underserved area. What is the most significant advantage of forming a PPP in this context?
a. The ability to bypass regulatory requirements that typically apply to healthcare organizations
b. Access to additional funding sources and resources that can be leveraged to expand services
c. The opportunity to prioritize profit over patient care due to private sector involvement
d. The potential to reduce the public sector's role in healthcare delivery

Answer: b. Access to additional funding sources and resources that can be leveraged to expand services. Explanation: Public-private partnerships allow healthcare organizations to access additional funding and resources from private sector partners, which can be critical for expanding services in underserved areas. This collaboration combines public sector reach with private sector efficiency, enhancing healthcare delivery.

536. A healthcare organization is considering a strategic alliance with a post-acute care provider to improve patient outcomes after discharge. Which key metric should the nurse executive monitor to evaluate the success of this alliance?
a. The number of patients referred to the post-acute care provider
b. The readmission rates of patients discharged to the post-acute care provider
c. The satisfaction scores of the post-acute care staff
d. The financial profitability of the post-acute care provider

Answer: b. The readmission rates of patients discharged to the post-acute care provider. Explanation: Monitoring readmission rates is critical to evaluating the success of a strategic alliance with a post-acute care provider. Reduced readmission rates indicate that the post-acute care provider is effectively managing patients' needs after discharge, contributing to better patient outcomes and continuity of care.

537. A nurse executive is developing a collaborative model with a pharmaceutical company to conduct clinical trials for a new medication. Which ethical consideration is most important to address in this collaboration?
a. Ensuring that the clinical trial is profitable for the healthcare organization
b. Allowing the pharmaceutical company to have sole control over patient selection

c. Protecting patient confidentiality and ensuring informed consent throughout the trial

d. Prioritizing the use of the new medication in the healthcare organization's formulary

Answer: c. Protecting patient confidentiality and ensuring informed consent throughout the trial. Explanation: In any clinical trial, ethical considerations such as patient confidentiality and informed consent are paramount. The nurse executive must ensure that these principles are upheld to protect patient rights and maintain the integrity of the trial.

538. A nurse executive is evaluating a potential strategic partnership with a community hospital that will include shared clinical services and resources. Which risk is most likely to affect the success of this partnership?

a. Differences in organizational culture between the two institutions

b. The cost of implementing shared electronic health record (EHR) systems

c. The distance between the academic medical center and the community hospital

d. The potential for increased competition between the two hospitals

Answer: a. Differences in organizational culture between the two institutions. Explanation: Differences in organizational culture can create significant challenges in strategic partnerships. If the two institutions have conflicting values, practices, or communication styles, it can hinder collaboration and compromise the success of the partnership.

539. A healthcare system is forming a strategic alliance with a medical device company to integrate new technology into clinical practice. What should the nurse executive prioritize to ensure the alliance delivers value to both parties?

a. Negotiating a significant discount on the medical devices to reduce costs

b. Securing exclusive rights to the technology for a competitive advantage

c. Establishing clear performance metrics and outcomes to evaluate the technology's impact on patient care

d. Limiting the partnership to a short-term contract to minimize risk

Answer: c. Establishing clear performance metrics and outcomes to evaluate the technology's impact on patient care. Explanation: To ensure the alliance delivers value, it is essential to establish clear metrics that measure the technology's impact on patient care. This approach ensures that both parties can objectively evaluate the effectiveness of the partnership and make data-driven decisions.

540. A nurse executive is involved in the creation of a public-private partnership (PPP) to build a new healthcare facility in a rural area. What is the most significant challenge associated with this type of partnership?

a. Managing the expectations of multiple stakeholders with diverse interests

b. Securing enough private sector investment to fully fund the project

c. Ensuring that the public sector retains ownership of the facility

d. Recruiting staff to work in the rural facility

Answer: a. Managing the expectations of multiple stakeholders with diverse interests. Explanation: PPPs often involve various stakeholders, including government agencies, private companies, and community groups, each with different priorities and interests. The nurse executive must effectively manage these expectations to ensure the partnership meets its objectives and benefits all parties involved.

541. A healthcare organization is exploring a collaborative model with a pharmaceutical company to provide patients with access to cutting-edge medications. Which strategy should the nurse executive implement to ensure the collaboration adheres to regulatory standards?
a. Allowing the pharmaceutical company to lead the clinical decision-making process
b. Ensuring that all promotional activities related to the medications are approved by the healthcare organization's legal and compliance teams
c. Requiring the pharmaceutical company to provide all necessary training materials for staff
d. Focusing the collaboration solely on high-profit medications to maximize revenue

Answer: b. Ensuring that all promotional activities related to the medications are approved by the healthcare organization's legal and compliance teams. Explanation: Adhering to regulatory standards is critical in collaborations with pharmaceutical companies. The nurse executive must ensure that all promotional activities are reviewed and approved by legal and compliance teams to avoid conflicts of interest and regulatory violations.

542. A nurse executive is negotiating a strategic partnership with a post-acute care provider to improve patient care transitions. What is the most important factor to consider during the negotiation process?
a. The ability to transfer all discharge planning responsibilities to the post-acute care provider
b. Ensuring that the post-acute care provider has experience with the specific patient populations served by the healthcare organization
c. Limiting the scope of the partnership to reduce financial risk
d. Negotiating a fixed fee for all services provided by the post-acute care provider

Answer: b. Ensuring that the post-acute care provider has experience with the specific patient populations served by the healthcare organization. Explanation: The success of a partnership in improving patient care transitions depends on the post-acute care provider's experience with the specific populations served by the healthcare organization. This alignment ensures that the provider can meet the unique needs of the patients and deliver high-quality care.

543. A healthcare organization is considering a strategic alliance with a community hospital to expand access to specialized services. What should the nurse executive prioritize to ensure that the alliance is financially sustainable?
a. Centralizing billing and revenue cycle management across both organizations
b. Setting up a joint governance structure to oversee the alliance
c. Developing a shared risk and revenue-sharing model that aligns financial incentives
d. Prioritizing low-cost service offerings to attract more patients

Answer: c. Developing a shared risk and revenue-sharing model that aligns financial incentives. Explanation: A shared risk and revenue-sharing model ensures that both organizations are financially invested in the success of the alliance. Aligning financial incentives helps both parties work collaboratively toward shared goals, promoting sustainability and long-term success.

544. A hospital is implementing a comprehensive pressure injury prevention program. Which of the following outcome measures would be MOST indicative of the program's long-term success?
a. Reduction in hospital-acquired pressure injury incidence rate
b. Increase in staff compliance with skin assessment protocols
c. Decrease in length of stay for patients with pressure injuries
d. Improvement in patient satisfaction scores related to comfort

Answer: a. Reduction in hospital-acquired pressure injury incidence rate. Explanation: The reduction in hospital-acquired pressure injury incidence rate is the most indicative measure of long-term success for a pressure injury prevention program. This outcome directly reflects the program's effectiveness in preventing new pressure injuries, which is the primary goal of such initiatives. While staff compliance (b) is important, it's a process measure rather than an outcome. Length of stay (c) for existing pressure injuries doesn't capture prevention effectiveness. Patient satisfaction related to comfort (d) is valuable but not specific to pressure injury prevention. The incidence rate provides a clear, quantifiable measure of the program's impact on patient outcomes, aligning with the core objective of pressure injury prevention and the principles of nursing-sensitive outcomes management.

545. In developing a fall prevention strategy for a long-term care facility, which of the following interventions would likely have the GREATEST impact on reducing fall rates?
a. Implementing a facility-wide exercise program
b. Installing bed alarms for all high-risk patients
c. Conducting comprehensive medication reviews
d. Increasing staffing ratios during night shifts

Answer: c. Conducting comprehensive medication reviews. Explanation: Conducting comprehensive medication reviews would likely have the greatest impact on reducing fall rates in a long-term care facility. Medications, particularly polypharmacy and certain drug classes (e.g., psychotropics, antihypertensives), are significant contributors to fall risk in older adults. Reviewing and optimizing medication regimens can address a root cause of falls that affects a large proportion of residents. While exercise programs (a) are beneficial, they may not be suitable for all residents. Bed alarms (b) have shown limited effectiveness in preventing falls and may increase agitation. Increased night staffing (d) can help but doesn't address underlying risk factors. Medication reviews offer a comprehensive approach to fall prevention by addressing a major modifiable risk factor, aligning with evidence-based practices in geriatric care and fall prevention strategies.

546. A hospital is launching a Catheter-Associated Urinary Tract Infection (CAUTI) reduction initiative. Which of the following strategies would be MOST effective in sustaining long-term improvements?
a. Implementing a nurse-driven catheter removal protocol
b. Conducting monthly CAUTI prevention training for all staff
c. Installing antimicrobial catheters as the facility standard
d. Increasing frequency of urinalysis for catheterized patients

Answer: a. Implementing a nurse-driven catheter removal protocol. Explanation: Implementing a nurse-driven catheter removal protocol would be most effective in sustaining long-term improvements in CAUTI reduction. This strategy empowers nurses to assess catheter necessity daily and remove catheters promptly when no longer indicated, addressing one of the primary risk factors for CAUTI - prolonged catheter use. It creates a sustainable, systemic change in practice. Monthly training (b) is valuable but may not lead to consistent practice changes. Antimicrobial catheters (c) don't address duration of use and may lead to antimicrobial resistance. Increased urinalysis (d) may lead to overtreatment of asymptomatic bacteriuria. The nurse-driven protocol aligns with evidence-based practices for CAUTI prevention, promoting timely catheter removal and reducing overall catheter days, which is crucial for long-term CAUTI reduction.

547. In evaluating a pain management quality improvement program, which of the following outcome measures would BEST reflect the program's effectiveness in improving patient care?
a. Increase in the use of non-pharmacological pain management techniques
b. Reduction in average pain scores across all patient populations
c. Decrease in opioid prescription rates at discharge
d. Improvement in patient-reported functional outcomes related to pain

Answer: d. Improvement in patient-reported functional outcomes related to pain. Explanation: Improvement in patient-reported functional outcomes related to pain would best reflect the effectiveness of a pain management quality improvement program in improving patient care. This measure goes beyond pain intensity to assess how pain management impacts patients' ability to function and quality of life, which aligns with contemporary, patient-centered approaches to pain management. Increased use of non-pharmacological techniques (a) is a process measure, not an outcome. Average pain scores (b) don't capture the complexity of pain management goals. Decreased opioid prescriptions (c) may be positive but don't necessarily indicate improved pain management. Patient-reported functional outcomes provide a more comprehensive view of pain management effectiveness, focusing on how pain control translates to meaningful improvements in patients' daily lives and activities.

548. A nurse executive is reviewing data from the hospital's pressure injury prevention program and notices that despite high compliance with skin assessment protocols, pressure injury rates have not significantly decreased. Which of the following actions would be MOST appropriate to address this issue?
a. Increase the frequency of staff training on skin assessment techniques
b. Implement more stringent documentation requirements for skin assessments
c. Conduct a root cause analysis of recent pressure injury cases
d. Purchase advanced pressure-redistribution mattresses for all beds

Answer: c. Conduct a root cause analysis of recent pressure injury cases. Explanation: Conducting a root cause analysis of recent pressure injury cases would be the most appropriate action to address the discrepancy between high compliance with skin assessments and persistent pressure injury rates. This approach allows for a deep dive into the specific factors contributing to pressure injuries despite preventive measures, potentially revealing gaps in the current prevention strategy or identifying patient populations at higher risk. Increasing training frequency (a) or stricter documentation (b) may not be effective if the current assessments are already being performed correctly. Purchasing advanced mattresses (d) may be helpful but doesn't address the root cause of why current measures are ineffective. The root cause analysis aligns with quality improvement principles, providing data-driven insights to refine and improve the pressure injury prevention program.

549. In implementing a fall prevention program in an acute care setting, which of the following interventions would be MOST effective in reducing falls among high-risk patients?
a. Implementing hourly rounding protocols
b. Providing non-slip socks to all patients

c. Installing bed exit alarms for high-risk patients

d. Increasing the use of physical restraints for agitated patients

Answer: a. Implementing hourly rounding protocols. Explanation: Implementing hourly rounding protocols would be the most effective intervention in reducing falls among high-risk patients in an acute care setting. Hourly rounding allows for regular assessment of patient needs, proactive assistance with toileting, positioning, and pain management, which addresses common reasons patients attempt to get up unassisted. Non-slip socks (b) provide minimal fall prevention benefit. Bed exit alarms (c) have not been consistently shown to reduce falls and may increase alarm fatigue. Increasing physical restraint use (d) is not recommended and can lead to other complications. Hourly rounding represents a proactive, patient-centered approach that addresses multiple fall risk factors simultaneously, aligning with best practices in fall prevention and patient safety.

550. A healthcare system is developing a CAUTI reduction bundle. Which of the following elements would have the GREATEST impact on reducing CAUTI rates?

a. Daily review of catheter necessity with prompt removal protocol

b. Use of silver-alloy catheters for all patients

c. Implementing a closed catheter system

d. Increasing frequency of perineal care for catheterized patients

Answer: a. Daily review of catheter necessity with prompt removal protocol. Explanation: Daily review of catheter necessity with a prompt removal protocol would have the greatest impact on reducing CAUTI rates. This practice directly addresses the primary risk factor for CAUTI - the duration of catheterization. By ensuring catheters are removed as soon as they are no longer medically necessary, it significantly reduces the opportunity for infection. Silver-alloy catheters (b) have shown mixed results in CAUTI prevention and don't address duration of use. Closed catheter systems (c) may reduce the risk of contamination but don't impact catheter duration. Increased perineal care (d) is important but less impactful than reducing catheter days. The daily review and prompt removal protocol aligns with evidence-based guidelines for CAUTI prevention, focusing on minimizing catheter use, which is the most effective strategy for reducing CAUTI incidence.

551. In evaluating a hospital-wide pain management program, a nurse executive notices significant variability in pain management practices across different units. Which of the following strategies would be MOST effective in standardizing pain management approaches while allowing for necessary customization?

a. Implementing unit-specific pain management protocols

b. Mandating the use of a single pain assessment tool across all units

c. Developing a tiered pain management algorithm with decision support

d. Centralizing pain management under a specialized pain service team

Answer: c. Developing a tiered pain management algorithm with decision support. Explanation: Developing a tiered pain management algorithm with decision support would be the most effective strategy for standardizing pain management approaches while allowing for necessary customization. This approach provides a structured framework for pain assessment and treatment that can be applied across units, while still allowing for individualization based on patient needs and unit-specific considerations. Unit-specific protocols (a) may perpetuate variability. Mandating a single assessment tool (b) doesn't address treatment variability. Centralizing under a specialized team (d) may not be feasible for all patients and could delay care. The tiered algorithm with decision support balances standardization with flexibility, promoting evidence-based practices while accommodating the diverse needs of different patient populations and clinical settings.

552. A long-term care facility is implementing a comprehensive fall prevention program. Which of the following outcome measures would BEST capture the program's impact on resident quality of life?
a. Reduction in the total number of falls per 1000 resident days
b. Increase in resident participation in mobility programs
c. Decrease in the use of physical restraints
d. Improvement in residents' fear of falling scores

Answer: d. Improvement in residents' fear of falling scores. Explanation: Improvement in residents' fear of falling scores would best capture the fall prevention program's impact on quality of life in a long-term care setting. Fear of falling is a significant factor affecting residents' mobility, social engagement, and overall well-being. Reduced fear can lead to increased activity and independence, key components of quality of life. While reduction in fall rates (a) is important, it doesn't directly measure quality of life impact. Increased participation in mobility programs (b) is positive but doesn't necessarily reflect reduced fear or improved quality of life. Decreased restraint use (c) is beneficial but may not directly correlate with residents' perceptions of safety and well-being. The fear of falling measure provides insight into the psychological impact of the fall prevention program, reflecting how it affects residents' confidence and willingness to engage in daily activities.

553. In developing a pain management quality improvement initiative for post-operative patients, which of the following approaches would be MOST aligned with current best practices in pain management?
a. Implementing standard opioid prescribing protocols for all surgical procedures
b. Focusing on achieving zero pain scores for all post-operative patients
c. Developing multimodal pain management pathways tailored to specific surgeries
d. Prioritizing non-pharmacological interventions over medication management

Answer: c. Developing multimodal pain management pathways tailored to specific surgeries. Explanation: Developing multimodal pain management pathways tailored to specific surgeries is most aligned with current best practices in pain management for post-operative patients. This approach recognizes that different surgical procedures have varying pain profiles and that effective pain management often requires a combination of pharmacological and non-pharmacological interventions. Standard opioid protocols (a) don't account for individual patient needs and may lead to over-or under-treatment. Aiming for zero pain scores (b) is unrealistic and may lead to overuse of pain medications. Prioritizing non-pharmacological interventions (d) over medications may be insufficient for post-operative pain control. Multimodal, surgery-specific pathways allow for comprehensive pain management strategies that can be tailored to individual patient needs while following evidence-based guidelines for different surgical procedures.

554. A nurse executive is leading the establishment of a data governance structure in a large healthcare organization. Which of the following roles is most critical to ensure accountability and oversight in the data governance framework?
a. Data Steward responsible for data entry accuracy.
b. Chief Data Officer responsible for overall data strategy and policy.
c. Data Analyst responsible for generating reports from the data.
d. IT Specialist responsible for maintaining data storage systems.

Answer: b. Chief Data Officer responsible for overall data strategy and policy. Explanation: The Chief Data Officer (CDO) plays a critical role in ensuring accountability and oversight by setting the organization's data strategy and policies. The CDO ensures that data governance aligns with organizational goals and regulatory requirements, making this role essential for an effective data governance framework. Data stewards, analysts, and IT specialists have important functions, but the CDO ensures strategic direction and compliance.

555. A nurse executive notices inconsistencies in clinical data across multiple departments. Which data quality management process would be most effective in resolving these issues?
a. Implementing a centralized data entry system to eliminate duplicate entries.
b. Conducting routine data audits to identify and correct inconsistencies.
c. Restricting access to data to reduce the risk of errors.
d. Training staff on data entry procedures to ensure consistency.

Answer: b. Conducting routine data audits to identify and correct inconsistencies. Explanation: Routine data audits are essential for identifying and correcting inconsistencies in clinical data, ensuring that the information is accurate, complete, and reliable. This proactive approach helps maintain high data quality across departments. While training and centralized systems are important, regular audits directly address the issue of data inconsistency.

556. A nurse executive is tasked with implementing a Master Data Management (MDM) system in the healthcare organization. Which of the following outcomes would best demonstrate the success of the MDM implementation?
a. Increased data storage capacity across the organization.
b. Consolidation of patient records into a single, accurate source.
c. Reduction in the time needed to generate patient care reports.
d. Enhanced security measures for protecting patient data.

Answer: b. Consolidation of patient records into a single, accurate source. Explanation: The primary goal of Master Data Management (MDM) is to create a single, accurate source of truth for key data entities, such as patient records. Successful MDM implementation results in the consolidation of disparate data sources, improving data accuracy and consistency across the organization. While storage, report generation, and security are important, the consolidation of data is the key indicator of MDM success.

557. A nurse executive is reviewing the data lineage for clinical data used in regulatory reporting. Why is data lineage important in this context?
a. It tracks the origin and movement of data, ensuring transparency and accuracy in regulatory reporting.
b. It defines the roles and responsibilities of staff involved in data management.
c. It provides real-time monitoring of data quality metrics.
d. It enhances the speed of data processing for regulatory submissions.

Answer: a. It tracks the origin and movement of data, ensuring transparency and accuracy in regulatory reporting. Explanation: Data lineage tracks the origin, movement, and transformation of data throughout its lifecycle. This transparency is crucial in regulatory reporting, as it ensures that the data used is accurate, traceable, and compliant with regulations. While roles, quality monitoring, and processing speed are important, data lineage is specifically critical for ensuring reporting integrity.

558. A nurse executive is implementing metadata management practices to support regulatory compliance. Which of the following actions would most effectively enhance the organization's metadata management?
a. Standardizing metadata definitions across all data sources.
b. Limiting access to metadata to only senior leadership.
c. Automating metadata collection through real-time data monitoring tools.
d. Storing metadata separately from clinical data to reduce complexity.

Answer: a. Standardizing metadata definitions across all data sources. Explanation: Standardizing metadata definitions ensures consistency and clarity across all data sources, which is essential for regulatory compliance and effective data management. This practice supports accurate data interpretation and reporting. While automation and storage considerations are important, standardization directly impacts the quality and usability of metadata.

559. A nurse executive is concerned about the accuracy of administrative data used for strategic decision-making. Which data governance structure should be prioritized to address this concern?
a. Establishing a cross-functional data governance committee to oversee data accuracy and integrity.
b. Implementing stricter access controls to limit data manipulation.
c. Creating a separate administrative data team to manage and validate data.
d. Increasing the frequency of training for staff involved in data entry.

Answer: a. Establishing a cross-functional data governance committee to oversee data accuracy and integrity. Explanation: A cross-functional data governance committee ensures that data accuracy and integrity are maintained across the organization by bringing together stakeholders from different departments to oversee data management practices. This structure supports collaborative decision-making and consistent data standards. While access controls, dedicated teams, and training are important, a governance committee ensures comprehensive oversight.

560. A healthcare organization is expanding its use of data analytics for clinical decision support. The nurse executive is concerned about the quality of the data being used. Which data quality management process would best address these concerns?
a. Implementing a data cleansing protocol to remove errors and inconsistencies from the dataset.
b. Increasing the number of data sources used for analytics to provide a broader perspective.
c. Limiting data collection to only those variables that are easily measurable.
d. Delegating data quality assurance to the IT department to streamline processes.

Answer: a. Implementing a data cleansing protocol to remove errors and inconsistencies from the dataset.
Explanation: Data cleansing is a critical process that ensures the data used in analytics is accurate, consistent, and free from errors. This process directly impacts the quality and reliability of clinical decision support. While broadening data sources and IT involvement are important, data cleansing specifically addresses data quality issues.

561. A nurse executive is leading the effort to document data lineage for all critical data elements in the organization. Which of the following challenges is most likely to arise during this process?
a. Difficulty in defining the roles of data stewards across departments.
b. Resistance from staff due to the perceived increase in workload.
c. Complexity in tracing data transformations across multiple systems.
d. Inadequate storage capacity for managing large volumes of lineage data.

Answer: c. Complexity in tracing data transformations across multiple systems. Explanation: Tracing data transformations across multiple systems is a complex task, particularly in large organizations with diverse data environments. This complexity makes documenting data lineage challenging, as it requires thorough understanding and mapping of data flows. While role definition, resistance, and storage are considerations, tracing transformations is the most significant challenge in lineage documentation.

562. A nurse executive is developing a data governance framework to ensure high data quality across the organization. Which of the following principles should be the foundation of this framework?
a. Data accessibility and availability for all users.
b. Centralized control over all data management activities.
c. Accountability for data quality assigned to specific roles and responsibilities.
d. Prioritization of financial data over clinical data to align with organizational goals.

Answer: c. Accountability for data quality assigned to specific roles and responsibilities. Explanation: Assigning accountability for data quality to specific roles ensures that there is clear ownership and responsibility for maintaining high data standards across the organization. This principle is foundational to effective data governance, as it drives consistent practices and accountability. While accessibility, control, and prioritization are important, accountability is the cornerstone of data quality management.

563. A nurse executive is evaluating the effectiveness of metadata management in supporting regulatory reporting. Which of the following outcomes would best demonstrate successful metadata management?
a. A decrease in the time required to generate regulatory reports.
b. Improved accuracy and consistency of data used in regulatory submissions.
c. Increased user satisfaction with the data management system.
d. Enhanced security measures for protecting metadata.

Answer: b. Improved accuracy and consistency of data used in regulatory submissions. Explanation: Successful metadata management results in improved accuracy and consistency of data, which is crucial for regulatory compliance. Accurate metadata ensures that the data used in reports is correctly interpreted and aligned with regulatory requirements. While report generation time, user satisfaction, and security are important, accuracy and consistency are key indicators of effective metadata management.

564. A nurse executive is leading the hospital's disaster response team and must implement a triage system during a mass casualty event. Which factor is most critical to consider when utilizing the START (Simple Triage and Rapid Treatment) method?
a. Prioritizing treatment for patients with minor injuries to ensure rapid discharge

b. Assigning the highest priority to patients with the most severe injuries, regardless of survival likelihood

c. Quickly assessing patients' breathing, circulation, and mental status to categorize them based on the urgency of care

d. Ensuring that all patients receive full medical evaluations before triage categorization

Answer: c. Quickly assessing patients' breathing, circulation, and mental status to categorize them based on the urgency of care. Explanation: The START method is designed to rapidly assess and categorize patients based on their need for immediate medical attention. By evaluating breathing, circulation, and mental status, responders can quickly determine which patients require urgent care and which can wait, optimizing resource allocation during a disaster.

565. During a disaster, a nurse leader is assigned to the hospital command center. What is the most important responsibility of the nurse leader in this role?
a. Directing clinical staff to specific patient care areas based on their specialties
b. Coordinating communication between the hospital command center and external agencies
c. Ensuring that all incoming patients are registered and billed appropriately
d. Monitoring supply inventory to prevent shortages during the disaster

Answer: b. Coordinating communication between the hospital command center and external agencies. Explanation: In the hospital command center, the nurse leader's primary responsibility is to coordinate communication with external agencies, such as emergency services, public health departments, and other hospitals. Effective communication ensures that resources are properly allocated, and that the hospital's response aligns with broader disaster management efforts.

566. Following a natural disaster, healthcare workers in a hospital are exhibiting signs of emotional distress. As a nurse executive, which action is most effective in providing post-disaster mental health support for the staff?
a. Mandating participation in group therapy sessions for all healthcare workers
b. Offering confidential one-on-one counseling services and peer support groups
c. Requiring staff to complete mental health assessments before returning to work
d. Providing financial incentives for staff to continue working despite emotional distress

Answer: b. Offering confidential one-on-one counseling services and peer support groups. Explanation: Providing confidential counseling and peer support groups helps healthcare workers process their experiences and access the mental health support they need. This approach fosters a supportive environment where staff can seek help without fear of stigma, promoting recovery and resilience.

567. A mass casualty incident has overwhelmed the local healthcare system, requiring difficult ethical decisions regarding the allocation of limited resources. What is the most ethical approach for a nurse leader to take in this situation?
a. Prioritizing treatment for patients based on their social status and community contributions
b. Allocating resources to those most likely to survive with immediate intervention, regardless of age or social status
c. Distributing resources equally among all patients, regardless of their condition
d. Reserving resources for patients with chronic illnesses who have limited access to healthcare

Answer: b. Allocating resources to those most likely to survive with immediate intervention, regardless of age or social status. Explanation: In a mass casualty incident, the ethical principle of utilitarianism often guides decision-making, where the focus is on maximizing the number of lives saved. Allocating resources to those most likely to survive with immediate intervention is consistent with this approach, ensuring that limited resources are used effectively to save as many lives as possible.

568. A nurse executive is involved in disaster preparedness planning and is tasked with integrating the JumpSTART triage method for pediatric patients. Which scenario would categorize a pediatric patient as a "yellow" or delayed in the JumpSTART system?
a. A child with a respiratory rate of 10 breaths per minute and cyanosis
b. A child with a minor laceration that is controlled with direct pressure
c. A child with open fractures and a palpable pulse but no respiratory distress
d. A child who is unresponsive, apneic, and does not resume breathing after a manual airway is opened

Answer: c. A child with open fractures and a palpable pulse but no respiratory distress. Explanation: In the JumpSTART triage system, a "yellow" or delayed category is used for patients who have serious but not life-threatening injuries and can wait for treatment. A child with open fractures and a stable pulse but no respiratory distress fits this category, as they require care but are not in immediate danger.

569. A disaster strikes during a shift change, causing confusion and uncertainty among staff. As a nurse leader, what is the most effective way to manage this situation to ensure continuity of care?
a. Instruct all staff members to leave the facility immediately to ensure their safety
b. Quickly designate roles and responsibilities based on available staff, and communicate the disaster plan clearly to everyone
c. Wait for the next shift to arrive before implementing the disaster response plan
d. Focus on securing the facility to prevent unauthorized access before addressing patient care

Answer: b. Quickly designate roles and responsibilities based on available staff, and communicate the disaster plan clearly to everyone. Explanation: In a disaster, clear communication and swift role assignment are crucial to maintaining order and ensuring patient care continues. By quickly designating roles and clearly communicating the disaster plan, the nurse leader can reduce confusion and ensure that the disaster response is effectively managed.

570. Following a disaster, the hospital's emergency department is overwhelmed with patients, and the usual admission process is no longer feasible. What should the nurse executive prioritize to manage patient flow effectively?
a. Implementing a simplified triage and registration process to expedite care
b. Redirecting all incoming patients to other healthcare facilities
c. Closing the emergency department to new patients until the situation stabilizes
d. Admitting only patients with private insurance to ensure financial reimbursement

Answer: a. Implementing a simplified triage and registration process to expedite care. Explanation: In a disaster, standard processes may need to be adjusted to manage high patient volumes effectively. A simplified triage and registration process allows for faster assessment and prioritization of care, ensuring that patients receive timely treatment even when the system is under strain.

571. A nurse leader is responsible for coordinating the hospital's disaster drills. Which drill scenario would best prepare staff for an actual mass casualty event?
a. A drill that focuses on the hospital's evacuation procedures due to a fire
b. A drill that simulates a mass casualty event with multiple trauma victims arriving simultaneously
c. A drill that emphasizes internal communication breakdowns during a power outage
d. A drill that tests the hospital's response to a hazardous material spill

Answer: b. A drill that simulates a mass casualty event with multiple trauma victims arriving simultaneously. Explanation: Simulating a mass casualty event with multiple trauma victims arriving simultaneously closely mirrors the challenges that staff would face during a real disaster. This type of drill prepares staff to manage patient flow, triage, and resource allocation under extreme conditions, enhancing their readiness for an actual event.

572. During a large-scale disaster, the nurse executive is tasked with making decisions about resource allocation. What is the most ethical framework to guide these decisions?
a. Deontological ethics, where the focus is on adherence to rules and duties regardless of outcomes
b. Utilitarian ethics, where the focus is on maximizing overall benefits and minimizing harm
c. Egoistic ethics, where the focus is on the self-interest of the decision-makers
d. Virtue ethics, where the focus is on the character and intentions of the individuals involved

Answer: b. Utilitarian ethics, where the focus is on maximizing overall benefits and minimizing harm. Explanation: In disaster scenarios, utilitarian ethics is often the most appropriate framework, as it prioritizes actions that maximize overall benefits and minimize harm. This approach is particularly relevant in resource allocation decisions, where the goal is to save as many lives as possible with the available resources.

573. After a disaster, a nurse leader notices signs of burnout among the healthcare team. What is the most effective initial intervention to address this issue?
a. Increasing the workload of unaffected staff members to allow those showing signs of burnout to rest
b. Mandating that all staff members attend stress management workshops
c. Conducting one-on-one meetings to assess individual needs and provide targeted support
d. Offering incentives for staff to work extra shifts to cover for those experiencing burnout

Answer: c. Conducting one-on-one meetings to assess individual needs and provide targeted support. Explanation: Individualized support is crucial in addressing burnout, as it allows the nurse leader to understand each team member's unique situation and provide appropriate resources. One-on-one meetings help identify specific needs and tailor interventions, promoting recovery and preventing further burnout.

574. A nurse executive is tasked with leading a community health needs assessment (CHNA) for a large urban area. Which of the following methodologies would most effectively capture the diverse health needs of this population?
a. Conducting surveys with a random sample of community residents.
b. Organizing focus groups with healthcare providers from local hospitals.
c. Analyzing hospital admission and discharge data to identify prevalent conditions.
d. Engaging community-based organizations to participate in key informant interviews.

Answer: d. Engaging community-based organizations to participate in key informant interviews. Explanation: Key informant interviews with community-based organizations allow for the gathering of in-depth insights from those who are directly involved with and knowledgeable about the community. This approach captures a broad range of health needs, especially in diverse populations, more effectively than random surveys, focus groups, or hospital data alone.

575. A nurse executive is leading the development of a school-based health center (SBHC) in a low-income community. Which of the following strategies would best ensure the sustainability of the SBHC?
a. Relying on grants and donations as the primary funding sources.
b. Partnering with local healthcare providers to offer pro bono services.
c. Establishing a sliding fee scale to generate consistent revenue from services provided.
d. Limiting services to only the most common health issues to reduce operational costs.

Answer: c. Establishing a sliding fee scale to generate consistent revenue from services provided. Explanation: A sliding fee scale ensures that the SBHC can generate revenue while remaining accessible to low-income families. This strategy balances sustainability with the center's mission to serve underserved populations, making it more reliable than relying solely on external funding or limiting services.

576. A nurse executive overseeing a home health and hospice program is facing challenges with staff retention. Which of the following strategies would most effectively address this issue?
a. Increasing the number of patient visits required per day to boost productivity.
b. Offering flexible scheduling options to accommodate work-life balance.
c. Implementing mandatory overtime to cover staffing shortages.
d. Reducing the caseload for each nurse to improve patient care quality.

Answer: b. Offering flexible scheduling options to accommodate work-life balance. Explanation: Flexible scheduling can significantly improve staff retention by accommodating nurses' work-life balance needs, which is a key factor in job satisfaction. Reducing caseloads might also help, but flexibility in scheduling directly addresses common reasons for turnover in home health and hospice care.

577. A nurse executive is developing a nurse-led community health worker (CHW) program to improve chronic disease management in a rural area. Which of the following components is most critical to the program's success?
a. Selecting CHWs from within the community they will serve.
b. Providing CHWs with advanced clinical training equivalent to that of registered nurses.
c. Ensuring CHWs have access to the latest healthcare technology.
d. Requiring CHWs to have formal healthcare credentials before participating.

Answer: a. Selecting CHWs from within the community they will serve. Explanation: CHWs who are selected from within the community they serve are more likely to be trusted and effective, as they understand local cultures, languages, and needs. Advanced clinical training and formal credentials, while beneficial, are not as critical to the program's success as community alignment and cultural competence.

578. A nurse executive is conducting a community health needs assessment and identifies significant disparities in access to care among different populations. Which of the following interventions would best address these disparities?
a. Expanding telehealth services to improve access for remote and underserved populations.
b. Increasing the number of healthcare providers in wealthier neighborhoods.
c. Focusing community health education efforts on populations with existing access to care.
d. Standardizing care protocols across all community clinics regardless of population needs.

Answer: a. Expanding telehealth services to improve access for remote and underserved populations. Explanation: Telehealth services can bridge the gap in access to care for remote and underserved populations, addressing disparities by providing more equitable healthcare access. Increasing providers in wealthier areas or standardizing care without considering specific needs would not address the root causes of disparities.

579. A nurse executive is tasked with improving the effectiveness of a school-based health center (SBHC) in addressing mental health issues among students. Which of the following approaches would be most effective?
a. Incorporating mental health screenings into routine physical exams.
b. Hiring additional primary care providers to manage mental health conditions.
c. Partnering with community mental health organizations to provide specialized services.
d. Limiting mental health services to crisis intervention only.

Answer: c. Partnering with community mental health organizations to provide specialized services. Explanation: Partnering with community mental health organizations brings in specialized expertise, ensuring that students receive comprehensive mental health care beyond what primary care providers can offer. Incorporating screenings is helpful, but specialized partnerships address the broader scope of mental health needs.

580. A nurse executive leading a home health and hospice program is considering implementing a new electronic health record (EHR) system. Which of the following factors is most critical in selecting an EHR system for this setting?
a. The ability of the EHR to interface with hospital systems to ensure continuity of care.
b. The cost of the EHR system and the availability of financial incentives.
c. The number of customizable features offered by the EHR.
d. The speed at which the EHR system can be implemented.

Answer: a. The ability of the EHR to interface with hospital systems to ensure continuity of care. Explanation: In home health and hospice settings, continuity of care is crucial. An EHR system that can interface with hospital systems ensures seamless transitions and comprehensive care management, making it the most critical factor in system selection. Cost, customization, and implementation speed are important but secondary to ensuring continuity of care.

581. A nurse executive is planning to expand a nurse-led community health worker (CHW) program into an urban area with high rates of diabetes. Which of the following strategies would most effectively support this expansion?
a. Recruiting CHWs with prior experience in diabetes care.
b. Focusing on CHW outreach in areas with existing healthcare services.
c. Developing a standardized care protocol for all CHWs to follow.
d. Providing CHWs with incentives based on the number of patients they serve.

Answer: a. Recruiting CHWs with prior experience in diabetes care. Explanation: Recruiting CHWs with experience in diabetes care ensures that they have the knowledge and skills needed to effectively manage and educate patients, leading to better outcomes. Standardized protocols and incentives are important but secondary to having a workforce with relevant expertise.

582. A nurse executive is conducting a community health needs assessment and finds that maternal and child health outcomes are particularly poor in a specific region. Which intervention would be most effective in addressing these outcomes?
a. Establishing a home visiting program for at-risk mothers and infants.
b. Increasing the number of pediatricians in the region's hospitals.
c. Implementing an awareness campaign on the importance of prenatal care.
d. Providing free childcare services to working mothers.

Answer: a. Establishing a home visiting program for at-risk mothers and infants. Explanation: Home visiting programs are evidence-based interventions that provide at-risk mothers and infants with the support they need, directly addressing poor maternal and child health outcomes. While increasing providers and raising awareness are helpful, direct support through home visits has a more immediate and impactful effect on health outcomes.

583. A nurse executive overseeing a home health program is faced with increasing demands for hospice care. Which strategy would best balance the needs of both home health and hospice patients?
a. Cross-training home health staff in hospice care principles to increase flexibility.
b. Segregating home health and hospice services to ensure specialized care.
c. Prioritizing hospice care due to its palliative nature and higher acuity.
d. Limiting the acceptance of new home health patients to focus on hospice care.

Answer: a. Cross-training home health staff in hospice care principles to increase flexibility. Explanation: Cross-training home health staff in hospice care allows for greater flexibility in meeting the needs of both patient populations, ensuring that care remains comprehensive and continuous. This approach maximizes resource use without sacrificing the quality of care for either group. Segregating services or limiting patients might reduce overall effectiveness and access.

584. A nurse executive is implementing a team-based care model in a large healthcare organization. Which factor is most critical to ensuring the successful implementation and sustainability of the model?
a. Assigning specific roles to team members based solely on their job titles
b. Establishing clear communication protocols and ensuring all team members are trained in these protocols
c. Limiting team meetings to reduce disruptions to clinical work
d. Focusing exclusively on individual performance metrics rather than team outcomes

Answer: b. Establishing clear communication protocols and ensuring all team members are trained in these protocols. Explanation: Effective communication is fundamental to the success of team-based care models. Clear protocols and comprehensive training ensure that all team members are on the same page, which enhances collaboration, minimizes errors, and improves patient outcomes.

585. During the implementation of a collaborative practice agreement (CPA) for advanced practice providers (APPs), the nurse executive encounters resistance from some physicians. What is the most effective strategy to address this interprofessional conflict?
a. Mandating compliance with the CPA without further discussion
b. Holding a meeting to discuss the benefits of the CPA and addressing any concerns from the physicians
c. Reducing the scope of practice for APPs to avoid conflicts with physicians
d. Allowing physicians to opt-out of the CPA if they disagree with it

Answer: b. Holding a meeting to discuss the benefits of the CPA and addressing any concerns from the physicians. Explanation: Addressing concerns through open communication and highlighting the benefits of the CPA can help resolve conflicts. Engaging physicians in the discussion fosters buy-in and collaboration, which is essential for the successful implementation of the CPA.

586. A healthcare organization is integrating the TeamSTEPPS (Team Strategies and Tools to Enhance Performance and Patient Safety) program to improve teamwork and communication. Which outcome would best indicate the success of the program?
a. An increase in the number of team meetings held each month
b. A reduction in medical errors and improved patient safety metrics
c. A higher number of staff members receiving TeamSTEPPS certification
d. A decrease in the amount of time spent on patient care rounds

Answer: b. A reduction in medical errors and improved patient safety metrics. Explanation: TeamSTEPPS is designed to enhance teamwork and communication with the goal of improving patient safety. A reduction in medical errors and better patient safety metrics are direct indicators of the program's success, reflecting improved team performance.

587. A nurse executive is leading the implementation of Crew Resource Management (CRM) training for clinical teams to enhance teamwork and decision-making. What is the most important element to focus on during CRM training?
a. Emphasizing the hierarchical structure of the team to ensure clear authority
b. Encouraging the use of standardized communication tools like SBAR (Situation, Background, Assessment, Recommendation)

c. Prioritizing individual accountability over team collaboration

d. Limiting training to senior staff members who have leadership responsibilities

Answer: b. Encouraging the use of standardized communication tools like SBAR (Situation, Background, Assessment, Recommendation). Explanation: CRM training emphasizes the importance of clear, structured communication in team settings. Tools like SBAR are essential for ensuring that critical information is accurately and efficiently conveyed, which is vital for effective decision-making and patient safety.

588. A healthcare organization is evaluating the effectiveness of its interprofessional team-based care model. Which metric would be most useful for this evaluation?

a. The number of team members who attend training sessions

b. The frequency of team meetings per month

c. Patient outcomes such as readmission rates and satisfaction scores

d. The level of individual productivity within each team

Answer: c. Patient outcomes such as readmission rates and satisfaction scores. Explanation: The ultimate goal of team-based care models is to improve patient outcomes. Metrics like readmission rates and patient satisfaction directly reflect the effectiveness of the team's collaborative efforts and provide meaningful data for evaluating the model's success.

589. A nurse executive is tasked with resolving an ongoing conflict between nursing staff and physical therapists over patient care responsibilities. Which conflict resolution strategy is most likely to foster long-term collaboration between the two groups?

a. Implementing a top-down decision that clearly delineates responsibilities

b. Facilitating a collaborative problem-solving session that includes both nursing staff and physical therapists

c. Assigning a mediator to enforce the existing care protocols without changes

d. Rotating responsibilities between the two groups on a weekly basis

Answer: b. Facilitating a collaborative problem-solving session that includes both nursing staff and physical therapists. Explanation: Collaborative problem-solving engages all parties in finding a mutually agreeable solution, which fosters understanding and cooperation. This approach not only resolves the immediate conflict but also builds a foundation for ongoing interprofessional collaboration.

590. A nurse executive is reviewing the collaborative practice agreement (CPA) for advanced practice providers (APPs) in the organization. Which of the following is most important to include in the CPA to ensure it supports effective interprofessional collaboration?

a. A detailed outline of billing procedures for services provided by APPs

b. Clear delineation of the APPs' scope of practice and the roles of collaborating physicians

c. A clause allowing physicians to unilaterally modify the CPA as needed

d. A provision that limits APPs' clinical responsibilities to reduce liability

Answer: b. Clear delineation of the APPs' scope of practice and the roles of collaborating physicians. Explanation: Clearly defining the roles and scope of practice for APPs and collaborating physicians is crucial for preventing misunderstandings and conflicts. This clarity supports effective collaboration by ensuring that all parties understand their responsibilities and how they will work together.

591. A healthcare organization is incorporating the TeamSTEPPS program into its training curriculum. Which key concept of TeamSTEPPS should be emphasized to enhance team communication and patient safety?
a. Maintaining strict adherence to the chain of command in all situations
b. Encouraging team members to speak up and voice concerns using the CUS (Concerned, Uncomfortable, Safety issue) technique
c. Limiting team communication to formal meetings to maintain professionalism
d. Focusing on individual achievements as the primary measure of success

Answer: b. Encouraging team members to speak up and voice concerns using the CUS (Concerned, Uncomfortable, Safety issue) technique. Explanation: The CUS technique empowers team members to voice concerns about potential safety issues, promoting a culture of openness and collaboration. This approach is central to TeamSTEPPS, as it enhances communication and helps prevent errors.

592. A nurse executive is evaluating the impact of Crew Resource Management (CRM) training on team performance in the operating room. What is the most effective method for assessing the training's impact?
a. Conducting anonymous surveys to gather staff opinions on the training
b. Analyzing changes in surgical outcomes and complication rates before and after the training
c. Monitoring attendance rates at CRM training sessions
d. Reviewing the number of surgical procedures completed each day

Answer: b. Analyzing changes in surgical outcomes and complication rates before and after the training. Explanation: CRM training aims to improve team performance and decision-making, particularly in high-stakes environments like the operating room. Analyzing surgical outcomes and complication rates provides objective data to assess whether the training has positively impacted patient safety and team effectiveness.

593. A nurse executive is implementing an interprofessional team-based care model in a new outpatient clinic. Which factor is most likely to pose a challenge to the success of this model?
a. The geographical location of the clinic in a rural area
b. Resistance from staff members who are accustomed to working independently
c. The availability of advanced practice providers to lead the team
d. The clinic's financial resources and reimbursement structure

Answer: b. Resistance from staff members who are accustomed to working independently. Explanation: Team-based care requires a shift from independent practice to collaborative work, which can be challenging for staff members used to working autonomously. Overcoming this resistance through training and change management strategies is crucial for the success of the team-based care model.

594. A large healthcare system is implementing an environmentally preferable purchasing program. Which of the following strategies would have the GREATEST impact on reducing the organization's environmental footprint?
a. Prioritizing local suppliers for all non-medical products
b. Implementing a comprehensive single-use device reprocessing program
c. Switching to 100% recycled paper products for administrative use
d. Mandating Energy Star certification for all new electronic equipment

Answer: b. Implementing a comprehensive single-use device reprocessing program. Explanation: Implementing a comprehensive single-use device reprocessing program would have the greatest impact on reducing a healthcare organization's environmental footprint. This strategy directly addresses the significant waste generated by single-use medical devices, reducing both waste and the need for new device production. It combines waste reduction with resource conservation. Prioritizing local suppliers (a) may reduce transportation emissions but doesn't address medical waste. Switching to recycled paper (c) is beneficial but has a smaller impact compared to medical waste reduction. Energy Star certification (d) is important but affects only energy consumption. Single-use device reprocessing tackles a major source of healthcare waste, aligning with circular economy principles and offering substantial environmental and cost benefits.

595. In developing a waste reduction strategy for a hospital's operating rooms, which of the following approaches would be MOST effective in minimizing landfill waste?
a. Implementing a comprehensive recycling program for packaging materials
b. Switching to reusable surgical gowns and drapes
c. Adopting a just-in-time inventory system for surgical supplies
d. Installing hand dryers to replace paper towels in scrub areas

Answer: b. Switching to reusable surgical gowns and drapes. Explanation: Switching to reusable surgical gowns and drapes would be most effective in minimizing landfill waste from operating rooms. This approach significantly reduces the volume of disposable textiles sent to landfills, which constitute a large portion of OR waste. Reusable textiles also decrease the environmental impact associated with producing and disposing of single-use items. A recycling program for packaging (a) is beneficial but doesn't address the larger volume of clinical waste. A just-in-time inventory system (c) may reduce expired supply waste but doesn't significantly impact overall waste volume. Hand dryers (d) address a minor waste stream compared to surgical textiles. Reusable gowns and drapes offer a comprehensive solution that aligns with waste hierarchy principles, prioritizing reduction over recycling or disposal.

596. A healthcare facility is developing an energy conservation strategy. Which of the following initiatives would likely yield the MOST significant long-term energy savings?
a. Implementing a building automation system for HVAC and lighting control
b. Replacing all lighting fixtures with LED bulbs
c. Installing solar panels on the facility's roof
d. Educating staff on energy-saving behaviors

Answer: a. Implementing a building automation system for HVAC and lighting control. Explanation: Implementing a building automation system for HVAC and lighting control would likely yield the most significant long-term energy savings for a healthcare facility. This system allows for optimized, real-time management of the largest energy consumers in healthcare settings - heating, cooling, and lighting. It can adjust based on occupancy, time of day, and external conditions, maximizing efficiency. While LED lighting (b) offers energy savings, it addresses only one aspect of energy use. Solar panels (c) generate clean energy but may not significantly reduce overall consumption. Staff education (d) is important but often yields less consistent results compared to automated systems. A building automation system provides comprehensive, ongoing energy management, aligning with best practices in healthcare facility energy conservation.

597. In addressing climate change adaptation for a coastal hospital, which of the following measures should be prioritized to ensure continuity of operations during extreme weather events?
a. Developing a comprehensive telemedicine program
b. Relocating critical infrastructure above potential flood levels
c. Increasing on-site renewable energy generation capacity
d. Implementing a staff carpooling incentive program

Answer: b. Relocating critical infrastructure above potential flood levels. Explanation: Relocating critical infrastructure above potential flood levels should be prioritized for climate change adaptation in a coastal hospital. This measure directly addresses the immediate threat of flooding due to sea-level rise and increased storm intensity, which are major climate change risks for coastal areas. It ensures the hospital can maintain critical operations during extreme weather events. A telemedicine program (a) enhances service delivery but doesn't protect physical infrastructure. Increasing renewable energy capacity (c) is beneficial for mitigation but doesn't directly address adaptation to flooding. A staff carpooling program (d) reduces emissions but doesn't improve resilience to extreme weather. Relocating critical infrastructure represents a crucial adaptation strategy, aligning with healthcare resilience planning for climate change impacts.

598. A hospital is launching a comprehensive recycling initiative. Which of the following strategies would be MOST effective in ensuring high compliance and proper waste segregation among staff?
a. Implementing color-coded waste bins with clear signage
b. Offering financial incentives for departments with highest recycling rates
c. Mandating annual waste management training for all staff
d. Publishing monthly waste audit results in staff newsletters

Answer: a. Implementing color-coded waste bins with clear signage. Explanation: Implementing color-coded waste bins with clear signage would be most effective in ensuring high compliance and proper waste segregation among staff. This strategy makes proper waste disposal intuitive and easily understandable, reducing confusion and errors in waste segregation. It provides constant visual cues that reinforce correct behaviors. Financial incentives (b) may drive improvement but can lead to competition rather than sustainable behavior change. Annual training (c) is important but may not provide daily reinforcement. Publishing audit results (d) increases awareness but doesn't provide immediate guidance during waste disposal. Color-coded bins with clear signage offer a practical, user-friendly solution that aligns with best practices in healthcare waste management and behavior change principles.

599. In developing an environmentally preferable purchasing policy for medical supplies, which criterion should be given the HIGHEST priority to balance environmental impact and patient safety?
a. Percentage of recycled content in product packaging
b. Distance from manufacturer to healthcare facility
c. Absence of harmful chemicals such as PVC or DEHP
d. Manufacturer's overall corporate sustainability rating

Answer: c. Absence of harmful chemicals such as PVC or DEHP. Explanation: The absence of harmful chemicals such as PVC or DEHP should be given the highest priority in an environmentally preferable purchasing policy for medical supplies. This criterion directly addresses both environmental impact and patient safety concerns. Chemicals like PVC and DEHP have been linked to health issues and environmental pollution. Recycled content in packaging (a) is beneficial but doesn't directly impact patient care. Manufacturing distance (b) affects transportation emissions but not product safety. Corporate sustainability ratings (d) are important but may not reflect specific product attributes. Prioritizing the absence of harmful chemicals aligns with healthcare's primary mission of "do no harm" while also addressing environmental concerns, representing a key intersection of health and sustainability in medical product selection.

600. A healthcare organization is striving to reduce its carbon footprint. Which of the following initiatives would have the MOST significant impact on reducing greenhouse gas emissions?
a. Implementing a comprehensive energy efficiency program
b. Transitioning to plant-based menu options in the cafeteria
c. Optimizing supply chain logistics to reduce transportation
d. Installing water-saving fixtures throughout the facility

Answer: a. Implementing a comprehensive energy efficiency program. Explanation: Implementing a comprehensive energy efficiency program would have the most significant impact on reducing greenhouse gas emissions for a healthcare organization. Energy consumption, particularly from fossil fuel sources, is typically the largest contributor to a healthcare facility's carbon footprint. A comprehensive program addressing heating, cooling, lighting, and equipment efficiency can substantially reduce energy use and associated emissions. While plant-based menu options (b) can reduce food-related emissions, their impact is smaller compared to facility-wide energy use. Supply chain optimization (c) is important but often has less impact than on-site energy consumption. Water-saving fixtures (d) are beneficial but primarily address water conservation rather than carbon emissions. An energy efficiency program offers the most direct and substantial approach to reducing greenhouse gas emissions in healthcare settings.

601. In developing a climate change mitigation strategy for a healthcare network, which of the following approaches would be MOST effective in achieving long-term emission reductions?
a. Purchasing carbon offsets for all organizational emissions
b. Implementing a green building standard for all new construction
c. Establishing a network-wide telehealth program to reduce patient travel
d. Transitioning the entire vehicle fleet to electric vehicles

Answer: b. Implementing a green building standard for all new construction. Explanation: Implementing a green building standard for all new construction would be most effective in achieving long-term emission reductions for a healthcare network. This approach ensures that future facilities are designed and built to maximize energy efficiency, utilize sustainable materials, and incorporate renewable energy sources from the ground up. It provides a long-term, systemic solution to reducing emissions. Purchasing carbon offsets (a) doesn't reduce actual emissions and may not drive organizational change. A telehealth program (c) can reduce patient travel emissions but doesn't address facility-related emissions. Transitioning to electric vehicles (d) is beneficial but addresses a smaller portion of healthcare emissions compared to building energy use. Green building standards offer a comprehensive, future-oriented strategy that aligns with sustainable healthcare infrastructure development.

602. A hospital is implementing a water conservation program. Which of the following measures would result in the LARGEST reduction in water consumption?
a. Installing low-flow faucets and showerheads in all patient rooms
b. Implementing water-efficient landscaping practices
c. Upgrading to water-efficient medical equipment (e.g., sterilizers, cooling systems)
d. Initiating a staff awareness campaign on water conservation

Answer: c. Upgrading to water-efficient medical equipment (e.g., sterilizers, cooling systems). Explanation: Upgrading to water-efficient medical equipment, such as sterilizers and cooling systems, would likely result in the largest reduction in water consumption for a hospital. These systems are often the biggest water consumers in healthcare settings, and modern, efficient models can significantly reduce water use without compromising functionality or safety. Low-flow fixtures (a) are beneficial but may have less impact compared to large equipment. Water-efficient landscaping (b) can save water but typically represents a smaller portion of a hospital's water use. Staff awareness campaigns (d) are important but may yield less consistent results compared to equipment upgrades. Focusing on major medical equipment addresses the largest water consumers, aligning with best practices in healthcare water conservation and offering substantial, measurable reductions in water use.

603. In addressing the environmental impact of pharmaceutical waste, which of the following strategies would be MOST effective in reducing both environmental contamination and medication waste?
a. Implementing a pharmaceutical take-back program for the community
b. Transitioning to unit-dose packaging for all medications
c. Developing a protocol for appropriate disposal of expired medications
d. Educating patients on proper storage and use of medications to reduce expiration

Answer: b. Transitioning to unit-dose packaging for all medications. Explanation: Transitioning to unit-dose packaging for all medications would be most effective in reducing both environmental contamination and medication waste. This approach minimizes the amount of unused medication that could potentially be disposed of improperly, reducing the risk of environmental contamination. It also helps prevent medication waste by providing only the necessary doses, reducing the likelihood of excess medication expiring before use. A take-back program (a) addresses disposal but not waste reduction. A disposal protocol (c) is important but doesn't prevent waste generation. Patient education (d) can help but may have limited impact on systemic waste. Unit-dose packaging addresses the issue at its source, aligning with waste reduction principles and offering a systemic solution to pharmaceutical waste in healthcare settings.

You've made it to the end of this ANCC Nurse Executive Advanced Exam Prep Study Guide, and that's an accomplishment worth celebrating. Whether you're feeling confident or still a bit uncertain, remember that every bit of effort you've put in here is a step closer to achieving your goal.

We've covered a lot together—from understanding leadership theories and quality improvement strategies to diving deep into financial management, human capital, and healthcare delivery. You've tackled practice questions, absorbed key concepts, and, most importantly, strengthened your ability to think like a Nurse Executive. The knowledge you've built is not just for passing an exam—it's the foundation you'll stand on as you lead with confidence and clarity in your career.

Now, as you prepare for the exam, keep in mind that the journey isn't about perfection; it's about progress. You might encounter a tricky question or a topic that tests your limits, but remember why you started this journey in the first place. Your dedication to advancing your career and your commitment to making a difference in the lives of your patients and colleagues is what truly matters.

If doubts creep in, know that you're not alone—every leader faces challenges. What sets you apart is your ability to push through those doubts, to keep learning, and to stay focused on the bigger picture. You've got the tools, the knowledge, and the mindset needed to succeed. Trust in the hard work you've done and the growth you've achieved along the way.

As you head into the exam, take a deep breath and believe in yourself. You've come so far, and you're more prepared than you might think. The exam is just one more step on your journey, and no matter the outcome, you're on a path to making a real impact as a Nurse Executive.

So go ahead—give it your best shot. We're rooting for you, and we know that with the passion and dedication you've shown, success is within your reach. Best of luck, and remember: you've got this!

Made in the USA
Las Vegas, NV
09 December 2024